The Apocalypse Revealed

Anonymous

Nabu Public Domain Reprints:

You are holding a reproduction of an original work published before 1923 that is in the public domain in the United States of America, and possibly other countries. You may freely copy and distribute this work as no entity (individual or corporate) has a copyright on the body of the work. This book may contain prior copyright references, and library stamps (as most of these works were scanned from library copies). These have been scanned and retained as part of the historical artifact.

This book may have occasional imperfections such as missing or blurred pages, poor pictures, errant marks, etc. that were either part of the original artifact, or were introduced by the scanning process. We believe this work is culturally important, and despite the imperfections, have elected to bring it back into print as part of our continuing commitment to the preservation of printed works worldwide. We appreciate your understanding of the imperfections in the preservation process, and hope you enjoy this valuable book.

THE AUTHOR'S PREFACE.

Not a few have laboured at the explication of the Apocalypse, but as they were unacquainted with the spiritual sense of the Word, they could not discern the arcana which it contains, seeing that these can only be unfolded by the spiritual sense: expositors have therefore formed various conjectures respecting it, in many instances applying its contents to the affairs of empires, and blending them, at the same time, with ecclesiastical matters. The Apocalypse, however, like the rest of the Word, treats not, in its spiritual sense, of mundane things, but of such as are heavenly, thus not of empires and kingdoms, but of heaven and the church.

It is to be observed that, after the last judgment, which was accomplished in the spiritual world, in the year 1757, and which forms the subject of a small treatise published in London in 1758, a new heaven was formed from among Christians, from those only, however, who admitted the Lord to be the God of heaven and earth, according to his own words in Matthew xxviii. 18; and likewise repented in the world of their evil works: from this heaven the New Church on earth, which is the New Jerusalem, descends, and will continue to descend. That this Church will acknowledge the Lord only is evident from these words in the Apocalypse: "There came unto me one of the seven angels, and talked with me, saying, Come hither, I will show thee the bride, the Lamb's wife; and he showed me that great city, the holy Jerusalem, descending out of heaven from God." And in another place: "Let us be glad and rejoice, for the time of the marriage of the Lamb is come, and his wife hath made herself ready; blessed are they which are called unto the marriage supper of the Lamb," chap. xix. 7, 9. That there will be a new heaven, and that the New Church will descend thence upon earth, is evident from the following words, in the same book: "I saw a new heaven and a new earth: and I saw the holy city, New Jerusalem, coming down from God out of heaven, prepared as a bride adorned for her husband; and he that sat upon the throne said, Behold, I make all things new; and he said unto me, Write, for these words are true and faithful," chap. xxi. 1, 2, 5; the new heaven means a new heaven from among Christians; the New Jerusalem means a new church upon earth, which will make one with that new heaven; the Lamb means the Lord as to the Divine Humanity.

To this something shall be added by way of illustration. The Christian heaven is below the ancient heavens; into this heaven, from the time of the Lord's abode in the world, were admitted those who worshipped one God under three persons, and who did not at the same time entertain an idea of three Gods; and this, by reason of a trinity of persons being received throughout the whole Christian world: but they, who entertained no other idea of the Lord's Humanity, than as of the humanity of another man, could not receive the faith of the New Jerusalem, which is, that the Lord is the only God in whom there is a trinity; these latter, therefore, were separated and removed; it was given me to see their separation and removal after the last judgment. For upon a just idea of God, the universal heaven, and the church universal on earth, are founded, and in general the whole of religion; for by that idea there is conjunction, and by conjunction, light, wisdom, and eternal happiness.

Any one may see that the Apocalypse could no how be explained but by the Lord alone, since every word of it contains arcana, which never could be known without some special illumination, and consequent revelation; wherefore it has pleased the Lord to open the sight of my spirit and to teach me. It must not therefore be supposed that I have given any explication of my own, nor that even of any angel, but only what I have had communicated to me from the Lord alone. The Lord said, moreover, by an angel unto John: "Seal not the words of the prophecy of this book," chap. xxii. 10; by which is signified, that they are to be manifested and laid open.

A COMPENDIUM

OF THE

DOCTRINES OF THE ROMAN CATHOLIC CHURCH AND RELIGION.

BABYLON, or the Roman Catholic Religion, being treated of in the Apocalypse, in chapter xvii., xviii., and xix., it is expedient, at the commencement of these explications, to say something concerning its doctrines, and that in the following order: On Baptism; on the Eucharist or Holy Supper; on Masses; on Repentance; on Justification; on Purgatory; on the Seven Sacraments; on the Saints; and on Power.

"I. ON BAPTISM, they teach: that Adam, after the sin of disobedience, was wholly changed for the worse, both as to soul and body; that this sin was transfused into the whole human race; that this original sin is only taken away by the merit of Christ; and that the merit of Christ is applied by the sacrament of baptism; and that thus the whole guilt of original sin is taken away by baptism; that concupiscence nevertheless remains in the baptized as an incentive to sins, but not sin itself; that thus they put on Christ, become new creatures, and obtain a full and complete remission of sins. Baptism is called the laver of regeneration and of faith. That the baptized, when they grow up, are to be questioned concerning the promises made by their sponsors; which is the SACRAMENT OF CONFIRMATION. That by reason of lapses after baptism, the sacrament of repentance is necessary.

"II. ON THE EUCHARIST OR HOLY SUPPER. That immediately after consecration, the real body and blood of Jesus Christ are truly and substantially comprehended under the form of bread and wine, together with his soul and divinity; the body under the form of bread, and the blood under the form of wine, by virtue of the words: but the body itself under the form of wine, and the blood under the form of bread, and the soul in both, by virtue of a natural connexion and concomitance, whereby the parts of the Lord Christ are united together, and the divinity by reason of its admirable hypostatic union with the body and soul; thus that they are as fully comprehended under one form as under both; in a word, that the whole and entire Christ exists under the form of the bread and under every part of that form; and the whole of him also under the form of the wine and all its parts; that therefore the two forms are separated, and the bread is given to the laity, and the wine to the clergy. That water is to be mixed with wine in the cup. That the laity are to receive the communion from the clergy, and the clergy from themselves. That the real body and the real blood of Christ, after consecration, is in the host in the consecrated particles; and that therefore the host is to be worshipped when it is shown and carried about. That this wonderful and singular conversion of the whole substance of the bread into body, and of the whole substance of the wine into blood, is called transubstantiation. That the communication of both forms, under certain conditions, may be granted by the pope. It is called supersubstantial bread, and the bread of angels, which these eat without any veils; it is called moreover spiritual food; also the antidote by which they are released from their sins.

"III. ON MASSES. It is called the sacrifice of the mass, because the sacrifice by which Christ offered up himself to God the Father, is represented thereby under the form of bread and wine; that thence it is a sacrifice truly propitiatory, pure, and altogether holy. That if the people do not communicate sacramentally, but only the minister, in such case the people communicate spiritually, because the ministers do it, not for themselves only, but for all the faithful who appertain to the body of Christ. The mass ought not to be performed in the vulgar tongue, because it contains the great learning of the faithful people; but that the ministers may declare something concerning it on the Lord's day. That it is ordained, that some things which are mystical should be pronounced with a lower, and other things with a louder, voice; and, for the purpose of giving a majesty to so great a sacrifice which is offered to God, there should be lights, incense, garments, and other things of a like nature for the occasion. That it is to be offered up for the sins, penalties, satisfactions, and all the necessities of the living, and also for the dead. That masses in honour of the saints are thanksgivings for their intercession when they are implored.

"IV. ON REPENTANCE. That besides baptism there is a sacrament of repentance, whereby the benefit of the death and merit of Christ is applied to those who lapse after baptism; therefore it is called a kind of laborious baptism. That the parts of repentance are contrition, confession, and satisfaction. That CONTRITION is the gift of God, and the impulse of the Holy Ghost, not yet inhabiting, but only moving the contrite person, therefore it is a disposing. That CONFESSION ought to be made of all mortal sins, even the most secret, and of the intentions; that sins which are withheld from confession are not forgiven, but that those which after search do not occur, are included in confession; that confession ought to be made at least once a year: that absolution of sins is to be given by the ministers of the keys, and that they are remitted on their saying, I ABSOLVE; that absolution is like the act of a judge when sentence is pronounced; that the more grievous sins are to be absolved by bishops, and the still more grievous by the pope. That SATISFACTION is made by satisfactory punishments imposed by the minister at discretion, according to the measure of the offence; that when eternal punishment is remitted, then temporal punishment is remitted also. That the power of INDULGENCES is left by Christ to the church, and that the use of them is highly salutary.

"V. ON JUSTIFICATION. That a translation cannot be effected from that state in which man is born a son of Adam, to a state of grace through the second Adam the Saviour, without the washing of regeneration and faith, or without baptism. That the second beginning of justification is from preventing grace, which is a calling, with which man co-operates by converting himself. That disposition is produced by *faith*, when man believes those things to be true which are revealed, to which he is freely moved; also by *hope*, when he believes that God is propitious for the sake of Christ; and by *charity*, in consequence whereof he begins to love his neighbour, and to hate sin. That justification, which follows, is not only remission of sins, but sanctification, and renovation of the inner man; that at this time the justified are not reputed just, but that they are just, receiving righteousness in themselves; and because they accept the merit of Christ's passion, justification is inserted by faith, hope, and charity. That faith is the beginning of human salvation, the foundation and root of justification, and that this is to be justified by faith: and because none of those things which precede justification, whether they be of faith or works, merit the grace of justification, that this is to be justified *gratis*, for there is a preventing grace; and that still man is justified by works, and not by faith alone. That the just may fall into light and venial sins, and that still they are just; and that therefore the just ought continually to labour by prayers, oblations, alms, fastings, lest they should fall, because they are born again to the hope of glory, and not to glory. That the just, if they fall from the grace of justification, may be justified again by the sacrament of repentance: that by any mortal sin grace is lost, but not faith, but that faith also is lost by infidelity, which is recession from religion. That the works of a justified man are merits; and that the justified, by such, which are done by them through the grace of God and the merit of Christ, merit everlasting life. That FREE-WILL was not lost and extinguished after the sin of Adam; and that man may co-operate, by assenting to the calling of God; and that otherwise he would be an inanimate body. They establish PREDESTINATION, by saying, that no one knows whether he is in the number of the predestinate, and among those whom God has chosen to himself, except by special revelation.

"VI. ON PURGATORY. That all the guilt from which men are to be purified by temporal punishment is not blotted out by justification, that therefore all go to purgatory to be purified, before they can be admitted into heaven. That the souls there detained are assisted by the suffrage of the faithful, and particularly by the sacrifice of the mass; and that this is diligently to be taught and preached." The torments there endured are variously described, but they are mere inventions and fictions.

"VII. ON THE SEVEN SACRAMENTS. That there are seven sacraments—baptism, confirmation, the eucharist, repentance, extreme unction, order, and matrimony; that there are neither more nor less; that one is of greater dignity than another; that they contain grace; and that from the work operated by them grace is conferred: that there were the same number of sacraments of the ancient law. Baptism, confirmation, the eucharist, and repentance have been treated of above. ON THE SACRAMENT OF EXTREME UNCTION: That it is founded on the epistle of James, chap. v., 14, 15; that it is to be administered to the sick at their lives' end, whence it is called the sacrament of the departing; that if they recover, it may be applied again; that it is to be performed with oil consecrated by the bishop, and with these words: 'May God grant thee his indulgence for whatsoever offence thou hast committed through the fault of the eyes, of the nostrils, or of the feeling.' ON THE SACRAMENT OF ORDER: That there are seven orders in the ministry of the priesthood, which differ in dignity, and all together are called the ecclesiastical hierarchy, which is like the order of an encampment; that inaugurations into the ministry are to be effected by unctions, and by transferring of the Holy Spirit upon them. That the secular power or consent, calling or authority of the magistrate is not requisite for the ordination of bishops and priests; that they who ascend to the ministry only by the appointment of their calling, are not ministers, but thieves and robbers, who do not enter in by the door. ON THE SACRAMENT OF MATRIMONY: That a dispensation of degrees and divorces belongs to the church. That the clergy are not to contract matrimony. That all of them may have the gift of chastity, and if any one saith he cannot, when nevertheless he had made a vow, let him be anathema, because God doth not refuse it to those who ask it properly, and doth not suffer any one to be tempted beyond what he is able to bear. That a state of virginity and celibacy is to be preferred to the conjugal state; besides other things of the same nature.

"VIII. ON THE SAINTS. That the saints reigning together with Christ offer up their prayers to God for men; that Christ is to be adored, and the saints to be invoked; that the invocation of saints is not idolatrous, nor derogatory to the honour of the one Mediator between God and men; it is called *Latria*. That images of Christ, of Mary the mother of God, and of the saints, are to be revered and honoured, not that it is to be supposed they possess any divinity or virtue, but because the honour which is paid to them is referred to the prototypes which they represent; and that by the images which they kiss and before which they kneel and uncover their heads, they adore Christ and venerate the saints. That the miracles of God are performed by the saints.

"IX. ON POWER. That the Roman Pontiff is the successor of the apostle Peter, and vicar of Jesus Christ, the head of the church, and the universal bishop; that he is superior to councils; that he hath the keys for opening and shutting heaven, consequently the power of remitting and retaining sins; that therefore he, as keeper of the keys of everlasting life, hath a right at once to earthly and heavenly empire; that moreover bishops and priests have such a power from him, because it was given also to the rest of the apostles, and that therefore they are called ministers of the keys. That it belongs to the church to judge of the true sense and interpretation of the Sacred Scriptures, and that they who oppose them are to suffer punishments established by law. That it is not proper for the laity to read the Sacred Scriptures, because the sense of them is only known to the church: thence its ministers boast that it is known to them."

X. The above doctrinals are selected from their councils and bulls, particularly from the council of Trent, and the papal bull confirming it, wherein all who think, believe, and act contrary to what was there decreed, which in general is as above adduced, are condemned to be excommunicated.

A COMPENDIUM

OF THE

DOCTRINES OF THE REFORMED CHURCH AND RELIGION.

The members of the Reformed Church being much treated of in the Apocalypse, in its spiritual sense, it is expedient, before entering upon its explication, to unfold their doctrines in the following order: On God; on Christ the Lord; on Justification by Faith, and on Good Works; on the Law and the Gospel; on Repentance and Confession; on Original Sin; on Baptism; on the Holy Supper; on Free-will; and on the Church.

"I. On God. Of God they believe according to the Athanasian Creed, which, as it is in the hands of every one, is not here inserted. That they believe in God the Father as the creator and preserver; in God the Son as the saviour and redeemer; and in the Holy Spirit as the illuminator and sanctifier, is also well known.

"II. On Christ the Lord. Concerning the person of Christ, the same doctrine is not taught by all the Reformed. The Lutherans teach that the Virgin Mary not only conceived and brought forth a real man, but also the real Son of God, whence she is justly called, and truly is, the mother of God. That in Christ there are two natures, a divine and a human, the divine from eternity, and the human in time; that these two natures are personally united, altogether in such a manner, that there are not two Christs, one the Son of God, and the other the Son of man; but that one and the same is the Son of God and the Son of man, not that these two natures are mixed together into one substance, nor that one is changed into the other, but that both natures retain their essential properties, which are also described as to their qualities: that their union is hypostatic, and that this is the most perfect communion, like that of the soul and body; that therefore it is justly said, that in Christ God is man and man God; that he did not suffer for us as mere man only, but as such a man, whose human nature hath so strict and ineffable a union and communion with the Son of God, as to become one person with him; that in truth the Son of God suffered for us, but yet according to the properties of human nature; that the Son of man, by whom is understood Christ as to his human nature, was really exalted to the right hand of God when he was taken into God, which was the case as soon as he was conceived of the Holy Spirit in the womb of his mother; that Christ always had that majesty by reason of his personal union, but that, in his state of exinanition, he only exercised it so far as he thought proper; but that after his resurrection he fully and entirely put off the form of a servant, and put his human nature or essence into a plenary assumption of the divine majesty; and that in this manner he entered into glory; in a word, that Christ is, and remains to all eternity, perfect God and man in one indivisible person; and the true, omnipotent, and eternal God: being also, with respect to his humanity, present at the right hand of God, he governs all things in heaven and upon earth, and also fills all things, is with us, and dwells and operates in us. That there is no difference of adoration, because by the nature which is seen, the divinity which is not seen, is adored. That the divine essence communicates and imparts its own excellences to the human nature, and performs its divine operations by the body as by its organ; that thus all the fulness of the Godhead dwells in Christ bodily, according to Paul. That the incarnation was accomplished that he might reconcile the Father to us, and become a sacrifice for the sins of the whole world, as well original as actual; that he was incarnate of the substance of the Holy Spirit, but that his human nature was produced from the Virgin Mary, which, as the Word, he assumed and united to himself; that he sanctifies those who believe in him, by sending the Holy Spirit into their hearts, to guide, comfort, and vivify them, and defend them against the devil and the power of sin. That Christ descended into hell, and destroyed hell for all believers; but in what manner these things were effected, he doth not wish them to scrutinize too curiously, but that the knowledge of this matter may be reserved for another age, when not only this mystery, but many other things also shall be revealed." These particulars are from Luther; the Augustan Confession; the Council of Nice; and the Smalcalden Articles. See the Formula Concordiæ.

"Some of the Reformed, who are also treated of in the Formula Concordiæ, believe that Christ, according to his human nature, by exaltation, received only created gifts and finite power, therefore that he is a man like any other, retaining the properties of the flesh; that therefore as to his human nature he is not omnipotent and omniscient; that although absent he governs, as a king, things remote from himself; that as God from eternity he is with the Father, and as a man born in time, he is with the angels in heaven; and that when it is said, in

Christ God is man and man God, it is only a figurative mode of speech: besides other things of a like nature.

"But this disagreement is adjusted by the Athanasian Creed, which is received by all the Christian world, where these words occur: 'The true faith is, that we believe and confess that our Lord Jesus Christ, the Son of God, is God and man; God, of the substance of the Father, begotten before the world, and man, of the substance of the mother, born in the world; perfect God and perfect man: who, although he be God and man, yet these are not two but one Christ; one, not by conversion of the divine Essence into body, but by the taking of his manhood into God; one altogether, not by confusion of substance, but by unity of person; for as the reasonable soul and body is one man, so God and man is one Christ.'

"III. ON JUSTIFICATION BY FAITH, AND ON GOOD WORKS. The justifying and saving faith of the clergy is this;—That God the Father turned himself away from the human race by reason of their iniquities, and so, from justice, condemned them to eternal death, and that he therefore sent his Son into the world to expiate and redeem them, and make satisfaction and reconciliation; and that his Son did this by taking upon himself the damnation of the law, and suffering himself to be crucified, and that thus by obedience he entirely satisfied God's justice, even to becoming justice himself; and that God the Father imputes and applies this, as his merit, to believers, and sends the Holy Spirit to them, who operates charity, good works, and repentance, as a good tree produces good fruits; and justifies, renews, regenerates, and sanctifies; and that this faith is the only medium of salvation, and that by it alone a man's sins are forgiven. They make a distinction between the act and the state of justification:—by the act of justification they understand the beginning of justification, which takes place in a moment, when man by that faith alone apprehends with confidence the merit of Christ; by the state of justification they understand the progress of that faith, which takes place by the interior operation of the Holy Spirit, which does not manifest itself except by certain signs, concerning which they teach various things; they speak also of good works manifested, which are done from the man and his will, and follow that faith; but they exclude them from justification, because the selfhood, and therefore the merit, of man is in them. This is a summary of modern faith, but its confirmations, and the traditions concerning it, are numerous and manifold; some of which also shall be adduced; which are, that men cannot be justified before God by their own strength, merits, and works, but gratuitously for Christ's sake, by faith; that by this faith they believe that they are received into grace, and their sins are remitted for his sake, who by his death made satisfaction for us, and that God the Father imputes this to believers for righteousness before him; that this faith, that Christ suffered and died for us, is not only an historical knowledge, but also a cordial assent, confidence, and trust, that sins are gratuitously remitted for Christ's sake, and that they are justified; and that at this time these three things concur, gratuitous promise, the merit of Christ as a price, and propitiation. That faith is the righteousness by which we are reputed just before God by reason of the promise; and that to be justified is to be absolved from sins, and that it may also be called a kind of quickening and regeneration; that faith is imputed to us for righteousness, not because it is so good a work, but because it apprehends the merit of Christ. That the merit of Christ is his obedience, passion, death, and resurrection; that it is necessary there should be something by which God can be approached, and that this is nothing else but faith, by which reception is effected. That faith, in the act of justification, enters by the word and by the hearing, and that it is not the act of man, but that it is the operation of the Holy Spirit, and that man does not co-operate any more than a statue of salt, a stock, or a stone, doing nothing from himself, and knowing nothing of it; but that after the act he co-operates, yet not with any will of his own in spiritual things; in things natural, civil, and moral, it is otherwise: but that they can so far proceed in things spiritual as to will what is good, and to feel delight in consequence, yet this is not from their own will, but from the Holy Spirit, and that thus they co-operate, not from their own powers, but from new powers and gifts begun in them by the Holy Spirit in their conversion; and that in real conversion a change, renovation, and motion are produced in the understanding and heart of man. That charity, good works, and repentance, do not enter into the act of justification, but that they are necessary in a state of justification, especially by reason of God's command, and that by them are merited the corporeal rewards of this life, but not the remission of sins, and the glory of everlasting life, because faith alone, without the works of the law, justifies and saves. That faith in act justifies man, but faith in state renovates him; that in renovation by reason of God's command, the works reputed good, as pointed out by the decalogue, are necessary to be performed, because it is the will of God that carnal lusts should be restrained by civil discipline, for which reason he has provided doctrine, laws, magistrates, and punishments; that, therefore, it is consequently false, that by works we merit remission of sins and salvation, and that works have any effect in preserving faith; and that it is also false, that man is reputed just on account of the rational justice or righteousness he may possess; and that reason can, from its own power, love God above all things and perform his law; in a word, that faith and salvation are not preserved and retained in men by good works, but only by the Spirit of God and by faith; but still that good works are testimonies that the Holy Spirit is present and dwells in them. They condemn as pernicious, this mode of speech—that good works are hurtful to salvation; because the interior works of the Holy Spirit are to be understood, which are good, not exterior works proceeding from man's own will, which are not good but evil, because they are meritorious. They teach, moreover, that Christ at the last judgment will pronounce sentence upon good and evil works as effects proper and not proper to the faith of man. This faith rules at this day in the whole reformed Christian world with the clergy, but not with the laity, except in a very few instances; for the laity by faith understand nothing else but believing in God the Father, the Son, and the Holy Spirit, and that he who lives well and believes well, will be saved; and of the Lord that he is the Saviour; for they are ignorant of the mysteries of justification of their preachers, who, although they preach such things, yet, with the laity who hear them, they enter in at one ear and go out at the other; their teachers, indeed, think themselves learned, from knowing them, and labour much in their schools and universities to make themselves masters of them; therefore it is said above, that that faith is the faith of the clergy. But yet the teachers teach this same faith differently in the different kingdoms in which the Reformed Church is established; in Germany, Sweden, and Denmark, they say, that the Holy Spirit operates by that faith, and justifies and sanctifies men, and afterwards successively renovates and regenerates them, but without the works of the law; and they who are in that faith from trust and confidence, are in grace with God the Father; and that then the evils which they do, appear indeed, but are constantly remitted. In England, they teach that that faith produces charity without man's knowledge, and that when man feels the Holy Spirit operate interiorly in himself, this operation also is the good of charity; and if he does not feel it, and yet does good for the sake of salvation, that it may be called good, but still that it derives somewhat from man, in that there is merit in it. Moreover, that such faith can operate this at the hour of death, yet they do not know how. In Holland, they teach, that God the Father, for the sake of the Son, justifies and purifies man interiorly by the Holy Spirit through that faith, but even to his own proper will, from which it turns back without touching it; some teach that it does indeed lightly touch it, and that the evils of man's will do not appear in the sight of God. But a few only of the laity know any thing of these mysteries of the clergy; the latter indeed are unwilling to publish them as they are in themselves, because they know that the laity have no relish for them.

"IV. ON THE LAW AND THE GOSPEL. That the law was

given by God, that it might be known what sin is, and that thus it might be restrained by threats and by fear, and afterwards by promise and the annunciation of grace; therefore the principal office of the law is, to reveal original sin and all the fruits of it, and to make known to how horrible a degree the nature of man is fallen and totally depraved; by this means it terrifies, humbles, and reduces man to despair of himself, and anxiously to desire aid: this effect of the law is called contrition, which is not active or factitious, but passive, and the torment of conscience; but the gospel is the whole doctrine concerning Christ and faith; and, therefore, concerning the remission of sins; consequently, a most joyful messenger, not reproving and terrifying, but comforting: by the law the wrath of God against all impiety is revealed, and man is condemned, therefore it causes man to look up to Christ, and to the gospel; they must both be preached, because they are connected. The gospel teaches that Christ took upon himself the curse of the law and expiated all sins, and that we consequently obtain remission by faith. That the Holy Spirit is given and received, and the heart of man renewed, not by the preaching of the law, but of the gospel; and that the Spirit afterwards makes use of the ministry of the law, to teach and show in the decalogue, what the good will and pleasure of God is; thus the Spirit mortifies and quickens. That a distinction is to be made between the works of the law, and the works of the Spirit, therefore the faithful are not under the law, but under grace, for that very reason. That the righteousness of the law does not justify, that is, does not reconcile nor regenerate, nor, by itself, make men accepted of God; but when the Holy Spirit is given, the fulfilling of the law follows. That the works of the second table of the decalogue do not justify, because by it we act with men, and not properly with God, and yet in justification we must act with God. That Christ without sin suffered the punishment of sin, and was made a sacrifice for us, whereby he took away that right of the law, that it might not condemn believers, because he is a propitiation for them, for the sake of which they are reputed just.

"V. On Repentance and Confession. That repentance consists of two parts; one is contrition, or terror struck into the conscience by reason of sin; the other faith, which is conceived from the gospel, and by the remission of sins, comforts the conscience and delivers from terrors. He who confesses himself to be nothing but sin, comprehends all sins, excludes none, and forgets none; thus sins are purged away, man is purified, rectified, and sanctified; because the Holy Spirit does not suffer sin to have dominion, but represses and restrains it. That the enumeration of sins ought to be free, as the person may choose or not choose; and that great stress is to be laid upon private confession and absolution; therefore if any one chooses, he may confess his sins, and receive absolution from the confessor, and that in such case his sins are remitted. The words which the minister is to make use of on this occasion are, 'May God be propitious to thee, and confirm thy faith; be it unto thee as thou believest, and I, by the commandment of the Lord, remit to thee thy sins:' but others say, 'I announce to thee the remission of thy sins:' that still, however, sins are not forgiven by repentance any more than by works; but by faith. Therefore, the repentance of the clergy is only a confession before God that they are sinners, and a prayer that they may persevere in faith. That expiations and satisfactions are not necessary, because Christ is expiation and satisfaction.

"VI. On Original Sin, they teach: That after the fall of Adam all men propagated according to nature born in sin, that is, without the fear of God, and with concupiscences; and that this condemns and brings eternal death upon those who are not born again by baptism and the Holy Spirit: that it is a privation of original righteousness, and at the same time an inordinate disposition of the parts of the soul, and a corrupt habit. That there is a difference between the nature itself into which man was created, which exists even after the fall, and remains a creature of God, and original sin; therefore, that there is a difference between corrupt nature, and the corruption which is inherent in nature, and by which nature is corrupt: that no one but God alone can separate the corruption of nature from nature itself; that this will manifestly be done in the blessed resurrection, because then nature itself, which encloses man in this world, will rise again without original sin, and enjoy eternal felicity; that the difference is as great as between the work of God and the work of the devil; that this sin did not invade nature in such a manner, as if Satan had created any evil substantially and commixed it with nature, but that concreate and original righteousness was lost: that original sin is an accident; and that by reason of it, man is, as it were, spiritually dead before God: that this evil is covered and pardoned by Christ alone: that the seed itself from which man is formed, is contaminated with that sin: that hence also it is, that man receives from his parents depraved inclinations and internal uncleanness of heart.

"VII. On Baptism. That baptism is not simply water, but that it is water taken by the divine command, and sealed with the Word of God, and thus sanctified: that the virtue, work, fruit, and end of baptism is, that men may be saved, and admitted into the Christian communion. That by baptism victory is offered over death and the devil; remission of sins; the grace of God; Christ with all his works; and the Holy Spirit with all his gifts; and eternal blessedness to all and every believer. Whether faith be given to infants, also, by baptism, is a question too deep to be solicitously inquired into. That immersion in water signifies the mortification of the old man, and the resurrection of the new; that therefore it may be called the laver of regeneration; and the true laver in the Word; also in the death and burial of Christ. That the life of a Christian is a daily baptism once begun in this manner: that the water does not effect this, but the Word of God, which is in and with the water, and the faith of God's Word added to the water; that hence it follows, that baptism in the name of God, is performed by men indeed, but is not from them, but from God himself. That baptism does not take away original sin, by extinguishing evil concupiscence, but only the guilt of it.

"But others of the Reformed believe, that baptism is an external laver of water, whereby an internal ablution from sin is signified; that it does not confer regeneration, faith, the grace of God, and salvation, but only signifies and seals them; and that they are not conferred in and with baptism, but afterwards as the person grows up; and that the elect alone obtain the grace of Christ and the gift of faith: and because salvation does not depend upon baptism, that therefore it is permitted to be performed by another for want of a regular minister.

"VIII. ON THE LORD'S SUPPER. They of the Reformed Church, who are called Lutherans, teach that in the holy supper or sacrament of the altar, the body and blood of Christ are really and substantially present, and are actually distributed and received with the bread and wine; that therefore the real body and the real blood of Christ are in, with, and under the bread and wine, and are given to Christians to eat and drink; and that therefore they are not simply bread and wine, but are included and bound in the Word of God, and that this causes them to be the body and blood of Christ; for when the Word accedes to the element, it becomes a sacrament; but yet that there is no transubstantiation, such as is that of the papists: that it is the food of the soul, nourishing and strengthening the new man: that it was instituted, to the end that faith might repair and receive its strength, to give remission of sins, and a new life, which Christ merited for us: that thus the body and blood of Christ are not only taken spiritually by faith, but also by the mouth, in a supernatural way, by reason of their sacramental union with the bread and wine: that the worthiness of this supper consists in obedience alone, and in the merit of Christ, which is applied by true faith. In a word, that the sacraments of the Lord's supper and of baptism, are testimonies of the will and grace of God towards men; and that the sacrament of the supper is a promise of remission of sins through faith; that it may move the heart to believe; and that the Holy Spirit may operate through the Word and the sacraments: that the consecration of the minister does not produce these effects, but that they are to be attributed to the sole omnipotent virtue of the Lord. That the unworthy, as well as the worthy, receive the real body and blood of Christ, as it hung upon the cross; but the worthy to salvation, the unworthy to condemnation; that they are worthy who have faith: that no one is to be forced to that supper, but every one may approach when urged by spiritual hunger.

"Others, however, of the Reformed Church teach, that in the holy supper the body and blood of Christ are only taken spiritually, and that the bread and wine are only signs, types, symbols, marks, figures, and similitudes; that Christ is not bodily present, but only in virtue and operation from his Divine Essence; but that in heaven there is a conjunction according to the communication of idioms: that the worthiness of this supper depends not only upon faith, but also upon preparation: that the worthy alone receive its virtue, but the unworthy bread and wine only. Although there are these disagreements in sentiment, yet all the Reformed agree in this: that it is altogether necessary that they should do the work of repentance, who desire to receive that holy supper worthily; the Lutherans insist that if they do not do repentance from evil works, and yet approach, they are eternally condemned; and the English, that otherwise the devil will enter into them as he did into Judas; this is evident from the prayers read before the communion.

"IX. On Free Will. They make a distinction between the state before the fall, after the fall, after the reception of faith and renovation, and after the resurrection. That man since the fall is entirely incapable of beginning, thinking, understanding, believing, willing, operating or co-operating any thing from his own power in matters of a spiritual and divine nature; or of applying or accommodating himself to grace; but that his natural will is only for those things which are contrary to God, and displease him; therefore that man in spiritual things is like a stock, but that still he has a capacity, not active, but passive, whereby he can be turned to good by the grace of God; that nevertheless there remains in man since the fall, the free-will and power either to hear or not to hear the Word of God, and that thus a spark of faith may be kindled in his heart, which embraces the remission of sins for Christ's sake, and imparts consolation. That nevertheless the human will enjoys the liberty of performing civil righteousness, and of making choice of such things as are within the province of reason.

"X. On the Church. That the church is the congregation and communion of saints, and that it is dispersed over the whole world among those who have the same Christ, and the same Holy Spirit, and the same sacraments, whether they have sin ilar or dissimilar traditions: and that it is principally a society of faith; and that this church alone is the body of Christ, and that the good are both really and nominally a church, but the wicked only nominally: that the wicked and hypocrites, because they are intermixed, are members of the church according to its external signs, provided they are not excommunicated, but that they are not members of the body of Christ. That ecclesiastical rites, which are called ceremonies, are matters of indifference (*adiaphori*), and that they are not the worship of God, nor a part of the worship of God; that therefore the church is at liberty to institute, change, and abrogate them, as, for instance, the distinctions of vestments, times, days, meats, and the like; and that therefore one church ought not to condemn another on account of things of this nature."

These are the doctrines of the Reformed Church and Religion in the abstract; but those which are taught by the Schwengfeldians, Pelagians, Manichæans, Donatists, Anabaptists, Arminians, Cinglians, Antitrinitarians, Socinians, Arians, and, at this day, by the Quakers and Moravians, are passed over, because they are reprobated and rejected by the Reformed Church as heretical.

THE APOCALYPSE.

CHAPTER I.

1. THE Revelation of Jesus Christ, which God gave unto him, to show unto his servants things which must shortly come to pass; and he signified [it] sending, by his angel, to his servant John,

2. Who bore witness of the Word of God, and of the testimony of Jesus Christ, whatsoever things he saw.

3. Blessed is he that readeth, and they that hear, the words of the prophecy, and keep those things which are written therein: for the time is at hand.

4. John to the seven churches which are in Asia: Grace be unto you, and peace, from Him who is, and who was, and who is to come; and from the seven spirits which are before his throne;

5. And from Jesus Christ, who is the faithful witness, the first-begotten from the dead, and the prince of the kings of the earth. To him that loved us, and washed us from our sins in his blood,

6. And hath made us kings and priests unto God and his Father: to him be glory and might for ever and ever. Amen.

7. Behold he cometh with clouds, and every eye shall see him, and they [also] who pierced him: and all the tribes of the earth shall wail because of him. Even so; Amen.

8. I am the Alpha and the Omega, the beginning and the end, saith the Lord, who is, and who was, and who is to come, the Almighty.

9. I John, who also am your brother, and companion in tribulation, and in the kingdom and patience of Jesus Christ, was in the island called Patmos, for the Word of God, and for the testimony of Jesus Christ.

10. I was in the spirit on the Lord's day; and I heard behind me a great voice, as of a trumpet,

11. Saying, I am the Alpha and the Omega, the First and the Last: and, what thou seest, write in a book, and send [it]

to the churches which are in Asia; unto Ephesus, and unto Smyrna, and unto Pergamos, and unto Thyatira, and unto Sardis, and unto Philadelphia, and unto Laodicea.

12. And I turned to see the voice that spoke with me: And, being turned, I saw seven golden candlesticks;

13. And in the midst of the seven candlesticks one like unto the Son of Man, clothed with a garment down to the foot, and girt about the paps with a golden girdle.

14. And his head and his hairs were white as wool is white, like unto snow; and his eyes were as a flame of fire;

15. And his feet were like unto fine brass, as if they burned in a furnace; and his voice as the voice of many waters.

16. And he had in his right hand seven stars; and out of his mouth went a sharp two-edged sword; and his face was as the sun shineth in his power.

17. And when I saw him, I fell at his feet as dead. And he laid his right hand upon me, saying unto me, Fear not; I am the First and the Last;

18. And am he that liveth, and was dead; and behold I am alive for ever and ever. Amen: and I have the keys of hell and of death.

19. Write the things which thou hast seen, and the things which are, and the things which shall be hereafter.

20. The mystery of the seven stars which thou sawest in my right hand, and the seven golden candlesticks. The seven stars are the angels of the seven churches; and the seven candlesticks, which thou sawest, are the seven churches.

THE SPIRITUAL SENSE.

THE CONTENTS OF THE WHOLE CHAPTER. That this revelation is from the Lord alone, and that it will be received by those who will be in his new church, which is the New Jerusalem, and acknowledge the Lord as the God of heaven and earth; the Lord is also described as to the Word.

THE CONTENTS OF EACH VERSE. V. 1, "The Revelation of Jesus Christ," signifies predictions from the Lord concerning himself and his church, what the latter will be in its end, and what it will be afterwards: "Which God gave unto him to show unto his servants," signifies for the use of those who are in faith originating in charity: "Things which must shortly come to pass," signifies that they will certainly be, lest the church perish: "And he signified.[it], sending, by his angel, to his servant John, signifies the things which are revealed from the Lord through heaven, to those who are in the good of life from charity and its faith: v. 2, "Who bore witness of the Word of God, and of the testimony of Jesus Christ," signifies who from the heart, and so in the light, receive divine truth from the Word, and acknowledge the Lord's Humanity to be divine: "Whatsoever things he saw," signifies their illustration in all the things which are in this revelation: v. 3, "Blessed is he that readeth, and they that hear, the words of the prophecy, and keep those things which are written therein," signifies the communion of those with the angels of heaven, who live according to the doctrines of the New Jerusalem: "For the time is at hand," signifies that the state of the church is such that it cannot endure any longer, so as to have conjunction with the Lord: v. 4, "John to the seven churches," signifies to all who are in the Christian world where the Word is, and by it the Lord is known, and who accede to the church: "Which are in Asia," signifies to those who are in the light of truth from the Word: "Grace be unto you, and peace," signifies divine salutation: "From Him who is, and who was, and who is to come," signifies from the Lord who is eternal and infinite, and who is Jehovah: "And from the seven spirits which are before his throne," signifies from the universal heaven, where the Lord is in his divine truth: v. 5, "And from Jesus Christ," signifies the Divine Humanity: "Who is the faithful witness," signifies that he is Divine Truth itself: "The first-begotten from the dead," signifies that he is Divine Goodness itself: "And the prince of the kings of the earth," signifies from whom proceeds all truth originating in good in the church: "To him that loved us, and washed us from our sins in his blood," signifies who, out of love and mercy, reforms and regenerates men by his divine truths from the Word: v. 6, "And hath made us kings and priests," signifies who gives those who are born of him, that is regenerated, to be in wisdom from divine truths, and in love from divine goods: "Unto God and his Father," signifies, and so images of his divine wisdom and of his divine love: "To him be glory and might for ever and ever," signifies, to whom alone belongs divine majesty and divine omnipotence to eternity: "Amen," signifies divine confirmation from the truth, thus from himself: v. 7, "Behold, he cometh with clouds," signifies that the Lord will reveal himself in the literal sense of the Word, and will open its spiritual sense at the end of the church: "And every eye shall see him," signifies that all who are in the understanding of divine truth from affection will acknowledge him: "And they [also] who pierced him," signifies that they also will see who are in falses in the church: "And all the tribes of the earth shall wail because of him," signifies that this will be when there are no longer any goods and truths in the church:

"Even so, Amen," signifies divine confirmation that so it will be: v. 8, "I am the Alpha and the Omega, the beginning and the end," signifies who is the self-subsisting and the only-subsisting from first principles to ultimates, from whom all things proceed; thus, who is the self-subsisting and only-subsisting love, the self-subsisting and only-subsisting wisdom, and the self-subsisting and only-subsisting life in himself; and consequently the self-subsisting Creator, Saviour, and Illuminator, from himself, and thence the All in all of heaven and the church: "Saith the Lord, who is, and who was, and who is to come," signifies, who is eternal and infinite, and who is Jehovah: "The Almighty," signifies, who is, lives, and has power from himself, and who governs all things from first principles by ultimates: v. 9, "I, John, who also am your brother, and companion," signifies those who are in the good of charity, and thence in the truths of faith: "In tribulation, and in the kingdom and patience of Jesus Christ," signifies, which in the church are infested by evils and falses, but which will be removed by the Lord at his coming: "Was in the isle called Patmos," signifies a state and place in which he could be illuminated: "For the Word of God, and for the testimony of Jesus Christ," signifies that divine truth from the Word might be received at heart and so in the light, and that the Lord's Humanity might be acknowledged to be divine: v. 10, "I was in the spirit on the Lord's day," signifies a spiritual state at that time from divine influx: "And I heard behind me a great voice as of a trumpet," signifies a manifest perception of divine truth revealed from heaven: v. 11, "Saying, I am the Alpha and the Omega, the First and the Last," signifies who is the self-subsisting and the only-subsisting from first principles, from whom all things proceed, &c., as above: "And what thou seest, write in a book," signifies that it may be revealed to posterity: "And send to the churches which are in Asia," signifies for those who are in the Christian world who are in the light of truth from the Word: "Unto Ephesus, and unto Smyrna, and unto Pergamos, and unto Thyatira, and unto Sardis, and unto Philadelphia, and unto Laodicea," signifies specifically according to the state of reception of each: v. 12, "And I turned to see the voice that spoke with me," signifies inversion of the state of those who are in good of life, with respect to the perception of truth in the Word, when they turn themselves to the Lord: "And being turned, I saw seven golden candlesticks," signifies the New Church, which will be in illustration from the Lord out of the Word: v. 13, "And in the midst of the seven candlesticks one like unto the Son of Man," signifies the Lord as to the Word, from whom that church is: "Clothed with a garment down to the foot," signifies the proceeding divine which is divine truth: "And girt about the paps with a golden girdle," signifies the proceeding, and at the same time, conjoining divine, which is divine good: v. 14, "And his head and his hairs were white as wool is white, like unto snow," signifies the divine love of the divine wisdom in first principles and in ultimates: "And his eyes were as a flame of fire," signifies the divine wisdom of the divine love: v. 15, "And his feet were like unto fine brass, as if they burned in a furnace," signifies divine good natural: "And his voice as the voice of many waters," signifies divine truth natural: v. 16, "And he had in his right hand seven stars," signifies all knowledges of goodness and truth in the Word from him: "And out of his mouth went a sharp two-edged sword," signifies the dispersion of falses by the Word, and by doctrine thence from the Lord: "And his face was as the sun shineth in his power," signifies the Divine Love and the Divine Wisdom, which are himself, and proceed from himself: v. 17, "And when I saw him, I fell at his feet as dead," signifies a defect of his own life from such presence of the Lord: "And he laid his right hand upon me," signifies life then inspired from him: "Saying unto me, Fear not," signifies resuscitation, and at the same time adoration from the most profound humiliation: "I am the First and the Last," signifies that he is eternal and infinite, therefore the only God: v. 18, "And am he that liveth," signifies who alone is life, and from whom alone life is: "And was dead," signifies that he was neglected in the church, and his Divine Humanity not acknowledged: "And behold, I am alive for ever and ever," signifies that he is life eternal: "Amen," signifies divine confirmation that this is truth: "And I have the keys of hell and death," signifies that he alone has power to save: v. 19, "Write the things which thou hast seen, and the things which are, and the things which shall be hereafter," signifies that all the things which are now revealed, are for the use of posterity: v. 20, "The mystery of the seven stars which thou sawest in my right hand, and the seven golden candlesticks," signifies arcana in visions concerning the new heaven and the new church: "The seven stars are the angels of the seven churches," signifies the new church in the heavens, which is the new heaven: "And the seven candlesticks which thou sawest, are the seven churches," signifies the New Church upon earth, which is the New Jerusalem descending from the Lord out of the new heaven.

THE EXPLANATION.

1. What the spiritual sense is, has hitherto been unknown. That there is such a sense in every particular of the Word, is shown in *the Doctrine of the New Jerusalem concerning the Sacred Scriptures*, n. 5—26, and that without it, the Word in many places cannot be understood: this sense does not appear in the literal sense, for it is in it as the soul in its body. It is well known, that there is what is spiritual, and what is natural, and that what is spiritual flows into what is natural, and renders itself visible and sensible in those forms which are the objects of sight and touch, and that what is spiritual, without such forms, is perceived no otherwise than as affection and thought, or as love and wisdom which are of the mind: that affection and thought, or love whose property it is to be affected, and wisdom whose property it is to think, are spiritual, is acknowledged; that these two faculties of the mind show themselves in the body in forms, which are called organs of sense and motion, is well known; also, that they make a one, and such a one as that what the mind thinks, that the mouth in an instant speaks, and what the mind wills, that the body in an instant does; hence it is evident, that there is a perfect union of things spiritual and natural in man. It is the same with every thing in the world, both generally and particularly; there is in them something spiritual, which is the inmost of the cause, and something natural, which is its effect, and these two make a one; and what is spiritual does not appear in what is natural, because it dwells in it as the soul in its body, and as the inmost of the cause in the effect, as was observed before. It is the same with the Word; that this is internally spiritual, because it is divine, cannot be denied by any one; but as what is spiritual does not appear in the sense of the letter, which is natural, therefore the spiritual sense has hitherto been unknown; nor could it have been known before genuine truths were revealed by the Lord, for in these that sense consists. For this reason the Apocalypse has not been understood before. But lest any doubt should remain, that such things are contained in it, the particulars must be explained, and demonstrated by similar passages in other parts of the Word. The explanation and demonstration now follow.

2. *The revelation of Jesus Christ*, signifies predictions from the Lord concerning himself and his church, what the latter will be in its end, and what it will be afterwards, as well in the heavens as upon earth. By the revelation of Jesus Christ are signified all predictions, which coming from the Lord, are called the revelation of Jesus Christ; that they relate to the Lord and his church, will appear from the explanations. The

Apocalypse does not treat of the successive states of the church, much less of the successive states of kingdoms, as some have hitherto believed, but from beginning to end it treats of the last state of the church in heaven and earth; and then concerning the last judgment; and after this the New Church, which is the New Jerusalem. That this New Church is the end and object of this work, is very evident, wherefore those things which are first mentioned refer to the state of the church, as to its quality immediately antecedent to its appearance. But in what series these matters are treated of, may be seen from the contents of each chapter; and more distinctly from the explanation of each particular verse.

3. *Which God gave unto him to show unto his servants*, signifies, for those who are in faith derived from charity, or in truths of wisdom derived from the good of love. By showing is signified to manifest, and by servants are here signified those who are in faith derived from charity; to them these things are manifested, because they understand and receive them: by servants, in a spiritual sense, are understood those who are in truths; and because truths originate in good, by servants are understood those who are in truths derived from good, therefore also, those who are in wisdom derived from love, because wisdom is of truth, and love is of good; also those who are in faith derived from charity, because faith also is of truth and charity is of good; and since the genuine spiritual sense is abstracted from person, therefore in it by servants are signified truths. Now truths being subservient to good by their teaching it, therefore, in general, and properly, by servant, in the Word, is meant what is subservient, or he or that which serves; in this sense not only the prophets are called the servants of God, but also the Lord as to his Humanity; that the prophets are called the servants of God, is evident from the following passages: "Jehovah hath sent unto you all his servants the prophets," Jer. xxv. 4. "He revealeth his secrets unto his servants the prophets," Amos iii. 7. "His laws which he set before us by his servants the prophets," Dan. ix. 10; and Moses is called "the servant of Jehovah," Malachi iii. 22;[*] the reason is because by a prophet in the spiritual sense is understood truth of doctrine, as explained below. And because the Lord was divine truth itself, which also is the Word, and is thence called the Prophet; and served in the world, and serves all to eternity by his teaching, therefore, he also, in many places, is called the servant of Jehovah; as in the following: "He shall see of the travail of his soul, and shall be satisfied; by his

---

[*] In the Hebrew Bible there are only three chapters in Malachi, and as our author quotes from the Hebrew text, it may be necessary to observe, that this text in our version is chap. iv. 4. In all like instances we shall alter it to the state of the English text.—EDITORS.

knowledge shall my righteous servant justify many," Isaiah liii. 11. "Behold, my servant shall deal prudently, he shall be exalted and extolled, and be very high," Isaiah lii. 13. "Behold, my servant, whom I uphold, mine elect, in whom my soul delighteth, I have put my spirit upon him," Isaiah xlii. 1, 19; this is spoken of the Lord: in like manner David is called a servant, where, by him, the Lord is understood; as in the following passages: "And I the Lord will be their God, and my servant David a prince among them," Ezek. xxxiv. 24. "David, my servant, shall be king over them, that they all shall have one shepherd," Ezek. xxxvii. 24. "I will defend this city to save it, for mine own sake, and for my servant David's sake," Isaiah xxxvii. 35. So also in Psalm lxxviii. 70—72, lxxxix. 3, 4, 20. That by David in these places is meant the Lord, may be seen in the *Doctrine of the New Jerusalem concerning the Lord*, n. 43, 44. The Lord himself says the same of himself: "Whosoever will be great among you, let him be your minister, and whosover will be chief among you, let him be your servant, even as the Son of man came not to be ministered unto, but to minister," Matt. xx. 26, 28, Mark x. 43—45, Luke xxii. 27, and so in Luke xii. 37. This the Lord says, because by servant and minister is understood one who serves and ministers by teaching, and, abstracted from person, divine truth, which was himself. Since, therefore, by servant is understood he who teaches divine truth, it is evident that by servants in this place in the Apocalypse are meant those who are in truths derived from good, or in faith derived from charity, because these can teach from the Lord, that is, the Lord can teach and minister by them. In this sense they are called servants in Matthew: "In the consummation of the age, who then is a faithful and wise servant, whom his Lord hath made ruler over his household, to give them their meat in due season: blessed is that servant whom his Lord when he cometh shall find so doing," xxiv. 45. And in Luke: "Blessed are those servants, whom the Lord when he cometh shall find watching: verily, I say unto you, that he shall gird himself, and make them to sit down to meat, and will come forth and serve them," xii. 37. In heaven all are called servants of the Lord, who are in his spiritual kingdom; but they who are in his celestial kingdom are called ministers; the reason is, because they who are in his spiritual kingdom, are in wisdom from divine truth; and they who are in his celestial kingdom are in love from divine good; and good ministers and truth serves. But in an opposite sense, by servants are meant those who serve the devil; these are in a state of real servitude; but they who serve the Lord are in a state of liberty; as the Lord also teaches in John viii. 32—36.

4. *Things which must shortly come to pass*, signifies that

they will certainly be, lest the church perish. By coming to pass shortly, is not meant that the things which are foretold in the Apocalypse, will happen immediately and speedily, but certainly; and that unless they do happen the church must perish. In the divine idea, and thence in the spiritual sense, there is no time, but instead of time, there is state; and because shortly relates to time, by it is signified certainly, and that it will come to pass before its time; for the Apocalypse was given in the first century, and since that seventeen centuries have now elapsed, from which it is evident, that by shortly is signified that which corresponds to it, and that is, certainly. The like is also involved in these words of the Lord: "Except those days should be shortened, there should no flesh be saved; but for the elect's sake, those days shall be shortened," Matt. xxiv. 22: by which also is understood, that except the church should come to an end before its time, it would totally perish; in that chapter the consummation of the age and the Lord's coming are treated of; and by the consummation of the age is meant the last state of the old church, and by the Lord's coming, the first state of the new. It was observed that in the divine idea there is no time, but a presence of all things past and future; wherefore it is said by David, "A thousand years in thy sight are but as yesterday," Psalm xc. 4: and again, "I will declare the decree, Jehovah hath said unto me, Thou art my son, this day have I begotten thee," Psalm ii. 7: this day denotes the presence of the Lord's advent. Thence also it is, that an entire period is called day in the Word, and its first state the dawning and the morning, and its last evening and night.

5. *And he signified [it], sending by his angel to his servant John*, signifies the things which are revealed from the Lord through heaven, to those who are in the good of life derived from charity and its faith. By signified [it], sending by his angel, in the spiritual sense, is meant things revealed from heaven, or through heaven from the Lord: for by angel in the Word is everywhere understood the angelic heaven, and in a supreme sense the Lord himself; the reason is, because no angel ever speaks with man in a state of separation from heaven; for there is such a conjunction of each individual with all in heaven, that every one speaks from the communion, although the angel is not conscious of it: for heaven in the sight of the Lord is as one man, whose soul is the Lord himself; wherefore the Lord speaks with man through heaven, as man does from his soul through his body with another; and this is done in conjunction with all and every thing of his mind, in the midst of which are the things which he speaks; but this arcanum cannot be unfolded in a few words; it is partly unfolded in *The Angelic Wisdom concerning the Divine Love and the Divine Wisdom:* hence it is evident, that by angel is signified heaven, and in

a supreme sense the Lord. The reason why by angel the Lord is understood in a supreme sense, is, because heaven is not heaven from any thing proper to the angels, but from the divine of the Lord,* from which is derived their love and wisdom, yea their life; hence it is that the Lord himself is called an angel in the Word. From these considerations it appears that the angel did not speak from himself with John; but the Lord out of the midst of heaven by him. By these words is meant, that this is revealed to those who are in the good of life derived from charity and its faith, because these are understood by John; for by the twelve disciples or apostles of the Lord, are understood all who are of the church in truths from good; and in an abstract sense, all things of the church; and by Peter, all who are in faith, and, abstractedly, faith itself; by James, they who are in charity, and, abstractedly, charity itself; and by John, they who are in the good of life from charity and its faith, and, abstractedly, good of life itself derived thence: that these things are meant by John, James, and Peter in the Word of the evangelists, may be seen in a *Treatise concerning the New Jerusalem and its Heavenly Doctrine*, n. 122. Since good of life, grounded in charity and its faith, constitutes the church, therefore, by the apostle John were revealed the arcana concerning the state of the church which are contained in his visions. That by all the names of persons and places in the Word are signified things of heaven and the church, is abundantly shown in the *Arcana Cœlestia*. From these considerations it may appear, that by signified [it], sending by his angel to his servant John, is understood, in the spiritual sense, what is revealed by the Lord through heaven to those who are in the good of life derived from charity and its faith; for charity through faith operates good, and not charity by itself, nor faith by itself.

6. *Who bore witness of the Word of God, and the testimony of Jesus Christ*, signifies who, from their heart, and so in the light, receive divine truth from the Word, and acknowledge the Lord's Humanity to be divine. It is said of John that he bore witness of the Word of God; but as by John are meant all who are principled in good of life from charity and its faith, as was said above, n. 5, therefore in the spiritual sense all these are understood: the angels, who are in the spiritual sense of the Word, never know any name of a person mentioned in the Word, but only that which the person represents and thence signifies, which, instead of John, is good of life, or good in act; consequently all in the aggregate who are in that good: these witness, that is, see, acknowledge, receive cordially in light, and confess the truths of the Word, especially that truth therein

---

* The words of our author, *Divino Domini*, may require the terms *sphere*, or *influence*, or *Holy Spirit*, to give them their full meaning: which the intelligent reader can apply, or not, as he thinks best.

that the Lord's Humanity is divine; which may appear from the passages quoted from the Word in great abundance in the *Doctrine of the New Jerusalem concerning the Lord*. By Jesus Christ and by the Lamb in the Apocalypse is understood, the Lord as to the Divine Humanity, and by God, the Lord as to his Divinity, from which are all things. With regard to the spiritual signification of *witnessing* or *testifying*, this is predicated of truth, because in the world the truth is to be testified or witnessed, and when it is testified, it is acknowledged; but in heaven truth testifies of itself because it is itself the light of heaven; for when the angels hear the truth, they instantly know and acknowledge it; and because the Lord is truth itself, as he himself teaches in John xiv. 6, he is in heaven the testimony of himself; hence it may appear, what is meant by the testimony of Jesus Christ; wherefore the Lord saith, "Ye sent unto John, and he bare witness unto the truth; but I receive not testimony from man," John v. 33; and in another place: "John came for a witness, to bear witness of the light; he was not that light; the Word which was with God, and was God, and was made flesh, was the true light, which lighteth every man," John i. 1, 2, 7, 8, 14, 34; and in another place: "Jesus said, Though I bare record of myself, yet my record is true, for I know whence I came, and whither I go," John viii. 14. "When the Comforter is come, even the spirit of truth, he shall testify of me," John xv. 26; by the Comforter, the spirit of truth, is meant the truth itself proceeding from the Lord, wherefore it is said of him, that he will not speak from himself, but from the Lord, John xvi. 13, 14, 15.

7. *Whatsoever things he saw*, signifies their illumination in all the things which are in this revelation. By whatsoever things he saw, in the spiritual sense, are not meant the things which John saw, for they were only visions, but the things which they see who are understood by John, who are such as are principled in good of life, grounded in charity and its faith, as was said above; these see in the visions of John, arcana concerning the state of the church, not so much when they read themselves, but when they see them revealed. To see signifies to understand; on this account in common discourse it is said, that any one sees a thing, and that he sees that it is a truth; for sight pertains as much to a man's spirit as to his body; but man with his spirit sees spiritual things, because from the light of heaven, but with his body he sees natural things, because this sees from the light of the world, and spiritual things are real things, but natural things are their forms: it is the spiritual sight of man which is called intellect. It is, therefore, evident what is meant, in the spiritual sense, by whatsoever things he saw; in like manner in what follows, where it is said that he saw them

8. *Blessed is he that readeth, and they that hear the words of the prophecy, and keep those things which are written therein*, signifies the communion of those with the angels of heaven, who live according to the doctrines of the New Jerusalem. By blessed, is here meant one who, as to his spirit, is in heaven; thus, one who, while he lives in the world, is in communion with the angels of heaven: for such a one, as to his spirit, is in heaven; by the words of this prophecy nothing else is understood than the doctrine of the New Jerusalem, for by prophet, in an abstract sense, is signified the doctrine of the church derived from the Word, thus here the doctrine of the New Church, which is the New Jerusalem; the same is signified by prophecy. By reading, hearing, and keeping the things which are written therein, is signified, to desire to know that doctrine; to attend to the things which are written in it, and to do them; in short, to live according to it: that they are not blessed who only read, hear and keep or retain in the memory the things which were seen by John, is clear, see below, n. 944. The reason why prophet signifies the doctrine of the church derived from the Word, and prophecy the same, is, because the Word was written by prophets, and in heaven a person is regarded according to that which belongs to his function and office; according to this, also, is every man, spirit, and angel, named in heaven; wherefore, when the word prophet is used, his function being to write and teach the Word, the Word is understood as to doctrine, or doctrine derived from the Word. Hence it is, that the Lord, being the Word itself, was called a prophet, Deut. xviii. 15—20, Matt. xiii. 57, chap. xxi. 1, Luke xiii. 33. To show, that by prophet is meant doctrine of the church derived from the Word, some passages shall be adduced, from which this may be collected. In Matthew: " In the consummation of the age many false *prophets* shall arise, and shall deceive many. There shall arise false Christs and false *prophets*, and, if it were possible, they shall deceive the very elect," xxiv. 11, 24; the consummation of the age is the last time of the church, which is at hand, when there are not false *prophets*, but false principles of doctrine. In the same: " He that receiveth a *prophet* in the name of a *prophet*, shall receive a *prophet's* reward; and he that receiveth a righteous man in the name of a righteous man, shall receive a righteous man's reward," x. 41; to receive a prophet in the name of a prophet, is to receive the doctrine of truth because it is true: and to receive a righteous man in the name of a righteous man, is to receive good for the sake of good; and to receive a reward, is to be saved according to reception; it is evident that no one receives a reward, or is saved, because he receives a prophet and a righteous man in the name of such. Those words cannot be understood by any one, without knowing what a prophet and a righteous man signify;

neither can the following: "That whosoever shall give to drink unto one of these little ones a cup of cold water only, in the name of a disciple, shall in no wise lose his reward;" by disciple is understood charity, and at the same time faith from the Lord. In Joel: "I will pour out my spirit upon all flesh, and your sons and your daughters shall *prophesy*," chap. ii. 28; speaking of the church which was to be established by the Lord, in which they would not prophesy, but receive doctrine, which is to prophesy. In Matthew: "Jesus said, Many will say to me in that day, Lord, Lord, have we not *prophesied* in thy name? but then will I profess unto them, I never knew you; depart from me, ye that work iniquity," chap. vii. 22, 23; who does not see, that they would not say that they have prophesied, but that they knew the doctrine of the church, and taught it? In the Apocalypse: "The time is come that the dead should be judged, and that thou shouldest give reward unto thy servants the *prophets*," chap. xi. 18; and in another place, "Rejoice over her, thou heaven, and ye holy apostles and *prophets*, for God hath avenged you on her," chap. xviii. 20: that a reward would not be given to the prophets alone, and that the apostles and prophets would not alone rejoice at the last judgment, is evident; but all who have received truths of doctrine, and have lived according to them; these, therefore, are understood by apostles and prophets. So in Moses: "Jehovah said unto Moses, See, I have made thee a god of Pharaoh, and Aaron thy brother shall be thy *prophet*," Exod. vii. 1: by God is understood divine truth as to reception from the Lord, in which sense the angels are also called gods, and by prophet is understood one who teaches and utters it, therefore Aaron is here called a prophet. The same is signified by prophet in other places, as in the following: "The law shall not perish from the priest, nor counsel from the wise, nor the Word from the *prophet*," Jerem. xviii. 18. "From the *prophets* of Jerusalem is profaneness gone forth into all the land," Jerem. xxiii. 15. "The *prophets* shall become wind, and the Word is not in them," Jerem. v. 13. "The priest and the *prophet* have erred through strong drink, they are swallowed up of wine, they stumble in judgment," Isaiah xxviii. 7. "The sun shall go down over the *prophets*, and the day shall be dark over them," Micah iii. 6. "From the *prophet* even unto the priest, every one dealeth falsely," Jerem. viii. 10; in these passages, by prophets and priests, in the spiritual sense, are not meant prophets and priests, but the universal church; by prophets, the church as to truth of doctrine, and by priests, the church as to good of life, both which were destroyed; these things are so understood by the angels in heaven; while, by men in the world, they are understood according to the sense of the letter. That the prophets represented the state of the church as to doctrine, and that the Lord represented it as to the Word itself, may be seen in *The Doctrine of the New Jerusalem concerning the Lord*, n. 15—17.

9. *For the time is at hand*, signifies that the state of the church is such, that it cannot endure any longer, so as to be in conjunction with the Lord. There are two essentials by which conjunction with the Lord, and thence salvation is effected, *the acknowledgment of one God*, and *repentance of life*; but at this day, instead of the acknowledgment of one God, there is an acknowledgment of three, and instead of repentance of life, there is only an oral confession of sin; and by these two there is not any conjunction: unless, therefore, a new church should arise, which acknowledges these two essentials, and lives accordingly, no one can be saved; on account of this danger the time is shortened by the Lord, according to his own words in Matthew: "For then shall be great tribulation, such as was not since the beginning of the world to this time, no, nor ever shall be; and except those days should be shortened, there should be no flesh saved," xxiv. 21, 22. That nearness of time, or its being at hand, is not understood, may be seen below, n. 947.

10. *John to the seven churches*, signifies to all who are in the Christian world where the Word is, and by it the Lord is known, and who accede to the church. By the seven churches are not to be understood seven churches, but all who are of the church in the Christian world; for numbers, in the Word, signify things, and seven, all things and all, and thence, also, what is full and perfect, and it occurs in the Word where any thing holy is treated of, and, in an opposite sense, where it treats of any thing profane; consequently, this number involves what is holy, and, in an opposite sense, what is profane. The reason why numbers signify things, or rather resemble certain adjectives to substantives denoting some quality in things, is, because number is, in itself, natural; for natural things are determined by numbers, but spiritual things by things and their states: therefore, he who is ignorant of the signification of numbers in the Word, and especially in the Apocalypse, must be ignorant of many arcana which are contained therein. Now, since seven signifies all things and all, it may appear that by seven churches are meant all who are in the Christian world where the Word is, and where consequently the Lord is known: these, if they live according to the Lord's precepts in the Word, constitute the true church. For this reason the sabbath was instituted on the *seventh* day, and the *seventh* year was called the sabbatarian year; and the *seven times seventh* year the jubilee, by which was signified every thing holy in the church: for this cause, also, a week, in Daniel, and elsewhere, signifies an entire period, from beginning to end, and is predicated of the church. The same is signified by seven in the following passages: as,

By the *seven* golden candlesticks, in the midst of which was one like unto the Son of Man, Apoc. i. 13. By the *seven* stars in his right hand, Apoc. i. 16, 20. By the *seven* spirits of God, Apoc. i. 4; iv. 5. By the *seven* lamps of fire, Apoc. iv. 5. By the *seven* angels, to whom were given *seven* trumpets, Apoc. viii. 2. By the *seven* angels having the *seven* last plagues, Apoc. xv. 6. By the *seven* vials full of the *seven* last plagues, Apoc. xvi. 1; xxi. 9. By the *seven* seals with which the book was sealed, Apoc. v. 1. In like manner in the following places: That their hands should be filled *seven* days, Exod. xxix. 35. That they should be sanctified *seven* days, Exod. xxix. 37. That when they were consecrated they should go clothed in the holy garments *seven* days, Exod. xxix. 30. That they were not to go out of the door of the tabernacle *seven* days, when they were initiated into the priesthood, Levit. viii. 33, 35. That an atonement was to be made *seven* times upon the horns of the altar, Levit. xvi. 18, 19. That the altar was to be sanctified with oil *seven* times, Levit. viii. 11. That the blood was to be sprinkled *seven* times before the vail, Levit. iv. 16, 17. And also *seven* times towards the east, Levit. xvi. 12—15. That the water of separation was to be sprinkled *seven* times towards the tabernacle, Numbers xix. 4. That the passover was celebrated *seven* days; and unleavened bread was eaten *seven* days, Exod. xii. 15; Deut. xvi. 4—7. In like manner, that the Jews were to be punished *seven* times more for their sins, Levit. xxvi. 18, 21, 24, 28. Wherefore David saith, Render unto our neighbour *seven-fold* into their bosom, Psalm lxxix. 12. Seven-fold is fully. Likewise in these places: "The words of Jehovah are pure words, as silver tried in a furnace of earth, purified *seven* times," Psalm xii. 6. "The hungry ceased, so that the barren hath borne *seven*, and she that hath many children is waxed feeble," 1 Sam. ii. 5. The barren is the church of the Gentiles, who had not the Word; she that had many children is the church of the Jews, who had the Word. "She who hath borne *seven* languisheth, she hath given up the ghost," Jerem. xv. 9. In like manner: "They that dwell in the cities of Israel shall go forth and set on fire and burn the weapons, and they shall burn them with fire *seven* years: they shall bury Gog, and *seven* months shall they be cleansing the land," Ezek. xxxix. 9, 12. "The unclean spirit will take with him *seven* spirits more wicked than himself," Matt. xii. 45. Profanation is here described, and by the seven spirits with which he would return, are signified all falses of evil; thus a plenary or total extinction of goodness and truth. By the *seven* heads of the dragon, and the *seven* crowns upon his head, Apoc. xii. 3, is signified the profanation of all goodness and truth. It is evident from what has been said, that seven involves what is holy or profane, and signifies all things and fulness.

11. *Which are in Asia*, signifies, to those who are in the light of truth from the Word. Since, by all the names of persons and places in the Word, things of heaven and the church are understood, as was before observed; so, therefore, Asia and the names of the seven churches therein, signify the same, as will appear from what follows. The reason why they who are in the light of truth from the Word, are understood by Asia, is, because the most ancient church, and, after it, the ancient, and then the Israelitish church, were established in Asia; also, because the ancient Word, and, after it, the Israelitish Word, was among them; and all the light of truth comes from the Word. That the ancient churches were in Asia, and that a Word which was afterwards lost, and lastly, the Word which is extant at this day, was among them, may be seen in *The Doctrine of the New Jerusalem concerning the Sacred Scripture*, n. 101, 102, 103. On this account it is, that by Asia are here signified all who are in the light of truth from the Word.

"Concerning this ancient Word, which was extant in Asia before the Israelitish Word, it is worth while to mention, that it is still preserved among the people who inhabit Great Tartary; I have conversed with spirits and angels in the spiritual world who came thence, who said that they possess a Word, and have possessed it from ancient times; and that in conformity to this Word, their divine worship is established; and that it consists of mere correspondences: they said that it contains the book of *Jasher*, which is mentioned in Joshua x. 12, 13, and 2 Sam. i. 17, 18, and also, that they possess the books mentioned by Moses, as *The Wars of Jehovah and the Propheticals*, Num. xxi. 14, 15, and 27—30; and when I read to them the words quoted thence by Moses, they examined whether they were extant there, and found them: from which circumstance it is very clear to me that the old Word is still preserved among them. In the course of the conversation, they said that they worship Jehovah, some as an invisible, and some as a visible God. Moreover they related that they do not suffer foreigners to come among them, except the Chinese, with whom they cultivate peace, because the emperor of China is from their country; and further, that they are so populous, that they do not believe any country in the world to be more so; which is very credible from the wall so many miles long, which the Chinese formerly built as a defence against any invasion from them. Seek for it in China, and peradventure you may find it there among the Tartars."

12. *Grace be unto you and peace*, signifies divine salutation. What is understood specifically by grace and peace, will be explained in what follows; that "peace be unto you" was the Lord's salutation to his disciples, thus the divine salutation, may be seen in Luke xxiv. 36, 37; John xx. 19, 20, 21; and

by command of the Lord, it was the salutation of the disciples to all to whom they should enter in, Matt. x. 11—13.

13. *From him who is, who was, and is to come*, signifies, from the Lord who is eternal and infinite, and who is Jehovah. That it is the Lord, appears clearly from what follows in this chapter, where it is said that he heard a voice from the Son of Man, saying, "I am the Alpha and the Omega, the First and the Last," verse 11, 13; and afterwards, "I am the First and the Last," verse 17; and in the following chapter, verse 8; and afterwards, chap. xxi. 6; xxii. 12; and in Isaiah: "Thus saith Jehovah, the King of Israel, and his Redeemer Jehovah of Hosts: I am the First, and I am the Last, and beside me there is no God," xliv. 6; also xlviii. 12; and he who is the First and the Last, is he who is, and who was, and who is to come. This also is to be understood by Jehovah; for the name of Jehovah signifies is, and he who is, or who is esse itself, the same is also he who was, and is to come, for in him the past and the future are present; hence he is without time eternal, and without place infinite: this also is acknowledged by the church in the Doctrine of the Trinity, called Athanasian, in which are these words: "The Father is eternal and infinite, the Son is eternal and infinite, and the Holy Spirit is eternal and infinite; but yet there are not three eternals and infinites, but one;" that this one is the Lord, is demonstrated in *The Doctrine of the New Jerusalem concerning the Lord.*

14. *And from the seven spirits which are before his throne*, signifies, from the universal heaven where the Lord is in his divine truth, and where his divine truth is received. By seven spirits are meant all who are in divine truth, and, in an abstract sense, the divine true or divine truth itself; that seven in the Word means all and every thing, may be seen above, n. 10; and that by throne is understood the universal heaven, will be seen presently; therefore by being before his throne, is meant where his divine truth is; for heaven is not heaven from any thing proper to the angels, but from the divine of the Lord, as is fully shown in *The Angelic Wisdom concerning the Divine Providence and the Divine Love.* That the Lord's throne signifies heaven, is evident from the following passages: "Thus saith Jehovah, Heaven is my *throne*," Isaiah lxvi. 1. "Jehovah hath prepared his *throne* in the heavens," Psalm ciii. 19. "He that sweareth by heaven, sweareth by the *throne* of God, and by him that sitteth thereon," Matt. xxiii. 22. "Above the firmament that was over the heads of the cherubim, was the likeness of a *throne*, as the appearance of a sapphire stone, and upon it the likeness as the appearance of a man," Ezek. i. 26; x. 1; by the firmament over the heads of the cherubim, is meant heaven; and in the Apocalypse: "To him that overcometh, will I grant to sit with me in my *throne*," iii. 21; in

my throne, is in heaven; specifically, where his divine truth reigns; thus also, where judgment is treated of, it is said, that the Lord will sit upon a throne, for judgment is performed by truths.

15. *And from Jesus Christ*, signifies the Divine Humanity. That by Jesus Christ and by the Lamb in the Word, is meant the Lord as to his Divine Humanity, may be seen above, n. 6.

16. *Who is the faithful witness*, signifies that he is Divine Truth itself. That witness is predicated of truth, and that the truth testifies of itself, thus the Lord, who is Divine Truth itself, and the Word, may be seen above, n. 6.

17. *The first-begotten from the dead*, signifies that he is Divine Goodness itself. What the first-begotten from the dead means, no one as yet knows; even the ancients disputed about the signification of it: they knew that by first-begotten is signified what is first and primary, from which is the all of the church; and it was believed by many, that it was truth in doctrine and in faith; but by few, that it was truth in act and operation, which is good of life. That this is the first and primary of the church, and thence in a strict sense is meant by first-begotten, will be seen presently; but first something shall be said on the opinion of those who believed, that truth in doctrine and in faith is the first and primary of the church, thus the first-begotten. They believed this, because it is first learnt, and because a church is a church by virtue of truth, though not before it forms a part of the life; until this happens, it is only in the thought of the understanding, and in the memory, and not in the act of the will; and truth, which is not truth in act or operation, has no life; it is only like a luxuriant tree having branches and leaves, but no fruit: and it is like knowledge without any application to use; and like the foundation upon which a house is built to be lived in. These things are first as to time, but they are not first as to end; and what is first as to end is primary; for habitation is the first as to end, but the foundation is the first as to time; use also is first as to end, and knowledge is first as to time; in like manner the first thing as to end, when a tree is planted, is the fruit, but the first things as to time are the branches and leaves. With the understanding it is similar, which is formed in man first, but to this end, that what a man sees with his understanding, he may bring into act; otherwise the understanding is like a preacher, who teaches well, but lives ill. Beside all truth is sown in the internal man, and rooted in the external; wherefore, unless the truth that is inseminated takes root in the external man, which is effected by doing it, it becomes like a tree planted, not in the ground, but upon it, which withers on exposure to the heat of the sun: the man who has acted up to the truth, takes this root with him after death; but not the man who had

only known and acknowledged it now as in faith. Many of the ancients made that which is first as to time, the first also as to end, that is, primary; therefore they said, that first-begotten signified truth in doctrine and faith in the church; not knowing that this is the first-begotten apparently, and not actually. But all they who have made truth in doctrine and in faith primary, are condemned, because in this there is nothing of action or operation, or nothing of life; therefore Cain, who was the first-begotten of Adam and Eve, was condemned: that by him is signified truth in doctrine and in faith, may be seen in the *Angelic Wisdom concerning the Divine Providence*, n. 242. And Reuben also, who was the first-begotten of Jacob, was condemned by his father, Genesis xlix. 3, 4, and his birthright taken from him, 1 Chron. v. 1; that by Reuben, in the spiritual sense, is meant truth in doctrine and in faith, will be seen presently. By the first-born of Egypt, which were all cut off, because condemned, nothing else is meant in the spiritual sense, but truth in doctrine and in faith separate from the good of life, which truth is in itself dead. By the goats in Daniel and in Matthew, none others are to be understood, but those who are in faith separate from life, concerning whom see *The Doctrine of the New Jerusalem concerning Faith*, n. 61—68. That they who were in faith separate from life, were rejected and condemned about the time of the last judgment, may be seen in *The Continuation concerning the Last Judgment*, n. 16, and following ones. From this brief account it may appear, that truth in doctrine and in faith is not the first-begotten of the church; but truth in act or operation, which is good of life; for the church is not in man, unless truth is in the life, and when truth is in the life, then it is good; for the thought of the understanding, and the memory, do not flow into the will, and through the will into act; but the will flows into the thought of the understanding, and into the memory, and acts; and what proceeds from the will, through the understanding, proceeds from affection, which is of love, through the thought, which is of the understanding, and is all called good, as it enters into the life; wherefore the Lord saith, that "he who doeth the truth cometh to the light, that his deeds may be made manifest, that they are wrought in God," John iii. 21. Because John represents the good of life, and Peter the truth of faith, as may be seen above, n. 5, therefore John leaned on the Lord's breast, and followed Jesus, but not Peter, John xxi. 18—21; the Lord also said of John, that he should tarry till he came, verse 22, 23; thus to this day, which is the Lord's coming; the good of life is therefore now taught by the Lord for those who are to be of his New Church, which is the New Jerusalem. In short, that is the first-begotten which truth first produces from good, thus what the understanding produces from the will; because truth is of the understanding, and good is of the will: this first is primary, because it is as the seed from which proceeds every thing else. So the Lord is the first-begotten from the dead, because he, as to his Humanity, is the truth itself united to the divine good, from whom all men, who in themselves are dead, are made alive. The same is understood in David: "I will make him my first-born higher than the kings of the earth," Psalm lxxxix. 27; speaking of the Lord's Humanity. It is on this account that Israel is called the first-born, Exod. iv. 22, 23: by Israel is understood truth in act, and by Jacob truth in doctrine; and because there is no church from the latter alone, therefore Jacob was named Israel; but in a supreme sense by Israel is meant the Lord. On account of this representation of the first-born, all the first-born and all the first-fruits were sanctified to Jehovah, Exod. xiii. 2, 12; xxii. 29. On account of this representation of the first-born, the Levites were taken instead of all the first-born in the Israelitish church; and it is said that thereby they belonged to Jehovah, Numbers iii. 12, 13—46, xviii. 15—18: for by Levi is signified truth in act, which is the good of life; and therefore the priesthood was given to his posterity, which will be treated of below. For the same reason a double portion of the inheritance was given to the first-born, and he was called the beginning of strength, Deut. xxi. 15—17. The reason why first-born signifies the primary of the church, is, because in the Word by natural births, spiritual births are signified, and then what first produces them in man, is understood by his first-born; for there is no church in him, until the truth of doctrine conceived in the internal man is brought forth in the external.

18. *And the prince of the kings of the earth*, signifies, from whom is derived all truth proceeding from good in the church. This follows from what has gone before, because by faithful witness, the Lord as to divine truth is signified; and by first-begotten, the Lord as to divine good; therefore by prince of the earth, is signified, that all good from truth in the church is from him; the reason why this is signified by prince of the kings of the earth, is, because by kings in the spiritual sense of the Word, are meant those that are in truths derived from good, and, abstractedly, truths from good; and by earth is understood the church: that this is the signification of kings and earth, may be seen below, n. 20 and n. 285.

19. *To him that loved us and washed us from our sins in his blood*, signifies, who out of love and mercy reforms and regenerates men by his divine truths from the Word. That to wash us from our sins is to purify from evils, thus to reform and regenerate, is evident; for regeneration is spiritual washing; but that by his blood, is not meant the passion of the cross, as many believe, but divine truth proceeding from him, may

appear from many passages in the Word, which it would be too tedious here to adduce, but they will be adduced below, n. 379, 653. In the mean time, see what is said and shown concerning the signification of the Lord's flesh and blood in the holy supper, as set forth in *The New Jerusalem and its Heavenly Doctrine*, n. 212—222; and concerning spiritual washing, which is regeneration, in the same, n. 202—209.

20. *And hath made us kings and priests*, signifies, who gives to those who are born of him, that is, who are regenerated, to be in wisdom from divine truths, and in love from divine goods. It is well known, that in the Word the Lord is called a king, and also a priest; he is called a king from his divine wisdom, and a priest from his divine love; therefore, they who are in wisdom from the Lord are called kings' sons, and also kings; and they who are in love from him, are called ministers and priests; for the love and wisdom in them is not from themselves, thus not their own, but the Lord's; hence it is that they are meant in the Word by kings and priests; not that they are such, but that the Lord is such in them, and causes them to be so called. They are also called born of him, sons of the kingdom, sons of the Father, and heirs; "born of him," John i. 12, 13, that is, born again, or regenerated, John iii. 3, and subsequent verses: "children of the kingdom," Matt. viii. 12, xiii. 38; "children of your Father which is in heaven," Matt. v. 45; "heirs," Psalm cxxvii. 3, 1 Sam. ii. 8, Matt. xxv. 34; and because they are called heirs, sons of the kingdom, and born of the Lord as their Father, they are denominated kings and priests: then also it is said that "they will sit with the Lord upon his throne," Apoc. iii. 21. There are two kingdoms into which the universal heaven is distinguished, the spiritual kingdom and the celestial kingdom; the spiritual kingdom is what is called the Lord's royalty, and as all who are therein are in wisdom from truths, therefore they are meant by kings, which the Lord will make those men who are in wisdom from him; and the celestial kingdom is what is called the Lord's priesthood, and all who are there, are in love from good, therefore they are meant by priests, which the Lord will make those men who are in love from him: in like manner, the Lord's church upon earth is distinguished into two kingdoms; concerning those two kingdoms, see the work *On Heaven and Hell*, n. 24, 226. He who does not know the spiritual signification of kings and priests, may be led into mistakes by many things which are recorded concerning them in the prophets and in the Apocalypse; as in the following instances in the prophets: "The sons of strangers shall build up thy walls, and their kings shall minister unto thee; thou shalt also suck the milk of the Gentiles, and shalt suck the breasts of kings; and thou shalt know that I Jehovah am thy Saviour and thy Redeemer," Isaiah

lx. 10, 16. "Kings shall be thy nursing fathers, and their queens thy nursing mothers," Isaiah xlix. 23; and in other places, as in Genesis xlix. 20; Psalm ii. 10; Isaiah xiv. 9; xxiv. 21; lii. 15; Jerem. ii. 26; iv. 9; lxix. 3; Lament. ii. 6, 9; Ezek. vii. 26, 27; Hosea iii. 4; Zephan. i. 8: by kings in these passages, kings are not understood, but they who are in divine truths from the Lord, and, abstractedly, divine truths, from which is derived wisdom. Neither are kings meant by the king of the south and the king of the north, who waged war with each other, Daniel xi. 1, and subsequent verses; but by the king of the south are meant those who are in truths, and by the king of the north those who are in falses. It is the same in the Apocalypse, where kings are frequently mentioned; as in the following passages: "And the sixth angel poured out his vial upon the great river Euphrates, and the water thereof was dried up, that the way of the kings of the east might be prepared," xvi. 12. "The kings of the earth have committed fornication with the great whore that sitteth upon many waters," xvii. 2. "For all nations have drunk of the wine of the wrath of the fornication of Babylon, and the kings of the earth have committed fornication with her," xviii. 3. "And I saw the beast, and the kings of the earth, and their armies gathered together to make war against him that sat on the white horse," xix. 19. "And the nations of them which are saved shall walk in the light of it, and the kings of the earth do bring their glory and honour into the New Jerusalem," xxi. 24; and in other places, as xvii. 9—14; xviii. 9, 10; by kings are here meant those who are in truths, and, in an opposite sense, those who are in falses; and, abstractedly, truths or falses; by the fornication of Babylon with the kings of the earth is meant the falsification of the truth of the church; that Babylon, or the woman who sat upon the scarlet-coloured beast, did not commit fornication with kings, but that she falsified the truths of the Word, is evident. It appears, therefore, that by kings, which the Lord will make those who are in wisdom from him, it is not to be understood that they will be kings, but that they will be wise; the evidence of which enlightened reason can discern. So in the following passages: "Thou hast made us unto our God kings and priests, and we shall reign upon the earth," Apoc. v. 10. That the Lord, by a king, meant truth, is evident from his own words to Pilate: "Pilate said unto him, Art thou not a king then? Jesus answered, Thou sayest that I am a king; to this end was I born, and for this cause came I into the world, that I should bear witness unto the truth; every one that is of the truth heareth my voice: Pilate saith unto him, What is truth?" John xviii. 37, 38; to bear witness unto the truth, means that he himself is truth; and because from it he called himself a king, Pilate said, what is truth, that is, truth is a king. That priests signify those who are in the good of love, and, abstracted from person, the goods of love, will appear in what follows.

21. *Unto God and his Father*, signifies, and thus images of his divine wisdom, and of his divine love. By God and Father, in the spiritual sense, two persons are not understood; but by God is understood the Divinity as to wisdom, and by Father the Divinity as to love; for there are two things in the Lord, divine wisdom and divine love, or divine truth and divine good; these two are understood in the Old Testament by God and Jehovah, and here, by God and the Father. Now because the Lord teaches, that he and the Father are one, and that he is in the Father and the Father in him (John x. 30; xiv. 10, 11), by God and the Father are not understood two persons, but only the Lord; the Divinity also is one and indivisible, therefore by Jesus Christ making us kings and priests unto God and his Father, is signified, that they appear in his sight as images of his divine wisdom and of his divine love; for in these two consists the image of God in men and angels. That the Divinity, which in itself is one, is expressed by various names in the Word, may be seen in the *Doctrine of the New Jerusalem concerning the Lord*. That the Lord himself is also the Father, is evident from the following places in Isaiah: "For unto us a child is born, unto us a son is given, and his name shall be called Wonderful, Counsellor, the Mighty God, the Everlasting *Father*, the Prince of Peace," ix. 5. In the same: "Thou, Jehovah, art our *Father*, our Redeemer, thy name is from everlasting," lxiii. 16; and in John, "If ye had known me, ye should have known my *Father* also, and from henceforth ye do know him, and have seen him: Philip saith unto him, Lord, show us the *Father;* Jesus saith unto him, He that hath seen me hath seen the *Father*, and how sayest thou then, Show us the *Father?* believe me, that I am in the *Father*, and the *Father* in me," xiv. 7, 8, 9, 11. See n. 960, below.

22. *To him be glory and might for ever and ever*, signifies, to whom alone belong divine majesty and divine omnipotence to eternity. By glory in the Word, where the Lord is treated of, is understood the divine majesty; this being predicated of his divine wisdom; and by might, is meant divine omnipotence, this being predicated of his divine love; and by for ever and ever, is meant eternity. That such is the meaning of glory, might, and ever and ever, when spoken of Jehovah or the Lord, may be confirmed from many passages in the Word.

23. *Amen*, signifies divine confirmation from the truth, thus from himself. Amen signifies truth; and because the Lord was truth itself, he so often said, Amen (verily), I say unto you, as in Matt. v. 18, 26; vi. 16; x. 23, 42; xvii. 20; xviii. 13, 18; xxv. 12; xxviii. 20; John iii. 11; v. 19, 24, 25; vi. 26, 32, 47,

53; viii. 34, 51, 58; x. 7; xiii. 16, 20, 21; xxi. 18, 25; and in the following passage in the Apocalypse: "These things saith the Amen, the faithful and true witness," iii. 14; that is, the Lord. That the Lord is truth itself, he himself teaches in John xiv. 6; xvii. 19.

24. *Behold he cometh with clouds*, signifies that the Lord will reveal himself in the literal sense of the Word, and will open its spiritual sense at the end of the church. He who does not know any thing of the internal or spiritual sense of the Word, cannot know what was meant by the Lord concerning his coming in the clouds of heaven; for he said unto the high priest, who adjured him to declare whether he was the Christ the Son of God, "Thou hast said; nevertheless I say unto you, hereafter shall ye see the Son of Man sitting on the right hand of power, and coming in the clouds of heaven," Matt. xxvi. 64; Mark xiv. 61, 62; and where the Lord speaks to his disciples of the consummation of the age, he says, "And then shall appear the sign of the Son of Man in heaven; and they shall see the Son of Man coming in the clouds of heaven with power and great glory," Matt. xxiv. 30; Mark xiii. 26. By the clouds of heaven in which he is to come, nothing else is meant but the Word in its literal sense; and by the glory in which they will see him, the Word in its spiritual sense. That this is the case, is difficult to be believed by those who do not think beyond the literal sense of the Word; with such, a cloud is a cloud, and thence comes their belief that the Lord will appear in the clouds of heaven, when the last judgment is at hand; but this idea falls to the ground, when it is known what is the meaning of cloud, and that it denotes divine truth in ultimates, and thus the Word in its literal sense. In the spiritual world there appear clouds as well as in the natural world; but the clouds in the spiritual world appear beneath the heavens, with those who are in the literal sense of the Word, darker or brighter according to their understanding and reception of the Word; the reason is, because the light of heaven there is divine truth, and darkness there proceeds from falses; consequently bright clouds are the divine truth veiled in appearances of truth, such as the Word is in the letter with those who are in truths; and dark clouds are the divine truth covered with fallacies and confirmed appearances, such as the Word is in the letter with those who are in falses: I have often seen those clouds, and it was evident whence and what they are. Now because the Lord, after the glorification of his humanity, was made divine truth, or the Word, even in ultimates, he said unto the high priest, that hereafter they should "see the Son of Man coming in *the clouds* of heaven." But his saying to his disciples, that in the consummation of the age the sign of the Son of Man should appear, and that they should see him coming in *the clouds* of

heaven with power and glory, signifies that at the end of the church, when the last judgment shall take place, he will appear in the Word, and reveal its spiritual sense, which is also accomplished at this day, because now is the end of the church, and the last judgment has taken place, as may appear from the *Treatise on the Last Judgment and its Continuation:* this, therefore, is what is meant in the Apocalypse, by "behold he cometh with *clouds:*" also in the following passages: "I looked, and behold, a white *cloud,* and upon the *cloud* one sat like unto the Son of Man," Apoc. xiv. 14. As also in Daniel: "I saw in the night visions, and behold one like the Son of Man with *clouds* of heaven," vii. 13; that by the Son of Man is meant the Lord as to the Word, may be seen in the *Doctrine of the New Jerusalem concerning the Lord,* n. 19—28. That by cloud in other parts of the Word, is meant, also, divine truth in ultimates, and thence the Word in the letter, may be seen in other passages where clouds are mentioned; as in these: "There is none like unto the God of Jeshurun, who rideth upon the heaven in thy help, and in his excellency on the *clouds,*" Deut. xxxiii. 26. "Sing unto God, sing praises to his name, extol him that rideth upon the *clouds,*" Psalm lxviii. 4. "Jehovah rideth upon a light *cloud,*" Isaiah xix. 1: to ride upon the clouds, signifies to be in the wisdom of the Word, for a horse signifies the understanding of the Word; who cannot see that Jehovah does not ride upon the clouds? "And he rode upon a cherub, and made *the clouds* of heaven his pavilion," Psalm xviii. 10, 11: here there is a similar signification; cherubs also signify the Word, as may be seen below, n. 239, 672; pavilion signifies a habitation. "Jehovah layeth the beams of his chambers in the waters, who maketh *the clouds* his chariot," Psalm civ. 3. Waters signify truths, chambers signify doctrinals, and chariot doctrine, all which, because they belong to the literal sense of the Word, are called clouds. "He bindeth up the waters in his thick *clouds,* and the *cloud* is not rent under them; he holdeth back the face of his throne, and spreadeth his *cloud* upon it," Job xxvi. 8, 9: this is to be understood in like manner, "God caused the light of his *cloud* to shine," Job xxxvii. 15. "Ascribe ye strength unto God, his excellency is over Israel, and his strength is in the *clouds,*" Psalm lxviii. 34. The light of a cloud signifies the divine truth of the Word, and strength signifies its divine power. "Thou, O Lucifer, hast said in thine heart, I will ascend above the heights of the *clouds;* I will be like the Most High," Isaiah xiv. 14. "Forsake ye Babylon, for her judgment reacheth unto heaven, and is lifted up even to the *clouds,*" Jer. li. 9. By Lucifer and Babylon are signified those who profane the goods and truths of the Word, therefore these truths are to be understood there by clouds. "Jehovah spread a *cloud* for a covering," Psalm cv. 39 "Jehovah will create upon every dwelling-place of Mount Zion, a *cloud* and smoke by day, for upon all the glory shall be a *defence*," Isaiah iv. 5 : here, also, by cloud, is meant the Word in its literal sense, which sense, as it includes and covers the spiritual sense, is called a covering upon the glory; that the literal sense of the Word is a covering, or defence, lest its spiritual sense should be violated, may be seen in *The Doctrine of the New Jerusalem concerning the Sacred Scripture*, n. 33; and that it is a defence, n. 97. Divine truth in ultimates, which is the same with the Word in its literal sense, is also represented by the cloud, in which Jehovah descended upon Mount Sinai, and promulgated the law, Exod. xix. 9; xxxiv. 5. Also by the cloud which covered Peter, James, and John, when Jesus was transfigured, concerning which it is written : " While Peter yet spake, behold a bright *cloud* overshadowed them, and behold a voice out of the *cloud* which said, This is my beloved Son, hear ye him," Matt. xvii. 5; Mark ix. 7; Luke ix. 34, 35. The Lord in this transfiguration caused himself to be seen as the Word; therefore a cloud overshadowed them, and a voice was heard out of the cloud, saying that he was the Son of God; a voice out of the cloud, means out of the Word. That by cloud, in an opposite sense, is meant the Word as to its literal sense falsified, will be seen elsewhere.

25. *And every eye shall see him*, signifies that all who are in the understanding of divine truth from affection will acknowledge him. In the spiritual sense, by eye, is not meant the eye, but the understanding; therefore, every eye shall see him, denotes that all who are in the understanding of divine truth from affection will acknowledge him, because they alone understand and acknowledge; the rest see indeed and also understand, but do not acknowledge; the former, then, are signified, because it follows, that they, also, who pierced him will see him, by whom are understood they who are in falses. That the eye signifies understanding, will be seen below, n. 48.

26. *And they also who pierced him*, signifies that they also will see who are in falses in the church. By piercing Jesus Christ, nothing else is meant but the destruction of his divine truth in the Word; this, also, is understood by " one of the soldiers piercing his side, and water and blood coming thereout," John xix. 34. Blood and water are divine truth, spiritual and natural, thus the Word in its spiritual and in its natural sense ; and to pierce the Lord's side is to destroy both by falses, as was also done by the Jews; for all the circumstances of the Lord's passion represented the state of the Jewish church as to the Word, on which subject, see *The Doctrine of the New Jerusalem concerning the Lord*, n. 15—17. The reason why piercing him, signifies to destroy the Word by falses, is, because this is said of Jesus Christ, who presently after is called the Son of Man,

and by the Son of Man is meant the Lord as to the Word, therefore to pierce the Son of Man, is to do the same to the Word.

27. *And all the tribes of the earth shall wail because of him*, signifies that this will be when there are no longer any goods and truths in the church. That the tribes of the earth signify the goods and truths of the church, will be seen in the explanation of the seventh chapter, where the twelve tribes of Israel are treated of; wailing signifies lamentation, by reason of their being dead. The same is meant here as by the Lord's words in Matthew: " Immediately after the tribulation of those days shall the sun be darkened, and the moon shall not give her light, and the stars shall fall from heaven; and then shall appear the sign of the Son of Man, and then shall *all the tribes of the earth mourn*," xxiv. 29, 30; these things are said of the consummation of the age, which is the end of the church; the sun shall be darkened, signifies that there is no longer any love and charity; the moon shall not give her light, signifies that there is no longer any intelligence and faith; the stars shall fall from heaven, signifies that there are no longer any knowledges of good and truth; all the tribes of the earth shall mourn, signifies that there are no longer any goods and truths; tribulation, signifies that state of the church.

28. *Even so, Amen*, signifies the divine confirmation that so it will be. This is evident from what was explained above, n. 19.

29. *I am the Alpha and the Omega, the Beginning and the End*, signifies who is the self-subsisting and only-subsisting from first principles to ultimates; from whom proceed all things; thus, who is the self-subsisting and only-subsisting love, the self-subsisting and only-subsisting wisdom, and the self-subsisting and only-subsisting life in himself; and, consequently, the self-subsisting and only-subsisting Creator, Saviour, and Illuminator, from himself; and thence the all in all of heaven and the church. These and many more things besides are contained in the above words, by which the Lord is described; that they are spoken of the Lord, and, indeed, of his Humanity, is very evident, for it follows, that John heard a voice, saying, " I am the Alpha and the Omega, the First and the Last; and I turned to see the voice that spake with me, and saw the *Son of Man* in the midst of seven candlesticks," chap. i. 10—13; who, also, a little further on, says, " I am the First and the Last, I am he that liveth and was dead," verse 17, 18; chap. ii 8. But that all the particulars above enumerated are contained in these words, cannot be confirmed briefly, for to confirm them, so as to be well comprehended, would require many volumes; still they are in part confirmed in *The Angelic Wisdom concerning the Divine Love and the Divine Wisdom*. The Lord calls himself the Alpha and the Omega, the Beginning and the End, because Alpha and Omega refer to his divine love, and

Beginning and End, to his divine wisdom; for there is, in every particular of the Word, a marriage of love and wisdom, or of good and truth; on which subject, see *The Doctrine of the New Jerusalem concerning the Sacred Scripture*, n. 80—90. The Lord is called the Alpha and the Omega, because alpha is the first letter and omega the last in the Greek alphabet, and therefore signify all in the aggregate; the reason is, because each letter of the alphabet, in the spiritual world, signifies something; and a vowel, being used for sound, somewhat of affection or love; from this origin, spiritual and angelic speech, and, also, the Scriptures, are derived; but this is an arcanum hitherto unknown; for there is a universal language which all angels and spirits use; and this has nothing in common with any language of men in the world: every man comes into this language after death; for it is inherent in every man from creation, therefore they all can understand each other in the spiritual world. It has been granted me frequently to hear that language, and also to speak it; and I have compared it with the languages in this world, and have found that it does not, even in the smallest particular, make one with any natural language upon the earth; it differs from these in its first principles, which are, that each letter of every word has a sense and signification peculiar to itself, as well in speaking as in writing: therefore it is that the Lord is called the Alpha and the Omega, which signifies that he is the All in all of heaven and the church; and as these two letters are vowels, they have relation to love, as was said above. Concerning this language, and the writing of it, as flowing from the spiritual thought of the angels, something may be seen in *The Angelic Wisdom concerning the Divine Love and the Divine Wisdom*, n. 295.

30. *Saith the Lord, who is, and who was, and who is to come;* that this signifies who is eternal and infinite, and who is Jehovah, may be seen above, n. 13, where the same is explained.

31. *The Almighty*, signifies who is, lives, and has power from himself, and who governs all things from first principles by ultimates. Since all things are from the Lord, and are created from the first principles which are from him; and since there is nothing made which does not thence derive its existence, as is abundantly shown in *The Angelic Wisdom concerning the Divine Love and the Divine Wisdom*, it follows, that he is omnipotent. Suppose a one from whom are all things; are not all things of that one, upon which they depend in their order, as the links of a chain upon their hook; or as the blood-vessels of the whole body upon the heart; or as all and every thing in the universe upon the sun? thus do all things depend upon the Lord, who is the sun of the spiritual world, from whom all the essence, life, and power, possessed by those who are under that sun, is derived; in a word, from him we live, and move, and

have our being, Acts xvii. 28: this is divine omnipotence. That the Lord rules all things from first principles by ultimates. is an arcanum never before revealed; but it is now explained in *The Doctrine of the New Jerusalem concerning the Lord, and concerning the Sacred Scripture*, in many places; and also in *The Angelic Wisdom concerning the Divine Providence*, n. 124; and concerning *The Divine Love*, n. 221. It is well known that the Divine being infinite, does not fall within the ideas of the thought of any man or angel, because these are finite, and what is finite is not capable of perceiving the infinite; still, that it may in some manner be perceived, it has pleased the Lord to describe his infinity by these words: I am the Alpha and the Omega, the Beginning and the End; who is, and who was, and who is to come, the Almighty; these words, therefore, include all things that ever angel or man can think, spiritually and naturally, concerning the Divine; which things, in general, are what were adduced above in an universal manner.

32. *I John, who also am your brother and companion*, signifies those who are in the good of charity, and thence in the truths of faith. It was observed above, n. 5, that the apostle John represented those who are in the good of charity; and they who are in the good of charity are, also, in the truths of faith, because charity is the life and soul of faith; hence it is, that John calls himself the brother and companion of those in the church to whom he wrote, for he wrote to the seven churches: by brother, in the spiritual sense of the Word, is meant one who is in the good of charity; and, by companion, one who is thence in the truths of faith; for all are, as it were, in consanguinity by charity, but in affinity by faith; for charity conjoins; not so faith, except it be from charity: when faith is from charity, then charity conjoins, and faith consociates; and since they make one, therefore the Lord commanded that all should be brethren, for he says, "One is your master, even Christ, but all ye are brethren," Matt. xxiii. 8; the Lord, also, calls those brethren who are in the good of charity, or in good of life; for he said, "My mother and my brethren are these, who hear the Word of God, and do it," Luke viii. 21; Matt. xii. 49; Mark iii. 33—35. By mother, is meant the church, and by brethren, those who are in charity; and as the good of charity is denoted by brother, therefore the Lord calls those who are principled therein, brethren, in Matthew, also, xxv. 40, and likewise disciples, Matt. xxviii. 10; John xx. 17; but it is not written that the disciples called the Lord brother, because brother denotes the good which is from the Lord: the case is comparatively as it is with kings, princes, and great men, who call those who are connected with them by blood or affinity, brethren, but yet the latter do not in their turn call them so; for the Lord says, "One is your master, even Christ,

but all ye are brethren," Matt. xxiii. 8; also, "Ye call me master and Lord; and ye say well, for so I am," John xiii. 13. The children of Israel called all those brethren who were descended from their father Jacob: and in a more extensive sense, those also who were descended from Esau; but such as were not descended from them they called companions. But as the Word, in its spiritual sense, treats only of those who are in the Lord's church, therefore in that sense, by brethren, they are meant who are in the good of charity from the Lord, and, by companions, they who are in the truths of faith; as in the following passages: "Thus shall ye say every one to his *companion*, and every one to his *brother*, What hath Jehovah answered?" Jer. xxxiii. 35. "Ye have not hearkened unto me in proclaiming liberty every one to his *brother*, and every man to his *companion*," Jer. xxxiv. 17. "He shall not exact it from his *companion*, or of his *brother*," Deut. xv. 2. "For my *brethren* and *companions*' sakes, I will now say," Psalm cxxii. 8. "They help every one his *companion*, and every one said to his *brother*, Be of good courage," Isaiah xli. 6; and, in an opposite sense, "Take ye heed every one of his *companion*, and trust not in any *brother*, for every *brother* will utterly supplant, and every *companion* will walk with slanders," Jer. ix. 4. "I will set the Egyptians against the Egyptians, and they shall fight every one against his *brother*, and every one against his *companion*," Isaiah xix. 2; and in other places. These passages are adduced, that it may be known why John calls himself brother and companion; and that by brother, in the Word, is meant one who is in charity or in good, and, by companion, one who is in faith or in truth. But as it is charity from which faith is derived, therefore none are called companions by the Lord, but brethren or neighbour; every one, indeed, is a neighbour according to the quality of good, Luke x. 36, 37.

33. *In tribulation, and in the kingdom and patience of Jesus Christ*, signifies which in the church are infested by evils and falses, but which will be removed by the Lord at his coming. By tribulation, is meant the state of the church when there are no longer any goods of charity and truths of faith, but instead of them, evils and falses; by the kingdom, is meant the church; and, by patience of Jesus Christ, is meant the Lord's advent; therefore these words, "In tribulation, and in the kingdom and patience of Jesus Christ," when collated into one sense, signify when the goods and truths of the church are infested by evils and falses, but which will be removed by the Lord at his coming. That by tribulation, is meant the state of the church when it is infested by evils and falses, is evident from the following passages: "In the consummation of the age, they shall deliver you up to be *afflicted*, and shall kill you. There shall be great *tribulation*, such as was not since the beginning of the world to this time, no, nor ever shall be.

Immediately after the *tribulation* of those days shall the sun be darkened, and the moon shall not give her light, and the stars shall fall from heaven," Matt. xxiv. 9, 21, 29; Mark xiii. 19, 24. That the kingdom signifies the church, will be seen in what follows.

34. *I was in the isle called Patmos*, signifies a state and place in which he could be illuminated. The reason why this revelation was made to John in Patmos, was, because it was an island in Greece, not far from the land of Canaan, and between Asia and Europe; and by isles are signified the nations more remote from the worship of God, but yet which will accede to it, because they are capable of being illuminated; the same is signified by Greece; but the church itself is signified by the land of Canaan; by Asia, they of the church who are in the light of truth from the Word; and, by Europe, they to whom the Word is about to come; hence it is, that by the isle of Patmos, is signified a state and place in which he could be illuminated. That by isles in the Word are signified the nations which are more remote from the worship of God, but which yet will accede to it, is evident from the following places: "Glorify Jehovah in the fires, even the name of the Lord God of Israel in the *isles* of the sea," Isaiah xxiv. 15. "He shall not fail nor be discouraged till he have set judgment in the earth, and the *isles* shall wait for his law. Sing unto Jehovah a new song, the *isles* and the inhabitants thereof, let them give glory unto Jehovah; and declare his praise in the *islands*," Isaiah xlii. 4, 10, 12. "Listen, O *isles*, unto me; and hearken, ye people from far," Isaiah xlix. 1. "The *isles* shall wait upon me, and on mine arm shall they trust," Isaiah li. 5. "The *isles* shall wait for me, and the ships of Tarshish," Isaiah lx. 9. "Hear the Word of Jehovah, O ye nations, and declare it in the *isles* afar off," Jer. xxxi. 10. "And men shall worship Jehovah every one from his place, even all the *isles* of the heathen," Zeph. ii. 11; and elsewhere. That the same is signified by Greece, is not so evident from the Word, because Greece is mentioned only in Daniel viii. 21; x. 20; xi. 2; as also in John xii. 20; Mark vii. 26. That by the land of Canaan is meant the Lord's church, which is thence called the Holy Land, and the heavenly Canaan, is evident from many passages in the Word; that by Asia are meant they in the church who are in the light of truth from the Word, may be seen above, n. 11; and that by Europe, they to whom the Word is about to come, is plain.

35. *For the Word of God, and for the testimony of Jesus Christ*, signifies that divine truth from the Word might be received from the heart and so in the light, and that the Lord's Humanity might be acknowledged to be divine; this was explained above, n. 6.

36. *I was in the spirit on the Lord's day*, signifies a spiritual

state at that time from divine influx. I was in the spirit, signifies the spiritual state in which he was when he was in visions, which state will be explained in what follows; on the Lord's day, signifies influx then received from the Lord; for in that day the Lord is present, because the day is holy; from which it is evident, that by being in the spirit on the Lord's day, is signified a spiritual state at that time from divine influx. Concerning the prophets it is written, that they were in the spirit or in vision, also that the Word came to them from Jehovah: when they were in the spirit or in vision, they were not in the body, but in their spirit, in which state they saw such things as are in heaven; but when the Word came to them, then they were in the body, and heard Jehovah speak; these two states of the prophets are carefully to be distinguished. In the state of vision the eyes of their spirit were opened, and the eyes of their body shut; and then they heard what the angels spake, or what Jehovah spake by the angels, and also saw the things which were represented to them in heaven; and then they sometimes seemed to themselves to be carried from one place to another, the body still remaining in its place; in this state was John when he wrote the Apocalypse; and sometimes, also, Ezekiel, Zechariah and Daniel; and then it is said that they were in vision, or in the spirit; for Ezekiel says, "The spirit took me up, and brought me in a *vision* by the *Spirit of God* into Chaldea, to them of the captivity: so the *vision* that I had seen went up from me," chap. xi. 1, 24. It is said also, that the *spirit* took him up, and that he heard behind him a voice of a great rushing and other things, iii. 12, 24; also, that the *spirit* lifted him up between the earth and the heaven, and brought him in the *visions of God* to Jerusalem, and he saw abominations, viii. 3, and subsequent verses. In like manner he was in a *vision of God*, or in the *spirit*, when he saw the four animals which were cherubs, i. and x.; as also when he saw the new earth and the new temple, and the angel measuring them, xl. to xlviii.; and that the *spirit* took him up, xliii. 5. The same was the case with Zechariah, in whom there was an angel at the time, when he saw the man riding among the myrtle trees, i. 8, &c.: When he saw four horns, and afterwards a man, in whose hand was a measuring line, ii. 1, 5, &c.: When he saw Joshua, the high priest, iii. 1, &c.: When he saw the candlestick and the two olive trees, iv. 1, &c.: When he saw the flying roll and the ephah, v. 1, 6: And when he saw the four chariots coming out from between two mountains, and horses, vi. 1. In a similar state was Daniel, when he saw four beasts coming up out of the sea, Dan. vii. 1, &c.: And when he saw the battle of the ram and the he-goat, viii. 1, &c. That he saw these things in *visions*, he himself saith, vii. 1, 2, 7, 13; viii. 2; x. 1, 7, 8; and that the angel Gabriel was seen by him in a *vision*, ix. 21. It was the same with John; as when he saw the Son of Man in the midst of the seven candlesticks, Apoc. i.: When he saw a throne in heaven, and him that sat thereon, and four animals round about the throne, iv.: When he saw the book sealed with seven seals, v.: When he saw four horses coming out of the book that was opened, vi.: When he saw the four angels standing upon the four corners of the earth, vii.: When he saw the locusts coming out of the bottomless pit, ix.: When he saw the angel in whose hand was a little book, which he gave him to eat, x.: When he heard the seven angels sound with their trumpets, xi.: When he saw the dragon, and the woman whom the dragon persecuted, and the former making war with Michael, xii.; and afterwards two beasts arising, one out of the sea, and the other out of the earth, xiii.: When he saw the seven angels having the seven last plagues, xv., xvi.: When he saw the great whore sitting upon the scarlet-coloured beast, xvii. 18; and afterwards, a white horse, and one sitting thereon, xix.; and lastly, a new heaven and a new earth, and then the New Jerusalem coming down out of heaven, xxi., xxii. That John saw these things in the *spirit*, and in a *vision*, he himself says, i. 10; iv. 2; ix. 17; xxi. 10; this also is understood by the expression, I saw, wherever it occurs. It appears, evidently, from these examples, that to be in the spirit, is to be in vision; which is effected by the opening of the sight of a man's spirit; which, when it is opened, the things which are in the spiritual world appear as clearly as the things which are in the natural world appear to the bodily sight. I can testify that it is so, from many years' experience. In this state the disciples were when they saw the Lord after his resurrection, wherefore it is said that their eyes were opened, Luke xxiv. 30, 31. Abraham was in a similar state when he saw the three angels, and discoursed with them. So were Hagar, Gideon, Joshua, and others, when they saw the angels of Jehovah; and, in like manner, the boy of Elisha, when he saw the mountain full of chariots and horses of fire about Elisha; for Elisha prayed and said, "Jehovah, I pray thee, *open* his eyes, that he may see; and Jehovah *opened* the eyes of the young man, and he saw," 2 Kings vi. 17. But as to the Word, it was not revealed in a state of the spirit or in vision, but was dictated by the Lord *viva voce* to the prophets; therefore, it is nowhere said that they spake it from the Holy Spirit, but from Jehovah; see *The Doctrine of the New Jerusalem concerning the Lord*, n. 53.

37 *And I heard behind me a great voice, as of a trumpet*, signifies manifest perception of divine truth revealed from heaven. A great voice, when heard from heaven, signifies divine truth, as will be seen below; the reason why it was heard as the sound of a trumpet, is, because when divine truth descends from heaven, it is sometimes so heard by the angels of the ultimate heaven, and then is manifestly perceived; therefore, by a voice as of a trumpet, is signified manifest perception

of the signification of trumpet, more will be seen below, n. 397, 519. That a great voice, when heard from heaven, signifies divine truth, is evident from the following passages: "The *voice of Jehovah* is upon the waters;" "the *voice of Jehovah* is powerful;" "the *voice of Jehovah* is full of majesty;" "the *voice of Jehovah* breaketh the cedars;" "the *voice of Jehovah* divideth the flames of fire;" "the *voice of Jehovah* shaketh the wilderness;" "the *voice of Jehovah* maketh the hinds to calve," Ps. xxix. 3—9. "Sing unto God, ye kingdoms of the earth, lo, he doth send out his *voice*, and that a mighty *voice*," Psalm lxviii. 32, 33. "Jehovah uttered his *voice* before his army, for his camp is very great, for he is strong that executeth his Word," Joel ii. 11. "Jehovah shall utter his *voice* from Jerusalem," Joel iii. 16. And since voice signifies divine truth from the Lord, therefore the Lord said, "That the sheep hear his *voice*, that they know his *voice;* and other sheep I have, them also I must bring, and they shall hear my *voice:* my sheep hear my *voice*, and I know them, and they follow me," John x. 3, 4, 16, 27. And in another place: "The hour is coming, and now is, when the dead shall hear the *voice* of the Son of Man, and they that hear shall live," John v. 25. Voice here denotes the divine truth of the Lord from his Word.

38. *Saying, I am the Alpha and the Omega, the First and the Last,* signifies who is the self-subsisting, and the only-subsisting, from first principles to ultimates, from whom are all things; therefore, who is the self-subsisting and only-subsisting love, the self-subsisting and only-subsisting wisdom, and the self-subsisting and only-subsisting life in himself; consequently the self-subsisting and only-subsisting Creator, Saviour, and Illuminator from himself; and thence the All in all of heaven and the church: who alone is infinite and eternal, and who is Jehovah; and that the Lord is He. That all these things, and infinitely more, are contained in these words, may be seen above, n. 13, 29. It was there said, that all the syllables or letters of the alphabet, in the spiritual world, signify things; and that thence originates the speech and writing of those who are there; and that therefore the Lord describes his divinity and infinity by Alpha and Omega; by which is signified that he is the All in all of heaven and the church. Now every letter signifying a thing in the spiritual world, and thence in the language of the angels; therefore David wrote the 119th Psalm, in order, according to the letters of the alphabet, beginning with Aleph and ending with Thau, as may appear from the initials of the verses; the like appears in Psalm cxi., but not so evidently. Therefore, also, Abram was called Abraham, and Sarai Sarah; which was done to the intent that in heaven, by Abraham and Sarah, they should not be understood, but the divine, as is also the case, for the letter H involves

infinity, being only an aspirate: more on this subject may be seen above, n. 29.

39. *And what thou seest, write in a book;* that this signifies that it may be revealed to posterity, is evident without explanation.

40. *And send [it] to the churches which are in Asia,* signifies for those in the Christian world, who are in the light of truth from the Word. That they are meant by the churches in Asia, may be seen above, n. 10, 11.

41. *Unto Ephesus, and unto Smyrna, and unto Pergamos, and unto Thyatira, and unto Sardis, and unto Philadelphia, and unto Laodicea,* signifies specifically according to the state of reception of each. That all states of reception of the Lord and of his church are signified by these seven names, in the spiritual sense, will be seen below; for John, when he received this command, was in a spiritual state, and in that state nothing is mentioned by name which does not signify some thing or state; therefore these things which were written by John, were not sent to any church in those places, but were told to their angels, by whom are understood those who receive. That by all the names of persons and places throughout the whole Word, are meant spiritual things, is abundantly shown in the *Arcana Cœlestia*, as what is meant by Abraham, Isaac, and Jacob; also by Israel, and by the names of his twelve sons; as also, what is meant by various places in the land of Canaan, and by places in the vicinity of that land; as what by Egypt, Syria, Assyria, and other places. It is the same with these seven names. But he who chooses to abide in the literal sense, let him do so, since that sense conjoins; only let him know, that by those names the angels perceive things and states of the church.

42. *And I turned to see the voice that spake with me,* signifies inversion of the state of those who are in good of life, with respect to the perception of truth in the Word, when they turn themselves to the Lord. John says that he heard a voice behind him (verse 10), and now, that he turned to see the voice and again, that being turned, he saw seven candlesticks; from which it is evident, that he heard a voice from behind, and that he turned himself, to see from whence it proceeded: that there is an arcanum in this, is evident; the secret is that before man turns himself to the Lord, and acknowledges him as the God of heaven and earth, he cannot see divine truth in the Word; the reason is, because God is one, both in person and in essence, in whom there is a trinity; and that God is the Lord; therefore, they who acknowledge a trinity of persons, look primarily to the Father, and indeed to the Holy Spirit, and rarely to the Lord, and if they do look up to the Lord, they think of his Humanity as of a common man; when a man does this, he can by no means be illuminated in the Word, for the Lord is

the Word, for it is from him and concerning him: therefore they who do not approach the Lord alone, see him and his Word behind them, and not before them; or backward, and not in front. This is the arcanum which lies concealed in these words: That John heard a voice behind him, and that he turned to see the voice, and, being turned, saw seven golden candlesticks, and in the midst of them the Son of Man; for the voice which he heard came from the Son of Man, who is the Lord. That the Lord alone is the God of heaven and earth, he now teaches in a manifest voice, for he says, "I am the Alpha and the Omega, the Beginning and the End, saith the Lord, who is, and who was, and who is to come," verse 8; and here, "I am the Alpha and the Omega, the First and the Last," verse 11; and afterwards, "I am the First and the Last," verse 17, and ii. 8. That by a voice, when from the Lord, Divine Truth is understood, may be seen above, n. 37. And that by John are understood they of the church, who are in good of life, n. 5, 6. From these things it may now appear, that by these words, "And I turned to see the voice which spake with me," is signified inversion of the state of those who are in good of life, as to the perception of truth in the Word, when they turn themselves to the Lord.

43. *And being turned, I saw seven golden candlesticks*, signifies the New Church, which will be in illumination from the Lord out of the Word. That the seven candlesticks are the seven churches, is said in the last verse of this chapter; and that by the seven churches are to be understood all who are in the Christian world, and accede to the church, may be seen above, n. 10; and specifically according to the state of reception of each, n. 41. The reason why the New Church is meant by the seven candlesticks is, because in it, and in the midst of it, the Lord is; for it is said, that in the midst of the seven candlesticks he saw one like unto the Son of Man, and by the Son of Man is meant the Lord as to the Word. They appeared to be golden candlesticks, because gold signifies good, and every church is a church from good, which is formed by truths; that gold signifies good, will be seen in what follows. Those candlesticks were not placed one close to another, or in contact, but at certain distances, forming a kind of circle, as is evident from these words in the subsequent chapter, "These things saith he, who walketh in the midst of the seven golden candlesticks," verse 1. Nothing is said of the lamps of those candlesticks; but in what follows it is said, that the holy Jerusalem, that is, the New Church, hath no need of the sun, neither of the moon, for the Lamb is the light [lamp] thereof, and the nations which are saved shall walk in his light, Apoc. xxi. 23, 24. And moreover, they need no lamp, for the Lord God giveth them light, xxii. 5; for they who will be of the Lord's New Church,

can only be candlesticks which will have their light from the Lord. By the golden candlestick in the tabernacle, was represented the church as to illumination from the Lord, concerning which candlestick, see Exod. xxv. 11 to the end; xxxvii. 17—20; Lev. xxiv. 3, 4; Numb. viii. 2, 3, 4; that it represented the Lord's church as to divine love spiritual, which is love towards the neighbour, may be seen in *The Arcana Cœlestia*, n. 9548, 9555, 9558, 9561, 9572, 9783; also, below, n. 493. By the candlestick in Zechariah iv., is also signified the New Church to be established by the Lord, because it signifies the new house of God, or the new temple; as is evident from what follows there; and by the house of God, or temple, the church is signified, and in a supreme sense, the Lord's Divine Humanity, as he himself teaches, John ii. 19—21, and elsewhere: but it shall be shown what is signified in its order, in the 4th chapter of Zechariah, when he saw the candlestick. By what is contained from verse 1 to 7, is signified the illumination of the New Church by the Lord, from the good of love by truth; the olive trees there signify the church as to the good of love: by the contents from verse 8 to 10, is signified that these things are from the Lord; by Zerubbabel, who is to build the house, thus the church, the Lord is represented; by what is contained from verse 11 to 14, is signified that in that church there will also be truths from a celestial origin: this explanation of that chapter was given me from the Lord through heaven.

44. *And in the midst of the seven candlesticks one like unto the Son of Man*, signifies the Lord as to the Word, from whom that church is. It is well known from the Word, that the Lord called himself *the Son of God*, and also *the Son of Man;* that by the Son of God he meant himself as to his Divine Humanity, and by the Son of Man, himself as to the Word, is fully demonstrated in *The Doctrine of the New Jerusalem concerning the Lord*, n. 19—28; and as it is there fully confirmed from the Word, it is unnecessary to add any further confirmation here. Now, as the Lord represented himself unto John as the Word, therefore as seen of him, he is called *the Son of Man*. He represented himself as the Word, because the New Church is the subject treated of, which is a church from the Word, and according to the understanding thereof; that the church is from the Word, and that such as its understanding of the Word is, such is the church, may be seen in *The Doctrine of the New Jerusalem concerning the Sacred Scripture*, n. 76—79. As the church is a church from the Lord through the Word, therefore *the Son of Man* was seen in the midst of the candlesticks; in the midst signifies in the inmost, from which the things which are round about, or which are without, derive their essence, in this instance, their light and intelligence,

that the inmost is the all in the things which are round about, or without, is abundantly shown in *The Angelic Wisdom concerning the Divine Love and the Divine Wisdom;* it is like light or flame in the centre, from which the circumference is illuminated and warmed. In the midst, has the same signification in the following passages in the Word: "Cry out and shout, thou inhabitant of Zion; for great is the Holy One of Israel *in the midst* of thee," Isaiah xii. 6. "God, my King of old, working salvation *in the midst* of the earth," Psalm lxxiv. 12. "We have thought of thy loving kindness *in the midst* of his temple," Psalm xlviii. 9. "God standeth in the congregation of the mighty; he judgeth *in the midst* of the gods," Psalm lxxxii. 1. They are called gods who are in divine truths from the Lord, and, abstractedly, the truths themselves. "Behold, I send an angel before thee, beware of him and obey his voice, for my name is *in the midst* of him," Exod. xxiii. 20, 21. The name of Jehovah is every thing Divine; in the midst, is in the inmost, and thereby in the all of him. The midst also signifies the inmost, and thence the all, in many other passages in the Word, where evils are also treated of, as in Isaiah xxiv. 13; Jerem. xxiii. 9; Psalm v. 9; ix. 4, 5; xxxvi. 2; lv. 7; lxii. 4. These passages are adduced in order to show, that in the midst of the candlesticks signifies in the inmost, from which the church and every thing belonging to it is derived; for the church and every thing that belongs to it is from the Lord through the Word. That candlesticks signify the New Church, may be seen above, n. 43.

45. *Clothed with a garment down to the foot,* signifies the proceeding divine, which is divine truth. The reason why a garment down to the foot signifies the proceeding divine, which is divine truth, is, because garments, in the Word, signify truths, thence *talaris,* which is an outer garment or vest, when the Lord is treated of, signifies the proceeding divine truth. That garments, in the Word, signify truths, is, because in heaven the angels are clothed according to the truths proceeding from their good; concerning which see the work on *Heaven and Hell,* n. 177—182. In what follows it will also be seen, that nothing else is understood by garments in the Word in its spiritual sense; therefore that nothing else is understood by the Lord's garments, when he was transfigured, which appeared white as the light, Matt. xvii. 1—4; Mark ix. 2—8; Luke ix. 28—36. Nor is any thing else understood by the Lord's garments which the soldiers divided, John xix. 23, 24. That similar things are represented, and therefore signified, by the garments of Aaron, may be seen in *The Arcana Cœlestia,* n. 9814, 10,068; particularly what is signified by the ephod, n. 9477, 9824, 10,005; what by the robe, n. 9825, 10,005; what by the coat, n. 9826, 9942; and what by the mitre, n. 9827: for Aaron represented

the priestly office of the Lord. Concerning the signification of garments in the Word, see below, n. 166, 328.

46. *And girt about the paps with a golden girdle*, signifies the proceeding, and, at the same time, the conjoining divine, which is divine good. That a golden girdle has this signification, is, because by the Lord's breast, and especially by the paps, his divine love is signified; thence, by the golden girdle which girded them, is signified the proceeding, and at the same time the conjoining divine, which is the divine good of his divine love: moreover gold signifies good; see below, n. 913. A zone or girdle, in the Word, likewise signifies a common band, whereby all things are kept in their order and connexion; as in Isaiah: "There shall come forth a rod out of the stem of Jesse, and righteousness shall be *the girdle* of his loins, and faithfulness *the girdle* of his reins," xi. 1—5; the rod coming out of the stem of Jesse is the Lord. That the girdle of the ephod and the belt of Aaron's coat, signified conjunction, may be seen in *The Arcana Cœlestia*, n. 9837, 9944. As a girdle signifies a band conjoining the goods and truths of the church, therefore when the church among the children of Israel was destroyed, Jeremiah the prophet was commanded to procure himself a girdle, and put it upon his loins, and then to hide it in a hole of a rock beside the Euphrates; and at the end of days, when he took it, behold it was rotten, and was profitable for nothing, Jerem. xiii. 1—12; by which was represented, that at that time there was no good in the church, and thence that truths were dissipated. The same is signified by girdle in Isaiah: "Instead of *a girdle* there shall be a rent," iii. 24; and also in other places. That by the paps or breasts divine love is signified, is evident from those passages in the Word where they are mentioned, as also from their correspondence with love.

47. *His head, and his hairs, were white like wool, as white as snow*, signifies the divine love of the divine wisdom in first principles and in ultimates. By the head of a man is signified the all of his life; and the all of man's life has relation to love and wisdom, therefore by the head is signified wisdom, and also love; but as there is no love without its wisdom, nor wisdom without its love, therefore it is the love of wisdom, which is understood by the head; and when the Lord is spoken of, it is the divine love of divine wisdom. But the signification of the head will be shown from the Word, below, n. 538, 565. Since, therefore, by the head is understood love, and also wisdom, in their first principles, it follows that by hair is to be understood love and wisdom in their ultimates; and because hairs are here spoken of the Son of Man, who is the Lord as to the Word, by his hairs are signified the divine good which is of love, and the divine truth which is of wisdom, in the ultimates of the Word;

and the ultimates of the Word are what are contained in its literal sense: that the Word in this sense is signified by the hairs of the Son of Man, or of the Lord, seems a paradox, but yet it is true; this may appear from the passages in the Word adduced in *The Doctrine of the New Jerusalem concerning the Sacred Scripture*, n. 35—49; where it is also shown, that the Nazarites in the Israelitish church represented the Lord as to the Word in ultimates, which is its literal sense; for Nazarite, in the Hebrew language, signifies hair, or a head of hair; hence the strength of Samson, who was a Nazarite from the womb, was in his hair; that in like manner divine truth is in its power, in the literal sense of the Word, may be seen in the abovementioned *Doctrine concerning the Sacred Scripture*, n. 37—49; therefore, also, the shaving of the head was strictly prohibited the high priest and his sons; and, for the same reason, forty-two children were torn in pieces by two bears, because they called Elisha, Baldhead. Elisha, as well as Elijah, represented the Lord as to the Word; bald signifies the Word without its ultimate, which, as was observed, is its literal sense, and bears signify that sense of the Word separated from its internal sense; they who separate them, appear also in the spiritual world, at a distance, like bears, whence it is evident why this was done to the children: therefore also to induce baldness was the greatest disgrace, and a mark of extreme grief. For which reason, when the Israelitish nation had perverted all the literal sense of the Word, this lamentation was made over them: "Her Nazarites were purer than snow, they were whiter than milk;—their visage is blacker than a coal, they are not known in the streets," Lament. iv. 7, 8. Also: "Every head was made bald, and every shoulder was peeled," Ezek. xxix. 18. And: "Shame shall be upon all faces, and baldness upon all their heads," Ezek. vii. 18. In like manner, Isaiah xv. 2; Jerem. xlviii. 37; Amos viii. 10. As the children of Israel dispersed by falses all the literal sense of the Word, therefore the prophet Ezekiel was commanded to represent this by shaving his head with a razor, and to burn with fire a third part of the hair, and smite a third part with a sword, and scatter a third part in the wind, and to collect some in his skirts, and afterwards cast them also into the fire, Ezek. v. 1—4. Therefore, also, it is said in Micah: "Make thee bald and poll thee for thy delicate children, enlarge thy baldness as the eagle; for they are gone into captivity from thee," i. 16. The delicate children are the genuine truths of the church from the Word. And as Nebuchadnezzar, king of Babylon, represented the Babylonian falsification of the Word, and destruction of all truth therein, therefore it came to pass that his hairs were grown like eagles' feathers, Dan. iv. 33. By reason that hairs signified that holy principle of the Word, it is said of the Nazarite, "That he should not shave *the hair* of his head, because the consecration of his God is upon his head," Numb. vi. 1—21; and therefore it was ordained, "That the high priest and his sons should not uncover their heads, lest they should die, and lest wrath should come upon all the people," Levit. x. 6. Now as by hairs is signified divine truth in its ultimates, which, in the church, is the Word in its literal sense, therefore, also, the same is said of the Ancient of Days in Daniel: "I beheld till the thrones were cast down, and the Ancient of Days did sit, whose garment was white as snow, and *the hair* of his head like pure wool," vii. 9; that the Ancient of Days is the Lord, appears evidently in Micah: "But thou Bethlehem Ephratah, though thou be little among the thousands of Judah, yet out of thee shall he come forth unto me that is to be ruler in Israel, whose goings forth have been from of old, from everlasting," v. 2; and in Isaiah, where he is called the Father of Eternity, ix. 5. From these passages, and many others, which are not adduced by reason of their abundance, it may appear, that by the head and hairs of the Son of Man, which were white like wool, as white as snow, is understood the divine of love and wisdom, in first principles and in ultimates; and as by the Son of Man, the Lord is understood as to the Word, it follows, that this also is understood in first principles and in ultimates; otherwise to what purpose would the Lord here in the Apocalypse, and the Ancient of Days in Daniel, be described as to the hair? That by hair, the literal sense of the Word is signified, appears evidently from those who are in the spiritual world; they who have held the literal sense of the Word in contempt, appear bald there; and on the contrary, they who have loved the literal sense of the Word, appear there with becoming hair. It is said white as wool, and as snow, because wool signifies good in ultimates, and snow, truth in ultimates; as also in Isaiah i. 18: for wool is from sheep, by which is signified the good of charity, and snow is from water, by which are signified the truths of faith.

48. *And his eyes were as a flame of fire*, signifies the divine wisdom of the divine love. By eyes, in the Word, is meant the understanding, and thence, by the eye-sight, intelligence; therefore, when spoken of the Lord, the divine wisdom is understood; but by a flame of fire, is signified spiritual love, which is charity; wherefore, when spoken of the Lord, the divine love is understood; hence, then, by his eyes being like a flame of fire, is signified the divine wisdom of the divine love. That the eye signifies the understanding, is, because they correspond; for as the eye sees from natural light, so does the understanding from spiritual light; wherefore to see is predicated of both. That by eye in the Word, the understanding is signified, is evident from the following passages: "Bring forth the blind people that have *eyes*, and the deaf that have ears," Isaiah xliii. 8. "In that

day shall the deaf hear the words of the book, and *the eyes* of the blind shall see out of obscurity," Isaiah xxix. 18. "Then *the eyes* of the blind shall be opened, and the ears of the deaf shall be unstopped," Isaiah xxxv. 5, 6. "I will give thee for a light of the Gentiles, to open the blind *eyes*," Isaiah xlii. 7. This is spoken of the Lord, who, when he comes, will open the understanding of those who are in ignorance of the truth. That this is meant by opening the eyes, is moreover evident from the following passages: "Make the heart of this people fat, and shut their *eyes*, lest they see with their *eyes*," Isaiah vi. 9, 10; John xii. 46. "Jehovah hath poured out upon you the spirit of deep sleep, and hath closed your *eyes*; the prophets, and your rulers, the seers, hath he covered," Isaiah xxix. 10; xxx. 10. "And shutteth his *eyes* from seeing evil," xxxiii. 15. "Hear this, O rebellious house, which have *eyes* to see and see not," Ezek. xii. 2. "Woe to the idle shepherd that leaveth the flock! the sword shall be upon his arm and upon his right *eye*, and his right *eye* shall be utterly darkened," Zech. xi. 17. "And this shall be the plague, wherewith Jehovah will smite all the people that have fought against Jerusalem; their *eyes* shall consume away in their holes," Zech. xiv. 12. "I will smite every horse with astonishment,—and every horse of the people with blindness," Zech. xii. 4. Horse, in the spiritual sense, denotes the understanding of the Word, n. 298. "Hear me, Jehovah, my God, lighten mine *eyes*, lest I sleep the sleep of death," Psalm xiii. 3. That in these passages, by eye is signified the understanding, every one sees. Hence it is evident what the Lord meant by eye in these places: "The light of the body is the *eye*; if therefore thine *eye* be single, thy whole body shall be full of light. But if thine *eye* be evil, thy whole body shall be full of darkness. If therefore the light that is in thee be darkness, how great is that darkness!" Matt. vi. 22, 23; Luke xi. 34. "And if thy right *eye* offend thee, pluck it out, and cast it from thee: for it is better for thee to enter into life with one *eye*, rather than having two *eyes* to be cast into hellfire," Matt. v. 29; xviii. 9. By eye in these places is not meant the eye, but the understanding of truth. As by eye is signified the understanding of truth, therefore it was among the statutes of the children of Israel, that a blind man, or one that hath a blemish in his eye, of the seed of Aaron, should not come nigh to offer sacrifice, nor enter within the vail, Levit. xxi. 18, 20; moreover, that any thing blind should not be offered as a sacrifice, Levit. xxii. 22; Malachi i. 8. From these considerations it is evident what is meant by eye, when predicated of a man; hence it follows, that by eye, when predicated of the Lord, his divine wisdom is understood, as also his divine omniscience and providence; as in these passages: "Open thine *eyes*, Jehovah, and see," Isaiah xxxvii. 18. "For I will set mine *eyes* upon them for good,—and I will build them," Jerem. xxiv. 6. "Behold *the eye* of Jehovah is upon them that fear him," Psalm xxxiii. 18. "Jehovah is in his holy temple,—his *eyes* behold, his *eye-lids* try the children of men," Psalm xi. 4. As by cherubs is signified the care and providence of the Lord that the spiritual sense of the Word should not be violated; therefore it is said of the four animals which were cherubs, that they were full of *eyes* before and behind, and their wings were full of *eyes* within, Apoc. iv. 6, 8: also, that the wheels upon which the cherubs were drawn, were full of *eyes* round about, Ezek. x. 12. That by a flame of fire is meant his divine love, will be seen in what follows, when flame and fire are mentioned; and because it is said, that his eyes were like a flame of fire, the divine wisdom of his divine love is signified. That in the Lord there is the divine love of divine wisdom, and the divine wisdom of divine love, and thus a reciprocal union of both, is revealed in *The Angelic Wisdom concerning the Divine Love and the Divine Wisdom*, n. 34—39; and elsewhere.

49. *And his feet were like unto fine brass, as if they burned in a furnace*, signifies divine good natural: the Lord's feet signify his divine natural; fire, or what burns, signifies good; and fine brass signifies the good of truth natural; therefore, by the feet of the Son of Man like unto fine brass, as if they burned in a furnace, is signified divine good natural. That his feet have this signification is from correspondence. There is in the Lord, and therefore from the Lord, the divine celestial principle, the divine spiritual, and the divine natural; the divine celestial is understood by the head of the Son of Man; the divine spiritual, by his eyes, and by his breast, which was girt about with a golden girdle; and the divine natural, by his feet; because these three are in the Lord, therefore also they are in the angelic heaven; the third or supreme heaven is in the divine celestial principle; the second or middle heaven is in the divine spiritual; and the first or ultimate heaven in the divine natural. In like manner, the church upon earth: for the universal heaven before the Lord is as one man, in which they who are in the Lord's divine celestial principle constitute the head; they who are in the divine spiritual constitute the body; and they who are in the divine natural constitute the feet: hence, also, in every man, by reason of his being created after the image of God, there are these three degrees, and, as these are opened, he becomes an angel either of the third, or of the second, or of the ultimate heaven: hence also it is, that in the Word there are three senses; the celestial, the spiritual, and the natural. This may be seen in *The Angelic Wisdom concerning the Divine Love and the Divine Wisdom*, particularly in the third part, which treats of these three degrees.

That the feet, the soles of the feet, and the heels, correspond to natural things in man, and therefore in the Word signify things natural, may be seen in *The Arcana Cœlestia*, n. 2162, 4938—4952. The divine natural good is also signified by feet in the following places; in Daniel: "I lifted up mine eyes, and looked, and behold a man clothed in linen, whose loins were girded with fine gold of Uphaz; his body also was like the beryl, and his eyes as lamps of fire, and his arms and his *feet* like in colour to polished brass," x. 5, 6. In the Apocalypse: "And I saw another mighty angel come down from heaven, and his *feet* as pillars of fire," x. 1. And in Ezekiel: "The *feet* of the cherubs sparkled like the colour of burnished brass," i. 7. The reason why the angels and cherubs had that appearance, was, because the Divine of the Lord was represented in them. The Lord's church being under the heavens, thus under the Lord's feet, it is therefore called his footstool, in the following places: "The glory of Lebanon shall come unto thee, to beautify the place of my sanctuary; and I will make the place of my *feet* glorious. And they shall bow themselves down at the *soles of thy feet*," Isaiah lx. 13, 14. "The heaven is my throne, and the earth is my *footstool*," Isaiah lxvi. 1. "The Lord hath not remembered his *footstool* in the day of his anger," Lament. ii. 1. "Worship at the *footstool* of Jehovah," Psalm xcix. 5. "Lo, we heard of it at Ephratah [Bethlehem]. We will go into his tabernacles; we will worship at his *footstool*," Psalm cxxxii. 6, 7; thence it is, that "they came and held the Lord's *feet* and worshipped him," Matt. xxviii. 9; Mark v. 22; Luke viii. 41; John xi. 32: also, that "Mary kissed his *feet*, and did wipe them with the hairs of her head," Luke vii. 37, 38, 44, 46; John xi. 2; xii. 3. As by feet is signified the natural principle, therefore the Lord said unto Peter, when he washed his feet, "He that is washed, needeth not save to wash his *feet*, but is clean every whit," John xiii. 10. To wash the feet, is to purify the natural man; and when this is purified, the whole man is also purified; as is abundantly shown in *The Arcana Cœlestia* and in *The Doctrine of the New Jerusalem*. The natural man, which is also the external man, is purified, when he shuns the evils which the spiritual or internal man sees to be evils and that they ought to be shunned. Now since the natural degree of man is understood by feet, and this perverts all things if it be not washed or purified; therefore the Lord says, "And if thy *foot* offend thee, cut it off; it is better for thee to enter halt into life, than having two *feet* to be cast into hell, into the fire that never shall be quenched," Mark ix. 45; here the foot is not understood, but the natural man. The same is understood by trampling under foot the good pasture, and troubling the waters with their feet, Ezek. xxxii. 13; xxxiv. 18, 19; Dan. vii. 7, 19; and in other places. Since by the

Son of Man is meant the Lord as to the Word, it is evident, that by his feet is also understood the Word in its natural sense; which is much treated of in *The Doctrine of the New Jerusalem concerning the Sacred Scripture;* as also that the Lord came into the world, that he might fulfil all things of the Word, and thereby be made the Word also in ultimates, n. 98 —100; but this arcanum is for those who will be in the New Jerusalem. The Lord's divine natural degree is also signified by the brazen serpent, which was set up by the command of Moses in the wilderness; by looking upon which, all who had been bit by serpents were healed, Numb. xxi. 6, 8, 9; that it signified the Lord's divine natural degree, and that they are saved who look up to it, the Lord himself teaches in John: "And as Moses lifted up the *serpent* in the wilderness, even so must the *Son of Man* be lifted up, that whosoever believeth in him should not perish, but have eternal life," iii. 14, 15: the reason why the serpent was made of brass, is, because brass, as also fine brass, signifies the natural degree as to good. See below, n. 775.

50. *And his voice as the voice of many waters,* signifies divine truth natural. That voice, when proceeding from the Lord, signifies divine truth, may be seen above, n. 37; that waters signify truths, and, specifically, natural truths, which are knowledges from the Word, is evident from many passages in the Word; of which only the following are adduced: "For the earth shall be full of the knowledge of Jehovah, as *the waters* cover the sea," Isaiah xi. 9. "Therefore with joy shall ye draw *waters* out of the wells of salvation," Isaiah xii. 3. "He that walketh righteously and speaketh uprightly;—bread shall be given him; his *waters* shall be sure," Isaiah xxxiii. 15, 16. "The poor and needy seek *water,* and there is none; and their tongue faileth for thirst;—I will open rivers in high places, and fountains in the midst of the valleys: I will make the wilderness a pool of *water,* and the dry land springs of *water,*—that they may see, and know, and consider, and understand together," Isaiah xli. 17, 18, 20. "For I will pour *water* upon him that is thirsty, and floods upon the dry ground, I will pour out my spirit upon thy seed," Isaiah xliv. 3. "Then shall thy light rise in obscurity;—and thou shalt be like a watered garden, and like a spring of *water* whose *waters* fail not," Isaiah lviii. 10, 11. "For my people have committed two evils; they have forsaken me, the fountain of living *waters,* and hewed them out cisterns, that can hold no *water,*" Jerem. ii. 13. "And their nobles have sent their little ones to *the waters:* they came to the pits and found no *water;* they returned with their vessels empty," Jerem. xiv. 3. "They have forsaken Jehovah, the fountain of living *waters,*" Jerem. xvi. 13. "They shall come with weeping; and with supplications will I lead them: I will cause them to walk by rivers of *waters* in a straight way,"

Jerem. xxxi. 9. "I will break the staff of bread; and they shall drink *water* by measure with astonishment: and consume away for their iniquity," Ezek. iv. 16, 17; xii. 18, 19; Isaiah li. 14. "Behold the days come, saith Jehovah God, that I will send a famine in the land, not a famine of bread, nor a thirst for *water*, but of hearing the words of Jehovah: and they shall wander from sea to sea; they shall run to and fro to seek the Word of Jehovah, and shall not find it. In that day shall the fair virgins and young men faint for thirst," Amos viii. 11—13. "And it shall be in that day that living *waters* shall go out from Jerusalem," Zech. xiv. 8. "Jehovah is my shepherd; he leadeth me beside the still *waters*," Psalm xxiii. 1, 2. "Behold he smote the rock, and *the waters* gushed out, and the streams overflowed," Psalm lxxviii. 20. "O God, thou art my God; early will I seek thee: my soul thirsteth for thee, in a dry and thirsty land where no *water* is," Psalm lxiii. 1. "Jehovah sendeth out his Word, he causeth his wind to blow, and the *waters* flow," Psalm cxlvii. 18. "Praise Jehovah, ye heavens of heavens, and ye *waters* that be above the heavens," Psalm cxlviii. 4. Jesus, as he sat at Jacob's well, said unto the woman, "Whosoever drinketh of this *water*, shall thirst again: but whosoever drinketh of the *water* that I shall give him, shall never thirst; but the *water* that I shall give him, shall be in him a well of *water* springing up into everlasting life," John iv. 6—14. Jesus said, "If any man thirst, let him come unto me, and drink. He that believeth on me, as the Scripture hath said, out of his belly shall flow rivers of living *water*," John vii. 37, 38. "I will give unto him that is athirst, of the fountain of the *water* of life freely," Apoc. xxi. 6. "And he showed me a river of *water* of life,—proceeding out of the throne of God, and of the Lamb," Apoc. xxii. 1. "And the Spirit and the Bride say, Come. And let him that heareth say, Come. And let him that is athirst, come. And whosoever will, let him take the *water* of life freely," Apoc. xxii. 17. By waters, in these passages, are understood truths: hence it is evident, that by the voice of many waters, is understood the divine truth of the Lord in the Word; as, also, in these places: "And, behold, the glory of the God of Israel came from the way of the east, and his voice was like a noise of *many waters:* and the earth shined with his glory," Ezek. xliii. 2. "And I heard a voice from heaven as *the voice of many waters*," Apoc. xiv. 2. "*The voice* of Jehovah is upon the *waters:* Jehovah is upon *many waters*," Psalm xxix. 3. When it is known, that by waters in the Word, are meant truths in the natural man, it may appear what was signified by washings, in the Israelitish church; and also what is signified by baptism; and likewise by these words of the Lord, in John: "Except a man be born of *water*, and of the spirit, he cannot enter into the kingdom of God," iii. 5. To be born of water, signifies to be born by truths; and of the spirit, signifies by a life according to them. That waters in an opposite sense signify falses, will be seen in what follows.

51. *And he had in his right hand seven stars*, signifies all knowledges of goodness and truth in the Word from him, which are thence with the angels of heaven and men of the church. About the angels, when they are beneath the heavens, there appear, as it were, little stars in great abundance; and in like manner, about spirits, who, when they lived in the world, had acquired to themselves knowledges of goodness and truth, or truths of life and doctrine from the Word. These stars appear fixed, with those who are in genuine truths from the Word; but wandering, with those who are in falsified truths. Concerning these little stars, as also concerning the stars which appear there in the firmament, I could relate wonderful things, but it does not belong to this work: hence it is evident that by stars are signified knowledges of goodness and truth from the Word. The Son of Man's having them in his right hand, signifies, that they are from the Lord alone through the Word. That seven signify all, may be seen above, n. 10. That knowledges of things good and true from the Word, are signified by stars, may also appear from these passages: "I will lay the earth desolate: For *the stars* of heaven and the constellations thereof shall not give their light," Isaiah xiii. 9, 10: the earth, which shall be laid desolate, is the church; which being vastated, the knowledges of things good and true in the Word do not appear. "And when I shall put thee out, I will cover the heaven and make *the stars* thereof dark: All the bright lights of heaven will I make dark over thee, and set darkness upon thy land," Ezek. xxxii. 7, 8: darkness upon the land, means falses in the church. "The sun and the moon are darkened, and *the stars* have withdrawn their shining," Joel ii. 10, 11; iii. 15. "Immediately after the tribulation of those days shall the sun be darkened, and the moon shall not give her light, and *the stars* shall fall from heaven," Matt. xxiv. 29; Mark xiii. 24. "And *the stars* of heaven fell unto the earth, even as a fig-tree casteth her untimely figs," Apoc. vi. 13. "And I saw *a star* fall from heaven unto the earth," Apoc. ix. 1. By stars falling from heaven are not to be understood stars, but that the knowledges of things good and true will perish. This is still more evident from its being said, that the tail of the dragon drew the third part of *the stars* from heaven, Apoc. xii. 4: also, that the he-goat cast down some of *the stars* and stamped upon them, Dan. viii. 8—11: therefore in the next verse, in Daniel, it is also said, that it cast down the truth to the ground, verse 12. The knowledges of things good and true, are also signified by stars, in these passages: "Jeho-

vah telleth the number of *the stars;* he calleth them all by their names," Psalm clxvii. 4. "Praise Jehovah all ye *stars* of light," Psalm cxlviii. 3. "*The stars* in their courses fought against Sisera," Judges v. 20. From hence it appears what is meant by these words in Daniel: "And they that be wise shall shine as the brightness of the firmament; and they that turn many to righteousness, as *the stars* for ever and ever," xii. 3. They that be wise, are such as are in truths; and they that turn many to righteousness, are such as are in goods.

52. *And out of his mouth went a sharp two-edged sword*, signifies the dispersion of falses by the Word, and by doctrine thence from the Lord. Sword very often occurs in the Word, and by it nothing else is signified but truth fighting against falses and destroying them; and, also, in an opposite sense, the false fighting against truths: for by wars in the Word, are signified spiritual wars, which are wars of truth against falsity, and of falsity against truth; wherefore, by weapons of war, such things are signified as are made use of in spiritual conflict. That the dispersion of falses by the Lord is here understood, is evident, because the sword was seen to go out of his mouth; and to go out of the mouth of the Lord, is to go out of the Word, for this the Lord spake with his mouth; and as the Word which is drawn from it is understood by the doctrine, this is also signified. It is called a sharp two-edged sword, because it penetrates the heart and soul. To show that by sword is here meant the dispersion of falses by the Word from the Lord, some passages shall be adduced in which sword is mentioned: "*A sword* upon the inhabitants of Babylon, and upon her princes, and upon her wise men. *A sword* is upon the liars, and they shall dote: *a sword* is upon her mighty men, and they shall be dismayed. *A sword* is upon their horses, and upon their chariots; *a sword* is upon her treasures, and they shall be robbed. A drought is upon her waters, and they shall be dried up," Jerem. 1. 35—38. These things are said of Babylon, by which those are understood who falsify and adulterate the Word; therefore by the liars who will dote, and the horses and chariots upon whom there is a sword, and the treasures which will be taken away, are signified the falses of their doctrines: that the waters upon which is a drought that they may be dried up, signify truths, may be seen above, n. 50. "Prophesy, and say, *A sword* is sharpened, and also furbished. It is sharpened to make a sore slaughter; and let *the sword* be doubled the third time; *the sword* of the slain; it is *the sword* of the great men that are slain, which entereth into their privy chambers," Ezek. xxi. 9—20. By sword is here also meant the devastation of truth in the church. "Jehovah will plead by *his sword* with all flesh, and the slain of Jehovah shall be

many," Isaiah lxvi. 16. They are called the slain of Jehovah here, and in other parts of the Word, who perish by falses. "The spoilers are come upon all high places through the wilderness: for *the sword of Jehovah* shall devour from the one end of the land, even to the other," Jerem. xii. 12. "We gat our bread with the peril of our lives, because of *the sword* of the wilderness," Lament. v. 9. "Woe to the idle shepherd that leaveth the flock! *the sword* shall be upon his arm and upon his right eye," Zech. xi. 17. The sword upon the right eye of the shepherd is the falsity of his understanding. "Even the sons of men, whose teeth are spears and arrows, and their tongue a sharp *sword*," Psalm lviii. 4. "Behold they belch out with their mouth: *swords* are in their lips," Psalm lix. 7. "The workers of iniquity, who whet their tongue like *a sword*," Psalm lxiv. 3. The same is signified by sword in other places, as in Isaiah xiii. 13, 15; xxi. 14, 15; xxvii. 1; xxxi. 7, 8; Jerem. ii. 30; v. 12; xi. 22; xiv. 13—18; Ezek. vii. 15; xxxii. 10—12. Hence it may appear what the Lord meant by sword in the following passages: "Jesus said, that he came not to send peace on earth, but *a sword*," Matt. x. 34. Jesus said, "He that hath a purse and a scrip, let him take it; and he that hath no *sword*, let him sell his garment and buy one. And his disciples said, Lord, behold, here are two *swords*. And he said unto them, It is enough," Luke xxii. 36, 38. "For all they that take *the sword*, shall perish with *the sword*," Matt. xxvi. 52. Jesus says, concerning the consummation of the age, "They shall fall by the edge of *the sword*, and shall be led away captive into all nations, and Jerusalem shall be trodden down of the Gentiles," Luke xxi. 24. The consummation of the age is the last time of the church; the sword is falsity destroying truth; the Gentiles are evils; Jerusalem which shall be trodden down, is the church. Hence, then, it is evident, that by a sharp sword going out of the mouth of the Son of Man, is signified the dispersion of falses by the Lord by means of the Word. The same is signified in the following passages in the Apocalypse: "And there was given unto him a great *sword* who sat upon the red horse," vi. 4. "And out of his mouth who sat upon the white horse goeth a sharp *sword*, that with it he should smite the nations. And the remnant were slain with *the sword* of him that sat upon the horse," xix. 15, 21. By him who sat upon the white horse, is understood the Lord as to the Word, which is plainly declared, verse 13, 16. The same is understood in David: "Gird *thy sword* upon thy thigh, O most Mighty, with thy glory and thy majesty. And in thy majesty ride prosperously because of truth. Thine arrows are sharp in the heart of the king's enemies," Psalm **xlv.** 3—5; speaking of the Lord. And in another place,

"Let the saints be joyful in glory, and a two-edged *sword* in their hand," Psalm cxlix. 5, 6. And in Isaiah, "Jehovah hath made my mouth a sharp *sword*," xlix. 2.

53. *And his face was as the sun shineth in his power*, signifies the divine love and the divine wisdom, which are himself, and proceed from himself. That by the face of Jehovah, or of the Lord, is understood the Divine Himself in his Essence, which is divine love and divine wisdom himself, will be thus seen in the explanations below, where mention is made of the face of God. The same is signified by the sun shining in his strength. That the Lord is seen as a sun in heaven before the angels, and that it is his divine love together with his divine wisdom, which have that appearance, may be seen in the work concerning *Heaven and Hell*, n. 116—125; and in *The Angelic Wisdom concerning the Divine Love and the Divine Wisdom*, n. 83—172. It remains here only to be confirmed from the Word, that the sun, when mentioned in reference to the Lord, signifies his divine love, and at the same time his divine wisdom; this may appear from the following places: "In that day the light of the moon shall be as the light of *the sun*, and the light of *the sun* shall be seven-fold, as the light of seven days," Isaiah xxx. 26. That day is the advent of the Lord, when the old church is destroyed, and a new one is about to be established; the light of the moon is faith from charity, and the light of the sun is intelligence and wisdom from love, and thus from the Lord. "Thy *sun* shall no more go down, neither shall thy moon withdraw itself; for Jehovah shall be thine everlasting light," Isaiah lx. 20. The sun which shall not set, is love and wisdom from the Lord. "The rock of Israel spake unto me:—And he shall be as the light of the morning when the *sun* riseth," 2 Sam. xxiii. 3, 4. The rock of Israel is the Lord. "His throne shall be as the *sun* before me," Psalm lxxxix. 36, 37. This is said of David: but by David is there meant the Lord. "They shall fear thee as long as the *sun* and moon endure. In his days shall the righteous flourish, and abundance of peace so long as the moon endureth: his name shall be continued as long as the *sun:* and men shall be blessed in him," Psalm lxxii. 5, 7, 17. This also is said of the Lord. As the Lord appears as a sun in heaven in the sight of the angels, therefore when he was transfigured, "his face did shine as the *sun*, and his raiment was white as the light," Matt. xvii. 2. And it is said of the strong angel who came down from heaven, that he was "clothed with a cloud,—and his face was as it were the *sun*," Apoc. x. 1: and of the woman, that she appeared "clothed with the *sun*," Apoc. xii. 1. The sun in these passages also signifies love and wisdom from the Lord; the woman is the church, which is called the New Jerusalem. Since, by the sun, is understood the Lord as to love and wisdom, it is

evident what is signified by the sun in the following places: "And it shall come to pass in that day—that the moon shall be confounded, and the *sun* ashamed, when Jehovah of hosts shall reign in mount Zion," Isaiah xxiv. 21, 23. "And when I shall have put thee out, I will cover the heavens and make the stars thereof dark; I will cover the *sun* with a cloud and the moon shall not give her light:—and I will set darkness upon thy land," Ezek. xxxii. 7, 8. "The day of Jehovah cometh, a day of darkness,—the *sun* and the moon shall be dark, and the stars shall withdraw their shining," Joel ii. 1, 10. "The *sun* shall be turned into darkness, and the moon into blood, before the great and terrible day of Jehovah come," Joel ii. 31. "The day of Jehovah is near in the valley of decision. The *sun* and the moon shall be darkened," Joel iii. 14, 15. "And the fourth angel sounded, and the third part of the *sun* was smitten,—and the third part of the stars,—and the day shone not for a third part of it," Apoc. viii. 12. "And the *sun* became black as sack-cloth of hair, and the moon became as blood," Apoc. vi. 12. "And the *sun* and the air were darkened by the smoke of the pit," Apoc. ix. 2. In these passages, by sun is not meant the sun of this world, but the sun of the angelic heaven, which is the divine love and the divine wisdom of the Lord; these are said to be obscured, darkened, covered, and to become black, when there are evils and falses in man. Hence it is evident, that the same is meant by the Lord's words, where he speaks of the consummation of the age, which is the last time of the church: "Immediately after the tribulation of those days shall the *sun* be darkened, and the moon shall not give her light, and the stars shall fall from heaven," Matt. xxiv. 29; Mark xiii. 24, 25. And in like manner in the following passages: "And the *sun* shall go down over the prophets, and the day shall be dark over them," Micah iii. 5, 6. "In that day—I will cause the *sun* to go down at noon, and I will darken the earth in the clear day," Amos viii. 9. "She that hath borne seven hath given up the ghost; her *sun* is gone down while it was yet day," Jerem. xv. 9; speaking of the Jewish church, which was to breathe out its soul, or, in other words, would perish: the sun shall set, signifies that there will be no longer any love and charity. What is said in Joshua, that the *sun* stood still upon Gibeon, and the moon in the valley of Ajalon, x. 12, 13, appears as if it was historical, but it is prophetic, being quoted from the book of Jasher, which was a prophetic book; for it is said, "Is not this written in the book of Jasher?" verse 13; the same book is also mentioned as prophetic by David, 2 Sam. i. 17, 18; something similar is also said in Habakkuk: "The mountains—trembled,—the *sun* and moon stood still in their habitation," iii. 10. "Thy *sun* shall no more go down; neither shall thy moon withdraw itself," Isaiah lx. 20

for to make the sun and moon stand still would be to destroy the universe. The Lord as to his divine love and his divine wisdom, being meant by the sun, therefore the ancients in their holy worship turned their faces to the rising sun; and also their temples, which custom still continues. That the sun and moon of this world are not understood in these places, is evident from its having been considered profane and abominable to adore them, as may be seen in Numb. xxv. 1—4; Deut. iv. 19; xvii. 3, 5; Jerem. viii. 1, 2; xliii. 10, 13; xliv. 17—19, 25; Ezek. viii. 16; for by the sun of this world is understood self-love and the pride of self-derived intelligence; and self-love is diametrically opposite to divine love; and the pride of self-derived intelligence is opposite to divine wisdom. To adore the sun of this world is also to acknowledge nature to be creative, and self-derived prudence to be effective of all things, which implies a negation of God, and a negation of the Divine Providence.

54. *And when I saw him, I fell at his feet as dead*, signifies that from such presence there was a defect or deprivation of his own life. Man's proper life cannot sustain the presence of the Lord, such as the Lord is in himself, nor such as he is intimately in his Word; for the Divine Love is just like the sun, which no one can bear as it is in itself, without being consumed. This is what is meant by saying that "no one can see God and live," Exod. xxxiii. 20; Judges xiii. 22. This being the case, the Lord appears to the angels in heaven as a sun, at a distance from them, as the sun of this world is from men; the reason is, because the Lord in himself is in that sun. But yet the Lord so moderates and tempers his Divine Essence as to enable man to sustain his presence, which is done by veilings or coverings; such was the case when he revealed himself to many in the Word; yea, by veils or coverings he is present in every one who worships him; as he himself says in John: "He that hath my commandments, and keepeth them;—I will manifest myself to him," xiv. 21, 23. "That he will be in them, and they in him," xv. 4, 5. Hence it is evident why John, when he saw the Lord in such glory, fell at his feet as dead; and also, why the three disciples, when they saw the Lord in glory, were heavy with sleep, and a cloud covered them, Luke ix. 32, 34.

55. *And he laid his right hand upon me*, signifies life then inspired from him. The reason why the Lord laid his right hand upon him, is, because communication is produced by the touch of the hands, for the life of the mind, and thence of the body, puts itself forth into the arms, and through them into the hands; on this account, the Lord touched with his hand those whom he restored to life and healed, Mark i. 31, 41; vii. 32, 33; viii. 22—27; x. 13, 16; Luke v. 12, 13; vii 14; xviii. 15; xxii. 51; and in like manner, "After his disciples saw Jesus transfigured, he touched them, and they fell on their faces,"

Matt. xvii. 6, 7. The origin of this is, because the presence of the Lord with man is adjunction, and thus conjunction by contiguity, and this contiguity is nearer and fuller in proportion as man loves the Lord, that is, does his commandments. From these few considerations it may appear, that by laying his right hand upon him, is signified inspiring him with his life.

56. *Saying unto me, Fear not*, signifies resuscitation, and at the same time adoration from the most profound humiliation. That it signifies resuscitation to life, is a consequence of what went before, n. 55; and that it signifies adoration from the most profound humiliation, is evident, for he fell at the Lord's feet; and as a holy fear seized him, the Lord said, on his being resuscitated, Fear not. Holy fear, which sometimes is joined with a sacred tremor of the interiors of the mind, and sometimes with horripilation,* supervenes, when life enters from the Lord in place of man's proper life; the proper life of man is to look from himself to the Lord, but life from the Lord is to look from the Lord to the Lord, and yet as if from himself; when man is in this latter life, he sees that he himself is not any thing, but only the Lord. Daniel also was in this holy fear, when he saw the man clothed in linen, whose loins were girded with fine gold of Uphaz, his body like the beryl, his face like lightning, his eyes like lamps of fire, and his arms and feet as the shining of polished brass, upon seeing whom Daniel also became as dead, and a hand touched him, and a voice said, *Fear not, Daniel*, Dan. x. 5—12. Something similar occurred to Peter, James, and John, when the Lord was transfigured, and appeared as to his face like the sun, and his garments as the light, upon which they also fell upon their faces, and were sore afraid, and then Jesus came and touched them, saying, *Be not afraid*, Matt. xvii. 5, 6, 7. The Lord also said unto the woman who saw him at the sepulchre, *Fear not*, Matt. xxviii. 10. Likewise the angel, whose face was like lightning, and his garment as snow, said unto those women, *Fear not ye*, Matt. xxviii. 3, 4, 5. The angel said to Zechariah also, *Fear not*, Luke i. 12, 13. In like manner the angel said to Mary, *Fear not*, Luke i. 30. The angel said to the shepherds also, when the glory of the Lord shone round about them, *Fear not*, Luke ii. 9, 10. A similar holy fear seized Simon, by reason of the draught of fishes; therefore he said, Depart from me, for I am a sinful man, O Lord; but Jesus said unto him, *Fear not*, Luke v. 8, 9, 10; besides other places. These are adduced that it may be known why the Lord said to John, Fear not, and that by it is denoted resuscitation and then adoration from the most profound humiliation.

57. *I am the First and the Last*, which signifies that He

---

* Erection of the hair caused by horror.

alone is eternal and infinite, therefore the only God, may appear from the explanation above, n. 13, 29, 38.

58. *And am he that liveth*, signifies, who alone is life, and from whom alone is life. Jehovah, in the Word of the Old Testament, calls himself the LIFE and the LIVING, because he alone lives; for he is love itself and wisdom itself, and these are life. That there is one only life, which is God, and that angels and men are recipients of life from him, is abundantly shown in *The Angelic Wisdom concerning the Divine Love and the Divine Wisdom*. Jehovah calls himself the *Living* and him that *Liveth*, in Isaiah xxxviii. 18, 19; Jerem. v. 2; xii. 16; xvi. 14, 15; xxiii. 7, 8; xlvi. 18; Ezek. v. 21. The Lord as to his Divine Humanity also is life, because the Father and he are one; therefore he says, "As the Father hath *life* in himself, so hath he given to the Son to have *life* in himself," John v. 26. "Jesus said, I am the resurrection and the *life*," John xi. 25. "Jesus said, I am the way, the truth, and the *life*," John xiv. 6. "In the beginning was the Word, and God was the Word; in him was *life*; and the Word was made flesh," John i. 1—4, 14. Because the Lord is alone life, it follows, that from him alone life is derived, therefore he says, "Because I *live*, ye shall live also," John xiv. 19.

59. *And was dead*, signifies that he was neglected in the church, and his Divine Humanity not acknowledged. By his becoming dead is not understood that he was crucified, and so died, but that he was neglected in the church, and his Divine Humanity not acknowledged, for so he became dead among men. His divinity from eternity is indeed acknowledged, but this is Jehovah himself; but his Humanity is not acknowledged to be divine, although the divine essence and the human in him are like soul and body, and therefore are not two but one, yea, one person, according to the doctrine received throughout the whole Christian world, which has its name from Athanasius. When, therefore, the divine in him is separated from the human, by saying that his Humanity is not divine, but like the human essence of any other man, in this case he is dead among men. But concerning this separation and consequent death of the Lord, more may be seen in *The Doctrine of the New Jerusalem concerning the Lord;* and in *The Angelic Wisdom concerning the Divine Providence*, n. 262, 263.

60. *And, behold, I am alive for ever and ever*, signifies that he is life eternal. Now as, who am alive, signifies that he alone is life, and from him alone life is derived, as above, n. 58, it follows that, Behold, I am alive for ever and ever, signifies that he alone is life to eternity, and consequently that eternal life is from him alone; for eternal life is in him, and consequently from him. For ever and ever, signifies eternity. That eternal life is from the Lord alone, is plain from the

following passages: "Jesus said, Whosoever believeth on me shall not perish, but have *everlasting life*," John iii. 16. "Every one that believeth in the Son hath *everlasting life*, but he who believeth not in the Son, shall not see *life*, but the wrath of God abideth on him," John vi. 40, 47, 48. "Verily, I say unto you, he that believeth on me hath *everlasting life*," John vi. 47. "I am the resurrection and *the life*; he that believeth in me, though he were dead, yet shall he live: and whosoever believeth in me, shall never die," John xi. 24, 26: and in other places. Hence, then, the Lord is called, He that is alive for ever and ever: as also in the following passages of the Apocalypse, iv. 9, 10; v. 14; x. 6; Dan. iv. 34.

61. *Amen*, signifies the divine confirmation that it is the truth. That amen is the truth, which is the Lord, may be seen above, n. 23.

62. *And have the keys of hell and death*, signifies that he alone has power to save. By keys is signified the power of opening and shutting; in this instance, the power of opening hell, that man may be brought forth, and of shutting it, lest, when he is brought forth, he should enter it again; for man is born in evils of all kinds, thus in hell, for evils are hell: he is brought out of it by the Lord, to whom belongs the power of opening it. The reason why by having the keys of hell and death, is not understood the power of casting into hell, but the power of saving, is, because it immediately follows after these words: "Behold, I am alive for ever and ever;" by which is signified that he alone is eternal life, n. 60; and the Lord never casts any one into hell, but man casts himself. By keys is signified the power of opening and shutting, in the Apocalypse also, iii. 7; ix. 1; xx. 1: also in Isaiah, xxii. 21, 22; in Matthew, xvi. 19; and in Luke, xi. 52. The power of the Lord is not only over heaven, but also over hell; for hell is kept in order and connexion by oppositions against heaven; for which reason, he who governs the one must necessarily govern the other; otherwise man could not be saved: to be saved is to be brought out of hell.

63. *Write the things which thou hast seen, and the things which are, and the things which shall be hereafter*, signifies that all the things now revealed are for the use of posterity; as may appear without explanation.

64. *The mystery of the seven stars which thou sawest in my right hand, and the seven golden candlesticks*, signifies arcana in visions concerning the new heaven and the new church. That by seven stars is signified the church in the heavens, and by seven candlesticks the church upon earth, will be seen in what now follows.

65. *The seven stars are the angels of the seven churches*, signifies the New Church in the heavens, which is the new hea

ven. The church exists in the heavens as well as upon earth; for the Word is in the heavens as well as upon earth, and there are doctrines and preachings from it: on which subject see *The New Jerusalem concerning the Sacred Scripture*, n. 70—75, and n. 104—113. That church is the new heaven, concerning which something is said in the preface. The reason why the church in the heavens, or the new heaven, is meant by the seven stars, is, because it is said, that the seven stars are the angels of the seven churches, and by angel is signified a heavenly society. In the spiritual world there appears a firmament full of stars, as in the natural world, and this appearance is from the angelic societies in heaven: each society there shines like a star to those who are below; hence they there know in what situation the angelic societies are. That seven does not signify seven, but all who are of the church there, according to the reception of each, may be seen above, n. 10, 14, 41; therefore, by the angels of the seven churches, is meant the universal church in the heavens, consequently the new heaven in the aggregate.

66. *And the seven candlesticks which thou sawest are the seven churches*, signifies the new church upon earth, which is the New Jerusalem descending from the Lord out of the new heaven. That the candlesticks are the church, may be seen above, n. 43; and whereas seven signify all, n. 10, by the seven candlesticks are not understood seven churches, but the church in the aggregate, which in itself is one, but various according to reception. Those varieties may be compared to the various jewels in the crown of a king; and they may also be compared to the various members and organs in a perfect body, which yet make a one. The perfection of every form consists in various things being suitably disposed in their order; hence it is, that the universal new church is described, as to its various particulars, by the seven churches, in what follows.

67. THE FAITH OF THE NEW HEAVEN AND NEW CHURCH, COMPREHENDED IN ONE UNIVERSAL IDEA, is this, that the Lord from eternity, who is Jehovah, came into the world to subdue the hells and glorify his Humanity; and that without this no flesh could have been saved; and that they will be saved who believe in him.

It is said, in a universal idea, because this is the universal of faith, and the universal of faith is what enters into all and every particular. It is a universal of faith, that God is one in person and in essence, in whom there is a trinity, and that the Lord is that God. It is a universal of faith, that no mortal could have been saved unless the Lord had come into the world. It is a universal of faith, that he came into the world that he might remove hell from man; and that he did remove it by successive combats against it and victories over it; whereby he finally subdued it, and reduced it to order, and under obedience to himself. It is also a universal of faith, that he came into the world to glorify the Humanity, which he assumed in the world, that is, to unite it with the all-begetting Divinity, from whom are all things; thus having subdued hell, he keeps it in order, and under obedience, to eternity. Now as neither of these could have come to pass except by means of temptations, even to the last and most extreme of all, which was the passion of the cross, therefore he endured it. These are the universals of faith concerning the Lord.

The universal of the Christian faith on man's part, is, to believe in the Lord; for by believing in him he has conjunction with him, and by conjunction, salvation. To believe in him is to have confidence that he will save; and because none can have such confidence but he who leads a good life, therefore this also is understood by believing in him.

These two universals of the Christian faith have been specifically treated of; the first, which relates to the Lord, in *The Doctrine of the New Jerusalem concerning the Lord;* and the second, which relates to man, in *The Doctrine of the New Jerusalem concerning Charity and Faith,* and in *The Doctrine of Life:* and both now in the explanations of the Apocalypse.

CHAPTER II.

1. UNTO the angel of the church of Ephesus write; These things saith he that holdeth the seven stars in his right hand, who walketh in the midst of the seven golden candlesticks.

2. I know thy works, and thy labour, and thy endurance, and how thou canst not bear them that are evil, and hast tried them that say they are apostles, and are not, and hast found them liars;

3. And hast borne, and hast endurance, and for my name's sake hast laboured, and hast not fainted.

4. Nevertheless I have somewhat against thee, that thou hast left thy first charity.

5. Remember therefore from whence thou art fallen; and repent, and do the first works; or else I will come unto thee quickly, and will remove thy candlestick out of its place, except thou repent.

6. But this thou hast, that thou hatest the works of the Nicolaitanes, which I also hate.

7. He that hath an ear, let him hear what the Spirit saith unto the churches: To him that overcometh will I give to eat of the tree of life, which is in the midst of the paradise of God.

8. And unto the angel of the church in Smyrna write; These things saith the First and the Last, who was dead, and is alive.

9. I know thy works, and tribulation, and poverty (but thou art rich), and I know the blasphemy of them that say they are Jews, and are not, but are the synagogue of Satan.

10. Fear none of those things which thou shalt suffer. Behold, the devil shall cast some of you into prison, that ye may be tried: and ye shall have tribulation ten days: be thou faithful unto death, and I will give thee a crown of life.

11. He that hath an ear, let him hear what the Spirit saith unto the churches: He that overcometh shall not be hurt of the second death.

12. And to the angel of the church in Pergamos write, These things saith He that hath the sharp sword with two edges.

13. I know thy works, and where thou dwellest, even where Satan's throne is: and thou holdest fast my name, and hast not denied my faith, even in those days wherein Antipas was my faithful martyr, who was slain among you where Satan dwelleth.

14. But I have a few things against thee, because thou hast there them that hold the doctrine of Balaam, who taught Balak to cast a stumbling-block before the children of Israel, to eat things sacrificed unto idols, and to commit fornication.

15. So hast thou also them that hold the doctrine of the Nicolaitanes; which thing I hate.

16. Repent, or else I will come unto thee quickly, and will fight against them with the sword of my mouth.

17. He that hath an ear, let him hear what the Spirit saith unto the churches: To him that overcometh will I give to eat of the hidden manna; and will give him a white stone, and in the stone a new name written, which no man knoweth saving he that receiveth it.

18. And unto the angel of the church in Thyatira write; These things saith the Son of God, who hath his eyes like unto a flame of fire, and his feet like fine brass.

19. I know thy works, and charity, and service, and faith, and thy endurance, and thy works; and the last to be more than the first.

20. Notwithstanding, I have a few things against thee, because thou sufferest that woman Jezebel, who calleth herself a prophetess, to teach, and to seduce my servants to commit whoredom, and to eat things sacrificed unto idols.

21. And I gave her time to repent of her whoredom; and she repented not.

22. Behold, I will cast her into a bed, and them that commit adultery with her into great tribulation, except they repent of their deeds.

23. And I will kill her children with death. And all the churches shall know that I am he that searcheth the reins and hearts; and I will give unto every one of you according to your works.

24. But unto you, I say, and unto the rest in Thyatira, as many as have not this doctrine, and who have not known the depths of Satan, as they speak; I will put upon you none other burden.

25. Nevertheless, that which ye have, hold fast till I come.

26. And he that overcometh and keepeth my works unto the end, to him will I give power over the nations;

27. And he shall rule them with a rod of iron, as the vessels of a potter shall they be broken to shivers: even as I received of my Father.

28. And I will give him the morning star.

29. He that hath an ear, let him hear what the Spirit saith unto the churches.

THE SPIRITUAL SENSE.

68. THE CONTENTS OF THE WHOLE CHAPTER. To the churches in the Christian world: to those therein who primarily regard truths of doctrine and not good of life, who are understood by the church of Ephesus, n. 72—90. To those therein who are in good as to life and in falses as to doctrine, who are understood by the church in Smyrna, n. 91—106. To those therein who place the all of the church in good works, and not any thing in truths, who are understood by the church in Pergamos, n. 107—123. And to those therein who are in faith originating in charity, as also to those who are in faith separated from charity, who are understood by the church in Thyatira, n. 124—152. All these are called to the New Church, which is the New Jerusalem.

THE CONTENTS OF EACH VERSE. v. 1, "Unto the angel of the church of Ephesus write," signifies to those and concerning those who primarily respect truths of doctrine, and not good of life: "These things saith he that holdeth the seven stars in his right hand," signifies the Lord, from whom, by the Word, proceed all truths: "Who walketh in the midst of the seven golden candlesticks," signifies from whom all illumination is received by those who are of his church: v. 2, "I know thy works," signifies that he sees all the interiors and exteriors of man at once: "And thy labour and thy endurance," signifies their study and patience: "And how thou canst not bear them that are evil," signifies that they cannot bear that evil should be called good, nor the reverse: "And hast tried them that say they are apostles, and are not, and hast found them liars," signifies that they scrutinize those things which are called goods and truths in the church, which nevertheless are evils and falses: v. 3, "And hast borne and hast endurance," signifies patience with them: "And for my name's sake hast laboured, and hast not fainted," signifies their study and endeavour to attain the things which belong to religion and its doctrine: v. 4, "Nevertheless I have somewhat against thee, that thou hast left thy first charity," signifies that this is against them, that they do not esteem good of life in the first place: v. 5, "Remember therefore from whence thou art fallen," signifies remembrance of their error: "And repent, and do the first works," signifies that they ought to invert the state of their life: "Or else I will come unto thee quickly, and will remove thy candlestick out of its place, except thou repent," signifies that otherwise, of a certainty, illumination will not be given them to see truths any longer: v. 6, "But this thou hast, that thou hatest the works of the Nicolaitanes, which I also hate," signifies that they know this by virtue of the truths they possess, and thence are not willing that works should be meritorious: v. 7, "He that hath an ear, let him hear what the Spirit saith unto the churches," signifies that he that understands, ought to obey what the divine truth of the Word teaches those who are to be of the New Church, which is the New Jerusalem: "To him that overcometh," signifies he who fights against evils and falses, and is reformed: "Will I give to eat of the tree of life," signifies appropriation of the good of love and charity from the Lord: "Which is in the midst of the paradise of God," signifies interiorly in the truths of wisdom and faith.

v. 8, "And unto the angel of the church in Smyrna write," signifies to those and concerning those who are in good as to life, but in falses as to doctrine: "These things saith the First and the Last," signifies the Lord, that he is the only God: "Who was dead and is alive," signifies that he is neglected in the church, and his Humanity not acknowledged to be divine, when yet as to that also he alone is life, and from him alone is life everlasting: v. 9, "I know thy works," signifies that the Lord sees all their interiors and exteriors at once: "And tribulation and poverty (but thou art rich)," signifies that they are in falses, and thence not in goods: "And I know the blasphemy of them that say they are Jews, and are not," signifies the false assertion that they possess the goods of love, when in fact they do not: "But are the synagogue of Satan," signifies, because they are in falses as to doctrine: v. 10, "Fear none of those things which thou shalt suffer," signifies, despair not when infested by evils and assaulted by falses: "Behold the devil shall cast some of you into prison," signifies that their good of life will be infested by evils from hell: "That ye may be tried," signifies by falses fighting against them: "And ye shall have tribulation ten days," signifies that it will endure its full time: "Be thou faithful unto death," signifies reception of truths until falses are removed: "And I will give thee a crown of life," signifies that they will then have eternal life, the reward of victory: v. 11, "He that hath an ear, let him hear what the Spirit saith unto the churches," signifies here, as before: "He that overcometh," signifies he that fights against evils and falses, and is reformed: "Shall not be hurt of the second death," signifies that afterwards they shall not yield to evils and falses from hell.

v. 12, "And to the angel of the church in Pergamos write," signifies to those and concerning those who place the all of the church in good works, and not any thing in truths of doctrine: "These things saith he that hath the sharp sword with two edges," signifies the Lord as to the truths of doctrine from the Word, by which evils and falses are dispersed: v. 13, "I know thy works," signifies here, as before: "And where thou dwellest, even where Satan's throne is," signifies their life in darkness: "And thou holdest fast my name, and hast not denied my faith," signifies when yet they have religion and worship according to it: "Even in those days wherein Antipas was my faithful martyr, who was slain among you where Satan dwelleth," signifies when all truth was extinguished by falses in the church: v. 14, "But I have a few things against thee," signifies that the things which follow are against them: "Because thou hast there them that hold the doctrine of Balaam, who taught Balak to cast a stumbling-block before the children of Israel, to eat things sacrificed unto idols, and to commit fornication," signifies that there are some among them who do hypocritical works, by which the worship of God in the church is defiled and adulterated: v. 15, "So hast thou also them that hold the doctrine of the Nicolaitanes, which thing I hate," signifies that there are some among them also who make works meritorious: v. 16, "Repent," signifies that they should take heed of such works: "Or else I will come unto thee quickly, and will fight against them with the sword of my mouth," signifies, if not, that the Lord will contend with them from the Word: v. 17, "He that hath an ear, let him hear what the Spirit saith unto the churches," signifies here, as before: "To him that overcometh," signifies here, the same as before: "Will I give to eat of the hidden manna," signifies the appropriation then of the good of celestial love, and thus conjunction of the Lord with those who operate: "And will give him a white stone," signifies truths affirmative and united to good: "And in the stone a new name written," signifies that thus they will have good of a quality such as they had not before: "Which no man knoweth saving he that receiveth it," signifies that it does not appear to any one, because it is written in their lives.

v. 18, "And unto the angel of the church in Thyatira write," signifies to those and concerning those, who are in faith grounded in charity, and thence in good works; and also to those and concerning those, who are in faith separated from charity, and thence in evil works: "These things saith the Son of God who hath his eyes like unto a flame of fire," signifies the Lord as to the divine wisdom of his divine love: "And his feet like fine brass," signifies divine good natural: v. 19, "I know thy works," signifies here, as before: "And charity and service," signifies the spiritual affection which is called charity, and its operation: "And faith, and thy endurance, and thy works," signifies truth and the desire of acquiring and teaching it: "And the last to be more than the first," signifies the increase thereof from the spiritual affection of truth: v. 20, "Notwithstanding, I have a few things against thee," signifies what follows: "Because thou sufferest that woman Jezebel," signifies that among them there are some in the church who separate faith from charity: "Who calleth herself a prophetess," signifies, and who make the doctrine of faith the sole doctrine of the church: "To teach and to seduce my servants to commit whoredom," signifies, from which it comes to pass that the truths of the Word are falsified: "And to eat things sacrificed unto idols," signifies the defilement of divine worship, and profanations: v. 21, "And I gave her time to repent of her whoredom, and she repented not," signifies that they who have confirmed themselves in that doctrine will not recede, although they see things contrary to it in the Word: v. 22, "Behold, I will cast her into a bed, and them that commit adultery with her into great tribulation," signifies that therefore they will be left in their doctrine with falsifications, and that they will be grievously infested by falses: "Except they repent of their deeds," signifies if they will not desist from separating faith from charity: v. 23, "And I will kill her children with death," signifies that all the truths of the Word will be turned into falses: "And all the churches shall know that I am he which searcheth the reins and hearts," signifies that the church shall know that the Lord sees the quality of every one's truth, and the quality of his good: "And I will give unto every one of you according to your works," signifies that he gives unto every one according to the charity and its faith which is in his works: v. 24, "But unto you I say, and unto the rest in Thyatira, as many as have not this doctrine," signifies to those with whom the doctrine of faith is separated from charity, and to those with whom the doctrine of faith is joined with charity: "And who have not known the depths of Satan as they speak," signifies they who do not understand their interiors, which are mere falses: "I will put upon you none other burden," signifies only that they should beware of them: v. 25, "Nevertheless, that which ye have, hold fast till I come," signifies that they should retain the few things which they know concerning charity, and thence concerning faith from the Word, and live according to them until the Lord's coming: v. 26, "And he that overcometh and keepeth my works unto the end," signifies those who are in charity and thence actually in faith, and remain in them to the end of their lives: "To him will I give power over the nations," signifies that they shall overcome the evils in themselves which are from hell: v. 27, "And he shall rule them with a rod of iron," signifies by truths from the literal sense of the Word, and at the same time by rational principles derived from natural light: "As the vessels of a potter shall they be broken to shivers," signifies as of little or no account: "Even as I received of my Father," signifies this from the Lord, who, when he was in the world, procured to himself all power over the hells, from the divine principle which was within him: v. 28, "And I will give him the morning star," signifies intelligence and wisdom: v. 29, "He that hath an ear, let him hear what the Spirit saith unto the churches," signifies here, as before.

THE EXPLANATION.

69. THIS and the following chapter treat of the seven churches, by which are described all those in the Christian church who have any religion, and out of whom the New Church, which is the New Jerusalem, can be formed; and this is formed by those who APPROACH THE LORD ONLY, AND AT THE SAME TIME PERFORM REPENTANCE FROM EVIL WORKS. The rest, who do not approach the Lord alone, from the confirmed negation of the divinity of his Humanity, and who do not perform repentance from evil works, are indeed in the church, but have nothing of the church in them.

70. Since the Lord alone is acknowledged as the God of heaven and earth, by those who are of his New Church in the

heavens, and by those who will be of his New Church upon earth; therefore, in the first chapter of the Apocalypse the Lord alone is treated of; and in the two following chapters, it is he alone who speaks to the churches, and he alone who will give the felicities of eternal life. That it is he alone who speaks to the churches is evident from these passages: "Unto the angel of the church of Ephesus write, *These things saith He that holdeth the seven stars in his right hand, who walketh in the midst of the seven golden candlesticks,*" ii. 1. "Unto the angel of the church in Smyrna write, *These things saith the First and the Last,*" ii. 8. "To the angel of the church in Pergamos write, *These things saith He which hath the sharp sword with two edges,*" ii. 12. "Unto the angel of the church in Thyatira write, *These things saith the Son of God, who hath his eyes like unto a flame of fire, and his feet are like fine brass,*" ii. 18. "Unto the angel of the church in Sardis, write, *These things saith He that hath the seven spirits of God, and the seven stars,*" iii. 1. "To the angel of the church in Philadelphia write, *These things saith He that is holy, He that is true, He that hath the key of David,*" iii. 7. "And unto the angel of the church of the Laodiceans write, *These things saith the Amen, the faithful and true Witness, the Beginning of the creation of God,*" iii. 14. These expressions are taken from the first chapter, in which the Lord alone is treated of, and where he is described by all these attributes.

71. That the Lord alone will give the felicities of eternal life to those who are and will be of his church, is evident from these passages: The Lord said to the church of Ephesus, "To him that overcometh *will I give to eat of the tree of life, which is in the midst of the paradise of God,*" ii. 7. Unto the church in Smyrna, "*I will give thee a crown of life.* He that overcometh shall not be hurt of the second death," ii. 10, 11. Unto the church in Pergamos, "To him that overcometh *will I give to eat of the hidden manna, and will give him a white stone, and in the stone a new name written, which no man knoweth saving he that receiveth it,*" ii. 17. Unto the church in Thyatira, "*To him will I give power over the nations, and I will give him the morning star,*" ii. 26, 28. Unto the church in Philadelphia, "Him that overcometh *will I make a pillar in the temple of my God;* and I will write upon him the name of my God, and the name of the city of my God, which is New Jerusalem, and my new name," iii. 12. Unto the church in Laodicea, "To him that overcometh *will I grant to sit with me in my throne,*" iii. 21. From these passages it is also evident, that the Lord alone is to be acknowledged in the New Church. Hence it is that this church is called *The Lamb's Wife,* Apoc. xix. 7, 9; xxi. 9, 10.

72. That the New Church, which is the New Jerusalem, is

to be formed of those who do repentance from evil works, is also manifest from the Lord's words to the churches: to that in Ephesus; "I know thy works;—nevertheless I have somewhat against thee, that thou hast left thy first charity. *Repent*, and do the first works; or else I will come unto thee quickly, and will remove thy candlestick out of his place, *except thou repent*," ii. 2, 4, 5. To the church in Pergamos; "I know thy works,—*repent*," ii. 13, 16. To the church in Thyatira; "I will deliver her into great tribulation, *except they repent* of their deeds,—and I will give unto every one of you according to his works," ii. 19, 22, 23. To the church in Sardis; "I have not found thy works perfect before God;—*repent*," iii. 1—3. To the church in Laodicea; "I know thy works;—be zealous, therefore, and *repent*," iii. 15, 19. But to proceed to the explanation.

73. *Unto the angel of the church of Ephesus write*, signifies, to those and concerning those, who primarily respect truths of doctrine and not good of life. It was shown above, n. 66, that by the seven churches are not meant seven churches, but the church in the aggregate, which in itself is one, but various according to reception; and that those varieties may be compared with the various members and organs in a perfect body, which yet make a one. They may also be compared with the various jewels in a king's crown; and hence it is that the universal New Church, with its various particulars, is described, in what now follows, by seven churches. That by the church of Ephesus, are understood those in the church who primarily respect truths of doctrine and not good of life, is clear from what is written to them, when understood in the spiritual sense. It is written to the angel of that church, because by an angel is understood an angelic society which corresponds to a church consisting of such, as above, n. 65.

74. *These things saith He that holdeth the seven stars in his right hand*, signifies the Lord, from whom, by the Word, proceed all truths. That He who holds the seven stars in his right hand, is the Lord; and that the seven stars in his right hand are all the knowledges of good and truth in the Word, which are thence from the Lord, with the angels of heaven and men of the church, may be seen above, n. 51. The knowledges of good and truth from the Word are truths.

75. *Who walketh in the midst of the seven golden candlesticks*, signifies, from whom all illumination is received by those who are of his church. That the seven candlesticks, in the midst of which was the Son of Man, signify the church, which is in illumination from the Lord, may be seen above, n. 43—66. He is here said to be walking, because to walk signifies to live, n. 167; and in the midst, signifies in the inmost and thence in all, n. 44, 383.

76. *I know thy works*, signifies that he sees all the interiors and exteriors of man at once. Works are often mentioned in the Apocalypse, but few know what is meant by works. This, however, is well known, that ten men may do works which externally appear alike, and which yet differ with them all; and this because they proceed from different ends and different causes, the end and the cause rendering the works either good or bad; for every work is a work of the mind, therefore such as is the quality of the mind, such is that of the work: if the mind be charity, the work becomes charity; but if the mind be not charity, the work is not charity: still, however, they may both appear externally alike. Works appear to men in their external form, but to angels in their internal form; and to the Lord their quality is apparent from inmost to outmost. Works in their external form appear like the outside of fruits, but works in their internal form appear like the inside of fruits, where there are innumerable eatable parts, and in the midst seeds, in which there are also things innumerable, which are too minute for the keenest eye to discern, yea, which are above the intellectual sphere of man: such are all works, the internal quality of which the Lord alone sees, and which the angels also perceive from the Lord, when performed by man. But on this subject more may be seen in *The Angelic Wisdom concerning the Divine Love and the Divine Wisdom*, n. 209—220, and n. 277—281; and also below, n. 141, 641, 868. From this it may appear, that by "I know thy works," is signified that the Lord sees all the interiors and exteriors of man at once.

77. *And thy labour and endurance;* that this signifies their study and patience, is evident without explanation.

78. *And how thou canst not bear them that are evil*, signifies that they cannot bear that evil shall be called good, nor the reverse, because this is contrary to the truths of doctrine. That this is the signification of these words, is evident from what follows, by which is signified that they scrutinize those things in the church which are called goods and truths, when yet they are evils and falses. To know goods, whether they be good or evil, pertains to doctrine, and is among its truths, but to do good or evil, pertains to life: this is said, therefore, of those who hold truths of doctrine in the first place, and not goods of life, n. 73. By them which are evil, in the spiritual sense, are not understood evil persons, but evils, because this sense is abstracted from persons.

79. *And hast tried them which say they are apostles, and are not, and hast found them liars*, signifies that they scrutinize those things which are called goods and truths in the church, which nevertheless are evils and falses. That this is what is signified, cannot be seen except by the spiritual sense, and consequently by knowing what is meant by apostles and liars: by

apostles are not understood apostles, but all who teach the goods and truths of the church, and, in an abstract sense, the goods and truths themselves of its doctrine. That apostles are not understood by apostles, clearly appears from these words addressed to them: "When the Son of Man shall sit on the throne of his glory, ye also shall sit upon twelve thrones judging the twelve tribes of Israel," Matt. xix. 28; Luke xxii. 30. Who does not see that the apostles neither will nor can judge any one, much less the twelve tribes of Israel, but that the Lord alone will do this according to the goods and truths of the doctrine of the church from the Word? In like manner from this passage: "And the wall of the city New Jerusalem had twelve foundations, and in them the names of the *twelve apostles* of the Lamb," Apoc. xxi. 14; because by the New Jerusalem, is signified the New Church, n. 880, 881; and by its foundations, all the goods and truths of its doctrine, n. 902, and following numbers. And also from this passage: "Rejoice over her, thou heaven, and ye holy *apostles* and prophets," Apoc. xviii. 20. What can the rejoicing of the apostles and prophets signify, unless by them are meant all who are in goods and truths of doctrine in the church? By the Lord's disciples are meant those who are instructed by the Lord in the goods and truths of doctrine; but by apostles they who, after they are instructed, teach them; for it is said, "Jesus sent his *twelve disciples* to preach the kingdom of God, and the *apostles*, when they were returned, told him all that they had done," Luke ix. 1, 2, 10; Mark vi. 7, 30. That by liars are meant they who are in falses, and, abstractedly, the falses themselves, may appear from many places in the Word, which, if they were adduced, would fill several pages; neither are lies, in the spiritual sense, any thing else but falses. From these considerations it may appear, that by "Thou hast tried them which say they are apostles, and are not, and hast found them liars," is signified that they scrutinize those things which are said to be good and true in the church, but which nevertheless are evil and false.

80. *And hast borne and hast endurance;* that this signifies their patience with them, is evident without explanation.

81. *And for my name's sake hast laboured, and hast not fainted*, signifies their study and endeavour to attain, and also to teach, the things which belong to religion and its doctrine. By the name of Jehovah or of the Lord, in the Word, is not meant his name, but all by which he is worshipped; and because he is worshipped in the church according to doctrine, by his name is meant the all of doctrine, and, in a universal sense, the all of religion. The reason why these things are meant by the name of Jehovah, is, because in heaven no other names are given but what involve the quality of any one, and the quality

of God is all by which he is worshipped. He that is not aware of this signification of name in the Word, can only understand name; in which alone nothing of worship nor of religion is involved. He that keeps in mind, therefore, the signification of the NAME OF JEHOVAH as here explained, whenever it occurs in the Word, will understand of himself what it means in the following places: "In that day shall ye say, Praise Jehovah, call upon his *name*," Isaiah xii. 4. "Jehovah, have we waited for thee: the desire of our soul is to thy *name*, by thee only will we make mention of thy *name*," Isaiah xxvi. 8, 13. "From the rising of the sun shall he call upon my *name*," Isaiah xli. 25. "From the rising of the sun even unto the going down of the same, my *name* shall be great among the Gentiles; and in every place incense shall be offered unto my *name*; for my *name* shall be great among the Gentiles: but ye have profaned my *name*, in that ye say, the table of Jehovah is polluted;—and ye have snuffed at my *name*—when ye brought that which was torn, and lame, and sick," Malachi i. 11—13. "For all people will walk in the *name* of his God, and we will walk in the *name* of Jehovah our God," Micah iv. 5. "Every one that is called by my *name*, for I have created him for my glory, I have formed him," Isaiah xliii. 7. "Thou shalt not take the *name* of Jehovah thy God in vain; for Jehovah will not hold him guiltless that taketh his *name* in vain," Deut. v. 11. They shall worship Jehovah in one place where he will *put his name*, Deut. xii. 5, 11, 13, 14; xvi. 2, 6, 11, 15, 16; besides many other places. Who may not perceive that in these, name alone is not understood? The same is signified in the New Testament by the name of the Lord, as in the following: Jesus said, "Ye shall be hated of all men for my *name's* sake," Matt. x. 22; xxiv. 9. "For where two or three are gathered together in my *name*, there am I in the midst of them," Matt. xviii. 20. "And every one that hath forsaken houses, or brethren, or sisters,—for my *name's* sake, shall receive an hundred-fold, and shall inherit everlasting life," Matt. xix. 29. "But as many as received him, to them gave he power to become the sons of God, even to them that believe on his *name*," John i. 12. "Many believed in his *name*," John ii. 23. "He that believeth not is condemned already, because he hath not believed in the *name* of the only-begotten Son of God," John iii. 18. They who believe will *have life in his name*, John xx. 31. "Blessed is he that cometh in the *name* of the Lord," Matt. xxi. 9; xxiii. 39; Luke xiii. 35; xix. 38. That the Lord, as to his Humanity, is the name of the Father, appears in these places: "Father, glorify thy *name*," John xii. 28. "Hallowed be thy *name*, thy kingdom come," Matt. vi. 9; also Exod. xxiii. 20, 21; Jerem. xxiii. 6; Micah v. 4. That name, applied to others, signifies the quality of worship, appears in the following passages: The shepherd of the sheep "calleth his own sheep by their *name*," John x. 3. "Thou hast a few *names* even in Sardis," Apoc. iii. 4. "I will write upon him the *name* of my God, and the *name* of the city of my God, which is New Jerusalem,—and my new *name*," Apoc. iii. 12; and in other places. Hence it may appear, that "for my name's sake thou hast laboured, and hast not fainted," signifies study and endeavour to acquire, and also to teach, the things which belong to religion and its doctrine.

82. *Nevertheless, I have somewhat against thee, that thou hast left thy first charity*, signifies that this is against them, that they do not esteem good of life in the first place, which, nevertheless, was and is done in the beginning of every church. This is said to the church, because by it are meant those in the church who primarily or in the first place respect truths of doctrine, and not goods of life, n. 73; when yet good of life is to be considered in the first place, that is, primarily; for in proportion as a man is in goods of life, in the same proportion he is really in truths of doctrine, and not *vice versâ*; the reason is, because goods of life open the interiors of the mind, and these being opened, truths appear in their own light, whence they are not only understood, but also loved; not so when doctrinals are primarily, or in the first place, respected; in this case truths may indeed be known, but not seen interiorly, and loved from spiritual affection; but this has been illustrated above, n. 17. Every church, at its beginning, respects goods of life in the first place, and truths of doctrine in the second; but as the church declines, it begins to respect truths of doctrine in the first place, and goods of life in the second; and at length in the end it respects faith alone, and then it not only separates the goods of charity from faith, but also omits them. From hence then it may appear, that by these words, "Thou hast left thy first charity," is signified that they do not esteem good of life in the first place, which nevertheless is, and has been done at the beginning of every church.

83. *Remember therefore from whence thou art fallen;* that this signifies remembrance of their error, is plain from what has just been said.

84. *And repent, and do the first works*, signifies that they ought to invert the state of their life. Every man respects truths of doctrine in the first place, yet so long as he does this, he is like unripe fruit; but he who is regenerated, after he has imbibed truths, respects good of life in the first place, and in proportion as he does so, he grows ripe like fruit; and in proportion as he ripens, in the same proportion the seed in him becomes prolific. These two states have been witnessed by me, in men who were become spirits: in the first state, they appeared turned to the valleys which are over hell; and in the second, to the paradises in heaven. It is this conversion of the

state of life which is here understood. That this is effected by repentance, and after it by good of life, is understood by "Repent, and do the first works."

85. *Or else I will come unto thee quickly, and will remove thy candlestick out of its place, except thou repent*, signifies that otherwise of a certainty illumination will not be given them to see truths any longer. By quickly is signified certainly, n. 4, 947; and by candlestick, the church as to illumination, n. 43, 66; hence, by removing it out of its place, is signified to remove illumination, that they may not see truths in their own light, and at length, that they may not see them any more. This follows from what was said above, n. 82, namely, that if truths of doctrine are respected primarily, or in the first place, they may indeed be known, but not interiorly seen, and loved from spiritual affection, therefore they successively perish; for to see truths from their own light, is to see them from man's interior mind, which is called the spiritual mind, and this mind is opened by charity; and when it is open, light and the affection of understanding truths flow in out of heaven from the Lord, which constitutes illumination. The man who is in this illumination, acknowledges truths as soon as he reads or hears them; but it is not so with the man whose spiritual mind is not opened, who is one that is not principled in the goods of charity, howsoever he may be principled in the truths of doctrine.

86. *But this thou hast, that thou hatest the works of the Nicolaitanes, which I also hate*, signifies that they know this by virtue of the truths they possess, and thence are not willing that works should be meritorious, because this is contrary to the merit and righteousness of the Lord. That the works of the Nicolaitanes are meritorious works, has been made known by revelation. It is said, that they hate those works, because the church from the truths of its doctrine knows this, and thence does not will it: therefore it is said, "this thou hast." Yet all those make works meritorious who put the truths of faith in the first place, and the goods of charity in the second; but not those who put the goods of charity in the first place the reason is, because genuine charity admits not of merit, for it loves to do good, existing in it and acting from it; and from good it looks to the Lord; and from truths it knows that all good is from him; it therefore has an aversion to merit. Now because they who respect the truths of faith in the first place, cannot do any other works than such as are meritorious, and yet know, from their truths, that such works ought to be detested, therefore this follows after its having been said, that if they do not esteem charity in the first place, they do works which ought to be held in aversion. It is asserted, that it is contrary to the merit and righteousness of the Lord; for they who place merit in works, claim righteousness to themselves:

for they say that justice is on their side because they have merit, when yet it is the greatest injustice, inasmuch as the Lord alone has merit, and alone does good in them. That the Lord alone is righteousness, is taught in Jeremiah: "Behold, the days come, that I will cause the branch of righteousness to grow up unto David, and this is his name whereby he shall be called, *Jehovah our righteousness*," xxxiii. 5, 6; xxxiii. 15, 16.

87. *He that hath an ear, let him hear what the Spirit saith unto the churches*, signifies that he who understands, ought to obey what the divine truth of the Word teaches those who are to be of the New Church, which is the New Jerusalem. By hearing, is signified both to perceive and to obey; because a person gives attention in order that he may perceive and obey: that both these are signified by hearing, is evident from common discourse, when we speak of hearing any one and of hearkening to him; the latter signifying to obey, and the former to perceive. That hearing has these two significations, is from correspondence; for they are in the province of the ears in heaven, who are in perception and at the same time in obedience. As both these things are signified by hearing, therefore the Lord so often said, "He that hath ears to hear, let him hear," Matt. xi. 15; xiii. 43; Mark iv. 9, 23; vii. 16; Luke viii. 8; xiv. 35: and the same is likewise said to all the churches, as is evident from verses 11, 17, 29, of this chapter, and from verses 6, 13, and 22, of the following. But by the Spirit which speaks to the churches, is signified the divine truth of the Word; and by the churches, the universal church in the Christian world. That by the Spirit of God, which is also the Holy Spirit, is understood divine truth proceeding from the Lord, may be seen in *The Doctrine of the New Jerusalem concerning the Lord*, n. 51; and as the universal church is understood, it is not said, what the Spirit saith to the church, but what the Spirit saith to the churches.

88. *To him that overcometh*, signifies he that fights against his evils and falses, and is reformed. Now as, in what is written to the seven churches, is described the state of all in the Christian church who are capable of receiving the doctrine of the New Jerusalem, and of living according to it, thus who are capable, by combats against evils and falses, of being reformed; therefore it is said to each, HE THAT OVERCOMETH: as here to the church of Ephesus, "To him that *overcometh* will I give to eat of the tree of life." To the church in Smyrna, "He that *overcometh* shall not be hurt of the second death," ii. 11. To the church in Pergamos, "To him that *overcometh* will I give to eat of the hidden manna," ii. 17. To the church in Thyatira, "He that *overcometh* and keepeth my works unto the end, to him will I give power over the nations," ii. 26. To the church in Sardis, "He that *overcometh*,

the same shall be clothed in white raiment," iii. 5. To the church in Philadelphia, "Him that *overcometh* will I make a pillar in the temple of my God," iii. 12. And to the church in Laodicea, "To him that *overcometh* will I grant to sit with me in my throne," iii. 21. He that overcometh, in these places, signifies he who fights against evils and falses, and thus is reformed.

89. *Will I give to eat of the tree of life*, signifies appropriation of the good of love and charity from the Lord. To eat, in the Word, signifies to appropriate; and the tree of life signifies the Lord as to the good of love; therefore by eating of the tree of life, is signified the appropriation of the good of love from the Lord. To eat signifies to appropriate, because as natural food, when it is eaten, is appropriated to the life of man's body, so spiritual food, when it is received, is appropriated to the life of his soul. The tree of life signifies the Lord as to the good of love, because nothing else is signified by the *tree of* LIFE in the garden of Eden; also because celestial and spiritual life is derived to man from the good of love and charity, which is received from the Lord. Tree is mentioned in many places, and by it is understood a man of the church, and in a universal sense the church itself, and by its fruit good of life; the reason is, because the Lord is the tree of life, from whom comes all good in the man of the church, and in the church: but of this in its proper place. It is said the good of love and charity, because the good of love is celestial good, which is that of love to the Lord, and the good of charity is spiritual good, which is that of love towards our neighbour. The nature and quality of these two kinds of good will be explained in what follows; they are treated of also in the work concerning *Heaven and Hell*, n. 13—19.

90. *Which is in the midst of the paradise of God*, signifies interiorly in the truths of wisdom and faith. In the midst signifies the inmost, n. 44, 383, here, the interior; the paradise of God signifies the truths of wisdom and faith; therefore the tree of life, which is in the midst of the paradise of God, signifies the Lord with the good of love and charity interiorly in the truths of wisdom and faith: good is also within truths, for good is the *esse* of life, and truth is the *existere* of life thence derived, as is abundantly shown in *The Angelic Wisdom concerning the Divine Love and the Divine Wisdom*. That the paradise of God means the truth of wisdom and of faith, is evident from the signification of garden in the Word: garden there signifies wisdom and intelligence, because trees signify men of the church, and their fruits goods of life; nothing else is signified by the garden of Eden, for by it is described the wisdom of Adam. The same is understood by the garden of God in Ezekiel: "With thy wisdom and thine intelligence thou

hadst gotten thee riches: thou hast been in Eden the *garden of God;* every precious stone was thy covering," xxviii. 4, 13; speaking of Tyre, by which is signified the church as to the knowledges of truth and good, thus as to intelligence; therefore it is said, In thy wisdom and thine intelligence thou hadst gotten thee riches: by a covering of precious stones are signified the truths of intelligence. Again: "Behold, the Assyrian was a cedar in Lebanon;—the cedars in the *garden of God* could not hide him: nor any tree in the *garden of God* was like unto him in his beauty. All the trees of Eden that were in the *garden of God* envied him," xxxi. 3, 8, 9. This is said of Egypt and Ashur, because by Egypt is signified science, and by Ashur rationality, by which comes intelligence; the like is signified by cedar. But because, by his rationality, he came into the pride of self-derived intelligence, therefore it is said of him, "To whom art thou thus like in glory and in greatness among the trees of Eden? yet shalt thou be brought down with the trees of Eden unto the nether parts of the earth: thou shalt lie in the midst of the uncircumcised," verse 18 of the same chapter; the uncircumcised are they who are without the good of charity. So in Isaiah: "Jehovah shall comfort Zion;—and he will make her wilderness like Eden, and her desert like the *garden of Jehovah,*" li. 3. Zion there is the church; the wilderness and the desert are the defect and ignorance of truth; Eden and the garden of God are wisdom and intelligence. Wisdom and intelligence are also signified by garden in Isaiah lviii. 11; lxi. 11; Jerem. xxxi. 12; Amos ix. 14; Numb. xxiv. 6. The man of the church is also like a garden as to intelligence, when he is in the good of love from the Lord, because the spiritual heat which vivifies him is love, and spiritual light is intelligence thence derived. It is well known that gardens in this world flourish by means of heat and light; it is the same in heaven: in heaven there appear paradisiacal gardens, with fruit-trees according to the wisdom of the inhabitants grounded in the good of love received from the Lord: but around those who are in intelligence and not in the good of love, there do not appear gardens, but grass; and around those who are in faith separated from charity, not even grass, but sand.

91. *And unto the angel of the church in Smyrna write,* signifies to those and concerning those, who are in good as to life, but in falses as to doctrine. That these are meant by the church in Smyrna, is clear from the things written to it when understood in the spiritual sense.

92. *These things saith the First and the Last,* signifies the Lord, that he is the only God. That the Lord calls himself the First and the Last, also the Beginning and the End, and Alpha and Omega, and He who is, and who was, and who is to come, may be seen, chap. i. 4, 8, 11, 17; and what they signify

above, n. 13, 29—31, 38, 57; where it is plain, that by the above is also understood, that he is the only God.

93. *Who was dead and is alive*, signifies that he is neglected in the church, and his Humanity not acknowledged to be divine, when yet as to that also he alone is life, and from him alone is life everlasting. That this is understood by these words, may be seen above, n. 58—60, where they are explained. Why these and the preceding things are said, is, because the primary falsity of those who are described by this church, is, that they do not acknowledge the Lord's Divine Humanity, and therefore do not approach him.

94. *I know thy works;* that this signifies that the Lord sees all their interiors and exteriors at once, is evident from the same explained above, n. 76; in the present case it denotes that he sees that they are in falses, and yet as to life in goods, which they believe to be goods of life, when yet they are not.

95. *And affliction and poverty (but thou art rich),* signifies that they are in falses, and thence not in goods. To know their affliction signifies to see that they are in falses, and to know their poverty signifies to see that they are not in goods; for in the Word, affliction is predicated of falses, as above, n. 33; and poverty of the defect of goods, neither is spiritual poverty any thing else. Poor and needy are often mentioned in the Word, and in the spiritual sense by poor is understood one who is not in truths, and by needy one who is not in goods. These words are also added, "but thou art rich," but in a parenthesis, because in some copies they are omitted.

96. *And I know the blasphemy of them that say they are Jews, and are not,* signifies the false assertion that they possess the goods of love, when yet they do not. Blasphemy here signifies false assertion; by Jews are not signified Jews, but they who are in the good of love, and, abstractedly, goods of love; so by the blasphemy of them which say they are Jews, and are not, is signified the false assertion that they possess the goods of love, when yet they do not. By Jews are meant they who are in the good of love, because in the Word by Judah, in a supreme sense, is meant the Lord as to the divine good of divine love, and by Israel, the Lord as to the divine truth of divine wisdom; hence by Jews are signified they who are in the good of love from the Lord, and by Israel they who are in divine truths from the Lord: that these are meant by Jews, may appear from many passages, which will be adduced below, n. 350; something may also be seen on this subject in *The Doctrine of the New Jerusalem concerning the Lord*, n. 51. In the abstract the goods of love are meant by Jews, because the spiritual sense is abstracted from persons, as may be seen above, n. 78, 79. He who is not aware, that by Jews, in the Word, are meant those who belong to the Lord's celestial church, by

reason of their being principled in love to him, is liable to fall into many mistakes when reading the prophetical part of the Word: but see below, n. 350.

97. *But are the synagogue of Satan*, signifies because they are in falses as to doctrine. It is called synagogue, because Jews are mentioned, and as they taught in synagogues, by synagogue is signified doctrine; and because by Satan is understood the hell of those who are in falses, therefore it is called the synagogue of Satan. Hell is called the devil and Satan, and by the hell which is called the devil, are understood such there as are in evils, properly who are in self-love; and by the hell which is called Satan, are understood such there as are in falses, properly who are in the pride of self-derived intelligence: the hells are called the devil and Satan, because all who are in them are called devils and Satans. Hence then it may appear, that by their being the synagogue of Satan, is signified that as to doctrine they are in falses. But as they who are in good as to life, and in falses as to doctrine, are here treated of, and as such know no other than that they are in good, and that their falses are truths, something shall be said respecting them. All the good of worship is formed by truths, and all truth is formed from good, therefore good without truth is not good, neither is truth, without good, truth; they appear indeed in their external form to be so, but still they are not. The conjunction of good and truth is called the heavenly marriage; from this is the church in man, and it is heaven in him; if therefore there are falses instead of truths in man, then he does good from a false ground, which is not good, for it is either pharisaical or meritorious, or natural connate good. But examples will illustrate this: he who is in this falsity, that he thinks he does good from himself, from his possessing the faculty of doing good; the good of such a man is not good, because he himself is in it, and not the Lord. He who is in this falsity, that he can do good which is in itself good, without a knowledge of what is evil in himself, so without repentance, although he appears to do good, yet he does not do good, because without repentance he is in evil. He who is in this falsity, that good purifies him from evils, and does not know any thing of the evils in which he is, such a man does no other good than spurious good, which is inwardly contaminated by his evils. He who is in this falsity, that there is a plurality of gods, the good which such a man does is divided good, and divided good is not good. He who is in this falsity, that he believes the divinity in the Lord's Humanity is not like the soul in the body, cannot do good from him, and good not from the Lord is not good, for it is contrary to these words of the Lord: "Except a man abide in me and I in him, he cannot bring forth any fruit; for without me ye can do nothing. If a man abide not in me, he is cast forth as

a branch and is withered, and is cast into the fire and burned," John xv. 4—6; and so in many other instances; for good derives its quality from truths, and truths derive their esse from good. Who does not know, that the church is no church without doctrine, and doctrine must teach how a man is to think of God and from God; and how he is to act from God and with God; therefore doctrine must be derived from truths, to act according to which, is what is called good; whence it follows, that to act according to falses is not good. It is thought, that in the good which a man does, there is not any thing derived from truths or falses, when yet the quality of good is not derived from any other source, for they cohere together like love and wisdom, and also like love and foolishness; it is the love of the wise man which does good, but the love of the fool does what is like good in externals, but totally unlike it in internals; therefore the good of a wise man is like pure gold, but the good of a fool is like gold covering dirt.

98. *Fear none of those things which thou shalt suffer*, signifies, despair not when ye are infested by evils and assaulted by falses, because they who are in goods as to life, and in falses as to doctrine, cannot but be so infested and assaulted. This is plain from what now follows.

99. *Behold, the devil shall cast some of you into prison*, signifies that their good of life will be infested by evils from hell. That this is signified by being cast into custody or into prison by the devil, is, because by the devil is meant the hell where they are who are in evils, and thus, abstractedly, the evil which is there and from thence, n. 97. To be cast into prison, denotes to be infested, because they who are infested by evils from hell are as if they were bound in prison, for they cannot think any thing but evil, when yet they will what is good; hence comes combat and interior anxiety, from which they cannot be released, being like persons who are in bonds; the reason is, because their good is not good so far as it coheres with falses, and so far as it coheres with falses evil is in it; therefore it is that which is infested. But this infestation does not exist in the natural world, but in the spiritual world, thus after death. It has often been permitted me to see their infestations; they lament, saying that they have done good, and desire to do good, and yet now they cannot, because of the evils which surround them. But still they are not all alike infested, but more severely according as they have confirmed themselves in falses, therefore it is said the devil shall cast *some of you* into prison. That the confirmation of what is false is hurtful, may be seen in *The Doctrine of the New Jerusalem concerning the Sacred Scripture*, n. 91—97. In the Word, by *prisoners* the same is signified as here by those who will be cast into prison, as in these places: I will " give thee for a covenant of the people,—to

bring out the *prisoners* from the *prison*, and them that sit in darkness out of the *prison-house*," Isaiah xlii. 6, 7 ; xlix. 8, 9. "Jehovah hath sent me,—to proclaim liberty to the *captives*, and the opening of the *prison* to them that are *bound*," Isaiah lxi. 1. "By the blood of thy covenant I have sent for thy *prisoners* out of the pit," Zech. ix. 11. "God—bringeth out those which are *bound with chains*," Psalm lxviii. 6. "Let the sighing of the *prisoner* come before thee," Psalm lxxix. 11. "To hear the groaning of the *prisoner*, to loose those that are appointed to die," Psalm cii. 20. "Jehovah looseth the *prisoners*," Psalm cxlvi. 7. It is plain that by prisoners in these places are not meant those who are imprisoned in the world, but those who are imprisoned by hell, thus by evils and falses. Similar is the signification of these words of the Lord: "I was in *prison*, and ye came unto me," Matt. xxv. 36. As the Lord brings out of prison, or delivers from infestation, those who have been in good as to life, though in falses as to doctrine, he says, "Fear none of those things which thou shalt suffer;" also, "Be thou faithful, and I will give thee a crown of life."

100. *That ye may be tried*, signifies by falses fighting against them. The reason why this is signified is, because all spiritual temptation is a combat of the devil and the Lord, which shall have possession of man; the devil or hell brings out his falses, and reproaches and condemns him, but the Lord brings out his truths, and withdraws him from falses, and delivers him. It is this combat which appears to man as in himself, because it is from evil spirits who are with him, and is called temptation. That spiritual temptation is nothing else, I know by experience, because in my temptations I have seen the infernals who brought them on, and have perceived the influx from the Lord, who delivered me.

101. *And ye shall have tribulation ten days*, signifies that this will endure its full time, that is, as long as they are willing to abide in falses. Affliction here signifies infestation, of which above, n. 33, 95, thus temptation; and ten days signify the duration of that state to the full: therefore it follows, "Be thou faithful unto death," by which is signified the reception and acknowledgment of truths, until by their means falses are removed, and as it were abolished. That ten days signify duration of state to the full is, because days signify states, and ten what is full; for times in the Word signify states, n. 947, and numbers designate their quality, n. 9. As ten signify what is full, they also signify much and many, also every thing and all, as may appear from these passages which follow: "Those men which have seen my glory,—have tempted me now these *ten* times," Numb. xiv. 22. "These *ten* times have ye reproached me," Job xix. 3. "Daniel was found *ten* times wiser than the astrologers," Dan. i. 20. "*Ten* women shall

bake your bread in one oven," Levit. xxvi. 26. "*Ten* men out of all languages of the nations, shall take hold of the skirt of him that is a Jew," Zech. viii. 23. Because ten signify many, and also all, therefore the things which were written upon the tables of the decalogue by Jehovah, are called the Ten Commandments, Deut. iv. 13; x. 4: the Ten Commandments signify all truths, for they include them. And because ten signify all and every thing, therefore the Lord compared the kingdom of heaven to *ten virgins*, Matt. xxv. 11. Likewise in the parable he said of the nobleman, that he gave his servants *ten talents* to trade with, Luke xix. 12, 18. Many are also signified by the *ten* horns of the beast which came up out of the sea, Dan. vii. 24, and by the *ten* horns, and the *ten* crowns upon the horns, of the beast which came up out of the sea, in the Apoc. xiii. 1; also by the *ten* horns of the dragon, Apoc. xii. 3, and by the *ten* horns of the scarlet-coloured beast, upon which the woman sat, Apoc. xvii. 3, 7, 12: by ten horns is signified much power. From the signification of the number ten, as denoting what is full, much, and all, it may be seen why it was ordained, that a tenth part of all the fruits of the earth should be given to Jehovah, and from Jehovah to Aaron and the Levites, Numb. xviii. 24, 28; Deut. xiv. 22; also, why Abram gave Melchizedek tithes of all, Gen. xiv. 18, 19; for by this was signified that all they had was from Jehovah, and sanctified, see Malachi iii. 10. From these considerations, it may now appear, that by having affliction ten days, is signified that their temptation will last its full time, that is, so long as they are willing to remain in falses; for falses are never taken away from a man against his will or consent, but with it.

102. *Be thou faithful unto death*, signifies reception and acknowledgment of truths, until falses are removed, and, as it were, abolished. By be thou faithful unto death, in the natural sense, is meant, that they must not depart from their fidelity to the end of life; but in the spiritual sense, that they must receive and acknowledge truths, until falses are removed by them, and, as it were, abolished, for this sense is properly for those who are in the spiritual world, who are not liable to death, therefore by death is here meant the end of their temptations. It is said, until they are, as it were, abolished, because falses and evils with man are not abolished, but removed, and when they are removed they appear as if they were abolished, because when evils and falses are removed, man is kept in goods and truths by the Lord.

103. *And I will give thee a crown of life*, signifies that they will then have eternal life, the reward of victory. Because temptations even unto death are here treated of, it is said that a crown of life will be given them, such as the martyrs had, who were faithful even unto death; and because the martyrs

wished for it, therefore after death crowns were given them, by which was signified the reward of victory; they still appear in their crowns in heaven, which it has been permitted me to see.

104. *He that hath an ear, let him hear what the Spirit saith unto the churches;* that this signifies that he who understands these things, ought to obey what the divine truth of the Word teaches those who are to be of the New Church, which is the New Jerusalem, is evident from the explanation of the same words above, n. 87.

105. *He that overcometh;* that this signifies he that fights against evils and falses, and is reformed, is evident from n. 88, where the same words occur, and are explained.

106. *Shall not be hurt of the second death*, signifies that afterwards they shall not yield to the evils and falses from hell. By the first death is meant the death of the body, and by the second death is meant the death of the soul, which is damnation, see below, n. 853, 873; and whereas by "Be thou faithful unto death," is signified that they ought to acknowledge truths till by their means falses are removed, n. 102, it follows, that by "not being hurt of the scond death," is signified that afterwards they shall not sink under evils and falses from hell, for thereby they are exempted from damnation.

107. *And to the angel of the church in Pergamos write*, signifies to those and concerning those, who place the all of the church in good works, and not any thing in the truths of doctrine. That these are meant by the church in Pergamos, is evident from what is written to it, when understood in the spiritual sense. But something must be premised concerning these, in order to make it known who they are in the church, and what is their quality: there are two kinds of men, of whom the Christian church at this day for the most part consists; one, who are in works alone, and in no truths; the other, who are in worship alone, and neither in works nor in truths: the former are here treated of; the latter in what is written to the church in Sardis, n. 154. They who are in works alone and in no truths, are like people who act and do not understand, and actions without understanding are inanimate; they appear to the angels like images carved out of wood; and they who have placed merit in their works, appear like the same images, but naked, without any covering whatever: they appear also like sheep without wool; and they who place merit in them, like such sheep covered with dirt; for all works are done from the will by the understanding, and in the understanding they receive life, and at the same time clothing; hence it is, as was observed, that they appear to the angels as things inanimate and naked.

108. *These things saith He that hath the sharp sword with two edges*, signifies the Lord as to the truths of doctrine from

the Word, by which evils and falses are dispersed. In the preceding chapter, where the SON OF MAN is described, who is the Lord as to the Word, it is said, that a sharp two-edged sword was seen to go out of his mouth, verse 16: that by it is signified the dispersion of falses by the Word, and by doctrine thence from the Lord, may be seen above, n. 52. This is said to those and concerning those, who place the all of the church in works alone, and not any thing in truths of doctrine; to whom, because they omit or lightly esteem truths of doctrine which yet are necessary, it is said in what follows: "Repent or else I will come unto thee quickly, and will fight against them with the *sword* of my mouth," verse 16 of this chapter.

. 109. *I know thy works;* that this signifies that the Lord sees all their interiors and exteriors at once, may be seen above, n. 76, where the same is explained; in this instance it denotes, that the Lord sees that they are in works alone, and not in doctrinals.

110. *And where thou dwellest, even where Satan's throne is,* signifies their life in darkness. That by Satan is meant the hell of those who are in falses, may be seen above, n. 97; and to be in falses, is to be in spiritual darkness: spiritual darkness, the shadow of death, and blindness, are nothing else but the states of those in hell, who are in the falses of evil; therefore, in the Word, falses are described thereby: from which it may appear, that by Satan's throne is signified mere darkness. But by darkness here, is not meant that they are in mere falses, but that they are in no truths of doctrine; for truths of doctrine, which are from the Word, are in light, therefore not to be in truths, is not to be in light, consequently to be in darkness. That truths are in the light of heaven, may be seen in the work concerning *Heaven and Hell,* n. 126—140; and in *The Doctrine of the New Jerusalem concerning the Sacred Scripture,* n. 73, 104—113. The Word in many places treats of those who are in darkness, in the shadow of death, and in thick darkness, whose eyes the Lord will open; and by them are meant the Gentiles, who have been in good works, but not in any truths, because they did not know the Lord, neither were possessed of the Word; exactly similar to these are they in the Christian world, who are in works alone and in no truths of doctrine, therefore they cannot be called any thing else but Gentiles; they know the Lord indeed, but yet do not approach him, and are in possession of the Word, but yet do not search for the truths it contains. By "I know where thou dwellest," is signified to know their nature and quality, because in the spiritual world every one dwells according to the quality of his affection. Hence it may appear, that by "thou dwellest where Satan's throne is," is signified the life of their good in darkness. For Satanic spirits have power through those in the spiritual

world who are in works alone, but none without them, for they draw them into connexion with themselves, provided any one of them says, I am thy neighbour, and on this account good offices ought to be extended to me; on hearing this they accede, and give him assistance, without inquiring who and what he is, since they are destitute of truths, by which alone one can be distinguished from another. This also is signified by "thou dwellest where Satan's throne is."

111. *And thou holdest fast my name, and hast not denied my faith*, signifies when yet they have religion and worship according to it, and also acknowledge the Word to be divine truth. That by the name of Jehovah, or of the Lord, is understood all by which he is worshipped, thus the all of religion, may be seen above, n. 81; here therefore it signifies that they have religion, and, according to religion, worship. By faith, here, is not meant that which exists in the church at this day, but divine truth, because faith is of truth and truth is of faith; nothing else is understood by faith in heaven, nor by the faith of God in the Word; hence it is that faith and truth are expressed in the Hebrew language by one and the same word, and are called *Amuna*. Since then by the faith of God is meant divine truth, and the Word is divine truth itself, it is evident that by "thou hast not denied my faith," is meant, that they acknowledge that the Word is divine truth.

112. *Even in those days wherein Antipas was my faithful martyr, who was slain among you where Satan dwelleth*, signifies when all truth was extinguished by falses in the church. By martyr is signified confession of the truth, the same as by witness above, n. 6, 16, because martyr and witness are expressed in the Greek language by one and the same word. Antipas is named from the spiritual or angelic language. Since by Antipas the martyr is signified a confesser of the truth, and, abstractedly, the truth itself, it is evident that, by the "days wherein Antipas was my faithful martyr, who was slain among you, where Satan dwelleth," is signified, when truth was extinguished by falses in the church. That by Satan is understood the hell where and from whence falses are, may be seen above, n. 97.

113. *But I have a few things against thee*, signifies that the things which follow are against them, as is evident without explanation.

114. *Because thou hast there them that hold the doctrine of Balaam, who taught Balak to cast a stumbling-block before the children of Israel, to eat things sacrificed unto idols, and to commit fornication*, signifies that there are some among them who do hypocritical works, by which the worship of God in the church is defiled and adulterated. That by these expressions are meant they who do works by which worship is defiled and adulterated, is evident from the historical parts of the Word

which relate to Balaam and Balak king of Moab; for Balaam was a hypocrite, and a diviner, and spake well of the children of Israel from Jehovah, when yet he cherished in his heart a desire to destroy them, which he also effected by the advice he gave Balak; from which it is evident that his works were hypocritical. That he was a diviner appears in Numbers xxii. 7; xxiv. 1; Josh. xiii. 22; that he spake in favour of the children of Israel, by blessing them, Numb. xxiii. 7—15, 18—24; xxiv. 5—9, 16—19; but that he spake these things from Jehovah, Numb. xxiii. 5, 12, 16; xxiv. 13. That he cherished in his heart a desire to destroy them, and also effected it by the advice given to Balak, Numb. xxxi. 16. The advice which he gave, Numb. xxv. 1, 9, 18. This was the stumbling-block which he cast before the children of Israel, concerning which it is written, "In Shittim the people began to commit whoredom with the daughters of Moab, and they called the people unto the sacrifices of their gods; and the people did eat and bowed down to their gods," especially they joined themselves unto Baalpeor: "and those that died in the plague were twenty-four thousand," Numb. xxv. 1, 9, 18. By the children of Israel is signified the church; by eating of their sacrifices, is signified the appropriation of what is holy; therefore by eating of the sacrifices of other gods, or things sacrificed unto idols, is signified the defilement and profanation of what is holy; by committing whoredom, is signified to adulterate and pervert worship; that by Moab, and therefore by the king, and his daughters, are also signified they who defile and adulterate worship, may be seen in *The Arcana Cœlestia*, n. 2468. From hence it is evident, that this is the spiritual sense of these words.

115. *So hast thou also them that hold the doctrine of the Nicolaitanes, which thing I hate*, signifies that there are some among them also who make works meritorious. That the works of the Nicolaitanes are meritorious works, may be seen above, n. 86. Among those who place the all of the church and of salvation in good works, and not any thing in truths of doctrine, as is the case with those who are meant by the church in Pergamos, there are some who do hypocritical works and also meritorious works, but not all, therefore it is said, "Thou hast there them that hold the doctrine of Balaam;" as also, "So hast thou also them that hold the doctrine of the Nicolaitanes;" and all works of worship are either good, or meritorious, or hypocritical, therefore the two latter are here spoken of, and good works afterwards in what follows.

116. *Repent*, signifies that they should take heed of such works, and do works which are good. That these things are signified by the injunction to repent, is, because the subject now relates to meritorious and hypocritical goods, of which they are to take heed who place the all of the church and of

salvation in good works, and not any thing in truths of doctrine; when yet truths of doctrine teach how and what is to be willed and taught, or loved and believed, that works may be good.

117. *Or else I will come unto thee quickly, and will fight against them with the sword of my mouth*, signifies, if not, that the Lord will contend with them from the Word, and convince them that their works are evil. But the explanation of these words may be seen above, n. 108.

118. *He that hath an ear, let him hear what the Spirit saith unto the churches*, signifies that he who understands these things, ought to obey what the divine truth of the Word teaches those who are to be of the New Church, which is the New Jerusalem, as appears above, n. 87, where the same words are explained.

119. *To him that overcometh*, signifies he that fights against his evils and falses, and is reformed, as is also evident from the explanation given above, n. 88.

120. *Will I give to eat of the hidden manna*, signifies wisdom, and at the same time the appropriation of the good of celestial love in works, and thus conjunction of the Lord with those who do them. By the hidden manna, which they will have who are in good works, and who at the same time adjoin the truths of doctrine to works, is meant hidden wisdom of a quality like that which they who are in the third heaven enjoy; for these, by reason of their having been in good works, and at the same time in truths of doctrine in the world, are in wisdom above other angels, but in hidden wisdom, for it is written in their lives more than in their memory; therefore that they are such, they do not talk of the truths of doctrine, but do them, and they do them because they know them, and also see them when others speak them. That the good of love is appropriated to them, and that the Lord conjoins himself with those who adjoin truths of doctrine to good works, and thus gives them wisdom in their good, and that this is giving them to eat of the hidden manna, may appear from these words of the Lord: " For the bread of God is he which cometh down from heaven, and giveth life unto the world. I am the bread of life: your fathers did eat *manna* in the wilderness and are dead. This is the bread which cometh down from heaven, that a man may eat thereof, and not die. I am the living bread, who came down from heaven;—if any man eat of this bread he shall live for ever," John vi. 31—51; from which it is evident, that the Lord himself is the hidden manna, which will be in their works, if they approach and worship him alone. Whether you say the Lord or the good of celestial love, and the wisdom of that love, it amounts to the same. But this is an arcanum which enters with difficulty into the natural idea of any one, so long as it is surrounded with a cloud from worldly things; but it does enter

when the mind is serene and in the sunshine, as may be seen in *The Angelic Wisdom concerning the Divine Love and the Divine Wisdom*, which treats on this subject from beginning to end.

121. *And will give him a white stone*, signifies truths affirmative and united to good. A white stone has this signification, because in judiciary proceedings, it was the custom to collect votes or suffrages by stones, and by white stones those which were on the affirmative side; that they are confirmatory truths which are signified, is, because white is predicated of truths, n. 167, 379; hence it is, that by white stone are signified truths supporting good; the reason why they are also united to good, is, because good invites and unites them to itself; for all good loves truth and conjoins to itself such as accords with it, especially the good of celestial love; this so unites truths to itself, that they altogether constitute a one; hence it is, that they see truths from good alone. These are understood by those who have the law written in their hearts, of whom it is said in Jeremiah, "I will put my law in their inward parts, and write it *in their hearts;*—and they shall teach no more every man his neighbour, and every man his brother, saying, Know Jehovah, for they shall all know me," xxxi. 34. Such are all who are in the third heaven; they do not speak of truths from the mere memory, but clearly see them when they hear others speaking of them, and especially when they are reading the Word; the reason is, because they are in the very marriage of goodness and truth. Such do they become in the world, who have approached the Lord alone, and have done good works, because they are according to the truths of the Word; concerning whom something may be seen in the work on *Heaven and Hell*, n. 25, 26, 270, 271.

122. *And in the stone a new name written*, signifies that thus they will have good of a quality such as they had not before. That name signifies the quality of a thing, may be seen above, n. 81, therefore here the quality of good: all the quality of good is from the truths that are united to it; for good without truths is like bread and meat without wine and water, which do not nourish; and also like fruit in which there is no juice: it appears also like a tree stripped of its leaves, on which there hang a few dry apples, left since autumn. This is also understood by these words of the Lord: "For every one shall be salted with fire, and every sacrifice shall be salted with salt. Salt is good, but if the salt have lost its saltness, wherewith will ye season it? Have salt in yourselves," Mark ix. 49, 50. Salt here is the desire of truth.

123. *Which no man knoweth saving he that receiveth it*, signifies that it does not appear to any one, because it is written in their lives. That truths united to good are not inscribed on their memories, but on their lives, may be seen above, n. 121,

122, and what is inscribed on the life alone, and not on the memory, does not appear to any one, not even to themselves, except from this circumstance, that they perceive whether a thing be true, and what the truth is, when they hear and read; for the interiors of their mind are open even unto the Lord; and because the Lord is in them, and he sees all things, therefore he causes them to see as from themselves; but yet out of their wisdom they know that they do not see truths from themselves, but from the Lord. Hence it may appear what is meant by the whole sentence, "I will give him to eat of the hidden manna, and will give him a white stone, and in the stone a new name written, which no man knoweth saving he that receiveth it:" the sum of its signification is, that they will be angels of the third heaven, if they read the Word, imbibe thence truths of doctrine, and approach the Lord.

124. *And unto the angel of the church in Thyatira write,* signifies, to those and concerning those, who are in faith grounded in charity, and thence in good works; and also to those and concerning those, who are in faith separate from charity, and thence in evil works. That both the former and the latter are described by the church in Thyatira, is evident from what is written to it, when understood in the spiritual sense.

125. *These things saith the Son of God, who hath his eyes like unto a flame of fire,* signifies the Lord as to the divine wisdom of his divine love. That this is the signification, may be seen explained above, n. 48.

126. *And his feet like fine brass,* signifies divine good natural, as is evident from the explanation given above, n. 49.

127. *I know thy works,* signifies that the Lord sees all their interiors and exteriors at once, as may be seen above, where these words are explained, n. 76.

128. *And charity and service,* signifies the spiritual affection which is called charity, and its operation. Charity is a spiritual affection, because charity is love towards our neighbour, and love towards our neighbour constitutes that affection: that ministry or service is its operation, follows from their being called ministers in the Word who serve the things which are of charity. The man who is a worshipper of God is sometimes called a servant, and sometimes a minister; and he is called a servant of God who is in truths, and he is called a minister of God who is in goods; the reason is, because truth serves good, and good ministers to truth: that he is called a servant who is in truths, may be seen above, n. 3; but that he is called a minister who is in good, is evident from these places: "But ye shall be named the priests of Jehovah; men shall call you the *ministers* of our God," Isaiah lxi. 6. "Then may also my covenant be broken with David my servant,—and with the

Levites the priests, *my ministers,*" Jerem. xxxiii. 21; they are called ministers, because priests represented the Lord as to divine good. "Bless the Lord all ye his hosts, ye *ministers* of his that do his pleasure," Psalm ciii. 21, 22. "Jehovah maketh his angels spirits; his *ministers* a flaming fire," Psalm civ. 4. Angel-spirits are they who are in truths, and angel-ministers they who are in goods; flaming fire also signifies the good of love. Jesus said, "Whosoever will be great among you, let him be your *minister;* and whosoever will be chief among you, let him be your *servant,*" Matt. xx. 26, 27; xxiii. 11, 12: minister is here predicated of good, and servant of truth. The same is signified by ministering and ministry in Isaiah lvi. 6; John xii. 26; Luke xii. 37; and in other places. Hence it is evident, that by charity and ministry, is signified spiritual affection and its operation; for good is of charity, and truth is of faith.

129. *And faith, and thy endurance, and thy works,* signifies truth, and the desire of acquiring and teaching it. That faith signifies truth, may be seen above, n. 111; and that in such case endurance signifies study and labour in acquiring and teaching it, follows of course.

130. *And the last to be more than the first,* signifies the increase thereof from the spiritual affection of truth, which is of charity. By their last works being more than the first, are understood all things of their charity and faith, for these are the interior things from which works proceed, n. 73, 76, 94: these things increase, when charity is regarded in the first place, and faith in the second: for charity is the spiritual affection of doing good, and from it comes the spiritual affection of knowing truth, good loving truth as meat does drink, for it desires to be nourished, and is nourished, by truths; hence it is, that they who are in genuine charity have a continual increase of truth. This then is what is signified by "I know thy last works to be more than the first."

131. *Notwithstanding, I have a few things against thee,* signifies that the following things may possibly be a stumbling-block to them. For what now follows relates to faith separated from charity, which may be a stumbling-block to those who are in faith grounded in charity.

132. *Because thou sufferest that woman Jezebel,* signifies that among them there are some in the church who separate faith from charity, and account the former alone to be saving. That faith separated from charity is meant by the woman Jezebel, is evident from what now follows, when it is unfolded by the spiritual sense in its series, and compared with that faith; for these were the evil doings of Jezebel the wife of Ahab: namely, that she went and served Baal, and built him an altar in Samaria, and made a grove, 1 Kings xvi. 31—33. That she

slew the prophets of Jehovah, 1 Kings xviii. 4, 23. That she was desirous to slay Elijah, xix. 1, 2. That by treacherously suborning false witnesses, she took away Naboth's vineyard, and put him to death, xxi. 6, 7, and following verses. That by reason of these her evil doings, it was foretold to her by Elijah, that the dogs should eat her, xxi. 13. That she was thrown down from the window where she stood with her face painted, and that some of her blood was sprinkled upon the wall, and upon the horses which trod her under foot, 2 Kings ix. 30, 32—34. As all the historical, as well as the prophetical parts of the Word, signify the spiritual things of the church, so also do these; and that they signify faith separated from charity, is evident from the spiritual sense, and from collating them together; for by going and serving Baal, and building him an altar, and making a grove, is signified to serve lusts of all kinds, or what amounts to the same, to serve the devil, without thinking of any evil lust, nor of any sin, as they who have no doctrine of charity and life, but only of faith. By slaying the prophets, is signified to destroy the truths of doctrine derived from the Word. By desiring to slay Elijah, is signified to desire to do the same to the Word. By taking away Naboth's vineyard and slaying him, is signified the church, for the vineyard is the church: by the dogs which did eat her, are signified lusts. By her being thrown down from the window, her blood being sprinkled upon the wall, and her being trod under foot by the horses, is signified their destruction, for each of those particulars has its signification; window signifies truth in the light; blood signifies what is false; wall signifies truth in ultimates, and horse signifies understanding of the Word. Hence it may be concluded, that these things, collated together, coincide with faith separate from charity, as may further appear from what follows in the Apocalypse, where this faith is treated of.

133. *Which calleth herself a prophetess*, signifies, and who make it the essential doctrine of the church, and build all theology upon it. That by prophet in the Word is signified doctrine of the church, may be seen above, n. 8, therefore the same is also signified by prophetess. That in the reformed Christian church, faith alone is received as the sole medium of salvation, and that thence works of charity, as not conducive to salvation, are separated from faith, is well known: hence it is, that the universal doctrine of the salvation of man, which is called theology, at this day constitutes that faith, consequently the woman Jezebel.

134. *To teach and to seduce my servants to commit whoredom*, signifies, from which it comes to pass that the truths of the Word are falsified. By to teach and to seduce the servants of the Lord, is meant those who are able and willing to be instructed in truths from the Word; that they are called servants

of the Lord who are in truths, may be seen above, n. 3, 128; and by committing whoredom, is signified to adulterate and falsify the Word: that this is the signification of committing whoredom, is, because in every particular of the Word there is a marriage of goodness and truth, and this marriage is broken when good is separated and taken away from truth. That in every particular of the Word there is a marriage of the Lord and the church, and thence a marriage of goodness and truth, may be seen in *The Doctrine of the New Jerusalem concerning the Sacred Scripture*, n. 80—90: for this reason it is, that to commit whoredom signifies to adulterate the good and falsify the truths of the Word; and because this is spiritual whoredom, therefore also they, who from their own reason have falsified the Word, after death, when they come into the spiritual world, become addicted to whoredom: and, what has hitherto been concealed from the world, they who have confirmed themselves in faith alone to the exclusion of works of charity, are in the lust of committing the adultery of a son with his mother; that they are in the lust of committing so abominable a kind of adultery, has often been perceived in the spiritual world: remember this, and inquire after death, and the truth of it will be confirmed to you: I could not venture to reveal this before, because it would have offended the ear. This adultery is signified by the adultery of Reuben with Bilhah his father's concubine, Gen. xxxv. 22; for by Reuben that faith is signified, for which cause he was cursed by his father Israel, and afterwards his birthright was taken from him; for his father Israel, prophesying concerning his sons, said of Reuben, "Reuben, thou art my first-born, my might, and the beginning of my strength,—unstable as water, thou shalt not excel, because thou wentest up to thy *father's bed; then defiledst thou it*: he went up to my couch," Gen. xlix. 3, 4: therefore his birthright was taken from him. "Reuben was the first-born of Israel;—but, forasmuch as he *defiled his father's bed*, his birthright was given unto the sons of Joseph," 1 Chron. v. 1. That by Reuben was represented truth grounded in good, or faith grounded in charity, and afterwards truth separated from good, or faith separated from charity, will be seen in the explanation of chap. vii. 5. That by whoredoms are signified adulterations of good and falsifications of truth in the Word, may appear from the following passages: "When Joram saw Jehu, he said, Is it peace, Jehu? and he answered, What peace, so long as the *whoredoms of thy mother Jezebel*, and her witchcrafts, are so many?" 2 Kings ix. 22. By the whoredoms of Jezebel are not meant any whoredoms of hers, but her actions, as stated above, n. 132. "And your children shall wander in the wilderness forty years, and bear your *whoredoms*," Numb. xiv. 33. "And the soul that turneth after such as have familiar spirits, and after wizards, and all that go a *whoring* after them, I will cut off," Levit. xx. 6. "Lest thou make a covenant with the inhabitants of the land, and they go a *whoring* after their gods," Exod. xxxiv. 15, 16. "But thou didst trust [O Jerusalem] in thine own beauty, and *playedst the harlot* because of thy renown, and pouredst out thy *whoredoms* on every one that passed by. Thou hast also committed *whoredom* with the Egyptians thy neighbours, great of flesh, and hast increased thy *whoredoms*. Thou hast *played the whore* also with the Assyrians, because thou wast insatiable in committing *whoredom*. Thou hast moreover multiplied thy *whoredom* in the land of Canaan unto Chaldea. But as a wife that committeth *adultery*, which taketh strangers instead of her husband. They give gifts *to all whores;* but thou givest thy gifts to all thy lovers,—that they may come unto thee on every side for thy *whoredom*. Wherefore, O *harlot*, hear the word of Jehovah," Ezek. xvi. 15, 16, 26, 28, 29, 32, 33, 35. Jerusalem in this passage is the Israelitish and Jewish church; by her whoredoms are meant adulterations and falsifications of the Word; and because in the Word by Egypt is signified the science of the natural man, by Ashur ratiocination thence derived, by Chaldea profanation of truth, and by Babylon profanation of good, therefore it is said that she committed whoredom with them. "There were two women, the daughters of one mother; and they committed *whoredoms* in Egypt; they committed *whoredoms* in their youth: one of them played the *harlot* when she was mine, and she doted on her lovers, on the Assyrians her neighbours. Thus she *committed her whoredoms* with them:—neither left she her *whoredoms* brought from Egypt. The other was more corrupt in her *inordinate love* than she, and in her *whoredoms*, more than her sister in her *whoredoms*. She increased her *whoredoms*,—and doted upon them, and sent messengers unto them into Chaldea. And the Babylonians came to her into the *bed of love*, and they defiled her with their *whoredom*," Ezek. xxiii. 2, 3, 5, 7, 11, 14, 16, 17: here the two daughters of one mother are likewise the Israelitish and Jewish church, whose adulterations and falsifications of the Word are described as above by whoredoms. So in the following places: "Thou hast *played the harlot* with many lovers; and hast polluted the land with thy *whoredoms* and with thy wickedness. Hast thou seen that which backsliding Israel hath done? she is gone up upon every high mountain, and there hath *played the harlot*. And her treacherous sister Judah feared not, but went and *played the harlot* also. And it came to pass through the lightness of her *whoredom*, that she defiled the land, and *committed adultery* with stones and with stocks," Jerem. iii. 1, 6, 8, 9: and in other places. "Run ye to and fro through the streets of Jerusalem, and see now and know,—if ye can find a man, if there be any that executeth judgment, that seeketh the truth. When I had fed them to the full, they then *committed whoredom*, and assembled themselves by troops in the *harlot's* houses," Jerem. v. 1, 7. "I have seen thine *adulteries*, and thy neighings, and the lewdness of thy *whoredoms*,—and thine abominations on the hills in the fields. Woe unto thee, O Jerusalem, wilt thou not be made clean?" Jerem. xiii. 27. "I have seen also in the prophets of Jerusalem a horrible thing, they *commit adultery*, and walk in lies," Jerem. xxiii. 14. "Because they have committed villany in Israel, and have committed *adultery* with their neighbours' wives, and have spoken lying words in my name," Jerem. xxix. 23. "So they sinned against me, therefore will I change their glory into shame; they shall *commit whoredom*, because they have left off to take heed to Jehovah. *Whoredom*, and wine, and new wine take away the heart. Therefore your daughters shall commit *whoredom*, and your spouses shall commit *adultery*," Hosea iv. 7, 13. "I know, Ephraim, thou committest *whoredom*, and Israel is defiled," Hosea v. 3. "I have seen a horrible thing in the house of Israel; there is the *whoredom* of Ephraim; Israel is defiled," Hosea vi. 10. Israel here is the church, and Ephraim is the understanding of the Word, from which, and according to which, the church exists; therefore it is said, Ephraim hath committed whoredom, and Israel is polluted. Because the church had falsified the Word, the prophet Hosea was commanded to take unto himself a harlot to wife, saying, "Go, take unto thee a wife of *whoredoms*, and children of *whoredoms;* for the land hath committed great *whoredom*, departing from Jehovah," Hosea i. 2; and again: "Go yet, love a woman beloved of her friend, yet an *adulteress*," Hosea iii. 1. As the Jewish church was of such a nature, therefore the nation of the Jews was called by the Lord an adulterous generation, Matt. xii. 39; xvi. 4; Mark viii. 38; and in Isaiah, a seed of adulterers, lvii. 3; and in Nahum: "Woe to the bloody city! it is all full of lies, and there is a multitude of slain. Because of the multitude of the *whoredoms* of the well favoured harlot,—that selleth nations through her *whoredoms*," iii. 1, 3, 4. As *Babylon* adulterates and falsifies the Word above all others in the Christian world, she is therefore called the *great whore*, and the following is said of her in the Apocalypse: Babylon hath "made all nations to drink of the wine of the wrath of her *fornication*," xiv. 8. "For all nations have drunk of the wine of the wrath of her *whoredom*, and the kings of the earth have committed *whoredom* with her," xviii. 3. The angel said, "I will show unto thee the judgment of the *great whore*,—with whom the kings of the earth have committed *whoredom*," xvii. 1, 2. "He hath judged the *great whore*, which did corrupt the earth with her *whoredom*," xix. 2. From these passages it manifestly appears, that to commit adultery and whoredom signify to adulterate and falsify the goods and truths of the Word.

135. *And to eat things sacrificed unto idols*, signifies the defilement of divine worship and profanations, as is clear from the explanation given above, n. 114; for they who adulterate things good, appropriate to themselves such as are unclean, by which they defile and profane divine worship.

136. *And I gave her time to repent of her whoredom, and she repented not,* signifies that they who have confirmed themselves in that doctrine, will not recede, although they see things contrary to it in the Word. By receding from whoredom, is here signified to recede from falsifying the Word: that they see things contrary to their doctrine, is evident from a thousand passages in the Word, where it is said that evils are to be shunned, and that good is to be done; also that they who do good go to heaven, and they who do evil to hell, as also that faith without works is dead and diabolical. But it may be asked, what part of the Word have they falsified, or where have they spiritually committed whoredom with the Word? It may be answered, that they have falsified the whole of the Word; for the whole Word is nothing else but the doctrine of love towards the Lord, and of love towards the neighbour, for the Lord says, that on the commandments concerning those two loves hang all the law and the prophets, Matt. xxii. 40. There is also in the Word the doctrine of faith, yet not of such faith as theirs, but of the faith of love.

137. *Behold I will cast her into a bed, and them that commit adultery with her into great tribulation,* signifies that therefore they will be left in their doctrine with falsifications, and that they will be grievously infested by falses. That by bed is signified doctrine, will be seen presently; that by committing adultery falsifications of truth are signified, may be seen above, n. 134, 136; and that by tribulation is signified infestation from falses, n. 33, 95, 100; and hence by great tribulation is signified grievous infestation. That a bed signifies doctrine, is from correspondence, for as the body rests in its bed, so does the mind rest in its doctrine: but by bed is signified the doctrine which every one acquires to himself either from the Word, or from his proper intelligence, for therein the mind reposes and, as it were, sleeps. The beds that are lain in, in the spiritual world, are of no other origin; for there every one's bed is conformable to the quality of his science and intelligence, the wise have such as are magnificent, the foolish have mean ones, and those of false-speakers are filthy. This is the signification of bed in Luke: "I tell you, in that night there shall be two men in one *bed:* the one shall be taken and the other left," xvii. 34; speaking of the last judgment; two in one bed, means two in one doctrine, but not in similar life. In John: Jesus saith

unto the sick man, "Rise, take up thy *bed*, and walk; and he took up his *bed*, and walked," v. 8, 9; and in Mark: "Jesus said unto the sick of the palsy, Son, thy sins be forgiven thee;" and he said unto the Scribes, "Whether is it easier to say, Thy sins be forgiven thee, or to say, Arise, take up thy *bed*, and walk?" then he said, "Arise, take up thy *bed*, and walk; and he took up the *bed*, and went forth before them all," ii. 5, 9, 11, 12; that here something is signified by bed, is evident, because Jesus said, Whether is it easier to say, Thy sins be forgiven thee, or to say, Take up thy bed and walk? by carrying his bed and walking, is signified to meditate in doctrine: it is so understood in heaven. Doctrine is also signified by bed in Amos: "As the shepherd taketh out of the mouth of the lion—so shall the children of Israel be taken out that dwell in Samaria, in the corner of a *bed*, and in Damascus in a *couch*," iii. 12: in the corner of a bed, and in a couch, means what is more remote from the truths and goods of doctrine. Bed and couch and bedchamber have a similar signification in other places, as in Isaiah xxviii. 20; lvii. 2, 7, 8; Ezek. xxiii. 41; Amos vi. 4; Micah ii. 1; Psalm iv. 4; Psalm xxxvi. 4; Psalm xli. 3; Job vii. 13; Levit. xv. 4, 5. Since by Jacob, in the propheticals of the Word, is signified the church as to doctrine, therefore it is said of him, that he "bowed himself upon the *bed's* head," Gen. xlvii. 31. That when Joseph came, he "sat upon the *bed*," Gen. xlviii. 2. That "he gathered up his feet into the *bed*, and yielded up the ghost," Gen. xlix. 33. The doctrine of the church being signified by Jacob, therefore sometimes, when I have thought of Jacob, there has appeared to me above, in front, a man lying in a bed.

138. *Except they repent of their deeds*, signifies, if they will not desist from separating faith from charity, and from falsifying the Word, as may appear without further explanation.

139. *And I will kill her children with death*, signifies that all the truths of the Word with them will be turned into falses. By children, in the Word, are signified truths, and in an opposite sense, falses; therefore to kill children, signifies to turn truths into falses, for by that means they perish; neither is any thing else understood by the slain and wounded of Jehovah: by killing her children with death, is also signified to condemn their falses. That children signify truths, and in an opposite sense falses, is, because in the spiritual sense of the Word by generations are meant spiritual generations, and in like manner by consanguinities and affinities; thus by their names, as by father, mother, sons, daughters, brethren, sisters, sons-in-law, daughters-in-law, and others; neither does spiritual generation give birth to any other sons and daughters, than truths and goods. See n. 512, 546, below.

140. *And all the churches shall know that I am He which*

searcheth the reins and hearts, signifies that the church shall know that the Lord sees the quality of every one's truth and the quality of every one's good. By the seven churches is signified the church universal, as before; and by searching the reins and hearts, is signified to see all the things which a man believes and loves, thus the quality of his truth and of his good that this is the signification of searching the reins and hearts, is from correspondence, for the Word in its literal sense consists of mere correspondences; the correspondence here is grounded in this circumstance, that as the reins [or kidneys] cleanse the blood from such impurities as are called urinous, and as the heart purifies the blood from such unclean things as are loathsome, so the truth of faith purifies man from falses, and the good of love from evils. From this cause the ancients placed love and its affections in the heart, and intelligence and its perceptions in the reins; as may appear from the following passages in the Word: "Behold, thou desirest truth in the *reins*, and in the hidden part thou shalt make me to know wisdom," Psalm li. 6. "Thou hast possessed my *reins*—my substance was not hid from thee when I was made in secret," Psalm cxxxix. 13, 15. "My *heart* was grieved, and I was pricked in my *reins*; so foolish was I and ignorant," Psalm lxxiii. 21, 22. "I Jehovah search the *heart*, I try the *reins*, even to give every man according to his ways," Jerem. xvii. 10. "Thou art near, in their mouth, and far from their *reins*; thou, O Jehovah,—hast seen me, and tried my *heart*," Jerem. xii. 2, 3. Jehovah is a judge of righteousness, trying the *reins* and the *heart*, Jerem. xi. 20; xx. 12. "Establish the just, for the righteous God trieth the *hearts* and *reins*," Psalm vii. 9. "Examine me, O Jehovah, and prove me, try my *reins* and my *heart*," Psalm xxvi. 2; by reins in these places are signified truths of intelligence and faith, and by heart, the good of love and charity. That heart signifies the love and its affections, may be seen in *The Angelic Wisdom concerning the Divine Providence*, n. 371, 393.

141. *And I will give unto every one according to your works*, signifies that he gives unto every one according to the charity and its faith which are in his works. That works are the continents of charity and faith, and that charity and faith without works are only like airy phantoms, which vanish as soon as they have appeared, may be seen above, n. 76.

142. *But unto you I say, and unto the rest in Thyatira, as many as have not this doctrine*, signifies, both to those with whom the doctrine of faith is separated from charity, and to those with whom the doctrine of faith is joined with charity, as is evident from what is said above, without further explanation.

143. *And who have not known the depths of Satan, as they speak*, signifies they who do not understand their interiors,

which are mere falses. That by Satan is understood the hell of those who are in falses, and, abstractedly, falses, may be seen above, n. 97; therefore by its depths are signified the interiors of doctrine separated from charity, which are mere falses. The depths and interiors of that doctrine are what are delivered in their books and lectures in universities, and thence in their sermons, the nature of which is pointed out in what is prefixed to the first chapter, where their doctrines are set forth; and particularly in what is adduced concerning Justification by Faith and concerning Good Works; where it may be seen asserted that the clergy alone are acquainted with the mysteries of that doctrine, but not the laity, therefore the latter principally are meant by those who have not known the depths of Satan.

144. *I will put upon you none other burthen*, signifies, only that they should beware of them. The reason is, because they confirm their falses by reasonings from the natural man, and by some things from the Word, which they falsify, for by these means they can seduce; they are like serpents in the grass who bite those that pass by; or like concealed poison which kills the unwary.

145. *Nevertheless, that which ye have, hold fast till I come*, signifies that they should retain the few things which they know concerning charity and thence concerning faith from the Word, and live according to them, until there be a new heaven and a new church, which are the Lord's coming; for these and no others receive the things which the doctrine of the New Jerusalem teaches concerning the Lord and charity.

146. *And he that overcometh and keepeth my works unto the end*, signifies those who fight against evils and falses and are reformed, and are in charity, and thence actually in faith, and continue in them to the end of their lives. That to overcome is to fight against evils and falses, may be seen above, n. 88; and that works are charity and thence faith in act, n. 76, 141; that to keep them unto the end, is to be in them, and remain in them to the end of life, is evident.

147. *To him will I give power over the nations*, signifies that they shall overcome evils in themselves which are from hell. That by nations in the Word are meant those who are in good, and, in an opposite sense, those who are in evil, thus, abstractedly, goods and evils, may be seen below, n. 483; therefore here by giving power over the nations, is signified to give them to overcome the evils from hell in themselves.

148. *And he shall rule them with a rod of iron*, signifies by truths from the literal sense of the Word, and at the same time by rational principles derived from natural light. It is said by a rod or staff of iron, because staff in the Word signifies power, and iron signifies natural truth, consequently the natural sense

of the Word, and at the same time the natural light of man; in these two consists the power of truth. That divine truth in the natural sense of the Word, which is its literal sense, is in its power, may be seen in *The Doctrine of the New Jerusalem concerning the Sacred Scripture*, n. 205—221; from this cause the literal sense is the basis, continent, and firmament of its spiritual sense, n. 27—36. And that all power is in the ultimates which are called things natural, may be seen in *The Angelic Wisdom concerning the Divine Love and the Divine Wisdom*, n. 205—221; consequently in the natural sense of the letter of the Word, and in the natural light of man; these therefore are the rod of iron by which he is to rule the nations, that is, to overcome the evils which are from hell. The same is signified by an iron rod in the following places: "Thou shalt break them with a *rod of iron*, thou shalt dash them in pieces like a potter's vessel," Psalm ii. 9. "And she brought forth a man-child who was to rule all nations with a *rod of iron*," Apoc. xii. 5. Out of the mouth of him that sat upon the white horse went "a sharp sword, that with it he should smite the nations; and he shall rule them with a *rod of iron*," Apoc. xix. 15. Jehovah "shall smite the earth with the *rod* of his mouth," Isaiah xi. 4.

149. *As the vessels of a potter shall they be broken to shivers*, signifies, as of little or no account. It is said the vessels of a potter, because by them are signified the things which are of self-derived intelligence, which are all falses, and in themselves of no account; so in David: "Thou shalt break them with a *rod of iron*, thou shalt dash them in pieces like a *potter's vessel*," Psalm ii. 9.

150. *Even as I received of my Father*, signifies that they shall receive this power from the Lord, who, when he was in the world, procured to himself all power over the hells, from the divine principle which was within him. That the Lord, when he was in the world, by admitting temptations in himself, and finally by the last of them, which was the passion of the cross, subdued the hells and glorified his Humanity, may be seen in *The Doctrine of the New Jerusalem concerning the Lord*, n. 29—36; as also above, n. 67; from which it may appear, that to receive from his Father, is to receive from the divine or divinity which was in him, for he said that the Father is in him and he in the Father; that the Father and he are one; as also the Father who is in me; and many other things to the same purpose.

151. *And I will give him the morning star*, signifies intelligence and wisdom. That by stars are signified knowledges of good and truth, may be seen above, n. 51; and because by them comes intelligence and wisdom, therefore these are signified by the morning star. It is called the morning star,

because intelligence and wisdom will be given them from the Lord, when he comes to establish the New Church, which is the New Jerusalem, for he says, "That which ye have, hold fast till I come," verse 25, by which is signified, that they must retain the few truths which they know concerning charity and its faith from the Word, and live according to them, until the new heaven and new church are formed, which constitute the coming of the Lord, n. 145. The morning star is mentioned, because by morning is signified the coming of the Lord, when there is a new church. That this is meant by morning, in the Word, appears from the following places: "Until the evening and *morning* two thousand three hundred, then shall the sanctuary be justified," Dan. viii. 14. "He calleth to me out of Seir, Watchman, what of the night? Watchman, what of the night? The watchman said, The *morning* cometh, and also the night," Isaiah xxi. 11, 12; by the evening and the night is signified the last time of the old church, and by the morning the commencement of the New Church. "The end is come,—the *morning* is come upon thee, O thou that dwellest in the land; behold the day it is come, the *morning* is gone forth," Ezek. vii. 6, 7, 10. "Every *morning* doth he bring his judgment to light, he faileth not," Zeph. iii. 5. "God is in the midst of her—God shall help her when the *morning* appeareth," Psalm xlvi. 5. "I wait for Jehovah—my soul doth wait for the Lord more than they that watch for the *morning*, I say more than they that watch for the *morning*; for with him is plenteous redemption, and he shall redeem Israel," Psalm cxxx. 5—8; and in other places. By morning in these passages is meant the Lord's coming, when he came into the world and established a new church; in like manner now. And because the Lord alone gives those who are to be of his new church intelligence and wisdom, and all things which the Lord gives are himself because they are of himself, therefore the Lord says that he himself is the morning star: "I am the root and offspring of David, *the bright and morning star*," Apoc. xxii. 16: he is called also the morning in 2 Samuel: "The God of Israel said, the Rock of Israel spake to me—he is as the light of the *morning—a morning* without clouds," xxiii. 3, 4.

152. *He that hath an ear, let him hear what the Spirit saith unto the churches*, signifies that he who understands these things, ought to obey what the Divine Truth of the Word teaches those who are to be of the New Church, which is the New Jerusalem, as above, n. 87.

153. To the above I will add a Memorable Relation, concerning the lot of those after death, who have confirmed themselves in faith alone unto justification, both in doctrine and life. I. When they are dead and revive as to their spirit, which commonly happens on the third day after the heart has ceased to

beat, they appear to themselves in a body like that which they had before in the world, so that they know no otherwise than that they are living in the former world; yet they are not in a material body, but in a spiritual body, this appearing to their senses, which are also spiritual, as if it was material, although it is not so. II. After some days they see that they are in a world where there are various societies instituted, which world is called the world of spirits, and is intermediate between heaven and hell: all the societies there, which are innumerable, are wonderfully arranged according to natural affections, good and evil; the societies arranged according to good natural affections communicate with heaven, and the societies arranged according to evil affections communicate with hell. III. The novitiate spirit, or the spiritual man, is conducted and introduced to various societies, both good and evil, and examination is made to discover whether he is affected by truths, and in what manner; and whether, and in what manner, he is affected by falses. IV. If he is affected by truths, he is withdrawn from evil societies, and introduced into good societies, and also into various ones, until he comes into a society corresponding with his own natural affection, where he enjoys the good which accords with that affection; and this until he has put off his natural affection and has put on a spiritual affection, and then he is elevated into heaven: but this takes place with those who in the world have lived a life of charity, and thus also a life of faith, which consists in believing in the Lord, and shunning evils as sins. V. But they who have confirmed themselves in doctrine and life in faith alone unto justification, by reason of their not being affected by truths, but by falses, and because they have rejected the goods of charity, which are good works, from the means of salvation, are withdrawn from good societies, and introduced into evil societies, and also into various ones, until they come into the society which corresponds to the concupiscences of their love; for he who loves falses cannot but love evils. VI. But as in the world they had feigned good affections in externals, although in their internals there was nothing but evil affections or concupiscences, they are at first kept by turns in externals; and they who in the world presided over companies of men, are here and there set over societies in the world of spirits, in general or in part according to the extent and importance of the offices they had formerly exercised: but as they neither love truth nor justice, nor are capable of being illuminated so as to know what truth and justice are in themselves, therefore after some days they are dismissed. I have seen such removed from one society to another, and some administration given them in each, but only to be as quickly and repeatedly dismissed. VII. After frequent dismissals, some out of weariness will not, and others from the fear of losing reputation do not, venture to seek for offices any further, but withdraw, and become disheartened: they are next led away into a desert, where there are cottages, into which they enter, and work of some kind is given them to do, and as they do it, they receive food, and if they do not do it, they are hungry and receive none, so that at length necessity compels them. Food there is similar to the food in this world, but it is from a spiritual origin, and is given from heaven from the Lord to all according to the uses they perform; to the idle, nothing is given, because they are useless. VIII. After a time they loathe work, and then they go out of the cottages; and if they have been priests, they have an inclination to build; and there appear then immediately heaps of hewn stones, bricks, rafters, and boards, also heaps of reeds and bulrushes, clay, lime, and bitumen, which when they see, the lust of building is kindled, and they begin to construct a house, taking now a stone, and then wood, now a reed, and then clay, and placing them irregularly one upon another, but in order as it seems to themselves; but what they build by day falls down by night; and the next day they gather materials from among the rubbish, and build again, and this they continue to do, until they are tired of building. From this cause it is, they collect together falses to confirm salvation by faith alone, and such falses cannot serve to build up a church in any other manner. IX. Afterwards from weary feeling they go away, and sit solitary and idle; and as the idle have no food given them from heaven, as was before observed, they begin to hunger, and think of nothing else but how they shall get food and satisfy their hunger. When they are in this state, there come to them some of whom they ask alms; and they say, Why do ye thus sit idle? come with us to our houses, and we will give you work to do, and food; and then they rise up with joy, and go with them to their houses, and there each has his work given him, and food for his work: but as all who have confirmed themselves in falses of faith are unable to do works of good use, but only works of evil use, neither do they do these faithfully, but only so as to save appearances for the sake of honour or interest, therefore they leave their work, and only love to converse, talk, walk about, and sleep; and then, because they cannot any longer be induced by their masters to work, they are cast out as useless. X. When they are cast out, their eyes are opened, and they see a way leading to a certain cavern; to which when they are come, a door is opened, and they enter, and inquire whether there is any food there, and when they receive for answer that there is, they ask leave to remain, and are told that they may, and are introduced and the door shut after them; and then comes the overseer of that cavern, and says to them, Ye cannot go out hence any more; behold your companions, they all labour, and as they labour food is given them from heaven; I tell you this for your information. And their companions also say, Our overseer knows what work every one is fit for, and assigns it to every one daily; on the day you finish it, food is given you, but if you do not, neither food nor clothing is granted; and if any one does evil to another, he is cast into a corner of the cavern, upon a certain bed of accursed dust, where he is miserably tormented, until such time as the overseer sees signs of repentance in him, and then he is released, and commanded to do his work. He is told also, that every one after his task is done is permitted to walk about, to converse, and afterwards to sleep; and he is carried into an interior part of the cavern, where there are harlots, from among whom each is permitted to take one to himself as a female companion, and promiscuous fornication is forbid under pain of chastisement. Of such caverns, which are nothing but eternal workhouses, the universal hell consists. It has been permitted me to enter into and have a view of some of them, to the end that I might make it known, and they all seemed vile, neither did any one of the inhabitants know who, or in what office he had been in the world; but the angel who was with me, told me, that such a one had been a servant in the world, another a soldier, a third a governor, a fourth a priest, this one in dignity, and that in opulence, and yet that none of them knew otherwise than that they had always been servants and companions, for this reason, because they were all interiorly alike, although they had been unlike exteriorly, and interiors associate all in the spiritual world. Such is the lot of those who have removed the life of charity, and who thence have not lived that life in the world.

With respect to the hells in general, they consist merely of such caverns and workhouses, but those inhabited by satans are of a different kind from those inhabited by devils; satans are they who have been in falses and thence in evils, and devils are they who have been in evils and thence in falses. Satans appear in the light of heaven like dead corpses, and some of them black like mummies; and devils appear in the light of heaven of a dark and fiery colour, and some of them black like soot; but they are all as to their faces and bodies, monstrous; yet in their own light, which is like the light of a coal-fire, they appear not as monsters, but men; this is granted them for the sake of consociation.

CHAPTER III.

1. And unto the angel of the church in Sardis write; These things saith He that hath the seven spirits of God, and the seven stars: I know thy works, that thou hast a name that thou livest and art dead.

2. Be watchful, and strengthen the things which remain, that are ready to die: for I have not found thy works full before God.

3. Remember therefore how thou hast received and heard; and hold fast, and repent. If therefore thou shalt not watch, I will come on thee as a thief, and thou shalt not know what hour I will come upon thee.

4. Thou hast a few names even in Sardis, which have not defiled their garments; and they shall walk with me in white; for they are worthy.

5. He that overcometh, the same shall be clothed in white raiment; and I will not blot out his name out of the book of life; and I will confess his name before my Father, and before his angels.

6. He that hath an ear, let him hear what the Spirit saith unto the churches.

7. And to the angel of the church in Philadelphia write; These things saith He that is holy, He that is true, He that hath the key of David, He that openeth and no one shutteth, and shutteth and no one openeth.

8. I know thy works: behold, I have set before thee an open door, and no one is able to shut it: for thou hast a little power, and hast kept my word, and hast not denied my name.

9. Behold, I will make them of the synagogue of Satan, who say they are Jews, and are not, but do lie; behold, I will make them to come and worship before thy feet, and to know that I have loved thee.

10. Because thou hast kept the word of my patience, I also will keep thee from the hour of temptation, which shall come upon all the world, to try them that dwell upon the earth.

11. Behold, I come quickly; hold fast that thou hast, that no one take thy crown.

12. Him that overcometh will I make a pillar in the temple of my God, and he shall go no more out; and I will write upon him the name of my God; and the name of the city of my God, the new Jerusalem, which cometh down out of heaven from my God; and my new name.

13. He that hath an ear, let him hear what the Spirit saith unto the churches.

14. And unto the angel of the church of the Laodiceans

write; These things saith the Amen, the faithful and true Witness, the beginning of the creation of God.

15. I know thy works, that thou art neither cold nor hot: I would thou wert cold or hot.

16. So, then, because thou art lukewarm, and neither cold nor hot, I will vomit thee out of my mouth.

17. Because thou sayest, I am rich, and increased with goods, and have need of nothing; and knowest not that thou art wretched, and miserable, and poor, and blind, and naked.

18. I counsel thee to buy of me gold tried in the fire, that thou mayest be rich; and white raiment that thou mayest be clothed, and that the shame of thy nakedness do not appear; and anoint thine eyes with eye-salve that thou mayest see.

19. As many as I love, I rebuke and chasten; be zealous, therefore, and repent.

20. Behold, I stand at the door and knock: If any man hear my voice, and open the door, I will come in to him, and will sup with him, and he with me.

21. To him that overcometh will I give to sit with me in my throne, even as I also overcame, and am set down with my Father in his throne.

22. He that hath an ear, let him hear what the Spirit saith unto the churches.

THE SPIRITUAL SENSE.

THE CONTENTS OF THE WHOLE CHAPTER. This chapter treats of those in the Christian church who are in dead worship, which is without charity and faith; who are described by the church in Sardis, n. 154—171: of those who are in truths from good from the Lord; who are described by the church in Philadelphia, n. 172—197: of those who believe alternately, sometimes from themselves, and sometimes from the Word, and thus profane holy things; who are described by the church in Laodicea, n. 198—223. All these being likewise called to the New Church of the Lord.

THE CONTENTS OF EACH VERSE. v. 1, "And unto the angel of the church in Sardis write," signifies to those and concerning those, who are in dead worship, or in worship which is without the good of charity, and without the truths of faith: "These things saith He that hath the seven spirits of God, and the seven stars," signifies the Lord, from whom are all truths, and all the knowledges of good and truth: "I know thy works," signifies that the Lord sees all their interiors and exteriors at once: "That thou hast a name that thou livest, and art dead," signifies that it may be seen and believed by themselves and by others, that they are spiritually alive, when yet they are spiritually dead: v. 2, "Be watchful," signifies to be in truths and in a life according to them: "And strengthen the things which remain, that are ready to die," signifies that the things which pertain to their worship may receive life: "For I have not found thy works full before God," signifies that the interiors of their worship are not in conjunction with the Lord: v. 3, "Remember therefore how thou hast received and heard," signifies that they should consider that all worship at first is natural, and afterwards by truths becomes spiritual, besides many other things: "And hold fast, and repent," signifies that they should attend to these things, and give life to their dead worship: "If therefore thou shalt not watch," signifies here the same as above: "I will come on thee as a thief, and thou shalt not know what hour I will come upon thee," signifies that the things which are of worship shall be taken from them, and that they shall not know when and how this is done: v. 4, "Thou hast a few names even in Sardis," signifies that among them there are also some who have life in their worship: "Which have not defiled their garments," signifies who are in truths, and have not defiled worship by evils of life and falses thence derived: "And they shall walk with me in white, for they are worthy," signifies that they shall live with the Lord, because they are in truths from him: v. 5, "He that overcometh, the same shall be clothed in white raiment," signifies that he who is reformed becomes spiritual: "And I will not blot out his name out of the book of life," signifies that he shall be saved: "And I will confess his name before my Father, and before his angels," signifies that they will be received who are in divine good and in divine truths from the Lord: v. 6, "He that hath an ear, let him hear what the Spirit saith unto the churches," signifies here, as before.

v. 7, "And to the angel of the church in Philadelphia write," signifies to those and concerning those, who are in truths originating in good from the Lord: "These things saith He that is holy, He that is true," signifies the Lord as to divine truth: "He that hath the key of David, He that openeth and no one shutteth, and shutteth and no one openeth," signifies who alone is omnipotent to save: v. 8, "I know thy works," signifies here, as above: "Behold, I have set before thee an open door," signifies that heaven is open to those who are in truths from good from the Lord: "And no one is able to shut it," signifies that hell cannot prevail against them: "For thou hast a little power," signifies because they know that they can do nothing from themselves: "And hast kept my word," signifies because they live according to the Lord's commandments in his Word: "And hast not denied my name," signifies that they are in the worship of the Lord: v. 9, "Behold, I will make them of the synagogue of Satan," signifies those who are in falses as to doctrine: "Who say they are Jews, and are not, but do lie," signifies who say that the church is among them, and yet it is not: "Behold, I will make them to come and worship before thy feet," signifies that many who are in falses as to doctrine, will receive the truths of the New Church: "And to know that I have loved thee," signifies that they shall see that they are loved and received into heaven by the Lord: v. 10, "Because thou hast kept the Word of my patience," signifies because they have fought against evils: "I also will keep thee from the hour of temptation, which shall come upon all the world, to try them that dwell upon the earth," signifies that they will be protected and preserved in the day of the last judgment: v. 11, "Behold I come quickly," signifies the Lord's coming: "Hold fast that thou hast," signifies that in the mean time they should remain in their truths and goods: "That no one take thy crown," signifies lest wisdom should perish, from which is eternal felicity: v. 12, "Him that overcometh," signifies they who persist in truths from good: "Will I make a pillar in the temple of my God," signifies that truths from good from the Lord, with those in whom they abide, sustain the church: "And he shall go no more out," signifies that they shall remain there to eternity: "And I will write upon him the name of my God," signifies that divine truth shall be written in their hearts: "And the name of the city of my God, the New Jerusalem," signifies that the doctrine of the New Church shall be written in their hearts: "Which cometh down out of heaven from my God," signifies which will be from the divine truth of the Lord such as it is in heaven: "And my new name," signifies the worship of the Lord alone, with other new things which were not in the former church: v. 13, "He that hath an ear, let him hear what the Spirit saith unto the churches," signifies here, as before.

v. 14, "And unto the angel of the church of the Laodiceans write," signifies to those and concerning those, in the church, who alternately believe, sometimes from themselves, and sometimes from the Word, and thus profane things holy: "These things saith the Amen, the faithful and true Witness," signifies the Lord as to the Word, which is divine truth from him: "The beginning of the creation of God," signifies the Word: v. 15, "I know thy works," signifies here, as before: "That thou art neither cold nor hot," signifies that they who are such, sometimes deny that the Word is divine and holy, and at other times acknowledge it: "I would thou wert cold or hot," signifies that it is better for them either from the heart to deny the holy things of the Word and of the church, or from the heart to acknowledge them: v. 16, "So then, because thou art lukewarm, and neither cold nor hot, I will vomit thee out of my mouth," signifies profanation and separation from the Lord: v. 17, "Because thou sayest, I am rich, and increased with goods," signifies that they think they possess in all abundance the knowledges of what is good and true, which are of heaven and the church: "And have need of nothing," signifies that they have no need of more wisdom: "And knowest not that thou art wretched," signifies that all things which they know do not at all cohere: "And miserable and poor," signifies that they are without truths and goods: "And blind and naked," signifies that they are without the understanding of truth, and without the will of good: v. 18, "I counsel thee to buy of me gold tried in the fire, that thou mayest be rich," signifies an admonition to acquire to themselves the good of love from the Lord by means of the Word, that they may become wise: "And white raiment, that thou mayest be clothed," signifies that they should acquire to themselves genuine truths of wisdom: "And that the shame of thy nakedness may not appear," signifies lest the good of celestial love should be profaned and adulterated: "And anoint thine eyes with eye-salve, that thou mayest see," signifies that their understandings may be healed: v. 19, "As many as I love, I rebuke and chasten," signifies that because they are now beloved, they cannot but be admitted to temptations: "Be zealous, therefore, and repent," signifies that this should be done from the affection of truth: v. 20, "Behold I stand at the door, and knock," signifies that the Lord is present to every one in the Word, and is there pressing to be received, and teaches how: "If any man hear my voice, and open the door," signifies he who believes in the Word and lives according to it: "I will come in to him, and will sup with him, and he with me," signifies that the Lord joins himself with them and they with him: v. 21, "To him that overcometh," signifies such as are in conjunction with the Lord by a life conformable to his precepts in the Word: "Will I give to sit with me in my throne," signifies that they will have conjunction with the Lord in heaven: "Even as I also overcame, and am set down with my Father in his throne," signifies as he and the Father are one and are heaven: v. 22, "He that hath an ear, let him hear what the Spirit saith unto the churches," signifies here, as before.

THE EXPLANATION.

154. *And unto the angel of the church in Sardis write*, signifies to those and concerning those, who are in dead worship, or in worship which is without the good of charity and without the truths of faith. That they who are in such worship are meant by the church in Sardis, is evident from what is written to it when understood in the spiritual sense. By dead worship is meant worship alone, which consists in going to church, hearing sermons, receiving the sacrament, reading the Word and pious books, talking about God, and about heaven and hell, and a life after death, and especially about piety, praying morning and evening, and yet not desiring to know the truths of faith, nor willing to do the good things of charity, believing that they shall have salvation by means of mere worship; when yet such worship without truths, and without a life conformable to them, is only the external sign of charity and faith, within which there may lie concealed all sorts of evils and falses, if charity and faith do not reside within; for of these genuine worship consists; otherwise worship is like the skin or surface of any kind of fruit, in which there lies concealed nothing but a rotten and worm-eaten substance, and therefore is dead. That such worship prevails in the church at this day, is well known.

155. *These things saith He that hath the seven spirits of God, and the seven stars*, signifies the Lord, from whom are all truths, and all the knowledges of good and truth. That by the seven spirits of God is understood the divine truth proceeding from the Lord, or divine verity, may be seen above, n. 14; and that by the seven stars are understood all the knowledges of what is good and true from the Word, n. 51, from which exists the church in heaven, n. 65. These things are now said by the Lord, because the subject treated of is concerning dead worship and concerning living worship, and worship derives its life from truths, and from a life according to them.

156. *I know thy works*, signifies that the Lord sees all their interiors and exteriors at once, as above, n. 76.

157. *That thou hast a name that thou livest, and art dead*, signifies that it may be seen and believed by themselves and others, that they are spiritually alive, when yet they are spiritually dead. By having a name, is signified to seem and to be thought to be such; in this instance, that they are living, when yet they are dead; for spiritual life, which is properly life, does not consist in worship alone, but is inwardly in worship, and inwardly there ought to be divine truths from the Word, and when man lives according to them, life is in the worship; the reason is, because the external derives its quality from internals, and the internals of worship are truths of life. These are they

who are meant by these words of the Lord: "And ye begin to stand without, and to knock at the door, saying, Lord, Lord, open unto us; and he shall answer and say unto you, I know you not whence you are. Then shall ye begin to say, We have eaten and drunk in thy presence, and thou hast taught in our streets; but he shall say, I tell you, I know you not whence ye are; depart from me, all ye workers of iniquity," Luke xiii. 25, 26, 27. I have also been permitted to hear many in the spiritual world say, that they have frequently received the sacrament, and thus have eaten and drunk what is holy, and have as often been absolved from their sins; that every sabbath day they have hearkened to their teachers; and have devoutly prayed at home morning and evening, besides other things: but when the interiors of their worship were laid open, they appeared full of iniquities, and infernal; therefore they were rejected; and when they asked the reason of it, they had for answer, that they were not at all solicitous about divine truths. And yet a life not according to divine truths, is not life such as they enjoy who are in heaven, and they who are not in the life of heaven, cannot bear the light of heaven, which is divine truth proceeding from the Lord as the sun there, much less can they bear the heat of heaven, which is divine love. But although they heard and also understood these things, yet when they were let into themselves, and their own worship, they said, What need is there of truths, and what are truths? and as they were no longer able to receive truths, they were left to their concupiscences, which lay hid within their worship, and these at length drove away from them all their worship of God; for the interiors accommodate the exteriors to themselves, and reject the things which are not in accordance with them; and the exteriors of all after death are rendered analogous with their interiors.

158. *Be watchful*, signifies that they should be in truths and in a life according to them. By watching, in the Word, nothing else is signified; for he who learns truths and lives according to them, is like one who is awakened out of sleep and becomes watchful; and he who is not in truths, but only in worship, is like one who sleeps and dreams. Natural life, considered in itself, or without spiritual life, is nothing else but sleep; but natural life, in which there is spiritual life, is watchfulness, and this cannot be acquired otherwise than by truths, which exist in their own light and in their own day, when man lives according to them. Such is the signification of watching in the following places: "*Watch*,—for ye know not what hour your Lord doth come," Matt. xxiv. 42. "Blessed are those servants whom the Lord when he cometh shall find *watching*:—Be ye therefore ready, for the Son of Man cometh at an hour when ye think not," Luke xii. 37, 40. "*Watch* ye, for ye know not when the master of the house cometh,—lest coming suddenly he find you

sleeping. What I say unto you, I say unto all, *Watch*," Mark xiii. 35, 36, 37. "While the bridegroom tarried, the virgins *slumbered* and *slept*," and the five foolish came and said, "Lord, Lord, open to us; but he answered and said, I know you not; *watch* therefore, for ye know neither the day nor the hour wherein the Son of Man cometh," Matt. xxv. 5, 11—13. Because the Lord's coming is called *morning*, n. 151, and then truths are opened, and there is light, therefore that time is called the *beginning of the watches*, in Lament. ii. 19, and the Lord is called *a Watcher*, Dan. iv. 13, and it is written in Isaiah, "Thy dead shall live,—*Awake*,—ye that dwell in the dust," xxvi. 19. But that the state of a man who is not in truths is called slumbering and sleeping, may be seen in Jerem. li. 39, 57; Psalm xiii. 3; Psalm lxxvi. 5; Luke viii. 23; and in other places.

159. *And strengthen the things which remain, that are ready to die*, signifies, that the things which pertain to their worship may receive life, and not be extinguished. How these things are to be understood, shall be explained. Dead worship is altogether similar to living worship in its external form, because they who are in truths do the same things, for they hear sermons, receive the holy supper, bow their knees in prayer morning and evening, besides other things which are common and customary in worship; therefore they who are in dead worship, have need of nothing more than to learn truths and bring them into life; so that the things which remain, and are ready to die, may be confirmed.

160. *For I have not found thy works full before God*, signifies that the interiors of their worship are not in conjunction with the Lord. That by works are understood the interiors and exteriors, and that by "I know thy works," is signified that the Lord sees all the interiors and exteriors of man at once, may appear above, n. 76; which are called full before God, when they are in conjunction with the Lord. It must be observed, that dead worship, or worship which is only external, causes the Lord's presence, but not conjunction with him; but external worship, in which the interiors are alive, causes both presence and conjunction; for the conjunction of the Lord is with the things in man which are from the Lord, which are truths from good, and unless these are in worship, works are not full before God, but are empty. A man is said to be empty in the Word, in whom there are nothing but falses and evils, as in Matt. xii. 44, and in other places; but a man is said to be full, in whom there are truths and goods.

161. *Remember therefore how thou hast received and heard*," signifies that they should consider that all worship at first is natural, and afterwards by truths out of the Word, and by a life according to them, becomes spiritual, besides many other things. These are the things that are to be understood by these words:

as also, that every one may know from the Word, from the doctrine of the church drawn from the Word, and from sermons, that truths ought to be learned, and that by truths men have faith, charity, and all things of the church. That this is the case, is abundantly shown in *The Arcana Cœlestia*: as for instance, that by truths comes faith, n. 4353, 4997, 7178, 10,367. That by truths comes love towards our neighbour or charity, n. 4368, 7623, 7624, 8034. That by truths comes love to the Lord, n. 10,143, 10,153, 10,310, 10,578, 10,648. That by truths come intelligence and wisdom, n. 3182, 3190, 3387, 10,064. That by truths regeneration is effected, n. 1553, 1904, 2046, 2189, 9088, 9954, 10,028. That by truths comes power against evils and falses, and against hell, n. 3091, 4015, 10,485. That by truths there is purification from evils and falses, n. 2799, 5954, 7044, 7918, 10,229, 10,237. That by truths the church exists, n. 1798, 1799, 3963, 4468, 4672. That by truths heaven exists, n. 1690, 9832, 9931, 10,303. That by truths comes the innocence of wisdom, n. 3183, 3495, 6013. That by truths there is conscience, n. 1077, 2053, 9113. That by truths there is order, n. 3316, 3417, 3570, 4704, 5339, 5343, 6028, 10,303. That by truths is the beauty of angels, and also of men as to the interiors which are their spirits, n. 353, 3080, 4983, 5199. That by virtue of truths man is man, n. 3175, 3387, 8370, 10,298. But all this by truths derived from good, and not by truths without good, and by good from the Lord, n. 2434, 4070, 4736, 5147. That every good is from the Lord, n. 1614, 2016, 2904, 4151, 9981, 5147. But who thinks this? Is it not at this day a matter of indifference what truths a man knows, provided he is in worship? And because few search the Word for the purpose of learning truths and living according to them, therefore nothing is known concerning worship, whether it be dead or living, and yet according to the quality of worship man himself is either dead or living; otherwise of what use would the Word be, and doctrine derived from it, or what would be the use of sabbaths and sermons, as well as of books of instruction, yea to what purpose would the church and religion be? That all worship in its beginning is natural, and afterwards by truths from the Word, and a life according to them, becomes spiritual, is well known; for man is born natural, but is educated in order that he may become civil and moral, and afterwards spiritual, being in this manner born again. These things therefore are signified by "Remember how thou hast received and heard."

162. *And hold fast and repent*, signifies that they should attend to these things and give life to their dead worship. That to observe is to attend to those things, which are understood by "Remember how thou hast received and heard," is evident; and that to repent is to give life to dead worship, by truths from the Word, and by a life according to them, follows of course.

163. *If therefore thou shalt not watch*, signifies, if they are not in truths and in a life according to them, as is evident from the explanation above, n. 158.

164. *I will come on thee as a thief, and thou shalt not know what hour I will come upon thee*, signifies that the things which are of worship shall be taken from them, and that they shall not know when and how this is done. It is said that the Lord will come like a thief, because man, who is in dead worship, is deprived of the external good of worship: for there is something of good in dead worship, because the worshipper thinks of God and of eternal life; still good without its truths is not good, but meritorious or hypocritical, evils and falses taking it away like a thief; this is done successively in the world, and after death fully, man in the mean time not knowing when and how. It is attributed to the Lord that he will come like a thief, but, in the spiritual sense, it is understood that hell will take away and steal it. This is similar to its being said in the Word, that God does evil to man, vastates him, revenges, is wrathful, and leads into temptation; when yet it is hell that does these things; the appearance before man causing it to be so expressed. That the talent and pound given to man to trade with, is taken away, if nothing is gained by it, may be seen in Matt. xxv. 26—30; Luke xix. 24—26: to trade and to gain signifies to acquire to one's self things true and good. Since good and truth are taken away from those who are in dead worship, as if it were done by a thief in the dark, therefore in the Word the same is sometimes likened to a thief, as in the following passages: "Behold, I come as a *thief*. Blessed is he that watcheth and keepeth his garments, lest he walk naked," Apoc. xvi. 15. "Watch therefore, for ye know not what hour your Lord doth come. But know this, that if the good man of the house had known in what watch the *thief* would come, he would have watched, and would not have suffered his house to be broken up," Matt. xxiv. 42, 43. "If *thieves* came to thee, if *robbers by night*, how art thou cut off, would they not have stolen till they had enough?" Obad. verse 5. "They shall run to and fro in the city, they shall run upon the wall, they shall climb up upon the houses, they shall enter in at the windows like a *thief*," Joel ii. 9. "They committed falsehood, and the *thief* cometh in, and the troop of *robbers* spoileth without," Hosea vii. 1. "Lay not up for yourselves treasures upon earth,—but in heaven,—where *thieves* do not break through nor steal," Matt. vi. 19, 20. The reason why man must watch, and be ignorant of the hour in which his Lord may come, is, that he may think and act as from himself, thus in freedom according to his reason, and that fear may not intrude, for every one, if he knew, would be in fear; and what man does from himself in a state of liberty remains to eternity, but what he does from fear, does not.

165. *Thou hast a few names even in Sardis*, signifies that among them there are also some who have life in their worship. By a few names are signified some who are such, as now follows: for name signifies the quality of any one; the reason is, because every one in the spiritual world is named according to his quality, n. 81. The quality of those who are now treated of, is, that they have life in their worship.

166. *Which have not defiled their garments*, signifies, who are in truths, and have not defiled worship by evils of life, and falses thence derived. By garments in the Word are signified truths which invest good, and, in an opposite sense, falses which invest evil; for man is either his own good or his own evil, the truths or falses thence proceeding are his garments. All angels and spirits appear clothed according to the truths of their good, or according to the falses of their evil; on which subject see the work concerning *Heaven and Hell*, n. 177—182; from which it is evident, that by not defiling their garments, is signified to be in truths, and not to render worship impure by evils of life and falses thence derived. That in the Word garments signify truths, and, in an opposite sense, falses, appears from the following places: "Awake, awake: put on thy strength, O Zion, put on thy *beautiful garments*, O Jerusalem," Isaiah lii. 1. "I *clothed* thee also with broidered work, I shod thee with badgers' skin, I girded thee about with fine linen. I decked thee also with ornaments. Thus wast thou decked with gold and silver, and thy *raiment* was of fine linen, and silk, and broidered work,—and thou wast exceeding beautiful. And of thy *garments* thou didst take, and deckedst thy high places with divers colours, and playedst the harlot thereupon; and madest to thyself images of men, and didst commit whoredom with them; and tookest thy broidered *garments* and coveredst them," Ezek. xvi. 10—18. The Jewish church is here described, in that truths were given to it by the Word, but that they falsified them: to commit whoredom is to falsify, n. 134. "The king's daughter is all glorious within; her *clothing* is of wrought gold; she shall be brought unto the king in *raiment* of needle-work," Psalm xlv. 13, 14. The king's daughter is the church as to the affection of truth. "Ye daughters of Israel, weep over Saul, who *clothed* you in scarlet with other delights, who put on ornaments of gold upon your *apparel*," 2 Sam. i. 24. These things are said of Saul, because by him, as king, is signified divine truth, n. 20. "I will punish the princes, and the king's children, and all such as are *clothed* with strange *apparel*," Zeph. i. 8. The enemy "shall strip thee of thy *clothes*, and take away thy fair jewels," Ezek. xxiii. 26. "Joshua was clothed with filthy *garments*, and stood before the angel," who said, "Take the filthy *garments* from off him,—and they clothed him with other *garments*," Zech. iii. 3—5. "And when the king came in to see the guests, he saw

there a man which had not on a *wedding garment,* and he saith unto him, Friend, how camest thou in hither not having a *wedding garment?*" Matt. xxii. 11—13. A wedding garment is divine truth from the Word. " Beware of false prophets, which come to you in sheep's *clothing,*" Matt. vii. 15. " No man putteth a piece of a new *garment* upon an old; otherwise the new maketh a rent in the old, and the piece of the—new agreeth not with the old," Luke v. 36. As garment signifies truth, therefore the Lord compares the truths of the former church, which were external and representative of things spiritual, to a piece of an old garment, and the truths of the new church, which were internal and spiritual, to a piece of a new garment. " Upon the seats I saw four and twenty elders sitting, clothed in white *raiment,*" Apoc. iv. 4. They who stood before the throne and before the Lamb, were " clothed in white *robes,*—these are they which—have washed their *robes,* and made them white in the blood of the Lamb," Apoc. vii. 9, 13, 14. " White *robes* were given unto every one of them" which were under the altar, Apoc. vi. 11. " The armies in heaven followed upon white horses, *clothed* in fine linen white and clean," Apoc. xix. 14. Because angels signify divine truths, therefore the angels which were seen in the Lord's sepulchre, appeared in white and shining *raiment,* Matt. xxviii. 3; Luke xxiv. 4. Since the Lord is divine good and divine truth, and truths are understood by garments, therefore when he was transfigured, " His face did shine as the sun, and his *raiment* was white as the light," Matt. xvii. 2; and " white and glistering," Luke ix. 29; and " shining, exceeding white as snow, so as no fuller on earth can white them," Mark ix. 3. Concerning the Ancient of Days, who also is the Lord, it is said, that his "*garment* was white as snow," Dan. vii. 9; and also of the Lord, " All thy *garments* smell of myrrh, aloes, and cassia," Psalm xlv. 8. " He washed his *garments* in wine, and his *clothes* in the blood of grapes," Gen. xlix. 11. " Who is this that cometh from Edom, with dyed *garments* from Bozrah? this that is glorious in his *apparel:* wherefore art thou red in thine *apparel;* and thy *garments* like him that treadeth in the wine-fat? And their blood shall be sprinkled upon my *garments,* and I will stain all my *raiment,*" Isaiah lxiii. 1—3. This also refers to the Lord; his garments there are the truths of the Word. He that sat upon the white horse, " was clothed with a *vesture* dipped in blood, and his name is called the Word of God," Apoc. xix. 13, 16. From the signification of garments it may be seen, why the Lord's disciples laid their *clothes* upon the ass and the colt, when the Lord entered into Jerusalem, and why the people then spread their *garments* in the way, Matt. xxi. 7—9; Mark xi. 7, 8; Luke xix. 35, 39; and what is signified by the soldiers dividing the Lord's *garments* into four parts, John xix. 23, 24; and consequently what is signified by these words in David: "They part my *garments* among them, and cast lots upon my *vesture*," Psalm xxii. 18. From the signification of garments it also appears why they rent their garments, when any one spake against the divine truth of the Word, Isaiah xxxvii. 1, and in other places: also why they washed their garments that they might be purified, Exod. xix. 14; Levit. xi. 24, 40; xiv. 8, 9; Numb. xix. 11, to the end: and why, on account of their trangressions against divine truths, they put off their garments and put on sackcloth, Isaiah xv. 3; xxii. 12; xxxvii. 1, 2; Jerem. iv. 8; vi. 26; xlviii. 37; xlix. 3; Lament. ii. 10; Ezek. xxvii. 31; Amos viii. 10; Jonah iii. 5, 6, 8. He who knows what garments signify in general and in particular, may know what was signified by the garments of Aaron and his sons, which were the ephod, the robe, the coat with embroidery of chequer-work, the girdle, the breeches, and the mitre. Because light signifies divine truth, and garment has the same signification, therefore it is said in David, Jehovah covereth himself "with *light* as with a *garment*," Psalm civ. 2.

167. *And they shall walk with me in white, for they are worthy*, signifies that they shall live with the Lord in his spiritual kingdom, because they are in truths from him. That this is the meaning of these words, is because to walk, in the Word, signifies to live, and to walk with God signifies to live with him; and because in white signifies in truths; for in the Word, white is predicated of truths, by reason of its deriving its origin from the light of the sun; and red is predicated of goods, in consequence of its deriving its origin from the fire of the sun; and black is predicated of falses, from its deriving its origin from the darkness of hell. They who are in truths from the Lord, are, by virtue of their being conjoined with him, called worthy, for all worth in the spiritual world is from conjunction with the Lord; from these considerations it is evident, that "they shall walk with me in white, for they are worthy," signifies that they shall live with the Lord, because they are in truths from him. It is said that they shall live with the Lord in his spiritual kingdom, because the universal heaven is divided into two kingdoms, the celestial and the spiritual, and they are in the celestial kingdom who are in the good of love from the Lord, and they are in the spiritual kingdom who are in the truths of wisdom from the Lord; and the latter are said to walk with the Lord in white; and they are also clothed in white garments. That to walk signifies to live, and that to walk with God signifies to live with him, because from him, appears from the following places: "Let us *walk* in the light of Jehovah," Isaiah ii. 5. "Thou hast delivered my feet from falling, that I may *walk* before God in the light of the living," Psalm lvi. 13. "Thou hast not been as my servant David who kept my commandments, and who *walked* after me with all his heart," 1 Kings

8. "Remember, O Jehovah,—how I have *walked* before thee in truth," Isaiah xxxviii. 3. If ye "will *walk* contrary unto me, and if ye will not—hearken unto me, then I will *walk* contrary unto you," Levit. xxvi. 23, 24, 27. They would not *walk* in the ways of Jehovah," Isaiah xlii. 24; Deut. xi. 22; xix. 9; xxvi. 17. "All people will *walk*, every one in the name of his God, and we will *walk* in the name of Jehovah," Micah iv. 5. "Yet a little while is the light with you; *walk* while ye have the light, —believe in the light," John xii. 35, 36; viii. 12. "The Pharisees and scribes asked him, Why *walk* not thy disciples according to the tradition of the elders?" Mark vii. 5. It is also said of Jehovah, that he walketh amongst them, that is, lives in them and with them: "I will set my tabernacle in the midst of them—and I will *walk* in the midst of you, and will be your God," Levit. xxvi. 11, 12. Hence it is evident, what is meant above by "These things saith He—who *walketh* in the midst of the seven golden candlesticks," Apoc. ii. 1.

168. *He that overcometh, the same shall be clothed in white raiment*, signifies that he who is reformed becomes spiritual. That he that overcometh, signifies he who is reformed, may be seen above, n. 88; and that to be clothed in white raiment, signifies to be made spiritual by means of truths, n. 166, 167. All those become spiritual who are in truths, and in a life according to them.

169. *And I will not blot out his name out of the book of life*, signifies that he shall be saved. What the signification of name is, has been shown before, and what the book of life is, will be explained below. That not to blot out his name out of the book of life, is to be saved, is plain to every one.

170. *And I will confess his name before my Father, and before his angels*, signifies that they will be received who are in divine good and in divine truths from the Lord, thus who have the life of heaven in themselves. That to confess the name is to acknowledge the quality of any one, or that it is such, is evident from the signification of name, as given above, n. 81, 122; by Father, is meant divine good, and by angels divine truths, both from the Lord. In the Word of the evangelists the Father is often mentioned by the Lord, by whom is everywhere meant Jehovah, from whom and in whom he was, and who was in him, and nowhere any divine principle separated from him: this is abundantly proved indeed in *The Doctrine of the New Jerusalem concerning the Lord;* and also in *The Angelic Wisdom concerning the Divine Providence*, n. 262, 263: that the Lord himself is the Father, may be seen, n. 21, 960. The Lord made mention of the Father, because by Father in the spiritual sense is signified good, and by God the Father the divine good of divine love; the angels never understand any thing else by Father when it is read in the Word, nor can they understand

any thing else, because no one in the heavens knows any Father, of whom they are said to be born, and whose children and heirs they are called, except the Lord: this is understood by the Lord's words in Matt. xxxii. 9. Hence it is evident that by confessing his name before the Father, is signified that they will be received among those who are in divine good from him. The reason why by angels are understood those who are in divine truths from the Lord, and, abstractedly, divine truths, is because angels are the recipients of divine good in the divine truths which they have from the Lord.

171. *He that hath an ear, let him hear what the Spirit saith unto the churches,* signifies that he who understands these things, ought to obey what the divine truth of the Word teaches those who are to be of the New Church, which is the New Jerusalem, as above, n. 87.

172. *And to the angel of the church in Philadelphia write,* signifies to those and concerning those who are in truths originating in good from the Lord. That these are meant by the church in Philadelphia, is clear from what is written to it, when understood in the spiritual sense.

173. *These things saith He that is holy, He that is true,* signifies the Lord as to divine truth. That it is the Lord, is evident; the reason why He that is holy, He that is true, is the Lord as to divine truth, is because the Lord is called holy from his divine truth, and righteous from his divine good; hence it is, that his proceeding divine, which is divine truth, is called the Holy Spirit, and the Holy Spirit here is He that is holy, He that is true. Holy often occurs in the Word, and everywhere relates to truth, and as all truth, which is true in itself, is grounded in good, and is from the Lord, it is that truth which is called holy; but good from which truth originates, is called righteous; hence it is, that the angels who are in the truths of wisdom, and are called spiritual, are named holy, and the angels who are in the good of love, and are called celestial, are named righteous; in like manner men in the church. It is also from this circumstance, that the prophets and apostles are called holy, for by the prophets and apostles are signified the doctrinal truths of the church. For the same reason also the Word is called holy, for the Word is divine truth; the law in the ark of the tabernacle was also called the holy of holies, and the sanctuary. In like manner Jerusalem is called holy, for by Jerusalem is signified the church, which is in divine truths. So likewise the altar, the tabernacle, and the garments of Aaron and his sons were called holy, after they were anointed with oil, for oil signifies the good of love which sanctifies, and every thing that is sanctified has relation to truth. That the Lord alone is holy, because he is divine truth itself, appears from the following passages: "Who shall not glorify thy name, O Lord, for

thou only art holy," Apoc. xv. 4. "Thy *Redeemer* is *the Holy One of Israel*, the God of the whole earth shall he be called," Isaiah liv. 5. "Thus saith Jehovah the *Redeemer* of Israel, and his *Holy One*," Isaiah xlix. 7. "As for our *Redeemer*, Jehovah of Hosts is his name, *the Holy One of Israel*," Isaiah xlvii. 4. "Thus saith Jehovah your *Redeemer*, the *Holy One of Israel*," Isaiah xliii. 1, 3. "In that day—they shall stay upon Jehovah the *Holy One of Israel* in truth," Isaiah x. 20; besides other places; as Isaiah i. 4; v. 19; xii. 6; xvii. 7; xxix. 19; xxx. 11, 12; xli. 16; xlv. 11, 15; xlviii. 17; lv. 5; lx. 9; Jerem. i. 29; Dan. iv. 10, 20; Psalm lxxviii. 41. As the Lord is holiness itself, therefore the angel said unto Mary, "That *holy* thing which shall be born of thee shall be called the Son of God," Luke i. 35; and the Lord said of himself, Father, "*sanctify* them through the truth, thy Word is truth;—for their sakes I *sanctify* myself; that they also might be *sanctified* through the truth," John xvii. 17, 19; hence it appears, that the truth, which is from the Lord, is holiness itself, because he alone is holy; on which subject the Lord says, "When He, the *Spirit of truth*, is come, he will guide you into all truth; for he shall not speak from himself—for he shall receive of mine—and shall show it unto you," John xvi. 13, 14, 15. "The Comforter, the *Holy Spirit*, he shall teach you all things," John xiv. 26. That the Holy Spirit is the life of the Lord's wisdom, thus the divine truth, may be seen in *the Doctrine of the New Jerusalem concerning the Lord*, n. 51. From hence it may appear, that He that is holy, He that is true, is the Lord as to his divine truth. That holy refers to truth, and righteous to good, is evident from those places in the Word where both expressions occur; as from the following: "He that is *righteous* let him be righteous still, and he that is *holy* let him be holy still," Apoc. xxii. 11. "*Just* and *true* are thy ways, thou King of *saints*," Apoc. xv. 3. To serve him "in *holiness* and *righteousness*," Luke i. 75. "Herod feared John, knowing that he was a *just* man and a *holy*," Mark vi. 20. "Fine linen is the *righteousness of the saints*," Apoc. xix. 8.

174. *He that hath the key of David, He that openeth and no one shutteth, and shutteth and no one openeth,* signifies, who alone is omnipotent to save. By David is meant the Lord as to divine truth; by key is signified the Lord's omnipotence over heaven and hell; and by opening that no one can shut, and by shutting that no one can open, is signified to lead forth out of hell and introduce into heaven, thus to save, in like manner as above, n. 62, where it is explained. That by David is meant the Lord as to divine truth, may be seen in *The Doctrine of the New Jerusalem concerning the Lord*, n. 43, 44. The same, which is here signified by the key of David, is also signified by the keys of Peter, Matt. xvi. 15—19, which may be seen explained below, n. 798, as also by these words to all the disciples,

"Whatsoever ye shall bind on earth shall be bound in heaven, and whatsoever ye shall loose on earth shall be loosed in heaven," Matt. xviii. 18; for the twelve disciples represented all things of the church as to its goods and truths, and Peter represented it as to truth, and truths and goods save man, consequently the Lord alone from whom they are derived. The same is also signified by the key of David which was given to Eliakim, concerning which it is thus written: "I will commit thy government into his hands, and he shall be a Father to the inhabitants of Jerusalem, and to the house of Judah, and the key of the house of David will I lay upon his shoulder, so he shall open and none shall shut, and he shall shut and none shall open," Isaiah xxii. 21, 22. He was over the king's house, and by the king's house is signified the church as to divine truth.

175. *I know thy works*, signifies that the Lord sees all their interiors and exteriors at once, as above, n. 76.

176. *Behold, I have set before thee an open door*, signifies that heaven is open to those who are in truths from good from the Lord. That by an open door is signified admission, is very evident: the door is said to be open to those who are of the church in Philadelphia, because by that church are understood those who are in truths from good from the Lord, and to them the Lord opens heaven. But on this subject something not before known shall be declared. The Lord alone is the God of heaven and earth, Matt. xxviii. 18; they therefore who do not directly approach him, cannot see the way to heaven, nor can they find the door, and if haply they are permitted to approach it, it is shut, and if they knock it is not opened. In the spiritual world there are actually ways which lead to heaven, and there are here and there gates, and they who are led to heaven by the Lord, take the ways which lead thither, and enter in at the gates. That there are ways there, may be seen in the work concerning *Heaven and Hell*, n. 479, 534, 590; and also gates, n. 429, 430, 583, 584; for all things which are seen in the heavens are correspondences, thus also ways and gates; for ways correspond to truths, and thence signify them, and gates correspond to admission, and thence signify it. Since the Lord alone leads man to heaven, and opens the door, therefore he calls himself the way and also the door: the way in John: "*I* am the *way*, and the truth, and the life," xiv. 6; the door in the same evangelist: "I am the *door* of the sheep—by me, if any man enter in, he shall be saved," x. 7, 9. Since there are both ways and doors in the spiritual world, and angelic spirits actually go those ways, and enter into heaven by doors, therefore inner doors, outer doors, and gates are frequently mentioned in the Word, by which is signified entrance; as in these places: "Lift up your heads, O ye *gates*, even lift them up, ye everlasting *doors*, and the King of Glory shall come in," Psalm xxiv. 7, 9. "Open ye the *gates*, that the

righteous nation, which keepeth the truth, may enter in," Isaiah xxvi. 2. The five prudent virgins "went in with him to the marriage, and the *door* was shut;" and the five foolish virgins came and knocked, but it was not opened, Matt. xxv. 10—12. Jesus said, "Strive to enter in at the strait *gate*, for many—will seek to enter in, and shall not be able," Luke xiii. 24; besides many others. Since a door signifies entrance, and the New Jerusalem signifies the church consisting of those who are in truths grounded in good from the Lord, therefore the New Jerusalem is described also as to its gates, upon which there were angels, and it is said, "They shall not be shut," Apoc. xxi. 12, 13, 25.

177. *And no one is able to shut it*, signifies that hell cannot prevail against them; for the Lord alone opens and shuts the doors to heaven, and the door, which he opens, is perpetually open to those who are in truths grounded in good from the Lord, and perpetually shut to those who are in falses grounded in evil; and since the Lord alone opens and shuts, it follows that hell cannot prevail against them: more may be seen on this subject above, n. 174.

178. *For thou hast a little power*, signifies because they know that they can do nothing from themselves. They who are in truths grounded in good from the Lord, know that they have not any power against evils and falses, thus against hell, from themselves, and they also know that they cannot, out of any power from themselves, do good and introduce themselves into heaven, but that all power is the Lord's, and thus is in them from the Lord, and in proportion as they are in truths grounded in good, in the same proportion they are in power from the Lord, which yet appears to them as their own: this then is what is meant by "For thou hast a little power."

179. *And hast kept my Word*, signifies because they live according to the Lord's commandments in his Word, as is evident without any explanation.

180. *And hast not denied my name*, signifies that they are in the worship of the Lord. That the name of Jehovah, or of the Lord, in the Word, signifies all by which he is worshipped, thus every doctrine of the church, and universally the whole of religion, may be seen above, n. 81; from which it is plain what is here signified by thou "hast not denied my name."

181. *Behold, I will make them of the synagogue of Satan*, signifies those who are in falses as to doctrine, as may be seen above, n. 97.

182. *Who say they are Jews, and are not, but do lie*, signifies who say that the church is among them, and yet it is not. By Jews here are meant they who are of the church, because the church was instituted among them, therefore also by their Jerusalem is still understood the church as to doctrine: but, specifically, by Jews are meant they who are in the good of

love, as above, n. 96, thus also the church, for from the good of love the church exists; that still there is no church among them, is signified by "and are not, but do lie."

183. *Behold, I will make them to come and worship before thy feet*, signifies that many who are in falses as to doctrine, provided they be not in falses grounded in evil, will receive and acknowledge the truths of the New Church. This is said of those who are of the synagogue of Satan, and say they are Jews, and are not, but do lie, by whom are meant such as are in falses as to doctrine, yet not in falses derived from evil, but in falses as to doctrine and yet in good as to life; the latter, and not the former, receive and acknowledge truths when they hear them; the reason is, because good loves truth, and truth, grounded in good, rejects what is false; to receive and acknowledge truths is signified by coming and worshipping at thy feet; not at their feet, but at the feet of the Lord, from whom truths are derived to them from good; therefore the following passage in David has a like signification: "Exalt ye Jehovah our God, and *worship at his footstool*," Psalm xcix. 5.

184. *And to know that I have loved thee*, signifies that they shall see that they who are in truths grounded in good, are beloved and received into heaven by the Lord: this follows in a series from the foregoing.

185. *Because thou hast kept the Word of my patience*, signifies because they have fought against evils, and then rejected falses. That the word of patience signifies spiritual combat, which is called temptation, is plain from what next follows; "I also will keep thee from the hour of *temptation* which shall come upon all the world," for he who is tempted in the world, is not tempted after death. Spiritual combat, which is temptation, is called the Word of the Lord's patience, because in temptations the Lord fights for man, and he fights by means of truths out of his Word.

186. *I also will keep thee from the hour of temptation which shall come upon all the world, to try them that dwell upon the earth*, signifies that they will be protected and preserved in the day of the last judgment. That their protection and preservation in the day of judgment is understood by these words, may be seen from what is written and related concerning *The Last Judgment* in the work on that subject, and afterwards in *The Continuation of the same*, from which it is manifest, that they who underwent it were let into temptation, and explored as to their qualities, and that such as were interiorly evil were rejected, and such as were interiorly good were saved; and they were interiorly good who were in truths grounded in good from the Lord.

187. *Behold, I come quickly*, signifies the Lord's coming, and then a new church from them. The Lord says here, "Behold, I come quickly," because by the foregoing words is under-

stood the last judgment, and the last judgment is also called the Lord's coming, as in Matthew: The disciples said unto Jesus, "What shall be the sign of thy *coming* and of the *consummation of the age?*" xxiv. 3. The consummation of the age is the last time of the church, when the last judgment is at hand. The reason why by these words, "Behold, I come quickly," a new church is also understood, is, because after a last judgment a church is established by the Lord; that church now is the New Jerusalem, into which will enter those who are in truths grounded in good from the Lord, to whom this is addressed.

188. *Hold fast that thou hast*, signifies that in the meantime they should remain in their truths and in their good, as is manifest without explanation.

189. *That no one take thy crown*, signifies lest wisdom should perish, from which comes eternal felicity. Wisdom in man is to be traced to no other source than good by truths from the Lord. The reason why man procures wisdom by truths, is, because the Lord joins or connects himself to man, and man to himself by them, and the Lord is wisdom itself; therefore wisdom perishes in man when he ceases to do truths, that is, to live according to them, for then he ceases to love wisdom, and thus to love the Lord. By wisdom is meant wisdom in things spiritual, from which, as from its source, is derived wisdom in other things, which is called intelligence, and by intelligence, science, which exists from the affection of knowing truths. A crown signifies wisdom, because wisdom holds the supreme place in man, and thus crowns him; neither does a king's crown signify any thing else, for king, in a spiritual sense, is divine truth, n. 20, and from divine truth comes all wisdom. Wisdom is also signified by crown in the following places: "There will I make the horn of David to bud—but upon himself shall his *crown* flourish," Psalm cxxxii. 17, 18. "And I will put a jewel in thy forehead, and ear-rings in thine ears, and a beautiful *crown* upon thy head," Ezek. xvi. 12; speaking of Jerusalem, by which is signified the church as to doctrine, therefore a crown of ornament denotes wisdom derived from divine truth or the Word. "In that day shall Jehovah of Hosts be for a *crown* of glory, and for a diadem of beauty unto the residue of his people," Isaiah xxviii. 5; speaking of the Lord, because it is said in that day; the crown of glory which he will be, is wisdom, and the diadem of beauty is intelligence; the residue of the people are they among whom his church will be. The same is signified by crown and diadem in Isaiah lxii. 1, 3; as also by the plate of gold upon Aaron's mitre, Exod. xxviii. 36, 37, which was also called the coronet. Likewise in these places: "Say unto the king, and to the queen, Humble yourselves, sit down, for your principalities shall come down, even the *crown* of your glory," Jerem. xiii. 18. "The joy of our heart is ceased—the *crown* is fallen from

our head," Lament. v. 15, 16. "He hath stript me of my glory, and taken the *crown* from my head," Job xix. 9. "Thou hast profaned his *crown* by casting it to the ground," Psalm lxxxix. 39. In these places, by crown is signified wisdom.

190. *Him that overcometh*, signifies they who persist in truths from good from the Lord, as appears from the series, and thus without explanation.

191. *Will I make a pillar in the temple of my God*, signifies that truths from good from the Lord, with those in whom they abide, sustain the Lord's church in heaven. By temple the church is signified, and by the temple of my God, the Lord's church in heaven; hence it is evident, that by pillar is signified that which sustains and strengthens the church, or the divine truth of the Word. By temple, in a supreme sense, the Lord is signified as to his Divine Humanity, more particularly as to divine truth; but, in a representative sense, by temple is signified the Lord's church in heaven, and likewise the Lord's church in the world. That temple, in a supreme sense, signifies the Lord as to his Divine Humanity, and more particularly as to divine truth, is evident from these places: "Jesus said unto the Jews, Destroy this *temple*, and in three days I will raise it up—but he spake of the *temple* of his body," John ii. 19, 21. "I saw no *temple* in the New Jerusalem, for the Lord God Almighty and the Lamb are the temple of it," Apoc. xxi. 22. "Behold,—the Lord whom ye seek shall suddenly come to his *temple*, even the messenger of the covenant," Malachi iii. 1. "I will bow down towards the *temple* of thine holiness," Psalm xxviii. 2 "Yet I will again look to thy *holy temple*,—and my prayer shall come in unto thee, into thy *holy temple*," Jonah ii. 4. 7. The holy temple of Jehovah, or the Lord, is his Divine Humanity, for that is bowed down to, looked to, and prayed to, and not the temple only, for the temple in itself is not holy; it is called the holy temple, because holiness is predicated of divine truth, n. 123. Neither by "the *temple* which sanctifieth the gold," Matt. xxiii. 16, 17, is any thing else understood but the Lord's Divine Humanity. That by temple, in a representative sense, is signified the Lord's church in heaven, appears from these places: "A voice from the *temple*, a voice of Jehovah," Isaiah lxvi. 6. "There came a great voice out of the *temple* of heaven," Apoc. xvi. 17. "The *temple* of God was opened in heaven, and there was seen in his *temple* the ark of his testament," Apoc. xi. 19. "The *temple* of the tabernacle of the testimony in heaven was opened; and the seven angels came out of the *temple*:—and the *temple* was filled with smoke from the glory of God," Apoc. xv. 5, 6, 8. "I called upon Jehovah, and cried unto my God: he heard my voice out of his *temple*," Psalm xviii. 6. "I saw Jehovah sitting upon a throne, high and lifted up, and his train filled the *temple*," Isaiah vi. 1. That temple signifies the church

in the world, is clear from these places: "Our holy—house is burnt up with fire," Isaiah lxiv. 11. "I will shake all nations,—and I will fill this house with glory;—the glory of this latter house shall be greater than of the former," Hag. ii. 7, 8. The church about to be re-established by the Lord is described by the new temple in Ezek. xl.—xlviii., and is understood by "the temple which the angel measured," Apoc. xi. 1, and also in Isaiah xliv. 28; Jerem. vii. 2, 3, 4, 9, 10, 11; Zech. viii. 9. The disciples came to Jesus, "to show him the buildings of the *temple*, and Jesus said unto them,—Verily I say unto you, there shall not be left one stone upon another that shall not be thrown down," Matt. xxiv. 1, 2; Mark xiii. 1—5; Luke xxi. 5—7. By temple here is signified the church at this day, and by its dissolution even to there not being one stone left upon another, is signified the end of this church, in that no truth whatever would be left; for when the disciples spoke to the Lord concerning the temple, the Lord foretold the successive states of this church to the end of it, or the consummation of the age, and by the consummation of the age is meant its last period, which is at this day: this was represented by that temple being utterly destroyed. Temple signifies these three, namely, the Lord, the church in heaven, and the church in the world, because these three make one, and cannot be separated, consequently one of them cannot be understood without the other; therefore whosoever separates the church in the world from the church in heaven, and these from the Lord, is not in the truth. The reason why the church in heaven is here understood, is, because the church in the world is treated of afterwards, n. 194.

192. *And he shall go no more out*, signifies that they shall remain there to eternity, as is evident without explanation.

193. *And I will write upon him the name of my God*, signifies that divine truth shall be written in their hearts. To write in or upon any one, signifies to inscribe, so that it may be in him as his own; and the name of my God signifies divine truth. Here it may be expedient to speak more particularly concerning the signification of "my God" as referring to divine truth. In the Word of the Old Testament, in innumerable places, "Jehovah God" occurs, as also separately, sometimes "Jehovah," and sometimes "God," and by Jehovah is meant the Lord as to divine good, and by God is meant the Lord as to divine truth; or what is the same, by Jehovah is meant the Lord as to divine love, and by God is meant the Lord as to divine wisdom; both terms are used for the sake of the celestial marriage in all the particulars of the Word, which is the marriage of love and wisdom, or the marriage of goodness and truth, concerning which marriage see *The Doctrine of the New Jerusalem concerning the Sacred Scripture*, n. 80—90. But in the Word of the New Testament it is not said Jehovah God, but the Lord God; for Lord,

in like manner as Jehovah, signifies divine good or divine love. From these considerations it may appear, that by the name of my God is signified the divine truth of the Lord. That name, when spoken of the Lord, denotes the all by which he is worshipped, may be seen above, n. 81; and the all by which he is worshipped, has relation to divine good and divine truth. As it is not known what is meant by these words of the Lord, "Father, glorify thy *name:* then came there a voice from heaven, saying, I have both glorified it, and will glorify it again," John xii. 28, therefore it shall be explained. The Lord, when he was in the world, made his Humanity divine truth, and when he went out of the world, he fully united divine truth to divine good, which was in him from conception; for the Lord glorified his Humanity, that is, made it divine, as he makes man spiritual; for he first introduces into man truths from the Word, and afterwards unites them to good, and by that union man is made spiritual.

194. *And the name of the city of my God, the New Jerusalem*, signifies that the doctrine of the New Church shall be written in their hearts. By the New Jerusalem is signified the New Church, and by the same, when it is called city, is signified the New Church as to doctrine; therefore by writing upon him the name of the city of my God, the New Jerusalem, is signified that the doctrine of the New Church shall be written in their hearts. That by the New Jerusalem is signified the church, and by the same, as a city, the church as to doctrine, may be seen below, n. 880, 881. A city signifies doctrine, because land, and in particular the land of Canaan, signifies the church in the aggregate, and thence by the inheritances into which the land of Canaan was divided, are signified the various things of the church, and, by the cities in them, doctrinals; so that the angels understand nothing else by cities when they are named in the Word; which has also been proved to me by much experience. Similar is the signification of mountains, hills, valleys, fountains, rivers, all which signify such things as belong to the church. That cities signify doctrinals, may in some measure appear from the following places: "The land shall be utterly emptied, and utterly spoiled; the earth mourneth and fadeth away: the *city* of confusion is broken down; in the *city* is left desolation, and the gate is smitten with destruction," Isaiah xxiv. 3, 4, 10—12. "The lion is come up from his thicket to make thy land desolate, and thy *cities* shall be laid waste. I beheld, and lo, the fruitful place was a wilderness, and all the *cities* thereof were broken down; the earth shall mourn,—the *whole city* shall flee," Jerem. iv. 7, 26—29. The land here is the church, and city is its doctrine; thus the devastation of the church by falses of doctrine is described. "The spoiler shall come upon every *city*, and no *city* shall escape; the valley shall perish, and the plain shall be

destroyed," Jerem. xlviii. 8: the same here. "Behold, I have made thee—a defenced *city*—against the whole land," Jerem. i. 18: this to the prophet, because prophet signifies doctrine of the church, n. 8. "In that day shall this song be sung in the land of Judah, We have a strong *city*, salvation will God appoint for walls and bulwarks," Isaiah xxvi. 1. "The great *city* was divided into three parts, and the *cities* of the nations fell," Apoc. xvi. 19. The prophet saw on a high mountain the structure of a *city* on the south, and an angel measured the wall, the gates, the chambers, the porch of the gate, and the name of the *city* was Jehovah there, Ezek. xl. 1, and following verses. "There is a river, the streams whereof shall make glad the *city of God*," Psalm xlvi. 4. "I will set the Egyptians against the Egyptians, and *city* against *city*, and kingdom against kingdom," Isaiah xix. 2. "Every kingdom divided against itself is brought to desolation, and every *city*—divided against itself shall not stand," Matt. xii. 25. In these places by cities, in the spiritual sense, are meant doctrines; as also in Isaiah vi. 11; xiv. 12, 17, 21; xix. 18, 19; xxv. 1—3; xxxiii. 8, 9; liv. 3; lxiv. 10; Jerem. vii. 17, 34; xiv. 18, 19; xxxii. 42, 44; xxxiii. 4; Zeph. iii. 6; Psalm xlviii. 2; lv. 9; cvii. 4, 7; Matt. v. 14, 15; and elsewhere. From the signification of city it may appear, what is meant by cities in this parable of the Lord: A certain nobleman, when he went into a far country to receive for himself a kingdom, gave unto his servants money to trade with; and when he was returned, he called his servants; "then came the first, saying, Lord, thy pound hath gained ten pounds; and he said unto him, Well, thou good servant,—*have thou authority over ten cities:* and the second came, saying, Lord, thy pound hath gained five pounds; and he said likewise to him, *Be thou also over five cities*," Luke xix. 12—19. By cities here, also, doctrinals or truths of doctrine are signified, and by being over them is meant to be intelligent and wise, thus to give authority over them is to give intelligence and wisdom; ten signifies much, and five, something: that by trading and gaining is meant to acquire intelligence by the exercise of one's faculties, is evident. That the holy city Jerusalem signifies the doctrine of the New Church, is plain from the description of it, Apoc. xxi.; for it is described as to its dimensions, also as to its gates, its wall, and its foundations, which, when Jerusalem signifies the church, cannot signify any other than things belonging to its doctrines; neither is the church a church from any other cause. Since by the city Jerusalem is meant the church as to doctrine, therefore it is called the "city of truth," Zech. viii. 3, 4, and in many places the "holy city," and that because holy is predicated of truths from the Lord, n. 173.

195. *Which cometh down out of heaven from my God*, signifies which will be from the divine truth of the Lord, such as it

is in heaven. As by my God is signified divine truth, n. 193, it follows, that by coming down out of heaven from my God, when it is said of the Lord, and of the doctrine of the New Church, is signified divine truth from the Lord, such as exists in heaven.

196. *And my new name*, signifies the worship of the Lord alone, with other new things which were not in the former church. That by the name of the Lord is signified every thing by which he is worshipped, may be seen above, n. 81, therefore here the worship of the Lord alone, with things new which were not in the former church. That in the New Church the Lord alone is worshipped, is evident from chap. xxi. 8, 9, where that church is called the "Lamb's Wife." That there are things new in that church, appears from chap. xxi. 5, where it is said, "Behold, I make all things *new*." Such therefore is the signification of *my new name*, which was to be written upon them.

197. *He that hath an ear, let him hear what the Spirit saith unto the churches*, signifies that he who understands, ought to obey what the divine truth of the Word teaches those who are to be of the New Church, which is the New Jerusalem, as above, n. 87.

198. *And unto the angel of the church of the Laodiceans write*, signifies to those and concerning those, in the church, who alternately believe, sometimes from themselves, and sometimes from the Word, and thus profane things holy. But concerning these something must be premised: there are to be found in the church those who believe and yet do not believe; thus they believe that there is a God, that the Word is holy, that there is eternal life, and many other things connected with the church and its doctrine; and still they do not believe them: they believe them when in their sensual natural [state], but they do not believe them when they are in their rational natural [state]; thus they believe them when they are in externals, therefore when they are in society and discourse with others; but they do not believe them when they are in internals, consequently when they are not in society with others, but are discoursing with themselves; concerning these it is said that they are neither cold nor hot, and that they shall be vomited out.

199. *These things saith the Amen, the faithful and true witness*, signifies the Lord as to the Word, which is divine truth from him. That amen is divine confirmation from truth itself, which is the Lord, so from the Lord, may be seen above, n. 23; and that a faithful and true witness, when spoken of the Lord, is the divine truth which is from him in the Word, n. 6, 16. Whether you say that the Lord testifies of himself, or that the Word testifies of him, it amounts to the same, because the *Son of Man*, who here speaks to the churches, is the Lord as to the Word, n. 44. These things are premised to this church, because those persons in the church are here treated of who both believe

from themselves and from the Word; and they who believe from the Word, believe from the Lord.

200. *The beginning of the creation of God,* signifies the Word. That the Word is the beginning of the creation of God, is not yet known in the church, because these words in John are not understood: "In the beginning was the Word, and the Word was with God, and the Word was God: all things were made by him, and without him was not any thing made that was made. In him was life, and the life was the light of men. He was in the world, and the world was made by him, but the world knew him not. And the Word was made flesh, and dwelt among us, and we beheld his glory, the glory as of the only-begotten of the Father," i. 1, 3, 4, 10, 14. He who understands these words in their interior sense, and at the same time compares them with what is written in *The Doctrine of the New Jerusalem concerning the Sacred Scripture*, as also with some things in *The Doctrine of the New Jerusalem concerning the Lord*, may see that the divine truth itself in the Word which was formerly in this world, as mentioned in n. 11, which likewise is in our Word at this day, is meant by the Word which was in the beginning with God, and which was God; but not the Word regarded merely as to the words and letters of the languages in which it is written, but as seen in its essence and life, which is from within in the senses or meaning of its words and letters; from this life does the Word vivify the affections of that man's will who reads it devoutly; and from the light of its life it illuminates the thoughts of his understanding, therefore it is said in John: "*In him [the Word] was life, and the life was the light of men.*" verse 4; this constitutes the Word, because the Word is from the Lord, and concerning the Lord, and thus the Lord. All thought, speech, and writing, derives its essence and life from him who thinks, speaks, and writes; the man, with all that he is, being therein; but in the Word, the Lord alone is. No one however feels and perceives the divine life in the Word but he who is in the spiritual affection of truth when he reads it, for he is in conjunction with the Lord through the Word; there being something intimately affecting the heart and spirit, which flows with light into the understanding and bears witness. The signification of what is said in John is similar to that conveyed by these words in the first chapter of Genesis: "In the beginning God created the heaven and the earth,—and the spirit of God moved upon the face of the waters; and God said, Let there be light, and there was light," verse 1—3. The spirit of God is divine truth, and also light; divine truth is the Word, therefore when the Lord calls himself the Word, he also calls himself the light, John i. 4, 8, 9. The same is also understood by this passage in David: "By the Word of Jehovah were the heavens made, and all the host of them by the breath [spirit] of his mouth," Psalm xxxiii. 6. In short, with-

out the divine truth of the Word, which in its essence is the divine good of the Lord's divine love, and the divine truth of his divine wisdom, man could not have life; by means of the Word there is a conjunction of the Lord with man, and of man with the Lord, and by that conjunction there is life: there must be something from the Lord, which it is in the power of man to receive, and by which there can be conjunction and thence life everlasting. From these considerations it may appear, that by the "Beginning of the creation of God," is understood the Word, and if you will believe it, the Word such as it is in its literal sense, for this sense is the aggregate of its interior sanctities, as is abundantly shown in *The Doctrine of the New Jerusalem concerning the Sacred Scripture*. And what is wonderful, the Word is so written, that it communicates with the universal heaven, and severally with each society there, which it has been given me to know by lively experience, as has been advanced elsewhere. That the Word in its essence is such, is moreover evident from these words of the Lord: "The words that I speak to you, they are spirit, and they are life," John vi. 63.

201. *I know thy works*, signifies that the Lord sees all their interiors and exteriors at once, as above, n. 76.

202. *That thou art neither cold nor hot*, signifies that they who are such, sometimes deny that the Word is divine and holy, and at other times acknowledge it. At one time to deny in heart the sanctity of the Word, and at another time to acknowledge it, is to be neither cold nor hot, for such persons are both for the Word and against it: they are also just the same with respect to God, at one time they deny, and at another time acknowledge him; in like manner as to every thing relating to the church; for which reason they are sometimes with those who are in hell, and at other times with those who are in heaven, and fly as it were between both, up and down, and wherever they fly, thither their countenances are turned. They become so, who have confirmed themselves in a belief of the existence of a God, of heaven and hell, and of life eternal, and afterwards recede from it; when the first confirmation returns, they acknowledge, but when it does not return, they deny: they recede because they afterwards think only of themselves and the world, continually aspiring to pre-eminence, and thereby immersing themselves in their selfhood; and thus hell swallows them up.

203. *I would thou wert cold or hot*, signifies that it is better for them either from the heart to deny the holy things of the Word and of the church, or from the heart to acknowledge them. The reason will be explained in the next article.

204. *So then because thou art lukewarm, and neither cold nor hot, I will vomit thee out of my mouth*, signifies profanation and consequent separation from the Lord. "I will vomit thee out of my mouth," signifies to be separated from the Lord

and such separation from the Lord consists in being neither in heaven nor in hell, but in a place apart, deprived of human life, where mere phantasies exist; the reason is, because they have mixed truths with falses, and goods with evils, thus holy things with profane, in such a manner as that they cannot be separated; and since man cannot then be prepared, either for heaven or hell, the whole of his rational life is destroyed, and the ultimates of life alone remain, which, when separated from the interiors of life, are mere phantasies. Concerning their state and lot more may be seen in *The Angelic Wisdom concerning the Divine Providence*, n. 226—228, 231, which will suffice to give an idea of them. It is said of them that they are vomited out, because the world of spirits, which is in the midst between heaven and hell, and into which every man first comes after death, and is there prepared, corresponds to the stomach, in which all the ingesta are prepared for being converted either into blood and flesh, or excrement and urine, the latter having a correspondence with hell, but the former with heaven; but the substances that are vomited out of the stomach are such as have not undergone that separation, but remain commixed. By reason of this correspondence, the expression vomited and vomit are used in the following passages: "Drink thou also, and let thy foreskin be uncovered; and the cup of the Lord's right hand shall be turned unto thee, and the shameful *vomiting* shall be on thy glory," Habak. ii. 15, 16. "Make ye him drunken, Moab also shall wallow in his *vomit*," Jerem. xlviii. 26. "All tables are full of *vomit* and filthiness," Isaiah xxviii. 8; besides other places, as Jerem. xxv. 27; Levit. xviii. 24, 25, 28. That warm water excites vomiting, is also from correspondence.

206. *Because thou sayest, I am rich and increased with goods*, signifies that they think they possess in all abundance the knowledges of what is good and true, which are of heaven and the church. To be rich and increased with goods, here signifies nothing else than to know and understand fully such things as belong to the church and to heaven, and are called spiritual and theological, because these are here considered; spiritual riches and abundance consist in nothing else. They who believe from themselves, and not from the Lord through the Word, think also that they know and understand every thing; the reason is, because their spiritual mind is shut, and their natural mind alone open; and this mind, devoid of spiritual light, sees no otherwise. That by riches and possessions in the Word are signified spiritual riches and possessions, which are knowledges of what is good and true, is evident from the following places: "With thy wisdom and with thy understanding thou hast gotten thee *riches*, and hast gotten gold and silver in thy *treasures;* by thy great wisdom thou hast increased thy *riches*," Ezek. xxviii. 4, 5; this is spoken of Tyre, by which is signified the church as to the know-

ledges of what is good and true: in like manner, "The daughter of Tyre shall be there with a gift, even the *rich among the people* shall entreat thy favour," Psalm xlv. 12. "The Lord will cast her out and he will smite her *wealth* in the sea," Zech. ix. 4. "They shall make a spoil of thy *riches*," Ezek. xxvi. 12. Ashur hath said, "By the strength of my hand I have done it, and by my wisdom, for I am prudent; and I—have robbed their *treasures*, and my hand hath found—the *riches* of the people," Isaiah x. 13, 14. Here Ashur signifies the rational faculty perverting the goods and truths of the church, these constituting the treasures and riches of the people, which he takes away. "I will give thee the *treasures* of darkness, and hidden *riches* of secret places," Isaiah xlv. 3. "Blessed is the man that feareth Jehovah, *wealth* and *riches* shall be in his house, and his righteousness endureth for ever," Psalm cxii. 1, 3. God "hath filled the hungry with good things, and the *rich* he hath sent empty away," Luke i. 53. "Woe unto you that are *rich*, for ye have received your consolation; woe unto you that are full, for ye shall hunger," Luke vi. 24, 25. By the rich here are understood those who were in possession of the knowledges of what is good and true, from their possessing the Word; who were the Jews: the same is meant by the rich man, who was clothed in purple and fine linen, Luke xvi. 19; and in like manner by the rich and riches in other places; as in Isaiah xxx. 6; Jerem. xvii. 11; Micah iv. 13; vi. 10; Zech. xiv. 14; Matt. xii. 35; xiii. 44; Luke xii. 21.

207. *And have need of nothing*, signifies that they have no need of more wisdom, as is evident from what has been said above, because it follows of course.

208. *And knowest not that thou art wretched*, signifies that they are not aware that all they know and think respecting the truths and goods of the church, is totally incoherent, and like uncemented walls. By being wretched is here signified a want of coherence, thus by those who are wretched, such as think incoherently concerning the things of the church; the reason is, because they of whom this is said, at one time deny God, heaven, eternal life, and the sanctity of the Word, and at another time acknowledge them; therefore what they build with one hand they pull down with the other; thus they are like those that build a house, and presently pull it down; or that clothe themselves in handsome garments, and presently tear them; their houses are therefore rubbish, and their garments rags: such is the nature of all their thoughts concerning the church and heaven, though they are not aware of it. This is also meant by wretchedness or misery in the following places: "Thy wisdom and thy knowledge it hath perverted thee, and thou hast said in thine heart, I am, and none else besides me; therefore shall *misery* come upon thee," Isaiah xlvii. 10, 11. "*Misery*

shall come upon *misery*, and the king shall mourn, and the prince shall be clothed with desolation," Ezek. vii. 26, 27. The king who shall mourn, and the prince who shall be clothed with desolation, are they who are in truths of the church. "There is no faithfulness in their mouth,—*misery* is in the midst of them," Psalm v. 9. Such also is the signification of the uncemented walls spoken of in Jerem. xlix. 27; Ezek. xiii. 11, 12; Hosea ii. 6.

209. *And miserable and poor*, signifies that they are without truths and goods. By the miserable and poor, in the spiritual sense of the Word, are meant they who are without the knowledges of things true and good, for they are spiritually miserable and poor; the same are understood hereby in the following places: "I am *miserable and poor*, yet the Lord thinketh upon me," Psalm xl. 17; lxx. 5. "Bow down thine ear, O Jehovah, hear me, for I am *miserable and poor*," Psalm lxxxvi. 1. "The wicked have drawn out their sword and have bent their bow, to cast down the *miserable and poor*," Psalm xxxvii. 14. The wicked hath "persecuted the *miserable and poor*, that he might even slay the broken in heart," Psalm cix. 16. God will "judge the *miserable* of the people, he shall save the children of the *poor:* he shall deliver the *poor* when he crieth, the *miserable* also, and him that hath no helper," Psalm lxxii. 4, 12. Jehovah delivereth "the *miserable* from him that is too strong for him, yea the *poor* and the needy from him that spoileth him," Psalm xxxv. 10. The wicked "deviseth wicked devices to destroy the *miserable* with lying words, even when the *poor* speaketh right," Isaiah xxxii. 7. "The *miserable* also shall increase their joy in Jehovah, and the *poor* among men shall rejoice in the Holy One of Israel," Isaiah xxix. 19. "Blessed are the *poor* in spirit, for theirs is the kingdom of heaven," Matt. v. 3. Not to mention other passages, as Isaiah x. 2; Jerem. xxii. 16; Ezek. xvi. 49; xviii. 12; xxii. 29; Amos viii. 4; Psalm ix. 18; lxix. 32, 33; lxxiv. 21; cix. 22; cxl. 12; Deut. xv. 11; xxiv. 14; Luke xiv. 13, 21, 23. By the poor and the needy are chiefly understood those who are not in the knowledges of what is good and true, and yet desire them, for by the rich are understood such as are possessed of the knowledges of things good and true, n. 206.

210. *And blind and naked*, signifies that they are without the understanding of truth, and the will of good. By the blind, in the Word, are meant those who are without truths, either from a defect thereof in the church and so from ignorance, or from the want of understanding them; and by the naked are meant those who are without good; for all spiritual good is acquired by means of truth. No others are understood by the blind in the following places: "In that day shall the deaf hear the words of the Book, and the eyes of the *blind* shall see out of—darkness," Isaiah xxix. 18. "Behold, your God will come, then the eyes of the *blind* shall be opened," Isaiah xxxv. 4, 5.

"I will give thee for a light of the Gentiles, to open the *blind* eyes," Isaiah xlii. 6, 7. "I will bring the *blind* by a way that they knew not, I will make their darkness light," Isaiah xlii. 16. "Bring forth the *blind* people that have eyes, and the deaf that have ears," Isaiah xliii. 8. "His watchmen are *blind*,—and cannot understand," Isaiah lvi. 10, 11. "He hath *blinded* their eyes, and hardened their heart, that they should not see with their eyes, nor understand with their heart," John xii. 40. "Jesus said, For judgment am I come into this world, that they which *see not* might see, and that they which see, might be made *blind*," John ix. 39. *Blind*, foolish, infatuated guides, Matt. xxiii. 16, 17, 19, 24. "*Blind*, leaders of the *blind*." Matt. xv. 14; Luke vi. 39. By reason of the signification of blind and blindness, it was forbid to offer for sacrifice any thing that was *blind*, Levit. xxi. 18; Deut. xv. 21. That they should not cast a stumbling-block before the *blind*, Levit. xix. 14. That he was cursed who made the *blind* to wander out of the way, Deut. xxvii. 18. Concerning the signification of naked and nakedness, see below, n. 213.

211. *I counsel thee to buy of me gold tried in the fire, that thou mayest be rich*, signifies an admonition to acquire to themselves the good of love from the Lord by means of the Word, that they may become wise. For to buy signifies to acquire to oneself; of me, signifies of the Lord by the Word; gold signifies good, and gold tried in the fire, the good of celestial love; and to be enriched thereby, signifies to become intelligent and wise. Gold signifies good, because metals in their order signify such things as are of good and truth, gold celestial and spiritual good, silver the truth of those goods, brass natural good, and iron natural truth. These are signified by the metals of which the statue of Nebuchadnezzar consisted, whose head was of *gold*, his breast and arms of *silver*, his belly and thighs of *brass*, his legs *iron*, his feet part *iron* and part *clay*, Dan. ii. 32, 33; by which are represented the successive states of the church as to the good of love and the truth of wisdom. From this succession of the states of the church, the ancients gave similar names to times, calling them ages of gold, silver, brass, and iron, and by the golden age they understood the earliest times, when the good of celestial love prevailed; celestial love is the love of the Lord from the Lord; from this love they at that time possessed wisdom. That gold signifies the good of love may be seen below, n. 913.

212. *And white raiment, that thou mayest be clothed*, signifies that they should acquire to themselves genuine truths of wisdom. That raiment or garments signify truths investing good, may be seen above, n. 166, and that white is spoken of truths, n. 167, therefore white raiment signifies the genuine truths of wisdom, and this, because gold purified in the fire

signifies the good of celestial love, the truths of this love being genuine truths of wisdom.

213. *That the shame of thy nakedness may not appear*, signifies lest the good of celestial love should be profaned and adulterated. No one can know what the shame of nakedness signifies, unless he knows that the members of generation in both sexes, which are also called the genitals, correspond to celestial love. That there is a correspondence of man and all his members with the heavens, may be seen in the work concerning *Heaven and Hell*, n. 87—102, and that the members of generation correspond to celestial love, in *The Arcana Cœlestia*, n. 5050—5062. As those members correspond to celestial love, which is the love of the third or inmost heaven, and man is born from his parents to loves which are opposite to that love, it is evident, that if he does not acquire to himself the good of love and the truth of wisdom from the Lord, signified by gold tried in the fire, and white raiment, he will appear in the opposite love, which is profane. This is signified by uncovering nakedness and revealing shame, in the following places: "Blessed is he that watcheth, and keepeth his garments, lest he walk *naked*, and they see his *shame*," Apoc. xvi. 15. "Sit in the dust, O virgin daughter of Babylon—and of the Chaldeans,—uncover thy locks, make bare the leg, uncover the thigh, pass over the rivers, thy *nakedness* shall be uncovered, yea thy *shame* shall be seen," Isaiah xlvii. 1, 2, 3. "Woe to the bloody city,—because of the multitude of its whoredoms, I will discover thy skirts upon thy face, and I will show the nations thy *nakedness*, and the kingdoms thy *shame*," Nahum iii. 1, 4, 5. "Plead with your mother—lest I strip her *naked*," Hosea ii. 2, 3. When I passed by thee,—I covered thy *nakedness*; then I washed thee,—and clothed thee, but thou didst commit whoredom, and hast not remembered thy youth, when thou wast naked and bare, therefore is thy *nakedness* discovered, Ezek. xvi. 6, and following verses. "Jerusalem hath grievously sinned, therefore —all despise her because they have seen her *nakedness*," Lament. i. 8. By Jerusalem, of whom these things are said, is understood the church, and committing whoredoms signifies to adulterate and falsify the Word, n. 134. "Woe unto him that giveth his neighbour drink, and maketh him drunken, that thou mayest look on their *nakedness*;—drink thou also, and let thy foreskin be uncovered," Habak. ii. 15, 16. He who knows what nakedness signifies, may understand what is signified by Noah's lying drunken with wine, and *naked*, in the midst of his tent, and that Ham saw and derided his *nakedness*; and that Shem and Japhet covered his *nakedness*, turning away their faces that they might not see it, Gen. ix. 21, 22, 23; also, why it was commanded that Aaron and his sons should not ascend by steps upon the altar, lest their *nakedness* should be discovered, Exod. xx. 26; and likewise, that they should "make them linen breeches, to

cover their nakedness," and that they should "be upon them when they came near unto the altar, and that otherwise they would bear iniquity and die," Exod. xxviii. 42, 43. By nakedness, in these places, are signified the evils to which man is born, which, because they are opposite to the good of celestial love, are in themselves profane, and are not removed otherwise than by means of truths and a life conformable to them; for linen signifies truth, n. 671. By nakedness is also signified innocence, and likewise ignorance of good and truth: innocence, in the following passage: "And they were both *naked*, the man and his wife, and were not ashamed," Gen. ii. 25. Ignorance of good and truth in this: "Is not this the fast that I have chosen? Is it not to deal thy bread to the hungry,—and when thou seest the *naked*, that thou cover him?" Isaiah lviii. 6, 7. "Hath given his bread to the hungry, and hath covered the *naked* with a garment," Ezek. xviii. 7. "I was an hungered, and ye gave me meat; I was—*naked*, and ye clothed me," Matt. xxv. 35, 36.

214. *And anoint thine eyes with eye-salve, that thou mayest see*, signifies, that their understanding may be healed, lest the genuine truths of wisdom should be profaned and falsified. That by the eyes is signified the understanding, and by the eye-sight intelligence and wisdom, may be seen, n. 48; and since by eye-salve a medicine for the same is signified, it follows that by "anoint thine eyes with eye-salve," is signified to heal the understanding, that it may see and know truths and advance thereby in wisdom; for unless this is the case, the genuine truths of the Word are profaned and adulterated.

215. *As many as I love, I rebuke and chasten*, signifies that such of them as do so are beloved by the Lord, and that then they cannot but be admitted to temptations that they may fight against themselves. That this is the sense of these words, is evident, for it is said, "As many as I love," by whom are meant they who buy of the Lord gold purified in the fire, and who anoint their eyes with eye-salve that they may see: it is said, "I rebuke and chasten" them, by which is meant temptation as to falses and evils; by rebuking, temptation as to falses, and by chastening, temptation as to evils. Such as are here treated of, could not but be led into temptations, because, without them, negations and confirmations against divine truths could not be extirpated. Temptations are spiritual combats against the falses and evils in one's self, thus against one's self: what temptations are, whence they proceed, and what good they produce, see the work concerning *The New Jerusalem and its Heavenly Doctrine*, n. 187—201.

216. *Be zealous, therefore, and repent*, signifies that this should be done from the affection of truth, and aversion of what is false. It is here said, "Be zealous," because it was said above, verse 15, "I would thou wert either cold or hot," here hot, for

zeal is spiritual heat, and spiritual heat is the affection of love, in this case the affection of the love of truth, and he who acts from the affection of the love of truth, acts also from aversion to what is false; therefore this is signified by repent. Zeal in the Word, when applied to the Lord, signifies love, and wrath; love, in John ii. 17; Psalm lxix. 10; Isaiah xxxvii. 32; lxiii. 15; Ezek. xxxix. 25; Zech. i. 14; viii. 2. Wrath, in Deut. xxxii. 16, 21; Psalm lxxix. 5, 6; Ezek. viii. 18; xxiii. 25; Zeph. i. 18; iii. 8. But zeal in the Lord is not wrath, it only appears so in externals; interiorly it is love. It appears so in externals, because the Lord seems to be angry when he rebukes man, especially when man's own evil punishes him. It is so permitted out of love, that his evil may be removed; just like a parent, who, if he loves his children, suffers them to be chastised for the sake of removing their evils. Hence it is evident, why Jehovah calls himself jealous, Deut. iv. 24; v. 9, 10; vi. 14, 15.

217. *Behold, I stand at the door, and knock*, signifies that the Lord is present to every one in the Word, and is there pressing to be received, and teaches how. Something similar to this is said by the Lord in Luke: "Be ye like unto men that wait for their Lord, when he will return from the wedding; that when he cometh and *knocketh, they may open unto him immediately,*" xii. 36. That door signifies admission and entrance, may be seen above, n. 176.

218. *If any man hear my voice, and open the door*, signifies he who believes in the Word and lives according to it. To hear his voice is to believe in the Word, for the divine truth of the Word is the voice of Jehovah, n. 37, 50; and to open the door is to live according to it, because the door is not opened, and the Lord received, by barely hearing his voice, but by living according to it, for the Lord says, "He that hath my commandments, and keepeth them, I will manifest myself to him, and we will come unto him, and make our abode with him," John xiv. 21—24. That man ought to open the door as from himself, by shunning evils as sins, and doing good, is shown in *The Doctrine of Life for the New Jerusalem;* and that this is the case, is also evident from the Lord's words here, "If any man open;" as also from his words in Luke xii. 36.

219. *I will come in to him, and will sup with him, and he with me*, signifies that the Lord joins himself with them and them with himself. To come in and sup with him, signifies to join himself to him, and, since there must be reciprocation that there may be conjunction, it is also said, "and he with me." That to be conjoined is signified by coming in and supping, appears from the Holy Supper instituted by the Lord, by means of which the Lord's presence is effected with those who hear his voice, that is, who believe in the Word, but his conjunction with those who live according to the Word: to live according to the

Word is to do the work of repentance, and to believe in the Lord. To sup, and the Lord's supper, are mentioned, because supper takes place in the evening, and by the evening is signified the last time of the church; therefore when the Lord departed out of the world, the last time of the church being then arrived, he supped with his disciples, and instituted the sacrament of the supper. That evening signifies the end of the old church and morning the beginning of the new, may be seen above, n. 13.

220. *To him that overcometh*, signifies such as are in conjunction with the Lord by a life conformable to his precepts in the Word, as is evident from what has been said above.

221. *Will I give to sit with me in my throne*, signifies that they will have conjunction with the Lord in heaven. That the Lord's throne is heaven, may be seen above, n. 14, therefore to sit with the Lord in his throne, signifies conjunction with him in heaven.

222. *Even as I also overcame, and am set down with my Father in his throne*, signifies in like manner as he and the Father are one, and are heaven. That the Father and the Lord are one, is fully shown in *The Doctrine of the New Jerusalem concerning the Lord*, and elsewhere. That heaven is not heaven from any property of the angels, but from the divine [principle] of the Lord, which is in the angels and about them, therefore by these words, in like manner as I " am set down with my Father in his throne," is signified like as he and the Father are one, and are heaven; throne signifies heaven, n. 14, 221. "Even as I also overcame," signifies that by temptations admitted into his human nature, and by the last of them, which was the passion of the cross, as also by the fulfilling of every thing in the Word, he overcame the hells and glorified his Humanity, that is, he united it to the Divinity which was in him by conception, and is called Jehovah the Father, on which subject see the above mentioned *Doctrine of the New Jerusalem concerning the Lord*, n. 8—11; n. 12—14; n. 29—36, and also above, n. 67. The reason why the Lord says, "To him that overcometh will I give to sit with me in my throne, even as I also overcame, and am set down with my Father in his throne," is, because the union of the Lord with the Father, that is, with the divinity within himself, took place, to the end that it might be possible for man to be joined to the divinity which is called the Father in the Lord; because it is impossible for man to have conjunction with the divinity of the Father immediately, but only mediately through his Divine Humanity, which is the divine natural [principle]; therefore the Lord says: "No man hath seen God at any time; the only-begotten Son, which is in the bosom of the Father, *he hath manifested him*," John i. 18; and in another place: "I am the *way*, the *truth*, and the *life*, no one cometh to the Father, but *by me*," John xiv. 6. The Lord's conjunction with man is by means

of his divine truth, and this in man is of the Lord, thus the Lord, and by no means man's, consequently is not man: man, indeed, feels it as his own, but still it is not his, for it is not united to him, but adjoined; not so the Father's divinity, this is not adjoined but united to the Lord's Humanity, as the soul is to its body. He who understands these things, may understand the following words of the Lord: "He that *abideth in me* and I in him, the same bringeth forth much fruit, for *without me* ye can do nothing," John xv. 5. "At that day ye shall know that I am in my Father, and *you in me, and I in you,*" John xiv. 20; and these: "Sanctify them through thy truth; thy Word is truth; for their sakes I sanctify myself, that they also might be sanctified through the truth: that they all may be one, as thou, Father, art in me, and I in thee, that they also may be *one in us; I in them and thou in me,*" John xvii. 17, 19, 21, 23.

223. *He that hath an ear, let him hear what the Spirit saith unto the churches,* signifies that he who understands, ought to obey what the divine truth of the Word teaches those who are to be of the New Church, which is the New Jerusalem, as above, n. 87.

224. To this I shall add the following Memorable Relation. I saw a number of spirits assembled, all upon their knees, praying to God to send his angels, that they might converse with them face to face, and open to them the thoughts of their hearts. And when they arose, there appeared three angels in white linen garments, standing before them, and they said, The Lord Jesus Christ has heard your prayers, and has therefore sent us to you; open unto us the thoughts of your hearts. And they answered, We have been told by our priests, that in matters of a theological nature the understanding avails nothing, but only faith, and that in such things intellectual faith is of no service to any one, because it is derived from man. We are Englishmen, and have heard many things from our holy priesthood, which we believed; but when we have conversed with others, who also called themselves the reformed, and with others who called themselves Roman Catholics, and likewise with sectaries, they all appeared to us learned, and yet, in many things, one did not agree with another, and still they all said, "Believe us;" and some of them, "We are God's ministers, and know." But as we know that the divine truths, which are called truths of faith, and which appertain to the church, are not derived to any one from his native soil, nor by inheritance, but out of heaven from God; and as these show the way to heaven, and enter into the life together with the good of charity, and so lead to eternal life, we became anxious, and prayed to God upon our knees. Then answered the angels, Read the Word, and believe in the Lord, and you will see the truths which should constitute your faith and

life; for all in the Christian world draw their doctrinals from the Word as the only fountain. But two of the company said, We have read, but did not understand; and the angels replied, You did not approach the Lord, and you have besides confirmed yourselves in falses; and added, What is faith without light, and what signifies thinking without understanding? there is nothing human in it; even magpies and ravens can learn to speak without understanding. We can affirm to you, that every man, whose soul desires it, is capable of seeing the truths of the Word in the light; there does not exist an animal that does not know the food proper to its life when it sees it, and man is a rational and spiritual animal, who sees the food of his life, not that of his body, but of his soul, which is the truth of faith, provided indeed he hungers after it, and seeks it of the Lord; whatsoever is not received also in the understanding, is not fixed in the memory in reality, but only verbally; therefore, when we have looked down out of heaven in the world, we have not seen any thing, but have only heard sounds, that are for the most part dissonant. But we will enumerate some things which the learned among the clergy have removed from the understanding, not knowing that there are two ways to the understanding, one from the world, and the other from heaven, and that the Lord withdraws the understanding from the world when he illuminates it; but if the understanding be closed by religion, the way into it from heaven is closed, and then man sees no more in the Word than a blind person: we have seen many such fall into pits, out of which they have never risen again. Examples must serve for illustration: are you not able to understand what charity is, and what faith is; that charity consists in doing well by your neighbour, and that faith consists in thinking well of God and of the essentials of the church, and therefore that he who does well and thinks well, that is, who lives well and believes well, will be saved? They replied, that these things they did understand. Then said the angels, Do you not understand, that repentance from sins is to be performed, in order that man may be saved, and that, unless a man actually repents, he abides in the sins into which he was born, and that the work of repentance consists in not willing evils because they are against God, and in examining himself once or twice a year, in seeing his evils, in confessing them before the Lord, imploring assistance, desisting from them, and leading a new life, and as far as he does this, and believes in the Lord, so far his sins are remitted? Then some of the company replied, This we understand, and thence also what remission of sins is. And then they solicited the angels to give them further information, and especially concerning God, the immortality of the soul, regeneration, and baptism. To this the angels replied, We will not say any thing but what you can understand, else our discourse will fall like rain upon sand, and upon the seed therein, which, notwithstanding its being watered from heaven, would pine and perish. Concerning GOD they said, All who come into heaven have their place allotted them there, and thence everlasting joy, according to their idea of God, because this idea reigns universally in every particular of worship; the idea of an invisible God is not determined to any god, nor does it terminate in any, therefore it ceases and perishes; the idea of God as a spirit, when a spirit is thought of as ether or air, is an empty idea; but the idea of God as a man is a just idea, for God is divine love and divine wisdom, with every quality belonging thereto, and the subject of these is man, and not ether or wind. The idea of God in heaven is the idea of the Lord, he being the God of heaven and earth, as he himself taught; let your idea of God be like unto ours, and we shall be consociated together. On saying these words, their faces became resplendent. Concerning the IMMORTALITY OF THE SOUL, they said, Man lives to eternity, because he is capable of being conjoined with God by love and faith, this indeed is possible with every one; that this possibility constitutes the immortality of the soul you may understand, provided you think of it with a little elevation of mind. Concerning REGENERATION; who does not see that every one is at liberty to think of God, or not to think of him, provided he be instructed that there is a God; so that every one has liberty in spiritual things, equally as in things civil and moral; the Lord gives this liberty to all continually; for which reason he becomes guilty, if he does not think of God; man is man by virtue of this possibility; but a beast is a beast from not having this possibility; therefore man is capable of reforming and regenerating himself as from himself, provided he acknowledges in his heart that he does it from the Lord: every one who does the work of repentance, and believes in the Lord, is reformed and regenerated; man must do both as from himself, but *as from himself* is from the Lord. It is true that man cannot contribute any thing thereto, no not in the least, nevertheless you were not created statues, but you were created men, that you might do that from the Lord as from yourselves; this is the only reciprocation of love and faith, that it is altogether the Lord's will that it should be done by man unto him: in a word, do it from yourselves, and believe that you do it from the Lord, thus do it as from yourselves. But then the English inquired, Whether to act as from oneself, is a faculty implanted in man from creation? The angel answered, It is not implanted or inherent, because to act from himself is of the Lord alone, but it is communicated continually, that is, adjoined continually, and then so far as man does good and believes what is true, as from himself, so far he is an angel of heaven; but so far as he does evil and thence believes what is false, which is done also as from himself, so far he is an angel of hell: that this also is as from himself surprises you, but still you see that it is so, when you pray that you may be preserved from the devil, lest he should seduce you, and enter into you, as he did into Judas, fill you with all iniquity, and destroy you, soul and body. But every one incurs guilt who believes that he acts from himself, whether it be good, or whether it be evil; but he does not incur guilt, who believes that he acts as from himself. Concerning BAPTISM, they said, That it is spiritual washing, which is reformation and regeneration, and that an infant is reformed and regenerated, when, on becoming an adult, he does the things which his sponsors promised for him, which are two, repentance and faith in God; for in the first place they promise that he shall renounce the devil and all his works; and secondly, that he shall believe in God. All infants in heaven are initiated into these two things, but with them the devil is hell, and God is the Lord: moreover baptism is a sign before the angels that a man is of the church. On hearing these things, some of the assembly said, This we understand. But a voice was heard from one side, exclaiming, We do not understand; and another voice, We will not understand; and inquiry was made from whence these voices proceeded, and it was found that they came from those who had confirmed themselves in falses of faith, and who wanted to be believed as oracles, and thus to be adored. Upon which the angels said, Be not surprised; there are a great many such at this day; they appear to us from heaven like images, made with so much art as to be able to move their lips, and utter sounds like organs, but without knowing whether the breath, by means of which they utter these sounds, comes from hell or from heaven, because they do not know whether a thing be false or true; they reason over and over again; they confirm over and over again without ever seeing whether it is so. But know, that human ingenuity can confirm whatsoever it pleases, so that it shall appear to be really true, therefore heretics and impious persons can do this, yea atheists can prove that there is no God, but only nature. Afterwards the assembly of Englishmen, being warmed with the desire of acquiring wisdom, said to the angels, So many different sentiments are entertained of the Holy Supper, tell us what is the truth? The angels replied, The truth is that the man who looks to the Lord and performs repentance, is conjoined with the Lord by means of that most holy rite, and introduced into heaven. But some of the company said, This is a mystery. To which the angels replied, It is a mystery, but nevertheless it is such a one as may be understood. The bread and wine do not produce this effect, for there is nothing holy in them, but material bread and heavenly bread correspond mutually to each other, and so do material wine and heavenly wine, and heavenly bread is the holy [principle] of love, and heavenly wine is the holy [principle] of faith, both from the Lord, and both the Lord; thence there is a conjunction of the Lord with man, and of man with the Lord, not with the bread and wine, but with the love and faith of the man who had done the work of repentance; and conjunction with the Lord is also introduction into heaven. And after the angels had given them some instruction concerning correspondence and its effects, some of the company said, Now for the first time do we understand. And when they said, We understand, behold a flame-coloured band, descending with light from heaven, consociated them with the angels, and their love for one another was mutual.

CHAPTER IV.

1. AFTER this I looked, and behold a door opened in heaven. And the first voice which I heard, as it were of a trumpet talking with me, said, Come up hither, and I will show thee things which must be hereafter.

2. And immediately I was in the spirit. And, behold, a throne was set in heaven, and one sat on the throne.

3. And he that sat was to look upon like a jasper and a sardine stone; and there was a rainbow round about the throne in sight like unto an emerald.

4. And round about the throne were four-and-twenty thrones; and upon the thrones I saw four-and-twenty elders sitting, clothed in white raiment; and they had on their heads crowns of gold.

5. And out of the throne proceeded lightnings, and thunderings, and voices: and there were seven lamps of fire burning before the throne, which are the seven spirits of God.

6. And before the throne there was a sea of glass like unto crystal: and in the midst of the throne and round about the throne, were four animals full of eyes before and behind.

7. And the first animal was like a lion, and the second animal like a calf, and the third animal had a face as a man, and the fourth animal was like a flying eagle.

8. And the four animals had each of them six wings about him; and they were full of eyes within; and they rest not day and night, saying, Holy, holy, holy, Lord God Almighty, who was, and who is, and who is to come.

9. And when the animals give glory, and honour, and thanks to Him that sat on the throne, who liveth for ever and ever,

10. The four-and-twenty elders fall down before Him that

sat on the throne, and worship Him that liveth for ever and ever, and cast their crowns before the throne, saying,

11. Thou art worthy, O Lord, to receive glory, and honour, and power, for thou hast created all things, and by thy will they are and were created.

THE SPIRITUAL SENSE.

THE CONTENTS OF THE WHOLE CHAPTER. The subject treated of is concerning the ordination and preparation of all things in heaven for judgment, to be executed from, and according to, the Word; likewise concerning the acknowledgment, that the Lord is the only judge.

THE CONTENTS OF EACH VERSE. v. 1, "After this I looked, and behold a door opened in heaven," signifies a manifestation of the ordination of the heavens preparatory to the last judgment from the Lord, about to be performed according to his divine truths in the Word: "And the first voice which I heard, as it were of a trumpet talking with me, said, Come up hither," signifies divine influx, and thence an elevation of the mind, followed by manifest perception: "And I will show thee things which must be hereafter," signifies revelations of things to come before the last judgment, and at it, and after it: v. 2, "And immediately I was in the spirit," signifies that he was let into a spiritual state, in which the things which exist in heaven manifestly appear: "And, behold, a throne was set in heaven," signifies a representation of judgment: "And one sat on the throne," signifies the Lord: v. 3, "And he that sat was to look upon like a jasper and a sardine stone," signifies the appearance of the Lord's divine wisdom and divine love in ultimates: "And there was a rainbow round about the throne in sight like unto an emerald," signifies the appearance of the same also round about the Lord: v. 4, "And round about the throne were four-and-twenty thrones, and upon the thrones I saw four-and-twenty elders sitting," signifies the ordination of all things in heaven preparatory to the judgment: "Clothed in white raiment," signifies from the divine truth of the Word: "And they had on their heads crowns of gold," signifies the things which are of wisdom derived from love: v. 5, "And out of the throne proceeded lightnings, and thunderings, and voices," signifies illumination, perception, and instruction from the Lord: "And there were seven lamps of fire burning before the throne, which are the seven spirits of God," signifies a new heaven from among Christians: v. 6, "And before the throne there was a sea of glass like unto crystal," signifies the new heaven composed of Christians, who are in general truths, derived from the literal sense of the Word: "And in the midst of the throne, and round about the throne, there were four animals," signifies the Word of God from its first principles to its ultimates, and its defences: "Full of eyes before and behind," signifies the divine wisdom therein: v. 7, "And the first animal was like a lion," signifies the divine truth of the Word as to its power: "And the second animal like a calf," signifies the divine truth of the Word as to affection: "And the third animal had a face as a man," signifies the divine truth of the Word as to its wisdom: "And the fourth animal was like a flying eagle," signifies the divine truth of the Word as to knowledge and thence understanding: v. 8, "And the four animals had each of them six wings about him," signifies the Word as to its powers and as to its defences: "And they were full of eyes within," signifies the divine wisdom in the Word in its natural sense, derived from its spiritual and celestial sense: "And they rest not day and night, saying, Holy, holy, holy, Lord God Almighty," signifies that the Word continually teaches of the Lord, and that he is the only God, and thence that he alone is to be worshipped: "Who was, and who is, and who is to come," signifies the Lord: v. 9, "And when the animals give glory, and honour, and thanks to him that sat on the throne," signifies that the Word ascribes all truth, and all good, and all worship to the Lord the judge: "Who liveth for ever and ever," signifies that the Lord alone is life, and that life eternal is from him alone: v. 10, "The four-and-twenty elders fall down before him that sat on the throne, and worship him that liveth for ever and ever," signifies the humiliation of all in heaven before the Lord: "And cast their crowns before the throne," signifies an acknowledgment that their wisdom is from him alone: v. 11, "Saying, Thou art worthy, O Lord, to receive glory, and honour, and power," signifies that the kingdom is the Lord's by merit and justice, because he is the divine truth and the divine good: "For thou hast created all things, and by thy will they are, and were created," signifies that all things of heaven and the church were made and formed, and men reformed and regenerated from the Lord's divine love by his divine wisdom, or from his divine good by his divine truth, which also is the Word.

THE EXPLANATION.

225. *After this I looked, and behold a door opened in heaven,* signifies a manifestation of the ordination of the heavens preparatory to the last judgment from the Lord, about

to be performed according to his divine truths in the Word. By an open door, when it relates to heaven, is signified admission, as above, n. 176; here, also, manifestation, because he says, "I looked and behold;" and because then were seen the things which are recorded in this chapter, which refer to the ordination of the heavens preparatory to the last judgment, about to be performed from the Lord according to his divine truths in the Word, therefore by "I looked, and behold a door opened in heaven," is signified a manifestation concerning them.

226. *And the first voice which I heard, as it were of a trumpet talking with me, said, Come up hither*, signifies divine influx, and thence an elevation of the mind, followed by manifest perception. That a voice, when heard from heaven, is influent divine truth, may be seen above, n. 37, 50, thus divine influx; and that by a voice as it were of a trumpet, is signified manifest perception, may also be seen above, n. 37; and by "Come up hither," is signified elevation of the mind; for in the spiritual world, the higher any one ascends so much the more does he come into purer light, by which the understanding is gradually opened, that is, the mind is elevated; therefore it also follows, that he was then in the spirit, by which is meant that he was let into a spiritual state, in which the things which are in the heavens manifestly appear. The voice was heard as it were a trumpet, because the subject treated of is the ordination of the heavens preparatory to the last judgment; and voices as of a trumpet are heard in heaven, when convocations and ordinations take place; therefore among the children of Israel with whom all things were representative of heaven and the church, it was also commanded, That they should make *trumpets* of silver, and that the sons of Aaron should blow with them for *the calling of assemblies*, and for *the journeying of the camps*, in *days of rejoicing*, in *festivals*, in the *beginnings of months, over burnt offerings*, for *a memorial*, and *going to war*, Numb. x. 1—11. But we shall speak of trumpets, and of sounding them, in the explanation of chap. viii., where the seven angels are mentioned, to whom were given seven trumpets.

227. *And I will show thee things which must be hereafter*, signifies revelations of things to come before the last judgment, and at it, and after it. These things are signified, because in the Apocalypse nothing else is treated of but the state of the church at its end, thus the things to come to pass before the last judgment, and at it, and after it, as above explained, n. 2.

228. *And immediately I was in the spirit*, signifies that he was let into a spiritual state, in which the things which exist in heaven manifestly appear. That to be in the spirit is to be let into a spiritual state by divine influx, as also what the nature of a spiritual state is, and that a man in that state sees as manifestly the things which are in the spiritual world, as in the

natural state of the body he sees the things which are in this world, may be seen above, n. 36.

229. *And, behold, a throne was set*, signifies a representation of judgment. That a throne signifies heaven may be seen, n. 14; that a throne also signifies judgment, is evident from the following places: "When the Son of Man shall come in his glory, and all the holy angels with him, then shall he sit on the *throne* of his glory," Matt. xxv. 31, and following verses; where the last judgment is treated of. Jehovah, "thou hast maintained my cause,—thou sattest in the *throne* judging right. Jehovah hath prepared his *throne* for judgment," Psalm ix. 4, 7. "I beheld,—and the Ancient of Days did sit,—his *throne* was like the fiery flame,—thousand thousands ministered unto him, and ten thousand times ten thousand stood before him; the judgment was set, and the books were opened," Dan. vii. 9, 10. "Jerusalem is builded as a city,—whither the tribes go up—for there sit *thrones* of judgment," Psalm cxxii. 3—5. "I saw *thrones*, and they sat upon them, and judgment was given unto them," Apoc. xx. 4. The throne built by Solomon, of which mention is made, 1 Kings x. 18—20, signified both royalty and judgment, because kings, when they executed judgment, sat upon thrones. It is said that a throne signifies a representation of judgment, because the things which John saw were visions which represented; they were seen as he has described them, but they were forms representative of things to come, as may appear from what follows; as that there were seen animals, a dragon, a beast, a temple, a tabernacle, an ark, and many other things. Similar were the things seen by the prophets, which are mentioned above, n. 36.

230. *And one sat on the throne*, signifies the Lord, as appears manifestly from what follows, and from passages in the Word where it is said that the Lord will execute judgment, as in Matt. xxv. 32, 33, and following verses; John v. 22, 27; and elsewhere.

231. *And he that sat was to look upon like a jasper and sardine stone*, signifies the appearance of the Lord's divine wisdom and divine love in ultimates. A stone, in the Word, signifies truth in ultimates, and a precious stone, truth transparent from good, n. 915. There are two colours fundamental of the rest in the spiritual world, red and white; white derives its origin from the light of the sun in heaven, thus from spiritual light, which is white; and red derives its origin from the fire of the sun there, thus from celestial light, which is flame-coloured. The spiritual angels, being in truths of wisdom from the Lord, are in that white light, therefore they are clothed in white; and the celestial angels, being in the good of love from the Lord, are in that flame-coloured light, therefore they are clothed in red; thence those two colours obtain also in precious

stones in heaven, where they are in great abundance. This is the reason why precious stones, in the Word, signify such things as are of the truth of wisdom, or of the good of love, and that a jasper, because it is white, signifies the things which are of the truth of wisdom, and a sardine stone, because it is red, the things which are of the good of love. These stones signify the appearance of the divine wisdom and the divine love in ultimates, because all precious stones in heaven derive their origin from the ultimates of the Word, and their transparency from the spiritual sense within those ultimates: that this is the case, may be seen in *The Doctrine of the New Jerusalem concerning the Sacred Scripture*, n. 44, 45. The ultimates of the Word are the truths and goods of its literal sense. That this is the origin of precious stones in heaven is difficult to be believed by any one in our world, because he does not know that all the things which exist in the spiritual world are correspondences, and that from thence all the things which exist in the natural world derive their spiritual origin. That this is the origin of precious stones in heaven has been permitted me to know from discourse with angels, and also to see it with my eyes, but the formation of them is from the Lord alone. But black colours, which are also two in number, derive their origin from hell; one in opposition to white, this blackness being with those who have falsified the truths of the Word; the other in opposition to red, this blackness being with those who have adulterated the good of the Word; the latter blackness is diabolical, but the former satanical. The signification of the jasper and sardine stone may be seen in the explanation of chap. xxi. 11, 18—20.

232. *And there was a rainbow round about the throne in sight like unto an emerald*, signifies the appearance of the same also round about the Lord. In the spiritual world there appear rainbows of many kinds, some of various colours, as upon earth, and some of one colour only; here of one colour only, because it is said like unto an emerald. This appearance was round about the Lord, because it is said round about the throne; round about him is also in the heaven of angels. The divine sphere which surrounds the Lord is from his divine love, and at the same time from his divine wisdom, which, when it is represented in the heavens, appears in the celestial kingdom red like a ruby, in the spiritual kingdom blue like the lazule stone, in the natural kingdom green like the emerald; everywhere with ineffable splendour and effulgence.

233. *And round about the throne were four-and-twenty thrones, and upon the thrones I saw four-and twenty elders sitting*, signifies the ordination of all things in heaven preparatory to the last judgment. He who is ignorant of the spiritual sense of the Word, and at the same time of the genuine truths of the church, may suppose, that when the last judgment takes

place, the Lord will sit upon a throne, and that there will be other judges also upon thrones around him; but he who is acquainted with the spiritual sense of the Word, and at the same time with the genuine truths of the church, knows that the Lord will not sit upon a throne, and that neither will there be other judges about him; and further, that neither will the Lord judge any one to hell, but that the Word will judge every one, the Lord himself directing that all things shall be done according to justice; the Lord says, indeed, "The Father *judgeth* no man, but hath committed all *judgment* unto the Son,—and hath given him authority to *execute judgment*, because he is the Son of Man," John v. 22, 27; but in another place he says, "I came not to *judge* the world, but to save the world; the *Word* that I have spoken, the same shall *judge* him in the last day," John xii. 47, 48: these two passages agree, when it is known that the Son of Man is the Lord as to the Word, see above, n. 44; therefore the Word will judge, under the Lord's direction. That by the twelve tribes of Israel and their elders are signified all who are of the Lord's church in the heavens and upon the earths, and, abstractedly, all the truths and goods therein, may be seen, n. 251, 349, 369, 808; and the same by the apostles, n. 79, 790, 903; hence it is plain what is signified by these words of the Lord: "Jesus said unto his disciples,—ye which have followed me,—when the Son of Man shall sit in the *throne* of his glory, ye also shall sit upon *twelve thrones judging* the twelve tribes of Israel," Matt. xix. 28; Luke xxii. 30. Twelve signifies all, and is predicated of the truths and goods of heaven and the church, n. 348; the same is signified by twenty-four; therefore the twelve apostles and the twenty-four elders signify all things of the church; and twelve, as also four-and-twenty thrones, signify the all of judgment. Who cannot understand, that the apostles and elders will not judge; and that neither are they able? From these considerations it may appear why thrones and elders are mentioned when the judgment is treated of; as also in Isaiah: "Jehovah will enter into *judgment* with the ancients of his people," iii. 14. In David: "Jerusalem is builded as a city,—whither the tribes go up,—for there are set *thrones* of *judgment*," Psalm cxxii. 3, 4, 5. And in the Apocalypse: "I saw *thrones*, and they sat upon them, and *judgment* was given unto them," xx. 4.

234. *Clothed in white raiment*, signifies from the divine truth of the Word. That white garments signify genuine truths of the Word, may be seen above, n. 166, 212.

235. *And they had on their heads crowns of gold*, signifies such things as are of wisdom derived from love. That a crown signifies wisdom, may be seen above, n. 189; and that gold signifies the good of love, n. 211, 913; hence a crown of gold signifies wisdom derived from love. As from this wisdom are

derived all the things of heaven and the church, which are signified by the four-and-twenty elders, n. 233; therefore crowns of gold were seen upon their heads. It is to be observed, that the spiritual sense is here abstracted from persons, as well as above, n. 78, 79, 96.

236. *And out of the throne proceeded lightnings, and thunderings, and voices*, signifies illumination, perception, and instruction from the Lord. Lightnings, by reason of the flash which strikes the eyes, signify illumination, and thunderings, by reason of the noise which affects the ears, signify perception, and when these two signify illumination and perception, then voices signify instruction. These were seen to proceed from the throne, because they proceed from the Son of Man, or the Lord as the Word, and from the Lord through the Word comes all illumination, perception, and instruction. Lightnings, thunderings, and voices, have a similar signification in other parts of the Word, as in these places: "Thou hast with thine arm redeemed thy people,—the skies sent out a *sound*, the *voice of thy thunder* was in the heavens, the *lightnings lightened* the world," Psalm lxxvii. 15, 17, 18. "The *lightnings* of Jehovah *enlightened* the world," Psalm xcvii. 3, 4. "Thou calledst in trouble, and I delivered thee, I answered thee in the secret place of *thunder*," Psalm lxxxi. 7. "I heard as it were the voice of a great multitude, and the voice of *mighty thunderings*, saying, Halleluia; for the Lord God Omnipotent reigneth," Apoc. xix. 6. As by lightnings, and thunderings, and voices, are signified illumination, perception, and instruction, therefore when Jehovah descended upon Mount Sinai, and promulgated the law, there were lightnings and voices, Exod. xix. 16. And when there came to the Lord a voice out of heaven, it was heard as thunder, John xii. 28, 29. And because James and John represented charity and its works, and from these is derived all perception of what is true and good, they were called by the Lord, Boanerges, that is, Sons of Thunder, Mark iii. 17. Hence it is evident, that lightnings, thunderings, and voices, have a similar signification in the following passages in the Apocalypse: I heard one of the four animals, "as it were a *voice* of *thunder*," vi. 1. "I heard a *voice* from heaven, as the *voice* of a great *thunder*," xiv. 2. When the angel cast the censer upon the earth, "there were *voices*, and *thunderings*, and *lightnings*," viii. 5. When the angel cried, "seven *thunders* uttered their voices," x. 3, 4. When the temple of God was opened in heaven, "there were *lightnings*, and *voices*, and *thunderings*," xi. 19: and the same in other places.

237. *And there were seven lamps of fire burning before the throne, which are the seven spirits of God*, signifies a new heaven from the Lord through the divine truth proceeding from him. Here by seven lamps the same is signified as by the seven

candlesticks, and also by the seven stars above. That by the seven candlesticks is meant a new church upon earth, which will be in illumination from the Lord, may be seen above, n. 43, and by the seven stars, a new church in the heavens, n. 65; and whereas the church is a church from the divine [principle] which proceeds from the Lord, which is divine truth, and is called the Holy Spirit, therefore it is said, which are the seven spirits of God. That by the seven spirits of God is signified that proceeding divine [principle], may be seen above, n. 14, 155.

238. *And before the throne there was a sea of glass like unto crystal*, signifies the new heaven composed of Christians who are in general truths derived from the literal sense of the Word. In the spiritual world there appear atmospheres, and also waters, like as in our world; the atmospheres, in which the angels of the supreme heaven dwell, are as it were ethereal; the atmospheres, in which the angels of the middle heaven dwell, are as it were aërial; and the atmospheres, in which the angels of the ultimate heaven dwell, are as it were aqueous or watery; and these last are the seas which appear at the boundaries of heaven, where they dwell who are in the truths of a general kind derived from the literal sense of the Word. That waters signify truths, may be seen above, n. 50; hence the sea, in which waters terminate and are collected, signifies divine truth in its boundaries. Since, therefore, by Him that sat on the throne is understood the Lord, n. 230, and by the seven lamps, which are the seven spirits of God before the throne, is understood the New Church, which will be in divine truth from the Lord, n. 237, it is evident that, by the sea of glass which was before the throne, is understood the church among those who are at the boundaries. It has also been permitted me to see the seas which bound the heavens, and to converse with those who were therein, and thus to know the truth of this matter from experience; they seemed to me to be in the sea, but they said that they were not in the sea, but in an atmosphere; from which it was manifest to me, that the sea is an appearance of the divine proceeding from the Lord in its boundaries. That there are seas in the spiritual world, is fully evident from their having been seen by John frequently, as well here as in chap. v. 13; vii. 1—3; viii. 8, 9; x. 2, 8; xii. 12; xiii. 1; xiv. 7; xv. 2; xvi. 3; xviii. 17, 19, 21; xx. 13. It is described as a sea of glass like unto crystal, from the lucidity of the divine truth proceeding from the Lord. Because divine truth at its boundaries causes the appearance of a sea in the spiritual world, therefore sea, in other parts of the Word, has a similar signification, as in these places: "And it shall be in that day, that living waters shall go out from Jerusalem, half of them toward the former *sea*, and half of them toward the hinder *sea*," Zech. xiv. 8.

Living waters from Jerusalem, are divine truths of the church from the Lord, therefore the sea is where they terminate. "Thy way, [O Jehovah,] is in the *sea*, and thy path in the great *waters*," Psalm lxxvii. 19. "Thus saith Jehovah, which maketh a way in the *sea*, and a path in the *mighty waters*," Isaiah xliii. 16. Jehovah hath laid the foundations of the world "upon the *seas*, and established it upon the *floods*," Psalm xxiv. 2. Jehovah hath "laid the foundations of the earth that it should not be removed for ever. Thou coveredst it with the *deep* [or *sea*] as with a garment," Psalm civ. 5, 6. The foundations of the earth being laid upon the sea, denotes that the church, which is meant by the earth, is founded upon common or general truths; for these are its bases and foundations. "And I will dry up the *sea* [of Babylon] and make her springs dry,—she is covered with the multitude of the *waves*," Jerem. li. 36, 42. Drying up the sea of Babylon and making her springs dry, signifies to extinguish every truth of its church from first principles to last. "They shall walk after Jehovah, then the children shall tremble *from the sea*," Hosea xi. 10. Children from the sea are they who are in general or ultimate truths. "Jehovah who buildeth his stories in the heavens,—and calleth for the *waters of the sea*, and poureth them out upon the face of the earth," Amos ix. 6. "By the Word of Jehovah were the heavens made,—he gathereth the *waters of the sea* together as a heap, he layeth up the depths in storehouses," Psalm xxxiii. 6, 7. "At my rebuke I dry up the *sea*, I make the rivers a wilderness," Isaiah l. 2: besides other places. As by sea is signified divine truth with those who are in the borders of heaven, therefore by Tyre and Zidon, from their being by the sea-side, is signified the church as to the knowledges of things good and true; and also by the isles of the sea are signified those who are in a more remote kind of divine worship, n. 34: and therefore the sea, in the Hebrew language, is called the west, that is, where the light of the sun declines towards evening, or truth into obscurity. That sea also signifies the natural degree of man separated from the spiritual, thus also hell, will be seen in what follows.

239. *And in the midst of the throne and round about the throne, there were four animals*, signifies the Word of God from its first principles to its ultimates, and its defences. I am well aware it will be thought surprising, that it should be said, the four animals signify the Word; that this is their signification, will however be seen in what follows. These animals are the same as the cherubs in Ezekiel, where they are also called animals in chap. i., but cherubs in chap. x., and were, in like manner as here, a lion, an ox, a man, and an eagle. In the Hebrew language they are there called *chajoth*, a word which indeed signifies animals, but is derived from *chaja*, which signifies life,

whence also the wife of Adam was called *Chaja*, Gen. iii. 20; animal in the singular number is also called *chaja* in Ezekiel, therefore those animals may also be called living [creatures]. Neither is there any thing extraordinary in the Word's being described by animals, since the Lord himself in many parts of the Word is called a lion, and very often a lamb, and they who are in charity from the Lord are called sheep; and the understanding also of the Word, in what follows, is called a horse. That the Word is signified by these animals or cherubs, is evident from this consideration, that they were seen in the midst of the throne and round about the throne, and in the midst of the throne was the Lord, and, as the Lord is the Word, they could not be seen anywhere else; that they were round about the throne also, was, because this denotes the angelic heaven, where also the Word is. That by cherubs is signified the Word, and its defence or guard, is shown in *The Doctrine of the New Jerusalem concerning the Sacred Scripture*, n. 97, where are the following words: "The literal sense of the Word serves as a defence for the genuine truths which lie within; and the defence consists in this, that the literal sense can be turned this way and that, or, in other words, can be explained according to every one's apprehension, without its internal being hurt or violated; for no harm ensues from the literal sense being understood differently by different people; but the danger is, when the divine truths which are within are perverted, for it is by this that the Word suffers violence. To prevent this, the literal sense keeps guard as it were, and serves indeed as a protection with those who are in falses from religion, but yet do not confirm them, for from these the Word suffers no violence. This defence is signified by cherubs, and is also described by them in the Word. This defence is signified by the cherubs, which, after the expulsion of Adam and his wife from the garden of Eden, were placed at its entrance; concerning which we read, when Jehovah God had driven out the man, "he placed at the east of the garden of Eden *cherubims*, and a flaming sword, which turned every way, to keep the way of the tree of life," Gen. iii. 23, 24. By cherubims is signified defence; by the way of the tree of life is signified admission to the Lord, which is given to men through the Word; by a flaming sword which turned every way, is signified divine truth in ultimates, which is as the Word in its literal sense, that allows of being turned this way and that. The same is understood by the *cherubims* made of gold over the two extremities of the mercy-seat, which was above the ark in the tabernacle, Exod. xxv. 18—21; because this was signified by cherubims, therefore Jehovah talked from between them with Moses, Exod. xxv. 22; xxxvi. 9; Numb. vii. 8, 9. Nor was any thing else understood by the *cherubims* over the curtains of the tabernacle, and over the vail, Exod. xxvi

31; for the curtains and vail of the tabernacle represented the ultimates of heaven and the church, thus also the ultimates of the Word. The same is signified by the *cherubims* in the middle of the temple of Jerusalem, 1 Kings vi. 22, 28; and by the *cherubims* carved upon the walls and doors of the temple, 1 Kings vi. 29, 32, 35; and also by the *cherubims* in the new temple, Ezek. xli. 18—20. Since by cherubims was signified defence, to secure the Lord, heaven, and the divine truth such as it is interiorly in the Word, from being approached immediately, but only mediately by ultimates, therefore it is said of the king of Tyre, "Thou sealest up the sum, full of wisdom and perfect in beauty. Thou hast been in Eden, the garden of God; every precious stone was thy covering; thou art the anointed *cherub* that covereth; and I will destroy thee, O *covering cherub*, from the midst of the stones of fire," Ezek. xxviii. 12—14, 16. By Tyre is signified the church as to the knowledges of truth and good, and thence, by its king, the Word where those knowledges are, and from whence they are derived. That the Word in its ultimate, which is its literal sense, is here signified by the king of Tyre, and its defence, by the cherub, is evident, for it is said, "Thou sealest up the sum," "every precious stone was thy covering," and, "thou art the anointed cherub that covereth;" by the precious stones which are also mentioned there, are signified the truths of the literal sense of the Word, n. 231. Because by cherubims is signified divine truth in its ultimates as a defence, therefore it is written in the Psalms of David, "Give ear, O Shepherd of Israel,—thou that dwellest between the *cherubims*, shine forth," lxxx. 1. "Jehovah sitteth between the *cherubims*," xcix. 1. "Jehovah bowed the heavens and came down, and rode upon a *cherub*," xviii. 10, 11. To ride upon cherubs, to sit upon them, and sit between them, means upon the ultimate sense of the Word. The divine truth in the Word, and its quality, is described by the cherubims in Ezekiel, in chap. i. ix. x., and as no one can know what the particulars by which they are described signify, without having the spiritual sense unfolded to him, therefore, as it has been discovered to me, I will explain, in a summary way, the signification of those things which are related concerning the four animals or cherubims in the first chapter of Ezekiel; which is as follows: "The divine external sphere of the Word is described, verse 4. It is represented as a man, verse 5. Its conjunction with things spiritual and celestial, verse 6. The natural sense of the Word, its quality, verse 7. The conjunction of the spiritual and celestial senses of the Word with the natural, its quality, verse 8, 9. The divine love of celestial, spiritual, and natural good and truth therein contained, jointly and severally, verse 10, 11. That they regard one end, verse 12. The sphere of the Word from the Lord's divine good and divine truth, from which the Word lives, verse 13, 14. The doctrine of goodness and truth in the Word and from the Word, verse 15—21. The divinity of the Lord above it and in it, verse 22, 23. And out of it, verse 24, 25. That the Lord is above the heavens, verse 26. That divine love and divine wisdom are his, verse 27, 28. This is a summary exposition of the above chapter."

240. *Full of eyes before and behind*, signifies the divine wisdom therein. By eyes, when spoken of man, is signified the understanding, and when of the Lord, the divine wisdom, n. 48, 125; the same when said of the Word, as in this instance, because the Word is from the Lord and concerning the Lord, and thus is the Lord. The like is said of the cherubims in Ezekiel, that they were *full of eyes*, x. 12. Before and behind, when it relates to the Word from the Lord, signifies the divine wisdom and divine love therein.

241. *And the first animal was like a lion*, signifies the divine truth of the Word as to its power. That a lion signifies truth in its power, here the divine truth of the Word as to its power, may appear from the power of the lion above every other beast of the earth, as also from lions in the spiritual world, where they are images representative of the power of divine truth; and likewise from the Word, where they signify divine truth in its power. What the power of the divine truth in the Word is, may be seen in *The Doctrine of the New Jerusalem concerning the Sacred Scripture*, n. 49, and in the work on *Heaven and Hell*, n. 228—233. Hence it is that Jehovah or the Lord is compared to a lion, and is also called a lion; as for instance: "The *Lion* hath roared, who will not fear? the Lord Jehovah hath spoken, who can but prophesy?" Amos iii. 8. "I will not return to destroy Ephraim, they shall walk after Jehovah: he shall roar as a *lion*," Hosea xi. 9, 10. "Like as the *lion* and the *young lion* roaring, so shall Jehovah of Hosts come down to fight for Mount Zion," Isaiah xxxi. 4. "Behold, the *Lion* of the tribe of Judah hath prevailed, the Root of David," Apoc. v. 5. "Judah is a *lion's* whelp, he stooped down, he couched as an *old lion*, who shall rouse him up?" Gen. xlix. 9. In these places the power of divine truth, as derived from the Lord, is described as a lion. To roar signifies to speak and act from power against the hells, which are desirous to carry man away, but from which the Lord snatches him, as a lion does his prey; to stoop or bend himself, is to put himself in power; Judah, in a supreme sense, signifies the Lord, n. 96, 266. The angel "cried with a loud voice as when a *lion* roareth," Apoc. x. 3. "He couched, he lay down as a *great lion*, who shall stir him up?" Numb. xxiv. 9. "Behold, the people shall rise up as a *great lion*, and lift up himself as a *young lion*," Numb. xxiii. 23, 24; speaking of Israel, by which

is signified the church, whose power, as consisting in divine truths, is thus described. In like manner: "And the remnant of Jacob shall be in the midst of many people as a *lion* among the beasts of the forest, as a *young lion* among the flocks of sheep," Micah v. 7, 8: besides many other places; as Isaiah xi. 6; xxi. 6—9; xxxv. 9; Jerem. ii. 15; iv. 7; v. 6; xii. 8; l. 17; li. 38; Ezek. xix. 3, 5, 6; Hosea xiii. 7, 8; Joel i. 6, 7; Nahum ii. 12; Psalm xvii. 12; Psalm xxii. 13; Psalm lvii. 4; Psalm lviii. 6; Psalm xci. 13; Psalm civ. 21, 22; Deut. xxxiii. 20.

242. *And the second animal like a calf*, signifies the divine truth of the Word as to affection. By the beasts of the earth are signified the various natural affections, for such indeed they are; and by a calf is signified the affection of knowing; in the spiritual world this affection is represented by a calf, therefore it is also signified by a calf in the Word, as in Hosea: We will render unto Jehovah the "*calves of our lips*," xiv. 2. Calves of the lips are confessions from the affection of truth. In Malachi: "But unto you that fear my name, shall the Sun of Righteousness arise, with healing in his wings, and ye shall go forth and grow up as *calves* of the stall," iv. 2. They are compared to calves of the stall, or fatted calves, because by them are signified those who are filled with the knowledges of things true and good from the affection of knowing them. In David: The voice of Jehovah maketh the cedars of Lebanon "to skip like a *calf*," xxix. 6. By the cedars of Lebanon are signified the knowledges of truth; hence it is said that the voice of Jehovah makes them to skip like a calf: the voice of Jehovah is divine truth, here affecting them. The Egyptians being fond of the sciences, they made to themselves calves as a sign of their affection for them; but after they began to worship calves as gods, then they came to signify, in the Word, the affections of knowing falses; as in Jerem. xlvi. 20, 21; Psalm lxviii. 30; and in other places: therefore the same is signified by the calf which the children of Israel made in the wilderness, Exod. xxxii., as also by the calves of Samaria, 1 Kings xii. 28—32; Hosea viii. 5; x. 5; therefore it is said in Hosea: They make them a molten image of silver, sacrificing man, they "kiss the *calves*," xiii. 2. To make them a molten image of silver signifies to falsify truth, to sacrifice man signifies to destroy wisdom, and to kiss calves signifies to acknowledge falses from affection. In Isaiah: "There shall the *calf* feed, and there shall he lie down and consume the branches thereof," xxvii. 10. The same is signified by calf in Jerem. xxxiv. 18, 19. Since all divine worship is from the affections of truth and good, and thence from the knowledge of them, therefore sacrifices, in which the worship of the church among the children of Israel chiefly consisted, were made of various beasts, such as lambs, goats, kids, sheep, he-goats, calves, oxen; calves were

offered, because they signified the affection of knowing things true and good, which is the first natural affection. This is what was signified by sacrifices of calves, Exod. xxix. 11, 12; Levit. iv. 3, 13, and following verses; viii. 14, and following verses; ix. 2; xvi. 3; xxiii. 18; Numb. vii. 15, and following verses; xv. 24, xxviii. 19, 20; Judges vi. 25—29; 1 Sam. i. 25; xvi. 2; 1 Kings xviii. 23—26, 33. The second animal appeared like a calf, because the divine truth of the Word, which is signified by it, affects men's minds, and thus instructs and imbues.

243. *And the third animal had a face as a man*, signifies the divine truth of the Word as to its wisdom. By man, in the Word, is signified wisdom, because he is born that he may receive wisdom from the Lord, and become an angel; therefore in proportion as any one is wise, in the same proportion he is a man. Wisdom, truly human, consists in knowing that there is a God, what God is, and what is of God; this the divine truth of the Word teaches. That by man is signified wisdom, is plain from the following places: "I will make *man* more precious than fine gold; even a *man* than the gold wedge of Ophir," Isaiah xiii. 12. Man [vir homo] in the first instance, means intelligence, and man [homo] in the second means wisdom. "The inhabitants of the earth are burned, and few *men* left," Isaiah xxiv. 6. "I will sow the house of Israel and the house of Judah with the seed of *man* and with the seed of beast," Jerem. xxxi. 27. "And ye, my flock, are *men*, and I am your God," Ezek. xxxiv. 31. "The waste cities shall be filled with the flocks of *men*," Ezek. xxxvi. 38. "I beheld the earth, and lo, it was without form and void; and the heavens, and they had no light; I beheld, and lo, there was no *man*," Jerem. iv. 23, 25. "Let the *men* that sacrifice kiss the calves," Hosea xiii. 2. The wall of the holy Jerusalem measured "one hundred and forty-four cubits, the measure of a *man*, that is of the *angel*," Apoc. xxi. 17: besides many other places, in which by man is signified one that is wise, and, in an abstract sense, wisdom.

244. *And the fourth animal was like a flying eagle*, signifies the divine truth of the Word as to knowledge, and thence understanding. By eagles various things are signified, and by flying eagles are signified knowledges from which understanding is derived, because when they fly they both see and have a cognizance of things; for they have sharp and penetrating eyes, and by eyes are signified the understanding, n. 48, 214: by flying is signified to perceive and instruct, and, in the supreme sense, in which it has relation to the Lord, it signifies to foresee and provide. That eagles, in the Word, have such a signification, appears from these places: "They that wait for Jehovah shall renew their strength; they shall mount up with wings as *eagles*," Isaiah xl. 31. To mount up with wings as eagles, is to be elevated into knowledges of truth and goodness and thence

into intelligence. "Doth the *eagle* mount up at thy command, and make her nest on high, from thence she seeketh the prey, and her eyes behold afar off," Job xxxix. 26, 29. The faculty of knowing, understanding, and providing, is here described by the eagle, and that this is not derived from man's own intelligence. "Jehovah who satisfieth thy mouth with good things so that thy youth is renewed like the *eagles*," Psalm ciii. 5. To fill the mouth with good, is to give understanding by means of knowledges; hence a comparison is made with the eagle. "A great *eagle*, with great wings, long-winged, full of feathers— came unto Lebanon, and took the highest branch of the cedar; and it was planted in a fruitful field, and it grew; and there was also another *great eagle*, to which the vine did bend its roots," Ezek. xvii. 1—8. Here by two eagles are described the Jewish and Israelitish churches, both as to the knowledges of truth and consequent intelligence. But eagles in an opposite sense signify knowledges of what is false, whereby the understanding is perverted, as in Matt. xxiv. 28; Jerem. iv. 13; Habak. i. 8, 9; and other places.

245. *And the four animals had each of them six wings about him*, signifies the Word as to its powers and as to its defences. That by the four animals the Word is signified, was shown above; that by wings are signified powers, and also defences, will be seen below. By six is signified all as to truth and good, for six is composed of three and two multiplied by each other, and by three is signified all as to truth, n. 505, and by two all as to good, n. 762. By wings are signified powers, because by them birds lift themselves up, and wings with birds are in the place of arms with men, and by arms are signified powers. Since by wings are signified powers, and each animal had six wings, it is evident, from what has been said above, what kind of power is signified by the wings of each, viz., that by the wings of the lion is signified the power of fighting against evils and falses from hell; this power is of the divine truth of the Word from the Lord: that by the wings of the calf is signified the power of affecting men's minds, for the divine truth of the Word affects those who read it devoutly: that by the six wings of the man is signified the power of acquiring wisdom by discovering what God is, and what is of God, for this is, strictly speaking, man's object in reading the Word: and that by the wings of the eagle is signified the power of discerning what is true and good, and thereby of acquiring intelligence. Concerning the wings of the cherubims in Ezekiel, it is written: That their *wings* kissed each other, and that they also covered their bodies, and that under them there was the appearance of the likeness of hands, i. 23, 24; iii. 13; x. 5, 21. By kissing each other, is signified to act in conjunction and unanimously; by covering their bodies, is signified to defend the interior truths which be-

long to the spiritual sense of the Word from violation; and by the hands under their wings are signified powers. Concerning the seraphim, it is also said: That they had "six *wings;* with twain he covered his face, with twain he covered his feet, and with twain he did fly," Isaiah vi. 2. By seraphim in like manner is signified the Word, properly doctrine from the Word, and by the wings with which they covered their faces and feet, in like manner are signified defences, and by the wings with which they flew, powers, as above. That by flying is signified to perceive and instruct, and in a supreme sense to foresee and provide, is also evident from the following places: "And he rode on a *cherub,* and did *fly,* yea, he did fly upon the *wings* of the wind," Psalm xviii. 11; 2 Sam. xxii. 11. "And I saw another angel *fly* in the midst of heaven, having the everlasting gospel," Apoc. xiv. 6. That by wings are signified defences, is plain from the following places: Jehovah shall cover thee under his *wings,* Psalm xci. 4. To be hid under the shadow of God's *wings,* Psalm xvii. 8. To confide under the shadow of his *wings,* Psalm xxxvi. 7; Psalm lvii. 1; Psalm lxii. 7. "I stretched out my *wing* over thee, and covered thy nakedness," Ezek. xvi. 8. "Shall the Sun of Righteousness arise with healing in his *wings,*" Malachi iv. 2. "As an eagle stirreth up her nest, fluttereth over her young, spreadeth abroad her *wings,* beareth them on her *wings,* so the Lord alone did lead him," Deut. xxxii. 11, 12. Jesus said, "O Jerusalem,—how often would I have gathered thy children together, even as a hen gathereth her chickens under her *wings,*" Matt. xxiii. 37; Luke xiii. 34.

246. *And they were full of eyes within,* signifies the divine wisdom in the Word, in its natural sense derived from its spiritual and celestial sense. That by the animals full of eyes before and behind is signified the divine wisdom in the Word, may be seen above, n. 240; in like manner here, by their wings being full of eyes. And whereas the divine wisdom of the Word in its natural sense is derived from its spiritual and celestial sense, which is concealed within, it is therefore said, that within they were full of eyes. Concerning the spiritual and celestial sense, which are contained in every particular of the Word, see *The Doctrine of the New Jerusalem concerning the Sacred Scripture,* n. 5—26.

247. *And they rest not day and night, saying, Holy, holy, holy, Lord God Almighty,* signifies that the Word continually teaches of the Lord, and that he is the only God, and thence that he alone is to be worshipped. The animals not resting day and night, signifies that the Word continually, and without intermission, teaches; and that it teaches what the animals say, namely, Holy, holy, holy, Lord God Almighty, that is, that the Lord is the only God, and thence that he alone is to be worshipped; this is what is signified by holy three times repeated,

for triplication involves every thing holy in him alone. That a divine trinity is in the Lord, is fully shown in *The Doctrine of the New Jerusalem concerning the Lord*; as also that the Word treats of the Lord alone, and that thence is its sanctity. That the Lord alone is holy, may be seen above, n. 173.

248. *Who was, and who is, and who is to come*, signifies the Lord. That it is the Lord is plain from chap. i. 4, 8, 11, 17, where the Son of Man is treated of, which is the Lord as to the Word, and there it is expressly said, that "*He is Alpha and Omega, the beginning and the end, the first and the last, who is, and who was, and who is to come, the Almighty;*" but what is signified by these words, is explained, n. 13, 29, 30, 31, 38, 57; it is here shown that the Lord is understood by "Holy, holy, holy, Lord God Almighty, who was, and who is, and who is to come."

249. *And when these animals give glory, and honour, and thanks to Him that sat on the throne*, signifies that the Word ascribes all truth, and all good, and all worship to the Lord the Judge. The animals are the Word, as has been shown; glory and honour, when applied to the Lord, mean, that all truth and all good are his and from him; thanks signify the all of worship; he that sat on the throne signifies the Lord as to judgment, as above: hence it is evident, that by the animals giving glory, and honour, and thanks to Him that sat on the throne, is signified that the Word ascribes all truth, and all good, and all worship, to the Lord the Judge. By giving the Lord glory and honour, nothing else is meant in the Word but to acknowledge and confess that all truth and all good is from Him, thus that he is the God alone, for his glory is from divine truth, and his honour is from divine good. Such is the signification of glory and honour in the following places: "Jehovah made the heavens, *glory* and *honour* are before him," Psalm xcvi. 5, 6. "Jehovah is a very great God, thou hast clothed thyself with *glory* and *honour*," Psalm civ. 1. "The works of Jehovah are great, *glory* and *honour* are his work," Psalm cxi. 2, 3. "*Glory* and *honour* hast thou laid upon him, for thou hast made him most blessed for ever," Psalm xxi. 5, 6; speaking of the Lord. "Gird thy sword upon thy thigh, O most mighty, with thy *glory* and *honour*; and in thy majesty ride prosperously because of truth," Psalm xlv. 4, 5. "Thou hast made him a little lower than the angels, thou hast crowned him with *glory* and *honour*," Psalm viii. 6. "The *glory* of Lebanon is given unto it, the *honour* of Carmel and Sharon: they shall see the *glory* of Jehovah, and the *honour* of our God," Isaiah xxxv. 1, 2; these things refer to the Lord; besides other places, as Psalm cxlv. 4, 5, 12; Apoc. xxi. 24, 26. Moreover, when divine truth is treated of in the Word, it is called glory, n. 629, and when divine good is treated of it is called honour.

250. *Who liveth for ever and ever*, signifies the Lord who alone is life, and from whom alone is life eternal, as seen above, n. 58, 60.

251. *The four-and-twenty elders fall down before Him that sat on the throne, and worship Him that liveth for ever and ever*, signifies the humiliation of all in heaven before the Lord. That by the four-and-twenty elders are meant all who are of the Lord's church, may be seen above, n. 233; here all who are of his church in heaven; the elders, as heads, represented all. That humiliation before the Lord is denoted, and from that humiliation, adoration, is evident without explanation.

252. *And cast their crowns before the throne*, signifies an acknowledgment that their wisdom is from Him alone. That crown signifies wisdom, may be seen above, n. 189, 235; therefore by casting their crowns before the throne, is signified to acknowledge that wisdom is not their own, but of the Lord in them.

253. *Saying, Thou art worthy, O Lord, to receive glory, and honour, and power*, signifies a confession that the kingdom is the Lord's by merit and justice, because he is divine truth and divine good. Confession is signified by saying; merit and justice are signified by thou art worthy, O Lord; that He is divine truth and divine good, is signified by glory and honour, as above, n. 249; that His is the kingdom, is signified by receiving power: these, therefore, collected into one sense, signify a confession that the kingdom is the Lord's by merit and justice, because He is divine truth and divine good.

254. *For thou hast created all things, and by thy will they are, and were created*, signifies that all things of heaven and the church were made and formed, and men reformed and regenerated from the divine love of the Lord by his divine wisdom, or from his divine good by his divine truth, which also is the Word. Such is the spiritual sense of these words, because by creating, is signified to reform and regenerate by divine truth; and by the will of the Lord is signified the divine good: whether you call it the divine good and divine truth, or the divine love and divine wisdom, it is the same, because all good is of love, and all truth is of wisdom. That from the divine love and divine wisdom all things of heaven and the church, yea and the world itself was created, is abundantly set forth in *The Angelic Wisdom concerning the Divine Love and the Divine Wisdom*; also that love and good is of the will, and wisdom and truth of the understanding; hence it appears, that by the Lord's will is understood his divine good or divine love. That to create, in the Word, signifies to reform and regenerate, is plain from the following places: "*Create* in me a clean heart, O God, and renew a right spirit within me," Psalm li. 10. "Thou openest thine hand, they are filled with good; thou sendest forth thy

Spirit, they are *created*," Psalm civ. 28, 30. "The people which shall be *created*, shall praise Jehovah," Psalm cii. 10. "Behold, I *create* new heavens and a new earth, rejoice for ever in that which I *create*: behold, I *create* Jerusalem a rejoicing," Isaiah lxv. 17, 18. "Jehovah that *created* the heavens, he that spread out the earth, he that giveth breath unto the people upon it, and spirit to them that walk therein," Isaiah xlii. 5; xlv. 12, 18. "Thus saith Jehovah that *created* thee, O Jacob, and he that *formed* thee, O Israel; I have redeemed thee, I have called thee by my name:—every one that is called by my name, for I have *created* him for my glory," Isaiah xliii. 1, 7. They were prepared "in the day that thou wast *created*; thou wast perfect in thy ways in the day that thou wast *created*, till iniquity was found in thee," Ezek. xxviii. 13, 15; speaking of the king of Tyre, by whom are signified they who are in intelligence from divine truth. "That they may see, and know, and consider, and understand together that the hand of Jehovah hath done this, and the Holy One of Israel hath *created* it," Isaiah xli. 19, 20.

255. Here I shall add this Memorable Relation. Lest any one should enter into the spiritual sense of the Word, and pervert the genuine truth which pertains to that sense, there are placed guards by the Lord, which are understood by cherubims in the Word, which are the four animals here: that such a watch is placed, was thus represented to me. I was permitted to see certain large purses, which seemed like bags, containing in them a large quantity of silver; and as they were open, it was perceived as though any one might take the silver out of them, and even carry it off: but near to the purses there sat two angels as guards: the place where they were deposited appeared like a manger in a stable; in the next apartment were seen some modest virgins with a chaste wife; and near that apartment stood two little children, and it was said, that they were to be treated not as children but in wisdom: and afterwards there appeared a harlot, and also a dead horse. On seeing which I was instructed, that by these was represented the literal sense of the Word, in which is the spiritual sense. The large purses full of silver signified the knowledges of truth and good in great abundance: their being open, and yet guarded by angels, signified that any one might take from thence the knowledges of truth, but that care is taken lest any one should falsify the spiritual sense, in which were nothing but truths. The manger in the stable, in which the purses lay, signified spiritual instruction for the understanding; this is the signification of a manger, and the same is signified by the manger in which the Lord lay when an infant, because a horse, who eats out of it, signifies the understanding of the Word. The modest virgins, who were

seen in the adjoining apartment, signified affections of truth, and the chaste wife, the conjunction of good and truth. The children signified the innocence of wisdom in the Word; they were angels from the third heaven, who all appear like little children. The harlot with the dead horse signified the falsification of the Word by many at this day, by which all the understanding of truth perishes; a harlot signifies falsification, and a dead horse no understanding of truth.

It has been permitted me to converse with many after death, who thought they should shine like stars in heaven, because, as they said, they had held the Word as sacred, had read it frequently, and collected many things from it; by which they had confirmed the tenets of their faith, and were therefore celebrated as men of learning in the world, for which reason they thought they should be Michaels or Raphaels: but many of them were explored, in order to ascertain from what love they had studied the Word, and it was found, that some had studied it from self-love, that they might appear great in the world, and be reverenced as heads of the church; but others from the love of the world, that they might acquire riches. When they were examined as to what they knew of the Word, it was found, that they knew nothing of genuine truth therefrom, but only such as is called truth falsified, which in itself is false, and this, in the spiritual world, is perceived as a stench by the angels; and it was told them that this befel them from their loving themselves and the world as ends, and not the Lord and heaven; and when self-love and the world are ends, then, when they read the Word, their mind dwells upon self and the world, and therefore they think constantly from their own selfhood, which is in darkness as to all things of heaven; in which state man cannot be abstracted from his own light, and so elevated into the light of heaven, nor thence receive any influx from the Lord through heaven. I also saw them admitted into heaven, and when they were found to be without truths, they were stripped of their garments and appeared in their nakedness and they who had falsified truths, were, by reason of their offensive smell, expelled, but still their pride remained with them, and a belief in their own merit. It was different with those who had studied the Word from the affection of knowing truth because it is truth, and is subservient to the uses of spiritual life, not only to a man's self, but also to his neighbour; these I saw taken up into heaven, and thus into the light, in which the divine truth is, and at the same time exalted to angelic wisdom and its felicity, which is life eternal.

CHAPTER V.

1. And I saw in the right hand of Him that sat on the throne, a book written within and on the back-side, sealed with seven seals.

2. And I saw a strong angel proclaiming with a loud voice, Who is worthy to open the Book, and to loose the seals thereof?

3. And no one in heaven, nor in earth, neither under the earth, was able to open the Book, neither to look thereon.

4. And I wept much because no one was found worthy to open and to read the Book, neither to look thereon.

5. And one of the elders saith unto me, Weep not; behold, the Lion which is of the tribe of Judah, the Root of David, hath prevailed to open the Book, and to loose the seven seals thereof.

6. And I beheld, and, lo, in the midst of the throne and of the four animals, and in the midst of the elders, stood a LAMB, as it had been slain, having seven horns and seven eyes, which are the seven spirits of God sent forth into all the earth.

7. And he came and took the Book out of the right hand of Him that sat upon the throne.

8. And when he had taken the Book, the four animals, and the four-and-twenty elders, fell down before the LAMB, having every one of them harps, and golden vials full of incense, which are the prayers of the saints.

9. And they sung a new song, saying, Thou art worthy to take the Book, and to open the seals thereof: for thou wast slain, and hast redeemed us to God by thy blood, out of every tribe, and tongue, and people, and nation;

10. And hast made us unto our God kings and priests: and we shall reign on the earth.

11. And I beheld, and I heard the voice of many angels round about the throne, and the animals, and the elders: and the number of them was myriads of myriads, and thousands of thousands;

12. Saying with a loud voice, Worthy is the LAMB that was slain to receive power, and riches, and wisdom, and honour, and glory, and blessing.

13. And every creature which is in heaven, and on the earth, and under the earth, and such as are in the sea, and all that are in them, heard I saying, Blessing, and honour, and glory, and power, be unto Him that sitteth upon the throne, and unto the Lamb, for ever and ever.

14. And the four animals said, Amen. And the four-and-twenty elders fell down, and worshipped Him that liveth for ever and ever.

THE SPIRITUAL SENSE.

The Contents of the whole Chapter. That the Lord in his Divine Humanity will execute judgment out of the Word and according to it, because he is himself the Word; and that this is acknowledged by all in the three heavens.

The Contents of each Verse. V. 1, "And I saw in the right hand of Him that sat on the throne, a Book written within and on the back-side," signifies the Lord as to his divinity from eternity, who is omnipotent and omniscient, and who is the Word: "Sealed with seven seals," signifies that it is entirely hid from angels and men: v. 2, "And I saw a strong angel proclaiming with a loud voice," signifies divine truth from the Lord most interiorly influencing both angels and men: "Who is worthy to open the Book, and to loose the seals thereof?" signifies, who has power to know the states of life of all in the heavens and on the earths, and to judge every one according thereto: v. 3, "And no one in heaven, nor in earth, neither under the earth, was able," signifies that no one in the superior heavens or inferior heavens was able: "To open the Book," signifies to know the states of the life of all, and to judge every one according thereto: "Neither to look thereon," signifies not in the least: v. 4, "And I wept much because no one was found worthy to open and read the Book, neither to look thereon," signifies grief of heart, because if no one could do it, all must perish: v. 5, "And one of the elders saith unto me, Weep not," signifies consolation: "Behold, the lion which is of the tribe of Judah, the Root of David, hath prevailed," signifies the Lord, who by his own power subdued the hells and reduced all things to order when he was in the world, by the divine good united to the divine truth in his Humanity: "To open the Book and to loose the seven seals thereof," signifies here as before: v. 6, "And I beheld, and, lo, in the midst of the throne, and of the four animals, and in the midst of the elders," signifies from the inmost and thence in all things of heaven, the Word, and the church: "Stood a Lamb, as it had been slain," signifies the Lord as to his Humanity, not acknowledged in the church to be divine: "Having seven horns," signifies his omnipotence: "And seven eyes," signifies his omniscience and divine wisdom: "Which are the seven spirits of God sent forth into all the earth," signifies that from divine wisdom is derived divine truth throughout the whole world, wheresoever there is any religion: v. 7, "And he came and took the Book out of the right hand of Him that sat upon the throne," signifies that the Lord as to his Divine Humanity is the Word, and this by virtue of the divinity within him, and that therefore he will execute judgment from his Divine Humanity: v. 8, "And when he had taken the Book," signifies when the Lord appointed to execute the judgment, and thereby to reduce all things in the heavens and upon the earths to order: "The four animals and the four-and-twenty elders fell down before the LAMB," signifies humiliation and adoration of the Lord from the superior heavens: "Having every one of them harps," signifies a confession of the Lord's Divine Humanity from spiritual truths: "And golden vials full of incense," signifies confession of the Lord's Divine Humanity from spiritual good: "Which are the prayers of saints," signifies thoughts which are of faith grounded in affections which are of charity with those who worship the Lord from spiritual good and truth: v. 9, "And they sung a new song," signifies an acknowledgment and glorification of the Lord, that he alone is the Judge, Redeemer, and Saviour, thus the God of heaven and earth: "Saying, Thou art worthy to take the Book, and to open the seals thereof," signifies here as before: "For thou wast slain, and hast redeemed us to God by thy blood," signifies deliverance from hell and salvation by conjunction with him: "Out of every tribe, and tongue, and people, and nation," signifies that they in the church, or in any religion, who are in truths as to doctrine, and in good as to life, are redeemed by the Lord: v. 10, "And hast made us unto our God kings and priests," signifies that from the Lord they are in wisdom from divine truths and in love from divine good: "And we shall reign on the earth," signifies, and will be in his kingdom, he in them and they in him: v. 11, "And I beheld, and I heard the voice of many angels round about the throne, and the animals, and the elders," signifies a confession and glorification of the Lord by the angels of the inferior heavens: "And the number of them was myriads of myriads," signifies all in truths and good: v. 12, "Saying with a loud voice, Worthy is the LAMB that was slain to receive power, and riches, and wisdom, and honour, and glory," signifies confession from the heart, that to the Lord as to his Divine Humanity belong omnipotence, omniscience, divine good, and divine truth: "And blessing," signifies all these in him, and from him in them: v. 13, "And every creature which is in heaven, and on the earth, and under the earth, and such as are in the sea, and all that are in them, heard I saying," signifies confession and glorification of the Lord by the angels of the lowest heaven: "Blessing, and honour, and glory, and power, be unto Him that sitteth upon the throne, and unto the Lamb for ever and ever," signifies that in the Lord from eternity, and thence in his Divine Humanity, is the All of heaven and the church, divine good, and divine truth, and divine power, and from him in them: v. 14, "And the four animals said, Amen," signifies divine confirmation from the Word: "And the four-and-twenty elders fell down and worshipped Him that liveth for ever and ever," signifies humiliation before the Lord, and, from humiliation, adoration of him, by all in the heavens, from whom and in whom is everlasting life.

THE EXPLANATION.

256. *And I saw in the right hand of Him that sat on the throne a Book, written within and on the back-side*, signifies the Lord as to his divinity from eternity, who is omnipotent and omniscient, and who is the Word; who also knows from him self the state of the life of all in the heavens and on the earths, as well in general as in every particular. By Him that sat on the throne is meant the Lord as to his divinity, from which his Humanity was derived, for it follows that the Lamb took the right hand of him that sat on the throne, verse 7, and by the Lamb is meant the Lord as to the Divine Humanity; by the Book written within and on the back-side is meant the Word in every particular and in every general respect; by within, in every particular respect, and by on the back-side, in every general respect: by within and on the back-side is also meant the interior sense of the Word, which is its spiritual sense, and its exterior sense, which is its natural sense; by right hand is himself as to his omnipotence and omniscience, because the exploration of all in the heavens and on the earths, upon whom judgment is to be executed, and their separation, is treated of. The Lord, as the Word, knows the states of life of all in the heavens and on the earths from himself, because he is divine truth itself, and divine truth itself knows all things from itself; but this is an arcanum, which is revealed in *The Angelic Wisdom concerning the Divine Love and the Divine Wisdom.* That the Lord as to his divinity from eternity was the Word, that is, divine truth, is evident from these words in John: "In the beginning was the *Word*, and the *Word* was with God, and *God was the Word*," i. 1; and that the Lord as to his Humanity also was made the Word, in the same evangelist: "And the *Word* was made flesh," i. 14. Hence it may appear what is meant by the Book being in the right hand of Him that sat on the throne, and by the Lamb taking it thence, verse 7. Since the Lord is the Word, and the Word is divine truth, which in common constitutes heaven and the church, and in particular each angel, that heaven may be in him, and man, that the church may be in him, and because the Word is here meant by the Book, out of which and according to which all were to be judged, therefore in many places occur these expressions, to be written in the Book, to be judged out of the Book, to be blotted out of the Book, where the state of any one's eternal

life is treated of, as in these places: The Ancient of Days did sit in judgment, "and the *books* were opened," Dan. vii. 10. Every people shall be delivered that "shall be found written in the *Book*," Dan. xii. 1. "My substance was not hid from thee, and in thy *book* all my members are written," Psalm cxxxix. 15, 16. Moses said, "*Blot me*, I pray thee, out of thy *book* which thou hast written. And Jehovah said unto Moses, Whosoever hath sinned against me will I *blot out of my book*," Exod. xxxii. 32, 33. "Let them be *blotted out* of thy *book* of the living, and not be written with the righteous," Psalm lxix. 28. "I saw that the *books* were opened, and another *book* was opened, which is the *book of life*, and the dead were judged out of those things which were written in the *book* according to their works, and whosoever was not found written in the *book of life*, was cast into the lake of fire," Apoc. xx. 12—14. There shall none enter into the New Jerusalem, but such as are "written in the Lamb's *book of life*," Apoc. xxi. 27. All shall worship the beast "whose names are not written in the Lamb's *book of life*," Apoc. xiii. 8; xvii. 8. That by the Book is understood the Word, may be seen in David: "In the *Volume of the Book* it is written of me," Psalm xl. 7; and Ezekiel: "I looked, and behold a hand was put forth unto me, and in it was a *roll of a Book*, written within and without," ii. 9, 10. The *Book* of the Words of Isaiah, Luke iii. 4. The *Book* of Psalms, Luke xx. 42.

257. *Sealed with seven seals*, signifies entirely hid from angels and men. That to be sealed with a seal signifies to be hid, is evident, hence to be sealed with seven seals signifies to be entirely or totally hid, for seven signifies all, n. 10, and therefore totally; that it was entirely hid from angels and men, is presently said in these words: "And no one in heaven, nor on earth, neither under the earth, was able to open and read the *Book*, neither to look thereon," verse 3, 4. Such is the Word to all to whom the Lamb, that is, the Lord, does not open it: but as the exploration of all before the last judgment is here treated of, it means the states of life of all both in general and in particular, which are entirely hid.

258. *And I saw a strong angel proclaiming with a loud voice*, signifies divine truth from the Lord most interiorly influencing the thoughts of angels and men, and searching them. By an angel proclaiming, is understood, in the spiritual sense, the Lord, because an angel does not preach and teach from himself, but from the Lord, but still as from himself. It is said a strong angel, to denote his acting with power, and that which is proclaimed with power penetrates deeply into the thought; a loud or great voice signifies divine truth from the Lord in its power or virtue: it signifies, also, diligent searching, because he asks, "Who is worthy to open the Book?" as now follows.

259. *Who is worthy to open the Book and to loose the seals*

thereof? signifies who has power to know the states of life of all in the heavens and on the earths, and to judge every one according thereto. "Who is worthy," signifies who is able or who has the power; "to open the Book and to loose the seals thereof," signifies here to know the states of life of all in the heavens and on the earths, and also to judge every one according to his state; for when the Book is opened, there is an examination into their quality, and then sentence or judgment is pronounced, comparatively as a judge does with a book of laws and acts from it. That by opening the Book, is signified a search into the quality of the states of life in all and every one, is evident from the following chapter, where is described what was seen, when the Lamb opened the seven seals in their order.

260. *And no one in heaven, nor in earth, neither under the earth, was able,* signifies that no one in the superior heavens or inferior heavens was able. In heaven, in earth, neither under the earth, mean in the superior and inferior heavens, in like manner as in the 13th verse, where it is said, "And every creature which is *in heaven, and on the earth, and under the earth,* and such as are in the sea, and all that are in them, heard I saying." Since he heard them all speaking, it is evident that they were angels and spirits who spake; for John was in the spirit, as he himself says in the preceding chapter (iv. verse 2), in which state no other earth appeared to him but the earth of the spiritual world; for there are earths there as well as in the natural world, as may appear from the description of that world in the work concerning *Heaven and Hell;* as also in *The Continuation concerning the Spiritual World,* n. 32—38. The superior heavens appear there upon mountains and hills, the inferior heavens in the earth beneath, and the ultimate heavens as it were under the earth; for the heavens are expanses, one above another, and each expanse is like the earth under the feet of those who are there: the uppermost expanse is like the top of a mountain, the next expanse is under it, but extending itself further on all sides round about, and the lowest expanse is still more extensive; and since this last is under the other, they who are there are under the earth. The three heavens also appear thus to the angels who are in the superior heavens, because to them there appear two heavens beneath them; in like manner they appeared to John, because he was with them, for he had ascended to them, as is evident from chap. iv. verse 1, where it is said, "Come up hither, and I will show thee things which must be hereafter." Such as are ignorant of the spiritual world and the earths there, can by no means know what is meant by under the earth, nor by the lower parts of the earth, in the Word, as in Isaiah: "Sing, O ye heavens, shout, ye *lower parts of the earth,* break forth into singing, ye mountains, for Jehovah hath redeemed Jacob," xliv. 23; and in other places. Who does

not see, that the earths of the spiritual world are here meant? for no man lives under the earth in the natural world.

261. *To open the Book*, signifies to know the states of the life of all, and to judge every one according thereto, as appears from the explanation above, n. 259.

262. *Neither to look thereon*, signifies not in the least. Since by opening the Book, is signified to know the states of the life of all, by looking on it is signified to see what the state of life of this or that person is, therefore by no one being able to open the Book nor to look thereon, is signified that they were not able in the least; for the Lord alone sees the state of every one from inmost to outmost, as also what a man has been from infancy to old age, and what he will be to eternity, and likewise what place he will have either in heaven or in hell; and this the Lord sees in an instant, and from himself, because he is the divine truth itself or the Word; but angels and men do not see this in the least, because they are finite, and the finite see only a few things, and those only external, and not these indeed from themselves, but from the Lord.

263. *And I wept much because no one was found worthy to open and read the Book, neither to look thereon*, signifies grief of heart, because if no one could do it, all must perish. That to weep much is to grieve at heart, is evident; the reason why he grieved at heart, was, because if this could not have been done, all must have perished; for if all things in the heavens and on the earths were not reduced to order by the last judgment, it could not be otherwise; for the Apocalypse treats of the last state of the church, when it comes to its end, the nature of which state is described by the Lord in these words: "For then shall be great tribulation, such as was not from the beginning of the world to this time, no, nor ever shall be; and except those days should be shortened, there should no flesh be saved," Matt. xxiv. 21, 22; speaking of the last time of the church, when judgment takes place. That such is the state of the church at this day, may be known solely from these considerations, that the greatest part of the Christian world is occupied by those who have transferred to themselves the divine power of the Lord, and would fain be worshipped as gods, and who invoke dead men, and scarce any of them the Lord; and that the rest of the church make God three, and the Lord two, and place salvation, not in amendment of life, but in certain words breathed out in a devout tone of voice; consequently not in repentance, but in a confidence that they are justified and sanctified, provided they do but fold their hands and look upwards, and utter some customary form of prayer.

264. *And one of the elders saith unto me, Weep not;* that this signifies consolation, is evident.

265. *Behold, the Lion hath prevailed*, signifies the Lord,

who by his own power subdued the hells, and reduced all things to order when he was in the world. That a lion signifies the divine truth of the Word as to its power, may be seen above, n. 241; and because the Lord is divine truth itself or the Word, he is called a Lion. That the Lord, when he was in the world, subdued the hells and reduced all things in the heavens to order, and likewise glorified his Humanity, may be seen above, n. 67; and how he did this, may be seen in *The Doctrine of the New Jerusalem concerning the Lord*, n. 12—14: hence it is evident, what is meant by " the Lion hath prevailed."

266. *Which is of the tribe of Judah, the Root of David*, signifies by the divine good united to the divine truth in his Humanity. By Judah, in the Word, is meant the church which is in the good of love to the Lord, and in a supreme sense the Lord as to the divine good of divine love; and by David is meant the Lord as to the divine truth of divine wisdom: that this is meant by David, may be seen in *The Doctrine of the New Jerusalem concerning the Lord*, n. 43, 48; and that the former is meant by Judah, may be seen, n. 96, 266, 350; hence it appears that by " Behold the Lion which is of the tribe of Judah, the Root of David, hath prevailed," is signified that the Lord overcame the hells and reduced all things to order by the divine good united to the divine truth in his Humanity. That this is the sense of these words, cannot be seen from the letter, but only that he it was who was born in the world of the tribe of Judah and lineage of David; still, however, these words contain in them a spiritual sense, in which by the names of persons are understood things, as has frequently been observed above, thus by Judah is not meant Judah, nor by David, David; but by Judah, the Lord as to divine good, and by David, the Lord as to divine truth; on this account the sense of this passage is as has been stated. The reason why this sense is here explained, is, because the Apocalypse as to its spiritual sense is now unfolded.

267. *To open the Book, and loose the seven seals thereof*, signifies to know the states of the life of all in the heavens and on the earths, and to judge every one according thereto, as above, n. 258, 259.

268. *And I beheld, and lo, in the midst of the throne, and of the four animals, and in the midst of the elders*, signifies from the inmost and thence in all things of heaven, the Word, and the church. In the midst signifies in the inmost, and thence in all things, n. 44; a throne signifies heaven, n. 14; the four animals or cherubs signify the Word, n. 239; and the four-and-twenty elders signify the church as to all things belonging thereto, n. 233, 251; from which it follows, that, in the midst of the throne, and of the four animals, and in the midst of the elders, signifies from the inmost in all things of heaven, the Word, and the church.

269. *Stood a Lamb standing as it had been slain*, signifies the Lord as to his Humanity, not acknowledged in the church to be divine. By Lamb, in the Apocalypse, is meant the Lord as to the Divine Humanity, and by a Lamb slain, is denoted that his Humanity is not acknowledged in the church to be divine; in like manner as in chap. i. verse 18, where it is said, "I *was made dead*, and behold I am alive for ever and ever;" by which is meant that the Lord is neglected in the church, and his Humanity not acknowledged to be divine, n. 59: that this is the case, may be seen below, n. 294. Since, therefore, the Lord as to the Divine Humanity is meant by the Lamb, and it is said of him, that he took the Book out of the right hand of Him that sat upon the throne, and afterwards that he opened it, and loosed the seven seals thereof, and since no mortal could do this, but God alone, it follows, that by the Lamb is meant the Lord as to the Divine Humanity, and by his being slain, that he is not acknowledged to be God as to his Humanity.

270. *Having seven horns*, signifies his omnipotence. A horn is frequently mentioned in the Word, and by it is everywhere signified power; therefore when a horn is predicated of the Lord, it signifies omnipotence. The reason why seven horns are mentioned, is, because seven signifies all, n. 10, thus omnipotence. That a horn signifies power, and when applied to the Lord, omnipotence, may appear from the following passages: "Ye which rejoice in a thing of naught, which say, Have we not taken to us *horns* by our own strength?" Amos vi. 13. I said unto the wicked, "Lift not up the *horn*, lift not up your *horn* on high: All the *horns* of the wicked will I cut off; but the *horns* of the righteous shall be exalted," Psalm lxxv. 4, 5, 10. Jehovah hath "set up the *horn* of thine adversaries," Lament. ii. 1. "The *horn* of Moab is cut off, and his arm is broken," Jerem. xlviii. 25. "Because ye have thrust with side and with shoulder, and push all the diseased [sheep] with your horns," Ezek. xxxiv. 21. Jehovah hath "exalted the *horn* of his people," Psalm cxlviii. 14. Jehovah the God of hosts is "the glory of our strength, and in his favour our *horn* shall be exalted," Psalm lxxxix. 17. The brightness of Jehovah God shall be as the light, "he had *horns* coming out of his hand, and there was the hiding of his power," Hab. iii. 4. "Mine arm also shall strengthen him— and in my name shall his *horn* be exalted," Psalm lxxxix. 21, 22, 24. "Jehovah is my strength, my rock, my *horn*," Psalm xviii. 2, 3; 2 Sam. xxii. 3. "Arise, O daughter of Zion, for I will make thine *horn* iron, and thou shalt beat in pieces many people," Micah iv. 13. Jehovah hath destroyed in his wrath "the strongholds of the daughter of Judah, and hath cut off all the *horn* of Israel," Lament. ii. 3. Powers are also signified by the "*horns* of the dragon," Apoc. xii. 3; by the *horns* of "the beast which came up out of the sea," Apoc. xiii. 1; by the *horns*

of the scarlet beast upon which the woman sat, Apoc. xvii. 3, 7, 12; by the *horns* of the ram and the he-goat, Dan. viii. 3, 4, 5, 7—12, 21, 25; by the *horns* of the beast which came up out of the sea, Dan. vii. 3, 7, 8, 20, 21, 23, 24; by the four *horns* which scattered Judah and Israel, Zech. i. 18; by the *horns* of the altar of burnt-offerings, and the altar of incense, Exod. xxvii. 2; xxx. 2, 3, 10: by these last was signified the power of divine truth in the church; and, on the other hand, that that power would perish, is signified by the *horns* of the altars in Bethel, Amos iii. 14: "I shall visit the transgressions of Israel, I will also visit the altars of Bethel, and the *horns* of the altar shall be cut off, and fall to the ground."

271. *And seven eyes*, signifies his omniscience and divine wisdom. That eyes, when spoken of the Lord, signify his divine wisdom, may be seen above, n. 48, 125, thus also his omniscience; and that seven signifies all, and is predicated of any thing holy, n. 10; hence by the seven eyes of the Lamb, is signified the divine wisdom of the Lord, which is also omniscience.

272. *Which are the seven spirits of God sent forth into all the earth*, signifies that from divine wisdom is derived divine truth throughout the whole world, wheresoever there is any religion. The seven spirits of God are the divine truth proceeding from the Lord as above, n. 14, 155. That being sent forth into all the earth, means throughout the whole world wheresoever there is any religion, is evident; for where there is any religion, mankind is taught that there is a God, and that there is a devil, and that God is good itself, and that all good is from him, and that the devil is evil itself, and that all evil is from him; and, as they are opposites, so evil, being from the devil, is to be shunned, and good, being from God, is to be done; consequently, in proportion as any one does evil, so far he loves the devil, and acts against God. Such divine truth exists throughout the whole world where there is any religion; so that it is only necessary to know what evil is, and this also is known by all who have any religion; for the precepts of every religion are similar to those contained in the decalogue, viz., that it is not lawful to kill, nor to commit adultery, nor to steal, nor to bear false witness. These are in general divine truths sent forth from the Lord into all the earth, see *The Doctrine of the New Jerusalem concerning the Sacred Scripture*, n. 101—118: therefore he who lives according to them on account of their being divine truths, or the commandments of God, and thence of religion, is saved; but he who only lives according to them because they are civil and moral truths, is not saved, for he that denies God may also so live, but not he that confesses God.

273. *And he came and took the Book out of the right hand of Him that sat upon the throne*, signifies that the Lord as to his Divine Humanity is the Word, and this by virtue of the divin-

ity within him, and that therefore he will execute judgment from his Divine Humanity. Here it manifestly appears, that He that sat upon the throne and the Lamb are one person, and that by Him that sat upon the throne is meant his divine principle whence are all things, and by the Lamb, his Divine Humanity; for it is said in the preceding verse, that he saw a Lamb standing in the midst of the throne, and in this, that he took the Book from Him that sat upon the throne. That the Lord will execute judgment from his Divine Humanity, because he is the Word, is evident from these passages: "And then shall appear the sign of the *Son of Man;* and they shall see the *Son of Man* coming in the clouds of heaven with power and glory," Matt. xxiv. 30. "When the *Son of Man* shall sit on his throne judging the twelve tribes of Israel," Matt. xix. 28. "The *Son of Man* shall come in the glory of his Father, and then shall he reward every man according to his works," Matt. xvi. 27. "Watch ye, therefore, and pray always, that ye may be accounted worthy to stand before the *Son of Man,*" Luke xxi. 36. "In such an hour as ye think not, the *Son of Man* cometh," Matt. xxiv. 44. "For the Father judgeth no man, but hath committed all judgment unto the *Son,*—because he is the *Son of Man,*" John v. 22, 27. The Son of Man is the Lord as to the Divine Humanity, and this is the Word, which was God, and was made flesh, John i. 1, 14.

274. *And when he had taken the Book,* signifies when the Lord appointed to execute the judgment, and thereby to reduce all things in the heavens and in the earths to order. By taking the Book and opening it, is signified to explore the states of life of all, and to judge every one according thereto, as above; therefore here by his taking the Book, is signified to be about to execute the last judgment; and as the last judgment is executed for the purpose of reducing all things to order in the heavens, and by the heavens, in the earths, this also is signified.

275. *The four animals and the four-and-twenty elders fell down before the Lamb,* signifies humiliation, and from humiliation, adoration of the Lord from the superior heavens. Now follows the glorification of the Lord on the above account, for, as was observed above, n. 263, did not the Lord accomplish the last judgment at this time, and thereby reduce all things in the heavens and in the earths to order, all would perish. The glorification of the Lord, which now follows, takes place first in the superior heavens, afterwards in the inferior heavens, and lastly in the lowest heavens; the glorification by the superior heavens, verses 8, 9, 10, by the inferior heavens, verses 11, 12, and by the lowest heavens, verse 13, and lastly confirmation and adoration by the superior heavens, verse 14. Therefore the superior heavens are signified by the four animals and the four-and-twenty elders; for by the cherubs, who are the four ani-

mals "in the midst of the throne," is signified the Lord as to the Word, but by the cherubs, or four animals "round about the throne," is signified heaven as to the Word; for it is said, "That in the midst of the throne, and round about the throne, were seen four animals, full of eyes before and behind," iv. 6; for the heavens are heavens by virtue of the reception of divine truth through the Word from the Lord. By the four-and-twenty elders are also signified the angels in the superior heavens, because those elders were proximately about the throne, iv. 4. That to fall down before the Lamb denotes humiliation, and, from humiliation, adoration, is evident.

276. *Having every one of them harps*, signifies a confession of the Lord's Divine Humanity from spiritual truths. It is well known that confessions of Jehovah were made in the temple at Jerusalem by singing, and at the same time by instruments of music, which corresponded; the instruments were principally trumpets and timbrels, and psalteries and harps; the trumpets and timbrels corresponded to celestial goods and truths, and the psalteries and harps to spiritual goods and truths; the correspondences were with their sounds. What celestial good and truth is, and what spiritual good and truth, may be seen in the work concerning *Heaven and Hell*, n. 13—19, and 20, 28. That harps signify confessions of the Lord from spiritual truths, may appear from these passages: "Praise Jehovah with the *harp*, sing unto him with the psaltery, and an instrument of ten strings," Psalm xxxiii. 2, 3. "I will praise thee on the *harp*, O God, my God," Psalm xliii. 3, 4. "I will also praise thee with the psaltery, I will sing unto thee with the *harp*, O thou Holy One of Israel," Psalm lxxi. 22. "Awake psaltery and *harp*, I will sing unto thee among the nations, O Lord," Psalm lvii. 8, 9; Psalm cviii. 2, 3. "Sing unto Jehovah with thanksgiving, sing praise upon the *harp* unto our God," Psalm cxlvii. 7. "It is a good thing to give thanks to Jehovah—upon the psaltery, and upon the *harp* with a solemn sound," Psalm xcii. 2—4. "Make a joyful noise unto Jehovah, all the earth, sing unto Jehovah with the *harp*, with the *harp* and the voice of a psalm," Psalm xcviii. 4—6: and in many other places; as Psalm xliii. 4; Psalm cxxxvii. 2; Job xxx. 31; Isaiah xxiv. 7—9; xxx. 31, 32; Apoc. xiv. 2, xviii. 22. Because the harp corresponded to confession of the Lord, and evil spirits could not endure it, therefore David by the *harp* caused the evil spirit to depart from Saul, 1 Sam. xvi. 14—16, 23. That they were not harps, but that confessions of the Lord were heard by John as harps, may be seen below, n. 661.

277. *And golden vials full of incense*, signifies confession of the Lord's Divine Humanity from spiritual good. The reason why incense signifies worship from spiritual goods, but in this instance confession from such goods, is, because the principal worship in the Jewish and Israelitish church consisted in the

offering of sacrifices and incense; wherefore there were two altars, one for sacrifices and the other for incense; the latter altar was within the tabernacle, and was called the golden altar, but the former was without the tabernacle, and was called the altar of burnt offerings; the reason was, because there are two kinds of good, from which all worship exists, celestial good and spiritual good; celestial good is the good of love to the Lord, and spiritual good is the good of love towards our neighbour; worship by sacrifices was worship from celestial good, and worship by incense was worship from spiritual good. Whether you call it worship or confession, it amounts to the same thing, for all worship is confession. What is signified by incense, is also signified by the vials in which the incense is contained, because the thing containing and the thing contained, like the instrumental and principal, act as one cause. Worship from spiritual good is signified by incense in the following places: "For from the rising of the sun even unto the going down of the same, my name shall be great among the Gentiles, and in every place *incense* shall be offered unto my name," Malachi i. 11. "They shall teach Jacob thy judgments, and Israel thy law: they shall put *incense* before thee, and whole burnt sacrifice upon thine altar," Deut. xxxiii. 10. "I will offer unto thee burnt-sacrifices of fatlings, with the *incense* of rams," Psalm lxvi. 13, 15. "And they shall come from the cities of Judah, bringing burnt-offerings, and sacrifices, and meat offerings, and *incense*," Jerem. xvii. 26. "All they from Sheba shall come; they shall bring gold and *incense*, and they shall show forth the praises of Jehovah," Isaiah lx. 6. By frankincense the same is signified as by incense, because frankincense was the principal aromatic used in offering incense. Therefore it is said in Matthew, that the wise men from the east opened their treasures, and offered to the Lord, then an infant, "gold, *frankincense*, and myrrh," ii. 11. The reason why they offered these three, was, because gold signified celestial good, frankincense spiritual good, and myrrh natural good, and from those three goods all worship is derived.

278. *Which are the prayers of saints*, signifies thoughts which are of faith, grounded in affections which are of charity, with those who worship the Lord from spiritual good and truth. By prayers are meant the things which are of faith, and at the same time the things which are of charity, with those who pour forth prayers, because prayers without such things are not prayers, but empty sounds. That saints mean those who are in spiritual goods and truths, may be seen above, n. 173. The reason why incense is called the prayers of saints, is, because fragrant odours correspond to affections of good and truth; hence it is, that "a grateful odour or sweet savour," and an "odour of rest to Jehovah," so often occur in the Word; as in Exod. xxix. 10, 25, 41; Levit. i. 9, 13, 17; ii. 2, 9, 10; iii. 5;

iv. 31; vi. 8, 15; viii. 28; xxiii. 8, 13, 18; xxvi. 31; Numb. xv. 7; xxix. 2, 6, 8, 13, 36; Ezek. xx. 41; Hosea xiv. 7. Prayers which are called incense have a similar signification in the following places in the Apocalypse: An angel stood at the altar having a golden vial, " and there was given unto him much *incense*, that he should offer it with the *prayers of all saints* upon the golden altar:—And the smoke *of* the *incense, with the prayers of the saints*, ascended up before God out of the angel's hand," viii. 3—5: and in the Psalms of David: " Give ear unto my voice; let my *prayer* be set forth before thee as *incense*," cxli. 1, 2.

279. *And they sung a new song*, signifies an acknowledgment and glorification of the Lord, that he alone is the Judge, Redeemer, and Saviour, thus the God of heaven and earth. These things are contained in the song which they sung, and the things which are contained are also signified; as an acknowledgment that the Lord is the Judge in this: "Thou art worthy to take the Book, and to open the seals thereof:" that he is the Redeemer, in this: "Because thou wast slain, and hast redeemed us in thy blood:" that he is the Saviour, in this: "Thou hast made us unto our God kings and priests, and we shall reign upon the earth:" that he is the God of heaven and earth, in this: "They fell down and worshipped him that liveth for ever and ever," verse 14. Since the acknowledgment of the Lord alone as the God of heaven and earth, and of the Divinity of his Humanity, and that in no other way could he be called a Redeemer and Saviour, was not before in the church, it is therefore denominated a new song. The reason why a song also signifies glorification, which is confession from joy of heart, is, because singing exalts, and causes affection to break out from the heart into sound, and show itself intensely in its life. Nor are the Psalms of David any other than songs; for they were set to music and sung, and therefore were also called songs in many places; as in Psalm xviii. 1; Psalm xxxiii. 1, 2; Psalm xlv. 1; Psalm xlvi. 1; Psalm xlviii. 1; Psalm lxv. 1; Psalm lxvi. 1; Psalm lxvii. 1; Psalm lxviii. 1; Psalm lxxv. 1; Psalm lxxxi. 1; Psalm lxxxvii. 1; Psalm lxxxviii. 1; Psalm xcii. 1; Psalm xcvi. 1; Psalm xcviii. 1; Psalm cviii. 1; Psalm cxx. 1; Psalm cxxi. 1; Psalm cxxii. 1; Psalm cxxiii. 1; Psalm cxxiv. 1; Psalm cxxv. 1; Psalm cxxvi. 1; Psalm cxxvii. 1; Psalm cxxviii. 1; Psalm cxxix. 1; Psalm cxxx. 1; Psalm cxxxii. 1; Psalm cxxxiii. 1; Psalm cxxxiv. 1. That songs were used for the sake of exalting the life of love, and the joy derived from it, is evident from the following passages: " O *sing* unto Jehovah a new *song*, make a joyful noise unto Jehovah all the earth, make a loud noise and rejoice," Psalm xcviii. 1, 4—8. "*Sing* unto Jehovah a new *song*,—let Israel rejoice in Him that made him, let them praise his name in the dance," Psalm cxlix.

1—3. "*Sing* unto Jehovah a new *song*,—lift up the voice," Isaiah xlii. 10, 12. "*Sing*, O ye heavens, shout ye lower parts of the earth, break forth into *singing*, ye mountains," Isaiah xliv. 23; xlix. 13. "*Sing* aloud unto God our strength, make a joyful noise unto the God of Jacob. Take a *psalm*," Psalm lxxxi. 2—4. "Joy and gladness shall be found in Zion, thanksgiving and the voice of *melody*," Isaiah li. 3; lii. 8, 9. "*Sing* unto Jehovah,—cry out and shout, thou inhabitant of Zion, for great is the Holy One of Israel in the midst of thee," Isaiah xii. 1—6. "My heart is fixed, I will *sing* and give praise. Awake up, my glory, I will praise thee, O Lord, among the nations, I will *sing* unto thee among the people," Psalm lvii. 8—10: and in many other places.

280. *Saying, Thou art worthy to take the Book, and to open the seals thereof*, signifies that he alone can know the states of life of all, and judge every man according to his own state respectively, as above, n. 256, 259, 261, 267, 273.

281. *For thou wast slain, and hast redeemed us to God by thy blood*, signifies deliverance from hell, and salvation by conjunction with him. It is not necessary to explain by the spiritual sense what is specifically signified by all the particulars here mentioned, as what by being slain, by redeeming us to God, and what by his blood, for they are arcana which do not appear in the literal sense; suffice it to know that it is redemption which is thus described; and since it is redemption it is deliverance from hell, and salvation by conjunction with the Lord, which are signified. Here it shall only be confirmed from the Word, that Jehovah himself came into the world, was born a man, and became the Redeemer and Saviour of all, who by a life of charity and its faith are in conjunction with his Divine Humanity, and that Jehovah is the Lord from eternity, consequently that the Divine Humanity of the Lord, with which there must be conjunction, is the Divine Humanity of Jehovah himself. Now therefore some passages shall be adduced, which prove that Jehovah and the Lord are one; and since they are one and not two, that the Lord from eternity, who is Jehovah himself, by the assumption of the Humanity, became the Redeemer and Saviour: this is evident from the following places: "Thou, O *Jehovah*, art our Father, our *Redeemer;* thy name is from everlasting," Isaiah lxiii. 16. "Thus saith the King of Israel and his *Redeemer, Jehovah of Hosts*, I am the First and I am the Last, and besides me there is no God," Isaiah xliv. 6. "Thus saith *Jehovah* thy *Redeemer*, and he that formed thee; I am *Jehovah* that maketh all things—alone by myself," Isaiah xliv. 24. "Thus saith *Jehovah* thy *Redeemer*, the Holy One of Israel, I am *Jehovah* thy God," Isaiah xlviii. 17. "*Jehovah* my Rock and my *Redeemer*," Psalm xix. 14. "Their *Redeemer* is strong, *Jehovah of Hosts* is his name," Jerem. l. 34.

"*Jehovah of Hosts* is his name, and thy *Redeemer* the Holy One of Israel, the God of the whole earth shall he be called," Isaiah liv. 5. "And all flesh shall know that I *Jehovah* am thy *Saviour* and thy *Redeemer*, the Mighty One of Jacob," Isaiah xlix. 26; lx. 16. "As for our *Redeemer, Jehovah of Hosts* is his name," Isaiah xlvii. 4. "With everlasting kindness will I have mercy on thee, saith *Jehovah* thy *Redeemer*," Isaiah liv. 8. "Thus saith *Jehovah* your *Redeemer*, the Holy One of Israel," Isaiah xliii. 14. "Thus saith *Jehovah* the *Redeemer* of Israel and his Holy One," Isaiah xlix. 7. "Thou hast *redeemed* me, *Jehovah God* of truth," Psalm xxxi. 5. "Let Israel hope in *Jehovah*, for with him there is plenteous *redemption*, and he shall *redeem* Israel from all his iniquities," Psalm cxxx. 7, 8. "Arise, [O Lord,] for our help, and *redeem* us for thy mercy's sake," Psalm xliv. 26. Thus saith Jehovah God, "I will *ransom* them from the power of the grave, I will *redeem* them from death," Hosea xiii. 4, 14. "Jehovah shall hear my voice, he shall *redeem* my soul," Psalm lv. 17, 18. Also in Psalm xlix. 15; Psalm lxix. 18; Psalm lxxi. 23; Psalm ciii. 1, 4; Psalm cvii. 2; Jerem. xv. 20, 21. That the Lord as to his Humanity is the Redeemer, is not denied in the church, because it is according to Scripture, and the following passages: "Who is this that cometh from Edom, travelling in the greatness of his strength?—and the year of my *redeemed* is come. He *redeemed* them," Isaiah lxiii. 1, 4, 9. "Say ye to the daughter of Zion, Behold, thy salvation cometh, behold, his reward is with him,—and they shall call them, The Holy People, the *Redeemed of Jehovah*," Isaiah lxii. 11, 12. "Blessed be the *Lord God* of Israel, for he hath visited and *redeemed* his people," Luke i. 68: besides other places. Many other passages, proving that the Lord from eternity, who is Jehovah himself, came into the world, and took upon him humanity, in order to redeem mankind, may be seen in *The Doctrine of the New Jerusalem concerning the Lord*, n. 37—46. Moreover Jehovah is called the Saviour in many places, which cannot be adduced by reason of their abundance.

282. *Out of every tribe, and tongue, and people, and nation*, signifies that they in the church or in any religion, who are in truths as to doctrine, and in good as to life, are redeemed by the Lord. By tribe is signified the church as to religion; by tongue is signified its doctrine, of which we shall speak presently; by people are signified they who are in truths of doctrine, and, abstractedly, truths of doctrine, n. 483; and by nation are signified they who are in the good of life, and, abstractedly, good of life, n. 483; from hence it appears that by these words, "Out of every tribe, and tongue, and people, and nation," such things are signified as were said above; see also n. 627. It shall now be proved that tongue, in the spir-

itual sense, signifies the doctrine of the church, or of any religion; this is evident from the following places: "My *tongue* also shall talk of thy righteousness all the day long," Psalm lxxi. 24. "Then shall the lame leap as a hart, and the *tongue* of the dumb shall sing, for in the wilderness shall waters break out," Isaiah xxxv. 6. "The *tongue* of the stammerers shall be ready to speak plainly," Isaiah xxxii. 4. It appears as if, in these instances, by tongue was meant speech, but in the spiritual sense that which is spoken is understood, which is truth of doctrine, which they will have from the Lord. In like manner, "I have sworn,—That unto me every knee shall bow, and every *tongue* shall swear," Isaiah xlv. 23. "It shall come, that I will gather all nations and *tongues*, and they shall come and see my glory," Isaiah lxvi. 18. "In those days it shall come to pass that ten men out of all *languages* of the nations, shall take hold of the skirt of him that is a Jew, saying, We will go with you, for we have heard that God is with you," Zech. viii. 23; speaking of the conversion of the Gentiles by the Lord to the truth of doctrine. But by tongues, in an opposite sense, are signified false doctrines in the following places: "Let not an *evil speaker* be established in the earth," Psalm cxl. 1. "Thou shalt keep them secretly in a pavilion from the strife of *tongues*," Psalm xxxi. 20. "Lo, I will bring a nation upon you,—whose *language* thou knowest not," Jerem. v. 15, 16. "To be sent to a people of a hard *language*," Ezek. iii. 5, 6. To a people of a "*stammering tongue*," Isaiah xxxiii. 19. It must be observed that tongue, as an organ, signifies doctrine, but, as speech, it also signifies religion. He who knows that a tongue signifies doctrine, may understand what is meant by those words which the rich man in hell addressed to Abraham, that he would send Lazarus that he might "dip the tip of his finger in water, and cool his *tongue*, and not be tormented with the flame," Luke xvi. 24. Water signifies truth, and tongue, doctrine; by the falses of which doctrine he was tormented, and not by the flame; for no one in hell is in flames, but flames there are appearances of the love of falsity; whilst fire is an appearance of the love of evil.

283. *And hast made us unto our God kings and priests*, signifies that from the Lord they are in wisdom from divine truths and in love from divine good, and thus images of his divine wisdom, and of his divine love; as above, n. 20, 21.

284. *And we shall reign on the earth*, signifies, and will be in his kingdom, he in them and they in him. By reigning on the earth, nothing else is meant, than being in the Lord's kingdom, and there one with him, according to these words of the Lord: "That all who believe in me, may be *one;* and may be *one* as thou Father art in me and I in thee, that they also may be *one in us:* And the glory which thou gavest me I have given

them, that they may be *one* even as *we are one*, I in them and thou in me, that where I am, they also may be with me," John xvii. 20—24. As, therefore, they are thus one with the Lord, and, together with the Lord, constitute a kingdom which is called the kingdom of God, it is evident that nothing else is signified by their reigning. The term reign is mentioned, because it was before said, "Thou hast made us kings and priests;" and by kings are signified they who are in wisdom by means of divine truths from the Lord; and by priests, they who are in love by means of divine good from him, n. 20; hence it is that the kingdom of the Lord is also called "the kingdom of the saints," Dan. vii. 18, 27; and it is said of the apostles, that together "with the Lord they should judge the twelve tribes of Israel," Matt. xix. 28; although the Lord alone judges and reigns; for he judges and reigns from divine good by divine truth, which is also from him in them; but who believes, that what is in them from the Lord is their own, is cast out of the kingdom, or, what is the same thing, out of heaven. The signification of reigning is the same in the following passages in the Apocalypse: "They shall be priests of God and of Christ, and shall *reign* with him a thousand years," xx. 6: and concerning those who are to enter into the New Jerusalem, it is said: "The Lamb shall enlighten them, and they shall *reign* for ever and ever," xxii. 5.

285. It is said, *They shall reign on the earth*, because by earth here and in other places is meant the Lord's church in the heavens and on the earths; the church, wherever it may be, is the Lord's kingdom. Lest, therefore, any one should believe that all who are redeemed by the Lord become kings and priests, and that they will reign on the earth, it must be proved from the Word that the earth signifies the church; this may appear from the following passages: "Behold, Jehovah maketh the *earth* empty, and maketh it waste, and turneth it upside down: the *land* shall be utterly emptied. The *earth* mourneth and fadeth away; the *earth* also is defiled under the inhabitants thereof. Therefore hath the curse devoured the *earth*, therefore the inhabitants of the *earth* are burned, and few men left. When this shall be in the midst of the *land* these shall be as the shaking of an olive tree. The windows from on high are open, and the foundations of the *earth* do shake. The *earth* is utterly broken down; the *earth* is clean dissolved; the *earth* is moved exceedingly. The *earth* shall reel to and fro like a drunkard," Isaiah xxiv. 1—23. "The lion is come up from his thicket to make thy *land* desolate: I beheld the *earth*, and lo, it was without form and void; Thus saith Jehovah, The whole *land* shall be desolate, for this shall the *earth* mourn," Jerem. iv. 7, 23—28. "How long shall the *land* mourn? the whole *land* is made desolate, because no man layeth it to heart,"

Jerem. xli. 4, 11—13. "The *earth* mourneth and languisheth, Lebanon is ashamed and hewn down," Isaiah xxxiii. 9. "And the *land* shall become burning pitch, and shall lie waste," Isaiah xxxiv. 9, 10. "I have heard from the Lord of Hosts a consumption even determined upon the whole *earth*," Isaiah xxviii. 2, 22. "Behold, the day of Jehovah cometh, to lay the *land* desolate, and the *earth* shall remove out of her place," Isaiah xiii. 9, 13. "Then the *earth* shook and trembled, and the foundations also of the hills moved," Psalm xviii. 7, 8. "Therefore will we not fear though the *earth* be removed; he uttereth his voice, the *earth* melted," Psalm xlvi. 3—7, 9. "Have ye not understood from the foundations of the *earth*?" Isaiah xl. 21, 23. "O God, thou hast cast us off,—thou hast made the *earth* to tremble; heal the breaches thereof, for it shaketh," Psalm lx. 2, 4. "The *earth* and all the inhabitants thereof are dissolved; I bear up the pillars of it," Psalm lxxv. 3, 4. "Woe to the *land* shadowing with wings: Go ye swift messengers to a nation scattered and peeled, whose *land* the rivers have spoiled," Isaiah xviii. 1, 2. "Through the wrath of Jehovah,—the *land* is darkened," Isaiah ix. 19. "For ye shall be a delightsome *land*," Malachi iii. 12. "I will give thee for a covenant of the people, to establish the *earth*; Sing, O heavens, and be joyful, O *earth*," Isaiah xlix. 8, 13. "I shall not see the Lord in the *land* of the living," Isaiah xxxviii. 11. "Which caused terror in the *land* of the living," Ezek. xxxii. 23—27. "Unless I had believed to see the goodness of Jehovah in the *land* of the living," Psalm xxvii. 13. "Blessed are the meek, for they shall inherit the *earth*," Matt. v. 5. "I am Jehovah that maketh all things, that stretcheth forth the heavens alone; that spreadeth abroad the *earth* by myself," Isaiah xliv. 23, 24; Zech. xii. 1; Jerem. x. 11—13; li. 15; Psalm cxxxvi. 6. "Let the *earth* open and bring forth salvation; thus saith Jehovah, who created the heavens and formed the *earth*," Isaiah xlv. 8, 12, 18, 19. "Behold, I create new heavens and a new *earth*," Isaiah lxv. 17; lxvi. 22; besides many other places, which, if they were adduced, would fill a volume. The reason why the earth signifies the church, is, because, in many instances, it means the land of Canaan, in which the church was planted; the heavenly Canaan is no other; as, also, because when the earth is named, the angels, who are spiritual, do not think of the earth, but of the human race that inhabit it and of their spiritual state, and their spiritual state is the state of the church. The earth has also an opposite sense, and in that it signifies damnation, because when there is no church in man, there is damnation; in this sense the earth is mentioned in Isaiah xiv. 12; xxi. 9; xxvi. 19, 21; xxix. 4; xlvii. 1; lxiii. 6; Lament. ii. 10; Ezek. xxvi. 20; xxxii. 24; Numb. xvi. 29—33; xxvi. 10; and in other places.

286. *And I beheld, and I heard the voice of many angels round about the throne, and the animals and the elders*, signifies a confession and glorification of the Lord by the angels of the inferior heavens. That there was a confession and glorification of the Lord by the angels of the three heavens, may be seen above, n. 275; and by the angels of the superior heavens, from verse 8 to 10; and therefore now by the angels of the inferior heavens, verses 11, 12; wherefore by the voice of the angels round about the throne, is meant the confession and glorification of the Lord by the angels of the inferior heavens. On this occasion he saw also the animals and elders together with them, because by the animals and elders are signified the angels of the superior heavens, n. 275, and the inferior heavens never act separately from the superior heavens, but in conjunction with them; for the Lord influences all the heavens immediately from himself; thus also the inferior heavens: and his influence is at the same time mediately through the superior heavens into the inferior. This is the reason, therefore, why he first saw and heard the animals by themselves, and afterwards in conjunction with the others.

287. *And the number of them was myriads of myriads, and thousands of thousands*, signifies all in truths and in good. By number, in the natural sense, is meant that which has relation to measure or weight, but by number, in the spiritual sense, that which has relation to quality: and here their quality is described by their being myriads of myriads, and thousands of thousands, for a myriad is predicated of truths, and a thousand of goods. The reason why a myriad is predicated of truths, and a thousand of goods, is because a myriad is the greater number, and a thousand a less, and truths are manifold, but goods are simple; and because where truths are treated of in the Word, goods are treated of also, on account of the marriage of good and truth existing in every particular, otherwise it would have been sufficient to have said myriads of myriads. Since these two numbers have such a signification, they are mentioned also in other places, as in the following: "The chariots of God are *two myriads*, even *thousands* of angels, the Lord is amongst them as in Sinai in the holy place," Psalm lxviii. 17. "I beheld, and the Ancient of Days did sit, *thousand thousands* ministered unto him, and *myriads of myriads* stood before him," Dan. vii. 9, 10. Moses saith of Joseph, "His horns are like the horns of unicorns, with them he shall push the people together to the ends of the earth; and they are the *myriads* of Ephraim, and the *thousands* of Manasseh," Deut. xxxiii. 17. "Thou shalt not be afraid for the pestilence that walketh in darkness, nor for the destruction that wasteth at noon-day, a *thousand* shall fall at thy side, and a *myriad* at thy right hand," Psalm xci. 5—7. "That our sheep may bring forth *thousands* and *myriads*

in our streets," Psalm cxliv. 13. "Will Jehovah be pleased with *thousands* of rams, or with *myriads* of rivers of oil?" Micah vi. 7. When the ark rested, Moses said, "Return, Jehovah, unto the *myriads* of the *thousands* of Israel," Numb. x. 36. In all these places myriads are spoken of truths, and thousands of goods.

288. *Saying with a loud voice, Worthy is the Lamb that was slain to receive power, and riches, and wisdom, and honour, and glory*, signifies confession from the heart, that to the Lord as to his Divine Humanity belong omnipotence, omniscience, divine good, and divine truth. To say with a loud voice, signifies confession from the heart: thou art worthy, signifies that in him are the things which follow; a Lamb signifies the Lord as to the Divine Humanity; power signifies divine power, which is omnipotence; riches, and wisdom, signify divine knowledge and wisdom, which are omniscience; honour and glory, signify divine good and divine truth. That riches signify knowledges of what is good and true, and thus science, may be seen above, n. 206; therefore, when said of the Lord, they signify omniscience; and that honour and glory, when spoken of the Lord, signify divine good and divine truth, see above, n. 249.

289. *And blessing*, signifies all these things in him, and from him in them. By blessing is meant every good which man receives from the Lord, or power and opulence, and all that is implied by them; but especially every spiritual good, or love and wisdom, charity and faith, and the joy and felicity resulting from them, which constitute eternal life; and since all these are from the Lord, it follows that they are in him, for if they were not in him, they could not be in others from him: hence it is, that, in the Word, the Lord is called the *Blessed*, and also *Blessing*, that is, *Blessing Itself*. That Jehovah, or the Lord, is called the Blessed, is evident from these places: "The high priest asked Jesus, Art thou the Christ, the Son of the *Blessed?*" Mark xiv. 61. Jesus said, "Ye shall not see me henceforth, till ye shall say, *Blessed* is he that cometh in the name of the Lord," Matt. xxiii 39; Luke xiii. 35. Melchisedek blessed Abram, and said, "*Blessed* be the most high God, who hath delivered thine enemies into thy hand," Gen. xiv. 18—20. "*Blessed* be Jehovah, the God of Shem," Gen. ix. 26. "*Blessed* be Jehovah, because he hath heard my voice," Psalm xxviii. 6. "*Blessed* be Jehovah, for he hath showed me his marvellous kindness," Psalm xxxi. 21. "*Blessed* be Jehovah, God of Israel, from everlasting to everlasting," Psalm xli. 13. In like manner, Psalm lxvi. 20; Psalm lxviii. 19, 35; Psalm lxxii. 18, 19; Psalm lxxxix. 52; Psalm cxix. 12; Psalm cxxiv. 6; Psalm cxxxv. 21; Psalm cxliv. 1; Luke i. 68. This is the reason why blessing is here mentioned, as also verse 12, and vii. 12; and likewise in the Psalms of David: "Glory and honour dost thou

lay upon him, for thou hast made him *Blessing* for ever," Psalm xxi. 5, 6 : speaking of the Lord. Hence it may be seen what is meant in the Word by blessing God, namely, to ascribe to him all blessing ; also to pray that he would bless, and to give thanks for having blessed ; as may appear from the following passages : The mouth of Zacharias was opened, and he spake, *blessing* God, Luke i. 64, 68. Simeon took up the infant Jesus in his arms, and *blessed God*, Luke ii. 28, 30, 31. " I will *bless* Jehovah, who hath given me counsel, Psalm xvi. 7. O "*bless* the name of Jehovah, show forth his salvation from day to day," Psalm xcvi. 1—3. " *Blessed* be the Lord from day to day, *bless* ye God in the congregations, even the Lord from the fountain of Israel," Psalm lxviii. 19, 26.

290. *And every creature which is in heaven, and on the earth, and under the earth, and such as are in the sea, and all that are in them, heard I saying*, signifies confession and glorification of the Lord by the angels of the lowest heaven. That this is a confession and glorification of the Lord by the angels of the lowest heaven, is evident from the series, because the confessions and glorifications of the Lord before mentioned, were by the angels of the superior and inferior heavens, n. 275, and following numbers, 286, and following numbers ; for there are three heavens, and innumerable societies in each, and each of them is called a heaven. That by every creature which is in heaven, and on the earth, and under the earth, and in the sea, are meant angels, is evident, for it says, " heard I saying," and they said, " Blessing, and honour, and glory, and power, be unto Him that sitteth upon the throne and unto the Lamb for ever and ever." Their being called creatures is conformable to the style of the Word, in which, by all created things, as well those which belong to the animal kingdom as those which belong to the vegetable kingdom, are signified various things in man, in general such things as belong to his will or affection, and such as pertain to his understanding or thought ; for they signify such things, because they correspond ; and since the Word is written by mere correspondences, similar things are said of the angels of heaven and men of the church ; in proof of which a few passages only shall be adduced, which are as follows : Jesus said unto his disciples, " Go ye into all the world, and preach the gospel to every *creature*," Mark xvi. 15. " Ask now the *beasts*, and they shall teach thee ; and the *fowls* of the air, and they shall tell thee ; or speak to the *earth*, and it shall teach thee, and the *fishes* of the sea shall declare unto thee ; who knoweth not in all these, that the hand of Jehovah hath wrought this ?" Job xii. 7, 10. " Let the *heaven* and *earth* praise Jehovah, the seas, and every thing that *creepeth* therein, for God will save Zion," Psalm lxix. 34, 35. " Praise Jehovah from the earth, ye *dragons* and all *deeps*," Psalm cxlviii. 7. " I

will utterly consume all things from off the land, I will consume *man* and *beast*, I will consume the *fowls* of the heaven, and the *fishes* of the sea," Zeph. i. 2, 3. The same in Isaiah l. 2, 3; Ezek. xxxviii. 19, 20; Hosea iv. 2, 3; Apoc. viii. 7—9. " Let the *heavens* rejoice, and the *earth* be glad; let the *sea* roar, and the fulness thereof; let the *field* be joyful, and all that is therein; then shall all the *trees* of the *wood* rejoice before Jehovah; for he cometh, for he cometh to judge the *earth*," Psalm xcvi. 11—13: and in many other places. It is said every created thing, by which is meant every reformed thing, or all the reformed, for to create signifies to reform and regenerate, n. 254. What is meant by "in heaven, in the earth, and under the earth," may be seen above, n. 260; and what by the sea, n. 238; hence it is evident what is signified by such things as are in the sea, and all that are in them; these things are meant in the Word by fishes of the sea, which are the sensual affections, these being the lowest affections of the natural man, for in the spiritual world such affections appear at a distance like fishes, and as if they were in the sea, because the atmosphere in which they are, appears watery, and therefore to those who are in the heavens and on the earth there, seems like a sea, as may be seen above, n. 238, and concerning fishes, n. 405.

291. *Blessing, and honour, and glory, and power, be unto Him that sitteth upon the throne and unto the Lamb for ever and ever*, signifies that in the Lord from eternity, and thence in his Divine Humanity, is the all of heaven and the church, divine good, and divine truth, and divine power, and from him in those who are in heaven and in the church. That the Lord from eternity is Jehovah, who took upon him the human nature in time, that he might redeem and save mankind, may be seen above, n. 281; therefore by Him that sat upon the throne, is meant the Lord from eternity, who is called the Father, and by the Lamb, the Lord as to the Divine Humanity, which is the Son; and because the Father is in the Son, and the Son in the Father, and they are one, it is evident that by both, or by Him that sat upon the throne and the Lamb, the Lord is meant; and because they are one, it is said that the Lamb also was in the midst of the throne, verse 6; also vii. 17. That blessing, when spoken of the Lord, is the all of heaven and of the church in him and from him, in those who are in heaven and in the church, may be seen above, n. 289. That honour and glory are divine good and divine truth, may also be seen above, n. 249: and that strength, when spoken of the Lord, is divine power, is evident. That all these are the Lord's, may appear from what is said in Daniel: "Behold, one like the Son of Man came to the *Ancient of Days;* and there was given him *dominion,* and glory, and the kingdom, that all people, nations, and languages, should serve him: his *dominion* is an everlasting

dominion, which shall not pass away, and his kingdom that which shall not be destroyed," vii. 13, 14. That the Ancient of Days is the Lord from eternity, appears from these words in Micah: "But thou, Bethlehem Ephratah, though thou be little among the thousands of Judah, yet out of thee shall He come forth unto me, that is to be ruler in Israel; and whose goings forth have been from *of old*, from the *days of everlasting*," v. 2: as also from these in Isaiah: "For unto us a Child is born, unto us a Son is given, and the government shall be upon his shoulder: and his name shall be called Wonderful, Counsellor, the Mighty God, *the Everlasting Father*, the Prince of Peace," ix. 6.

292. *And the four animals said, Amen*, signifies divine confirmation from the Word. That the four animals or cherubs signify the Word, may be seen above, n. 239; and that amen signifies divine confirmation from truth itself, n. 23, 28, 61, thus from the Word.

293. *And the four-and-twenty elders fell down and worshipped Him that liveth for ever and ever*, signifies humiliation before the Lord, and from humiliation, adoration of him by all in the heavens, in whom and from whom is everlasting life, as above, n. 251, and n. 58, 60

294. To the above I will add this Memorable Relation. In the natural world the speech of man is twofold, because his thought is twofold, exterior and interior; for a man can speak from interior thought and at the same time from exterior thought, and he can speak from exterior thought and not from interior, yea, contrary to interior thought, whence come dissimulation, flattery, and hypocrisy. But in the spiritual world man's speech is not twofold, but single; a man there speaks as he thinks, otherwise the sound is harsh and offends the ear; but yet he may be silent, and so not publish the thoughts of his mind; a hypocrite, therefore, when he comes into the company of the wise, either goes away, or retires to a corner of the room and withdraws himself from observation, and sits silent. On one occasion there was a numerous assembly in the spiritual world, who were discoursing on this subject, and saying, that not to be able to speak but as one thinks, must be a hard thing for those who might be in company with the good, but yet who have not thought justly concerning God and the Lord. In the midst of the assembly were those of the reformed church, and many of the clergy, and next to them were papists and monks; and they all at first said that it was not a hard thing at all; "What need is there to speak otherwise than one thinks, and if one should happen not to think justly, can he not shut his mouth and keep silence?" And one of the clergy said, "Who does not think justly of God and the Lord?" But some of the com-

pany said, "Let us make the experiment." And they who had confirmed themselves in the idea of a trinity of persons in the Godhead, especially from these words in the Athanasian doctrine, "There is one person of the Father, another of the Son, and another of the Holy Ghost; and as the Father is God, so also the Son is God, and the Holy Ghost is God," were desired to say, "*One God;*" but they could not; they distorted and folded their lips in many ways, but could not articulate any other words than such as were consonant with the ideas of their thought, which were ideas of three persons, and thence of three gods. They who had confirmed themselves in faith separate from charity, were then desired to name "*Jesus;*" but they could not; yet they could all say Christ, and also God the Father. This they were surprised at, and inquired into the cause, which they found to be this, viz., that they had prayed to God the Father for the Son's sake, and had not prayed to the Saviour himself; for Jesus signifies Saviour. They were then desired, by thinking of the Lord's Divine Humanity, to say, "*Divine Human;*" but none of the clergy that were present could do so, though some of the laity could, wherefore the matter was taken into serious consideration; and then, I. The following texts from the evangelists were read to them: "The Father hath given *all things* into the Son's hand," John iii. 35. "The Father hath given the Son *power* over all flesh," John xvii. 2. "All *power* is given unto me in heaven and in earth," Matt. xxviii. 18; and they were directed to keep in mind, that Christ, both as to his Divinity and as to his Humanity, is the God of heaven and earth, and thus to pronounce "*Divine Human;*" but still they could not; and they said that they were thus enabled, indeed, to entertain the thought of it by virtue of their understanding concerning it, but not the acknowledgment, and that on this account they were not able. II. Afterwards was read to them out of Luke, i. 32, 34, 35, that the Lord as to the human nature was the Son of Jehovah God, and that every where in the Word he is called, as to his Humanity, the Son of God, and also the Only-begotten, and they were desired to keep this in mind; and likewise that the only-begotten Son of God born in the world cannot but be God, as the Father is God, and to utter the words, "*Divine Human.*" But they said, "We cannot, by reason that our spiritual thought, which is interior, does not admit into the thought which is next to the speech any other than similar ideas, and that thence they could perceive, that it is not permitted them to divide their thoughts, as it was in the natural world." III. Then were read to them these words of the Lord to Philip: "Philip said, Lord, show us the Father, and the Lord said, He who seeth me seeth the Father; believest thou not that I am in the Father, and the Father in me?" John xiv. 8—11; and other places; as "That he and the Father are one," John x. 30, and the like; and it was enjoined them to keep this in mind, and say, "*Divine Human;*" but as their thought was not rooted in the acknowledgment that the Lord was God as to his human nature also, therefore they could not; they twisted and folded their lips even to indignation, and would have forced their mouths to utter and extort it, but it was not in their power. The reason was, because the ideas of thought, which flow from acknowledgment, make one with words uttered by the tongue, with those who are in the spiritual world, and where such ideas do not exist, there are no words, for ideas become words in speaking. IV. Moreover there was read to them from the doctrine of the church received throughout the whole world, the following passage, taken from the Athanasian Creed: "That the divine and human nature in the Lord are not two but one, yea, one person, united altogether like soul and body;" and it was said to them, From this you may possibly have an idea grounded in the acknowledgment that the Lord's human nature is divine, seeing that his soul is divine, for it is a doctrine of your own church, acknowledged by you when in the world. Moreover the soul is essence itself, and the body its form, and the essence and form make one, like being and existence, and like the efficient cause of the effect, and the effect itself; they retained that idea, and were wont to have uttered "*Divine Human;*" but it was not in their power; for their interior idea concerning the Lord's Humanity exterminated and expunged this new adventitious idea, as they called it. V. Again there was read to them this passage out of John: "The Word was with God, and God was the Word; and the Word was made flesh," i. 1, 14; and the following from Paul: "In Christ Jesus dwelleth all the fulness of the Godhead bodily," Coloss. ii. 9: and they were desired to think firmly, that God, who was the Word, was made flesh, and that every thing divine, or all the divinity, dwells in him bodily, as they might, perhaps, by these means be able to pronounce "*Divine Human;*" but still they could not, avowing openly that they could not entertain an idea of a divine human being, because God is God, and man is man, and God is a spirit, and of a spirit we have never thought any otherwise than as of air or ether. VI. At length it was said to them, "Ye know that the Lord said, 'Abide in me, and I in you; he who abideth in me, and I in him, the same beareth much fruit, for without me ye can do nothing,'" John xv. 4, 5. And as some of the English clergy were present, there was read to them this passage out of one of their prayers before the Holy Sacrament: "For when we spiritually eat the flesh of Christ, and drink his blood, then we dwell in Christ, and Christ in us." "If now you will but think that this cannot take place, except the Lord's Humanity be Divine, you may pronounce '*Divine*

Human,' from an acknowledgment in thought;" but still they could not; so deeply was the idea impressed on their minds that the Lord's Divinity was one thing and his Humanity another, and that his Divinity was like the Divinity of the Father, and his Humanity like the humanity of another man. But it was said to them, "How can you entertain such a thought? Is it possible for a rational mind ever to think that God is three, and the Lord two?" VII. Afterwards they turned to the Lutherans, saying, "That the Augustan Confession, and Luther, taught that the Son of God and the Son of Man in Christ are one person, and that he, as to his human nature also, is the true, omnipotent, and eternal God, and that as to this nature also, being present at the right hand of God Almighty, governs all things in heaven and earth, fills all things, is with us, and dwells and operates in us; and that there is no distinction of adoration, because by the nature which is seen, the divinity which is not seen is adored, thus that in Christ God is Man and Man God." On hearing this, they said, "Is it so?" And they looked round, and presently they said, "This is what we did not know before, therefore we are not able." But one or two of them said, "We have read and written concerning these things, but yet when we thought of them in ourselves from ourselves, they were only words of which we had no interior idea." VIII. At length, turning to the papists, they said, "Possibly you can name the '*Divine Human,*' because you believe that in your eucharist, in the bread and wine and in every part, there is the whole of Christ, and also adore him as God, when you show and carry about the host; and likewise because you call Mary the mother of God, consequently you acknowledge that she brought forth God, that is, the Divine Human." They then attempted to pronounce it from those ideas of their thought concerning the Lord, but could not, by reason of their entertaining a material idea of his body and blood; and by reason of the assertion that the human and not the divine power is transferred by him to the pope. Then a certain monk got up, and said, "That he could think of the Divine Human, from the most Holy Virgin Mary, the mother of God, and the same of the saint of his monastery." And another monk came, and said, "From my idea of the matter, I could rather call his holiness, the pope, the divine human, than Christ;" but then some other monks pulled him back, and said, "Are you not ashamed of yourself?" After this heaven was seen open, and there appeared tongues, as of flame, descending and influencing some; and they then celebrated THE DIVINE HUMANITY OF THE LORD, saying, "Remove the idea of three gods, and believe that in the Lord dwells all the fulness of the Godhead bodily, and that the Father and he are one, as the soul and body are one, and that God is not air or ether, but that he is a Man, and then you will be brought into conjunction with heaven, and thereby have power from the Lord to pronounce the name of 'Jesus,' and utter the words 'Divine Human.'"

CHAPTER VI.

1. And I saw when the Lamb opened one of the seals, and I heard one of the four animals say, as with a voice of thunder, Come and see.

2. And I saw, and behold, a white horse: and he that sat on him had a bow; and a crown was given unto him: and he went forth conquering and to conquer.

3. And when he had opened the second seal, I heard the second animal say, Come and see.

4. And there went out another horse that was red, and power was given to him that sat thereon to take peace from the earth, and that they should kill one another: and there was given unto him a great sword.

5. And when he had opened the third seal, I heard the third animal say, Come and see. And I beheld, and lo, a black horse; and he that sat on him had a pair of balances in his hand.

6. And I heard a voice in the midst of the four animals say, A measure of wheat for a penny, and three measures of barley for a penny; and see thou hurt not the oil and the wine.

7. And when he had opened the fourth seal, I heard the voice of the fourth animal say, Come and see.

8. And I looked, and behold, a pale horse: and his name that sat on him was Death, and hell followed with him. And power was given unto them over the fourth part of the earth, to kill with sword, and with hunger, and with death, and with the beasts of the earth.

9. And when he had opened the fifth seal, I saw under the altar the souls of them that were slain for the Word of God, and for the testimony which they held.

10. And they cried with a loud voice, saying, How long, O Lord, holy and true, dost thou not judge and avenge our blood on them that dwell on the earth?

11. And white robes were given unto every one of them; and it was said unto them, that they should rest yet for a little season, until their fellow-servants also, and their brethren, that should be killed as they were, should be fulfilled.

12. And I beheld when he opened the sixth seal, and lo, there was a great earthquake; and the sun became black as sackcloth of hair, and the moon became as blood.

13. And the stars of heaven fell unto the earth, even as a fig-tree casteth her untimely figs, when she is shaken of a mighty wind.

14. And the heaven departed as a scroll, when it is rolled together: and every mountain and island were moved out of their places.

15. And the kings of the earth, and the great men, and the rich men, and the chief captains, and the mighty men, and every bond-man, and every free-man, hid themselves in the dens and in the rocks of the mountains;

16. And said to the mountains and rocks, Fall on us, and hide us from the face of Him that sitteth on the throne, and from the wrath of the Lamb;

17. For the great day of his wrath is come, and who shall be able to stand?

THE SPIRITUAL SENSE.

THE CONTENTS OF THE WHOLE CHAPTER. The subject treated of is concerning the exploration of those, on whom the last judgment is to be executed; and exploration is made to discover the quality of their understanding of the Word, and thence the quality of their state of life. That they consisted of such as were in truths originating in good, verses 1, 2; of such as were without good, verses 3, 4; of such as were in contempt of truth, verses 5, 6; and of such as were totally devastated, both as to good and truth, verses 7, 8. Of the state of those who were preserved by the Lord from the wicked in the inferior earth, and were to be delivered at the time of the last judgment, verses 9, 10. Of the state of those who were in evils and thence in falses, the nature of that state at the day of the last judgment, verses 12—17.

THE CONTENTS OF EACH VERSE. V. 1, "And I saw when the Lamb opened one of the seals," signifies exploration from the Lord of all those upon whom the last judgment was about to be executed, as to their understanding of the Word, and thence as to their state of life: "And I heard one of the four animals say, as with a voice of thunder," signifies, according to the divine truth of the Word: "Come and see," signifies a manifestation concerning those who were first in order: v. 2, "And I saw, and behold, a white horse," signifies the understanding of truth and good from the Word with these: "And he that sat on him had a bow," signifies that they had the doctrine of truth and good from the Word, by virtue of which they fought against the falses and evils which are from hell: "And a crown was given unto him," signifies his token of combat: "And he went forth conquering, and to conquer," signifies victory over evils and falses to eternity: v. 3, "And when he had opened the second seal, I heard the second animal say, Come and see," signifies the same here as above: v. 4, "And there went out another horse that was red," signifies the understanding of the Word destroyed as to good, and thence as to life, in these: "And power was given to him that sat thereon to take peace from the earth," signifies the taking away of charity, spiritual security, and internal tranquillity: "And that they should kill one another," signifies intestine hatreds, infestations from the hells, and internal restlessness: "And there was given unto him a great sword," signifies the destruction of truth by falses of evil: v. 5, "And when he had opened the third seal, I heard the third animal say, Come and see," signifies the same here as above: "And I beheld, and lo, a black horse," signifies the understanding of the Word destroyed in these as to truth, and thus as to doctrine: "And he that sat on him had a pair of balances in his hand," signifies the estimation of good and truth, of what kind it was with these: v. 6, "And I heard a voice in the midst of the four animals say," signifies the divine protection of the Word by the Lord: "A measure of wheat for a penny, and three measures of barley for a penny," signifies, because the estimation of good and truth is so small as scarcely to amount to any thing: "And see thou hurt not the oil and the wine," signifies that it is provided by the Lord, that the holy goods and truths which lie interiorly concealed in the Word, shall not be violated and profaned: v. 7, "And when he had opened the fourth seal, I heard the voice of the fourth animal say, Come and see," signifies the same here as above: v. 8, "And I looked, and behold, a pale horse," signifies the understanding of the Word destroyed both as to good and as to truth: "And his name that sat on him was Death, and hell followed with him," signifies the extinction of spiritual life and thence damnation: "And power was given unto them over the fourth part of the earth, to kill," signifies the destruction of all good in the church: "With sword, and with hunger, and with death, and with the beasts of the earth," signifies by falses of doctrine, by evils of life, by the love of self, and by lusts: v. 9, "And when he had opened the fifth seal," signifies exploration from the Lord into the state of life of those who were to be saved at the day of the last judgment, and were in the mean time reserved: "I saw under the altar the souls of them that were slain for the Word of God, and for the testimony which they held," signifies those who were rejected by the wicked on account of their life being conformable to the truths of the Word, and their acknowledgment of the Lord's Divine Humanity, and who were guarded by the Lord that they might no be seduced: v. 10, "And they cried with a loud voice," signifies grief of heart: "Saying, How long, O Lord, holy and true, dost thou not judge and avenge our blood on them that dwell on the earth?" signifies by reason that the last judgment was protracted, and that they who offer violence to the Word and to the Lord's Divine Humanity were not removed: v. 11, "And white robes were given unto every one of them," signifies their communication and conjunction with angels who are in divine truths: "And it was said unto them, that they should rest yet for a little season, until their fellow-servants also, and their brethren, that should be killed as they were, should be fulfilled," signifies that the last judgment should yet be protracted a little, till they should be collected, who should be rejected in like manner by the wicked: v. 12, "And I beheld, when he had opened the sixth seal," signifies exploration from the Lord of their state of life, who were interiorly evil, upon whom the last judgment was to be executed: "And lo, there was a great earthquake," signifies the state and terror of the church with those totally changed: "And the sun became black as sackcloth of hair, and the moon became as blood," signifies the adulteration of all the good of love in them, and the falsification of all the truth of faith: v. 13, "And the stars of heaven fell unto the earth," signifies the dispersion of all the knowledges of good and truth: "Even as a fig-tree casteth her untimely figs, when she is shaken of a mighty wind," signifies by the ratiocination of the natural man separated from the spiritual: v. 14, "And the heaven departed as a scroll when it is rolled together," signifies separation from heaven and conjunction with hell: "And every mountain and island were moved out of their places," signifies that all the good of love and truth of faith departed: v. 15, "And the kings of the earth, and the great men, and the rich men, and the chief captains, and the mighty men, and every bond-man, and every free-man," signifies those who, before separation, were in the understanding of truth and good, in the science of the knowledges thereof, in erudition, either from others or from themselves, and yet not in a life conformable thereto: "Hid themselves in the dens and in the rocks of the mountains," signifies that they were now in evils and in falses of evil: v. 16, "And said to the mountains and rocks, Fall on us, and hide us from the face of Him that sitteth on the throne, and from the wrath of the Lamb," signifies confirmations of evil by means of falsity and of falsity from evil, until they did not acknowledge any divinity in the Lord: v. 17, "For the great day of his wrath is come, and who shall be able to stand?" signifies that they were made such of themselves by separation from the good and faithful on account of the last judgment, which otherwise they would not be able to abide.

THE EXPLANATION

295. *And I saw when the Lamb opened one of the seals*, signifies exploration from the Lord of all those upon whom the last judgment was about to be executed, as to their understanding of the Word, and thence as to their state of life. This is signified, because now follows in order the exploration of all upon whom the last judgment was about to be performed, as to their states of life, and this from the Lord according to the Word. Such then is the signification of the Lamb's opening the seals of the Book. That to open the Book, and loose the seals thereof, signifies to know the states of the life of all, and to judge every one according to his own respectively, may be seen above, n. 259, 265, 266, 267, 273, 274.

296. *And I heard one of the four animals say, as with a voice of thunder*, signifies according to the divine truth of the Word. That by the four animals, or cherubs, is understood the Word, may be seen above, n. 239, 275, 286, and by a voice of thunder, the perception of divine truth, n. 236. It is here said a voice of thunder, because by this animal is meant the lion, by which is signified the divine truth of the Word as to its power, n. 241; hence it is, that this animal is said to have spoken as with a voice of thunder; for it is said afterwards, that the second animal spake, then the third, and the fourth.

297. *Come and see*, signifies a manifestation concerning those who were first in order. It has been observed above, that in this chapter is described the exploration of all upon whom the last judgment was to be executed, as to their states of life, and this from the Lord according to the Word, n. 295; here therefore is described the exploration of the first in order, as to their understanding of the Word, and consequent state of life. That the church exists from the Word, and that the nature and quality of every church is determined by the understanding it has of the Word, may be seen in *The Doctrine of the New Jerusalem concerning the Sacred Scripture*, n. 76—79.

298. *And I saw, and behold, a white horse*, signifies the understanding of truth and good from the Word with these. By horse is signified the understanding of the Word, and by a white horse the understanding of truth from the Word; for white is predicated of truths, n. 167. That a horse signifies the understanding of the Word, is shown in a particular tract concerning *The White Horse;* but as a few passages only are there quoted, others shall be here adduced by way of further confirmation. This is very manifest indeed, from the circumstance of horses being seen to go out of the Book which the Lamb had opened, and from the animals saying, Come and see; for by the animals is signified the Word, n. 239, 275, 286; so likewise

by the Book, n. 257; and by the Son of Man, who is here the Lamb, the Lord as to the Word, n. 44. From these considerations it is at once evident, that nothing is here meant by horse but the understanding of the Word. This may appear more manifestly still from the following passages in the Apocalypse: "I saw heaven opened, and behold, a *white horse*, and He that sat upon him is called the *Word of God*, and he hath on his vesture and on his thigh a name written, King of kings and Lord of lords. And his armies in the heavens followed him upon *white horses*," xix. 11, 13, 14, 16. That a horse signifies the understanding of the Word, may also appear from the following places: "Was thy wrath against the sea, O Jehovah, that thou didst ride upon *thine horses*, and thy chariots of salvation? Thou didst walk through the sea with *thine horses*, through the heap of great waters," Habak. iii. 8, 15. Jehovah's *horses' hoofs* are counted like flint, Isaiah v. 28. "In that day—I will smite *every horse* with astonishment, and his rider with madness,—and will smite *every horse* of the people with blindness," Zech. xii. 4. "In that day there shall be upon the *bells of the horses*, holiness unto Jehovah," Zech. xiv. 20. "Because God hath deprived her of wisdom, neither hath imparted to her understanding. What time she lifteth up herself on high she scorneth *the horse* and his rider," Job xxxix. 17, 18. "And I will cut off *the horse* from Jerusalem,—and he shall speak peace to the heathen," Zech. ix. 10. "At thy rebuke, O God of Jacob, both the chariot and *horse* are cast into a dead sleep," Psalm lxxvi. 6. "And I will overthrow the throne of kingdoms, and I will overthrow the chariots and those that ride in them, and the *horses* and their riders shall come down," Haggai ii. 22. "And with thee will I destroy kingdoms; and with thee will I break in pieces *the horse* and his rider," Jerem. li. 20, 21. Gather yourselves on every side to my sacrifice;—thus shall ye be filled at my table with *horses* and chariots, and I will set my glory among the nations," Ezek. xxxix. 17, 20, 21. "Gather yourselves together unto the supper of the great God; that ye may eat the flesh of *horses*, and of them that sit on them," Apoc. xix. 17, 18. "Dan shall be a serpent by the way, that biteth the *horse heels*, so that his rider shall fall backward. I have waited for thy salvation, O Jehovah," Gen. xlix. 17, 18. "Gird thy sword upon thy thigh, O most Mighty, and *ride* prosperously because of truth," Psalm xlv. 3, 4. "Sing unto God, extol Him that *rideth* on the heavens," Psalm lxviii. 5 "Behold, Jehovah *rideth* upon a swift cloud," Isaiah xix. 1, 2 Sing praises unto the Lord which "*rideth* upon the heaven of heavens which were of old," Psalm lxviii. 34. God *rode* upon a cherub, Psalm xviii. 10. "Then shalt thou delight thyself in Jehovah, and I will cause thee to *ride* upon the high places of the earth," Isaiah lviii. 14. "Jehovah alone did lead him, and made him to *ride* upon the high places of the earth," Deut. xxxii. 12, 13. "I will make Ephraim to *ride*," Hosea x. 11. Ephraim also signifies the understanding of the Word. Because Elijah and Elisha represented the Lord as to the Word, therefore they were called the chariot of Israel and his horsemen: Elisha said to Elijah, "My father, my father, the *chariot of Israel* and the *horsemen* thereof," 2 Kings ii. 12; and king Joash said to Elisha, "O my father, the *chariot of Israel* and the *horsemen* thereof," 2 Kings xiii. 14. "Jehovah opened the eyes of Elisha's young man, and he saw; and, behold, the mountain was full of *horses* and *chariots* of fire round about Elisha," 2 Kings vi. 17. A chariot signifies doctrine drawn from the Word, and a horseman, one that is wise by means of it. The same is signified by the *four chariots* which came out from between the mountains of brass, and by the *four horses* in them, which were red, black, white, and grisled, which are also called the four spirits, and are said to have gone forth from standing before the Lord of all the earth, Zech. vi. 1—8, 15. In these places, by horses is meant the understanding of the Word, or the understanding of truth from the Word; and in like manner in other places. It may appear still more clearly from the mention that is made of horses in an opposite sense, in which they signify the understanding of the Word and of truth falsified by reasonings, and likewise destroyed; as also self-derived intelligence; as in the following places: "Woe to them that go down to Egypt for help; and stay on *horses*,—but look not unto the Holy One of Israel.—Now the Egyptians are men and not God, and their *horses*, flesh and not spirit," Isaiah xxxi. 1, 3. "Thou shalt in any wise set him king over Israel whom Jehovah thy God shall choose: but he shall not multiply *horses* to himself, nor cause the people to return to Egypt to the end that he should multiply *horses*," Deut. xvii. 15, 16. This is said, because by Egypt is signified science and reasoning from self-derived intelligence, and thus the falsification of the truth of the Word, which is here expressed by a horse. "Ashur shall not save us, we will not ride upon *horses*," Hosea xiv. 3. "Some trust in chariots, and some in *horses*, but we will remember the name of the Lord our God," Psalm xx. 7. "A *horse* is a vain thing for safety," Psalm xxxiii. 17. "Jehovah delighteth not in the strength of the *horse*," Psalm cxlvii. 10. "Thus saith Jehovah God, the Holy One of Israel,—in confidence shall be your strength; but ye said, No; for we will flee upon *horses;* we will *ride* upon the swift," Isaiah xxx. 15, 16. "Jehovah will make Judah as a goodly *horse*. The riders on *horses* shall be confounded," Zech. x. 3, 4, 5. "Woe to the bloody city, it is all full of lies,—the prancing of *horses*, and of the jumping chariots; the *horseman* lifteth up," Nahum iii. 1—4. "I will bring upon Cyrus—the king of Babylon,—with *horses*, and with chariots, and with *horsemen* ;—by reason of the abundance of his *horses* their dust shall cover thee; thy walls shall shake at the noise of the *horsemen* and of the chariots; with the hoofs of his *horses* shall he tread down all thy streets," Ezek. xxvi. 7—11. By Tyre is signified the church as to the knowledges of truth, here such as are falsified in her, which are denoted by the horses of Babylon: besides other places; as Isaiah v. 26, 28; Jerem. vi. 22, 23; viii. 16; xlvi. 4, 9; l. 37, 38, 42; Ezek. xvii. 15; xxiii. 5, 20; Habak. i. 6, 8, 9, 10; Psalm lxvi. 11. 12. The understanding of the Word destroyed is also signified by the red, black, and pale horse, mentioned below. That it is from appearances in the spiritual world that a horse signifies the understanding of truth from the Word, see the small tract concerning *The White Horse*.

299. *And he that sat on him had a bow*, signifies that they had the doctrine of truth and good from the Word, by virtue of which they fought against the falses and evils which are from hell, thus against hell. By him that sat on the white horse, as mentioned in Apoc. xix. 13, is meant the Lord as to the Word; but by him that sat on this white horse, is understood a man-angel as to the doctrine of truth and good from the Word, thus from the Lord; in like manner as by the Lord's army in heaven, who "followed the Lord upon *white horses*," Apoc. xix. 14. Of Him that sat on the white horse, Apoc. xix., it is said, that out of his mouth went forth a sharp sword, that with it he should smite the nations; and by the sword out of his mouth, is signified the divine truth of the Word fighting against falses and evils, n. 52, 108, 117; but here it is said that he who sat on this white horse had a bow, and by a bow is signified the doctrine of truth and good drawn from the Word fighting against evils and falses. To fight against falses and evils is also to fight against the hells, because evils and falses are from thence, therefore this also is signified. That a bow, in the Word, signifies doctrine combating, in both senses, may appear from these passages: "Whose *arrows* are sharp, and all their *bows* bent, the horses' hoofs shall be counted like flint," Isaiah v. 28. "The Lord bent his *bow* like an enemy," Lament. ii. 4. "Thou, O Jehovah, didst ride upon thine horses, thy *bow* was made quite naked," Habak. iii. 8, 9. Who "gave the nations before him and made him rule over kings? he gave them as dust to his sword, and as driven stubble to his *bow*," Isaiah xli. 2. In these places a bow, because it is applied to Jehovah or the Lord, signifies the Word, from which the Lord fights in man against evils and falses. "And I will cut off the chariot from Ephraim, and the horse from Jerusalem, and the battle *bow* shall be cut off; and he shall speak peace to the heathen," Zech. ix. 10. "For lo, the wicked bent their *bow*, they make ready their *arrow* upon the string, that they may privily *shoot*

at the upright of heart," Psalm xi. 2. "The *archers* have sorely grieved Joseph, and *shot* at him, and hated him; but his *bow* abode in strength, and the arms of his hands were made strong by the hands of the Mighty One of Jacob," Gen. xlix. 23, 24. "Put yourselves in array against Babylon round about; all ye that bend the *bow*, shoot at her, spare no *arrows*, for she hath sinned against Jehovah," Jerem. l. 14, 29. David lamented over Saul "to teach the children of Judah the use of the *bow*," 2 Sam. i. 17. In that lamentation the combat of truth against falses is treated of. "Thus saith Jehovah of Hosts; Behold, I will break the *bow* of Elam, the chief of their might," Jerem. xlix. 35. "Jehovah hath made me a polished *shaft*, in his *quiver* hath he hid me," Isaiah xlix. 2. "Lo, children are an heritage of Jehovah,—happy is the man that hath his *quiver* full of them," Psalm cxxvii. 3, 4, 5. Children here, as in other places, signify truths of doctrine. "In Salem also is the tabernacle of Jehovah,—there brake he the *arrows of the bow*, the shield, the sword and the battle," Psalm lxxvi. 2, 3, 4 "Jehovah maketh wars to cease unto the ends of the earth, he breaketh the *bow*, and cutteth the spear in sunder, he burneth the chariots in the fire," Psalm xlvi. 9; Ezek. xxxix. 8, 9; Hosea ii. 18. In these places a bow signifies the doctrine of truth contending against falses, and, in an opposite sense, false doctrine contending against truths; therefore arrows and shafts signify truths or falses. As war, in the Word, signifies spiritual war, therefore warlike arms, such as the sword, spear, shield, target, bow and arrows, signify such things as are proper thereto.

300. *And a crown was given unto him*, signifies his token of combat. A crown signifies a token of combat, because in ancient times kings wore crowns in battle, as may appear from history, and partly from 2 Sam. i. 10, where the man says to David concerning Saul, that when he was fallen in battle, "he took the *crown* that was upon his head, and the bracelets that were upon his arm;" as also from what is said of the king of Rabbah and David, 2 Sam. xii. 29, 30. And as temptations are spiritual combats which the martyrs sustained, therefore crowns were given them as tokens of victory, n. 103. Hence it appears, that by a crown is here signified the token of their combat; therefore it follows, "And he went forth conquering, and to conquer."

301. *And he went forth conquering and to conquer*, signifies victory over evils and falses to eternity. It is said conquering and to conquer, because he who in spiritual combats, which are temptations, conquers in this world, conquers to eternity, for the hells cannot assault any one who has conquered them.

302. *And when he had opened the second seal*, signifies exploration from the Lord of those upon whom the last judgment was to be executed, respecting their states of life. The signi

fication here is similar to what was shown before, n. 295, only with the difference mentioned in what follows.

303. *I heard the second animal say*, signifies according to the divine truth of the Word, as above, n. 296.

304. *Come and see*, signifies a manifestation concerning the second in order, as may appear from the explanation above, n. 297, but there concerning the first in order, and here concerning the second.

305. *And there went out another horse that was red*, signifies the understanding of the Word destroyed as to good, and thence as to life in these. By a horse is signified the understanding of the Word, n. 298; and by a red horse is signified good destroyed. That white is predicated of truths, because it proceeds from the light of the sun of heaven, and that red is predicated of goods because it proceeds from the fire of the sun of heaven, may be seen above, n. 167, 231. But the reason why red is predicated of good destroyed, is, because an infernal redness is signified, proceeding from infernal fire, which is the love of evil; this kind of redness is hideous and abominable, there being nothing alive therein, but all dead; hence it is, that by a red horse is signified the understanding of the Word destroyed as to good. This may also appear from the description of him below; that "it was given him to take peace from the earth, that men should kill one another:" the second animal also, being like unto a calf, by which is signified the divine truth of the Word as to affection, n. 241, said, "Come and see," and thus showed that there was no affection of good, and thence no good in them. That red is spoken of love, as well the love of good as of evil, may appear from the following places: "He washed his garments in wine, and his clothes in the blood of grapes; his eyes shall be *red* with wine, and his teeth white with milk," Gen. xlix. 11, 12; speaking of the Lord. "Who is this that cometh from Edom? Wherefore art thou *red* in thine apparel, and thy garments like him that treadeth in the wine-fat?" Isaiah xliii. 1, 2; also of the Lord. "Her Nazarites were purer than snow, they were whiter than milk, they were more *red* than rubies," Lament. iv. 7; in these passages red is predicated of the love of good; in those which follow, of the love of evil: "The shield of his mighty men is made *red*, the valiant men are in *scarlet*, the chariots shall be with flaming *torches*, they shall seem like *torches*," Nahum ii. 3, 4. "Though your sins be as *scarlet*, they shall be as white as snow, though they be *red* like *crimson*, they shall be as wool," Isaiah i. 18. Nor is any thing else signified by the *red dragon*, Apoc. xii. 3; and by the *red horse* standing among the myrtle trees, Zech. i. 8. The same is predicated of the colours which in their ground are red, as is predicated of scarlet and purple.

306. *And power was given to him that sat thereon to take peace from the earth*, signifies the taking away of charity, spiritual security, and internal tranquillity. By peace are signified all things in their aggregate which come from the Lord, and thence all things of heaven and the church, and the beatitudes of life that are in them; these are what belong to peace in the supreme or inmost sense. It follows therefore that peace is charity, spiritual security, and internal tranquillity; for when man is in the Lord, he is in peace with his neighbour, which is charity; in protection against the hells, which is spiritual security; and when he is in peace with his neighbour, and in protection against the hells, he is in internal tranquillity from evils and falses. Since therefore all this is from the Lord, it may appear what is signified in general and in particular by peace in the following places: "For unto us a Child is born, unto us a Son is given; and the government shall be upon his shoulder: and his name shall be called Wonderful, Counsellor, The Mighty God, The Everlasting Father, The *Prince of Peace*. Of the increase of his government and *peace* there shall be no end," Isaiah ix. 6, 7. Jesus said, "*Peace* I leave with you, my *peace* I give you," John xiv. 27. Jesus said, "These things have I spoken unto you, that in *me* ye might have *peace*," John xvi. 33. "In his days shall the righteous flourish, and abundance of *peace*," Psalm lxxii. 7. "And I will make with them a covenant of *peace*," Ezek. xxxiv. 25, 27; xxxvii. 25, 26; Malachi ii. 4, 5. "How beautiful upon the mountains are the feet of him that bringeth good tidings,—that publisheth *peace*,—that saith unto Zion, Thy King reigneth," Isaiah lii. 7. "Jehovah bless thee, and lift up his countenance upon thee, and give thee *peace*," Numb. vi. 24—26. "Jehovah will bless his people with *peace*," Psalm xxix. 11. "Jehovah will deliver my soul in *peace*," Psalm lv. 18. "And the work of righteousness shall be *peace*, and the effect of righteousness is *quietness*, and *assurance* for ever. And my people shall dwell in a *peaceable* habitation and in *sure* dwellings, and in *quiet resting-places*," Isaiah xxxii. 17, 18. Jesus said unto the seventy whom he sent, "Into whatsoever house ye enter, first say, *Peace* be to this house; and if the Son of *Peace* be there, your *peace* shall rest upon it," Luke x. 5, 6; Matt. x. 12—14. "But the meek shall inherit the earth, and shall delight themselves in the abundance of *peace:* behold the upright, for the end of that man is *peace*," Psalm xxxvii. 11, 37. Zacharias prophesying, said, "The day-spring from on high hath visited us,—to guide our feet into the way of *peace*," Luke i. 78, 79 "Depart from evil and do good: seek *peace*, and pursue it,' Psalm xxxiv. 14. "Great *peace* have they that love thy law,' Psalm cxix. 165. "O that thou hadst hearkened to my commandments! then had thy *peace* been as a river: There is no

peace, saith Jehovah, unto the wicked," Isaiah xlviii. 18, 22. "Jehovah will speak *peace* unto his people: Righteousness and *peace* shall kiss each other," Psalm lxxxv. 9, 10. "There is no *peace* in my bones because of my sin," Psalm xxxviii. 3. "He hath filled me with bitterness, and thou hast removed my soul far off from *peace;* I forgat prosperity," Lament. iii. 15, 17; besides many other passages; from which it may be seen, that the above-mentioned things are understood by peace; keep in mind spiritual peace, and you will clearly perceive that this is the case; so likewise in these verses: Isaiah xxvi. 12; liii. 5; liv. 10, 13; Jerem. xxxiii. 6, 9; Haggai ii. 9; Zech. 8, 19; Psalm iv. 7, 8; Psalm cxx. 6, 7; Psalm cxxii. 6—9, Psalm cxxviii. 5, 6; Psalm clxvii. 14. That peace is what inmostly affects all good with blessedness, may be seen in the work concerning *Heaven and Hell*, n. 284—290.

307. *And that they should kill one another*, signifies intestine hatreds, infestations from the hells, and internal restlessness. These things are signified, when by the taking away peace is signified the taking away charity, spiritual security, and internal tranquillity, and when by the red horse is signified the understanding of the Word destroyed as to good; for these things happen when there is no longer any good; and there is no longer any good when it is not known what good is. That intestine hatreds take place when there is no charity, likewise infestations from the hells when there is no spiritual security, and internal disquietude when there is no rest from evils and their concupiscences or lusts, is evident; this is the case after death at least, if not in the world. That to kill, has such a signification, is plain from the signification of a sword, in what follows.

308. *And there was given unto him a great sword*, signifies the destruction of truth by falses of evil. That a sword, a dagger, and knife, signify truth combating against falses and destroying them, and in an opposite sense, falsity combating against truths, and destroying them, may be seen above, n. 52; here a great sword signifies the falses of evil destroying the truths of good. They are called falses of evil, because there are falses which are not falses of evil, and the latter do not destroy truths, but the former. That such is the signification of a great sword, is evident from its being said that presently a black horse was seen, by which is signified the understanding of the Word destroyed as to truth, and truth is destroyed by nothing but evil.

309. *And when he had opened the third seal*, signifies exploration from the Lord of those upon whom the last judgment was to be executed, as to the states of their life. The same is here signified by these words as before, n. 295, only with the difference explained below.

310. *And I heard the third animal say*, signifies according to the divine truth of the Word, as above, n. 296.

311. *Come and see*, signifies a manifestation concerning the third class, or concerning those who are the third in order, as may appear from the explanation above, n. 297, only there the first class in order are treated of, but here the third.

312. *And I beheld, and lo, a black horse*, signifies the understanding of the Word destroyed as to truth, thus as to doctrine among these. That a horse signifies the understanding of the Word, was shown above; the reason why black signifies what is not true, thus falsity, is, because black is the opposite of white, and white is predicated of truth, n. 167, 232, 233; white also derives its origin from light, and black from darkness, thus from the absence of light, and light is truth. But in the spiritual world there exists darkness from a twofold origin, one from the absence of flaming light, which light is enjoyed by those who are in the Lord's celestial kingdom, and the other from the absence of white light, which is the light enjoyed by those who are in the Lord's spiritual kingdom; the latter blackness has the same signification as darkness, but the former as thick darkness: there is a difference between these two kinds of blackness, the one is abominable, the other not so much so; it is the same with the falsities which they signify. They who appear in the abominable kind of blackness are called devils, such holding truth in abomination as much as owls do the light of the sun; but they appear in that kind of blackness, which is not so abominable, who are called satans; these do not abominate truth, but are averse to it; the latter may therefore be compared to birds of night, and the former to horned owls. That black, in the Word, is applicable to falsity, may appear from these places: "Her Nazarites were purer than snow,—their visage is *blacker than a coal*," Lament. iv. 7, 8. "The day shall become *dark* over the prophets," Micah iii. 6. "In the day when thou goest down into hell, I will make Lebanon *black* over thee," Ezek. xxxi. 15. "The sun became *black* as sackcloth of hair," Apoc. vi. 12. The sun, the moon, and the stars, became *black*, Jerem. iv. 27, 28; Ezek. xxxii. 7; Joel ii. 3; iii. 25; and elsewhere. The reason why the third animal displayed a black horse, was, because it had a face like a man, by which is signified the divine truth of the Word as to wisdom, n. 243, therefore this animal showed that there was no longer any truth of wisdom among those who constituted the third class.

313. *And he that sat on him had a pair of balances in his hand*, signifies the estimation of good and truth, of what kind it was with these. By the pair of balances in his hand, is signified the estimation of good and truth; for all measures and weights, in the Word, signify the estimation of the thing treated

of. That measures and weights have such a signification, is evident from the following passage in Daniel: There appeared a hand-writing before Belshazzar king of Babylon, when he was drinking wine out of the vessels of gold and of silver which were taken out of the temple in Jerusalem, "Mene, mene, tekel, upharsin," that is, thou art *numbered*, thou art *numbered, weighed*, and *divided;* whereof this is the interpretation: "mene, God hath numbered thy kingdom and put an end to it; tekel, thou art weighed in the balance and found wanting; peres, thy kingdom is divided and given to the Medes and Persians," v. 1, 2, 26, 28; by drinking out of the vessels of gold and silver of the temple in Jerusalem, and at the same time worshipping other gods, is signified the profanation of good and truth, as also by Babel; by mene, or to number, is signified to know his quality as to truth; by tekel, or to weigh, is signified to know his quality as to good; by peres, or to divide, is signified to disperse. That the quality of truth and good is signified by measures and balances in the Word, is evident in Isaiah: "Who hath *measured* the waters in the hollow of his hand, and *meted* out the heavens with the span, and comprehended the dust of the earth in a *measure*, and *weighed* the mountains in *scales* and the hills in a *balance?*" xl. 12. And in the Apocalypse: "The angel *measured* the wall of the Holy Jerusalem a hundred and forty-four cubits, which is the *measure* of a man, that is, of an angel," xxi. 17.

314. *And I heard a voice in the midst of the four animals say*, signifies the divine protection of the Word by the Lord. That the four animals signify the Word from first principles in ultimates, and the defences, lest its interior truths and goods should be violated, may be seen above, n. 239; and because those defences are from the Lord, therefore the voice was heard in the midst of the four animals; in the midst of them, means the Word as to its internal spiritual sense, which is guarded by the Lord. That the guarding of it is signified, is plain from what the voice says: "A measure of wheat for a penny, and three measures of barley for a penny, and see thou hurt not the oil and the wine," which signifies that since good and truth are held in little or no estimation, it will be provided that the holy goods and truths, which lie interiorly concealed in the Word, shall not be violated and profaned; and this is provided of the Lord by this result, that they come at length to know nothing concerning good, and thence nothing concerning truth, but mere evil and falsity; for they who know goods and truths can violate, yea, they can profane them, but not so they who do not know them. That such is the operation of the Divine Providence in guarding the Word from violation, may be seen in *The Angelic Wisdom concerning the Divine Providence*, n. 221 –233, n. 257, the end; n. 258, the beginning.

315. *A measure of wheat for a penny, and three measures of barley for a penny*, signifies because the estimation of good and truth is so small as scarcely to amount to any thing. By chœnix,* which denotes the measure and quantity measured, is signified quality, as above, n. 314; by wheat and barley is signified good and truth; and by a penny, which is a very small coin, that they are held in little or no estimation. It is said three measures of barley, because three signify all, and are predicated of truths, n. 515. The reason why wheat and barley signify good and truth, in this instance the good and truth of the church from the Word, is, because all things which belong to the field and the vineyard, signify such things as are of the church, on account of a field signifying the church as to its good and consequent truth, and a vineyard, the church as to its truth and consequent good; therefore where these are mentioned in the Word, the angels, who perceive all things spiritually, understand nothing else; as in Joel: "The *field* is wasted, the land mourneth; for the *corn* is wasted; the new *wine* is dried up, the *oil* languisheth. Be ye ashamed, O ye husbandmen; howl, O ye vine-dressers, for the *wheat* and for the *barley;* because the *harvest* of the *field* is perished," i. 10—12. All these expressions signify such things as belong to the church. That wheat and barley signify the good and truth of the church, may be seen from these places: John saith concerning Jesus, that he will "gather his *wheat* into the garner, and burn up the chaff with unquenchable fire," Matt. iii. 11, 12. Jesus said, "Let the tares and the *wheat* grow together, and in the time of harvest I will say to the reapers, Gather ye together first the tares, to burn them, but gather the *wheat* into my barn," Matt. xiii. 24—30. I have heard the consummation and decision from Jehovah God; "he layeth up the principal *wheat*, and appointed *barley;* for his God doth instruct him to discretion, and doth teach him," Isaiah xxviii. 21—26. Jehovah shall lead thee to "a land of *wheat* and *barley*," Deut. viii. 7, 8. A land of wheat and barley here is the land of Canaan, by which the church is signified. "Therefore they shall come and sing in the height of Zion, and shall flow together to the goodness of Jehovah, for *wheat* and for wine," Jerem. xxxi. 12. Jehovah shall satisfy thee "with the *fat of kidneys, of wheat*," Deut. xxxii. 13, 14; Psalm lxxxi. 14, 16; Psalm cxlvii. 12—14. Jehovah said unto the prophet Ezekiel, that he should make himself cakes of *barley* mixed with dung, and eat them, iv. 12, 15; and commanded the prophet Hosea to take a woman that was an adulteress; whom he bought for "a homer of *barley*, and half a homer of *barley*," iii. 1, 2: which things were done by those

---

* Chœnix, a Grecian measure, which contained as much corn as would serve a man one day It has been reckoned to be about a *pint and a half* English corn measure.

prophets, that they might represent the falsifications of truth in the church, for barley denotes truths, and barley mixed with dung denotes truths falsified and profaned; an adulterous woman also signifies truth falsified, n. 134.

316. *And see thou hurt not the oil and the wine*, signifies that it is provided by the Lord that the holy goods and truths, which lie interiorly concealed in the Word, shall not be violated and profaned. Oil signifies the good of love, and wine, truth from that good, therefore oil signifies holy good, and wine holy truth; see thou hurt them not, signifies that it is provided by the Lord that they shall not be violated and profaned; for this was heard from the midst of the four animals, thus from the Lord, n. 314; what is said by the Lord, the same is also provided for by him: that it is so provided, may be seen above, n. 314 and n. 255. That oil signifies the good of love, will be seen below, n. 778, 779; but that wine signifies truth from that good, is evident from the following places: "Ho, every one that thirsteth, come ye to the waters, and he that hath no money, come ye, buy and eat, yea come, buy *wine* and milk without money," Isaiah lv. 1. "And it shall come to pass in that day, that the mountains shall drop down new *wine*, and the hills shall flow with milk," Joel iii. 18; Amos ix. 13, 14. "And gladness is taken away from Carmel, and in the *vineyards* there shall be no singing:—the treaders shall tread out no *wine*, I have made their *vintage* shouting to cease," Isaiah xvi. 10; Jerem. xlviii. 32, 33. By Carmel is signified the spiritual church, because there were vineyards there. "Howl, all ye drinkers of *wine*, because of the new *wine;* for it is cut off from your mouth; howl, O ye *vine-dressers*," Joel i. 5, 10, 11. Nearly the same words occur in Hosea ix. 2, 3; Zeph. i. 13; Lament. ii. 11, 12; Micah vi. 15; Amos v. 11; Isaiah xxiv. 6, 7, 9, 10. "He washed his garments in *wine* and his clothes in the *blood of grapes;* his eyes shall be red with *wine*," Gen. xlix. 11, 12; speaking of the Lord: wine signifies divine truth. This is the reason why the holy supper was instituted by the Lord, in which the bread signifies the Lord as to his divine good, and the wine the Lord as to his divine truth, and with the recipients the bread signifies holy good, and the wine, holy truth, from the Lord: therefore he said, "I say unto you, I will not drink henceforth of this *fruit of the vine*, until that day when I drink it new with you in my Father's kingdom," Matt. xxvi. 29; Luke xxii. 18. Because bread and wine had this signification, therefore, also, Melchisedek, going to meet Abram, "brought forth *bread and wine;* and he was the priest of the most high God, and he blessed Abram," Gen. xiv. 18, 19. Similar is the signification of *the cakes* and *drink-offering*, in the sacrifices, concerning which see Exod. xxix. 40; Levit. xxiii. 12, 13, 18, 19; Numb. xv. 2—15; xxviii. 6, 7, 18, to the end; xxix. 1—7, and following verses.

The cakes were of wheat flour, and were therefore instead of bread, and the drink-offering was of wine. From which it may appear what is meant by these words of the Lord: "Neither do men put *new wine* into old bottles,—but they put *new wine* into new bottles, and both are preserved," Matt. ix. 17; Luke v. 37. New wine is the divine truth of the New Testament, thus of the new church, and old wine is the divine truth of the Old Testament, thus of the old church. Similar is the signification of these words, spoken at the marriage in Cana of Galilee: "Every man at first setteth forth good *wine*, and when men have well drunk, then that which is worse; but thou hast kept the good wine until now," John ii. 1—10. The like is also signified by wine in the Lord's parable of the man that was wounded by robbers, into whose wounds the Samaritan poured *oil* and *wine*, Luke x. 33, 34: for by him that was wounded by robbers, are meant they who are spiritually wounded by the Jews by evils and falses, to whom the Samaritan gave assistance by pouring oil and wine into his wounds, that is, by teaching good and truth, and, so far as he was able, by healing. Holy truth is also signified by new wine and wine in other parts of the Word; as in Isaiah ix. 21, 22; xxv. 6; xxxvi. 17; Hosea vii. 4, 5, 14; xiv. 6—8; Amos ii. 8; Zech. ix. 15, 17; Psalm civ. 14—16. Hence it is that a *vineyard*, in the Word, signifies a church that is in truths from the Lord. That wine signifies holy truth, may also appear from its opposite sense, in which it signifies truth falsified and profaned; as in these places: "Whoredom, and *wine*, and *new wine*, take away the heart. Their *wine* is sour, they have committed whoredom continually," Hosea iv. 11, 17, 18. Whoredom signifies the falsification of truth, as do wine and new wine. "For in the hand of Jehovah there is a cup, and the *wine* is red; it is full of mixture, and he poureth out of the same, but the dregs thereof all the wicked of the earth shall wring them out and drink them," Psalm lxxv. 8. "Babylon is a cup of gold in the hand of Jehovah that made all the earth drunken: the nations have drunken of her *wine*; therefore the nations are mad," Jerem li. 7. "Babylon is fallen, because she made all nations drink of the *wine* of the wrath of her fornication. If any man worship the beast,—the same shall drink of the *wine* of the wrath of God, which is poured out without mixture into the cup of his indignation," Apoc. xiv. 8—10. "Babylon hath made all nations drink of the *wine* of her fornication," Apoc. xviii. 3. "Great Babylon came in remembrance before God, to give unto her the cup of the *wine* of the fierceness of his wrath," Apoc. xvi. 19. "The inhabitants of the earth have been made drunk with the *wine* of her fornication," Apoc. xvii. 1, 2. By the *wine* which Belshazzar, king of Babylon, and his princes, and his wives, and his concubines, drank out of the vessels of the temple of Jerusalem, and at the same time "praised the gods of gold, and of silver, of brass, of iron, of wood, and of stone," Dan. v. 2—5, nothing is meant but the holy truth of the Word and of the church profaned; wherefore the hand-writing then appeared upon the wall, and the king was slain that night, verses 25, 30. Wine signifies truth falsified also in Isaiah v. 11, 12, 21, 22; xxviii. 1, 3, 7; xxix. 9; lvi. 11, 12; Jerem. xiii. 12, 13; xxiii. 9, 10. The same is signified by the drink-offering which they offered to idols, Isaiah lxv. 11; lvii. 6; Jerem. vii. 18; xliv. 17—19; Ezek. xx. 28; Deut. xxxii. 38. That wine should signify holy truth, and, in an opposite sense, truth profaned, is from correspondence; for the angels, who perceive all things spiritually, understand nothing else, when man reads about wine in the Word; such a correspondence is there between the natural thoughts of men and the spiritual thoughts of angels. It is the same with the wine in the holy supper, and hence it is, that introduction into heaven is effected by the holy supper, n. 224, at the end.

317. *And when he had opened the fourth seal*, signifies exploration from the Lord of those upon whom the last judgment was to be executed, as to their states of life, as above, n. 296, 303, only with the difference explained below.

318. *I heard the voice of the fourth animal say*, signifies according to the divine truth of the Word, as above, n. 296, 303.

319. *Come and see*, signifies a manifestation concerning the fourth class, or those who were fourth in order, as is evident from the explanation above, n. 297; but there it is applied to the first class, here to the fourth.

320. *And I looked, and behold, a pale horse*, signifies the understanding of the Word destroyed both as to good and as to truth. A horse signifies the understanding of the Word, n. 298, and paleness signifies a want of vitality. In the Word, this want of vitality is predicated of those who are not in the good of life grounded in the truths of doctrine; for the Word, in its literal sense, is not understood without doctrine, and doctrine is not perceived without a life according to it; the reason is, because a life according to doctrine which is from the Word, opens the spiritual mind, when light flows into it from heaven and illustrates and imparts perception. That this is the case, he is not aware of who knows truths of doctrine, and yet does not live according to them. The reason why the fourth animal showed a pale horse, was, because that animal was like a flying eagle, and therefore it signified the divine truth of the Word, as to knowledges, and as to the understanding derived from them, n. 244; therefore it indicated, that among those who were now seen there were no knowledges of good and truth from the Word, nor any understanding of them, and such in the spiritual world appear pale, as if devoid of life.

321. *And his name that sat on him was Death, and hell followed with him,* signifies the extinction of spiritual life, and thence damnation. By death is here signified spiritual death, which is the extinction of spiritual life; and by hell is signified damnation, which is a consequence of that death. Every man, indeed, has by creation, and therefore by birth, spiritual life, but that life is extinguished when he denies God, the sanctity of the Word, and eternal life; it is extinguished in the will, but remains in the understanding, or rather in the faculty of understanding. By this man is distinguished from the brute. As death signifies the extinction of spiritual life, and hell the consequent damnation, therefore death and hell in some places are named together; as in these: "I will ransom them from the power of *hell*, I will redeem them from *death:* O *death*, I will be thy plagues; O *hell*, I will be thy destruction," Hosea xiii. 14. "The sorrows of *death* compassed me;—the sorrows of *hell* compassed me; the snares of *death* prevented me," Psalm xviii. 5, 6; Psalm cxvi. 3. "Like sheep they are laid in *hell; death* shall feed on them, and their beauty shall consume in *hell.* But God will redeem my soul from the power of *hell*," Psalm xlix. 14, 15. "I have the keys of *hell* and *death*," Apoc. i. 18.

322. *And power was given them over the fourth part of the earth, to kill,* signifies the destruction of all good in the church. Since death signifies the extinction of man's spiritual life, and hell signifies damnation, it follows that to kill, here, means to destroy the life of a man's soul; the life of the soul is spiritual life; a fourth part of the earth signifies all the good of the church; the earth is the church, n. 285. That a fourth part denotes all good, cannot be known by any one, unless he knows what numbers in the Word signify. The numbers two and four, in the Word, are predicated of goods, and signify them; and the numbers three and six, of truths, and signify them; thus a fourth part, or simply a fourth, signifies all good, and a third part, or simply a third, signifies all truth; therefore to kill a fourth part of the earth, here signifies to destroy all the good of the church. That power was not given to him that sat upon the pale horse to kill a fourth part of the habitable earth, is evident. Besides, four, in the Word, signifies the conjunction of good and truth. That four has these significations, may indeed be proved out of the Word; as by *the four animals or cherubs*, Ezek. i. vii. x.; Apoc. v. By the *four* chariots between the two mountains of brass, Zech. vi. 2. By the *four* winds, Zech. ii.; and by the *four* horns of the altar, Exod. xxvii. 1—9; Apoc. ix. 13. By the "*four* angels standing on the *four* corners of the earth, holding the *four* winds of the earth," Apoc. vii. 1; Matt. xxv. 31; as also "by visiting their sins upon the *third* and *fourth* generation," Numb. xiv. 18; and in

other places by the third and fourth generation. By these, and by many other passages in the Word, I say, it might be proved that four is predicated of goods, and signifies them, and also the conjunction of good and truth; but since this would not appear without a prolix explanation of those passages, it is sufficient to mention, that nothing else is understood in heaven by four and by a fourth part.

323. *With sword, and with hunger, and with death, and with the beasts of the earth*, signifies by falses of doctrine, by evils of life, by the love of self, and by lusts. That by a sword is signified truth combating against evils and falses, and destroying them, and, in an opposite sense, falsity combating against goods and truths, and destroying them, may be seen above, n. 52, 108, 117; here therefore by sword, the destruction of all good in the church being treated of, are signified falses of doctrine. That hunger signifies evils of life, will be confirmed below. The reason why death signifies the self-love of man, is, because death signifies extinction of spiritual life, and thence natural life separated from spiritual life, as above, n. 321, and this life is the life of man's self-love; for from it man loves nothing but himself and the world, and thence also he loves all kinds of evils, which, from the love of that life, are delightful to him. That beasts of the earth signify lusts originating from that love, will be seen below, n. 567. Now something shall be said concerning the signification of hunger. Hunger signifies deprivation and rejection of the knowledges of truth and good, arising from evils of life; it also signifies ignorance of the knowledges of truth and good arising from a deficiency thereof in the church; and it signifies likewise a desire to know and understand them. I. That famine signifies a deprivation and rejection of the knowledges of truth and good, arising from evils of life, and thence evils of life, may appear from the following passages: "They shall be consumed by the *sword* and by *famine*, and their carcasses shall be meat for the fowls of heaven, and for the beasts of the earth," Jerem. xvi. 4. "These two things shall come unto thee, desolation and destruction, and the *famine* and the *sword*," Isaiah li. 19. "Behold, I will punish them: the young men shall die by the *sword*, their sons and their daughters shall die by *famine*," Jerem. xi. 22. "Deliver up their children to the *famine*, and pour out their blood by the force of the *sword;* and let their men be put to *death*," Jerem. xviii. 21. "I will send upon them the *sword*, the *famine*, and the *pestilence*, and will make them like vile figs that cannot be eaten, they are so evil. And I will persecute them with the *sword, famine*, and *pestilence*," Jerem. xxix. 17, 18. "I will send the *sword*, the *famine*, and the *pestilence*, till they be consumed from off the land," Jerem. xxiv. 10. "I proclaim a liberty for you,—to the *sword*, to the *pestilence*, and

to the *famine;* and I will make you to be removed into all the kingdoms of the earth," Jerem. xxxiv. 17. "Because thou hast defiled my sanctuary,—a third part of thee shall die with the *pestilence*, and with *famine* shall they be consumed, and a third part shall fall by the *sword*, when I shall send upon them the evil arrows of *famine*, which shall be for their destruction," Ezek. v. 11—13, 16. "The *sword* is without, and *pestilence* and *famine* within," Ezek. vii. 15. "For all the evil abominations of the house of Israel, they shall fall by the *sword*, and by the *famine*, and by the *pestilence*," Ezek. vi. 11. "I will send my four sore judgments upon Jerusalem, the *sword*, the *famine*, and the *noisome beast*, and the *pestilence*, to cut off from it man and beast," Ezek. xiv. 13, 15, 21: besides other places; as Jerem. xiv. 12, 13, 15, 16; xlii. 13, 14, 16—18, 22; xliv. 12, 13, 27; Matt. xxiv. 7, 8; Mark xiii. 8; Luke xxi. 11. The sword, famine, pestilence, and beasts, in those places, have a signification similar to that of the sword, hunger, death, and the beasts of the earth, here mentioned; for in the Word there is a spiritual sense in every single expression, in which sense a sword denotes the destruction of spiritual life by falses; hunger, the destruction of spiritual life by evils; beasts of the earth, the destruction of spiritual life by lusts of falsity and evil; and pestilence and death denote plenary consummation, and thus damnation. II. That hunger signifies ignorance of the knowledges of good and truth arising from a deficiency of such knowledges in the church, is also evident from various passages in the Word; as from Isaiah v. 13; viii. 19—22; Lament. ii. 19; v. 8—10; Amos viii. 11—14; Job v. 17, 20; and other places. III. That famine or hunger signifies a desire to know and understand the truths and goods of the church, is plain from the following: Isaiah viii. 21; xxxii. 6; xlix. 10; lviii. 6, 7; 1 Sam. ii. 4, 5; Psalm xxxiii. 18, 19; Psalm xxxiv. 10, 11; Psalm xxxvii. 18, 19; Psalm cvii. 8, 9, 35—37; Psalm cxlvi. 7; Matt. v. 6; xxv. 35, 37, 44; Luke i. 53; John vi. 35; and others.

324. *And when he had opened the fifth seal*, signifies an exploration from the Lord of their states of life, who were to be saved at the day of the last judgment, and in the mean time were reserved. That these are here treated of, is evident from what now follows. But it is to be observed, that these, and the like, are treated of throughout the twentieth chapter, the explanation of which may be seen, n. 839—874, manifesting who they are, and why reserved.

325. *I saw under the altar the souls of them that were slain for the Word of God, and for the testimony which they held*, signifies those who were hated, abused, and rejected by the wicked on account of their life being conformable to the truths of the Word, and their acknowledgment of the Lord's Divine

Humanity, and who were guarded by the Lord that they might not be seduced. Under the altar, signifies the lower earth, where they were guarded by the Lord; an altar signifies the worship of the Lord from the good of love; by the souls of them that were slain, are not here signified the martyrs, but they who are hated, abused, and rejected by the wicked in the world of spirits, and who might be seduced by the dragonists and heretics; for the Word of God and for the testimony which they held, signifies for living according to the truths of the Word, and acknowledging the Lord's Divine Humanity. Testimony in heaven is not given to any but to those who acknowledge the Lord's Divine Humanity, for it is the Lord who testifies, and gives the angels to testify; "For the *testimony of Jesus* is the spirit of prophecy," Apoc. xix. 10. Since they were under the altar, it is evident they were guarded by the Lord; for they who led, in any sort, a life of charity, were all guarded by the Lord against sustaining any injury from the wicked; and after the last judgment, when the wicked were removed, they were set free and elevated into heaven. I have frequently seen them, since the last judgment, liberated from the lower earth and translated into heaven. That by the slain are meant they who are rejected, slandered, and hated by the wicked in the world of spirits, and who might be seduced, and also who desire to know truths, but cannot, by reason of falses in the church, may appear from these passages: "Thus saith Jehovah God, Feed the flock of the *slaughter*, whose possessors *slay* them:—and I will feed the flock of *slaughter*, even you, O poor of the flock," Zech. xi. 4, 5, 7. "We are *killed* all the day long; we are counted as sheep for the *slaughter;* O Jehovah, arise, cast us not off for ever," Psalm xliv. 22, 24. "Jacob shall cause them which are to come to take root, or is he *slain* according to the *slaughter* of them that were *slain* by him?" Isaiah xxvii. 6, 7. "For I have heard a voice of the daughter of Zion,—woe is me, now; for my soul is wearied because of *murderers*," Jerem. iv. 3. "They shall deliver you up to be afflicted, and shall *kill* you, and ye shall be hated of all nations for my name's sake," Matt. xxiv. 9; John xvi. 33: this the Lord said to his disciples; but by disciples are meant all who worship the Lord, and live according to the truths of his Word; these the wicked in the world of spirits continually desire to kill; but because there they cannot kill the body, they continually desire to kill the soul; and since they are not able to do this, they burn with such hatred against them, that nothing delights them more than to do them mischief: this is the reason why they were guarded by the Lord, and when the wicked were cast into hell, which happened after the last judgment, they were brought out of their places of security: but see the explanation of chap. xx., n. 846, which treats of this subject. That to slay or kill, in the

Word, signifies to destroy souls, which is to kill spiritually, is evident from many places there, as also from the following: Isaiah xiv. 19—21; xxvi. 21; Jerem. xxv. 33; Lament. ii. 21; Ezek. ix. 1, 6; Apoc. xxviii. 24.

326. *And they cried with a loud voice*, signifies grief of heart, as is evident from what now follows.

327. *Saying, How long, O Lord, holy and true, dost thou not judge and avenge our blood on them that dwell on the earth?* signifies, by reason that the last judgment was protracted, and they who offer violence to the Word and to the Lord's Divine Humanity were not removed. "How long, O Lord, holy and true, dost thou not judge," signifies, why is the last judgment protracted? "and avenge our blood," signifies, why in justice are they not condemned, who have offered them violence for acknowledging the Lord's Divine Humanity, and living in conformity to the truths of his Word? by blood is signified violence offered to them, n. 379; by "them that dwell on the earth," are meant the wicked in the world of spirits, from whom they were guarded that they might not be hurt.

328. *And white robes were given unto every one of them*, signifies that there was given them a communication and conjunction with the angels who were in divine truths. Garments signify truths, n. 166, and white garments genuine truths, n. 212. Garments have this signification, because all in the heavens are clothed according to the truths they possess; every one is clothed according to conjunction with angelic societies; therefore when conjunction is granted, they immediately appear clothed in a similar manner; hence it is, that by white robes being given them, is signified that communication and conjunction was given them with angels who were in divine truths. Robes, mantles, and cloaks, signify truths in common, because they are a common covering to the body. He who is aware of this their signification, may know the arcana which are contained in the following passages: That Elijah, when he found Elisha, "cast his *mantle* upon him," 1 Kings xix. 19. That Elijah with his *mantle* divided the waters of Jordan, 2 Kings ii. 8. And in like manner Elisha, 2 Kings ii. 14. That the *mantle* of Elijah fell from him when he was taken up into heaven, and that Elisha took it up, 2 Kings ii. 12, 13; for by Elijah and Elisha the Lord was represented as to the Word, and therefore their mantle signified the divine truth of the Word in general. As also what was signified by the *robe* of Aaron's ephod, at the border of which there were pomegranates of blue and purple, and golden bells, Exod. xxviii. 31—35; that it signified divine truth in common, may be seen in *The Arcana Cœlestia*, n. 9825. Cloaks and mantles have a similar signification in the following passages: "All the princes of the sea shall come down, and lay away their *robes*," Ezek.

xxvi. 16. The scribes and Pharisees make broad the borders of their *garments*, that they may be seen of men, Matt. xxiii. 5. "My people is risen up as an enemy, ye pull off the *robe* with the *garment* from them that pass by," Micah ii. 8; and in other places.

329. *And it was said unto them, that they should rest yet for a little season, until their fellow-servants also and their brethren, that should be killed as they were, should be fulfilled*, signifies that the last judgment should yet be protracted a little, till they should be collected from all quarters, who would, in like manner, be hated, abused, and rejected by the wicked for acknowledging the Lord's Divine Humanity, and living in conformity to the truths of his Word. That this is the signification, appears from what has been said above. Similar is the signification of this passage in Isaiah: "Thy dead men shall live; Awake and sing, ye that dwell in the dust: Come, my people, enter thou into thy chambers, and shut thy door after thee: hide thyself as it were for a little moment, until the indignation be overpast. For, behold, Jehovah cometh out of his place, to pursue the inhabitants of the earth for their iniquity: the earth also shall disclose her blood, and shall no more cover her slain," xxvi. 19—21. But, as was observed before, this subject, and others of a similar nature, are treated of in chapter xx., which is explained, n. 839—874.

330. *And I beheld when he had opened the sixth seal*, signifies exploration from the Lord of their state of life, who were interiorly evil, and on whom the last judgment was to be executed. That these are treated of is evident from what now follows; but that they may be understood, two arcana are to be revealed: First, that the last judgment was executed only on such as appeared in their external form as Christians, and orally professed the things of the church, but in their internal form, or in their hearts, were against them; and, as such, they were therefore in conjunction with the ultimate heaven as to their exteriors, but with hell as to their interiors. Secondly, that as long as they were in conjunction with the ultimate heaven, so long the internals of their will and their love were closed, for which reason they did not appear wicked to others; but when they were separated from the ultimate heaven, then their interiors were disclosed, and found to be totally in opposition to their exteriors, from which they dissembled and feigned that they were angels of heaven, and that the places they inhabited were heavens. These heavens, so called, were those which passed away at the time of the last judgment, Apoc. xxi. 1. But more on this subject may be seen in the small tract on *The Last Judgment*, n. 70, 71, and in *The Continuation of the Last Judgment*, n. 10.

331. *And, lo, there was a great earthquake*, signifies an

entire change of the state of the church with these, and their terror. Earthquakes signify changes of state in the church, because the earth signifies the church, n. 285; and because in the spiritual world, when the state of the church is perverted anywhere, and there is a change, an earthquake takes place, and as this is a prelude to their destruction, the effect is terror; for the earths in the spiritual world are in appearance like the earths in the natural world, n. 260; but as the earths there, like all other things in that world, are from a spiritual origin, therefore changes occur according to the state of the church among the inhabitants, and when the state of the church is perverted, they quake and tremble, yea, sink down and are moved out of their places. That this was the case, when the last judgment was at hand and accomplished, may be seen in the tract on *The Last Judgment.* Hence it may appear what is meant by quakings, concussions, and commotions of the earth, in the following places: "There shall be famines, pestilences, and *earthquakes* in divers places," Matt. xxiv. 7; Mark xiii. 8; Luke xxi. 11; this is said of the last judgment. "In the fire of my wrath have I spoken, Surely in that day there shall be a great *earthquake*, and all the men that are upon the face of the earth shall *shake*, and the mountains shall be thrown down," Ezek. xxxviii. 18—20. "And there was a great *earthquake*, such as was not since men were upon the earth," Apoc. xvi. 18. "I will shake the heavens, and the earth shall be *removed* out of her place, in the wrath of Jehovah of Hosts," Isaiah xiii. 12, 13. "And the foundations of the earth do *shake*, the earth is *moved exceedingly*, for the transgression thereof shall be heavy upon it," Isaiah xxiv. 18—20. "Then the foundations of the world were *moved* at thy rebuke, O Jehovah," Psalm xviii. 17, 18. The mountains *quake* at the presence of Jehovah, and the rocks are *thrown down*, Nahum i. 5, 6: and so in other places; as Jerem. x. 10; xlix. 21; Joel ii. 10; Haggai ii. 6, 7; Apoc. xi. 19; and elsewhere. But these things are to be understood as having taken place in the spiritual world, and not in the natural world; in this respect they signify such things as are explained above.

332. *And the sun became black as sackcloth of hair, and the moon became as blood*, signifies the adulteration of all the good of love in them, and the falsification of all the truth of faith. That the sun signifies the Lord as to divine love, and thence the good of love from him; and in an opposite sense, a denial of the Lord's divinity, and thence adulteration of the good of love, may be seen above, n. 53. And as the sun signifies the good of love, the moon therefore signifies the truth of faith; for the sun is red from fire, and the moon is white by virtue of the light from the sun; and fire signifies the good of love, and light, the truth from that good: concerning the moon, see also the

passages adduced above, n. 53. It is said the sun became black as sackcloth of hair, because adulterated good in itself is evil, and evil is black; and the reason why it is said the moon became as blood, is, because blood signifies divine truth, and in an opposite sense, divine truth falsified, as may be seen below, n. 379, 684. Nearly the same is said of the sun and moon in Joel: "The *sun* shall be turned into *darkness*, and the *moon* into *blood*, before the great and the terrible day of Jehovah," ii. 31.

333. *And the stars of heaven fell unto the earth*, signifies the dispersion of all the knowledges of good and truth. That stars signify the knowledges of good and truth, may be seen above, n. 51; that to fall from heaven to the earth means to be dispersed, or to disappear, is evident; in the spiritual world, also, stars appear to fall from heaven to the earth there, when the knowledges of good and truth perish.

334. *Even as a fig-tree casteth her untimely figs, when she is shaken of a mighty wind*, signifies by ratiocinations of the natural man separated from the spiritual. It is said to have this signification, when yet it is a comparison, because all comparisons in the Word are also correspondences, and in the spiritual sense they cohere with the subject treated of, as in the present instance; for a fig, from correspondence, signifies the natural good of man in conjunction with his spiritual good, but here, in an opposite sense, the natural good of man separated from his spiritual good, which is not good; and as the natural man, when separated from the spiritual, perverts from ratiocinations the knowledges of good and truth, which are signified by the stars, it follows that this is signified by a fig-tree shaken by a mighty wind. That wind and storm signify ratiocination, is evident from many passages in the Word, but it is not necessary to adduce them here, because it is a comparison. The reason why a fig-tree signifies the natural good of man, is, because every tree signifies something of the church in man, therefore also man with respect thereto: by way of confirmation we select these passages: All the hosts of heaven "shall fall down, as the leaf falleth off from the vine, and as a falling *fig* from the *fig-tree*," Isaiah xxxiv. 4. "I will surely consume them, there shall be no grapes on the vine, nor *figs* on the *fig-tree*, and the leaf shall fade," Jerem. viii. 13. "All thy strongholds shall be like *fig-trees* with the first ripe *figs;* if they be shaken, they shall even fall into the mouth of the eater," Nahum iii. 12; besides other places; as Isaiah xxxiv. 2, 3, 5, 8; xxxviii. 21; Jerem. xxix. 17, 18; Hosea ii. 12; ix. 10; Joel i. 7, 12; Zech. iii. 10; Matt. xxi. 18—21: xxiv. 32, 33; Mark xi. 12—15, 19—25; Luke vi. 44; xiii. 6—9; in which places nothing else is meant by a fig-tree.

335. *And the heavens departed as a scroll when it is rolled together*, signifies separation from heaven and conjunction with

hell. It is said that heaven departed as a scroll rolled together, because the interior understanding, and hence the thought, of man, is as heaven; for his understanding can be elevated into the light of heaven, and in such elevation can think with the angels concerning God, concerning love and faith, and concerning eternal life: but if his will is not at the same time elevated into the heat of heaven, the man is not conjoined with the angels of heaven, thus is not a heaven. That this is the case, may be seen in *The Angelic Wisdom concerning the Divine Love and the Divine Wisdom*, Part the Fifth. By virtue of this faculty of the understanding, the wicked, who are here treated of, could be in consociation with the angels of the ultimate heaven; but when these were separated from the former, their heaven departed as a scroll rolled together. By a scroll rolled together is meant parchment rolled up, because their books were skins, and the comparison is made with a book, because a book denotes the Word, n. 256; therefore when it is rolled up like a skin, nothing that it contains is apparent, and it is as though it were not. On this account the like is said in Isaiah: "And all the host of heaven shall be dissolved, and the heavens shall be rolled together as a *scroll*, and shall fall down as the leaf falleth from the fig-tree," xxxiv. 4. Hosts are the goods and truths of the church derived from the Word, n. 447. From these considerations it may appear, that by the heavens departing as a scroll rolled together, is signified separation from heaven, and conjunction with hell. That separation from heaven is conjunction with hell, is evident.

336. *And every mountain and island were moved out of their places*, signifies that all the good of love and truth of faith departed. That this is the signification of these words no one could discover without the spiritual sense; they have this signification however, because by mountains are understood those who are in the good of love, by reason that the angels dwell upon mountains; such as are in love to the Lord dwelling on high mountains, and such as are in love towards their neighbour dwelling on lower ones; wherefore by every mountain is signified every good of love. By islands are meant those who are more remote from the worship of God, see above, n. 34; here those who are in faith, and not so much in the good of love, therefore, in an abstract sense, every island signifies every truth of faith; by being moved out of their places is signified to recede. It is owing to the circumstance of the angels dwelling upon mountains and hills, that mountains and hills in the Word signify heaven and the church, where there exists love to the Lord and love to the neighbour, and, in an opposite sense, hell, where there exists self-love and the love of the world. That by mountains and hills are signified heaven and the church, where there exists love to the Lord and love to the

neighbour, and thus where the Lord is, is evident from the following places: "I will lift up mine eyes to the *hills*, from whence cometh my help," Psalm cxxi. 1. "Behold upon the *mountains* the feet of him that bringeth good tidings, that publisheth peace," Nahum i. 15; Isaiah lii. 7. "Praise Jehovah, *mountains* and all *hills*," Isaiah cxlviii. 9: The *hill of God* is as the *hill* of Bashan, *a high hill* is the *hill* of Bashan. Why leap ye, ye *high hills?* the *hill* which Jehovah desireth to dwell in, yea, Jehovah will dwell in it for ever," Psalm lxviii. 15, 16. "Ye *mountains* that ye skipped like rams; and ye little *hills* like lambs? Tremble, thou earth, at the presence of the Lord," Psalm cxiv. 4, 7. "And I will bring forth a seed out of Jacob, and out of Judah an inheritor of my *mountains*, and mine elect shall inherit it, and my servants shall dwell there," Isaiah lxv. 9. At the consummation of the age; "then let them which be in Judea flee into the *mountains*," Matt. xxiv. 16. "Thy righteousness, O Jehovah, is like the great *mountains*," Psalm xxxvi. 6. Jehovah will go forth to battle, "and his feet shall stand in that day upon the *Mount of Olives*, which is before Jerusalem on the east," Zech. xiv. 4. Because the Mount of Olives signified divine love, therefore the Lord in the day-time taught in the temple, but "at night he went out and abode in the *Mount of Olives*," Luke xxi. 37; xxii. 39; John viii. 1. And for the same reason the Lord discoursed with his disciples upon that *mount* concerning his coming and the consummation of the age, Matt. xxiv. 3; Mark xiii. 3, and following verses. And also went from thence to Jerusalem and suffered, Matt. xxi. 1; xxvi. 30; Mark xi. 1; xiv. 26; Luke xix. 29, 37; xxi. 37; xxii. 39. Because a mountain signified heaven and love, Jehovah descended upon the *top of Mount Sinai*, and promulgated the law, Exod. xix. 20; xxiv. 17. And for the same reason the Lord was transfigured before Peter, James, and John, upon a *high mountain*, Matt. xvii. 1. And on this account Zion was upon a mountain, and also Jerusalem, and they are called the *Mountain of Jehovah* and *the Mountain of Holiness*, in many parts of the Word. Mountains and hills have a similar signification in other places; as in Isaiah vii. 25; xxx. 25; xl. 9; xliv. 23; xlix. 11, 13; iv. 12; Jerem. xvi. 15, 16; Ezek. xxxvi. 8; Joel iii. 18; Amos iv. 12, 13; ix. 13, 14; Psalm lxxx. 9, 10; Psalm civ. 6—10, 13. That those loves are signified by mountains and hills, may appear still more evidently from their opposite sense, in which they signify infernal loves, which are self-love and the love of the world, as is manifest from the following passages: The day of Jehovah shall come upon "all the *high mountains*, and upon all the *hills* that are *lifted* up," Isaiah ii. 12, 14. "Every valley shall be exalted, and every *mountain* and *hill* shall be made low," Isaiah xl. 3, 4. "The *mountains* flowed down at thy presence," Isaiah lxiv. 1, 3. "Behold, I am against thee, O destroying *mountain*, which destroyest all the earth, and will make thee a *burnt mountain*," Jerem. li. 25. "I beheld the *mountains*, and lo, they trembled, and all the *hills* moved lightly," Jerem. iv. 23, 24. "For a fire is kindled in mine anger,—and it shall set on fire the foundations of the *mountains*," Deut. xxxii. 22. "I will make waste *mountains* and *hills*," Isaiah xlii. 15. "Behold, (O Jacob,) I will make thee a new sharp threshing instrument having teeth, thou shalt thresh the *mountains*, and beat them small, and shalt make the *hills* as chaff,—and the wind shall carry them away," Isaiah xli. 15, 16. "Give glory to Jehovah your God, before your feet stumble upon the *mountains* of *twilight*," Jerem. xiii. 16. Nor is any thing else meant by the *seven mountains*, upon which the woman sat, which was Babylon, Apoc. xvii. 9 ; besides other places ; as Isaiah xiv. 13 ; lii. 7 ; Jerem. ix. 10 ; Ezek. vi. 3 ; xxxiv. 6 ; Micah vi. 1, 2 ; Nahum i. 4, 5 ; Psalm xlvi. 3, 4. From the above it is evident what is to be understood by every mountain and island being moved out of their places ; as also in what follows, by "And every island fled away, and the *mountains* were not found," Apoc. xvi. 20; n. 714.

337. *And the kings of the earth, and the great men, and the rich men, and the chief-captains, and the mighty men, and every bond-man, and every free-man*, signifies those who before separation were in the understanding of truth and good, in the science of the knowledges thereof, in erudition, either from others or from themselves, and yet not in a life conformable thereto. That such is the signification of the above words in their order, can only be known by those who are acquainted with the meaning of kings, of great men, rich men, chief-captains, mighty men, bond-men, and free-men, in the spiritual sense; for by kings, in this sense, are signified they who are in truths; by great men, they who are in goods; by rich men, they who are in the knowledges of truth; by chief-captains, they who are in the knowledges of good; by mighty men, they who are in erudition; by servants, they who are in such things from others, thus from the memory; by free-men, they who are in such things from themselves, thus from judgment. But to prove the signification of all these names from the Word would be too prolix; what is signified by kings has been shown before, n. 20, and what by rich men, n. 206; what by great men, is evident from Jerem. v. 5; Nahum iii. 10; Jonah iii. 7 ; for great is predicated of good, n. 896, 898; that mighty men, and bond-men, and free-men, are such as are in erudition, either from others or from themselves, will be seen below. It is said, they who are in these things, and yet not in a life according to them, because wicked men, yea, the worst of men, may be in the science and in the understanding of the knowledges of good

and truth, and also in much erudition, but as they are not in a life according to them, they are in fact not in them; for what is only in the understanding, and not at the same time in the life, is not in a man, but without, as it were in an outer court; but that which is at the same time in the life, is in a man, it is within him as in a house; therefore the latter are preserved, and the former rejected.

338. *Hid themselves in the dens and in the rocks of the mountains*, signifies that they were now in evils and in falses of evil. To hide themselves in the dens and in the rocks of the mountains, signifies to be in evils and in falses of evil, because they who in the sight of the world have appeared to be in the good of love, and yet were in evil, after death hide themselves in dens; and they who have pretended to be principled in the truths of faith, and yet were in falses of evil, hide themselves in the rocks of the mountains. The entrances appear like holes in the earth, and like clefts in the mountains, into which they crawl like serpents, and there hide themselves. That such are their abiding places I have frequently seen. Hence it is that by dens or caves are signified the evils with such, and by holes and clefts the falses of evil, in the following places: In that day "they shall go into the *holes of the rocks* and into the *caves of the earth*, when Jehovah ariseth to shake terribly the earth," Isaiah ii. 19. In that day they shall "go into the *clefts of the rocks* and into the *tops of the rugged rocks* for fear of Jehovah," Isaiah ii. 21. "To dwell in the *cliffs* of the valleys, in *caves* of the earth, and in the rocks," Job xxx. 6. "The pride of thine heart hath deceived thee, thou that dwellest in the *clefts* of the rock," Obad. verse 3. In that day "they shall come and shall rest in the desolate valleys, and in the *holes* of the rocks," Isaiah vii. 19. "Because the palaces shall be forsaken—the forts and towers shall be for *dens* for ever," Isaiah xxxii. 14. "The pride of thine heart hath deceived thee, O thou that dwellest in the *clefts* of the rock," Jerem. xlix. 16. "And they shall hunt them from every mountain and hill, and out of the *holes* of the rocks; they are not hid from my face, neither is their iniquity hid from mine eyes," Jerem. xvi. 16, 17. In that day "the sucking child shall play on the *hole* of the asp, and the weaned child shall put his hand on the cockatrice *den*," Isaiah xi. 8.

339. *And said to the mountains and rocks, Fall on us, and hide us from the face of Him that sitteth on the throne, and from the wrath of the Lamb*, signifies confirmations of evils by falsity, and of falsity from evil, until they did not acknowledge any thing divine in the Lord. Mountains signify the loves of evil, thus evils, n. 336, and rocks signify the falses of faith; by falling upon them and hiding them, is signified to be defended against influx from heaven; and as this is done by confirma

tions of evil by falsity, and by confirmations of falsity from evil, therefore these are signified; by hiding themselves from the face of Him that sitteth on the throne, and from the wrath of the Lamb, is signified until they do not acknowledge any thing divine in the Lord; by Him that sitteth on the throne is meant the Lord's divinity, from whence are all things; and by the Lamb is meant himself as to the Divine Humanity; the Lord as to both was upon the throne, as has been shown above. It is said from his face and from his anger, because all they who are in dens and rocks, dare not set foot out of them, nor even put forth a finger, by reason of the pain and torment consequent on doing so; this is owing to the hatred which they bear against the Lord, even to their not being able to name him; and the divine sphere of the Lord fills all things, which they cannot remove from themselves, but by confirmations of evil by falsity, and of falsity from evil; the delights of the wicked occasion this. Similar is the signification of this passage in Hosea: "And they shall say to the *mountains*, Cover us, and to the *hills*, Fall on us," x. 8: and in Luke: "Then shall they begin to say to the *mountains*, Fall on us; and to the *hills*, Cover us," xxiii. 30. That this is the spiritual sense of these words, cannot appear in the letter, but the spiritual sense is rendered apparent by this consideration, that when a last judgment is executed, they who are in evil, and desire to be in good, experience great sufferings in the beginning; whereas they suffer less on such an occasion who confirm themselves in their evil by falses, for these last cover their evil by falses, but the former lay bare their evil, and in this case cannot support the divine influx, as is seen in what follows. The dens and caves into which they cast themselves, are correspondences.

340. *For the great day of his wrath is come, and who shall be able to stand?* signifies that they were made such of themselves by means of their separation from the good and faithful on account of the last judgment, which otherwise they would not be able to abide. The great day of the wrath of the Lamb, signifies the day of the last judgment; and who shall be able to stand? signifies their inability to support it by reason of their torment; for when the last judgment is at hand, the Lord, together with heaven, approaches, and of those who are below in the spiritual world, none can support the Lord's coming, but those who are interiorly good, and they are interiorly good, who shun evils as sins, and look to the Lord. That the day of the Lord's anger signifies the last judgment is evident from the following passages: "Before the fierce *anger* of Jehovah come upon you, before the *day* of Jehovah's *anger* come upon you, —it may be ye shall be hid in the *day* of Jehovah's *anger*," Zeph. ii. 2, 3. "Behold the *day of Jehovah* cometh, cruel both with wrath and fierce *anger*," Isaiah xiii. 9, 13. "The great

day of Jehovah is near, a *day of wrath*, a day of trouble and distress, a day of clouds and thick darkness," Zeph. i. 14, 15. "*Thy wrath* is come, and the time of the dead that they should be judged, and that thou shouldest give reward unto thy servants, and shouldest destroy them that destroy the earth," Apoc. xi. 18. "Kiss the Son, lest he be angry and ye perish in the way, when his *wrath* is kindled but a little. Blessed are all they that put their trust in Him," Psalm ii. 12.

341. To the above I will add this Memorable Relation. I saw some of the English clergy assembled, to the number of six hundred, who prayed to the Lord that they might be permitted to ascend to a society of the superior heaven; which being granted them, they ascended. And when they entered, to their great joy they saw their king, the present king's grandfather,* who went up to two bishops that were among them, whom he had known in the world, and entering into discourse with them, asked them, "How came you here?" To which they replied, that they had made supplication to the Lord, and it was granted them. He said to them, "Why to the Lord, and not to God the Father?" And they answered, that they were so instructed below. Upon which he said, "Did I not sometimes tell you in the world, that the Lord ought to be approached, and also that charity is primary? What reply did you then make concerning the Lord?" And it was given them to recollect, that they had made answer, "That when the Father is approached, the Son also is approached." But the angels who were about the king said, "You are mistaken, you did not think so, nor is the Lord approached, when application is made to the Father; but God the Father is approached, when application is made to the Lord, because they are one, like soul and body. Who applies to a man's soul, that he may thus have access to his body? When a man is addressed as to his body which is seen, is not his soul also addressed, which is not seen?" To this they were silent; and the king went up to the two bishops, with two gifts in his hand, saying, "These are gifts from heaven." They were celestial forms of gold which he was about to present to them, when a dusky cloud covered them, and separated them, and they descended by the way that they had come up; and wrote these things in a book.

The rest of the English clergy, who heard that their companions had been permitted to ascend to the superior heaven, assembled at the foot of a mountain, where they waited for their return. On their return they saluted their brethren, and related what had happened to them in heaven, and that the king had presented the bishops with two celestial forms of gold, beautiful to behold; but that they fell out of their hands.

* This was written in the reign of George III., who was grandson to George II.

They then retired into a grove, which was nigh at hand, and discoursed among themselves, looking about to see if any one heard them; though they were heard nevertheless. Their discourse was about unanimity and concord, and then about supremacy and dominion. The bishops spoke, and the rest assented. And on a sudden, to my surprise, they no longer appeared as many, but as one great figure whose face resembled that of a lion, having on his head a turreted mitre, on which was a crown: and he spake in a lofty tone, and walked proudly; and, looking behind, he said, "Who else has a right to supremacy but me!" The king looked down from heaven, and saw them, first all as one, and afterwards as several unanimous; but most of them, as he said, in a secular habit.

CHAPTER VII.

1. AND after these things I saw four angels standing on the four corners of the earth, holding the four winds of the earth, that the wind should not blow on the earth, nor on the sea, nor on any tree.

2. And I saw another angel ascending from the rising of the sun, having the seal of the living God. And he cried with a loud voice to the four angels, to whom it was given to hurt the earth and the sea,

3. Saying, Hurt not the earth, neither the sea, nor the trees, till we have sealed the servants of our God in their foreheads.

4. And I heard the number of them that were sealed; a hundred and forty and four thousand, sealed out of all the tribes of the children of Israel.

5. Of the tribe of Judah were sealed twelve thousand. Of the tribe of Reuben were sealed twelve thousand. Of the tribe of Gad were sealed twelve thousand.

6. Of the tribe of Aser were sealed twelve thousand. Of the tribe of Nephtalim were sealed twelve thousand. Of the tribe of Manasses were sealed twelve thousand.

7. Of the tribe of Simeon were sealed twelve thousand. Of the tribe of Levi were sealed twelve thousand. Of the tribe of Issachar were sealed twelve thousand.

8. Of the tribe of Zabulon were sealed twelve thousand. Of the tribe of Joseph were sealed twelve thousand. Of the tribe of Benjamin were sealed twelve thousand.

9. After this, I beheld, and, lo, a great multitude which no man can number, of all nations, and tribes, and people, and tongues, stood before the throne, and before the Lamb, clothed with white robes, and palms in their hands;

10. And cried with a loud voice, saying, Salvation to our God that sitteth upon the throne, and unto the Lamb.

11. And all the angels stood round about the throne, and about the elders, and the four animals, and fell before the throne on their faces, and worshipped God,

12. Saying, Amen; blessing, and glory, and wisdom, and thanksgiving, and honour, and power, and might, be unto our God, for ever and ever, amen.

13. And one of the elders answered, saying unto me, Who are these that are arrayed in white robes? and whence came they?

14. And I said unto him, Sir, thou knowest. And he said unto me, These are they that come out of great tribulation, and have washed their robes, and made them white in the blood of the Lamb.

15. Therefore are they before the throne of God, and serve him day and night in his temple: and He that sitteth on the throne shall dwell among them.

16. They shall hunger no more, neither thirst any more; neither shall the sun light on them, nor any heat.

17. For the Lamb which is in the midst of the throne shall feed them, and shall lead them unto living fountains of waters: and God shall wipe away all tears from their eyes.

THE SPIRITUAL SENSE.

THE CONTENTS OF THE WHOLE CHAPTER. This chapter treats of those who are and will be in the Christian heaven; and first of their separation from the wicked, verses 1 to 3: afterwards, of those who are in love to the Lord and thereby in wisdom, of whom the superior heavens consist, verses 4 to 8; and of those who are in charity and its faith from the Lord, because they have fought against evils, of whom are the inferior heavens, verses 9 to 17.

THE CONTENTS OF EACH VERSE. V. 1, "And after these things, I saw four angels standing on the four corners of the earth," signifies the universal heaven now in the effort to execute the last judgment: "Holding the four winds of the earth, that the wind should not blow on the earth, nor on the sea, nor on any tree," signifies a withholding and restraining by the Lord, of a nearer and thence more powerful influx into the inferior things, where the good were in conjunction with the wicked: v. 2, "And I saw another angel ascending from the rising of the sun," signifies the Lord providing and regulating

"Having the seal of the living God," signifies who alone knows all and every one, and can distinguish and separate them one from another: "And he cried with a loud voice to the four angels, to whom it was given to hurt the earth and the sea, (v. 3,) saying, Hurt not the earth, neither the sea, nor the trees," signifies the preventing and withholding by the Lord of a nearer and stronger influx into inferior things: "Till we have sealed the servants of our God in their foreheads," signifies before they are separated who are in truths originating in good from the Lord: v. 4, "And I heard the number of them that were sealed, a hundred and forty and four thousand," signifies all who acknowledge the Lord to be the God of heaven and earth, and are in truths of doctrine from the good of love, from him through the Word: "Sealed out of all the tribes of the children of Israel," signifies the Lord's heaven and church composed of them: v. 5, "Of the tribe of Judah were sealed twelve thousand," signifies celestial love, which is love to the Lord, and this with all who will be in the new heaven and the new church: "Of the tribe of Reuben were sealed twelve thousand," signifies wisdom derived from celestial love, with them who are there: "Of the tribe of Gad were sealed twelve thousand," signifies uses of life, which are of wisdom derived from that love, with those who were there: v. 6, "Of the tribe of Aser were sealed twelve thousand," signifies mutual love with them: "Of the tribe of Nephtalim were sealed twelve thousand," signifies a perception of use, and what use is with them: "Of the tribe of Manasses were sealed twelve thousand," signifies the will of serving, and of action, with them: v. 7, "Of the tribe of Simeon were sealed twelve thousand," signifies spiritual love, which is love towards the neighbour, with them: "Of the tribe of Levi were sealed twelve thousand," signifies the affection of truth derived from good, from whence comes intelligence, with them: "Of the tribe of Issachar were sealed twelve thousand," signifies good of life with them: v. 8, "Of the tribe of Zabulon were sealed twelve thousand," signifies the conjugial love of good and truth with them: "Of the tribe of Joseph were sealed twelve thousand," signifies the doctrine of good and truth with them: "Of the tribe of Benjamin were sealed twelve thousand," signifies the life of truth derived from good according to doctrine with them: v. 9, "After this I beheld, and, lo, a great multitude which no man could number," signifies all the rest who are not among the above-recited, and yet are in the new heaven and new church of the Lord, and who constitute the ultimate heaven and the external church, whose quality no one knows but the Lord alone: "Of all nations, and tribes, and people, and tongues," signifies all in the Christian world, who are in religion from good, and in truths from doctrine: "Stood before the throne and before the Lamb," signifies, hearing the Lord and doing his precepts : " Clothed with white robes, and palms in their hands," signifies communication and conjunction with the superior heavens, and confession from divine truths: v. 10, " And cried with a loud voice, saying, Salvation to our God that sitteth upon the throne and unto the Lamb," signifies an acknowledgment from the heart that the Lord is their Saviour: v. 11, " And all the angels stood round about the throne, and about the elders, and the four animals," signifies all in the universal heaven : " And fell before the throne on their faces, and worshipped God," signifies the humiliation of their heart, and, from humiliation, adoration of the Lord : v. 12, " Saying, Amen," signifies divine verity and confirmation therefrom : " Blessing, and glory, and wisdom, and thanksgiving," signifies the divine spiritual things of the Lord : " And honour, and power, and might," signifies the divine celestial things of the Lord : " Be unto our God for ever and ever," signifies these things in the Lord, and from the Lord to eternity : " Amen," signifies the consent of all : v. 13, " And one of the elders answered, saying unto me, Who are these that are arrayed in white robes? and whence came they? (v. 14,) And I said unto him, Sir, thou knowest," signifies a desire of knowing and the will of interrogating, and the answer and information : " And he said unto me, These are they that come out of great tribulation," signifies that they are those who have been in temptations, and have fought against evils and falses : " And have washed their robes," signifies who have cleansed their religious principles from the evils of falsity: " And made them white in the blood of the Lamb," signifies, and purified them from the falses of evil by truths, and thus have been reformed by the Lord: v. 15, " Therefore are they before the throne of God, and serve him day and night in his temple : and He that sitteth on the throne shall dwell among them," signifies that they are in the presence of the Lord, and constantly and faithfully live according to the truths which they receive from him in his church: v. 16, " They shall hunger no more, neither thirst any more," signifies that hereafter there shall be no deficiency of goods and truths with them : " Neither shall the sun light on them, nor any heat," signifies that hereafter they shall have no lusts to evil nor to the false of evil : v. 17, " For the Lamb which is in the midst of the throne shall feed them," signifies that the Lord alone will teach them : " And shall lead them unto living fountains of waters," signifies, and lead them by the truths of the Word to conjunction with himself: " And God shall wipe away all tears from their eyes," signifies that they shall no longer be in combats against evils and their falses, and thereby in sorrow, but in goods and truths, and thence in joys celestial from the Lord.

THE EXPLANATION.

342. *And after these things I saw four angels standing on the four corners of the earth,* signifies the universal heaven now in the effort to execute the last judgment on those who were in the world of spirits. Many things now follow concerning the state of the spiritual world previous to the last judgment, which no one could know but by revelation from the Lord. And since it has been granted me to see in what manner the last judgment was performed, and also the changes which preceded it, and the arrangements which ensued; I am thereby enabled to explain the signification of all the particulars contained in this and the following chapters. By the four angels is here signified the universal heaven; by the four corners of the earth is signified the universal world of spirits, which is in the midst between heaven and hell; for the last judgment was executed on those who were in the world of spirits, but not on any one in heaven, nor on any one in hell. The reason why the angels signify heaven, is, because an angel, in the supreme sense, means the Lord as to the Divine Humanity, n. 344; and as heaven is heaven from the Lord, by the angels is also signified heaven. The four angels here signify the universal heaven, because they were seen standing on the four corners of the earth, and by the four corners are signified the four quarters. The reason why the above words signify the effort of the universal heaven to execute a last judgment, is, because the Lord, when the judgment was at hand, caused the heavens to draw near over the world of spirits, and by this approach of the heavens, such a change of state in the interiors of the minds of those who were below, was effected, that they saw nothing but terrors before their eyes. That corners signify quarters, and thence four corners all quarters, may appear from the following passages: "Ye shall measure from without the city, the *corner* towards the *east,* the *corner* towards the *south,* the *corner* towards the *west,* and the *corner* towards the *north,*" Numb. xxxv. 5. "Thou shalt make the boards for the tabernacle for the *south side* [*corner*], and for the *north side* [*corner*]," Exod. xxvi. 18, 20, 23. "And a court for the *south side* [*corner*], for the *north side* [*corner*], for the *west side* [*corner*], and for the *east side* [*corner*]," Exod. xxvii. 9, 11—13. The four quarters are also called the four corners frequently in Ezekiel, as in chap. xlvii. 18—20, and xlviii. Because corners signify quarters, therefore they signify all things, as all things relating to heaven or hell, or to good and truth, as is plain from these passages: Satan shall go out to "deceive the nations which are in the four *quarters* of the earth," Apoc. xx. 8. "I have cut off the nations: their *corners* are desolate," Zeph. iii. 6. "Israel was

gathered together as one man,—and the *corners* of all the people stood up," Judges xx. 1, 2. "A sceptre shall rise out of Israel, and shall smite the *corners* of Moab," Numb. xxiv. 17. "A day of the trumpet and alarm—and against the high *corners*," Zeph. i. 16. "I would scatter them into *corners*," Deut. xxxii. 26. That a corner signifies the ultimate which sustains things superior, as a foundation does a house, and thus also all things, appears from these passages: "Behold, I lay in Zion for a foundation a stone, a tried stone, a precious *corner stone*," Isaiah xxviii. 16. "And they shall not take of the stone for a *corner*," Jerem. li. 26. "And Judah shall be a *corner stone*," Zech. x. 4. "The stone which the builders refused is become the head of the *corner*," Psalm cxviii. 22; Matt. xxi. 42; Mark xii. 10; Luke xx. 17, 18.

343. *Holding the four winds of the earth, that the wind should not blow on the earth, nor on the sea, nor on any tree*, signifies a withholding and restraining by the Lord of a nearer and thence more powerful influx into inferior things, where the good were in conjunction with the wicked. It is to be noted that the last judgment takes place when the wicked are multiplied, below the heavens in the world of spirits, to such a degree that the angels in the heavens cannot subsist in their state of love and wisdom; for in this case they have no support and foundation to rest upon; and as this is occasioned by the increase of the wicked below, therefore the Lord, in order to preserve their state, flows in with his divinity more and more strongly, and this continues till they can no longer be preserved by any influx, without a separation of the wicked, that are below, from the good, which is effected by the letting down and drawing near of the heavens, and thence by a stronger influx, until it at length becomes insupportable to the wicked, upon which they flee away, and cast themselves into hell. This is also what is signified in the foregoing chapter by these words: "And said to the mountains and rocks, Fall on us, and hide us from the face of Him that sitteth upon the throne, and from the wrath of the Lamb: for the great day of his wrath is come; and who shall be able to stand?" Apoc. vi. 16. But to proceed to the explanation. By the four winds is signified the influx of the heavens; by the earth, the sea, and every tree, are signified all inferior principles and the things that are therein; by the earth and sea, all inferior principles; and by every tree, all things therein. That wind signifies influx, properly the influx of truth into the understanding, may appear from the following passages: "Thus saith the Lord Jehovah, Come from the four *winds*, O spirit, and breathe upon these slain, that they may live," Ezek. xxxviii. 9, 10. There were seen four chariots, at which there were four horses, "these are the four *winds* of the heavens," Zech vi. 1. 5 "Ye must be born again. The *wind* bloweth where it

listeth, but thou canst not tell whence it cometh, and whither it goeth," John iii. 7, 8. The Maker of the earth "hath established the world by his wisdom,—and bringeth forth the *wind* out of his treasures," Jerem. x. 12, 13; li. 15, 16; Psalm cxxxv. 7. Jehovah " causeth his *wind* to blow, and the waters flow. He showeth his Word unto Jacob, his statutes and judgments unto Israel," Psalm cxlvii. 17—19. "Stormy *wind* fulfilling his Word," Psalm cxlviii. 8. Jehovah " maketh his angels *winds*," Psalm civ. 3, 4. Jehovah " did fly upon the wings of the *wind*," Psalm xviii. 10, 11; Psalm civ. 3. The wings of the wind are divine truths which flow in: therefore the Lord is called "The *breath* of our nostrils," Lament. iv. 20; and it is written, that he *breathed into the nostrils* of Adam the soul of lives, Gen. ii. 7; also, that "He *breathed* on his disciples, and said, Receive ye the Holy Ghost," John xx. 21, 22. The Holy Ghost (or Spirit) is the divine truth proceeding from the Lord, whose influx into the disciples was represented, and thus signified, by his breathing upon them. That wind and respiration signify the influx of divine truth into the understanding, is from the correspondence of the lungs with the understanding, on which subject see *The Angelic Wisdom concerning the Divine Love and the Divine Wisdom*, n. 371—429. As, therefore, a nearer and stronger divine influx through the heavens disperses truths among the wicked, therefore wind signifies the dispersion of truth among them, and thence their conjunction with hell, and destruction; as may be seen from these passages: "And upon Elam will I bring the four *winds* from the four quarters of heaven, and will scatter them," Jerem. xlix. 36. "Thou shalt fan them, and the *wind* shall carry them away, and the *whirlwind* shall scatter them," Isaiah xli. 16. "The *breath of Jehovah*, like a stream of brimstone, doth kindle it," Isaiah xxx. 33. The contrivers of iniquity perish " by the *blast of God*, and by the *breath of his nostrils* are they consumed," Job iv. 8, 9. "The foundations of the world were discovered at thy rebuke, O Jehovah, at the *blast of the breath of thy nostrils*," Psalm xviii. 15. "I saw in my vision,—and behold, the four *winds* of the heavens strove upon the great sea. And four great beasts came up," Dan. vii. 2, 3, and following verses. " Behold, *a whirlwind of Jehovah* is gone forth in fury—it shall fall grievously upon the head of the wicked," Jerem. xxiii. 19; xxx. 23. "So persecute them with thy *storm*, and make them afraid with thy *tempest*," Psalm lxxxiii. 15. "The way of Jehovah is in the *whirlwind* and the *storm*," Nahum i. 3; besides other places; as Jerem. xxv. 32; Ezek. xiii. 13; Hosea viii. 7; Amos i. 14; Zech. ix. 14; Psalm xi. 6; Psalm l. 3; Psalm lv. 8; Psalm cvii.; where it is thus written: "For he commandeth and raiseth the *stormy wind*. He maketh the *storm* to a calm, so that the waves thereof are still," verse 25,

39: hence it may appear what is the signification of these words in their spiritual sense. Jesus in the ship "rebuked the *wind*, and said unto the sea, Peace, be still, and there was a great calm," Mark iv. 39, 40; Luke viii. 23, 24. By the sea is here signified hell, and by the wind influx thence. Nor is any thing but strong influx signified by the east wind, Ezek. xvii. 10; Jerem. xviii. 17; xix. 12; Hosea xiii. 15, 39; Psalm xlviii. 7: nor by the same wind which dried up the Rea Sea, Exodus xiv. 21; concerning which it is thus written by Moses: "And with the *blast of thy nostrils* the waters were gathered together—as a heap,—thou didst *blow* with thy *wind*, the sea covered them," Exod. xv. 8, 10. From what has been said, it may now be seen, that by holding the four winds that the wind should not blow on the earth, is signified to withhold and prevent a nearer and stronger influx into inferior things.

344. *And I saw another angel ascending from the rising of the sun*, signifies the Lord providing and regulating. An angel here means the Lord as to his divine love, because he ascended from the east, and from the east or rising of the sun, is from divine love, for in the spiritual world the Lord is the sun and the east, and is so called as to that love. That he was providing and moderating, is evident from his command to the four angels, not to hurt the earth and the sea, till the servants of God were sealed on their foreheads. That the Lord's Divine Humanity is meant by an angel, in the supreme sense, is manifest from these passages: "The *angel of the faces of Jehovah* saved them; in his love and in his pity he redeemed them, and he bare them, and carried them all the days of old," Isaiah lxiii. 9. "The *angel* which redeemed me from all evil bless the lads," Gen. xlviii. 16. "The Lord whom ye seek, shall suddenly come to his temple, even the *angel of the covenant*, whom ye delight in," Malachi iii. 1. "Behold, I send an *angel* before thee to keep thee in the way, beware of him, and obey his voice,—for my name is in him," Exod. xxiii. 20—23. Angel and Sent, in the Hebrew language, are expressed by one and the same word; hence it is that the Lord so often calls himself the Sent of the Father, by which is to be understood the Divine Humanity. But an angel, in a relative sense, denotes every one who receives the Lord, both in heaven and in the world.

345. *Having the seal of the living God*, signifies who alone knows all and every one, and can distinguish and separate them one from another. Since they were sealed on their foreheads with a seal, therefore by having the seal of the living God, as spoken of the Lord, is meant to know all and every one, and to be able to distinguish and separate the servants of God from those who are not.

346. *And he cried with a loud voice to the four angels, to whom it was given to hurt the earth and the sea, saying, Hurt not*

the earth, neither the sea, nor the trees, signifies the preventing and withholding by the Lord of a nearer and stronger influx into inferior things. That this is the signification of these words, is evident from the explanation above, n. 343. In a literal sense, it was the four angels that withheld influx, but, in a spiritual sense, it was the Lord. Not to hurt the earth, the sea, nor the trees, signifies that they should not operate by a vehement, but by a moderate, influx; for the Lord, by various degrees of influx into the heavens, disposes, regulates, tempers, and moderates all things there and in the hells, and, through the heavens and the hells, all things in the world.

347. *Till we have sealed the servants of our God in their foreheads*, signifies before they are separated who are in truths originating in good from the Lord, thus who are interiorly good. By sealing them in their foreheads, is not meant to set a seal there, but to distinguish and separate those who are in the good of love from the Lord; for the forehead signifies the good of love. That they who are in truths from good from the Lord are meant, follows from such being understood by the servants of God, n. 3. The reason why the forehead signifies the good of love, is, because the face is the image of man's affections, and the forehead is the highest part of the face; the brain, from which is the origin of all things of man's life, being immediately under the forehead. As the forehead signifies love, good love in the good, and evil love in the evil, therefore by sealing them on their foreheads, is signified to distinguish and separate one from another according to the love. Similar is the signification of this passage in Ezekiel: "Go through the midst of Jerusalem, and *set a mark upon the foreheads* of the men that sigh over the abominations," ix. 4—6. As the forehead signifies love, therefore concerning the plate of gold on the mitre of Aaron, on which was engraven *Holiness to Jehovah*, it is written, That it should be on the region of the faces of the mitre, that it might be over the *forehead* of Aaron, and that it should always be upon the *forehead* of Aaron, that he might be accepted of Jehovah, Exod. xxviii. 36—38. And moreover it was commanded that these words, "And thou shalt love Jehovah thy God with all thy heart, and with all thy soul," were to be upon the hand and upon the *forehead*, Deut. vi. 5, 8; xi. 18. That they should have the name of the Father written on their *foreheads*, Apoc. xiv. 1. And the name of God and of the Lamb in their *foreheads*, Apoc. xxii. 4. It may be observed, that the Lord looks at the angels in the forehead, whilst they look at the Lord through the eyes; by reason that the Lord views all from the good of love, and desires that they, on their part, should view him from the truths of wisdom: in this manner conjunction is effected. The forehead, in an opposite sense, signifies evil love in these places: Who have the mark of the beast on

their *foreheads*, Apoc. xiii. 16; xiv. 9; xx. 4; and also the name of Babylon upon her *forehead*, Apoc. xvii. 5. The *forehead* of an adulterous woman, Jerem. iii. 3. Obdurate of *forehead*, and hard of heart, Ezek. iii. 7, 8. "Thou art obstinate, and thy *forehead* is brass," Isaiah xlviii. 4.

348. *And I heard the number of them which were sealed, a hundred and forty and four thousand*, signifies all who acknowledge the Lord to be the God of heaven and earth, and are in truths of doctrine from the good of love from him through the Word. That these are signified by a hundred and forty and four thousand out of the twelve tribes of Israel, is, because the twelve tribes of Israel signify the church, as composed of those who are in good and truth from the Lord, and acknowledge him as the God of heaven and earth. By the number one hundred and forty-four thousand, all these are understood; for by this number the same is signified as by twelve, since it arises by multiplying twelve into twelve, and then by multiplying it by one hundred and by one thousand; and any number whatever multiplied into itself, and then by ten, one hundred, or one thousand, has the same signification as the original number; therefore the number one hundred and forty-four thousand signifies the same as one hundred and forty-four, and this the same as twelve, because twelve multiplied by twelve make one hundred and forty-four; so likewise the twelve thousand sealed out of each tribe, being multiplied by twelve, make one hundred and forty-four thousand. The number twelve signifies all, and is predicated of truths from good, because twelve is the product of three and four multiplied by each other, and the number three signifies every thing as to truth, and the number four every thing as to good; hence twelve, in this instance, signifies every thing as to truth derived from the good of love. That all numbers signify the adjuncts of things determining their quality or quantity, may appear manifest from numbers in the Apocalypse, which, were they without some specific signification, would yield no sense whatever in many places. From what has been said it may be seen, that by one hundred and forty-four thousand sealed, and by twelve thousand out of each tribe, is not to be understood that so many were sealed and elected out of the tribes of Israel, but all who are in truths of doctrine derived from the good of love from the Lord. This is what is signified in general by the twelve tribes of Israel, and also by the Lord's twelve apostles; but, in particular, some truth derived from good is signified by each tribe and by each apostle. But the signification of each particular tribe shall be explained presently. Since the twelve tribes signify all truths of doctrine derived from the good of love from the Lord, they also signify all things of the church; on which account the twelve tribes of Israel represented the church, as did also the twelve apostles.

As twelve is predicated of the truths and goods of the church, therefore the New Jerusalem, by which is understood the Lord's New Church, is described by the number twelve in every particular, as that the length and breadth of the city was *twelve thousand furlongs;* that the wall thereof was *one hundred and forty-four cubits;* one hundred and forty-four is twelve multiplied by twelve; that there were *twelve gates;* and the gates were of *twelve pearls;* that over the gates there were *twelve angels;* and the names written of the *twelve tribes* of Israel; that the wall had *twelve foundations;* and in them the names of the *twelve apostles* of the Lamb; and they consisted of *twelve precious stones;* as also that the tree of life was there, bearing *twelve fruits* according to the *twelve months.* Concerning all these particulars, see chapters xxi. and xxii. From such as are here treated of the new heaven is formed, and the new church is forming by the Lord; for they are the same who are mentioned in chapter xiv., where it is written of them: "And I looked, and, lo, a Lamb stood on the Mount Zion, and with him *one hundred and forty-four thousand.*—And they sung, as it were, a new song before the throne, and no man could learn that song but the *hundred and forty-four thousand,* which were redeemed from the earth,—for they are virgins,—which follow the Lamb whithersoever he goeth," verses 1, 3, 4. Because the twelve tribes signify the Lord's church as to all its truths and goods, therefore the number twelve became a number of the church, and was used in its holy ceremonies and solemnities. In the breast-plate of judgment, in which were the urim and thummim, and *twelve precious stones*, Exod. xxviii. 21. That *twelve breads* of faces were put upon the table in the tabernacle, Levit. xxiv. 5, 6. That Moses built an altar at the foot of Mount Sinai, and erected *twelve pillars*, Exod. xxiv. 4. That *twelve men* were sent to explore the land of Canaan, Deut. i. 23. That *twelve men* brought *twelve stones* out of the midst of Jordan, Josh. iv. 1—9, 20. That *twelve princes* at the dedication of the altar brought *twelve chargers of silver, twelve bowls of silver, twelve censers of gold, twelve oxen, twelve rams, twelve lambs,* and *twelve he-goats*, Numb. vii. 84, 87. That Elijah took *twelve stones*, and built an altar, 1 Kings xviii. 31. That Elijah found Elisha ploughing with *twelve yoke of oxen*, and himself among the *twelve*, and that then he cast his mantle upon him, 1 Kings xix. 19. That Solomon placed *twelve oxen* under the brazen sea, 1 Kings vii. 25, 44. That he made a throne, and *twelve lions* standing at the steps of it, 1 Kings x. 19, 20. That on the head of the woman who was clothed with the sun there was a crown of *twelve stars*, Apoc. xii. 1. From what has been said it may now be evident, that by one hundred and forty-four thousand sealed, twelve thousand out of each tribe, are not understood so many in number of the Jews and Israelites, but alof the new Christian heaven, and the New Church, who will be in truths of doctrine derived from the good of love through the Word from the Lord.

349. *Of all the tribes of the children of Israel,* signifies the Lord's heaven and church composed of them. By a tribe is signified religion as to good of life, and by every tribe is signified the church as to every good of love and as to every truth from that good in which good of life originates; for there are two things which constitute a church—good of life, and truth of doctrine; the marriage of these is the church. The twelve tribes of Israel represented, and thence signified the church as to that marriage, and each tribe some universal truth of good or good of truth therein. But what each tribe signifies has not been revealed to any one, nor could be revealed, lest, by an ill-connected explanation, the sanctity which lies concealed in their several conjunctions into one, should be profaned, for their signification is determined by their conjunction. They have one signification in the series in which they are named according to their nativities, Gen. xxix., xxx., xxxv. 18; where the series of them is as follows: Reuben, Simeon, Levi, Judah, Dan, Naphtali, Gad, Aser, Issachar, Zebulun, Joseph, Benjamin. They have another signification in the series in which they are mentioned when they came to Egypt, which is as follows: Reuben, Simeon, Levi, Judah, Issachar, Zebulun, Gad, Aser, Joseph, Benjamin, Dan, Naphtali, Gen. xlvi. 9—21. Another, in the series in which they are blessed by their father Israel, which is this: Reuben, Simeon, Levi, Judah, Zebulun, Issachar, Dan, Gad, Aser, Naphtali, Joseph, Benjamin, Gen. xlix. Another, in the series in which they are blessed by Moses, which is, Reuben, Judah, Levi, Benjamin, Joseph, Ephraim, Manasses, Zebulun, Gad, Dan, Naphtali, Aser, Deut. xxxiii: here Ephraim and Manasses are mentioned, and not Simeon and Issachar. Another, in the series in which they encamped and journeyed, which was this: the tribe of Judah, Issachar, and Zebulun to the east; the tribe of Reuben, Simeon, and Gad to the south; the tribe of Ephraim, Manasses, and Benjamin to the west; the tribe of Dan, Aser, and Naphtali to the north; and the tribe of Levi in the middle, Numb. ii. 1 to the end. Another, in the series in which they are mentioned in other places; as Gen. xxxv. 23—26; Numb. i. 5—16; x. 1 to the end; xiii. 4—15; xxvi. 5—56; xxxiv. 17—28; Deut. xxvii. 12, 13; Josh. xv.—xix.; Ezek. xlviii. 1 to the end. So, therefore, when Balaam saw Israel dwelling according to their *tribes,* he said, "How goodly are thy tents, O Jacob, and thy tabernacles, O Israel," Numb. xxiv. 1, 2, 3, 5. In the breast-plate of judgment, which was the urim and thummim, wherein were twelve precious stones, according to the names of the sons of Israel (Exod. xxviii. 15—29), the signification of the tribes in their

series was determined by the interrogation, to which they required an answer. But what they signify in the series in which they are here mentioned in the Apocalypse, this being different also, shall be explained presently. That tribes signify religion, and the twelve tribes the church as to all things relating to it, is, because tribe and sceptre, in the Hebrew language, are one and the same word, and the sceptre is the kingdom, and the Lord's kingdom is heaven and the church.

350. *Of the tribe of Judah were sealed twelve thousand*, signifies celestial love, which is love to the Lord, and this with all who will be in the Lord's new heaven and new church. By Judah, in a supreme sense, is signified the Lord as to celestial love; in a spiritual sense, the Lord's celestial kingdom and the Word; and, in a natural sense, the doctrine of the celestial church from the Word. But here by Judah is signified celestial love, which is love to the Lord; and because it is mentioned first in the series, it signifies that love with all who will be of the Lord's new heaven and new church; for the tribe first named is the all in the rest, it is as their head, and as a universal entering into all things that are consequent, collecting, qualifying, and affecting them. Love to the Lord is such a universal principle. That twelve thousand signify all who are in that love, may be seen above, n. 348. It is well known that the twelve tribes of Israel, after Solomon's time, were divided into two kingdoms, the Jewish and Israelitish; the Jewish kingdom represented the Lord's celestial kingdom or priesthood; and the Israelitish kingdom, the Lord's spiritual kingdom or royalty; the latter, however, was destroyed when there was nothing spiritual left among them; but the Jewish kingdom was preserved, on account of the Word, and because the Lord was to be born there. But when they had wholly adulterated the Word, and thus could not know the Lord, then their kingdom was also destroyed. From hence it may appear, that by the tribe of Judah is signified celestial love, which is love to the Lord; but by reason of their character being such as to the Word, and as to the Lord, therefore by the tribe of Judah is also signified the opposite love, which is self-love, properly the love of dominion from the love of self, which love is called diabolical love. That by Judah and his tribe is signified the celestial kingdom and its love, which is love to the Lord, is evident from these places: "*Judah*, thou art he whom thy brethren shall praise:—The sceptre shall not depart from *Judah* —until Shiloh come, and unto him shall the gathering of the people be; binding his foal unto the vine, and his ass's colt unto the choice vine; he washed his garments in wine; his eyes shall be red with wine, and his teeth white with milk," Gen. xlix. 8—12. "And my servant David shall be their prince for ever. Moreover I will make a covenant of peace with them,

it shall be an everlasting covenant with them; and I will set my sanctuary in the midst of them for evermore," Ezek. xxxvii. 26, 27. "Sing and rejoice, O daughter of Zion; and Jehovah shall inherit *Judah*, his portion in the holy land," Zech. ii. 10, 12. "Keep thy solemn feasts, O *Judah*, perform thy vows; for the wicked shall no more pass through thee, he is entirely cut off," Nahum i. 15. "The Lord shall suddenly come to his temple,—then shall the offering of *Judah and Jerusalem* be pleasant unto Jehovah, as in the days of old," Malachi iii. 1, 4. "*Judah* shall dwell for ever, and *Jerusalem* from generation to generation," Joel iii. 20. "Behold, the days come, that I will raise unto David a righteous branch;—in his days shall *Judah* be saved," Jerem. xxiii. 5, 6. "*Judah* was his sanctuary, and Israel his dominion," Psalm cxiv. 2. "And I will bring forth a seed out of Jacob, and out of *Judah* an inheritor of my mountains; and mine elect shall inherit it," Isaiah lxv. 9. "Behold, the days come, that I will make a new covenant with the house of *Judah*; but this shall be the covenant,—I will put my law in their inward parts, and write it in their hearts," Jerem. xxxi. 27, 31, 33, 34. "In those days, ten men shall take hold of the skirt of a man of *Judah*, saying, We will go with you, for we have heard that God is with you," Zech. viii. 22, 23. "For as the new heavens and the new earth, which I will make, shall remain before me,—so shall your seed and your name remain: and kings shall be thy nursing fathers, and their queens thy nursing mothers; they shall bow down to thee with their face toward the earth, and lick up the dust of thy feet," Isaiah lxvi. 20, 22; xlix. 22, 23. From these and many other passages, too numerous to be adduced, it is very evident, that by Judah is not meant Judah, but the church; not to mention the Lord's entering into a new and eternal covenant with that nation, and making them his inheritance and his sanctuary for ever; and the kings of the Gentiles and their princes bowing down to them, licking the dust of their feet, and such like. That by the tribe of Judah, regarded in itself, is meant the diabolical kingdom which has its origin in the love of dominion from self-love, may appear from these passages: "I will hide my face from them, I will see what their end shall be; for they are a froward generation, children in whom there is no faith; for they are a nation void of counsel; for their vine is of the vine of Sodom, and of the fields of Gomorrah; their grapes are grapes of gall, their clusters are bitter, their wine is the poison of dragons and the cruel venom of asps. Is not this laid up in store with me, and sealed up among my treasures?" Deut. xxxii. 20—34. "Understand, therefore, that Jehovah thy God giveth thee not this good land for thy righteousness, or for the uprightness of thine heart: for thou art a stiff-necked people," Deut. ix. 5, 6. "According to the number of thy cities are thy gods, *O Judah*, ac cording to the number of the streets of *Jerusalem* have ye set up altars to burn incense unto Baal," Jerem. ii. 28; xi. 13. " Ye are of your father the devil, and the lusts of your father ye will do," John viii. 44. They are said to be *full of hypocrisy, iniquity, and uncleanness,* Matt. xxiii. 27, 28. *An adulterous generation,* Matt. xii. 39; Mark viii. 38. And *Jerusalem, their dwelling-place, is called Sodom,* Isaiah iii. 9; Jerem. xxiii. 14; Ezek. xvi. 46, 48; Apoc. xi. 8: besides other places, where it is said, that that nation is utterly ruined, and Jerusalem doomed to destruction; as in Jerem. v. 1; vi. 6, 7; vii. 17, 18, and following verses; viii. 6—8, and following verses; ix. 10, 11, 13, and following verses; xiii. 9, 10, 14; xiv. 16; Lament. i. 8, 9, 17; Ezek. iv. 1 to the end; xii. 18, 19; xv. 6, 7, 18; xvi. 1—63; xxiii. 1—49.

351. *Of the tribe of Reuben were sealed twelve thousand,* signifies wisdom derived from celestial love, with those who will be in the Lord's new heaven and new church. By Reuben, in a supreme sense, is signified omniscience; in a spiritual sense, wisdom, intelligence, and science, also faith; and, in a natural sense, sight; but here by Reuben is signified wisdom, because it follows after Judah, by whom is signified celestial love, and celestial love produces wisdom; for love does not exist without its consort, which is science, intelligence, and wisdom. The consort of natural love is science, that of spiritual love is intelligence, and that of celestial love is wisdom. That these things are signified by Reuben, follows from his being named from sight, and spiritual-natural sight is science, spiritual sight is intelligence, and celestial sight is wisdom. Reuben was also the first-born of Jacob, and therefore was called by Israel his " might, the beginning of my strength, the excellency of dignity, and the excellency of power," Gen. xlix. 3; such indeed is wisdom derived from celestial love. And as Reuben from his primogeniture represented, and thence signified, the wisdom of the men of the church, he therefore exhorted his brethren not to kill Joseph, and was grieved when Joseph was not found in the pit, Gen. xxxvii. 21, 22. And on this account his tribe *encamped on the south,* and was called *the Camp of Reuben,* Numb. ii. 10—16; the south also signifies wisdom derived from love: therefore they who are in that wisdom dwell to the south in heaven, as may be seen in the work on *Heaven and Hell,* n. 148—150. This wisdom is signified by Reuben in the prophecy of Deborah and Barak by these words, " For the divisions of *Reuben* were great thoughts of heart, Why abodest thou among the sheepfolds to hear the bleatings of the flocks? For the divisions of *Reuben* there were great searchings of heart," Judges v. 15, 16; the divisions of Reuben are knowledges of every kind, which have relation to wisdom. As all the tribes have an opposite signification also, the tribe of Reuben, in this

sense, signifies wisdom separated from love, and thence also faith separated from charity; wherefore he was cursed by his father Israel, Gen. xlix. 3, 4; and deprived of his birthright, 1 Chron. v. 1, see above, n. 17; and an inheritance was given him on the other side Jordan, and not in the land of Canaan; and instead of Reuben and Simeon, the sons of Joseph, Ephraim and Manasseh, were acknowledged, Gen. xlviii. 5; nevertheless he retained the representation and thence the signification of wisdom.

352. *Of the tribe of Gad were sealed twelve thousand*, signifies uses of life, which are of wisdom derived from that love, also with those who will be in the Lord's new heaven and new church. By Gad, in a supreme sense, is signified omnipotence; in a spiritual sense, good of life, which also is use; and, in a natural sense, work; in this instance uses of life, because it follows after Reuben and Judah, and celestial love by wisdom produces uses. There are three things which cohere and cannot be separated—love, wisdom, and use of life; if one is separated, the other two fall to the ground, as may be seen in *The Angelic Wisdom concerning the Divine Love and the Divine Wisdom*, n. 241, 297, 316. That by Gad is signified uses of life, which is also called fruit, may appear from his name as denoting a troop or a heap, Gen. xxx. 11; as also from his father Israel's blessing, Gen. xlix. 19; and from the blessing given him by Moses, Deut. xxxiii. 20, 21; and likewise from his inheritance, Numb. xxxii. 1 to the end; xxxiv. 14; Deut. iii. 16, 17; xxxiii. 20, 21. Also from the signification of Gad in an opposite sense, Isaiah lxv. 11; Jerem. xlix. 1—3. It must be observed, that all the tribes of Israel are here divided into four classes, as in the urim and thummim, and in their encampments, and that each class contains three tribes, by reason that three cohere as one, as love, wisdom, and use, and as charity, faith, and work; for, as was said, if one is wanting, the other two are not any thing.

353. *Of the tribe of Aser were sealed twelve thousand*, signifies mutual love, which is the love of performing good uses to the community or society, with those who will be of the Lord's new heaven and new church. By Aser, in a supreme sense, is signified eternity; in a spiritual sense, eternal beatitude; and, in a natural sense, the affection of good and truth; but here by Aser is signified the love of performing uses, which exists with those who are in the Lord's celestial kingdom, and is there called mutual love; this love desends proximately from love to the Lord, because the love of the Lord is to perform uses to the community, and to each society in the community, and he performs these by means of men who are principled in love to him. That Aser has the above signification, may in some measure be seen from his father Israel's blessing: "Out

of Aser; his bread shall be fat, and he shall yield royal dainties," Gen. xlix. 30; and from his blessing by Moses: "Let Aser be blessed with children, let him be acceptable to his brethren, and as thy days so shall thy strength be," Deut. xxxii. 24, 25. Moreover the name denotes beatitude, and they who are in the love of performing uses to the community and to society, enjoy beatitude above all others in heaven.

354. *Of the tribe of Nephtalim were sealed twelve thousand*, signifies a perception of use, and what use is, with those who will be in the Lord's new heaven and new church. By Nephtalim, in a supreme sense, is signified the proper power of the Lord's Divine Humanity; in a spiritual sense, temptation and victory; and, in a natural sense, resistance on the part of the natural man; for the name denotes wrestlings. But Nephtalim here signifies a perception of use, and what use is, because it follows in the series after Aser, by whom is signified the love of uses; and also because they who have conquered in temptation, have an interior perception of uses; for by temptations the interiors of the mind are opened. The perception which they have is described in Jeremiah xxxi. 33, 34; they feel in themselves what is good, and see in themselves what is true. That the tribe of Nephtalim signifies angels and men as to that perception, may be confirmed from the Word: *Nephtalim* "is in the high places of the field," Judges v. 18; high places of the field are the interiors of the church as to perception. *Nephtalim* "is satisfied with favour, and full with the blessing of Jehovah; possess thou the west and the south," Deut. xxxiii, 23; to possess the west, is to possess the good that is subservient to love, and to possess the south, is to possess the light of wisdom, which constitutes that perception. "*Nephtalim* is a hind let loose, he giveth goodly words," Gen. xlix. 21; describing the state after temptation as to the spontaneous eloquence which results from perception. It is also recorded of one of the tribe of *Nephtalim*, that he was filled with wisdom, intelligence and knowledge, and executed all Solomon's work about the temple in brass, 1 Kings vii. 14. The historical parts of the Word, as to names and tribes, are equally as significative as the prophetical.

355. *Of the tribe of Manasses were sealed twelve thousand*, signifies the will of serving and of action, with those also who will be of the Lord's new heaven and new church. There are three things which follow in order, love to the Lord, wisdom, and use, as was said above, n. 352; so also here, mutual love, understanding or perception, and will or action; these likewise make one, so that if one of them is wanting, the other two are not any thing; the will or willingness to serve with the action, is the effect, thus the ultimate, in which the two former are and co-exist. The reason why Manasses has this signification,

is, because Joseph, who was the father of Manasses and Ephraim, signifies the spiritual principle of the church; and the spiritual principle of the church is the good of the will, and at the same time the truth of the understanding; hence it is that Manasses signifies the voluntary principle of the church, and Ephraim its intellectual principle. Manasses signifies the voluntary principle of the church, because Ephraim signifies its intellectual principle, as appears manifestly in Hosea, where Ephraim is so frequently mentioned; and as Manasses signifies the voluntary principle of the church, he also signifies action, for the will is the endeavour in all action, and where there is endeavour, there is action, when it is possible. Mention is made of Manasses in several places, as when he was born, Gen. xli. 50—52; when he was accepted of Jacob as if instead of Simeon, Gen. xlviii. 3—5; and blessed by him, Gen. xlviii. 15, 16; and by Moses, Deut. xxxiii. 17; and moreover in Isaiah ix. 18—20; Psalm lx. 9; Psalm lxxx. 2; Psalm cviii. 9; from which it may in some measure be seen, that by Manasses is signified the voluntary principle of the church.

356. *Of the tribe of Simeon were sealed twelve thousand*, signifies spiritual love, which is love towards the neighbour, or charity with those who will be of the Lord's new heaven and new church. By Simeon, in a supreme sense, is signified providence; in a spiritual sense, love towards the neighbour or charity; and, in a natural sense, obedience and hearing. In the two foregoing series they are treated of who are in the Lord's celestial kingdom; but in this series they are treated of who are in the Lord's spiritual kingdom; the love of the latter is called spiritual love, which is love towards the neighbour, and charity. The reason why Simeon and his tribe represented this love, and therefore signify it in the Word, is, because he was born after Reuben, and immediately before Levi, and by these three, Reuben, Simeon, and Levi, in their order, is signified truth in the understanding, or faith; truth in the will, or charity; and truth in act, or good works; in like manner as by Peter, James, and John. That Simeon and his tribe might therefore represent truth in the will, which is both charity and obedience, he was named from hearing, and to hear signifies both to understand truth and to will or obey it;—to understand it when it is said to *hear* any one, and to will and obey it, we say to *hearken* to any one, or to listen. Here it may be expedient to say something concerning love towards our neighbour, or charity: love towards our neighbour, is the love of obeying the Lord's commandments, which are chiefly those contained in the second table of the decalogue, as, thou shalt not kill; thou shalt not commit adultery; thou shalt not steal; thou shalt not bear false witness; thou shalt not covet the things which are thy neighbour's. The man who will not do such things because

they are sins, loves his neighbour; for he does not love the neighbour who hates him, and from hatred desires to kill him; he does not love the neighbour who desires to commit adultery with his wife; nor does he love the neighbour who desires to steal and make depredations on his goods, and so on. This, also, Paul teaches in the following words: "For he that *loveth another*, hath fulfilled the law. For this, Thou shalt not commit adultery, Thou shalt not kill, Thou shalt not steal, Thou shalt not bear false witness, Thou shalt not covet, and if there be any other commandment, it is briefly comprehended in this saying, namely, Thou shalt *love thy neighbour as thyself*: therefore *charity* is the fulfilling of the law," Rom. xiii. 8—10.

357. *Of the tribe of Levi were sealed twelve thousand*, signifies the affection of truth derived from good, from whence comes intelligence with those who will be of the Lord's new heaven and new church. By Levi, in a supreme sense, is signified love and mercy; in a spiritual sense, charity in act, which is good of life; and, in a natural sense, consociation and conjunction; for the name denotes to *adhere*, by which, in the Word, is signified conjunction through love. But by Levi is here signified the love or affection of truth, and thence intelligence, because it follows after Simeon, and in this series forms the intermediate. Since Levi represented these things, therefore this tribe was appointed to the priesthood, Numb. iii. 1, to the end; Deut. xxi. 5; and in other places. That the tribe of Levi signifies the love of truth, which is the essential love from which the church is a church, and thence intelligence, may appear from these places: The *sons of Levi* are chosen by Jehovah to minister unto him, and to bless in his name, Deut. xxi. 5; to bless in the name of Jehovah is to teach; which they alone can do, who are in the affection of truth, and thence in intelligence. "For they have observed thy Word, and kept thy covenant;—they shall teach Jacob thy judgments, and Israel thy law," Deut. xxxiii. 8—12. "The Lord shall suddenly come to his temple, and he shall sit as a refiner and purifier of silver, and he shall purify the *sons of Levi*, and purge them as gold and silver," Malachi iii. 1—4; to purify the sons of Levi, is to purify those who are in the affection of truth. As that affection flourishes from intelligence, therefore the staff of Levi, upon which was written the name of Aaron, blossomed and yielded almonds, Numb. xvii. 6—8.

358. *Of the tribe of Issachar were sealed twelve thousand*, signifies good of life with those who will be of the Lord's new heaven and new church. By Issachar is signified, in a supreme sense, the divine good of truth, and the truth of good; in a spiritual sense, celestial conjugial love, which is the love of good and truth; and, in a natural sense, remuneration; but here the good of life, because in this class it is the third in

order, and the third in any class signifies the ultimate, which is produced from the two former, as the effect from its cause; and the effect of spiritual love, which is love towards the neighbour, and is signified by Simeon, through the affection of truth, which is signified by Levi, produces good of life, which is Issachar: he was also named from *hire*, Gen. xxx. 17, 18, thus from remuneration, and good of life has remuneration in itself. Something of this sort is also signified by Issachar in his blessing by Moses: "Rejoice Zebulon in thy going out, and *Issachar* in thy tents. They shall call the people unto the mountain; there shall they offer sacrifices of righteousness: for they shall suck of the abundance of the sea, and of treasures hid in the sand," Deut. xxxiii. 18, 19. But by Issachar, in his blessing by his father Israel, Gen. xlix. 14, 15, is signified meritorious good of life, as may be seen in *The Arcana Cœlestia*, n. 6388.

359. *Of the tribe of Zabulon were sealed twelve thousand*, signifies the conjugial love of good and truth also with those who will be of the Lord's new heaven and new church. By Zabulon, in a supreme sense, is signified the union of the essential divinity and the Divine Humanity in the Lord; in a spiritual sense, the marriage of good and truth with those who are in heaven and in the church; and, in a natural sense, conjugial love itself; therefore here, by Zabulon is signified the conjugial love of good and truth; he was also named from *cohabitation* Gen. xxx. 19, 22; and cohabitation is predicated of married pairs whose minds are joined into one, for such conjunction is spiritual cohabitation. The conjugial love of good and truth, which is here signified by Zabulon, is the conjugial love of the Lord and his church; the Lord is the good of love itself, and gives to the church to be truth from that good; and cohabitation is effected, when the man of the church receives good from the Lord in truths; in this case the marriage of good and truth takes place with man, which constitutes the church itself, and he becomes a heaven; hence it is that the kingdom of God, that is, heaven and the church, is so often compared in the Word to a marriage.

360. *Of the tribe of Joseph were sealed twelve thousand*, signifies the doctrine of good and truth with those who will be of the Lord's new heaven and new church. By Joseph is signified the Lord as to the divine spiritual priciple: in a spiritual sense, the spiritual kingdom; and, in a natural sense, fructification and multiplication; but by Joseph is here signified the doctrine of good and truth, which is with those who are in the Lord's spiritual kingdom. Joseph has this signification, because he is named after the tribe of Zabulon, and before the tribe of Benjamin, thus in the middle; and the tribe which is first named in a series or class, signifies some love which is of the will; and the tribe which is named after it signifies something

of wisdom which relates to the understanding; and the tribe which is named last signifies some use or effect derived from them. Thus each series is full or complete. As Joseph signified the Lord's spiritual kingdom, therefore he was made governor in Egypt, Gen. xli. 38—44; Psalm cv. 17—23; where each particular signifies such things as relate to the Lord's spiritual kingdom. The spiritual kingdom is the Lord's royalty; and the celestial kingdom is his priesthood. Joseph, in the present instance, signifies the doctrine of good and truth, because he is here in the place of Ephraim; and by Ephraim is signified the intellectual principle of the church; see *The Doctrine of the New Jerusalem concerning the Sacred Scripture*, n. 79; and the intellectual principle of the church is in every respect derived from the doctrine of good and truth from the Word. The reason why Joseph is here in the place of Ephraim, is, because Manasseh, who was Joseph's other son, and signified the voluntary principle of the church, was before reckoned among the tribes, n. 355. The intellectual principle of the church being derived from the doctrine of good and truth, therefore that intellectual principle, and also that doctrine, are signified by Joseph in the following passages: "*Joseph* is a fruitful bough, even a fruitful bough by a well; but his bow abode in strength; he shall be blessed with the blessings of heaven above, and with the blessings of the deep that lieth under," Gen. xlix. 22, 26: a well signifies the Word, and a bow doctrine, n. 299. "And of *Joseph* he said, Be his land blessed of Jehovah, for the precious things of heaven; for the dew, and for the deep that concheth beneath; and for the precious things brought forth by the sun, and for the precious things put forth by the moon, and for the precious things of the earth and fulness thereof," Deut. xxxiii. 13—17; by those precious things are signified the knowledges of good and truth, from which doctrine is derived. Who "drink wine in bowls, but are not grieved for the affliction of *Joseph*," Amos vi. 5, 6. "And I will strengthen the house of Judah, and I will save the house of *Joseph*, and they of Ephraim shall be like a mighty man, and their heart shall rejoice as through wine," Zech. x.. 6, 7; here also Joseph signifies doctrine, and wine, the truth of it from good, n. 316.

361. *Of the tribe of Benjamin were sealed twelve thousand*, signifies the life of truth derived from good according to doctrine, with those who will be in the Lord's new heaven and new church. When by Zabulon is signified the conjugial love of good and truth; and by Joseph, the doctrine of good and truth; then by Benjamin, because he is third in the series, is signified the life of truth derived from good. Benjamin has this signification, because he was born last, and was called by his father Jacob, the *son of his right hand*, Gen. xxxv. 18; and by a son

of the right hand is signified truth derived from good; therefore also his tribe dwelt round about Jerusalem, where the tribe of Judah was, and the city of Jerusalem signified the church as to doctrine, and its circuit, such things as are derived from doctrine; see Joshua xviii. 11—28; Jerem. xvii. 26; xxxii. 8, 44; xxxiii. 13; and other places.

362. In the enumeration of the tribes of Israel neither Dan nor Ephraim is named; the reason is, because Dan was the last of the tribes, and his tribe dwelt in the most remote part of the land of Canaan, and thus could not signify any thing in the Lord's new heaven and new church, where there will only be such as are celestial and spiritual; wherefore Manasseh is put in the place of Dan, whilst Joseph is put in the place of Ephraim; see above, n. 360.

363. *After this I beheld, and, lo, a great multitude, which no man could number*, signifies all the rest who are not among the above-recited, and yet are in the Lord's new heaven and new church, being those who compose the ultimate heaven and the external church, whose quality no one knows but the Lord alone. That by a great multitude are signified those who are not enumerated above, and yet are in the Lord's heaven and church, is plain from verses 9, 10, 13—17, where it is said, tha they "stood before the throne and before the Lamb, clothed in white robes, and palms in their hands; and that they serve him in his temple; and he that sitteth on the throne shall dwell among them;" besides many other things. By numbering, in a spiritual sense, is signified to know the nature and quality of any thing; that such is the signification of numbering, will be seen in the next paragraph. But who they are in particular, who are meant by those that are called a great multitude, cannot be known without first revealing an arcanum; the arcanum is this: the universal heaven, together with the church on the earths, in the sight of the Lord, is as one man; and because it is as one man, there are some who constitute the head, and thus the face with all its organs of the senses; and there are some who constitute the body with all its members: those who are enumerated above constitute the face with all its organs of the senses; but these now mentioned, are they who constitute the body with all its members. That this is the case has been revealed to me; as also, that they who constitute the first class of the tribes, verse 5, are those who correspond to the forehead down to the eyes; that they who are of the second class, verse 6, are those who correspond to the eyes, together with the nostrils; the third class, verse 7, those who correspond to the ears and cheeks; and the fourth class, verse 8, those who correspond to the mouth and tongue. The Lord's church is also internal and external; they who are meant by the twelve tribes of Israel are such as constitute the Lord's internal church, but

they who are now mentioned are such as constitute the external church, and cohere as one with the above recited, as inferior things with superior, thus as the body does with the head; therefore the twelve tribes of Israel signify the superior heavens and also the internal church, but these signify the inferior heavens and the external church. That these are also called a great multitude, see below, n. 803, and n. 811.

364. To number, in a spiritual sense, signifies to know the quality of a thing, because number, in the Word, does not signify number, but its quality, n. 10; in this passage therefore, by "a great multitude which no man could number," in a natural sense, is meant what the words import, that there was a great multitude; but, in a spiritual sense, is meant that none but the Lord alone knows their quality: for the Lord's heaven consists of innumerable societies, and these societies are distinguished according to the varieties of affections in general; in like manner all in each society, are distinguished in particular. The Lord alone knows the quality of the affection of each individual, and disposes all in order according thereto. By numbering, the angels understand, to know this quality. The same is meant, in the Word, in these passages: When Belshazzar was drinking wine out of the vessels of the temple of Jerusalem, there was written upon the wall, "Thou art *numbered*, thou art *numbered*," Dan. v. 2, 5, 25. "I shall go to the gates of the grave, I am *numbered*," Isaiah xxxviii. 10. "A tumultuous noise of the kingdoms, Jehovah of hosts *numbereth* the host of battle," Isaiah xiii. 4. "Behold, who hath created these things, that bringeth out their host by *number?*" Isaiah xl. 26. Jehovah who *numbereth* the host of the stars, Psalm cxlvii. 4. "The flocks shall pass again under the hands of him that *numbereth* them," Jerem. xxxiii. 13. "My steps are *numbered*," Job xiv. 16. The houses and towers of Zion and of Jerusalem are *numbered*, Isaiah xxii. 9, 10; xxxiii. 18, 19; Psalm xlviii. 12—14; to number is the same as to know their quality. From the signification of numbers and of numbering, it may appear, why a punishment was denounced against David for numbering the people or tribes of Israel, and why he said to the prophet Gad, "I have sinned greatly in that I have done," 2 Sam. xxiv. 1, to the end. And why, when the people were numbered by Moses as to all their tribes, it was commanded, that every one should give an expiation of his soul to Jehovah in *numbering*, that there be no plague among them in *numbering* them, Exod. xxx. 12; the reason was, because to number signified to know their quality as to their spiritual state, thus as to the state of the church understood by the twelve tribes of Israel, which the Lord alone knows.

365. *Of all nations, and tribes, and people, and tongues*, signifies all in the Christian world, who are in religion from good.

and in truths from doctrine. By all nations and tribes, are meant those who are in religion from good, who are of the ultimate or lowest heaven, n. 363; by nations, those who are in good, n. 920, 921; and by tribe, religion, n. 349; by people and tongues are meant those who are in truths from doctrine; by people, those who are in truths, n. 483; and by tongue, doctrine, n. 282. By "out of all nations, tribes, people, and tongues," taken together in a spiritual sense, are therefore signified all who are in religion from good, and in truths from doctrine.

366. *Stood before the throne, and before the Lamb*, signifies hearing the Lord, and doing his precepts. By standing before God, is signified to hear and do what he commands, as they do who stand before a king. The same is signified by standing before God, in other parts of the Word; thus: The angel said to Zacharias, "I am Gabriel, that *stand* in the presence of God," Luke i. 19. "There shall not want a man to *stand* before me for ever," Jerem. xxxv. 19. "These are the two anointed ones that *stand* before the Lord of the whole earth," Zech. iv. 14. He hath "separated the tribe of Levi to *stand* before Jehovah," Deut. x. 8; and in other places.

367. *Clothed with white robes, and palms in their hands*, signifies communication and conjunction with the superior heavens, and confession from divine truths. That to be clothed with white robes, signifies to have communication and conjunction with the heavens, may be seen above, n. 328. The reason why to hold palms in their hands signifies confession from divine truths, is, because palms signify divine truths; for every tree signifies somewhat of the church, and palms signify divine truth in ultimates, which is the divine truth of the literal sense of the Word; for this reason on all the walls of the temple of Jerusalem, within and without, and also upon the doors, were carved cherubs and *palm trees*, 1 Kings vi. 29, 32. The same in the new temple, mentioned in Ezekiel xli. 18—20. By cherubs is signified the Word, n. 239, and by palm trees, divine truths therein. That by palm trees are signified the divine truths of the Word, and by palms in their hands confessions from them, may appear from its being commanded at the feast of tabernacles that they should "take boughs of goodly trees and branches of *palm trees*, and should rejoice before Jehovah," Levit. xxiii. 39, 40. That when Jesus went to Jerusalem to the feast, "they took branches of *palm trees*," and went to meet him, crying, "Blessed is he that cometh in the name of the Lord," John xii. 12, 13; by which was signified confession from divine truths concerning the Lord. A palm tree signifies divine truth also in David: "The righteous shall flourish like the *palm tree*—those that be planted in the house of Jehovah shall flourish in the courts of our God," Psalm xcii. 12, 13; in like manner in other

places. Because Jericho was a city near Jordan, and by the river Jordan was signified that which is first in the church, and this is divine truth, such as it is in the literal sense of the Word, therefore it was called the *City of Palm Trees*, Deut. xxxiv. 3; Judges i. 16; iii. 13; for Jordan was the first boundary or entrance into the land of Canaan, and by the land of Canaan is signified the church.

368. *And cried with a loud voice, saying, Salvation to our God that sitteth upon the throne, and unto the Lamb,* signifies an acknowledgment from the heart that the Lord is their Saviour. To cry with a loud voice, signifies acknowledgment from the heart; "Salvation to our God that sitteth upon the throne, and unto the Lamb," signifies that the Lord is salvation itself, and that the salvation of all is from him, thus that he is the Saviour. By him that sitteth upon the throne and the Lamb, is meant the Lord alone; by him that sitteth upon the throne, his divinity from which he came forth; and by the Lamb, his Divine Humanity; as may also be seen above, n. 273: they are both named, because from his divinity, from whence he came forth by his Divine Humanity, he was the Saviour; that they are one, is evident from the passages where the Lamb is mentioned as being *in the midst of the throne*, chap. v. 6; vii. 17. The Lord in many parts of the Word is called Salvation, by which is understood that he is the Saviour; as, "My *salvation* shall not tarry, and I will place *salvation* in Zion," Isaiah xlvi. 13. "Say ye to the daughter of Zion, Behold, thy *salvation* cometh," Isaiah lxii. 11. "I will also give thee for a light to the Gentiles, that thou mayest be my *salvation* unto the end of the earth," Isaiah xlix. 6. "This is Jehovah, we have waited for him, we will be glad and rejoice in his *salvation*," Isaiah xxv. 9. Salvation, in the Hebrew language, is called Joschia, which is Jesus.

369. *And all the angels stood round about the throne, and about the elders and the four animals,* signifies all in the universal heaven hearing and doing what the Lord commands. By the animals and elders are meant the angels of the superior heavens, as above, and also below, n. 808; but by angels are here meant the angels of the inferior heavens, and thus all in the universal heaven. To stand, signifies to hear and do what he commands, n. 366.

370. *And fell before the throne on their faces, and worshipped God,* signifies the humiliation of their heart, and, from humiliation, adoration of the Lord. That to fall upon their faces and worship, denotes humiliation of heart and thence adoration, is evident. Humiliation before the Lord and adoration of him, is signified by falling before the throne and worshipping God, because by God is understood his divinity, which is the divinity whence he came forth, and at the same time, his Divine Human

ity, n. 286; for both together are one God, because they are one person.

371. *Saying, Amen*, signifies divine truth and confirmation therefrom; as may be seen above, n. 23, 28, 61.

372. *Blessing, and glory, and wisdom, and thanksgiving*, signifies the divine spiritual things of the Lord. All acknowledgment and confession of the Lord comprehends, in general, these two points: that he is divine love itself and divine wisdom itself, and consequently that love, and every thing of the nature of love, with those who are in heaven and in the church, is from him: in like manner wisdom, and all that pertains thereto. Whatsoever proceeds from the Lord's divine love, is called divine celestial, and what from his divine wisdom, is called divine spiritual. The divine spiritual principle of the Lord is understood by glory, wisdom, and thanksgiving; and his divine celestial principle, by honour, power, and might, which follow. The blessing which goes before, signifies both, as may be seen above, n. 289. That glory is predicated of divine truth, thus of the divine spiritual principle, see n. 249. That wisdom has relation to the same, is evident. That thanksgiving has also a like reference, is, because it is performed from divine truth; for man gives thanks therefrom and thereby.

373. *And honour, and power, and might*, signifies the divine celestial things of the Lord. In the preceding article it is said that these three, honour, power, and might, in the Word, when applied to the Lord, are predicated of the divine celestial principle, or of the divine love, or of his divine good. That honour is so predicated, may be seen, n. 249; and might, n. 22; and that power is so likewise, may be rendered evident by a reference to the passages in the Word where it is mentioned. It is to be observed, that in all the particulars of the Word there is a marriage of good and truth, and that there are expressions which have relation to good, and expressions which have relation to truth; but these expressions can only be distinguished by those who study the spiritual sense. From that sense it appears what expressions have relation to good or love, and what to truth or wisdom; and from many passages it has been given to know, that honour, power, and might, occur when the subject treated of is concerning divine good. That this is very evident with respect to power, may be seen in Matt. xiii. 54; xxiv. 30; Mark xiii. 25, 26; Luke i. 17, 35; ix. 1; xxi. 27; and elsewhere. That in all the particulars of the Word there is a marriage of the Lord and the church, and thence a marriage of good and truth, may be seen in *The Doctrine of the New Jerusalem concerning the Sacred Scripture*, n. 80—90.

374. *Be unto our God for ever and ever*, signifies these things in the Lord and from the Lord to eternity; as is evident

from what was said above: and also that for ever and ever, means to eternity.

375. *Amen*, signifies the consent of all. In this verse amen is said at the beginning, and again at the end; when it is said at the beginning it signifies truth, and thence confirmation, n. 371; but when at the end, it signifies the confirmation and consent of all that it is the truth.

376. *And one of the elders answered, saying unto me, Who are these that are arrayed in white robes? and whence came they? And I said unto him, Sir, thou knowest*, signifies the desire of knowing, and the will of interrogating, and the answer and information. The reason why John was questioned concerning these things, is, because it is common in all divine worship, that man should first will, desire, and pray, and that the Lord should then answer, inform, and do; otherwise man does not receive any thing divine. Now as John saw those who were arrayed in white robes, and was desirous to know and to ask who they were, and as this was perceived in heaven, therefore he was first questioned and then informed. The same occurred to the prophet Zechariah, when he saw several things represented to him, as may appear from chap i. 9; ii. 2, 4; iv. 2, 5, 11, 12; v. 2, 6, 10; vi. 4. Besides, we frequently read in the Word, that the Lord answers such as call and cry unto him; as in Psalm iv. 2; Psalm xvii. 6; Psalm xxx. 8, 9; Psalm xxxiv. 6; Psalm xci. 15; Psalm cxx. 1: also, that he gives on being asked, Matt. vii. 7, 8; xxi. 22; John iv. 13, 14; xv. 7; xvi. 23, 27. But yet the Lord gives them to ask, and what to ask; therefore the Lord knows it beforehand; but still the Lord wills that man should ask first, to the end that he may do it as from himself, and thus that it should be appropriated to him; otherwise, if the petition itself were not from the Lord, it would not be said in those places, that they should receive whatsoever they asked.

377. *And he said unto me, These are they that come out of great tribulation*, signifies that they are those who have been in temptations, and have fought against evils and falses. That tribulation is infestation from evils and falses, and spiritual combat against them, which is temptation, see n. 33, 95, 100, 101.

378. *And have washed their robes*, signifies, and who have cleansed their religious principles from the evils of falsity. By washing, in the Word, is signified to cleanse from evils and falses; and by robes are signified common or general truths, n. 328. General truths are the knowledges of goodness and truth derived from the literal sense of the Word, and according to which men have lived, and thence constitute religious principles; and as every thing of a religious nature relates to good and truth, therefore robes are twice mentioned, thus, have

washed their robes and whitened their robes. Robes, or religious principles, are cleansed only with those who fight against evils, and so reject falses; thus by temptations, which are signified by great affliction, n. 377. That to be washed signifies to be cleansed from evils and falses, and so to be reformed and regenerated, may be seen evidently from the following passages: "When the Lord shall have *washed* away the filth of the daughters of Zion, and shall have *purged* away the blood of Jerusalem by the spirit of judgment, and by the spirit of burning," Isaiah iv. 4. "*Wash* you, make you clean, put away the evil of your doings from before mine eyes; cease to do evil," Isaiah i. 16. "O Jerusalem, *wash* thine heart from wickedness, that thou mayest be saved," Jerem. iv. 14. "*Wash* me thoroughly from mine iniquity,—and I shall be whiter than snow," Psalm li. 2, 7. "For though thou *wash* thee with nitre, and take thee much soap, yet thine iniquity is marked before me," Jerem. ii. 22. "If I *wash* myself with snow-water, and make my hands never so clean, yet shalt thou plunge me in the ditch, and mine own clothes shall abhor me," Job ix. 30, 31. "He *washed* his garments in wine, and his clothes in the blood of grapes," Gen. xlix. 11. This is said of the celestial church, to which they belong who are in love to the Lord; and, in a supreme sense, it refers to the Lord: wine, and the blood of grapes, is divine truth spiritual and celestial. I *washed* thee with waters, and *washed* away the blood from off thee, Ezek. xvi. 9; speaking of Jerusalem: waters are truths, and bloods are the adulterations of truth. From these considerations, it may appear what was represented, and thence signified, by washings in the Israelitish church; as that Aaron should *wash* himself before he put on the garments of his ministry, Levit. xvi. 4, 24. And before he went to the altar to minister, Exod. xxx. 18—21; xl. 30, 31. In like manner, the Levites, Numb. viii. 6, 7. In like manner, others, who were made unclean by sins; yea, that they *washed vessels*, Levit. xi. 32; xiv. 8, 9; xv. 5—12; xvii. 15, 16; Matt. xxix. 26, 27. That they were sanctified by *washings*, Exod. xxix. 4; xl. 12; Levit. viii. 6. That Naaman from Syria *washed* himself in Jordan, 2 Kings v. 10, 14. Therefore, that they might wash themselves, the brazen sea and many vessels for *washing* were placed near the temple, 1 Kings vii. 23—39. And that the Lord *washed* the disciples' feet, John xiii. 10. And commanded the blind man to *wash* himself in the pool of Siloam, John ix. 6, 7, 11, 15. From which it may appear, that washing, among the children of Israel, represented spiritual washing, which is purification from evils and falses, and consequent reformation and regeneration. And from what has been said, it is also evident what was signified by John's baptizing in Jordan, Matt. iii.; Mark i. 4—13; and by these words of John concerning the Lord, That he would *baptize* with the

Holy Spirit and with fire, Luke iii. 16; John i. 33; and of himself, That he *baptized* with water, John i. 26: the meaning of which is, that the Lord washes or purifies man by the divine truth and the divine good, and that John represented this by his baptism: for the Holy Spirit is divine truth, fire is divine good, and water is the representative of both; for water signifies the truth of the Word, which becomes good by a life according to it, n. 50.

379. *And made them white in the blood of the Lamb*, signifies, and have purified them from the falses of evil by truths, and thus are reformed by the Lord. There are evils of the false, and falses of evil; evils of the false with those who from religion believe that evils do not condemn, provided they confess with their lips that they are sinners; and falses of evil with those who confirm evils in themselves. By robes are here signified, as above, n. 378, general truths from the Word, which constitute their religious principles. It is said, they made white their robes in the blood of the Lamb, because white is predicated of truths, n. 167, 231, 232; thus, that they purified themselves from falses by truths: it also signifies that they were reformed by the Lord; because all who have fought against evils in the world, and have believed in the Lord, after their departure out of the world, are taught by the Lord, and are withdrawn from the falsities of their religion by truths, and thus are reformed: the reason is, because they who shun evils as sins, are in the good of life; and good of life desires truths, and acknowledges and accepts them; but evil of life never. By the blood of the Lamb here, and in other parts of the Word, it is believed that the Lord's passion of the cross is signified; but the passion of the cross was the last temptation, by which the Lord fully overcame the hells, and fully glorified his Humanity, by which two processes he saved man; see *The Doctrine of the New Jerusalem concerning the Lord*, n. 22—24, and n. 25—27; also above, n. 67. And because the Lord thus fully glorified his Humanity, that is, made it divine, therefore nothing else can be meant by his flesh and blood but the divinity in him and from him; by flesh, the divine good of the divine love; and by blood, divine truth from that good. Blood is mentioned in many parts of the Word, and everywhere signifies, in a spiritual sense, the divine truth of the Lord, which also is the divine truth of the Word; and, in an opposite sense, the divine truth of the Word falsified or profaned, as may appear from the following passages. First; that blood signifies the divine truth of the Lord, or of the Word, is manifest from these considerations: that blood was called the blood of the covenant, and covenant is conjunction, and this is effected from the Lord by his divine truth; as in Zechariah: "By the *blood* of thy *covenant* I have sent forth thy prisoners out of the pit," ix. 11; and

in Moses: Moses, after that he had read the book of the law in the ears of the people, sprinkled half of the *blood* upon the people, " and said, Behold the *blood of the covenant*, which Jehovah hath made with you concerning all these Words," Exod. xxiv. 3—8. "And Jesus took the cup, and gave it to them, saying, Drink ye all of it; for this is my *blood of the new covenant*," Matt. xxvi. 27, 28; Mark xiv. 24; Luke xxii. 20. By the blood of the new covenant or testament, nothing else is signified but the Word, which is called a Covenant and Testament, Old and New, thus the divine truth therein. As this is signified by blood, therefore the Lord gave them the wine, saying, This is my blood; and wine signifies divine truth, n. 316: it is also on this account called the *blood of grapes*, Gen. xlix. 11; Deut. xxxii. 14. This is again evident from these words of the Lord: " Verily, verily, I say unto you, except ye eat the flesh of the Son of Man, and *drink his blood*, ye have no life in you. For my flesh is meat indeed, and my *blood* is drink indeed. He that eateth my flesh and *drinketh my blood*, dwelleth in me, and I in him," John vi. 50—58. That by blood is here meant divine truth, appears manifestly, because it is said that he who drinks, has life, and dwells in the Lord, and the Lord in him. That divine truth and a life conformable to it effects this, and that the holy supper confirms it, might be known in the church. Since blood signifies the divine truth of the Lord, which is also the divine truth of the Word, and this is the Old and New Covenant or Testament itself, therefore blood was the most holy representative in the Israelitish church, in which all and singular things were correspondences of spiritual things; as, That they should take the *paschal blood*, " and strike it on the two side-posts and the upper door-post of the houses," that the plague might not come upon them, Exod. xii. 7, 13, 22. That the *blood of the burnt-offering* should be sprinkled upon the altar, on the foundations of the altar, upon Aaron, his sons, and their garments, Exod. xxix. 12, 15, 20, 21; Levit. i. 5, 11, 15; iii. 2, 8, 13; iv. 25, 30, 34; v. 9; viii. 15, 24; xvii. 6; Numb. xviii. 17; Deut. xii. 27: as also on the vail which was over the ark, on the mercy seat, and on the horns of the altar of incense, Levit. iv. 6, 7, 17, 18; xvi. 12—15. The same is signified by the blood of the Lamb in the following passage in the Apocalypse: " And there was war in heaven; Michael and his angels fought against the dragon, and overcame him by the *blood of the Lamb*, and by the word of their testimony," xii. 7, 11: for it cannot be supposed that Michael and his angels overcame the dragon by any thing else but the divine truth of the Lord in the Word; for, in heaven, the angels cannot think at all of blood; nor do they think of the Lord's passion, but of the divine truth and of his resurrection: wherefore, when man thinks of the Lord's blood, the angels perceive his divine truth; and when he thinks of the Lord's passion, they perceive his glorification, and then his resurrection only. It has been granted me to know that this is the fact, by much experience. That blood signifies divine truth is also evident from these words in David: God "shall save the souls of the needy, and precious shall their *blood* be in his sight. And he shall live, and to him shall be given of the gold of Sheba," Psalm lxxii. 13—16. Blood precious in the sight of God denotes divine truth with them; gold of Sheba is wisdom derived from it. In Ezekiel: "Gather yourselves on every side to my sacrifice upon the mountains of Israel, that ye may eat flesh and drink *blood;* ye shall drink the *blood* of the princes of the earth, and ye shall drink *blood till ye be drunken,* of my sacrifice which I have sacrificed to you. And I will set my glory among the heathen," xxxix. 17—21. By blood here cannot be meant blood, because it is said that they shall drink the blood of the princes of the earth, and that they shall drink blood till they be drunken; but the true sense of the Word results, when by blood is understood divine truth. The Lord's church also is there treated of, which he was about to establish among the Gentiles. Secondly, that blood signifies divine truth, may be clearly seen from its opposite sense, in which it signifies the divine truth of the Word falsified or profaned, as is evident from the following passages: Who "stoppeth his ears from hearing *blood*, and shutteth his eyes from seeing evil," Isaiah xxxiii. 15. "Thou shalt destroy them that speak leasing, Jehovah will abhor the *bloody* and deceitful man," Psalm v. 6. Every one that is written among the living in Jerusalem, when the Lord shall have washed away the filth of the daughters of Zion, and shall have purged the *blood* of Jerusalem from the midst thereof, by the spirit of judgment, and by the spirit of burning, Isaiah iv. 3, 4. "In the day thou wast born,—I saw thee polluted in thine own *blood;* I said unto thee, In thine own *blood*, live; I washed thee, and washed away the *lood* from off thee," Ezek. xvi. 5, 6, 9, 22, 36, 38. "They have wandered as blind men in the streets, they have polluted themselves with *blood*, so that men could not touch their garments," Lament. iv. 13, 14. "And garments rolled in *blood*," Isaiah ix. 5. "Also in thy skirts is found the *blood* of the souls of the poor innocents," Jerem. ii. 33, 34. "Your hands are full of *blood*. Wash you, make you clean; put away the evil of your doings," Isaiah i. 15, 16. "For your hands are defiled with *blood*, and your fingers with iniquity; your lips have spoken lies,—they make haste to shed innocent *blood*," Isaiah lix. 3. "For Jehovah cometh out of his place to visit the inhabitants of the earth for their iniquity; the earth also shall disclose her *blood*," Isaiah xxvi. 20. "But as many as received him, to them gave he power to become the sons of God;—which were born not of *blood*," John i. 12, 13. In Babylon " was found the *blood* of the prophets and saints," Apoc. xviii. 24. " The sea became as the *blood* of a dead man,—and the fountains of water became *blood*," Apoc. xvi. 3, 4; Isaiah xv. 6, 9; Psalm cv. 23, 28, 29. The same is signified by the rivers, collections, and lakes of water in Egypt being turned into *blood*, Exod. vii. 15, 25. The moon shall be turned into *blood* before the coming of the great day of Jehovah, Joel ii. 3. "The moon became as *blood*," Apoc. vi. 12. In these places, and many others, blood signifies the truth of the Word falsified, and also profaned; which yet may be seen more manifestly still by reading those passages in the Word in their series. Since therefore by blood, in an opposite sense, is signified the truth of the Word falsified or profaned, it is evident that by blood, in a genuine sense, is signified the truth of the Word not falsified.

380. *Therefore are they before the throne of God, and serve him day and night in his temple: and He that sitteth on the throne shall dwell among them*, signifies that they are in the presence of the Lord, and constantly and faithfully live according to the truths which they receive from him in his church, and that the Lord constantly gives good in their truths. Therefore are they before the throne of God, signifies that they are in the Lord's presence; and serve him day and night, signifies that they constantly and faithfully live according to the truths, that is, the precepts, which they receive from him; by serving the Lord nothing else is signified; in his temple signifies in the church, n. 191; He that sitteth on the throne shall dwell among them, signifies that the Lord constantly introduces good with the truths which they receive from him; that this is signified by dwelling among them, is, because, in the Word, to dwell, is predicated of good, and to serve, of truth. This arcanum may now be made known, viz., that the marriage of the Lord with the church consists in this, that the Lord flows into angels and men with the good of love, and that angels and men receive him, or the good of his love, in truths; that hereby a marriage of good and truth is effected, which marriage constitutes the church itself, and makes heaven with them. Such being the nature of the Lord's influx and reception of him, therefore the Lord looks at angels and men in the forehead, and they look at the Lord through the eyes; for the forehead corresponds to the good of love, and the eyes correspond to truths from that good, which thus by conjunction become truths of good. But the Lord's influx with truths into angels and men, is not as the influx of good into them, for it is mediate, flowing from good, as light does from fire, being received by them in the understanding, and only so far in the will as they do truths. This then constitutes the marriage of love and wisdom, or of

good and truth from the Lord, with those who receive them in the heavens and in the earths. This arcanum was disclosed for the sake of making it known how it is to be understood, that the Lord constantly gives good in their truths.

381. *They shall hunger no more, neither thirst any more*, signifies that hereafter there shall be no deficiency of goods and truths with them. By not hungering is signified to have no lack of good, and by not thirsting is signified to have no lack of truth; for to hunger is predicated of bread and meat, and to thirst, of wine and water; and by bread and meat is signified good, and by wine and water is signified truth: see above, n. 323.

382. *Neither shall the sun light on them, nor any heat*, signifies that hereafter they shall have no lust to evil, nor to the false of evil. The sun shall not light upon them, signifies that they shall have no lust to evil; neither shall any heat light on them, signifies that they shall have no lust to falsity. That the sun signifies divine love and thence the affections of good; and, in an opposite sense, diabolical love and thence the lust to evil, may be seen above. n. 53. But the reason why heat signifies lust to the false of evil, is, because falsity is produced from evil, as heat is from the sun; for when the will loves evil, the understanding loves falsity, and burns with the lust of confirming it, and evil confirmed in the understanding, is the falsity of evil; consequently the falsity of evil is evil in its form. Heat, and to burn or be hot, have a like signification in the following places: "Blessed is the man that trusteth in Jehovah,—and he shall not see when heat cometh," Jerem. xvii. 7, 8. "For thou hast been a refuge to the needy from the storm; a shadow from its *heat ;—*even the *heat* with the shadow of a cloud," Isaiah xxv. 4, 5. "In their *heat—*I will make them drunken,—that they may sleep a perpetual sleep," Jerem. li. 39. "They are all *hot* as an oven, there is none among them that calleth unto me," Hosea vii. 7. "He beholdeth not the way of the vineyards. Drought and *heat* consume the snow waters," Job xxiv. 18, 19. "And the fourth angel poured out his vial upon the sun; and power was given unto him to scorch men with *great heat,—*and they blasphemed the name of God," Apoc. xvi. 8, 9. "That thou mayest say to the prisoners, Go forth ;—They shall not hunger nor thirst, neither shall the *heat* nor sun smite them," Isaiah xlix. 9, 10.

383. *For the lamb which is in the midst of the throne shall feed them*, signifies that the Lord alone will teach them. By the Lamb in the midst of the throne, is signified the Lord as to his Divine Humanity in the inmost, and thus in all things of heaven; in the midst is in the inmost, and thereby in all things, n. 44; the throne is heaven, n. 14; and the Lamb is the Lord as to his Divine Humanity, n. 269, 291; and he who is in the

inmost, and thus in all things of heaven, alone feeds, that is, teaches all. If it be asked, how can he alone feed all? be it known that he is God, and because in the universal heaven he is as a soul in its body, for heaven is from him as one man. To feed means to teach, because the church, in the Word, is called a flock, and the men of the church are called sheep and lambs, hence to feed signifies to teach, and a pastor, or feeder, one that teaches; and this in many places; as: "In that day shall thy *cattle* feed in large pastures," Isaiah xxx. 23. "He shall *feed his flock* as a shepherd," Isaiah xl. 11. "They shall *feed* in the ways, and their *pastures* shall be in all high places," Isaiah xlix. 9. Israel "shall *feed* on Carmel and Bashan," Jerem. l. 19. "I will seek out my sheep, I will *feed them* in a good pasture, and in a fat pasture upon the mountains of Israel," Ezek. xxxiv. 12—14. "*Feed* thy people,—let them *feed* in Bashan and Gilead," Micah vii. 14. "The remnant of Israel shall *feed* and lie down," Zeph. iii. 13. "Jehovah is *my shepherd*, I shall not want, he maketh me to lie down in green pastures," Psalm xxiii. 1, 2. The Lord hath chosen David to *feed* Jacob and Israel, and he *fed* them, Psalm lxxviii. 70—72. Jesus said unto Peter, *Feed my lambs*, and a second and a third time he said, *Feed my sheep*, John xxi. 15—17.

384. *And shall lead them unto living fountains of waters*, signifies, and lead them by the truths of the Word to conjunction with himself. Since by a living fountain of waters is signified the Lord, and also the Word, and by waters are signified truths, n. 50, and since by the divine truths of the Word, when they are brought into the life, or by living according to them, conjunction is effected with the Lord, therefore by leading them to living fountains of waters, is signified to lead by the truths of the Word to conjunction with the Lord. That by a fountain and fountains is signified the Lord, and also the Word, is evident from these passages: "All my *fountains* are in thee, O Jehovah," Psalm lxxxvii. 7. "They have deserted Jehovah, the *Fountain of living waters*," Jerem. ii. 13. "And thou shalt make them drink of the river of thy pleasures, for with thee is the *fountain of life*," Psalm xxxvi. 9, 10. "In that day shall a *fountain* be opened to the inhabitants of Jerusalem," Zech xiii. 1. Israel dwelt securely solitary at the *fountain of Jacob*, Deut. xxxiii. 28. When the Lord was sitting at the *fountain of Jacob*, he said unto the woman, "The water that I shall give shall become a *fountain* of water springing up into everlasting life," John iv. 5—20. "Joseph is a fruitful bough by a *fountain*," Gen. xlix. 22. "Bless the Lord from the *fountain* of Israel," Psalm lxviii. 26. "Therefore with joy shall ye draw waters out of the *fountains* of salvation," Isaiah xii. 3. Unto him that is athirst will I give of the *fountain* of the water of life freely," Apoc. xxi. 6. "I will cause them to walk by the

fountains of waters in the straight way," Jerem. xxxi. 9. Expressions similar to these and the above in the Apocalypse, occur also in Isaiah: "THEY SHALL NOT HUNGER NOR THIRST, NEITHER SHALL THE HEAT NOR SUN SMITE THEM, FOR HE THAT HATH MERCY ON THEM SHALL LEAD THEM EVEN BY THE FOUNTAINS OF WATER," Isaiah xlix. 10.

385. *And God shall wipe away all tears from their eyes*, signifies that they shall no longer be in combats against evils and their falses, and thereby in sorrow, but in goods and truths, and thence in celestial joys from the Lord. That these things are signified by the Lamb wiping away all tears from their eyes, is, because above, in verse 14, it is said that these are they which come out of great affliction, by which is signified that they are such as have been in temptations, and fought against evils, n. 377; and they who afterwards are not in combats against evils, the same are in goods and truths, and thence in celestial joys. The following passage in Isaiah has a similar signification: "He will swallow up death in victory, and the Lord Jehovah will wipe away the tears from all faces: And it shall be said in that day, Lo, this is our God, we have waited for him, and he will save us. This is Jehovah, we have waited for him, we will be glad and rejoice in his salvation," xxv. 8, 9.

386. To the above I will add this Memorable Relation. On a time, when looking around in the spiritual world, I heard a noise like that of the gnashing of teeth, and also a beating noise, and a sort of hoarse sound blended with them: and I inquired what was meant by them; and the angels who were with me said, "There are colleges which we call *diversoria*,* where disputations take place; these disputations are so heard at a distance, but on coming near to them they are only heard as disputations." I drew near, and saw some huts, constructed of reeds stuck together with mud; and I would fain have looked through a window, but there was none; for it was not allowed to enter by the door, because the light would thus have flowed in from heaven, and confounded them. But suddenly a window was made on the right side; and then I heard them complain that they were in darkness. Shortly afterwards a window was made on the left side, and that on the right was closed; upon which the darkness gradually dispersed, and they seemed to themselves to be in the light. After this I was permitted to go in at the door and hear. There was a table in the middle, and benches round about; but they all seemed to me to stand upon the benches, and to dispute sharply with one another concerning FAITH and CHARITY: on one side, that faith was the essential of the church; on the other, that charity was. They

* A house of resort.

who made faith the essential, said, "Have we not to do with God by faith, and with man by charity? is not faith therefore heavenly, and charity earthly? are we not saved by what is heavenly, and not by what is earthly? Again, cannot God give faith from heaven, because it is heavenly, and must not man procure to himself charity, because it is earthly? and what man procures for himself, is not of the church, and therefore is not saving: can any one be justified in the sight of God by works, which are called works of charity? Believe us, we are not only justified, but also sanctified by faith alone, provided that faith be not defiled by things meritorious, which are derived from works of charity:" not to mention more arguments to the same purpose. But they who made charity the essential of the church, strenuously denied these things, saying, "That charity saves, and not faith; are not all dear to God, and does he not will the good of all? how can God effect this, except by men? does God only give to men to talk with one another about such things as relate to faith, and not to do to men those things which relate to charity? do you not see that it is absurd in you to say that charity is earthly? charity is heavenly, and because you do not perform the good of charity, your faith is earthly; how do you receive faith but as a stock or a stone? you say by the hearing of the Word only; but how can the Word operate by being heard only, and this too upon a stock or a stone? possibly you are quickened without knowing it; but of what avail is this quickening, except in being enabled to say that faith alone saves? but what faith is, and what a saving faith, you know not." But there then arose one, who, by the angel that was talking with me, was called a syncretist;[*] he took off a turban from his head, and placed it on the table; but suddenly put it on again, because he was bald. He said, "Attend! you are all in error; it is true that faith is spiritual, and charity, moral; but yet they are joined together; and this by the Word, by the Holy Spirit, and by effect, without man's knowledge, which indeed may be called obedience, but in which man has no share. I have long considered this with myself, and have at length discovered, that man may receive faith from God, which may be spiritual, but that he cannot be moved by God to charity, which may be spiritual, but as a statue of salt." On saying this, he was applauded by those who were in faith alone, but disapproved by those who were in charity: and the latter said, with indignation, "Hear, friend! you do not know that there is a spiritual moral life, and that there is a moral life merely natural; a spiritual moral life with those who do good

---

[*] Syncretist—a name given to some Platonic Christians in the fifteenth century, who steered a middle course between the opposite factions among the followers of Aristotle and Plato; a sect held in great veneration, for a long time, among the mystics. *Vide* Mosheim's Ecclesiastical History, Cent. 15, Ch. 11. Part 2.

from God, and yet as if from themselves; and a moral life merely natural with those who do good from hell, and yet as if from themselves."

It was said above, that the disputation was heard as a gnashing of teeth, and as a beating noise, with which a hoarse sound was blended. The disputation heard as a gnashing of teeth, was by those who were in faith alone; but the disputation heard as a beating noise, was by those who were in charity alone; and the hoarse sound that was blended with them was from the syncretist. The sound of them was so heard at a distance, because, when in the world, they all spent their time in disputations, and did not shun any evil, and therefore performed no spiritual moral good; and, moreover, they were entirely ignorant, that the all of faith is truth, and the all of charity, good, and that truth without good is not truth in spirit, and that good without truth is not good in spirit, and that thus one makes or completes the other. The reason why darkness ensued when a window was made on the right side, is, because light from heaven flowing-in on that side affects the will; and the reason why there was light when the window on the right side was shut, and another was made on the left, is, because light flowing-in from heaven on the left side affects the understanding, and man may be in the light of heaven as to his understanding, provided the will be closed as to its evil.

CHAPTER VIII.

1. And when he had opened the seventh seal, there was silence in heaven about the space of half an hour.

2. And I saw the seven angels, who stood before God; and to them were given seven trumpets.

3. And another angel came and stood at the altar, having a golden censer: and there was given unto him much incense, that he should offer it with the prayers of all saints upon the golden altar which was before the throne.

4. And the smoke of the incense, which came with the prayers of the saints, ascended out of the hand of the angel before God.

5. And the angel took the censer, and filled it with the fire of the altar, and cast it unto the earth: and there were voices, and thunderings, and lightnings, and an earthquake.

6. And the seven angels that had the seven trumpets prepared themselves to sound.

7. The first angel sounded, and there followed hail and fire, mingled with blood; and they were cast upon the earth; and

the third part of the trees was burnt up, and all green grass was burnt up.

8. And the second angel sounded, and as it were a great mountain burning with fire was cast into the sea: and the third part of the sea became blood.

9. And the third part of the creatures which were in the sea, and had life, died; and the third part of the ships were destroyed.

10. And the third angel sounded, and there fell from heaven a great star burning as it were a lamp: and it fell upon the third part of the rivers, and upon the fountains of waters:

11. And the name of the star is called Wormwood: and the third part of the waters became wormwood; and many men died of the waters, because they were made bitter.

12. And the fourth angel sounded, and the third part of the sun was smitten, and the third part of the moon, and the third part of the stars; so that the third part of them was darkened, and the day shone not for a third part of it, and the night likewise.

13. And I beheld, and I heard an angel flying in the midst of heaven, saying with a loud voice, Woe, woe, woe, to the inhabiters of the earth, by reason of the other voices of the trumpet of the three angels that are yet to sound.

THE SPIRITUAL SENSE.

THE CONTENTS OF THE WHOLE CHAPTER. The reformed church is here treated of, as to the quality of those therein who are in faith alone: the preparation of the spiritual heaven for communication with them, verses 1—6. The exploration and manifestation of those therein, who are in the interiors of that faith, verse 7; of those who are in its exteriors, verses 8, 9; what they are in regard to the understanding of the Word, verses 10, 11. That they are in falses and thence in evils, verses 12, 13.

THE CONTENTS OF EACH VERSE. V. 1, "And when he had opened the seventh seal," signifies exploration from the Lord of the state of the church, and thence of the life of those who are in his spiritual kingdom, being those who are in charity and its faith; in this case who are in faith alone: "There was silence in heaven about the space of half an hour," signifies that the angels of the Lord's spiritual kingdom were greatly amazed, when they saw those who said they were in faith, in such a state: v. 2, "And I saw the seven angels who stood before God," signifies the universal spiritual heaven in the presence of the

Lord, hearing and doing his commands: "And to them were given seven trumpets," signifies the exploration and discovery of the state of the church, and thence of the life of those who are in faith alone: v. 3, "And another angel came and stood at the altar, having a golden censer," signifies spiritual worship, which is performed from the good of charity by the truths of faith: "And there was given him much incense, that he should offer it with the prayers of all saints upon the golden altar which was before the throne," signifies propitiation lest the angels of the Lord's spiritual kingdom should be hurt by the spirits of the satanic kingdom that were beneath: v. 4, "And the smoke of the incense which came with the prayers of the saints ascended up out of the hand of the angels before God," signifies the protection of them by the Lord: v. 5, "And the angel took the censer, and filled it with the fire of the altar, and cast it unto the earth," signifies spiritual love, in which there is celestial love, and its influx into inferior things, where they were who were in faith separated from charity: "And there were voices, and thunderings, and lightnings, and an earthquake," signifies that after a communication was opened with them, there were heard reasonings concerning faith alone, and confirmations in favour of it: v. 6, "And the seven angels that had the seven trumpets prepared themselves to sound," signifies that they were prepared and ready to explore the state of the church and thence the state of life with those whose religion is faith alone: v. 7, "The first angel sounded," signifies the exploration and manifestation of the quality of the state of the church with those who are interiorly in that faith: "And there followed hail and fire mingled with blood," signifies falsity from infernal love destroying good and truth, and falsifying the Word: "And they were cast upon the earth, and the third part of the trees was burnt up," signifies that with them all the affection and perception of truth, which constitute the man of the church, had perished: "And all green grass was burnt up," signifies, thus all that is alive in faith: v. 8, "And the second angel sounded," signifies the exploration and manifestation of what the state of the church is with those who are exteriorly in that faith: "And as it were a great mountain burning with fire was cast into the sea," signifies the appearance of infernal love with them: "And the third part of the sea became blood," signifies that all general truths with them were falsified: v. 9, "And the third part of the creatures which were in the sea that had life, died," signifies that they who have lived and do live this faith cannot be reformed and receive life: "And the third part of the ships were destroyed," signifies that all the knowledges of good and truth from the Word, serving for the use of life, were destroyed with them: v. 10, "And the third angel sounded," signifies the exploration and manifestation of the state of the church with those whose religion is faith alone, as to the affection and reception of truths from the Word : "And there fell from heaven a great star, burning as it were a lamp," signifies the appearance of self-derived intelligence from a pride springing from infernal love : " And it fell upon the third part of the rivers, and upon the fountains of waters," signifies that thence all the truths of the Word were totally falsified: v. 11, " And the name of the star is called Wormwood ; and the third part of the waters became wormwood," signifies the infernal falsity from which their self-derived intelligence is derived, by which all the truths of the Word are falsified : "And many men died of the waters, because they were made bitter," signifies the extinction of spiritual life from the falsified truths of the Word : v. 12, " And the fourth angel sounded," signifies the exploration and manifestation of the state of the church with those whose religion is faith alone, as being in the evils of falsity, and in the falsities of evil : "And the third part of the sun was smitten, and the third part of the moon, and the third part of the stars, so that the third part of them was darkened," signifies that by reason of evils from falsities and of falsities from evils, they did not know what love is, or what faith is, or any truth : " And the day shone not for a third part of it, and the night likewise," signifies that there is no longer any spiritual truth nor natural truth serviceable for doctrine and life from the Word with them : v. 13, " And I beheld, and I heard an angel flying in the midst of heaven," signifies instruction and prediction from the Lord : " Saying with a loud voice, Woe, woe, woe, to the inhabiters of the earth, by reason of the other voices of the trumpet of the three angels which are yet to sound," signifies deep lamentation over the damned state of those in the church, who in doctrine and life have confirmed themselves in faith separate from charity.

THE EXPLANATION.

387 THERE are two kingdoms into which the universal heaven is divided, the CELESTIAL KINGDOM and the SPIRITUAL KINGDOM. The celestial kingdom consists of those who are in love to the Lord and thence in wisdom ; and the spiritual kingdom consists of those who are in love towards their neighbour, and thence in intelligence ; and as love towards our neighbour is at this day called charity, and intelligence, faith, the latter kingdom consists of those who are in charity, and thence in faith. Now, because heaven is divided into two kingdoms, hell also is

divided into two kingdoms that are opposite to them; into a DIABOLICAL KINGDOM and into a SATANICAL KINGDOM. The diabolical kingdom consists of those who are in the love of dominion from self-love, and thence in foolishness; for this love is opposite to celestial love, and its foolishness is opposite to celestial wisdom: but the satanical kingdom consists of those who are in the love of dominion from the pride of self-derived intelligence, and thence in insanity; for this love is opposite to spiritual love, and its insanity is opposite to spiritual intelligence. By foolishness and insanity are meant foolishness and insanity in things celestial and spiritual. The same things which are said of heaven are to be understood of the church on earth, for they make one. Concerning these two kingdoms, see the work on *Heaven and Hell*, n. 20—28, and many other places. Now, as the Apocalypse treats only of the state of the church at its end, as was observed in the preface, and at n. 2, therefore what now follows treats of those who are in the two kingdoms of heaven, and of those who are in the two kingdoms of hell, and of their quality; from this chapter, viz., viii. to xvi., of those who are in the spiritual kingdom, and in the satanical kingdom opposite to it; in chap. xvii. and xviii., of those who are in the celestial kingdom, and in the diabolical kingdom opposite to it; and afterwards of the last judgment; and, lastly, of the New Church which is the New Jerusalem; this bringing all that goes before to a conclusion, by reason of its constituting the final purpose. In many parts of the Word the devil and satan are mentioned, and by both is meant hell; it is so named, because all in one hell are called devils, and all in the other are called satans.

388. *And when he had opened the seventh seal*, signifies exploration from the Lord of the state of the church, and thence of the state of life of those who are in his spiritual kingdom, being those who are in charity and its faith; in this case, who are in faith alone. That this is the signification of these words, may appear from all the particulars of this chapter when understood in a spiritual sense; for this chapter and the following to capter xvi. treat of those who are in the spiritual kingdom, or those who are in love towards their neighbour and thence in intelligence, as was said above, n. 387. But since, at this day, the word charity is used instead of love towards our neighbour, and faith instead of intelligence; and here there is not any exploration of those who are in charity and thence in faith, because these belong to such as are in heaven; therefore exploration is here made of those who are in faith alone. Faith alone is also faith separated from charity, there being no conjunction: see below, n. 417. That to open the seal signifies to explore states of life, or, what is the same thing, the states of the church and thence of life, see above, n. 295, 302, 309, 317, 324.

389. *There was silence in heaven about the space of half an hour*, signifies that the angels of the Lord's spiritual kingdom were greatly amazed, when they saw those, who said they were in faith, in such a state. By silence in heaven, nothing else is meant but amazement there in regard to those who say they are in faith, and are nevertheless in such a state; for their state is described in what follows, the quality of which will be rendered evident by the explanation. By half an hour is signified greatly, because by an hour is signified a full state. That time signifies state, will be seen below.

390. *And I saw the seven angels who stood before God*, signifies the universal spiritual heaven in the presence of the Lord, hearing and doing his commands. By seven angels is signified the universal heaven, because seven signifies all, or every thing, thence the total, and the universal, n. 10; and by angels, in a supreme sense, is signified the Lord, and, in a relative sense, heaven, n. 5, 66, 342, 344; here, the spiritual heaven, as may appear from what was said above, n. 387, 388. That to stand before God signifies to hear and do his commands, see above, n. 366.

391. *And to them were given seven trumpets*, signifies the exploration and discovery of the state of the church, and thence of the life of those who are in faith alone. Here, by trumpets the same thing is signified as by sounding, because they sounded with them, and by sounding with trumpets is signified to call together upon solemn occasions, which were various; in this case, for the purpose of exploring and discovering the quality of those who are in faith alone, thus the quality of those who are at this day of the reformed churches. "It should be observed, that the church in the reformed world is at this day divided into three, from the three leaders, Luther, Calvin, and Melancthon, and that these three churches differ in various things; but in this point, that man is justified by faith without the works of the law, they all agree, which is remarkable." That by sounding with trumpets is signified to call together, will be seen below, n. 397.

392. *And another angel came and stood at the altar, having a golden censer*, signifies spiritual worship, which is performed from the good of charity by the truths of faith. By the altar at which the angel stood, and by the golden censer which he had in his hand, is signified the worship of the Lord from spiritual love, which worship exists from the good of charity by the truths of faith. With the children of Israel there were two altars, one without the tent, and the other within it; the altar without the tent was called the *altar of burnt-offering*, because burnt-offerings and sacrifices were offered upon it; the altar within the tent was called the *altar of incense*, as also the *golden altar*. There were two altars, because the worship of the Lord

is performed from celestial love and from spiritual love; from celestial love by those who are in his celestial kingdom, and from spiritual love by those who are in his spiritual kingdom; concerning these two kingdoms, see above, n. 387. Concerning the two altars, see the following passages in Moses: on the altar of burnt-offering, Exod. xx. 24 to the end; xxvii. 1—9; xxxix. 36—43; Levit. vii. 1—5; viii. 11; xvi. 18, 19, 33, 34. On the altar of incense, Exod. xxx. 1—10; xxxii. 6; xxxvii. 25—29; xl. 5, 26; Numb. vii. 1. That altars, censers, and incense, were seen by John, was not because such things exist in heaven, these being only representative of the worship of the Lord there; the reason is, because such things were instituted among the children of Israel, and are therefore often mentioned in the Word; and that church was a representative church, for all things connected with their worship did represent, and do consequently now signify, the divine celestial and spiritual things of the Lord, which relate to his church in the heavens and in the earths. The same is therefore signified by the two altars spoken of in the Word, in the following passages: "O send out thy light and thy truth, let them lead me; let them bring me to thy holy hill.—Then will I go unto the *altar of God*, unto God my exceeding joy," Psalm xliii. 3, 4. "I will wash my hands in innocency; so will I compass thine *altar*, O Jehovah; that I may publish with the voice of thanksgiving," Psalm xxvi. 6, 7. "The sin of Judah is written with a pen of iron, it is graven upon the table of their heart, and upon the horns of your *altars*," Jerem. xvii. 1, 2. "God is Jehovah, which hath showed us light; bind the sacrifice with cords unto the horns of the *altar*," Psalm cxviii. 27. "In that day shalt thou be an *altar* to Jehovah in the midst of the land of Egypt," Isaiah xix. 19. The altar of Jehovah in the midst of the land of Egypt, signifies the worship of the Lord from love in the natural man. "The thorn and the thistle shall come up on their *altars*," Hosea x. 7, 8: by which is signified worship from evils and from the falses of evil. Besides other places; as Isaiah xxvii. 9; lvi. 6, 7; lx. 7; Lament. ii. 7; Ezek. vi. 3, 4, 6, 13; Hosea viii. 11; x. 1, 2; Amos iii. 14; Psalm li. 18, 19; Psalm lxxxiv. 3—5; Matt. v. 23, 24; xxiii. 18—20. Since the worship of the Lord was represented and thence signified by the altar, it is evident that by altar here in the Apocalypse nothing else is understood: and also elsewhere: as, "I saw under the *altar* the souls of them that were slain for the Word of God," Apoc. vi. 9. "The angel stood saying, Rise, and measure the temple of God and the *altar*, and them that worship therein," Apoc. xi. 1. "And I heard another angel out of the *altar*, say,—True and righteous are thy judgments," Apoc. xvi. 7. As representative worship, which was performed for the most part upon two altars, was abolished by the Lord when he came into the world, from the circumstance of his having himself opened the interiors of the church; therefore it is said in Isaiah, "At that day shall a man look to his Maker, and his eyes shall have respect to the Holy One of Israel. And he shall not look to the *altars*, the work of his hands," xvii. 8.

393. *And there was given him much incense, that he should offer it with the prayers of all saints upon the golden altar which was before the throne*, signifies propitiation, lest the angels of the Lord's spiritual kingdom should be hurt by the spirits of the satanic kingdom, that were beneath. By the incense and by the golden altar is signified the worship of the Lord from spiritual love, n. 277, 392; by prayers are signified those things which relate to charity and thence to faith in worship, n. 278; and by saints are meant those who are of the Lord's spiritual kingdom; and by the righteous, those who are of the Lord's celestial kingdom, n. 173: from which it may appear, that they who are in the Lord's spiritual kingdom are here treated of. That much incense offered with the prayers of all saints upon the golden altar signifies propitiation, lest they should be hurt by the spirits of the satanic kingdom who were beneath them, is, because propitiations and expiations were made by incense, especially when dangers threatened; as may appear from the following passages: When the congregation murmured against Moses and Aaron, and were affected with a plague, Aaron took fire from off the altar, and put *incense* into a censer, and ran in among the living and the dead to make atonement, "and the plague was stayed," Numb. xvi. 46—48. Moreover, the *altar of incense* was placed in the tabernacle, before the mercy-seat, that was over the ark, and *incense* was offered on it every morning when the lamps were dressed, Exod. xxx. 1—10. And it was commanded, that as often as Aaron entered within the vail, he should offer *incense*, and the cloud of *incense* should cover the mercy-seat, lest he should die, Levit. xvi. 11—13. Hence it may appear, that propitiations in the representative Israelitish church were made by offering incense: in like manner here, that they might not be hurt by the satanic spirits who were beneath them.

394. *And the smoke of the incense which came with the prayers of the saints, ascended up out of the hand of the angel before God*, signifies the protection of them by the Lord. By the smoke of the incense ascending before God is signified what is accepted and grateful; wherefore the like is said by David: "Let my prayers be set forth before thee as *incense*," Psalm cxli. 2; the reason was, because the smoke of the incense was fragrant, from the spices of which it was composed, which were stacte, onyche, galbanum, and frankincense, Exod. xxx. 34; and the fragrances of those spices correspond to such things as are of spiritual love or charity, and thence of faith; for in

heaven most fragrant odours are sensibly perceived corresponding to the perceptions of the angels originating from their love; therefore it is also said in many parts of the Word, that Jehovah smelled an odour of rest. That protection from the Lord is signified, follows from what was said above, n. 393.

395. *And the angel took the censer, and filled it with the fire of the altar, and cast it unto the earth,* signifies spiritual love, in which is celestial love, and its influx into inferior things, where they were who are in faith separated from charity. That by a censer, as well as by incense, is signified worship from spiritual love, is evident from what was shown above; and also from this consideration, that in the Word, the thing containing signifies the same as the thing contained, as a cup and platter signify the same as wine and meat, Matt. xxiii. 25, 26; Luke xxii. 20; and in other places. By the fire of the altar of burnt-offering, is signified divine celestial love, because by that altar was signified worship from that love, as may be seen above, n. 392; and by fire, in a supreme sense, is signified divine love, n. 494. Spiritual love, which is charity, derives its essence from celestial love, which is love to the Lord; without this love there is nothing vital in spiritual love or charity, for spirit and life is from no other source than from the Lord. This was represented in the Israelitish church by their not being allowed to take fire from any other place to put into the censer when they offered incense, than from the altar of burnt-offering; as may appear in Moses, Levit. xvi. 12, 13; Numb. xvii. 11, 12: and that the two sons of Aaron were consumed by *fire* from heaven, because they offered *incense* with strange *fire*, that is, with fire not taken from the altar, Levit. x. 1, 2; therefore it was also ordained, that *fire* should burn constantly on the altar of burnt-offering, and should not be put out, Levit. vi. 9; and this by reason that the fire of that altar signifies the divine love of the Lord, and thence love to the Lord. By casting the censer upon the earth is signified influx into lower spheres (or degrees).

396. *And there were voices, and thunderings, and lightnings, and an earthquake,* signifies that after a communication was opened with them, there were heard reasonings concerning faith alone, and confirmations in favour of it, and that the state of the church with them was perceived to be tottering towards destruction. That lightnings, thunderings, and voices, signify illustrations, perceptions, and instructions, by influx from heaven, see above, n. 236; but here, with those who were in faith alone, who have no illustration, perception, and instruction, by influx from heaven. By voices, thunderings, and lightnings, are signified reasonings about faith alone, and argumentations and confirmations in favour of it; by earthquakes are signified changes of the state of the church, n. 331, in this case, that the state of the church among them was perceived to be tottering

towards destruction; for earthquakes take place in the world of spirits, when the state of the church in societies is perverted and inverted. The reason why the censer was thrown unto the earth by the angel, before the seven angels began to sound with their trumpets, was, that by influx a communication might be opened between those who were in the spiritual heaven, with those beneath who were in faith alone; from which communication there arose reasonings and confirmations in favour of it, which were also heard and perceived; wherefore it is said that after a communication was opened, they were heard and perceived.

397. *And the seven angels that had the seven trumpets prepared themselves to sound*, signifies that they were prepared and ready to explore the state of the church, and thence the state of life, with those whose religion is faith alone. What is meant by trumpets, appears from the statute respecting the use of them among the sons of Israel, concerning which it is thus written in Moses: Jehovah spake unto Moses to make *trumpets* of silver for the calling of the assembly, and for the journeying of the camps; and that they should blow with them in days of gladness, and festivals and new moons, and over burnt-offerings and sacrifices; also, that when they went to war against enemies that infested them, they should blow an alarm with the *trumpets*, and that then they should come into remembrance before Jehovah God, and should be preserved from their enemies, Numb. x. 1—11. From these words it may be seen what is signified by blowing with trumpets. That by the seven angels sounding, is here signified the exploration and manifestation of what the state of the church is with those whose religion consists in faith alone, is evident from the particulars of this chapter, and from the particulars of the chapters that follow as far as the sixteenth inclusive, when understood in the spiritual sense. From the use of trumpets among the sons of Israel may also be seen what is signified by trumpets, and by sounding with them, in the following places: "Blow ye *the trumpet* in Zion, and *sound* an alarm in my holy mountain, for the day of Jehovah cometh," Joel ii. 1, 2. "And Jehovah shall be seen over them, and his arrow shall go forth as the lightning, and the Lord Jehovah shall *blow the trumpet*," Zech. ix. 14. "Jehovah shall go forth as a lion and *sound*," Isaiah xlii. 13. "And it shall come to pass in that day, that the *great trumpet* shall be blown, and they shall come which were ready to perish in the land of Assyria, and the outcasts in the land of Egypt, and shall worship Jehovah in the holy mountain at Jerusalem," Isaiah xxvii. 13. "And he shall send his angels with a *great sound of a trumpet*, and they shall gather together his elect from the four winds, from one end of heaven to the other," Matt. xxiv. 31. "Blessed is the people who know the *joyful sound*; they shall walk, O

Jehovah, in the light of thy countenance," Psalm lxxxix. 15. "When the morning stars sang together, and all the sons of God *shouted for joy*," Job xxxviii. 7. Since the sounds of trumpets signify such things, and as, in the Israelitish church, all things were represented to the life according to correspondences and their consequent significations, therefore it came to pass, when Jehovah came down upon Mount Sinai, that there were voices, and lightnings, and a heavy cloud, and a vehement voice of a *trumpet*, and a voice of a *trumpet* going and strengthening itself greatly, and the people in the camp trembled greatly, Exod. xix. 16—25. And for the same reason it came to pass, that when the three hundred with Gideon *blew with their trumpets* against Midian, then the sword of a man was against his companion, and they fled, Judges vii. 16—22: in like manner, that twelve thousand of the sons of Israel with vessels of holiness and *trumpets* in their hands overcame Midian, Numb. xxxi. 1—8; as also, that the wall of Jericho fell down, after the seven priests with seven *trumpets* compassed the city seven times, Joshua vi. 1—20. Wherefore it is said in Jeremiah, *Sound the trumpet* against Babylon round about, her walls are destroyed, l. 15; and in Zephaniah, "A day of clouds and thick darkness, a day of the *trumpet* and alarm against the fenced cities," i. 15, 16.

398. *The first angel sounded*, signifies exploration and manifestation of the quality of the state of the church with those who are interiorly in that faith. By sounding is signified to explore and make manifest, n. 397. The reason why by the sounding of this first angel, is meant the exploration and manifestation of the state of the church with those who are interiorly in that faith, is, because its operation was felt upon the earth, as appears from what follows; and the operation of the sounding of the second angel was felt upon the sea, the earth and the sea, throughout the Apocalypse, when named together, meaning the church universal; by the earth, the church as consisting of those who are in its internals, and by the sea, the church as consisting of those who are in its externals: for the church is internal and external; internal with the clergy, and external with the laity; or internal with those who have studied its doctrinals interiorly, and have confirmed them from the Word, and external with those who have not. Both are understood by the earth and the sea in the following passages in the Apocalypse: "That the wind should not blow upon the *earth*, nor on the *sea*," vii. 1. "Hurt not the *earth*, neither the *sea*," vii. 3. "The angel descending out of heaven set his right foot upon the *sea*, and his left upon the *earth*," x. 2, 8; also in verse 6. "I saw a beast rise out of the sea,—and another beast coming up out of the *earth*," xiii. 1, 11. "Worship him who made heaven, and *earth*, and the *sea*," xiv. 7. "The first

angel poured out his vial upon the *earth*, and the second angel his upon the sea," xvi. 2, 3. The earth and sea signify the church internal and external, thus the church universal, because, in the spiritual world, they who are in the internals of the church appear upon dry land, and they who are in its externals, as on the sea; but the sea is only an appearance from the general truths in which they are principled. That earth signifies the church, may be seen, n. 285: so also does the world; see n. 551.

399. *And there followed hail and fire mingled with blood*, signifies falsity from infernal love destroying good and truth, and falsifying the Word. By hail is signified falsity destroying good and truth; by fire is signified infernal love; and by blood is signified the falsification of truth. That hail signifies falsity destroying good and truth, will be seen below; that fire means love in both senses, celestial and infernal, may be seen, n. 468; that blood means the divine truth of the Lord, which is also the Word, and, in the opposite sense, the Word falsified, n. 379. On joining these together into one sense, it is plain, that by there followed hail and fire mingled with blood, is signified falsity from infernal love destroying good and truth, and falsifying the Word. This is signified, because such things appear in the spiritual world when the sphere of the Lord's divine love and divine wisdom descends from heaven into the societies below, where falsities derived from infernal love exist, and the Word is falsified thereby. Hail and fire together have a like signification in the following places: "At the brightness that was before him his thick clouds passed, *hail-stones and coals of fire:* and the Highest gave his voice, *hail-stones and coals of fire;* yea, he sent out his arrows and scattered them," Psalm xviii. 12—14. "And I will plead against him with pestilence and with blood, and I will rain upon him great *hail-stones, fire,* and brimstone," Ezek. xxxviii. 22. "And Jehovah shall cause his glorious voice to be heard,—and with the *flame* of a devouring *fire,*—and *hail-stones,*" Isaiah xxx. 30. He gave them *hail* for rain, and *flaming fire* in their land,—and brake the trees of their coasts, Psalm cv. 32, 33. The *hail* smote their vine, and their sycamore trees with grievous *hail*, and their cattle with burning *coals;* he sent in the burning of his anger a sending forth of evil angels, Psalm lxxviii. 47—49. These words are applied to Egypt. In Moses we read concerning them, that "he stretched forth his rod, and Jehovah gave voices and *hail;* and there was *hail and fire* together walking in the midst of *grievous hail:* and the hail smote every herb of the field, and brake every tree of the field," Exod. ix. 22—35. All the miracles that were wrought in Egypt signified the evils and falses derived from infernal love, which prevailed with the Egyptians; each miracle signifying some particular evil and

falsity: for with them there was a representative church, as in like manner with many kingdoms of Asia, but it became idolatrous and magical; by the Red Sea is signified hell, in which at last they perished. Something similar is signified by the *hail-stones* by which more of the enemy perished than by the sword, Josh. x. 11. The same, also, is meant by hail in the following places: " Woe to the crown of pride,—behold, the Lord hath a mighty and strong one, like an inundation of *hail:* and the *hail* shall sweep away the refuge of lies," Isaiah xxviii. 1, 2, 17. " When it shall *hail*, coming down on the forest," Isaiah xxxii. 19. " And the temple of God was opened in heaven,—and there were lightnings, and voices, and thunderings, and an earthquake, and *great hail*," Apoc. xi. 19. " And there fell upon men a *great hail* out of heaven, about the weight of a talent," Apoc. xvi. 21. " Hast thou seen the treasures of *hail*, which I have reserved against the day of battle and war?" Job xxxviii. 22, 23. " Say unto them which daub with untempered mortar, that it shall fall; there shall be an overflowing shower, and ye, O *great hail-stones*, shall fall," Ezek. xiii. 11. To daub with untempered mortar means to confirm falsity, to make it appear like truth; they therefore who do so are called hail-stones.

400. *And they were cast upon the earth, and the third part of the trees was burnt up*, signifies that with those who are in the internals of the church and in faith alone, every affection and perception of truth, which constitute a man of the church, had perished. By the earth, upon which were cast hail and fire mingled with blood, is signified the church with those who are in its internals and in faith alone. That these are the clergy, may be seen above, n. 398. By the third part is signified all as to truth, and by the fourth part, all as to good, n. 322. That by three is signified all, full, and totally, will be seen below, n. 505; thence, by a third, which is a third part, the same is signified. By being burnt up is signified to perish, in the present case, by falsity derived from infernal love, which is meant by hail and fire mingled with blood, see above, n. 399. By a tree is signified man; and as man is man by virtue of affection, which is of the will, and by virtue of perception, which is of the understanding, therefore these also are signified by a tree. There is also a correspondence between man and a tree; wherefore in heaven there appear paradises of trees, which correspond to the affections and consequent perceptions of the angels; and, likewise, in some places in hell there are forests of trees, which bear evil fruits, correspondent with the concupiscences and consequent thoughts of those who are there. That trees in general signify men as to their affections and consequent perceptions, may appear from the following places: " And all the *trees of the field* shall know, that I Jehovah have brought down

the high *tree*, have exalted the low *tree*, have dried up the green *tree*, and have made the dry *tree* to flourish," Ezek. xvii. 24. "Blessed is the man that trusteth in Jehovah,—for he shall be as a *tree* planted by the waters—neither shall cease from yielding fruit," Jerem. xvii. 7, 8. "Blessed is the man whose delight is in the law of Jehovah; and he shall be like a *tree* planted by the rivers of water, that bringeth forth fruit in his season," Psalm i. 3. Praise Jehovah, ye *fruitful trees*, Psalm cxlviii. 9. "The *trees* of Jehovah are full of sap," Psalm civ. 16. "And now also the axe is laid at the root of the *trees*, therefore every *tree* which bringeth not forth good fruit, is hewn down," Matt. iii. 10; vii. 16, 21. "Either make the *tree* good and its fruit good; or else make the *tree* corrupt and its fruit corrupt: for the tree is known by his fruit," Matt. xii. 33; Luke vi. 43, 44. "Behold, I will kindle a fire in thee, and it shall devour every green *tree* and every dry *tree*," Ezek. xx. 47. Since a tree signifies man, therefore it was ordained, that the fruit of a *tree* serving for food in the land of Canaan should be circumcised, Levit. xix. 23—25; as also, when any city is besieged, they shall not put forth an axe against any *tree* with good fruit, Deut. xx. 20, 21; and that at the feast of tabernacles they should take fruit of the *tree of honour*, and rejoice before Jehovah, Levit. xxiii. 40, 41; besides other passages, which are not here adduced by reason of their abundance.

401. *And all green grass was burnt up*, signifies, thus all that is alive in faith. By being burnt is signified to perish, as above, n. 400: by green grass, in the Word, is signified that good and truth of the church or of faith, which first springs up in the natural man; the same also is signified by the herb of the field; and because faith has its life from good and truth, therefore by all green grass being burnt up, is signified that every thing alive in faith has perished; and every thing alive in faith perishes when there is no affection of good and perception of truth, of which above. This signification of grass is also owing to correspondence; wherefore they who separate faith from charity, not only in doctrine but also in life, in the spiritual world live in a desert, where there is not even grass. As a fruit-tree signifies man as to the affections of good and perceptions of truth, so green grass signifies man as to that principle of the church which is first conceived and also born in him, and grass which is not green signifies the same destroyed. In general all things which grow in gardens, woods, fields, and plains, signify man as to something of the church, or what is the same, something of the church in him; the reason is, because they correspond. That grass has this signification, may appear from these passages: "The voice said, Cry. And he said, What shall I cry? *All flesh is grass*,—the *grass* withereth, and the flower fadeth, because the spirit of Jehovah bloweth upon it

surely the people is *grass*. The *grass* withereth and the flower fadeth, but the Word of our God shall stand for ever," Isaiah xl. 5—8. "The inhabitants were as the *grass of the field*, and as the *green herb*, as the *grass on the house-tops*, a field blasted before the corn is grown up," Isaiah xxxvii. 27; 2 Kings xix. 26. "I will pour out my blessing upon thine offspring, and they shall spring up as among the *grass*," Isaiah xliv. 3, 4; and in other places; as in Isaiah li. 12; Psalm xxxvii. 2; Psalm ciii. 15; Psalm cxxix. 6; Deut. xxxii. 2. That by what is green or flourishing, is signified what is alive or has life in it, is evident in Jerem. xvii. 8; l. 11; Ezek. xvii. 24; xxi. 3; Hosea xiv. 9; Psalm xxxvii. 35; Psalm lii. 10; Psalm xcii. 11. The same as what is here described in the Apocalypse came to pass in Egypt, for by hail and fire mingled, every tree and every *herb of the field* was burnt up, Exod. ix. 29—35; Psalm lxxxviii. 47—49; Psalm cv. 32, 33.

402. *And the second angel sounded*, signifies the exploration and manifestation of what the state of the church is with those who are exteriorly in that faith. That to sound with a trumpet signifies to explore and make manifest the state of the church, and thence of the life of those whose religion is faith alone, may be seen above, n. 397. It is said of those who are exteriorly in that faith, because they are here treated of who are in the sea, and previously they were treated of who were on the earth; and by these latter are meant such as are in the internals of the church, who are the clergy, and by the former are meant such as are in the externals of the church, who are the laity, as may be seen above, n. 398, who in the spiritual world appear as it were in the sea, n. 238, 290.

403. *And as it were a great mountain burning with fire was cast into the sea*, signifies the appearance of infernal love with those who are in the externals of the church, and in faith alone. By the sea is signified the church with those who are in externals, and in faith alone; and they who are in externals are called, in common language, the laity, because they who are in internals are called the clergy, n. 397, 402. A mountain signifies love, n. 336, and a mountain burning with fire signifies infernal love, n. 494, 599; this is the appearance of this love with those who are here treated of, and is so seen by the angels; the reason is, because faith alone is faith separated from charity, n. 388: and where there is not charity, that is, love towards our neighbour, which is spiritual love, there is infernal love; an intermediate love does not exist except among the lukewarm, mentioned in Apoc. iii. 15, 16.

404. *And the third part of the sea became blood*, signifies that all general truths with them were falsified. By the third part is signified all, n. 400; by blood is signified the falsification of the truth of the Word, n. 379; by the sea is signified the

church with those who are in its externals, and in faith alone, n. 397, 402. General truths are falsified with such because they are principled in them alone, for they are not acquainted with the particulars of that faith, as the clergy are; it is from the general truths in which they are principled, that they appear as in a sea, in the spiritual world; the reason is, because waters signify truths, n. 50, the sea being their general receptacle, n. 238.

405. *And the third part of the creatures which were in the sea that had life, died*, signifies that they who have lived and do live this faith cannot be reformed and receive life. By the third part is signified all of them, as above; by creatures are meant those who are capable of being reformed, n. 290; the reason is, because to create signifies to reform, n. 254. By having lives, is signified to be capable of receiving life by reformation; by their death, is signified that they who live that faith alone cannot receive life; the reason why they cannot, is, because all are reformed by faith united to charity, thus by the faith of charity, and no one by faith alone, for charity is the life of faith. Since the affections and consequent perceptions and thoughts of spirits and angels, in the spiritual world, appear at a distance in the forms of animals or creatures upon the earth, which are called beasts, of creatures in the air which are called birds, and of creatures in the sea which are called fishes, therefore in the Word mention is so often made of beasts, birds, and fishes, by which nothing else is understood; as in these passages: "The Lord hath a controversy with the inhabitants of the earth, because there is no truth, nor mercy, nor knowledge of God in the land,—and every one that dwelleth therein shall languish with the *beasts of the field, and with the fowls of the heaven; yea, the fishes of the sea*, also, shall be taken away," Hosea iv. 1, 3. "I will consume man and *beast —the fowls of the heaven and the fishes of the sea*, and the stumbling blocks with the wicked," Zeph. i. 3. "There shall be a great shaking in the land of Israel, so that the *fishes of the sea, and the fowls of the heaven, and the beast of the field*, —shall shake at my presence," Ezek. xxxviii. 18—20. "Thou madest him to have dominion over the works of thy hands; thou hast put all things under his feet,—*the beasts of the field, the fowl of the air, and the fish of the sea*, and whatsoever passeth through the paths of the seas," Psalm viii. 6—8; speaking of the Lord. "But ask,—now, the *beasts*, and they shall teach thee; and the *fowls of the air*, and they shall tell thee;—*and the fishes of the sea* shall declare unto thee. Who knoweth not in all these that the hand of Jehovah hath wrought this?" Job xii. 7—9; besides many other places. But by fishes or creatures of the sea, are here meant the affections and consequent thoughts of those men who are principled in general

truths, and are therefore more attracted by what is natural than by what is spiritual; these are understood by fishes in the passages above cited, and also in the following: "Behold, at my rebuke I dry up the sea, I make the rivers a wilderness: their *fish* sinketh, because there is no water, and dieth for thirst," Isaiah l. 2. "The king of Egypt is a great dragon that lieth in the midst of his rivers, which hath said,—My river is mine own, and I have it for myself, and I will cause the *fish of thy rivers* to stick to thy scales,—and I will leave thee in the wilderness, thee and all the *fish of thy rivers*," Ezek. xxix. 3—5. This is said to the king of Egypt, because by Egypt is signified what is natural separated from what is spiritual, and therefore by the fishes of his rivers are meant those who are in doctrinals, and thereby in faith separated, which faith is only science; on account of this separation, one of the miracles that were performed there was as follows: That their waters were turned into blood, and that thereby the *fish* died, Exod. vii. 17—25; Psalm cv. 29. Wherefore dost thou make man as the *fishes of the sea*, every man draweth and gathereth into the net, Habak. i. 14—16; fishes here denote those who are in general truths, and in faith separated from charity; but fishes denote those who are in general truths and in faith conjoined with charity, in Ezekiel: He said unto me, "Behold, these waters issued from under the threshold of the house eastward; —and it shall come to pass, that every thing that liveth, which moveth, whithersoever the river shall come, shall live: *and there shall be a very great multitude of fish;* and it shall come to pass, that the fishers shall stand upon it to spread forth nets; their *fish* shall be according to their kinds, *exceeding many like the fish of the great sea*," xlvi. 1, 9, 10. In Matthew: Jesus said. "The kingdom of heaven is like unto a net that was cast into the sea, and they gathered *fishes*, the good into vessels, but cast the bad away," xiii. 47—49. And in Jeremiah: "I will bring again the children of Israel into their land, and, behold, I will send for many *fishers*, and they shall fish them," xvi. 15, 16. He that knows therefore, that such persons and things are signified by fishes, may see why the Lord chose *fishers* for his disciples, and said, "Follow me, and I will make you *fishers* of men," Matt. iv. 18, 19; Mark i. 16, 17. That the disciples, by the blessing of the Lord, caught a great multitude of *fishes*, and the Lord said unto Peter, "Fear not, from henceforth thou shalt *catch men*," Luke v. 2—10. Why the Lord, when they would have required tribute of him, commanded Peter to go to the sea, and draw up a *fish*, and give the piece of money found in it for him and himself, Matt. xvii. 24—27. Why the Lord, after his resurrection, gave his disciples a *fish* and bread to eat, John xxi. 2—13; and commanded them, "Go ye into all the world, and preach the gospel to *every creature*," Mark

xvi. 15; for the nations whom they converted were only principled in general truths, or in natural truth more than in spiritual.

406. *And the third part of the ships were destroyed*, signifies that all the knowledges of good and truth from the Word, serving for use of life, were destroyed with them. The third part signifies all, as above, n. 400, 404, 405; ships signify the knowledges of what is good and true from the Word serving for use of life. Ships have this signification, because they traverse the sea, and bring such necessaries as are of use to the natural man exclusively, and the knowledges of good and truth are the necessaries which are of use to the spiritual man, from these the doctrine of the church is derived, and, according to this doctrine, life. Ships signify these knowledges, because they are what contain things, and in the Word, in many places, the thing containing is taken for the thing contained, as the cup for the wine; the platter for meat; the tabernacle and the temple for the holy things in them; the ark for the law; the altar for worship, and so on. Ships signify the knowledges of what is good and true, in the following passages: "Zebulon shall dwell at the haven of the sea, and he shall be for an haven of *ships*," Gen. xlix. 13. By Zebulon is meant the conjunction of good and truth. O Tyre, the "builders have perfected thy beauty, they have made all thy *ship-boards* of fir-trees of Senir: they have taken the cedars from Lebanon to make *masts* for thee; of the oaks of Bashan have they made thine *oars;* thy *pole* have they made of ivory, a *daughter of steps* from the isles of Chittim; the inhabitants of Zidon and Arvad were thy *mariners*, thy wise men were thy *pilots*, all the *ships of the sea* and their *mariners* were in thee to occupy thy merchandise; the *ships of Tarshish* did sing of thee in thy market: and thou wast replenished and made very glorious in the midst of the seas," Ezek. xxvii. 4—9, 25; speaking of Tyre, because by Tyre, in the Word, is signified the church as to the knowledges of truth and good, as may appear from the particulars mentioned respecting it in this and the eighteenth chapter, when understood in a spiritual sense; and as the knowledges of the truth and good of the church are signified by Tyre, therefore a ship is described as to its particulars, and by each is signified some quality of those knowledges conducive to intelligence; for what can the Word have in common with the ships of Tyre and its commerce? The devastation of that church is afterwards thus described: "The suburbs shall shake at the sound of the cry of thy *pilots. And all that handle the oar*, the *mariners* and *pilots* of the sea, shall *come down from their ships*, and shall cry bitterly," Ezek. xxvii. 28—30; as also in Isaiah xxiii. 14, 15. In like manner the devastation of Babylon as to all the knowledges of truth, is described in what follows in the

Apocalypse: "For in one hour so great riches is come to nought, and every *ship-master*, and all the company in *ships*, and *mariners*, cried, saying, Alas, alas, that great city (Babylon), wherein were made rich all that had *ships* in the sea," xviii. 17, 19; see the explanation below. By ships are also signified the knowledges of good and truth in the following passages: "Now my days are swifter than a post, they flee away, they see no good. They are passed away as the swift *ships*," Job ix. 25, 26. "They who go down to the sea in *ships*, that do business in great waters. These see the works of Jehovah, and his wonders in the deep," Psalm cvii. 23, 24. "Surely the isles shall wait for me, and the *ships of Tarshish* first, to bring thy sons from far," Isaiah lx. 9. "For lo, the kings were assembled, they passed by together. Fear took hold upon them there. Thou breakest the *ships of Tarshish* with the east wind," Psalm xlviii. 4, 7, 8. Howl, ye *ships of Tarshish*, Isaiah xxiii. 1, 14; besides other places; as Numb. xxiv. 24; Judges v. 17; Psalm civ. 26; Isaiah xxxiii. 21.

407. *And the third angel sounded*, signifies the exploration and manifestation of the church with those whose religion is faith alone, what they are as to the affection and reception of truths from the Word. That this is signified, will appear from what follows, when understood in a spiritual sense.

408. *And there fell from heaven a great star, burning as it were a lamp*, signifies the appearance of self-derived intelligence from a pride springing from infernal love. The reason why by the falling from heaven of a great star, is signified the appearance of self-derived intelligence from a pride springing from infernal love, is, because it was seen to burn as a lamp; and because the name of it was Wormwood, as follows; and by a star, and also by a lamp, is signified intellignce, here self-derived intelligence, because it seemed to burn, and all self-derived intelligence burns from pride; and the pride of it proceeds from infernal love, which is signified by a mountain burning with fire, n. 403. By wormwood is signified infernal falsity, from which that intelligence exists, and of which it is composed. That a star signifies intelligence, may be seen, n. 151, 954; so likewise does a lamp or candle, n. 796.

409. *And it fell upon the third part of the rivers, and upon the fountains of waters*, signifies that thence all the truths of the Word were totally falsified. By rivers are signified truths in abundance, because by waters are signified truths, n. 50: and by fountains of waters is signified the Word, n. 384. The truths of the Word were altogether falsified, because it is said in what follows, that the third part of the waters became wormwood; and by wormwood is signified infernal falsity, n. 410. That rivers signify truths in abundance, may appear from the following passages: "Behold, I will do a new thing; I give

waters in the wilderness, and *rivers* in the desert, to give drink to my people, my chosen," Isaiah xliii. 19, 20. "For I will pour water upon him that is thirsty, and *rivers* upon the dry ground; I will pour my spirit upon thy seed, and my blessing upon thine offspring," Isaiah xliv. 3. "Then—shall the tongue of the dumb sing, for in the wilderness shall waters break out, and *rivers* in the desert," Isaiah xxxv. 6. "I will open *rivers* in high places, and fountains in the midst of the valleys: I will make the wilderness a pool of waters, and the dry land springs of water," Isaiah xli. 18. Jehovah hath laid the foundations of the world "upon the seas, and established it upon the *rivers*," Psalm xxiv. 2. "I will set his hand also in the sea, and his right hand in the *rivers*," Psalm lxxxix. 25. "Was Jehovah displeased against the *rivers?* was thine anger against the *rivers?* was thy wrath against the sea, that thou dost ride upon thine horses?" Habak. iii. 8. The *river* whose "streams shall make glad the city of God," Psalm xlvi. 3—5. "And he showed me a pure *river* of water of life proceeding out of the throne of God and the Lamb," Apoc. xxii. 1. "He clave the rocks in the wilderness, and gave them drink as out of the great *depths*. He clave the rock, and *rivers* gushed out," Psalm lxxviii. 15, 16, 20; Psalm cv. 41. "And the waters shall fail from the sea, and the *river* shall be wasted and dried up," Isaiah xix. 5—7; xlii. 15; l. 2; Nahum i. 4; Psalm cvii. 33; Job xiv. 10, 11. Jesus said, If any one come unto me, as the Scripture hath said, "out of his belly shall flow *rivers* of living waters," John vii. 37, 38; besides other places; as in Isaiah xxxiii. 21; Jerem. xvii. 7, 8; Ezek. xxxi. 3, 4; xclii. 1—12; Joel iii. 18; Zech. ix. 10; Psalm lxxx. 11; Psalm xciii. 3—5; Psalm xcviii. 7, 8; Psalm cx. 7; Numb. xxiv, 6, 7; Deut. viii. 7. But that rivers, in an opposite sense, signify falses in abundance, may appear from these passages: He shall send ambassadors in the sea to the "nation trodden down, whose land the *rivers* have spoiled," Isaiah xviii. 2. "If Jehovah had not been for us, then the waters had overwhelmed us, and the *river* had gone over our soul," Psalm cxxiv. 2, 4, 5. "When thou passest through the waters I will be with thee, and through the *rivers*, they shall not overflow thee," Isaiah xliii. 2. "The sorrows of death compassed me, and the *rivers* of ungodly men made me afraid," Psalm xviii. 4. "And the serpent cast out of his mouth water as a *river* after the woman, that he might cause her to be carried away of the *river*," Apoc. xii. 15, 16. "Behold, Jehovah bringeth up upon them the waters of the *river* strong and many, and it shall overflow and go over, and shall reach even to the neck," Isaiah viii. 7, 8. "And the *rivers* came, and the winds blew and beat upon that house, and it fell not, for it was founded upon a rock," Matt. vii. 25, 27; Luke vi. 48, 49; here also rivers denote falses in abundance, because by a rock is signified the Lord as to divine truth. By rivers or floods are also signified temptations, because temptations are inundations of falses.

410. *And the name of the star is called Wormwood; and the third part of the waters became wormwood*, signifies the infernal falsity from which their self-derived intelligence is derived, and by which all the truths of the Word are falsified. By a star is signified self-derived intelligence springing from a pride in infernal love, n. 408; by name is signified its quality, n. 81, 122, 165; by wormwood is signified infernal falsity concerning which something will be said presently; by waters are signified truths, n. 50; here, the truths of the Word, because the subject relates to faith; by the third part is signified all, as above: from these particulars taken together the sense results as delivered above. Wormwood signifies infernal falsity, from its intense bitterness, whereby it renders meat and drink abominable; such falsity is signified therefore by wormwood, in the following passages: "Behold, I will feed this people with *wormwood*, and I will give them water of gall to drink," Jerem. ix. 14, 15. "Thus saith Jehovah concerning the prophets; Behold, I will feed them with *wormwood*, and I will make them drink the *water of gall*; for from the prophets of Jerusalem is profaneness gone forth into all the earth," Jerem. xxiii. 15. "Ye who turn judgment *into gall*, and the fruit of righteousness into *wormwood*," Amos v. 7; vi. 12. "Lest there should be among you a root that beareth *gall* and *wormwood*," Deut. xxix. 18. Since the Jewish church have falsified all the truths of the Word, like the church here treated of, and since the Lord by all the circumstances of his passion represented the same, by permitting the Jews to treat him as they did the Word, he himself being the Word, therefore they gave him vinegar mingled *with gall*, which is like wormwood, but, tasting it, he would not drink, Matt. xxvii. 34; Mark xv. 23; Psalm lxix. 21. As this was the character of the Jewish church, it is therefore thus described: "He hath filled me with bitterness, and hath made me drunken with *wormwood*," Lament. iii. 15, 18, 19.

411. *And many men died of the waters, because they were made bitter*, signifies the extinction of spiritual life with many from the falsified truths of the Word. Many men died, signifies extinction of spiritual life; for man from the spiritual life within him is called alive, but from natural life separated from spiritual life, he is called dead; of the waters because they were made bitter, signifies by the falsified truths of the Word: that waters mean the truths of the Word, may be seen above, n. 410. The reason why bitter signifies what is falsified, is, because the bitter of wormwood is understood, and by wormwood is signified infernal falsity, n. 410. The spiritual life in a Christian is from no other source than from the truths of the Word, for in them there

is life; but when the truths of the Word are falsified, and man understands and views them according to the false notions of his religion, then spiritual life in him is extinguished; the reason is, because the Word communicates with heaven, therefore when it is read by man, the truths therein ascend to heaven, and the falses to which truths are adjoined or conjoined, tend towards hell, whence there is a rending asunder, whereby the life of the Word is extinguished. But this is the case only with those who confirm falses by the Word, but not with those who do not confirm them. I have seen such rendings asunder, and have heard the noise like that of wood split by fire on a hearth. Bitter signifies what is falsified also in the following places: "Woe unto them that call evil good, and good evil, that put *bitter* for sweet, and sweet for *bitter*," Isaiah v. 20, 22. "They shall not drink wine with a song; strong drink shall be *bitter* to them that drink it," Isaiah xxiv. 9. The like is signified by the little book that was eaten, which was sweet in the mouth, and by which the belly was made *bitter*, Apoc. x. 9, 10; and by this: "And when they came to Marah, they could not drink of the waters, for they were *bitter*; and Jehovah showed him a wood, which when he had cast into the waters, they were made sweet," Exod. xv. 23—25. Wood, in the Word, signifies good. The same is also signified by the wild gourds* which were put into the pottage, by reason of which the sons of the prophets cried out, There is death in the pot, which Elisha healed by putting in meal, 2 Kings iv. 38—41. Meal signifies truth from good.

412. *And the fourth angel sounded*, signifies the exploration and manifestation of the state of the church with those whose religion is faith alone, as being in the evils of falsity, and in the falsities of evil. That this is the signification of these words, is evident from what follows, when understood in a spiritual sense. To sound signifies here, as before, n. 398, 402, 407, to explore and make manifest.

413. *And the third part of the sun was smitten, and the third part of the moon, and the third part of the stars, so that the third part of them was darkened*, signifies that by reason of evils from falsities and of falsities from evils, they did not know what love is, or what faith is, or any truth. By the third part is signified all, n. 400; by the sun is signified love, n. 53; by the moon is signified intelligence and faith, n. 332; by stars are signified the knowledges of truth and good from the Word, n. 51; by being darkened is signified not to be seen and known by reason of evils from falses and of falses from evils. Evils from falses exist with those who assume the falses of religion, and confirm them till they appear as truths, and when they live according to them they do evils from falses, or the evils of falsity; but falses from

---

* Colocynthis—a *kind of wild gourd*, the apple of which is called *Coloquintida*

evils exist with those who do not consider evils as sins, and still more with those who by reasonings from the natural man, and also from the Word, confirm in themselves, that evils are not sins, such confirmations constitute the falses from evils, and are called the falses of evil. That such is the signification of darkness follows, because light signifies truth, and the extinction of light makes darkness. By way of confirmation, some passages shall first be adduced, where similar things are mentioned as are here said in the Apocalypse, of the sun, the moon, and the stars, and of the darkness consequent upon their extinction: "*The sun shall be turned into darkness, and the moon into blood,*" before the great and terrible day of Jehovah cometh, Joel ii. 31. "*For the stars of heaven and the constellations thereof shall not give their light, the sun shall be darkened in his going forth, and the moon shall not cause her light to shine,*" Isaiah xiii. 10. "And when I shall put thee out I will cover the heaven, I *will cover the sun with a cloud, and the moon shall not give her light, all the bright lights of heaven will I make dark over thee,* and set *darkness* upon thy land," Ezek. xxxii. 7, 8. The day of Jehovah is near; "*the sun and the moon shall be black, and the stars shall withdraw their shining,*" Joel ii. 10. "Immediately after the tribulation of those days, *shall the sun be darkened, and the moon shall not give her light, and the stars shall fall from heaven,*" Matt. xxiv. 29; Mark xiii. 24, 25. Who cannot see, on elevating his mind, that in these places, the sun, moon, and stars of the world are not understood? That by darkness falses of various kinds are signified, is evident from the following passages: "Woe unto you that desire the day of Jehovah! it is *darkness* and not light; shall not the day of Jehovah be *darkness* and not light? even *very dark*, and no brightness in it?" Amos v. 18, 20. "The day of Jehovah is a day of *darkness and gloominess*, a day of clouds and *thick darkness*," Zeph. i. 15. "And in that day if one look unto the land, behold *darkness*, and the light is darkened in the heavens thereof," Isaiah v. 30; viii. 22. "For behold, *darkness* covereth the earth, and *gross darkness* the people," Isaiah lx. 2. "Give glory unto Jehovah your God, before he cause *darkness*, and while ye look for light, he make it *gross darkness*," Jerem. xiii. 16. "We wait for light, but behold *obscurity;* for brightness, but we walk in *darkness;*— we stumble at noon-day as in the night; we are in desolate places as dead men," Isaiah lix. 9, 10. "Woe unto them—that put *darkness* for light, and light for *darkness*," Isaiah v. 20. "The people that walked in *darkness* have seen a great light," Isaiah ix. 2; Matt. iv. 16. "The day-spring from on high hath visited us, to give light to those who sit in *darkness* and in the shadow of death," Luke i. 79. "And if thou draw out thy soul to the hungry, then shall thy light rise in *obscurity*, and thy *darkness* be as the noon-day," Isaiah lviii. 10. "And in that day—the eyes of the blind shall see out of *obscurity* and out of *darkness,"* Isaiah xxix. 18; xlii. 16; xlix. 9. Jesus said, "I am the light of the world; he that followeth me shall not walk in *darkness*, but shall have the light of life," John viii. 12. "Walk while ye have the light, lest *darkness* come upon you: I am come a light into the world, that whosoever believeth on me, should not abide in *darkness*," John xii. 35, 46. "When I sit in *darkness*, Jehovah shall be a light to me," Micah vii. 8. "And this is the condemnation, that light is come into the world, and men loved *darkness* rather than light," John iii. 19; i. 4, 5. "If, therefore, the light which is in thee be *darkness*, how great is the *darkness*," Matt. vi. 23; Luke xi. 34—36. "But this is your hour, and the power of *darkness*," Luke xxii. 53. By darkness in these places is signified falsity proceeding either from ignorance of the truth, or from a false principle of religion, or from a life of evil. Concerning those who are in the falses of religion, and thence in evils of life, the Lord says, that they shall be cast into outer *darkness*, Matt. viii. 12; xxii. 13; xxv. 30.

414. *And the day shone not for a third part of it, and the night likewise*, signifies that there is no longer any spiritual truth nor natural truth, serviceable for doctrine and life, from the Word with them. By the day not shining, is meant that there was no light from the sun; and by the light, in like manner, is meant that there was no light from the moon and stars. By light, in general, is signified divine truth, which is truth from the Word; by the light of the sun, divine truth spiritual; and, by the light of the moon and stars, divine truth natural, both from the Word. The divine truth, in the spiritual sense of the Word, is like the light of the sun by day; and the divine truth, in the natural sense of the Word, is like the light of the moon and stars by night; the spiritual sense of the Word also flows into its natural sense as the sun does with its light into the moon, which gives forth the light of the sun in a mediate manner. In the same way does the spiritual sense of the Word illuminate men, even those who know nothing at all concerning it, whilst they read the Word in its natural sense; but it illuminates the spiritual man, as the sun's light does the eye; and the natural man, as the light of the moon and stars illuminate his eye. Every one receives illumination according to the spiritual affection of truth and good, and at the same time according to genuine truths, by which he has opened his rational faculty. The same is understood by day and night, in the following passages: "And God said, Let there be *light* in the firmament of the heaven, to divide the *day* from the *night:* And God made two great *lights*, the greater *light* to rule the *day*, and the lesser *light* to rule the *night;* he made the *stars* also: And God set them in the firmament of the heaven, to give *light* upon the earth, and to rule over the *day* and over the *night*, and to divide the light from the dark

ness," Gen. i. 14—19. Jehovah made great luminaries, "the *sun* to rule by *day*, the *moon* and *stars* to rule by *night*," Psalm cxxxvi. 7—9. "The *day* (O Jehovah) is thine, the *night* also is thine; thou hast prepared the light and the sun," Psalm lxxiv. 16. "Jehovah giveth the *sun* for a light by *day*, and the ordinances of the *moon* and of the *stars* for a light by *night*," Jerem xxxi. 35. "If ye can break my covenant of the *day* and my covenant of the *night*, and that there shall not be *day* and *night* in their season; then may also my covenant be broken with David my servant: If my covenant be not with *day* and *night*, and if I have not appointed the ordinances of heaven and earth, then will I cast away the seed of Jacob and David my servant," Jerem. xxxiii. 20, 21, 25, 26. These passages are adduced for the sake of showing that a darkening of both kinds of light is meant.

415. *And I beheld, and I heard an angel flying in the midst of heaven*, signifies instruction and prediction from the Lord. By an angel, in a supreme sense, is meant the Lord, and thence also something from the Lord, n. 344; and by flying in the midst of heaven and saying, is signified to perceive and understand, and when applied to the Lord, to foresee and provide, n. 245; but here, to instruct and foretell.

416. *Saying with a loud voice, Woe, woe, woe, to the inhabiters of the earth, by reason of the other voices of the trumpet of the three angels which are yet to sound*, signifies deep lamentation over the damned state of those in the church, who in doctrine and life have confirmed themselves in faith separated from charity. By woe is signified lamentation over the evil in any one, and thence over his unhappy state; here, over the damned state of those who are treated of in the next chapter, and afterwards; and by woe, woe, woe, is signified extreme lamentation; for triplication constitutes the superlative, because three signifies all and full, n. 505. By the inhabiters upon earth, are meant they who are in the church where the Word is, and the Lord known thereby: that earth signifies the church may be seen above, n. 285. By the voices of the trumpet of the three angels which are yet to sound, is signified the exploration and manifestation of the state of the church and of life with those, who by doctrine and life have confirmed in themselves faith separated from charity, over whose state lamentation is made. Woe signifies lamentation over the present or future calamity, unhappiness, or damnation of others, in these passages: "*Woe* unto you, scribes and Pharisees, hypocrites!" Matt. xxiii. 13—17, 23, 25, 27, 29. "*Woe* unto that man by whom the Son of Man is betrayed," Luke xxii. 22. *Woe* unto him by whom scandals come, Luke xvii. 1. *Woe* unto them that join house to house. *Woe* unto them that rise up early in the morning that they may follow strong drink. "*Woe* unto them that draw iniquity with

cords of vanity. *Woe* unto them that call evil good. *Woe* unto them that are wise in their own eyes. *Woe* unto them that are mighty to drink wine," Isaiah v. 8, 11, 18, 20—22; and in many other places.

417. To the above I will add this Memorable Relation. I saw in the spiritual world two flocks, one of GOATS, and the other of SHEEP; I wondered who they were, for I knew that animals, seen in the spiritual world, are not animals, but correspondences of the affections and consequent thoughts of those who are there. Wherefore I approached towards them, and as I drew near, the likenesses of animals disappeared, and instead of them were seen men. And it was shown, that they who formed the flock of goats, were those who had confirmed themselves in the doctrine of justification by faith alone; and they who formed the flock of sheep, were those who believed that charity and faith are a one, as good and truth are a one. And then I entered into discourse with those who had been seen as goats, and said, "Why are you thus assembled?" They consisted chiefly of clergy, who gloried in their fame for erudition, because they knew the arcana of justification by faith alone. They replied that they were assembled to sit in council, because they had heard that what is said by Paul, Rom. iii. 28, that man is justified by faith without the works of the law, is not rightly understood, because Paul, by the works of the law, meant the works of the Mosaic law, which were intended for the Jews; which we also clearly see from his words to Peter, whom he rebuked for judaizing, when yet he knew that no one is "justified by the *works of the law*," Gal. ii. 14—16; as, also, from his making a distinction between the law of faith and the law of works; and between Jews and Gentiles, or circumcision and uncircumcision, meaning by circumcision, Judaism, as everywhere else; and likewise from his summing up with these words: "Do we then make void the *law* through faith? God forbid; yea, we establish the *law;*" he says all these things in one series, Rom. iii. 27—31; and further, he observes in the preceding chapter: "For not the hearers of the *law* are just before God, but *the doers of the law* shall be justified," Rom. ii. 13; also, that God "will render to every man according to his *deeds*," Rom. ii. 6; and that, "For we must all appear before the judgment-seat of Christ; that every one may receive the *things done* in his body, whether they be good or bad," 2 Cor. v. 10; besides many other things to the same purpose, from which it is evident that Paul rejects faith without good works, equally with James, ii. 17—26. That the works of the Mosaic law, which were for the Jews, were meant by Paul, we are additionally confirmed n by this consideration, that all the statutes for the Jews in Moses are called the law, thus the works of the

law, which we perceive from these passages: "This is the *law* of the meat-offering," Levit. vi. 9, and following. "This is the *law* of the burnt-offering," Levit. vii. 1. "This is the *law* of the peace-offering," Levit. vii. 7, 11, and following. "This is the *law* of the burnt-offering, of the meat-offering, of the sin-offering, and of the trespass-offering, of the consecrations," Levit. vii. 37. "This is the *law* of the beasts and of the fowl," Levit. xi. 46, and following. "This is the *law* for her that hath borne a male or a female," Levit. xii. 7. "This is the *law* of the plague of leprosy," Levit. xiii. 59; xiv. 2, 32, 54, 57. "This is the *law* of him that hath an issue," Levit. xv. 32. "This is the *law of jealousies*," Numb. v. 29, 30. This is the *law* of the Nazarite, Numb. vi. 13, 21. This is the *law* of purification, Numb. xix. 14. This is the *law* concerning the red heifer, Numb. xix. 2. The *law* for the king, Deut. xvii. 15—19. Yea, the whole Book of Moses is called "the Book of the *Law*," Deut. xxxi. 9, 11, 12, 26; also in the Evangelists, Luke ii. 22; xxiv. 44; John i. 45; vii. 22, 23; viii. 5; and other places. To this they added, also, what they had seen in Paul, that the law of the Decalogue was to be practised in the very life, and that it is fulfilled by charity, which is love towards the neighbour, Rom. xiii. 8—10; thus not by faith alone. They affirmed that this was the reason of their being convened together. But that I might not disturb them, I retired; upon which they again appeared, at a distance, like goats, and sometimes as lying down, and at others as standing; but they turned themselves away from the flock of sheep: they appeared as if they were lying down, when deliberating, but as standing up, when they came to a conclusion. But, keeping my eyes fixed upon their horns, I was surprised to see that the horns upon their foreheads sometimes appeared to extend forward and upward, then to be bent backward, and at last to be thrown back entirely; upon which they all suddenly turned round to the flock of sheep, but still appeared as goats; wherefore I drew near to them again, and inquired, "What now?" They replied, that they had come to this conclusion, that faith alone produces the goods of charity, which are called good works, as a tree produces fruit. But then thunder was heard, and lightning seen from above; and presently there appeared an angel, standing between the two flocks, who cried to the flock of sheep, "Do not give ear to them; they have not receded from their former faith, which is, that God the Father hath compassion for the sake of the Son; which faith is not faith in the Lord; neither is faith a tree, but man is a tree; but do the work of repentance, and look to the Lord, and you will have faith; faith before that, is not a faith in which there is any life." Then the goats, whose horns were directed backward, approached the sheep; but the angel standing between them, divided the sheep into two flocks, and said to those on the left, "Join yourselves to the goats; but I must tell you, that a wolf will come, which will snatch them away, and you along with them."

418. But after the two flocks of sheep had separated, and they on the left hand had heard the threatening words of the angel, they looked at one another, and said, "Let us confer with our former associates;" and then the left-hand flock spake to the right, saying, "Why have you receded from your pastors? are not faith and charity a one, as a tree and its fruit are one? for the tree by its branch is continued unto the fruit; take away any thing from the branch which flows by continuity into the fruit, and will not the fruit perish? ask our priests if it is not so." And upon their putting the question, the priests looked round to the rest, who made signs with their eyes to intimate that they had spoken correctly, and then they replied that it was;—faith is preserved by the fruit;—but they would not say faith is continued into the fruit. One of the priests, who was among the sheep on the right-hand, then got up, and said, "They have told you that it is so, but they have told their companions that it is not so; for they think otherwise." Wherefore they inquired, "How do they think, then,—do they not think as they teach?" He said, "No; they think that every good of charity, which is called a good work, done by man for the sake of salvation or eternal life, is not good but evil, by reason that man desires to save himself by his own works, by claiming to himself the righteousness and merit of the only Saviour; and that it is so with every good work, in which man feels his own will; therefore among themselves they call good works from man, not blessed, but cursed; and say that they merit hell rather than heaven." But the flock on the left-hand said, "You speak falsehoods against them; do they not manifestly preach to us charity and its works, which they call works of faith manifested before us?" He replied, "You do not understand their discourses; no one but a clergyman, who may be present, does attend to and understand them; they think only of moral charity, and its civil and political goods, which they call the goods of faith, which yet are not at all so; for a man may be an atheist, and perform these works in the same manner, and under the same form; wherefore they are unanimous in saying that no one is saved by works at all, but by faith alone; but this shall be illustrated by comparisons. An apple-tree bears apples; but if a man does what is good for the sake of salvation, as the tree produces apples by continuity, then those apples are rotten within, and full of worms. They say, also, that a vine produces grapes; but that if a man were to bring forth spiritual goods as a vine does grapes, he would bring forth wild grapes." But then they asked, "What is the nature of their goods of charity or works, which are the fruits

of faith?" He replied, "They are invisible, being inwardly in man from the Holy Spirit, concerning which man knows nothing." But they said, "If man knows nothing concerning them, there must surely be some conjunction, or how could they be called works of faith? perhaps those insensible goods are then insinuated into the voluntary works of man by some mediating influx, as by some affection, aspiration, inspiration, incitement and excitement of the will; or by some tacit perception in thought and consequent exhortation, contrition, and thus by conscience, and thence by impulse and obedience to the Decalogue and the Word, as an infant, or as a wise man, or by something else of a similar nature." But he replied, "No! and if they say it is effected by such means because by faith, still they word their discourses in such a manner as that the result after all is, that they do not proceed *from faith;* some, however, do maintain such things, *though as the signs of faith*, but not *as the ties thereof with charity*. Some have nevertheless thought of a conjunction by the Word. Is there not thus conjunction," said they, "when man voluntarily acts according to the Word?" But he replied, "This is not what they think; they ascribe it to the hearing the Word, thus not to the understanding of the Word, lest any thing should manifestly enter by the understanding into the thought and will of man; since they assert that every thing voluntary in man is meritorious, and that, in spiritual things, man cannot begin, will, think, understand, believe, operate and co-operate any thing, any more than a stock: but yet it is different with the influx of the Holy Spirit by faith into the speech of the preacher, because these are acts of the mouth, and not acts of the body; likewise because man acts by faith with God, but by charity with men." But when one of them heard that it was done merely by hearing the Word, and not by understanding the Word, he said, with indignation, "Is this effect produced then by the understanding of the Word,—by the Holy Spirit alone, whilst man, throughout the church service, turns himself away, or sits as deaf as a post, or sleeps, or as merely feeling an exhalation from the Bible? What can be more ludicrous?" After this, a certain man of the flock on the right-hand, who excelled the rest in judgment, requested to speak, and said, "I heard a certain person say, 'I have planted a vineyard, now will I drink wine even to intoxication.' But another asked, 'Do you mean to drink the wine out of your own cup with your own right hand?' And he said, 'No! but out of an invisible cup from an invisible hand.' And the other replied, 'Of a certainty then you will not be intoxicated.' Presently the same man said, 'But hear me, I beseech you; I say unto you, drink wine from the Word understood; do you not know that the Lord is the Word? is not the Word from the Lord? is he not therefore in it; if then you do good from the Word, do you not do it from the Lord,—from his mouth and will? and if you at the same time look to the Lord, he will also lead you, and will cause you to do it, and this he will do through you, and you as from yourselves. Who can say, when doing any thing by the authority of a king, of his word and will, I do this from myself, from my own mouth or command, and from my own will?" After this he turned to the clergy, and said, "Ye ministers of God, seduce not the flock." On hearing these things, the greater part of the flock on the left-hand receded, and joined themselves to the flock on the right; some of the clergy also then said, "We have heard what we did not know before; we are pastors; we will not leave the sheep." And they receded along with them, and said, "That man spoke a true word: who can say, when he does any thing from the Word, thus from the Lord, from his will and command, I do this from myself? Who that does any thing from the will and command of a king, says, I do this from myself? Now we see the Divine Providence, why a conjunction of faith and works has not been discovered, which the body of ecclesiastics might acknowledge; it could not be discovered, because no such conjunction can exist; for theirs is not a faith in the Lord, who is the Word, and therefore neither is it a faith from the Word." But the other priests went away, flourishing their caps, and crying out, "Faith alone! faith alone for ever, notwithstanding!"

CHAPTER IX.

1. And the fifth angel sounded, and I saw a star fall from heaven unto the earth: and to him was given the key of the bottomless pit.

2. And he opened the bottomless pit; and there arose a smoke out of the pit, as the smoke of a great furnace: and the sun and the air were darkened by reason of the smoke of the pit.

3. And there came out of the smoke locusts upon the earth: and unto them was given power, as the scorpions of the earth have power.

4. And it was commanded them that they should not hurt the grass of the earth, neither any green thing, neither any tree; but only those men, who had not the seal of God in their foreheads.

5. And to them it was given that they should not kill them, but that they should be tormented five months: and

their torment was as the torment of a scorpion when he striketh a man.

6. And in those days shall men seek death, and shall not find it; and shall desire to die, and death shall flee from them.

7. And the shapes of the locusts were like unto horses prepared unto battle: and on their heads were as it were crowns like gold, and their faces were as the faces of men.

8. And they had hair as the hair of women, and their teeth were as the teeth of lions.

9. And they had breast-plates, as it were breast-plates of iron; and the sound of their wings was as the sound of chariots of many horses running to battle.

10. And they had tails like unto scorpions; and there were stings in their tails: and their power was to hurt men five months.

11. And they had a king over them, the angel of the bottomless pit; whose name in the Hebrew tongue is Abaddon, but in the Greek tongue he hath his name Apollyon.

12. One woe is past; behold, there come two woes more hereafter.

13. And the sixth angel sounded: and I heard a voice from the four horns of the golden altar which is before God,

14. Saying to the sixth angel who had the trumpet, Loose the four angels that are bound at the great river Euphrates.

15. And the four angels were loosed; who were prepared for an hour, and a day, and a month, and a year, to slay the third part of men.

16. And the number of the armies of horsemen were two myriads of myriads: and I heard the number of them.

17. And thus I saw the horses in the vision, and them that sat on them, having breast-plates of fire, and of jacinth, and of brimstone: and the heads of the horses were as the heads of lions: and out of their mouths issued fire, and smoke, and brimstone.

18. By these three was the third part of men killed, by the fire, and by the smoke, and by the brimstone, which issued out of their mouths.

19. For their power is in their mouth: for their tails were like unto serpents, and had heads, and with them they hurt.

20. And the rest of the men who were not killed by these plagues, yet repented not of the works of their hands, that they should not worship demons, and idols of gold, and silver, and brass, and stone, and wood; which neither can see, nor hear, nor walk:

21. Neither repented they of their murders, nor of their sorceries. nor of their fornication, nor of their thefts.

THE SPIRITUAL SENSE.

The Contents of the whole Chapter. Of the exploration and manifestation of the states of life of those in the reformed church, who are called learned and wise from the confirmation of faith separated from charity, and of justification and salvation by it alone; these are treated of from verse 1—13. Of the exploration and manifestation of those therein, who are not so learned and wise, and are in faith alone, and who live as they like; from verse 13—20. Lastly, of those therein, who know nothing but that faith is the all by which man is saved, and not any thing besides, verses 20, 21.

The Contents of each Verse. V. 1, "And the fifth angel sounded," signifies the exploration and manifestation of the states of life of those in the reformed church, who are called learned and wise from their confirmation of faith separated from charity, and of justification and salvation by it alone: "And I saw a star fall from heaven unto the earth," signifies divine truth spiritual flowing from heaven into the church as existing with such persons, and effecting exploration and manifestation: "And to him was given the key of the bottomless pit," signifies the opening of their hell: v. 2, "And he opened the bottomless pit, and there arose a smoke out of the pit, as the smoke of a great furnace," signifies the falses of the concupiscences of the natural man springing forth from their evil loves: "And the sun and the air were darkened by reason of the smoke of the pit," signifies that thereby the light of truth was turned into thick darkness: v. 3, "And there came out of the smoke locusts upon the earth," signifies that from them were derived falses to the extreme or lowest degrees, such as prevail with those who have become sensual, and see and judge of all things by the senses and their fallacies: "And unto them was given power, as the scorpions of the earth have power," signifies the power of persuading that their falses are truths: v. 4, "And it was commanded them that they should not hurt the grass of the earth, neither any green thing, neither any tree; but only those men who had not the seal of God in their foreheads," signifies the divine providence of the Lord, that they should not be able to take away any truth and good of faith, nor any affection and perception of them, from any others than such as are not in charity and thence not in faith: v. 5, "And to them it was given that they should not kill them, but that they should be tormented five months," signifies that neither from these should they be able to take away the faculty of understanding and willing truth and good, but that they should only be able to bring on stupor for a short time: "And their torment was as the torment of a scorpion when he striketh a man," signifies that this is from their persuasive power: v. 6, "And in those days shall men seek death, and shall not find it; and shall desire to die, and death shall flee from them," signifies that it is their desire that, in matters of faith, the understanding should be shut up and the will closed, by which means spiritual light and life are extinguished, and that yet this cannot be done: v. 7, "And the shapes of the locusts," signifies the form and appearance of those who have confirmed in themselves faith separated from charity: "Were like unto horses prepared unto battle," signifies that because they can reason, they appear to themselves to combat from the understanding of truth from the Word: "And on their heads were as it were crowns like gold," signifies that they appeared to themselves as conquerors: "And their faces were as the faces of men," signifies that they appeared to themselves to be wise: v. 8, "And they had hair as the hair of women," signifies that they appeared to themselves to be in the affection of truth: "And their teeth were as the teeth of lions," signifies that sensual things, which are the ultimates of the life of the natural man, appeared with them to have power over all things: v. 9, "And they had breast-plates, as it were breast-plates of iron," signifies that argumentations from fallacies, by which they fight and prevail, appeared to them so powerful that they could not be refuted: "And the sound of their wings was as the sound of chariots of many horses running to battle," signifies their reasonings as if they were from truths of doctrine from the Word fully understood, for which they must ardently fight: v. 10, "And they had tails like unto scorpions," signifies the truths of the Word falsified, by means of which they induce stupor: "And there were stings in their tails, and their power was to hurt men five months," signifies subtile falsifications of the Word, by which for a short time they darken and fascinate the understanding, and thus deceive and captivate: v. 11, "And they had a king over them, the angel of the bottomless pit, whose name in the Hebrew tongue is Abaddon, but in the Greek tongue he hath his name Apollyon," signifies that they are in the satanic hell who are in falses from concupiscences, and by a total falsification of the Word have destroyed the church: v. 12, "One woe is past; behold, there come two woes more hereafter," signifies further lamentations over the state of the church.

V. 13. "And the sixth angel sounded," signifies the exploration and manifestation of their state of life in the reformed church who are not so wise, and yet place the all of religion in faith, and think of it alone, and live as they like: "And I heard a voice from the four horns of the golden altar which is before God, saying to the sixth angel who had the trumpet," signifies a command from the Lord out of the spiritual heaven to those who were to explore and make manifest: v. 14, "Loose the four angels that are bound at the great river Euphrates," signifies that external restraints should be removed from them, that the interiors of their minds might appear: v. 15, "And the four angels were loosed," signifies that when external restraints were removed, the interiors of their minds appeared: "Who were prepared for an hour, and a day, and a month, and a year, to slay the third part of men," signifies that they were perpetually in the effort to take away spiritual light and life from men of the church: v. 16, "And the number of the armies of horsemen were two myriads of myriads," signifies reasonings concerning faith alone, with which the interiors of their minds were filled, from the great abundance of the mere falses of evil: "And I heard the number of them," signifies that the quality of them was perceived: v. 17, "And thus I saw the horses in the vision, and them that sat on them," signifies that it was then discovered that the reasonings of the interiors of their minds concerning faith alone were imaginary and visionary, and that they themselves were infatuated with them: "Having breast-plates of fire, and of jacinth, and of brimstone," signifies their imaginary and visionary argumentations from infernal love and self-derived intelligence, and from the concupiscences thence proceeding: "And the heads of the horses were as the heads of lions," signifies phantasies concerning faith alone as if it were in power: "And out of their mouths issued fire, and smoke, and brimstone," signifies that in their thoughts and discourses, viewed interiorly, there is nothing, and from them there proceeds nothing, but the love of self and of the world, and the pride of self-derived intelligence, and the concupiscences of evil and falsity springing from these two sources: v. 18, "By these three was the third part of men killed, by the fire, and by the smoke, and by the brimstone, which issued out of their mouths," signifies that from these it is that the men of the church perish: v. 19, "For their power was in their mouth," signifies that they only prevail by their discourse in confirmation of faith: "For their tails were like unto serpents, and had heads, and with them they do hurt," signifies the reason, because they are in a sensual and inverted state, speaking truths with their lips, but falsifying them by the principle which constitutes the head of their religion, and thus they deceive: v. 20, "And the rest of the men who were not killed by these plagues," signifies those in the reformed church who are not so spiritually dead from visionary reasonings, and from self-love, and from the pride of self-derived intelligence, and from the concupiscences thence proceeding, as those before mentioned, and yet make faith alone the head of their religion: "Yet repented not of the works of their hands," signifies that neither did they shun the things that are proper to themselves, which are evils of every kind, as sins: "That they should not worship demons," signifies that thus they are in the evils of their concupiscences, and make one with their like in hell: "And idols of gold, and silver, and brass, and stone, and of wood," signifies that thus they are in worship grounded in mere falses: "Which neither can see, nor hear, nor walk," signifies, in which there is nothing of spiritual and truly rational life: v. 21, "Neither repented they of their murders, nor of their sorceries, nor of their fornication, nor of their thefts," signifies that the heresy of faith alone induces on their hearts stupidity, tergiversation, and hardness, so that they do not think any thing of the precepts of the decalogue, nor indeed of any sin that it ought to be shunned because it is in favour of the devil and against God.

THE EXPLANATION.

419. *And the fifth angel sounded*, signifies the exploration and manifestation of the states of life of those in the reformed church, who are called learned and wise from their confirmation of faith separated from charity, and of justification and salvation by it alone. That these are treated of in what now follows as far as verse 13, is evident from the particulars, understood in a spiritual sense. That by sounding is signified to explore and make manifest the state of the church, and thence the state of life with those whose religion consists in faith alone, may be seen above, n. 397.

420. *And I saw a star fall from heaven unto the earth*, signifies divine truth spiritual flowing from heaven into the church as existing with such persons, and effecting exploration and manifestation. By a star is here signified divine truth spiritual, because it fell from the spiritual heaven, concerning which, above, n. 387, 388; and by the earth is here signified the church with those who are in its internals, as above, n. 398. By divine truth spiritual is meant intelligence derived from spiritual love, which is love towards the neighbour; and as that intelligence at this day is called faith, and that love, charity, it is faith derived from charity, or rather it is the truth of faith derived from the good of charity, which is here signified by a star. The same is signified by a star in the singular number, Apoc. ii. 28; xxii. 16; for by stars, in the plural number, are signified the knowledges of good and truth, n. 51, and by these intelligence is acquired. That it is divine truth exploring and manifesting, is evident from what follows.

421. *And to him was given the key of the bottomless pit*, sig-

nifies the opening of their hell. By a key is signified the power of opening, and also the act of opening, n. 62, 174, 840. And by the bottomless pit is signified the hell where they are who have confirmed themselves in justification and salvation by faith alone, who are all of the reformed church: but in the present case, they who in their own eyes, and thence in the eyes of many others, appear as learned and erudite, when yet in the sight of the angels in heaven they appear destitute of understanding as to those things which pertain to heaven and the church; because they who confirm that faith even to its interiors, close the superior degrees of their understanding, till at length they are unable to see any spiritual truth in light; the reason is, because the confirmation of falsity is the negation of truth; therefore when they hear any spiritual truth, which is a truth of the Word serviceable to those who are of the church for doctrine and life, they keep their minds fixed in the falses which they have confirmed, and then they either veil over the truth they have heard with falses, or reject them as a mere sound, or yawn at it and avert themselves; and this in the degree in which they are in the pride of their own erudition; for pride glues falses together, so that at last they cohere like the concretions formed from the foam of the sea; therefore the Word is hid from them as a book sealed with seven seals. What their quality is, and what their hell, shall also be described, because it has been permitted me to see it, and to discourse with those who are therein, and also to see the locusts that came out of it. "That pit, which is like the aperture of a furnace, appears in the southern quarter, and the abyss beneath is of large extent towards the east; there is light in it, but if light from heaven be admitted into it, it becomes darkness, wherefore the pit is closed above. Huts, arched as it were with brick, appear therein, divided into various little cells, in each of which there is a table, with paper and books lying upon it. Every one sits at his own table, who in the world had confirmed justification and salvation by faith alone, making charity an act merely natural-moral, and its works only works of civil life, whereby men may attain reward in the world; but if they are done for the sake of salvation, they condemn them, and this severely, because human reason and will are in them. All who are in this abyss have been learned and erudite in the world; and among them there are some metaphysicians and scholastics, who are esteemed there above the rest. When it was granted me to enter into discourse with them, I recognised some of them: but this is their lot on their first admission;—they sit in the foremost cells; but as they confirm faith by excluding works of charity, they leave their first habitations, and enter into cells nearer to the east, and so on successively till towards the end, where those are who confirm these tenets from the

Word; and as they then cannot but falsify the Word, their huts disappear, and they see themselves in a desert, whereupon what is described above, n. 153, happens to them. There is also an abyss beneath the one just mentioned, where they are who in like manner have confirmed justification and salvation by faith alone, but who by themselves in their spirit have denied God, and in their hearts have laughed at the holy things of the church; here they do nothing but quarrel, tear their garments, climb upon the tables, and kick and abuse one another; and because no one is there permitted to do mischief to the body of another, they menace with their faces and fists. Filthiness and impurity here prevail; but these are not treated of in this place."

422. *And he opened the bottomless pit, and there arose a smoke out of the pit as the smoke of a great furnace*, signifies the falses of the concupiscences of the natural man springing forth from their evil loves. By the bottomless pit, is signified the hell above described, n. 421; by the smoke from thence, are signified the falses from concupiscences; and because the smoke as of a great furnace is mentioned, the falses of concupiscences springing forth from evil loves are understood, for fire signifies love, n. 468; and the fire of hell, evil love, n. 490. A great furnace has a like signification, because it smokes from fire. Infernal spirits are not in any material fire, but in spiritual fire, which is their love; therefore they do not feel any other fire; on which subject see the work on *Heaven and Hell*, n. 134, 566—575. All love, in the spiritual world, when it is excited, appears at a distance as fire,—within the hells, as red-hot fire, and without, as the smoke of a fire, or as the smoke of a furnace. The falses of the concupiscences springing forth from evil loves, are also described as smoke from a fire and from a furnace, in other parts of the Word, as in these passages: Abraham "looked towards Sodom and Gomorrah,—and beheld, and lo, the *smoke of the country* went up as the *smoke of a furnace*," Gen. xix. 28. "The sun went down, and it was dark, and behold, *a smoking furnace*, and a burning lamp, that passed between those pieces," Gen. xv. 17. "And now, they sin, more and more, therefore they shall be as the *smoke out of the chimney*," Hosea xiii. 2, 3. "But the wicked shall perish, into *smoke* shall they consume away," Psalm xxxvii. 20. "And I will show wonders in the heavens, and in the earth, blood, and fire, and pillars of *smoke*," Joel ii. 30. "And shall cast them into a *furnace of fire*, there shall be wailing and gnashing of teeth," Matt. xiii. 41, 42, 49, 51; and in other places.

423. *And the sun and the air were darkened, by reason of the smoke of the pit*, signifies that thereby the light of truth was turned into thick darkness. By the sun and the air is here signified the light of truth, for by the sun is signified love, and by

the light proceeding from it, divine truth; wherefore when it is said that when the sun is darkened, and at the same time the air, it signifies that divine truth had become thick darkness: that this was from the falses of concupiscences, is signified by its being effected by the smoke of the pit.

424. *And there came out of the smoke locusts upon the earth*, signifies that from them were derived falses to the extreme or lowest degrees, such as prevail with those who have become sensual, and see and judge of all things from their senses and from the fallacies thereof. They are called falses in the extreme or lowest degrees, which occupy the extreme or lowest principles of man's life, and are termed sensual, concerning which we shall speak presently; these are signified by locusts, in the Word: but it is to be observed, that they did not appear like the locusts of the field, which leap about and lay waste meadows and corn fields, but like pigmies or little men, which is evident also from their description, in that they had crowns on their heads, and faces like men, hair like women, teeth like lions, breast-plates of iron, and a king over them;—the angel of the bottomless pit. That little men were also called locusts by the ancients, may be concluded from this passage: The spies who were sent to search the land of Canaan, said, "And there we saw the giants, the sons of Anak, *and we were in their eyes as locusts*," Numb. xiii. 33. "It is Jehovah that sitteth upon the circle of the earth, *and the inhabitants thereof are as locusts*," Isaiah xl. 22. But as falses in extremes or lowest principles, such as prevail among them, are signified by locusts in the Word, therefore they are called locusts, as also crowned and commanders, in Nahum: "There shall the fire devour thee, it shall eat thee up like the canker-worm; make thyself many as the canker-worm, make thyself many as the *locusts;* thy crowned are as the *locusts*, and thy captains as the *locust of locusts*," iii. 15—17. It is in consequence of falses in extreme or lowest principles consuming the truths and goods of the church, as they spring up in man, that they are signified by locusts, which consume the grass and herb of the field, as may be evident from these passages: "Thou shalt carry much seed out into the field, for the *locust* shall consume it," Deut. xxviii. 38. "That which the palmer-worm hath left hath the *locust* eaten, and that which the *locust* hath left hath the canker-worm eaten, and that which the canker-worm hath left hath the *caterpillar* eaten," Joel i. 4, 5. "And I will restore to you the years that the *locust* hath eaten, the canker-worm, the *caterpillar*, and the palmer-worm have eaten," Joel ii. 24, 25. The same is signified by the locusts in Egypt, concerning which it is thus written in Moses: "And Moses stretched forth his rod over the land of Egypt, and the east wind brought the *locusts*. And the *locusts* went up over all the land of Egypt;—before them there

were no such *locusts*,—and they did eat every herb of the land:" and afterwards, " Moses stretched forth his rod, and the *locusts* were cast into the Red Sea," Exod. x. 13, and subsequent verses; and in David: He gave their produce to the *caterpillar*, and their labour to the *locust*, Psalm cv. 34, 35. By the miracles in Egypt is described the vastation of the church; and by this miracle, vastation by falses in extreme or lowest principles; and the extreme or lowest principles of man's life, when the interiors on which they depend are closed, are infernal; for this reason it is that it is said the locusts were cast into the Red Sea, by which is signified hell.

As few at this day know what is meant by the sensual principle, and what the quality of the sensual man is; and as locusts signify such, the following extracts are therefore adduced concerning it from the *Arcana Cœlestia*. "That the sensual principle is the ultimate of the life of man's mind, adhering and cohering to his five bodily senses, n. 5077, 5767, 9121, 9216, 9331, 9730. That he is called a sensual man who judges of all things by his bodily senses, and who believes nothing but what he can see with his eyes, and touch with his hands; saying that these are something, and rejecting the rest, n. 5094, 7693. That the interiors of his mind, which see from the light of heaven, are closed, so that he sees nothing of truth there, which is of heaven and the church, n. 6564, 6844, 6845. That such a man thinks in extreme or lowest principles, and not interiorly from any spiritual light, n. 5089, 5094, 5564, 7693. In short, that they are in a dense natural light, n. 6201, 6310, 6464, 6844, 6845, 6612, 6614, 6622, 6524. That thence interiorly they are against the things which are of heaven and the church, but that exteriorly they can speak in favour of them, and ardently, according to the dominion they exercise by means of them, n. 6201, 6316, 6844, 6845, 6948, 6949. That the learned and erudite, who have confirmed themselves deeply in falses, and still more they who have confirmed themselves against the truths of the Word, are sensual above all others, n. 6316. That sensual men reason acutely and subtilly, because their thought is so near their speech that it is almost in it, and as it were in their lips, and because they place all intelligence in speech from memory only; also that some of them can dextrously confirm falses, and that after confirmation they believe them to be truths, n. 195, 196, 5700, 10236. But that they reason and confirm things from the fallacies of the senses, by which the vulgar are captivated and persuaded, n. 5084, 6948, 6949, 7693. That sensual men are more cunning and malicious than others, n. 7693, 10236. That the avaricious, adulterous, and the voluptuous and deceitful, are especially sensual, although in the eyes of the world they do not appear so, n. 6310. That the interiors of their minds are filthy and unclean, n. 6201. That by these they communicate with the hells, n. 6311. That they who are in the hells are sensual, and the more so in proportion to the depths to which they have fallen, n. 4623, 6311. That the sphere of infernal spirits conjoins itself with the sensual principle of man from behind, n. 6312. That they who have reasoned from sensual things only, and thence against the genuine truths of the church, were called by the ancients, serpents of the tree of knowledge, n. 195, 196, 197, 6398, 6399, 10313. Moreover the sensual principle or faculty of man, and the sensual man, are described, n. 10236 : and the extension of things sensual in man, n. 9731. That sensual things ought to be in the last place, and not in the first, and that in a wise and intelligent man they are in the last place, and subject to the interiors; but that in a foolish man, they are in the first place, and govern; these are they who are properly called sensual, n. 5077, 5125, 5128, 7645. If sensual things are in the last place, a way is opened by them to the understanding, and truths are corrected by a mode of extraction, n. 5580. That those sensual things are in close contact with the world, and admit the things which flow from the world, and, as it were, sift them, n. 9726. That man by means of those sensual things, communicates with the world, and, by means of rational things, with heaven, n. 4009. That sensual things supply such as are subservient to the interiors of the mind, n. 5077, 5081. That there are sensual things which minister to the intellectual part; and such as minister to the voluntary part, n. 5077. That unless the thought be elevated above sensual things, man enjoys but little wisdom, n. 5089. That a wise man thinks about sensual things, n. 5089, 5094. That man, when his thought is elevated above sensual things, comes into a clearer light, and, at length, into heavenly light, n. 6183, 6313, 6315, 9407, 9730, 9922. That elevation above sensual things, and abstraction from them, was known to the ancients, n. 6313. That man, by his spirit, might perceive the things which are done in the spiritual world, if he could be withdrawn from sensual things, and be elevated into the light of heaven by the Lord, n. 4622. The reason is, because the body does not think, but the spirit of man in the body; and in proportion as it thinks in the body, in the same proportion it thinks obscurely and in darkness; and in proportion as it does not think in the body, in the same proportion it thinks clearly and in the light; but in spiritual things, n. 4622, 6614, 6622. That the sensual scientific principle is the ultimate of the understanding, and the sensual delight, the ultimate of the will, n. 9996. What the difference is between the sensual things common to beasts, and the sensual things not common to them, n. 10236. That there are sensual men not wicked, by reason that their interiors are not closed correspondently, concerning whose state in another life, see n. 6311."

425. *And unto them was given power, as the scorpions of the earth have power*, signifies the power of persuading that their falses are truths. By a scorpion is signified deadly persuasion; and, by a scorpion of the earth, persuasion in things relating to the church; the earth signifying the church, n. 285; for a scorpion, when he stings a man, induces a stupor upon the limbs, which, if it be not cured, is followed by death; their persuasion produces a corresponding effect upon the understanding. Such is also the signification of scorpion in these passages: "And thou, son of man, be not afraid of them, neither be afraid of their words, though briers and thorns be with thee, and thou dost dwell among *scorpions*, nor be dismayed at their looks, though they be a rebellious house," Ezek. ii. 6. Jesus said unto the seventy whom he sent forth, "Behold, I give unto you power to tread on serpents and *scorpions*, and on all the power of the enemy; and nothing shall by any means hurt you," Luke x. 10.

426. *And it was commanded them that they should not hurt the grass of the earth, neither any green thing, neither any tree; but only those men who had not the seal of God in their foreheads*, signifies the divine providence of the Lord, that they should not be able to take away any truth and good of faith, nor any affection and perception of them, from any others than such as are not in charity and thence not in faith. By its being commanded them, is signified the Lord's divine providence, because it was commanded from heaven; by not hurting the grass of the earth nor any green thing, is signified not to be able to take away any truth and good of faith; for by grass is signified the truth of faith, which is what first springs up in man, n. 401; and, by green thing, is signified the living principle of faith, which is derived from good, n. 401; by not hurting any tree, is signified not to be able to take away the affection and perception of truth and good; for by a tree is signified man as to these qualities, n. 400; by those men who had not the seal of God in their foreheads, are signified they who are not in charity, and thence in faith; for the forehead signifies love and charity, n. 347; and to have the seal, signifies to know and distinguish them from others, n. 345. The reason why they who have confirmed faith alone, to the very arcana of justification and salvation by it, cannot take away any truth and good of faith, nor the affection and perception of them, from any but those who are not in the faith of charity, is, because they are scarcely comprehended by any one but the priest who teaches and preaches them. The layman hears them, but they enter in at one ear and go out at the other; which the priest himself, who utters those arcana, may know of a certainty from this circumstance, that he himself spent the whole force of his genius in acquiring a knowledge of them in his youth, and afterwards in retaining

them in adult age, likewise from his considering himself as a man of extraordinary learning: what then must be the case with a layman, who simply thinks of faith from charity, when he hears these mysteries? From what has been said, it may be seen that faith alone, as being competent to justification, is the faith of the clergy, and not of the laity, save such of them as live unconcernedly, who imbibe no more from their arcana than that faith alone saves; that they cannot do good from themselves, nor fulfil the law; and that Christ suffered for them; besides some other universals of a similar nature.

427. *And to them it was given that they should not kill them, but that they should be tormented five months*, signifies that from the divine providence of the Lord, they are not able to take away from those, who are not in the faith of charity, the faculty of understanding and willing what is true and good, but that they should only be able to induce stupor for a short time. By its being given them, is signified that it is so ordered from the divine providence of the Lord, as above; not to have power to kill them, signifies not to be able to take away from those who are not in the faith of charity, the faculty of understanding and willing what is true and good, for when this faculty is taken away, man is spiritually killed; by tormenting them five months, is signified to induce stupor for a short time; five signifies a little, or a short time, and to torment, signifies to induce stupor, because this is what is signified by a scorpion, n. 425; and by the torment, as it were, of a scorpion, is signified as follows, n. 428. That the faculty of understanding truth and of willing it, or rationality and liberty, cannot be taken away from man, is amply shown in the *Angelic Wisdom concerning the Divine Providence*, n. 73, 74, 82—86, 92—98, 138—149, 322. That five months signify a little, and a short time, is owing to the signification of five, as denoting a little; for times, whether they be hours, days, weeks, or months, or years, do not signify time, but state; and numbers determine its quality, n. 4, 10, 348, 947. That five signifies something, and also a little, may appear from these places: A thousand shall flee at the rebuke of *five*, Isaiah xxx. 17. "And *five* of you shall chase a hundred," Levit. xxvi. 8. Jesus said, "The kingdom of heaven is like unto ten virgins, of which *five* were wise and *five* were foolish," Matt. xxv. 1, 2. By ten virgins are signified all in the church; by five are signified a certain part or some of them. The like is signified by ten and five in the parable where there were given unto the servants talents that they should trade, and one with his talent gained ten talents, and another, *five*, Luke xix. 13—20. Ten talents signify much, and five talents, a little; not to mention other passages; as in Isaiah xvii. 6; xix. 18, 19; Matt. xiv. 15—22.

428. *And their torment was as the torment of a scorpion*

when he striketh a man, signifies that this is from their power of persuasion. This follows from what was said, n. 427; for by torment is signified the stupor, which their persuasion induces upon the understanding, as the scorpion does upon the body when he stings it; a scorpion signifies that faculty of persuasion, n. 425. In the spiritual word there exists a power of persuasion which takes away the understanding of truth, and induces stupor, and thus distress, upon the mind; but this power of persuasion is unknown in the natural world.

429. *And in those days shall men seek death, and shall not find it; and shall desire to die, and death shall flee from them*, signifies that it is the desire of those who are in the doctrine of faith separated, that in matters of faith the understanding should be shut up and the will closed, and thus that they should not have any spiritual light and life; but that it is nevertheless provided by the Lord that the understanding should not be shut up, nor the will closed, lest spiritual light and life in man should be extinguished. In those days, signifies the last state of the church, when the doctrine of faith alone is universally received; men shall seek death, signifies that they will desire that, in matters of faith, the understanding should be shut up; and shall not find it, signifies that it is provided of the Lord, that this should not be done: and shall desire to die, signifies that they will also wish to have the will closed in them; and death shall flee from them, signifies that it is provided that neither should take place; for thus spiritual light and life would be extinguished, and man would spiritually die; to seek, is predicated of the understanding; and to desire, of the will; and death, of both. That this is the signification of these words, is evident; otherwise, what meaning could there be in men's seeking death in those days and not finding it, and desiring to die and death fleeing from them? for by death, no other death is meant but spiritual death, which is induced when the understanding is removed from the things that are to be believed; for in this case man knows not whether he thinks and does what is true, or what is false, thus whether he thinks and acts with the angels of heaven, or with the devils of hell.

430. *And the shapes of the locusts*, signifies the form and appearances of those who have confirmed in themselves faith separated from charity. By shapes, is signified their appearances in a representative image; by locusts, are signified falses in extreme or lowest principles, n. 424; and as falses make one with those who are in falses, they also are signified by locusts. That they who have confirmed themselves in faith alone, or that the falses in which they are principled, are meant by locusts, appeared evident to me from this circumstance, that the presbyters who were in that faith, embraced the locusts that were seen, and kissed them, and were desirous of introducing them

into their houses; for the images, which are forms representative of the affections and thoughts of angels and spirits in the spiritual world, appear as if they were alive, in like manner as the animals, birds, and fishes, mentioned above.

431. *Were like unto horses prepared unto battle*, signifies that because they can reason, they appear to themselves to combat from the understanding of truth from the Word. By a horse, is signified the understanding of the Word, n. 298; by war, is signified spiritual war, which consists in reasonings and argumentations, n. 500, 586; by like, or similitudes, are signified appearances, as above, n. 430.

432. *And on their heads were as it were crowns like gold*, signifies that they appeared to themselves as conquerors. By crowns on their heads like gold, are signified tokens of victory, because formerly kings wore crowns of gold in battle, n. 300; for it is said that they were seen like horses, that is, on horses prepared for war, n. 431, for they had the faces of men, as follows; and they are in the persuasion that they are invincible.

433. *And their faces were as the faces of men*, signifies that they appeared to themselves to be wise. By man, in the Word, is signified to be wise and intelligent, n. 243; and by his face, wisdom and intelligence; hence it is, that by their faces being as the faces of men, is signified that they appeared to themselves to be wise. They are also called wise, learned, and erudite, although they are among the foolish virgins, who had no oil in their lamps, Matt. xxv. 1, 2. Oil signifies love and charity; and among the foolish means among those who hear the Lord, that is, read the Word, and do not do it, Matt. vii. 26.

434. *And they had hair as the hair of women*, signifies that they appeared to themselves to be in the affection of truth. By man, in the Word, is signified the understanding of truth; and by woman, the affection of truth, because man by birth is understanding, and woman, affection; on which subject, see *The Treatise concerning Conjugial Love*. By hair, in the Word, is signified the ultimate of man's life, which is the sensual principle, see n. 424; this is what gives them the appearance of being in the affection of truth, when yet they are in the affection of falsity; for this they believe to be truth. That a woman signifies the affection of truth, may appear from many passages in the Word; hence it is, that the church is called a wife, a woman, a daughter, and a virgin, the church being a church by virtue of the love or affection of truth; for from this comes the understanding of truth. The church is called a woman in these passages: "There were *two women* of one mother, and they committed whoredoms in Egypt, Ahola which is Samaria, and Aholiba which is Jerusalem," Ezek. xxiii. 2—4. "Jehovah hath called thee as a *woman* forsaken and grieved in spirit, and a *wife of youth*," Isaiah liv. 6, 7. "Jehovah hath created a new thing in the

earth, a *woman* shall compass a man," Jerem. xxxi. 21, 22. By the *woman* clothed with the sun, whom the dragon persecuted, Apoc. xii., is signified the New Church, which is the New Jerusalem. By women are signified the affections of truth, by virtue of which the church is a church, in many passages, as in the following: "The *women* of my people have ye cast out of their pleasant houses," Micah ii. 9. The families of houses shall mourn apart, and the *women* apart, Zech. xii. 12, 13. "Rise up, ye *women* that are at ease, give ear unto my speech," Isaiah xxxii. 9. "Wherefore commit ye this great evil to cut off from you *man and woman?*" Jerem. xliv. 7. "I will break in pieces *man and woman*," Jerem. li. 22. By man and woman, here and elsewhere, is signified, in a spiritual sense, the understanding of truth, and the affection of truth.

435. *And their teeth were as the teeth of lions*, signifies that sensual things, which are the ultimates of the life of the natural man, appeared with them to have power over all things. Teeth signify the ultimates of the life of the natural man, which are called sensual things; concerning which, see above, n. 424. Sensual things are of two kinds, one kind having relation to the will, and the other to the understanding; the sensual things of the will are signified by the hair of women, of which above, n. 434; and the sensual things of the understanding are signified by teeth; the latter, or what is the same, sensual men who are in falses from confirmation, seem to themselves to be in power over all things, so as to be altogether invincible; wherefore the teeth of the locusts, by which such sensual things are signified, were as the teeth of lions, for by a lion is signified power, n. 241. That teeth signify the ultimates of man's life, which are called sensual things, and which, when separated from the interiors of the mind, are in mere falses, and do violence to truths even to destroying them, may appear from the following passages: "My soul is among *lions*, whose *teeth* are spears and arrows," Psalm lvii. 4. "Break their *teeth*, O God, in their mouth, break out the *great teeth of the young lions*," Psalm lviii. 6. "For a nation is come up upon my land, strong,—whose *teeth are the teeth of a lion*, and he hath the *cheek-teeth of a great lion*," Joel i. 6. "Jehovah hath broken the *teeth* of the ungodly," Psalm iii. 7. There came up out of the sea a beast dreadful and terrible, and exceedingly strong, which had great iron *teeth*, it devoured and brake in pieces, Dan. vii. 7. "Blessed be Jehovah, who hath not given us a prey to their *teeth*," Psalm cxxiv. 6. Since sensual men do not see any truth in its own light, but ratiocinate and dispute about every thing, by questioning its identity; and since these disputes in the hells are heard without as the gnashing of teeth, being in themselves the collisions of falsity and truth, it is evident what is signified by the *gnashing of teeth*, Matt. viii. 12; xiii. 42, 50; xxii. 13; xxiv. 51; xxv.

30; Luke xiii. 28; and partly what by *gnashing with the teeth*. Psalm iii. 7; Psalm xxxv. 15, 16; Psalm xxxvii. 12; Psalm cxii. 10; Micah iii. 5; Lament. ii. 16.

436. *And they had breast-plates, as it were breast-plates of iron*, signifies argumentations from fallacies, by which they fight and prevail, which appeared to them so powerful that they could not be refuted. By breast-plates are signified defences, because they protect the breast; here, defences of falsities, which are effected by argumentations grounded in fallacies, by which a false principle is defended; for from a false principle nothing but falses can flow: if truths are advanced, they are only viewed outwardly or superficially, thus also sensually, and are consequently falsified, and, with such persons, become fallacies. The reason why breast-plates have this signification, is, because wars, in the Word, signify spiritual wars, and thence the implements of war signify the various things relating to such wars; as in Jeremiah: " Harness the horses; and get up, ye horsemen, and stand forth with your *helmets;* furbish the *spears*, and put on the *brigandines*," xlvi. 4. In Isaiah: " For he put on righteousness as a *breast-plate*, and an *helmet* of salvation upon his head," lix. 17. In David: " Under his wings shalt thou trust, his truth shall be thy *shield* and *buckler*," Psalm xci. 4; besides other places; as in Ezekiel xxiii. 24; xxxviii. 4; xxxix. 9; Nahum ii. 4; Psalm v. 12; Psalm xxxv. 2, 3. Their breast-plates being as it were of iron, signifies that their argumentations seemed to them so strong that they could not be refuted; for iron, from its hardness, signifies what is strong.

437. *And the sound of their wings was as the sound of chariots of many horses running to battle*, signifies their reasonings as if they were from truths of doctrine from the Word fully understood, for which they must ardently fight. The sound of wings signifies reasonings, because to fly signifies to perceive and instruct, n. 245, 415; chariots signify doctrinals, as will be seen presently; horses signify the understanding of the Word, n. 298; and many horses, what is plenary: that running to battle signifies ardour for contest, is evident. That a chariot signifies doctrine, is plain from these passages: " The *chariots* of God are twenty thousand thousands of angels, the Lord is among them," Psalm lxviii. 17. " Jehovah maketh the clouds his *chariot;* who walketh upon the wings of the wind," Psalm civ. 2, 3. " Thou didst ride (O Jehovah) upon thine horses, and *thy chariots* are salvation," Habak. iii. 8. " For behold, Jehovah will come with fire, and with his *chariots* like a whirlwind," Isaiah lxvi. 15. " Thus shall ye be filled at my table with horses and *chariots;* and I will set my glory among the heathen," Ezek. xxxix. 20. " And I will cut off the *chariot* from Ephraim, and the horse from Jerusalem," Zech. ix. 10

"And I will overthrow the throne of kingdoms, and I will overthrow the *chariots*, and those that ride in them," Haggai ii. 22. "Go, set a watchman, let him declare what he seeth; and he saw a *chariot*, with a couple of horsemen, and a *chariot* of camels, and a *chariot* of men, and he said, Babylon is fallen, is fallen," Isaiah xxi. 6—8. And Elijah and Elisha represented the Lord as to the Word, and thence signified doctrine from the Word, as did all the prophets, n. 8, therefore they were called *the chariots of Israel and the horsemen thereof;* and for the same reason Elijah was seen taken into heaven in a *chariot of fire*, and there were seen by Elisha's young man *chariots and horses of fire* round about him, 2 Kings ii. 11, 12; vi. 17; xiii. 14; besides other places where chariots occur; as in Isaiah xxxi. 1; xxxvii. 24; lxvi. 20; Jerem. xvii. 25; xxii. 4; xlvi. 2, 3, 8, 9; l. 37, 38; li. 20, 21; Ezek. xxvi. 7, 8, 10, 11; Dan. xi. 40; Nahum iii. 1—3; Joel ii. 1, 2, 5.

438. *And they had tails like unto scorpions*, signifies the truths of the Word falsified, by means of which they induce stupor. By the tail is signified the ultimate of the head, because the brain is continued through the back-bone to the tail, therefore the head and tail make one, as the first and last; when, therefore, by the head, faith alone justifying and saving is signified, by the tail is signified the sum of all the confirmations thereof, which are from the Word, thus which are the truths of the Word falsified. Every one, who from his own intelligence assumes a principle of religion, and establishes it as the head, also assumes confirmations from the Word, and makes them the tail, thus induces a stupor upon others, and so hurts them; therefore it is said, that "they had *tails* like unto scorpions;" and presently after, "that there were stings in their *tails*, and that their power was to hurt men;" for by a scorpion is signified the power of persuasion inducing stupor upon the understanding, n. 425. That the tail is a continuation of the brain through the back-bone to its termination, any anatomist will tell you; or merely observe a dog or any other animal with a tail, and encourage and coax him, and you will see that the ridge of his back will become smooth, and his tail move correspondently; but that, on the contrary, he will set his back up if you provoke him. The primary tenet of the understanding, which is assumed as a principle is signified by the head, and the ultimate thereof by the tail, in these passages also: "Therefore Jehovah will cut off from Israel *head and tail*, the ancient and the honourable, he is the *head*, and the prophet that teacheth lies, he is the *tail*," Isaiah ix. 14, 15. Egypt shall not have any work to make *head and tail*, Isaiah xix. 15. By the seven *heads* of the dragon, and by his *tail*, with which he drew a third part of the stars of heaven, and cast them to the earth, Apoc. xii. 4; as also by the tails like serpents, hav

ing heads with which they do hurt, verse 19 of this chapter, nothing else is signified. Inasmuch as by the tail is signified the ultimate, and the ultimate being the complex or aggregate of all, therefore Jehovah said to Moses, Take the serpent by the *tail;* and he took it, and it became a rod, Exod. iv. 3, 4; and therefore it was commanded, that they should take off the *tail* entire near the back-bone, and sacrifice it together with the fat that was upon the entrails, kidneys, intestines, and liver, Levit. iii. 9—11; viii. 25; ix. 19; Exod. xxix. 22. That the ultimate is the continent and complex, or that which contains and comprehends all prior things, may be seen in *The Doctrine of the New Jerusalem concerning the Sacred Scripture,* n. 38, 65; and in *The Wisdom of Angels concerning the Divine Love and the Divine Wisdom,* n. 209—216, n. 217—222.

439. *And there were stings in their tails: and their power was to hurt men five months,* signifies subtle falsifications of the Word, by which, for a short time, they darken and fascinate the understanding, and thus deceive and captivate. By stings in their tails are signified subtle falsifications of the Word;—by stings, subtilty; and by tails, the truths of the Word falsified, n. 438. By their power to hurt, is signified that by means of these they can induce stupor, that is, they can darken and fascinate the understanding, and thus deceive and captivate; for their tails were like scorpions, and by scorpions such things are signified, n. 425. By five months, is signified for a short time, as above, n. 427: this takes place when they quote and apply any thing from the Word; for the Word is written according to correspondences, and correspondences are in part appearances of truth, containing within them genuine truths. If these truths are not known in the church, many things may be taken from the Word, which at first appear in accordance with heresy; but when genuine truths are known in the church, then the appearances of truth are rendered manifest, and genuine truths come to view. But before this is done, a heretic, by various things drawn from the Word, may obscure and fascinate the understanding, and thus deceive and captivate. That this is done by those who assert that man's sins are remitted, or, in other words, that he is justified by an act of faith, concerning which no one knows any thing, and this in a moment, and if not before, even at the hour of death, might be illustrated by examples, were this the place to do so. By stings are signified falses of a hurtful nature derived from evil, also in Amos: "Lo, the days shall come upon you, when they shall take you away with *stings,*" iv. 2. And in Moses: That they should drive out the inhabitants of the land, lest they should be thorns in their eyes, and *stings* in their sides, Numb xxxiii. 55. Thorns, briers, brambles, and thistles, also signify falses of evil, on account of their prickles.

440. *And they had a king over them, the angel of the bottomless pit; whose name in the Hebrew tongue is Abaddon, but in the Greek tongue he hath his name Apollyon,* signifies that they are in the satanic hell who are in falses derived from concupiscences, and, by a total falsification of the Word, have destroyed the church. By their king, the angel of the bottomless pit, is not signified any angel who is a king there, but the false principle reigning therein; for by a king, in a genuine sense, is signified one who is in truths from the affection of good, and, abstractedly, that truth itself, n. 20; and thence, in the opposite sense, by a king is signified one who is in falses from concupiscence of evil, and, abstractedly, that false itself. By the bottomless pit is signified the satanic hell, where they are, n. 387, 428; by name is signified the quality of the state, n. 81, 122, 165; Abaddon, in the Hebrew tongue, signifies a destroying and a destroyer; so does Apollyon, in the Greek tongue; and this is the false principle in extreme or lowest principles, which, by the total falsification of the Word, has destroyed the church. By Abaddon, in the Hebrew text, is signified destruction or perdition, in these places: "Shall thy faithfulness be declared in *destruction?*" Psalm lxxxviii. 11. "Hell is naked before him, and *destruction* hath no covering," Job xxvi. 6. "For it is a fire that consumeth to *destruction*," Job xxxi. 12. "*Destruction* and Death say," Job xxviii. 22. In other places, hell and the devil are called *Destruction or Perdition, and Destroyer*, Isaiah liv. 16; Ezek. v. 16; ix. 1; Exod. xii. 13; though another term is used,

441. *One woe is past; behold, there come two woes more hereafter,* signifies further lamentations over the devastation of the church. That woe signifies lamentation over calamity, unhappiness, and damnation, see n. 416; here, then, by two woes to come, are signified further lamentations over the state of the church.

442. *And the sixth angel sounded,* signifies the exploration and manifestation of their state of life in the reformed church who are not so wise, and yet place the all of religion in faith, and think of it alone and of nothing beyond it, and the customary worship, and so live as they like. That these are treated of to the end of this chapter, will appear from the explanation of what follows. That to sound signifies to explore and lay open the state of the church, and thence of the life of those whose religion consists in faith alone, may be seen above, n. 397.

"These who are now treated of, are altogether distinct from those referred to thus far in this chapter, the falses of whose faith were seen in the form of locusts: this is the ground of distinction; the latter, or those already described, are studious in exploring the arcana of justification by faith, and also in giving the signs of it, and its testimonies, which, with them are the goods of moral and civil life; insisting that the precepts of the Word are indeed in themselves divine, but that with man they become natural, because they proceed from his will, and have no conjunction with his spiritualities of faith; and because they confirm these things by rational considerations, which savour of erudition, they dwell in the southern quarter of the bottomless pit, according to the description above, n. 421. But they who are treated of in what follows to the end of the chapter, do not study those arcana, but only make bare faith the all of religion, and nothing besides it and the customary worship, and so live at their ease. I have been permitted to see and converse with these also; they live in the northern quarter, in huts that are scattered about, and constructed of reeds and rushes plastered over with lime, without any floor but the ground. The more ingenious, who, by means of natural light, know how to establish that faith by reasonings, and can prove that it has nothing at all to do with life, dwell in front, the more simple behind them, and the more stupid toward the western part of that tract: the multitude of them is so great that it is incredible. They are instructed by angelic spirits, but they who do not receive the truths of faith, and live according to them, are let down into the hell which is under them, and confined there."

443. *And I heard a voice from the four horns of the golden altar which is before God, saying to the sixth angel which had the trumpet*, signifies a command from the Lord out of the spiritual heaven to those who were to explore and make manifest. By a voice is signified a divine command; by the golden altar, or altar of incense, is signified the spiritual heaven, n. 277, 392; by the four horns of that altar is signified its power, n. 270; here, the power of loosing the four angels bound at the river Euphrates, as follows: by the sixth angel who had the trumpet, is signified to those to whom the office of exploring and laying open these things was committed, n. 442.

444. *Loose the four angels that are bound at the great river Euphrates*, signifies that external restraints should be removed from them, that the interiors of their minds might appear. That this is the signification of these words, no one can know, and scarcely can suspect, unless he knows what is meant by the great river Euphrates, and what by the four angels bound there. By Euphrates, in the Word, are signified the interiors of man's mind, which are called things rational, which, with those who are in truths derived from good, are full of wisdom, but in those who are in falses derived from evil, are full of insanity. The reason why these are signified in the Word by the river Euphrates, is, because that river divided the land of Canaan from Assyria; and by the land of Canaan was signified the church;

and by Assyria, its rational principle; and thence by the river which bounded it, are signified the interiors of the mind which are called things rational, in both senses: for there are three things which constitute a man of the church, the spiritual principle, the rational or intellectual, and the natural, which is also the scientific. The spiritual principle of the church was signified by the land of Canaan and its rivers; the rational or intellectual principle of the church, by Ashur or Assyria and its river Euphrates; and the natural, which is also the scientific principle of the church, by Egypt and its river Nile: but concerning these more may be seen below, n. 503. By the four angels bound at the river Euphrates, are signified those interiors with the men of the church which are said to be bound, because they are not openly avowed; for they are infernal spirits, who are meant by these four angels, since it is said of them, in what follows, n. 446, that they were prepared to kill the third part of men, and the interiors of men make one with spirits, either infernal or celestial, because they cohabit: by loosing them is signified to remove external restraints, that the interiors of their minds may appear. Such is the signification of these words. By Euphrates are signified the interiors of man's mind bordering upon or bounding the spiritual things of his church, as may appear from those places in the Word where Ashur or Assyria is mentioned; but Euphrates occurs in an opposite sense, in which it signifies the interiors full of falses and thence of insanities, in these passages: "Behold the Lord bringeth up upon them the waters of the *river*, strong and many, even the *king of Assyria*. And he shall pass through Judah; he shall overflow, and go over," Isaiah viii. 7, 8. "And now what hast thou to do in the way of Egypt, to drink the waters of Sihor? or what hast thou to do with the way of *Assyria*, that thou shouldest drink the waters of the *river?*" Jerem. ii. 18. "And Jehovah shall utterly destroy the tongue of the Egyptian sea; and shake his hand over the *river Euphrates*," Isaiah xi. 15. "And the sixth angel poured out his vial upon the great *river Euphrates*, and the water thereof was dried up," Apoc. xvi. 12. The prophet was commanded to put a girdle upon his loins, and to hide it afterwards in a hole of a rock beside the *Euphrates*, and after a short time when he took it, behold it was rotten, nor was it useful for any thing, Jerem. xiii. 1—7, 11. And he was also commanded, when he had done reading the Book, to cast it into the midst of the *Euphrates*, and to say, Thus shall Babylon sink, and not rise again, Jerem. li. 63, 64; by these things were represented the interiors of the state of the church with the children of Israel. That the river of Egypt, the Nile, and the river of Assyria, the Euphrates, were the boundaries of the land of Canaan, appears from this passage: "Jehovah made a covenant with Abram, saying, Unto thy seed will I give this land, from *the river of Egypt unto the great river Euphrates,*" Gen. xv. 18. That the Euphrates was a boundary, may be seen, Exod. xxiii. 31; Deut. i. 7, 8; xi. 24; Joshua i. 4; Micah vii. 12.

445. *And the four angels were loosed*, signifies that when external restraints were removed, the interiors of their minds appeared. This follows from what was said above.

446. *Who were prepared for an hour, and a day, and a month, and a year, to slay the third part of men*, signifies that they were perpetually in the effort to take away spiritual light and life from men of the church. Being prepared signifies to be in the endeavour; by an hour, a day, a month, and a year, is signified continually and perpetually, in like manner as by at all times; to slay signifies to take away spiritual light and life from men of the church, n. 325; and the third part signifies all, n. 400.

447. *And the number of the armies of horsemen were two myriads of myriads*, signifies reasonings concerning faith alone, with which the interiors of their minds were filled, from the great abundance of mere falses of evil. By armies are signified goods and truths; and, in the opposite sense, evils and falses; here, the falses of evil, of which below. By horsemen are signified reasonings concerning faith alone; because by a horse is signified the understanding of the Word, n. 298; and also the understanding of the Word destroyed, n. 305, 312, 321; therefore by horsemen are signified reasonings from the understanding of the Word destroyed: in the present instance, concerning faith alone; because they who are principled therein are treated of. By two myriads of myriads are not meant the precise number, but a great abundance; two are mentioned, because two are predicated of good, and, in the opposite sense, of evil, n. 322; and myriads are predicated of truths, and, in the opposite sense, of falses, n. 336. Hence it may be seen, that by the number of the armies of horsemen, two myriads of myriads, are signified reasonings concerning faith alone, with which the interiors of their minds were filled, from the great abundance of mere falses of evil. That by armies, in the Word, are signified the goods and truths of heaven and the church, and, in the opposite sense, evils and falses, may appear from those places where the sun, moon, and stars, are called armies or hosts; and by the sun is signified the good of love; by the moon, the truth of faith; and by the stars, knowledges of what is good and true; and the contrary, in the opposite sense, n. 51, 53, 332, 413; both the former and the latter are called armies or hosts, in these passages: "Praise Jehovah all ye *his hosts*, praise ye him sun and moon, praise him all ye stars of light," Psalm cxlviii. 2, 3. "My hands have stretched out the heavens, and all their *host* have I commanded," Isaiah xlv

12. "By the word of Jehovah were the heavens made, and all the *host of them* by the breath of his mouth," Psalm xxxiii 6. The heavens and the earth were finished, and all the *host of them*, Gen. ii. 1. The horn of the goat grew even " to the *host of heaven*, and it cast down some of the *host* and of the stars to the ground, yea, he magnified himself even to the prince of the *host:*—and an *host* was given him against the daily sacrifice by reason of transgression, and it cast down the truth to the ground: then I heard one saint speaking, How long is the sanctuary and the *host* to be trodden under foot?" Dan. viii. 10—14. " Jehovah shall utter his voice before his *army*," Joel ii. 11. On the house tops they offered incense to all the *host of heaven*, Jerem. xix. 13. Lest thou worship and serve the sun, the moon, the stars, and all the *host of heaven*, Deut. iv. 19; xvii. 3; Jerem. viii. 2; in like manner in Isaiah xiii. 4; xxxiv. 4; xl. 26; Jerem. xxxiii. 22; Zech. ix. 15; Apoc. xix. 14. Because the host of heaven signifies the goods and truths of heaven and the church, therefore the Lord is called *Jehovah Zebaoth*, that is, Jehovah of hosts: and, for the same reason, the ministry of the Levites was called *military service*, Numb. iv. 3, 23, 30, 39; and it is written in David: "Bless Jehovah, all ye his *hosts*, ye ministers of his that do his pleasure," Psalm ciii. 21. Evils and falses in the church are signified in Isaiah by the *army of the Gentiles*, xxxiv. 2; and by the *army* of the king of the north, with which he came against the king of the south, Dan. xi. 13, 15, 20. The king of the north is the false of evil in the church, and the king of the south is the truth of good there. It is said by the Lord, " When ye shall see Jerusalem compassed with *armies*, then know that the desolation thereof is nigh," Luke xxi. 20. By Jerusalem is here signified the church, and by armies the evils and falses which would lay it waste; speaking of the consummation of the age, which is the last time of the church. Evils and falses are signified by an army, in Joel: " And I will restore to you the years that the locust hath eaten, the cankerworm, the caterpillar, and the palmer-worm, my great *army*, which I sent among you," ii. 25. That by the locust and the other things is signified the false in extreme or lowest principles, see above, n. 424.

448. *And I heard the number of them*, signifies that the quality of them was perceived, which was as follows. To hear signifies to perceive; number signifies the quality and state of a thing, n. 10, 348, 364: it denotes the quality of their state, as given below, because it is described in what now follows, wherefore it is said, And *thus* I saw.

449. *And thus I saw the horses in the vision, and them that sat on them*, signifies that then it was discovered that the reasonings of the interiors of their minds concerning faith alone,

were imaginary and visionary, and that they themselves were infatuated with them. To see signifies to discover their quality; by horses are signified the reasonings of the interiors of their minds concerning faith alone; in the present case, imaginary and visionary reasonings, because it is said, that he saw them in vision. By those that sit on horses are signified such as are intelligent from the Word understood, but here, such as are infatuated by imaginary and visionary notions, which are contrary to the Word. Because the interiors of their minds appeared under such forms as signify imaginary and visionary reasonings concerning faith alone, a few of them, which I have heard from their own mouths, shall be made public; thus, for instance: " Was not faith alone, after the grievous fall of man, made the only medium of salvation? How can we appear before God without that medium? Is it not the only medium? Are we not born in sins, and is not our nature entirely corrupted by the transgression of Adam? Can there be any other means of being healed but by faith alone? What can our works contribute towards this? Who can do any good work from himself, —who can purify, forgive, justify, and save himself? Does there not lurk, in every work that man does from himself, merit and self-righteousness? And if, haply, we should do any thing that was good, could we do all, and fulfil the law? Besides, if any one sins against one commandment, he sins against all, because they cohere. Why did the Lord come into the world, and suffer so grievously on the cross, but to take away from us damnation and the curse of the law, to reconcile God the Father, and become merit and righteousness alone, which might be imputed to man through faith? otherwise, what good end could be answered by his coming? Since, then, Christ suffered for us, and fulfilled the law for us, and took away its right of condemnation, can evil, in this case, any longer condemn, and can good save us? therefore we who have faith, are at full liberty to think, will, speak, and do whatever we please, provided we do no injury to our reputation, honour, and interest, nor incur the penalties of the civil law, which would be a disgrace and hurt to us." Some, who wander further north, said, " That good works, which are done for the sake of salvation, are hurtful, pernicious, and cursed;" among these, also, there were some Presbyters. These things are what I heard, but they mumbled and muttered many more, which I did not hear. They spoke, also, indecently with all licentiousness, and were lascivious, both in words and actions, without fear for any wicked deed, except out of pretence, for the sake of appearing honest. Such are the interiors of the mind, and thence the exteriors of the body of those, who place the all of religion in faith alone. But all those things, which were uttered by them, fall to the ground, if the Lord himself—the Saviour—is immediately ap proached, and believed in, and good is done, each for the sake of salvation, and by man as from himself, with a belief, however, that it is from the Lord: unless these things are done *as* by man, neither faith nor charity can be given at all; nor, consequently, can religion nor salvation.

450. *Having breast-plates of fire, and of jacinth, and of brimstone*, signifies their imaginary and visionary argumentations from infernal love and self-derived intelligence, and the concupiscences thence proceeding. By breast-plates are signified argumentations, by which they fight for faith alone, n. 436; by fire is signified celestial love, and in the opposite sense, infernal love, n. 452, 465, 495; by jacinth is signified intelligence from sipiritual love, and, in the opposite sense, intelligence from infernal love, which is self-derived intelligence, of which below; and by brimstone is signified concupiscences derived from that love through self-intelligence, n. 452: hence it follows, that by breast-plates of fire, of jacinth, and of brimstone, such things are signified. The reason why their argumentations in favour of faith alone are thus described, is, because all they who believe themselves justified, that is, absolved from sin, by faith alone, never think of repentance; and an impenitent man is in mere sins, and all sins are derived from, and thence partake of the nature of infernal love, of self-intelligence, and the concupiscences springing from them; and they who are principled in these things, not only act from them, but also speak, yea, think and will, and consequently reason and argue from them; these constitute, indeed, the very man, because they are his very life; but then a man devil, and an infernal life. They who live a moral life, only for the sake of themselves and the world, do not know this; the reason is, because their interiors are infernal, whilst their exteriors are similar to the exteriors of those who live a Christian life: let them know, however, that every one, when he dies, comes into his interiors, because he becomes a spirit, this being the internal man; and then the interiors accommodate the exteriors to themselves, and they become alike: wherefore the morality of their life in the world then becomes as the scales of fishes which are wiped away. The case is quite different with those who hold the precepts of moral life to be divine, and then those also of a civil nature, by reason of their having relation to love towards the neighbour. A jacinth signifies intelligence derived from spiritual love, because its colour partakes of the redness of fire and the whiteness of light; and by fire is signified love; and by light, intelligence: this intelligence is signified by blue in the *coverings and vails of the tabernacle*, Exod. xxvi. 31, 36; xxvii. 16; in *Aaron's ephod*, Exod. xxviii. 6, 15; by the cloth of *blue* or *hyacinth* which was placed over the ark, the table, the candlestick, and the altar, when they journeyed, Numb. iv. 6, 7, 9, 11, 12; by the *fringe of blue thread*

on the borders of their garments, Numb. xv. 38, 39; and by the hyacinthine or blue colour, in Ezekiel xxvii. 7, 24. But intelligence derived from the affection of infernal love, is signified by blue in Ezekiel: Aholah, or Samaria, played the harlot, and doted on her lovers, the neighbouring Assyrians, clothed in *blue*, horsemen riding upon horses, xxiii. 4—6: hereby the church is described, which, by reasonings from self-derived intelligence, had falsified the truths of the Word. And in Jeremiah: "But they are altogether brutish and foolish: the stock is a doctrine of vanities. Silver spread into plates is brought from Tarshish, the work of the workmen and of the hands of the founder, *blue* and purple is their clothing, they are all the work of the wise," x. 8, 9. The work of the workmen and of the hands of the founder, and all the work of the wise, signify, in this passage, that they were the offspring of self-derived intelligence.

451. *And the heads of the horses were as the heads of lions*, signifies phantasies concerning faith alone, as if it were in power. By heads are signified the imaginary and visionary notions about faith alone, with those who are here treated of collectively, which are called phantasies; by horses are signified the reasonings of the interiors of their minds, which are such, n. 449; by lions are signified power, n. 241; but then it is power from fallacies, inasmuch as they are sensual, and the sensual reason from fallacies, by which they persuade and captivate, n. 424. That their arguments in favour of faith alone are imaginary and visionary, any one may see, who elevates his mind a little. What are faith in act and faith in state, as conceived by them, but visionary things? Who is there among them that knows any thing concerning faith in act; and what avails faith in state, when no good enters from man into faith in act? What is remission of sins and consequent momentaneous salvation, but a result of visionary thought? That it is the fiery flying serpent in the church, see *The Wisdom of Angels concerning the Divine Providence*, n. 340. What is the conceit of immunity, merit, righteousness, and sanctification by imputation, but a visionary thing? see *The Doctrine of the New Jerusalem concerning the Lord*, n. 18. What is the Divine Operation in internals, without man's co-operation in externals as from himself? For to separate the internal from the external so that there can be no conjunction of them, is merely visionary, see below, n. 606. Such a visionary thing is faith separated from charity; for charity in works is the very foundation and continent of faith; it is its ground and soil, also its essence and life; in a word, faith from charity constitutes a man; but faith, without charity, is a spectre, and a creature of the imagination, like a bubble of water floating in the air. But perhaps some may say, If you remove the understanding from faith, you will not see visionary things;

but be it known, that he who can remove the understanding from faith, may obtrude a thousand visionary things upon every religious tenet, as has been done for ages past by the Roman Catholics.

452. *And out of their mouths issued fire, and smoke, and brimstone*, signifies that in their thoughts and discourses, viewed interiorly, there is nothing, and from them there proceeds nothing but the love of self and of the world, which is the proprium or selfhood of the will; the pride of self-derived intelligence, which is the proprium of the understanding, and the concupiscences of evil and falsity, which is the common proprium springing from the two former. Out of their mouths, means out of their thoughts and discourses; by fire is signified the love of self and of the world, which love is the proprium of man's will, n. 450, 465, 495; by smoke is signified the pride of self-derived intelligence, which is the proprium of his understanding, proceeding from the love of self and of the world, as smoke does from fire, n. 422; and by brimstone is signified the concupiscence of evil and falsity, which is the common proprium flowing from the two former. These things, however, do not appear from their discourses before men in the world, but manifestly before the angels in heaven; therefore it is said, that when viewed interiorly, they are such. Fire signifies infernal love, and brimstone, the concupiscences flowing from that love through the pride of self-derived intelligence, in the following passages: I will cause it to rain *fire and brimstone* upon him, Ezek. xxxviii. 22. "Jehovah shall rain upon the wicked *fire and brimstone*," Psalm xi. 6. "For it is the day of Jehovah's vengeance—and the streams thereof shall be turned into pitch, and the dust thereof into *brimstone*, the *smoke thereof* shall go up for ever," Isaiah xxxiv. 8—10. "But the same day that Lot went out of Sodom, it rained *fire and brimstone* from heaven;—even thus shall it be in the day when the Son of Man is revealed," Luke xvii. 29, 30; Gen. xix. 24. "If any man worship the beast and his image,—he shall be tormented with *fire and brimstone*," Apoc. xiv. 9, 10. "And the beast, and with him the false prophet and the devil, were cast alive into a lake of *fire burning with brimstone*," Apoc. xix. 20; xx. 10; xxi. 8. "The breath of Jehovah like a stream of *brimstone* doth kindle it," Isaiah xxx. 33. "And that the whole land thereof is *brimstone*, and salt and *burning*, that it is not sown, neither shall it bring forth any grass like the overthrow of Sodom and Gomorrah," Deut. xxix. 21, 23. *Brimstone* shall be scattered over the habitation of the wicked, Job xviii. 15.

453. *By these three was the third part of men killed, by the fire, and by the smoke, and by the brimstone, which issued out of their mouths*, signifies that from these it is, that the men of the church perish. A third part of men being killed, signifies that

the men of the church perish by the three things just now mentioned, n. 452; for by being killed, is signified to be killed spiritually, which is to perish as to the soul; and by a third part is signified all who are principled in those falses, which have been frequently enumerated above; what is signified by fire, smoke, and brimstone, and what by issuing out of their mouths, may be seen above, n. 452. To these falses may be ascribed the circumstance, that throughout Christendom it is not known that the fire here spoken of denotes the love of self and of the world, and that this love is the devil; also that the smoke issuing from this fire denotes the pride of self-derived intelligence, and that this pride is Satan; as also that brimstone kindled by this fire, by means of that pride, denotes the concupiscences of evil and falsity; and that these concupiscences are the crew of the devil and Satan, of which hell consists; and when ignorance prevails respecting these things it cannot be known what is a sin, for sin derives all its delight and pleasantness from them.

454. *For their power is in their mouth*, signifies that they only prevail by their discourse in confirmation of faith. By power in their mouth is signified power in discourse confirming doctrine; for neatness and elegance of language, pretended zeal, ingenious confirmation of what is false, especially from the appearances of truth in the Word, authority, closure of the understanding, and the like, effect every thing, whilst truth and the Word effect nothing; for truth shines before none, and the Word teaches none, but those who are principled in charity and thence in faith.

455. *For their tails were like unto serpents and had heads, and with them they hurt*, signifies the reason, because they are in a sensual and inverted state, speaking truths with their lips, but falsifying them by the principle which constitutes the head or chief doctrine of their religion, and thus they deceive. The same is here signified as above, by the locusts, n. 438, 439; but it is there said, that they had tails like scorpions, whereas here, like serpents, for they who are described by the locusts, speak and persuade from the Word, the sciences, and from erudition; but these only from arguments, which are appearances of truth and fallacies; and they who use such arguments ingeniously, and as it were wisely, do indeed deceive, but not in so great a degree. By serpents, in the Word, are signified sensual things, which are the ultimates of man's life, as above, n. 424; the reason is, because all animals signify the affections of man, wherefore also the affections of angels and spirits, in the spiritual world, appear at a distance as animals, and affections, merely sensual, as serpents; and this because serpents creep on the ground and lick the dust, and sensual things are the lowest of the understanding and will, being in close contact with the world, and nourished by its objects and delights, which only

affect the material senses of the body. Noxious serpents, which are of many kinds, signify the sensual things that are dependent on the evil affections which constitute the interiors of the mind with those who are insane through the falses of evil; and harmless serpents signify the sensual things that are dependent on the good affections, which constitute the interiors of the mind with those who are wise by virtue of the truths of good. Sensual things dependent on evil affections, are signified by serpents in these places: "They shall lick the dust like a *serpent*," Micah vii. 17. "And dust shall be the *serpent's* meat," Isaiah lxv. 25. Unto the *serpent* it was said, "Upon thy belly shalt thou go, and dust shalt thou eat all the days of thy life," Gen. iii. 14. The sensual principle is so described, because, communicating as it does with hell, where all are sensual, it, in things spiritual, changes celestial wisdom into infernal insanity. "Rejoice not thou, whole Palestina,—for out of the *serpent's* root shall come forth a cockatrice, and his fruit shall be a fiery flying serpent," Isaiah xiv. 29. "They hatch *cockatrice'* eggs,—he that eateth of their eggs dieth, and that which is crushed breaketh out into a viper,' Isaiah lix. 5. Because the sons of Israel desired to return into Egypt, they were bit by *serpents*, Numb. xxi. 1—10. To return into Egypt, signifies from spiritual to become sensual; therefore it is said, The hirelings of Egypt turned themselves away, " the voice thereof shall go like the voice of a *serpent*," Jerem. xlvi. 22. Because Dan was the last of the tribes, and thence signified the ultimate of the church, which is the sensual principle subject to the interiors, therefore it is said of him, "*Dan shall be a serpent* by the way that biteth the horses' heels, so that his rider shall fall backward," Gen. xlix. 17. By the horses' heels are signified the ultimates of the understanding, which are sensual; by biting is signified to adhere to them; by horseman, or rider, is signified the defect of knowledge from them whereby truths are perverted, for which reason it is said, His rider shall fall backward. As sensual men are crafty and cunning, like foxes, therefore the Lord says, Be ye wise as *serpents*, Matt. x. 16; for the sensual man speaks and reasons from appearances and fallacies, and if he has a talent for disputation can ingeniously confirm every falsity, and also the heresy of faith alone; though in discerning truth it is scarcely possible for any one to be so dull and slow of comprehension.

456. *And the rest of the men who were not killed by these plagues*, signifies those in the reformed church who are not so spiritually dead from visionary reasonings and from self-love, and from the pride of self-derived intelligence, and from the concupiscences thence proceeding, as the former, and yet make faith alone the head of their religion. By the rest of the men are meant they who are not as the former, but yet make faith alone the head of their religion; who were not killed, signifies

who are not so spiritually dead; by these plagues are meant self-love, the pride of self-derived intelligence, and the concupiscences of evil and falsity flowing from them; these three being signified by fire, smoke, and brimstone, concerning which above, n. 432, 453. That such is the signification of plagues, will be seen below. But something must first be said respecting this class of persons, whom also it has been granted me to see and to converse with. "They dwell in the northern quarter towards the west, where some of them have cottages with roofs, and some without roofs; their beds are of bulrushes, their garments of goat's hair. In the light flowing-in from heaven their faces appear stupid and also livid. The reason is, because they know nothing more about religion than that there is a God, that there are three persons, that Christ suffered for them on the cross, and that it is faith alone by which they are saved; and likewise by worship in temples, and by prayers at stated times: as to any thing else relating to religion and its doctrine, they pay no attention whatever; for the worldly and corporeal things, with which their minds are filled and overcharged, close up their ears against their admission. There are many of the Presbyters among them, whom I asked, 'What do you think, when you read in the Word of works, of love and charity, of fruits, of the precepts of life, of repentance, in short, of things that are to be done?' They replied, That they did indeed read them, and thus saw them; but still they did not see them, because they kept their minds fixed upon faith alone, and therefore thought that all these were faith, and did not perceive that they were effects of faith. That such ignorance and stupidity prevails with those who have embraced faith alone, and made it the all of their religion, is scarcely credible; nevertheless it has been permitted me to have abundant experience of the fact." That by plagues are meant spiritual plagues, by means of which man dies as to his spirit or soul, is evident from these passages: "Thy bruise is desperate, thy *plague* is grievous, for I will restore health unto thee, I will heal thee of thy *plagues*," Jerem. xxx. 12, 14, 17. "Every one that goeth by Babylon, shall hiss at all her *plagues*," Jerem. l. 13. "In one day shall *plagues* come upon Babylon, death and mourning," Apoc. xviii. 8. "I saw seven angels having the seven last *plagues*, for in them is filled up the wrath of God," Apoc. xv. 1. "Ah! sinful nation, a people laden with iniquity,—from the sole of the foot even unto the head, there is no soundness in it, but wounds, and bruises, and recent *plagues*: they have not been closed, nor bound up, nor mollified with ointment," Isaiah i. 4, 6. "In the day that Jehovah bindeth up the breach of his people, and healeth the stroke of their *plague*," Isaiah xxx. 26; besides other places; as in Deut. xxviii. 59; Jerem. xlix. 17; Zech. xiv. 12, 15; Luke vii. 21; Apoc. xi. 6; xvi. 21.

457. *Yet repented not of the works of their hands*, signifies that neither did they shun the things that are proper to themselves, which are evils of every kind, as sins. By the works of a man's hands, are signified the things proper to man, which are evils and consequent falses, because by hand are signified those things, in the aggregate, which proceed from man; for the powers of the mind, and thence of its body, are determined to the hands and there terminate; wherefore by hands, in the Word, is signified power: consequently, by the works of a man's hands, the things proper to him are signified, which are evils and falses of all kinds; the things proper to his will are evils, and the things proper to his understanding are falses flowing from them. It is said of those who are here treated of, that they repented not; the reason is, because they who make faith alone the all of religion, say in themselves, What need is there of repentance, when by faith alone sins are remitted, and we are saved? Of what avail are our own works in this matter? I know that I was born in sin, and that I am a sinner; if I confess this, and pray that my faults may not be imputed to me, is not the work of repentance then performed, and what need is there for any thing more? Thus he has no thought at all about sins, and comes at length not to know that there is any such thing as sin; wherefore he is continually borne along within them and into them, by the delight and pleasantness which flow from them, in like manner as a ship is carried by a fair wind and tide toward the rocks, whilst the pilot and mariners are asleep. By the works of men's hands, in the Word, in its natural sense, are meant graven images, molten images, and idols; but, in the spiritual sense, they signify evils and falses of every kind, which are the things proper to man; as in these passages: Provoke me not to anger by the *works of your hands;* if ye provoke me to anger by the *works of your hands*, to your own hurt, "I will recompense them according to their deeds, and according to the *works of their own hands*," Jerem. xxv. 6, 7, 14. "For the children of Israel have provoked me to anger with the *work of their hands*," Jerem. xxxii. 30; xliv. 8. "And I will utter my judgments against them touching all their wickedness, because they have worshipped the *works of their own hands*," Jerem. i. 16. In that day their eyes shall look up to the Holy One of Israel, and not to altars—the *work of their hands*, and which their *fingers have made*, Isaiah xvii. 7, 8; xxxi. 7; xxxvii. 19; Jerem. x. 9. That the work of man's hands is his selfhood, and thence evil and falsity, may appear manifestly from this consideration, that on this account it was forbidden to build the altar and temple with hewn stones, or to lift up an iron tool upon them, for this would signify the work of men's hands: "And if thou wilt make me an altar of stone, thou shalt not build it of hewn stone, for if thou lift up thy *tool*

upon it, thou hast polluted it," Exod. xx. 25. Joshua built an altar of stones, over which he did not *lift up any iron*, Joshua viii. 30, 31. The temple of Jerusalem was built of "stone made ready, so that there was neither hammer nor axe, nor any *tool of iron* heard, while it was building," 1 Kings vi. 7. All things which are done by the Lord, are also called the works of his hands, which are proper to him, and in themselves are goods and truths, as in these passages: The *works of Jehovah's hands* are truth and judgment, Psalm cxi. 7. "Thy mercy, O Jehovah, endureth for ever, forsake not the *works of thine own hands*," Psalm cxxxviii. 8. "Thus saith Jehovah, the Holy One of Israel and his Maker, Ask me of things to come, concerning my sons, and concerning the *work of my hands* command ye me," Isaiah xlv. 11. "Thy people shall be all righteous,—the branch of my planting, the *work of my hands*," Isaiah lx. 21. "But now, O Jehovah, thou art our Father; we are clay, and thou our potter, and we all are the *work of thy hands*," Isaiah lxiv. 8.

458. *That they should not worship demons*, signifies that thus they are in the evils of their concupiscences, and make one with their like in hell. By demons are signified the concupiscences of evil springing from the love of the world; the reason is, because in hell they are called demons who are in those concupiscences; and men also, who are in the same, become demons after death; there is also a conjunction between them and such men; for every man is conjoined with spirits as to his affections, even to their making a one; from which circumstance it is evident, that to worship demons, is to sacrifice to those concupiscences from the love of them. Therefore he who invokes faith alone, as the head of his religion, or as his idol, remains in evil, by reason of his not searching out any evil in himself which he considers a sin, and consequently is not desirous of removing it by repentance; and as every evil is composed of concupiscences, being nothing but a fascicle or bundle of them, it follows, that he who does not search out any evil in himself, and shun it as a sin against God, which can only be done by repentance, becomes a demon after death. Nothing but such concupiscences are signified by demons in the following passages: "They sacrificed unto *devils*, not to God," Deut. xxxii. 17. The children of Israel no longer sacrificed to the *devils*, after which they went a whoring, Levit. xvii. 7; Psalm cvi. 37. "The wild beast of the desert and of the islands (Ziim and Ijim) shall meet, and the *demon of the woods* shall cry to his fellow," Isaiah xxxiv. 14. "But the wild beasts of the desert (Ziim) shall lie there, and their houses shall be full of doleful creatures (Ochim), and the daughters of the owl shall dwell there, and the *demons of the woods* shall dance there," Isaiah xiii. 21. By Ziim, Ijim, Ochim, and the daughters of the owl,

are signified various concupiscences; wood demons are such concupiscences as appertain to priapuses and satyrs. *Babylon is become the habitation of devils, and the hold of every unclean spirit,* Apoc. xviii. 2. The demons which the Lord cast out, were such concupiscences, when they lived in the world, concerning which, see Matthew viii. 16, 28; ix. 32, 33; x. 8; xii. 22; xv. 22; Mark i. 32—34; Luke iv. 33—38, 41; viii. 2, 26, 40; ix. 1, 37—44—50; xiii. 32.

459. *And idols of gold, and silver, and brass, and stone, and wood,* signifies that thus they are in worship grounded in mere falses. By idols, in the Word, are signified the falses of worship, and therefore to worship them signifies worship from falses; and by adoring idols of gold, silver, brass, stone, and wood, is signified worship from falses of all kinds, and, taken collectively, worship from mere falses; moreover, the materials of which idols were made, their forms, and their garments, among the ancients, represented the falses of religion, from which their worship was performed; idols of gold signified falses concerning divine things; idols of silver, falses concerning spiritual things; idols of brass, falses concerning charity; idols of stone, falses concerning faith; and idols of wood, falses concerning good works. All these falses exist in those who do not do the work of repentance, that is, shun evils as sins against God. Graven images and molten images, which were idols, have this signification, in the spiritual sense, in the following passages: "Every man is brutish in his knowledge: every founder is confounded by the *graven image:* for his *molten image* is falsehood, and there is no breath in them. They are vanity, and the work of errors: in the time of their visitation shall they perish," Jerem. x. 14, 15; li. 17, 18. *Graven images* are the work of the hands of the workman, they speak not, they are altogether brutish and foolish, the *wood* is a discipline of vanities, the whole a work of cunning men, Jerem. x. 3—5, 8—10. "What profiteth the *graven image,* that the maker and a teacher of lies hath graven it, that the maker of his work trusteth therein; and there is no breath at all in the midst of it," Habak. ii. 18—20. "In that day a man shall cast his *idols of silver and his idols of gold,* which they made each one for himself to worship, to the moles and to the bats," Isaiah ii. 18, 20. "And have made them *molten images* of their silver, and *idols* according to their own understanding, the work of the craftsmen," Hosea xiii. 2. "Then will I sprinkle clean water upon you, and ye shall be clean from all your filthiness, and from all your *idols,*" Ezek. xxxvi. 25. Clean water is truth; idols are the falses of worship. "Ye shall defile also the covering of your *graven images of silver,* and the ornament of thy *molten images of gold,* thou shalt cast them away as a menstruous cloth, thou shalt say unto it, Get thee hence," Isaiah xxx. 22. Nor is any thing else but

the falses of religion and thence of worship signified by the *gods* of *gold*, of *silver*, of *brass*, of *iron*, of *wood*, and of *stone*, which Belshazzar king of Babylon praised (worshipped) when he drank wine with his princes, his wives, and his concubines, out of the vessels of gold and of silver from the temple in Jerusalem, Dan. v. 1—5, and following verses; besides many other places; as in Isaiah x. 10, 11; xxi. 9; xxxi. 7; xl. 19, 20; xli. 29; xlii. 17; xlviii. 5; Jerem. viii. 19; l. 38, 39; Ezek. vi. 4, 5; xiv. 3—6; Micah i. 7; v. 13; Psalm cxv. 4, 5; Psalm cxxxv. 15, 16; Levit. xxvi. 30. By idols, the falses of worship from self-derived intelligence are strictly signified; the manner in which man fashions them, and afterwards accommodates them, so as to appear like truths, is fully described in Isaiah xliv. 9, 10.

460. *Which neither can see, nor hear, nor walk,* signifies in which there is nothing of spiritual and truly rational life. The reason why this is said, is, because idolaters believe that their idols see and hear, for they make them gods: still this is not the meaning of these words; but, that in the falses of worship there is nothing of spiritual nor truly rational life, for by seeing and hearing is signified to understand and perceive, n. 7, 25, 87; and by walking is signified to live, 167; therefore by these three things is signified spiritual and truly rational life: this is signified, because by idols are signified the falses of worship, in which there is nothing of spiritual and rational life. That idols do not see, and hear, and walk, is a thing too obvious to be here mentioned, were there not some inward signification involved within it. The like is also said of idols in other parts of the Word, as in these passages: "They have not known nor understood, for he hath shut their eyes—that they cannot see, and their hearts that they cannot understand," Isaiah xliv. 18, 20. They speak not, neither do they walk, Jerem. x. 3—10. "They have mouths but they speak not, eyes have they but they see not," Psalm cxv. 5; Psalm cxxxv. 15, 16; by which like things are signified, because by idols are signified the falses of worship; and in falses of worship there is nothing of life which is really life.

461. *Neither repented they of their murders, nor of their sorceries, nor of their fornication, nor of their thefts,* signifies that the heresy of faith alone induces on their hearts stupidity, tergiversation, and hardness, so that they do not think any thing of the precepts of the decalogue, nor indeed of any sin, that it ought to be shunned because it is in favour of the devil and against God. What murders, adulteries, and thefts, signify in every sense, may be seen in *The Doctrine of Life for the New Jerusalem from the Precepts of the Decalogue,* where it is explained; therefore it is unnecessary to repeat it here; but what is signified by sorceries, shall be explained in the following article. Faith alone induces stupidity, tergiversation, and hard-

ness of heart, in those who are in the reformed church, because the good of life does not constitute religion where faith alone prevails: and if religion does not consist in good of life, then the second table of the decalogue, which is the table of repentance, is like a blank, whereon nothing is written. That the second table of the decalogue is a table of repentance, is evident, because it is not there said that good works are to be done, but that evil works are not to be done, as, Thou shalt not kill, thou shalt not commit adultery, thou shalt not steal, thou shalt not bear false witness, thou shalt not covet thy neighbour's goods; and if these things do not constitute religion, the result is as here stated: "Neither repented they of their murders, nor of their sorceries, nor of their fornication, nor of their thefts." That good of life does not constitute religion where faith alone prevails, will be clearly shown in what follows.

462. Since at this day it is not known what is meant by *sorceries*, it shall briefly be explained. *Sorceries* are mentioned in the above passage, in place of the eighth precept in the decalogue, THOU SHALT NOT BEAR FALSE WITNESS, for the three other evils, which are murders, fornications, and thefts, are there named. To bear false witness signifies, in the natural sense, to act the part of a false witness, to lie and defame; and in the spiritual sense, to confirm and persuade that what is false is true, and that what is evil is good; from which it is evident, that by sorcery is signified to persuade to what is false, and thus to destroy truth. Sorceries were in use among the ancients, and were performed in three ways: first, by keeping the hearing and thus the mind of another continually intent upon his words and sayings, without retaining aught from them; and, at the same time, by an aspiration and inspiration of thought conjoined with affection, by means of the breath, into the sound of the voice, whereby the hearer is incapable of thinking any thing from himself; in this manner did the lovers of falsehood pour in their falses with violence. Secondly, they infused a persuasion, which was done by detaining the mind from every thing of a contrary nature, and directing the attention exclusively to the idea involved in that which was uttered by themselves, hence the spiritual sphere of his mind dispelled the spiritual sphere of the mind of another, and stifled it: this was the kind of spiritual fascination which the magi of old made use of, and which was spoken of as the tying up and binding the understanding. The latter kind of sorcery pertained only to the spirit or thought, but the former to the lips or speech also. Thirdly, the hearer kept his mind so fixed in his own opinion, that he almost shut his ears against hearing any thing from the speaker, which was done by holding the breath, and sometimes by a tacit muttering, and thus by a continual negation of his adversary's sentiment. This kind of sorcery was practised by those who heard

others, but the two former by those who spake to others. These three kinds of sorceries prevailed among the ancients, and prevail still among infernal spirits; but with men in the world there remains only the third kind, and this with those, who from the pride of their own intelligence, have confirmed in themselves the falses of religion; for these, when they hear things contrary, admit them no further into their thought than to mere contact, and then from the interior recess of their mind they emit as it were fire which consumes them, about which the other knows nothing except by conjecture drawn from the countenance and the sound of the voice in the reply, provided the sorcerer does not, by dissimulation, restrain that fire, or what is the same, the anger of his pride. This kind of sorcery operates at the present day, to prevent truths from being accepted, and, with many, to their not being understood. That in ancient times many magical arts prevailed, and among these, sorceries, is evident from Moses: "When thou art come into the land, thou shalt not learn to do after the abominations of those nations, there shall not be found among you one that maketh his son or his daughter to pass through the fire, or that useth divinations, or an observer of times, or an enchanter, or a witch, or a *charmer of incantations*, and a consulter with familiar spirits, or a wizard, or a necromancer; for all these things are an abomination unto Jehovah," Deut. xviii. 9—11. A persuasion of the false, and consequently the destruction of truth, is signified by sorceries in these passages: "Thy wisdom and thy knowledge hath perverted thee, therefore shall evil come upon thee; stand now with thine *incantations*, and with the multitude of thy *sorceries*," Isaiah xlvii. 10—12. "By the *sorceries* of Babylon all nations were deceived," Apoc. xviii. 23. "Without are dogs, *sorcerers*, whoremongers, murderers," Apoc. xxii. 15. Joram said to Jehu, "Is it peace? and he answered, What peace, so long as the whoredoms of thy mother Jezebel, and her *sorceries* are so many?" 2 Kings ix. 22. By her whoredoms are signified falsifications, n. 134; and, by her incantations and sorceries, destructions of truth by means of false persuasions. On the other hand, incantation signifies the rejection of falsity by truths, which was also effected by tacitly thinking and whispering, from a zeal for truth in opposition to falsehood, as is plain from these passages: Jehovah will take away from Jerusalem the mighty man, the man of war, the counsellor, the cunning artificer, the skilful in *incantation*, Isaiah iii. 1—3. "Their poison is like the poison of the deaf adder, she stoppeth her ears that she may not hear the voice of silent murmuring, the charmers of *the incantations* of the wise," Psalm lviii. 5, 6. "Behold, I send serpents, cockatrices among you, against which there is no *incantation*," Jerem. viii. 17. "In trouble have they visited thee, they poured out a *secret prayer*," Isaiah xxvi. 16.

463. To the above I will add this Memorable Relation. I was once looking towards the sea-coast, in the spiritual world, when I observed a grand dock or arsenal for shipping: I walked towards it, and, taking a nearer view, I saw vessels of various sizes, laden with all kinds of merchandise, which was liberally distributed to all comers, by some boys and girls that sat on the decks. And I heard those boys and girls say, "We are in expectation of seeing our beautiful turtles, which will soon rise out of the sea, and come to us." And lo! I saw turtles of different sizes, both great and small, on whose shells and scales there sat young turtles, which looked towards the islands that surrounded the coast. The parent turtles had two heads, one of large size, covered over with a shell, like that which covered their bodies, so that they were of a glowing polish, and the other of small size, such as turtles generally have, which they drew back into the fore part of the body, and inserted it, in a manner scarcely discernible, into the larger head. I kept my eyes fixed on one of the large shining heads, and observed that it had a face like that of a man, and that it talked with the boys and girls that were sitting on the decks, and licked their hands; whereupon the boys and girls gently stroked them, and gave them food and dainties, with various precious articles, as silk for clothes, almug wood for tables, purple for ornaments, and scarlet for colouring. Having made these observations, I was desirous to learn what each thing represented, because I knew that all appearances in the spiritual world are correspondences, and represent something spiritual coming down from heaven: and immediately angels entered into conversation with me from heaven, and said, "Thou knowest already what is represented by a dock or arsenal for shipping, and also what by ships, and by boys and girls on their decks; but thou dost not know what is signified by the turtles. Understand, therefore, that the turtles represent such of the clergy as entirely separate faith from charity and its good works, affirming, in their own minds, that there is no sort of conjunction between them whatever, but that the Holy Spirit, through faith in God the Father, for the sake of his Son's merits, enters into man, and purifies his interiors, till it reaches to man's own will, of which will they make, as it were, an oval plane, supposing that when the operation of the Holy Spirit approaches that plane, it turns itself about on its left side, and never enters into contact with it, and that thus the interior or superior part of the human faculties is intended for God, and the exterior or inferior part for man; and, consequently, that nothing which man does appears in God's sight, whether it be good or evil, the good not appearing because it is meritorious, nor the evil because it is evil, whence if either were to appear, the man would inevitably perish; but as they are there kept out of sight, they suppose

that it is allowable for a man to will, to think, to speak, and to act, as he pleases, having nothing to guard against but worldly censures and punishments." I then asked, whether such persons assert also, that it is allowable to think of God as not being omnipresent and omniscient: and the angels replied, "This also is allowable according to their maxims, since God, with such as have obtained faith, and are thereby purified and justified, does not look at any thing belonging to their thought and will; and they still retain, in the inner chamber or superior regions of their mind, or faculties, that faith which they had received in its first act or operation, which act, they insist, may some time or other return, without their knowing any thing of the matter. These tenets are what are represented by the small head, which they draw into the fore part of the body, and also insert in the great head, whilst they talk with the laity; for their discourses with such persons do not proceed from the small head, but from the great one, which appears in front, with a face resembling that of a man: and they converse with them from the Word about love, charity, good works, the commandments of the decalogue, and repentance; in which discourses they quote from the Word almost all that is said on these subjects, but at times they put the small head into the great one, and think with themselves in the former, that these duties are not to be performed for the sake of God and salvation, but only with a view to the public good, or private advantage. Since, however, their discourses on such occasions are pleasing and elegant, particularly when they speak about the gospel, the operation of the Holy Spirit, and the nature of salvation; therefore they appear to their hearers like handsome and comely persons, of a wisdom superior to the rest of mankind; and this is the reason why, as thou observedst, the boys and girls on the decks of the ships gave them delicate food and other things of value. These, then, are they whom thou sawest represented as turtles. In the world where thou livest, they are hardly to be distinguished from other people, save in this respect, that they fancy themselves wiser than others, and treat the rest of mankind with contempt, even those who profess the same doctrine respecting faith as themselves, but do not dive so deep into its mysteries. They carry about them a particular mark or badge, in their clothes, by which they are known to one another. I shall not tell thee," said my angelic instructor, "what are their sentiments in regard to other subjects connected with their faith, as election, free-will, baptism, and the holy supper; which are such as they never divulge, but yet are known to us in heaven. This, however, being their nature and quality in the world, and no one being permitted, after death, to think one thing and say another, therefore when they come into another world, where they cannot refrain from uttering all their wild and extravagant conceits, they are considered as insane; and they are expelled from all societies, and are at length cast down into the bottomless pit, mentioned in the Revelation ix. 2, where they become corporeal spirits, and appear like Egyptian mummies; for the interiors of their minds contract a hard callous covering, by reason of the barrier which they themselves had placed between the two regions of their minds while in the world. The infernal society, consisting of such spirits, is in the neighbourhood of that of the Machiavelists; and they are continually passing from one to the other, and calling one another fellow-companions; but they do not stay long with each other, because there is a diversity between them, arising from the circumstance, that some sort of religious impression, connected with their notion concerning the act of justification by faith, had been cherished by the former, whilst the Machiavelists had rejected every thing of the kind."

After I had seen these spirits expelled from the societies, and collected together, in order to be cast down into the bottomless pit, I observed a ship flying in the air, having seven sails, and in it officers and sailors clad in purple garments, with caps magnificently adorned with laurel, who exclaimed, with a loud voice, "Lo, we are in heaven! we are the truly learned, distinguished above others by our purple robes, and our grand laurel wreaths, because we are the chief of the wise from all the clergy in Europe." I was wondering what this exhibition could mean, when I was informed that it arose from the conceited images, and ideal thoughts called phantasies, that proceeded from those who had before appeared as turtles, and who were now expelled from every society, as persons insane, and collected in a body into one place. I was straightway seized with a desire to converse with them, and accordingly walked towards the place where they were assembled, and paid my respects to them, and said, "Are ye the people who have separated the internals of men from their externals, and the operation of the Holy Spirit as being within faith, from its co-operation with man's, as having nothing to do with faith, and who have thus separated God from man? Have ye not, by so doing, not only separated charity and its works from faith, as many other teachers among the clergy have done, but also faith itself, as to its manifestation in the sight of God, from man? But, in discussing this subject with you, which do you prefer, that I should draw my arguments from reason, or from the Sacred Scriptures?" And they said, "Begin with reason." So I proceeded, saying, "How is it possible for the internal and external of man to be separated from each other? Who does not, or cannot, see plainly by virtue of a perception common to all men, that all the interiors of man proceed and are continued to his exteriors, and even to his most external, in order to produce their effects and perform their works? Do not internal things exist for the sake of external, that they may be terminated by them, and subsist in them, and thus exist, just as a column does upon its pedestal? How plain is it to see, that unless there was such a continuation and consequent conjunction, the things most external must be dissolved and melt to nothing, like bubbles in the air? Who can deny that the interior operations of God in man are myriads of myriads, utterly unknown to man himself? And what signifies it, if they be unknown or not, provided only that what is extreme and most external be known, in which man, with his thought and will, is together with God? But let us illustrate this matter by an example: Is a man at all acquainted with the operations of his faculty of speech, as, how the lungs draw in the air, and thereby fill the vesicles, the bronchia, and the lobes; how they emit it into the trachea, and there convert it into sound; how the sound is modified in the glottis by the assistance of the larynx; and how the tongue afterwards articulates it, and the lips complete the articulation, in order to its becoming speech? Do not all these interior operations, of which man is altogether unconscious, exist for the sake of the last or most external, which is articulate discourse? If you remove or separate any one of those internal operations, so as to destroy its connexion with the last, or most external, would it not be as impossible for man to speak, as for a stock or a stone? Take another example;—the two hands are the ultimate or extreme parts of the human body; but do not the interior, which are continued to them, descend from the head through the neck, and also through the breast, the shoulders, the arms, and the fore-arms? Are there not innumerable muscular textures, innumerable orders of moving fibres, innumerable collections of nerves and blood-vessels, with several bony articulations with their ligaments and membranes, of which man is utterly unconscious? And yet, are not all and every one of these unknown parts necessary to the operation of the hands? Supposing those interior parts to be reflected back to the right or left about the elbow-joint, and not to be continued below, would not the hand, in such case, necessarily fall from the joint, and putrefy, like something inanimate that was separated from all connexion with the source of its life? Doubtless, under such circumstances, it would be with the hand as it is with the body, when a man is beheaded. Just so would it be also with the human mind, and with its two lives, the will and the understanding, supposing the divine operations, which relate to faith and charity, should stop in the middle of their course, and not proceed by continued connexion to the man himself; in such case, man would be not only a brute-animal, but a rotten branch broken off from its parent stock. Thus far I have explained to you the dictates of reason, in regard to this subject; I shall now show you, if ye are disposed to hear me, that the Sacred Scripture inculcates the same doctrine; for does not the Lord say, 'Abide in me, and I in you: I am the vine, ye are the branches: He that abideth in me, and I in him, the same bringeth forth much fruit?' John vii. 4, 5. Does not fruit mean the good works, which the Lord operates by man; and which man operates of himself from the Lord? Again, the Lord says, 'Behold! I stand at the door and knock; if any man will open the door, I will come into him and sup with him, and he with me,' Rev. iii. 20. Does not the Lord give pounds and talents to the intent that men should trade with them and make profit of them, and in proportion to such profit should receive eternal life? Matt. xv. 14—34; Luke xix. 13—26. And again: Does not he give to every one according to the work which he does in his vineyard? Matt. xx. 1—17. But these are only a few passages, selected out of many; for it would be easy to fill sheets with extracts from the Word, insisting that man ought to bear fruit like a tree; that he ought to work in obedience to the commandments; that he ought to love God and his neighbour, and the like. I am well aware, however, that your own intelligence, grounded in your proprium or selfhood, cannot have any thing in common with the contents of the Word, according to their true and proper sense, and, therefore, notwithstanding you can introduce such passages into your discourse, yet the ideas you attach to them are such as pervert them; and this is a necessary consequence of your removing all things that are of God from man, as to communication and conjunction: what more can you reject, unless you also abandon all things belonging to worship?" After I had ended these words, the assembly appeared to me in the light of heaven, which detects and manifests the true nature and quality of every one; and then they no longer seemed floating aloft in a ship, as if exalted into heaven, nor clothed in purple, nor crowned with laurel wreaths, but in a sandy place, in tattered garments, having their loins girt about with nets like those used by fishermen, through which their nakedness appeared: and then they sunk down to the society bordering on the Machiavelists.

CHAPTER X.

1. AND I saw another mighty angel coming down from heaven, clothed with a cloud; and a rainbow was over his head, and his face was as it were the sun, and his feet as pillars of fire.

2. And he had in his hand a little book open. And he set his right foot upon the sea, and his left upon the earth,

3. And cried with a loud voice, as when a lion roareth. And when he cried, seven thunders uttered their voices.

4. And when the seven thunders had uttered their voices, I was about to write: and I heard a voice from heaven saying unto me, Seal up those things which the seven thunders uttered, and write them not.

5. And the angel whom I saw standing upon the sea and upon the earth lifted up his hand to heaven,

6. And sware by him that liveth for ever and ever, who created heaven, and the things that therein are, and the earth, and the things that therein are, and the sea, and the things that are therein, that there should be time no longer:

7. But in the days of the voice of the seventh angel, when he is about to sound, the mystery of God should be finished; as he hath declared to his servants the prophets.

8. And the voice which I heard from heaven, spake unto me again, and said, Go, take the little book, which is open in the hand of the angel who is standing upon the sea and upon the earth.

9. And I went unto the angel, and said unto him, Give me the little book. And he said unto me, Take it, and eat it up; and it shall make thy belly bitter, but it shall be in thy mouth sweet as honey.

10. And I took the little book out of the angel's hand, and ate it up; and it was in my mouth sweet as honey; and when I had eaten it, my belly was bitter.

11. And he said unto me, Thou must prophesy again before many peoples, and nations, and tongues, and kings.

THE SPIRITUAL SENSE.

THE CONTENTS OF THE WHOLE CHAPTER. The exploration and manifestation of those who are in the reformed church is still treated of; in the present chapter, what their belief is concerning the Lord, as to his being the God of heaven and earth, as he himself taught in Matthew xxviii. 18; and as to his Humanity being divine; that these articles of belief are not received in those churches; and that it is no easy matter for them to be received, so long as a belief in justification by faith alone is so strongly fixed in their hearts.

THE CONTENTS OF EACH VERSE. V. 1, "And I saw another mighty angel coming down from heaven," signifies the Lord in divine majesty and power: "Clothed with a cloud, and a rainbow was over his head," signifies his divine natural and his divine spiritual principles: "And his face was as it were the sun," signifies divine love, and at the same time divine wisdom: "And his feet as pillars of fire," signifies the Lord's divine natural principle, as to divine love, which sustains all things: v. 2, "And he had in his hand a little book open," signifies the Word as to this doctrinal point therein, that the Lord is the God of heaven and earth, and that his Humanity is divine: "And he set his right foot upon the sea, and his left upon the earth," signifies that the Lord has the universal church under his auspices and dominion: v. 3, "And cried with a loud voice, as when a lion roareth," signifies grievous lamentation by reason of the church being taken from him: "And when he cried, seven thunders uttered their voices," signifies that the Lord revealed throughout the universal heaven what was in the little book: v. 4, "And when the seven thunders had uttered their voices, I was about to write: and I heard a voice from heaven, saying unto me, Seal up those things which the seven thunders uttered, and write them not," signifies that these things indeed are made manifest, but that they will not be received till after they wh are meant by the dragon, the beast, and the false prophet, are cast out of the world of spirits, because there would be danger were they to be received before: v. 5, "And the angel whom I saw standing upon the sea and upon the earth lifted up his hand to heaven (v. 6), and sware by him that liveth for ever and ever," signifies the attestation and testification of the Lord by himself: "Who created heaven, and the things that therein are, and the earth, and the things that therein are, and the sea, and the things that are therein," signifies, who vivifies all that are in heaven and that are in the church, and every thing in general and in particular with them: "That there should be time no longer," signifies that there cannot be any state of the church, or any church, except one God be acknowledged, and that the Lord is that God: v. 7, "But in the days of the voice of the seventh angel, when he is about to sound," signifies the final exploration and manifestation of the state of the church which must perish, unless a new one be established by the Lord: "The mystery of God should be finished, as he hath declared to his servants the prophets," signifies that then it will appear, that it is foretold in the Word of both Testaments, but has hitherto been concealed, that after the last judgment is executed upon those who have devastated the church, the Lord's kingdom will come: v. 8, "And the voice which I heard from heaven, spake unto me again, and said, Go, take the little book, which is open in the hand of the angel who is standing upon the sea and upon the earth," signifies a command from heaven, that they should admit that doctrine, but that it should be made manifest by John how it would be received in the church, before they who are meant by the dragon, the beast, and the false prophet, are removed: v. 9, "And I went unto the angel, and said unto him, Give me the little book," signifies a motion, or inclination of the mind, with many, to receive the doctrine: "And he said unto me, Take it, and eat it, and it shall make thy belly bitter, but it shall be in thy mouth sweet as honey," signifies that reception from the acknowledgment that the Lord is the Saviour and Redeemer, is grateful and pleasing, but that the acknowledgment that he alone is the God of heaven and earth, and that his Humanity is divine, is unpleasing and difficult to relieve by reason of falsifications: v. 10, "And I took the little book out of the angel's hand, and ate it up; and it was in my mouth sweet as honey; and when I had eaten it, my belly was bitter," signifies that so it came to pass, and was thus manifested: v. 11, "And he said unto me, Thou must prophesy again before many peoples, and nations, and tongues, and kings," signifies that because it is so, the quality of those who are in faith alone must be further shown.

THE EXPLANATION.

464. IN this and the following chapter the Lord is treated of as being the God of heaven and earth, and that as to his Humanity also he is God; consequently that he is Jehovah himself. That this is the subject treated of in these two chapters, may be seen from their contents, as understood in a spiritual sense, and from their conclusion, chap. xi. 15—17.

465. *And I saw another mighty angel coming down from heaven*, signifies the Lord in divine majesty and power. That this angel is the Lord, is evident from the description of him, as being encompassed with a cloud, a rainbow over his head, his face as the sun, his feet like columns of fire, and that he set his feet upon the sea and upon the earth; as also that he cried with a loud voice as when a lion roareth, and spake as thunder. He was seen as an angel, because he appears in the heavens and below the heavens, when he manifests himself, as an angel; for he fills some angel with his Divinity in accommodation to the reception of those to whom he gives to see him. His presence itself, such as he is in himself or in his own essence, cannot be supported by any angel, much less by any man; wherefore he appears above the heavens as a sun, at a distance from the angels, as the sun of this world is from men; there he dwells in his Divinity from eternity, and at the same time in his Divine Humanity, which are a one like soul and body. He

is here called a mighty angel from his divine power: and it is said, another angel, by reason of another divine attribute of his, different from the former, being here described.

466. *Clothed with a cloud; and a rainbow was over his head*, signifies his divine natural and divine spiritual principles. By the cloud with which he was clothed, is signified the divine natural principle; wherefore the Word in its natural sense, which also is from him, thus is his, and himself, is signified by cloud, n. 24; by a rainbow is signified the divine spiritual principle, and as this is above the natural, therefore the rainbow appeared over his head. It must be observed, that the Lord is present with men in his divine natural principle, but, with the angels of his spiritual kingdom, in his divine spiritual principle, and with the angels of his celestial kingdom, in his divine celestial principle; still he is not divided, but appears to every one according to his quality. The Lord's divine spiritual principle is also signified by the rainbow in Ezekiel: "And above the firmament (of the cherubs) was the likeness of a throne," and upon it the appearance of a man; and from the fire of his loins there was as it were the appearance of the *bow* which is in the cloud in the day of rain, "this was the appearance of the glory of Jehovah," i. 26, 28, 29. By a throne is signified heaven; by the man upon it, the Lord; by the fire of his loins, celestial love; and by the rainbow, divine truth spiritual, which also is of his divine wisdom. By the rainbow, of which it is written in Moses: "*I have set my bow in the cloud*, and it shall be for a token of a covenant between me and the earth," and when it shall be seen in the cloud, "I will remember my covenant," Gen. ix. 12—17, nothing else is meant but divine truth spiritual in the natural degree, with the man who is regenerated; for man, when he is regenerated, from natural becomes spiritual; and inasmuch as there is then a conjunction of the Lord with him, therefore it is said, that the bow in the cloud should be for a sign of a covenant; covenant signifying conjunction. That there is no conjunction of the Lord with man by rainbows, in the world, is evident.

467. *And his face was as it were the sun*, signifies divine love, and at the same time divine wisdom, as is evident from the explanation above, n. 53; where the same is said of the Son of Man.

468. *And his feet as pillars of fire*, signifies the Lord's divine natural principle as to divine love, which sustains all things. This also appears from the explanation above, at n. 49; where it is said of the Son of Man, that "*his feet* were like fine brass, as though they burned in a furnace." The reason why his feet seemed like pillars of fire is, because the Lord's divine natural principle, which in itself is the Divine Humanity which he took upon him in the world, sustains his Eternal Divinity, as the

body does the soul, and as the natural sense of the Word sustains its spiritual and celestial sense; on which subject see *The Doctrine of the New Jerusalem concerning the Sacred Scripture*, n. 27—49. That the feet signify what is natural, may be seen, n. 49; and that a pillar signifies support, n. 191. Fire signifies love, because spiritual fire is nothing else; therefore it is usual to pray, that heavenly fire may be kindled in the heart; that is, celestial love. That there is a correspondence between fire and love, may be known from this circumstance, that man grows warm from love, and grows cold from the privation thereof, there being nothing else that constitutes vital heat, but love in both senses; the origin of correspondences is from two suns, one in the heavens which is pure love, and the other in the world which is pure fire; hence, also, is derived the correspondence between all spiritual and natural things. Since fire signifies divine love, therefore Jehovah was seen by Moses on Mount Horeb in the bush on *fire*, Exod. iii. 1—3. And descended upon Mount Sinai in *fire*, Deut. iv. 36. And therefore the seven lamps of the candlestick in the tabernacle were *lighted up* every evening, that they might *burn* before Jehovah, Levit. xxiv. 2—4. And for the same reason, the *fire burned* continually upon the altar, and was never put out, Levit. vi. 9. And they took *fire* from the altar to put into their censers when incense was offered, Levit. xvi. 12, 13; Numb. xvi. 6, 12. Hence it was that Jehovah went before the children of Israel by night in a *pillar of fire*, Exod. xiii. 21, 22. That there was a *fire* by night over the tabernacle, Exod. xl. 38; Psalm cv. 37, 39; Isaiah iv. 5, 6. That *fire from heaven* consumed the burnt-offering upon the altar, as a sign of the Lord's being well pleased, Levit. ix. 24; 1 Kings xviii. 38. That the burnt-offering was called an offering made by *fire to Jehovah*, and an offering by *fire of an odour of rest to Jehovah*, Exod. xxix. 18; Levit. i. 9, 13, 17; ii. 2, 9, 10, 12; iii. 5, 16; iv. 31; v. 12; vi. 30; xxi. 6; Numb. xxxviii. 2; Deut. xviii. 1. That the eyes of the Lord seemed as a *flame of fire*, Apoc. i. 14; ii. 18; xix. 12; Dan. x. 5, 6. That seven *lamps of fire* burned before the throne, Apoc. iv. 5. Hence it is evident, what is signified by *lamps with oil* and without oil, Matt. xxv. 1—11. By oil is understood fire, and thus love; as also in many other passages. That fire, in an opposite sense, signifies infernal love, is evident from so many passages in the Word, that it is needless to adduce them by reason of their abundance: something may be seen on this subject in the work on *Heaven and Hell*, n. 566—575.

469. *And he had in his hand a little book open*, signifies the Word as to this doctrinal point therein, that the Lord is the God of heaven and earth, and that his Humanity is Divine. That by the Book, which the Lamb took from Him that sat on

the throne, and the seven seals of which he loosed, Apoc. v. 1, 7; vi. 1, is meant the Word, may be seen above, n. 256, 259, 295, and following; therefore by the little book in the hand of the angel, who also is the Lord, n. 465, nothing else is here meant but the Word as to some essential therein. That this is the doctrinal point in the Word, which teaches that the Lord is the God of heaven and earth, and that his Humanity is Divine, is evident from the spiritual sense of all the particulars in this and the following chapter, and also from the natural sense of the next or 11th chapter, verses 15—17. The little book is said to be open because that doctrine appears manifestly in the Word, and is evident to every one who reads it with attention. This is the subject now treated of, because it is the very essential of the New Church; the reason is, because on the knowledge and acknowledgment of God depends the salvation of every one; for, as was observed in the Preface, "The universal heaven, and the universal church on earth, and, in general, all religion, has its foundation in a just idea of God; because hereby there is conjunction, and by conjunction, light, wisdom, and eternal happiness." Since the Lord is the very God of heaven and earth, therefore no one, who does not acknowledge him, is admitted into heaven, for heaven is his body; but stands without, and is bit by serpents, that is, by infernal spirits, for whose bite there is no cure but that which the sons of Israel experienced by looking up to the brazen serpent, Numb. xxi. 1—10; by which is meant the Lord as to his Divine Humanity, as is plain from this passage in John: "And as Moses lifted up the *serpent* in the wilderness, even so must the *Son of Man* be lifted up; that whosoever believeth in him, should not perish, but have eternal life," John iii. 14, 15.

470. *And he set his right foot upon the sea, and his left upon the earth*, signifies that the Lord has the universal church, as well those therein who are in its externals, as those who are in its internals, under his auspices and dominion. By the sea and the earth is signified the universal church; by the sea, the external church, that is, they who are in its externals; and by the earth, the internal church, that is, they who are in its internals, n. 398. By setting his feet upon them, is signified to hold all in subjection to himself, consequently, under his divine auspices and dominion. Since the Lord's church on earth is beneath the heavens, therefore it is called his foot-stool, as in these places: "And cast down from heaven unto the earth the beauty of Israel, and remembered not his *foot-stool*," Lament. ii. 1. "And the earth is my *foot-stool*," Isaiah lxvi. 1. "We will go into his tabernacles: we will worship at his *foot-stool*," Psalm cxxxii. 7. Swear not at all; neither by heaven, for it is God's throne; nor by the *earth*, for it is his *foot-stool*, Matt. v. 34, 35. "I will make the *place of my feet* glorious," Isaiah lx

13. "Thou madest him to have dominion over the works of thy hands; thou hast put all things under his *feet*," Psalm viii. 6; speaking of the Lord. He set his right foot upon the sea, and his left upon the earth, because they who are in the externals of the church, have not so strongly confirmed themselves in falses, as they who are in its internals.

471. *And cried with a loud voice, as when a lion roareth*, signifies grievous lamentation by reason of the church being taken from him. That by crying with a loud voice as a lion roareth, is signified a grievous lamentation respecting the church, and this by reason of its being taken from him, is evident from what is explained in the foregoing chapter, where the states of life of those who are of the church were explored and laid open, which were lamentable; also from its being said in this chapter, that the angel sware by him that liveth for ever and ever, that there should be time no longer, by which is signified that there would be no church; and, in the following chapter, that the beast, which came up out of the bottomless pit, slew his two witnesses; and especially from his not being acknowledged and approached, although he is the God of heaven and earth. Lamentation concerning these things is signified by his roaring as a lion, for a lion roars when he sees his enemies and is assaulted by them, and when he sees his whelps and prey taken from him; so does the Lord, comparatively, when he sees his church taken from him by devils. That this is what is signified by roaring as a lion, may appear from these passages: "Like as the *lion* and the *young lion* roaring on his prey, when a multitude of shepherds is called forth against him, so shall Jehovah of hosts come down to fight for Mount Zion," Isaiah xxxi. 4. "Therefore is the anger of Jehovah kindled against his people, *his roaring is like a lion's, he roareth like the young lions*, yea, he shall war and lay hold of the prey: behold, darkness and sorrow, and the light is darkened in the heavens thereof," Isaiah v. 25—30. "Jehovah shall *roar* from on high, and utter his voice from his holy habitation, *he shall mightily roar* upon his habitation," Jerem. xxv. 30, 31. "Jehovah also shall *roar* out of Zion, and utter his voice from Jerusalem," Joel iii. 16. "I will not return to destroy Ephraim,—they shall walk after Jehovah; he shall *roar* like a lion; when he shall *roar*," Hosea xi. 9, 10. "The lion hath *roared*, who will not fear? the Lord Jehovah hath spoken, who can but prophesy?" Amos iii. 7, 8. God *roareth* with his voice, "he thundereth marvellously with his voice," Job xxxvii. 4, 5. That roaring signifies grievous lamentation, is evident from the following: "My bones waxed old through my *roaring* all the day long," Psalm xxxii. 3. "I am feeble and sore broken, I have *roared* by reason of the disquietness of my heart," Psalm xxxviii. 9. "For my sighing cometh

before I eat, and my *roarings* are poured out like the waters," Job iii. 24.

472. *And when he cried, seven thunders uttered their voices,* signifies that the Lord revealed throughout the universal heaven what was in the little book. This signification is evident, because it presently follows, that he was about to write what the seven thunders uttered, but was enjoined from heaven to seal it up and not to write it; and afterwards to eat up the little book; and that in his mouth it was sweet as honey, but that it made his belly bitter; by which is signified that such things were in it as could not yet be received: the reason may be seen in the following article. But I will show what was in the little book; it contained those things, for instance, which are to be found in *The Doctrine of the New Jerusalem concerning the Lord*, from beginning to end, which are as follows: That the whole Sacred Scripture relates to the Lord, and that the Lord is the Word, n. 1—7. That by the Lord's fulfilling all things of the law, is meant, that he fulfilled all things of the Word, n. 8—11. That the Lord came into the world to subdue the hells and glorify his Humanity, and that the passion of the cross was the last combat, by which he fully conquered the hells, and fully glorified his Humanity, n. 12—14. That the Lord, by the passion of the cross, did not take away sins, but that he bore them, n. 15—17. That the imputation of the Lord's merit is nothing else but the remission of sins after repentance, n. 18. That the Lord, as to his Divine Humanity, is called the Son of God, and, as to the Word, he is called the Son of Man, n. 19—28. That the Lord made his Humanity Divine from the Divinity in himself; and that thus he became one with the Father, n. 29—36. That the Lord is God himself, from whom the Word is derived, and concerning whom it treats, n. 37—44. That there is one God, and that the Lord is that God, n. 45. That the Holy Spirit is the Divinity proceeding from the Lord, and that it is the Lord himself, n. 46—54. That the doctrine of the Athanasian faith agrees with the truth, if only by a trinity of persons is understood a trinity of person, which is in the Lord, n. 55—61.

The reason why it is said that seven thunders uttered their voices, is, because what the Lord speaks, as it descends through the heavens into the lower spheres, is heard as thunder; and as he speaks through the whole heaven at once, and thus fully, they are called seven thunders, for by seven are signified all, all things, and the whole, n. 10, 391; therefore also by thunder is signified instruction and the perception of truth, n. 236; in this instance, the revealing and manifestation thereof likewise. That a voice from heaven is heard as thunder, when it proceeds from the Lord, is evident from these passages: Jesus said, "Father, glorify thy name. Then came there a voice from heaven, saying, I have both glorified it, and will glorify it again;" the multitude heard this as *thunder*, John xii. 28—30. God roareth with his voice, " he *thundereth* with a voice of his excellency," Job xxxvii. 4, 5 "Jehovah *thundered* from heaven, and the Most High uttered his voice," 2 Sam. xxii. 14. "I heard a voice from heaven as the voice of *great thunder*," Apoc. xiv. 2. Thou didst call upon me, "and I answered thee in the secret place of *thunder*," Psalm lxxxi. 7.

473. *And when the seven thunders had uttered their voices, I was about to write: And I heard a voice from heaven saying unto me, Seal up those things which the seven thunders uttered, and write them not*, signifies that these things indeed are made manifest, but that they will not be received till after they who are meant by the dragon, the beast, and the false prophet, are cast out of the world of spirits, because there would be danger were they to be received before. The voices which the seven thunders uttered, are the things just mentioned above, n. 472, which are three times mentioned, because they contain the very essentials of the New Church. By writing, in the natural sense, is signified to commit to paper, and thus to record any thing for the information of posterity, but, in the spiritual sense, by writing is signified to commit to the heart for reception; hence by sealing them up and not writing them, is signified that they will not be committed to the heart and received, till after the dragon, the beast, and the false prophet, are cast out of the world of spirits, because there would be danger if they were received before: the reason is, because by the dragon, the beast, and the false prophet, are signified they who are in faith separated from charity, and these constantly and tenaciously adhere to their belief, that God the Father is to be approached, and not the Lord immediately, and that the Lord is not the God of heaven and earth as to his Humanity; therefore if the above-mentioned doctrine, n. 472, which has been and still is made manifest, as is signified by the *little book being opened*, were to be received by any others than such as are in charity and its faith, who also are those who are signified by John, n. 5, 17, before the dragon is cast out, it would be rejected not only by them, but, through their means, by the rest; and if not rejected, still it would be falsified, yea, profaned. That this is the case, evidently appears from what now follows in the Apocalypse, when seen in its proper series, as, that they slew the Lord's two witnesses, chap. xi.; that the dragon stood by the woman who was about to be delivered, that he might devour her child; and that after he had fought with Michael he persecuted the woman, chap. xii.; and that the two beasts which came up, one out of the sea, and the other out of the earth, acted in conjunction with him, chap. xiii.; as also that he gathered together his followers to battle

at the place called Armageddon, chap. xvi.; and, finally, that they assembled the nations, Gog and Magog, to battle, chap. xx. 8, 9. But that the dragon, the beast, and the false prophet, were cast into the lake of fire and brimstone, chap. xx. 10; and this being effected, the New Church, which is to be the Lamb's wife, came down out of heaven, chap. xxi., xxii. Such is the signification of these words, "Seal up those things which the seven thunders uttered, and write them not;" and also of the following in this chapter: "In the days of the voice of the seventh angel the mystery of God will be finished, as he hath declared to his servants the prophets," verse 7; and by these words in the next chapter: "And the seventh angel sounded, and there were great voices in heaven, saying, The kingdoms of this world are become the kingdoms of our Lord and of his Christ," verse 15; and likewise by many things to the same effect in the subsequent chapters. Something may be seen on this subject in *The Doctrine of the New Jerusalem concerning the Lord*, n. 61.

474. *And the angel whom I saw standing upon the sea and upon the earth lifted up his hand to heaven, and sware by him that liveth for ever and ever*, signifies the attestation and testification of the Lord by himself. By the angel who stood upon the sea and upon the earth is understood the Lord, n. 470; by lifting his hand up to heaven is signified this attestation, that there should be time no longer, verse 6; by swearing is signified this testification, that in the days of the voice of the seventh angel the mystery of God should be consummated, verse 7; by him that liveth for ever and ever is meant the Lord himself, as above, chap. i. 18; iv. 9, 10; v. 14; Dan. iv. 31. That the Lord testifies by himself will be seen presently. From what has been said, it is evident, that by these words, "and the angel whom I saw standing upon the sea and upon the earth, lifted up his hand to heaven, and sware by him that liveth for ever and ever," is signified the attestation and testification of the Lord by himself. That Jehovah swears, or testifies, by himself, is evident from these passages: "*I have sworn by myself*, the word is gone out of my mouth—and shall not return," Isaiah xlv. 23. "*I have sworn by myself*, that this house shall become a desolation," Jerem. xxii. 5. *Jehovah hath sworn by his soul*, Jerem. li. 14; Amos vi. 8. *Jehovah hath sworn by his holiness*, Amos iv. 2. "*Jehovah hath sworn by his right hand*, and by the arm of his strength," Isaiah lxii. 8. "Behold, *I have sworn by my great name*," Jerem. xliv. 26. Jehovah, that is, the Lord, swearing by himself, signifies that divine truth testifies, for he is divine truth itself, and this testifies from itself and by itself. Besides which, that Jehovah swears may also be seen in Isaiah xiv. 24; liv. 9; Psalm lxxxix. 3, 35; Psalm xcv. 11; Psalm cx. 4; Psalm cxxx. 11. Jehovah

is said to swear, because the church instituted among the sons of Israel was a representative church, and the Lord's conjunction with the church was thence represented by a covenant, such as takes place between two who swear to their compact; therefore, as swearing was used for the purpose of ratifying a covenant or compact, it is said that Jehovah sware; by which, nevertheless, it is not meant that he really did swear, but that divine truth testifies or bears testimony to the things asserted. That an oath was used to ratify covenants, appears from these passages: "*I have sworn* unto thee, and entered into a covenant, and thou becamest mine," Ezek. xvi. 8. "To remember his holy covenant, the *oath which he sware*," Luke i. 72, 73; Psalm cv. 9; Jerem. xi. 5; xxxii. 22; Deut. i. 35; x. 11; xi. 9, 21; xxvi. 3, 15; xxxi. 20; xxxiv. 4. As a covenant was representative of the conjunction of the Lord with the church, and, reciprocally, of the church with the Lord; and as the oath had relation to the covenant, and man was to swear from the truth therein, thus also by it, therefore the children of Israel were permitted to swear by Jehovah, and thus by divine truth, Exod. xx. 7; Levit. xix. 12; Deut. vi. 13; x. 20; Isaiah xlviii. 1; lxv. 16; Jerem. iv. 2; Zech. v. 4; but after the representative rites of the church were abolished, oaths as used in covenants were abolished also by the Lord, Matt. v. 33—37; xxiii. 16—22.

475. *Who created heaven, and the things that therein are, and the earth, and the things that therein are, and the sea, and the things that are therein*, signifies who vivifies all that are in heaven and that are in the church, and all and every thing in general and in particular appertaining to them. By creating, in the natural sense, is signified to create; but, in the spiritual sense, by creating is signified to reform and regenerate, n. 254, 290; which is also to vivify or make alive. By heaven is meant heaven where are the angels; by the earth and the sea is signified the church; by the earth, they who are in its internals; and by the sea, they who are in its externals, n. 398, 470. By the things that are therein, are signified all and singular the things appertaining to them.

476. *That there should be time no longer*, signifies that there cannot be any state of the church, or any church, except one God be acknowledged, and that the Lord is that God. By time is signified state; and, because the church is here treated of, the state of the church is signified. Therefore there shall be time no longer, signifies that there will not be any state of the church. That it also means that there is not any church, except one God be acknowledged, and that the Lord is he, follows as a consequence. But what is the case at this day? That there is one God is not denied, but that the Lord is that God

is denied; and yet there is not one God, in whom is a trinity at the same time, but the Lord: that the church exists from him, who is the Saviour and Redeemer, is not denied; but that he, as the Saviour and Redeemer, ought to be approached immediately, is denied. Hence it is evident, that a church would perish, did not a new one come into existence, which acknowledges the Lord alone to be the God of heaven and earth, and, for this reason, immediately approaches him, see Matt. xxviii. 18; therefore these words, there shall be time no longer, that is, there shall be no church, relate to what follows in this chapter, verse 7; and this again, to what is written in chap. xi., verse 15; where it is said that there will be a church which will originate from the Lord alone. By time is signified state, because in the spiritual world time is not measured by days, weeks, months, and years, but by states, which are progressions of the life of those who are there, from which they remember things past; on which subject see the work on *Heaven and Hell*, n. 162—169, where time in heaven is treated of. The reason why the state of the church is here meant by time, is because day and night, morning and evening, summer and winter, constitute time in this world, and when understood in a spiritual sense, they constitute states of the church; therefore when these states no longer exist, there is no church; and there is then no church, when there is no longer any good and truth, thus when the light of truth is turned into thick darkness, and the heat of good into cold; this is what is meant by there not being time any longer. Similar is the signification of the following passages in the Word: The fourth beast will think to *change the times*, Dan. vii. 25. "But it shall be *one day* which is known to Jehovah, not day nor night," thus there would be no time, Zech. xiv. 10. "I will cause the sun to go down at noon, and I will darken the earth in the *clear day*," thus again there would be no time, Amos viii. 9. "Behold, one evil is come, an end is come, the end is come, the *morning* is come unto thee, O thou that dwellest in the land, the *time* is come," Ezek. vii. 5—7; the morning is the beginning of a new church, n. 151, therefore it is said, the time is come.

477. *But in the days of the voice of the seventh angel, when he is about to sound*, signifies the final exploration and manifestation of the state of the church, which must perish, unless a new one be established by the Lord. That by sounding a trumpet is signified to explore and lay open the state of life of those who are of the church, consequently the state of the church, may be seen above, n. 397; and as seven angels sounded, by the voice of the seventh angel is signified the final exploration and manifestation, by which it appears that the church must perish, unless a new one be established by the Lord; that it

must perish, is meant by there being time no longer, n. 476; and that a new church is to be established by the Lord, is meant by what now follows.

478. *The mystery of God should be finished; as he hath declared to his servants the prophets*, signifies that then it will appear that it is foretold in the Word of both Testaments, but has hitherto been concealed, that after the last judgment is executed upon those who have devastated the church, the Lord's kingdom will come. By being finished is signified to be fulfilled, to come to an end, and then to appear again; by the mystery of God declared to the prophets, is signified that which is foretold by the Lord in the Word, and hitherto concealed; by declaring is signified to announce the Lord's advent, and also that of his kingdom, for the term here used signifies to declare glad tidings (*evangelium*). That this will come to pass, after the last judgment is executed upon those who have devastated the church, is also foretold in the Word, therefore this also is signified; from which it may appear, that all this is understood by these words. It may be expedient here to premise something of what is foretold in the Word of both Testaments, concerning the coming of the Lord, and of his kingdom. In the Word of the Old Testament, which is called prophetic, in the spiritual sense, and also where this shines forth, in the natural sense, the Lord alone is treated of, that is to say, his advent in the fulness of time; which is, when there shall no longer be any good of charity and truth of faith in the church, which state of the church is called the consummation, devastation, desolation, and decision: it also treats of his combats with the hells and his victories over them, which likewise constitute the last judgment executed by him; and afterwards of the creation of a new heaven, and the establishment of a new church, or the Lord's kingdom that is to come; these things are also treated of in the Word of the New Testament, which is called apostolic, and particularly in the Apocalypse. That it is the Lord's kingdom, the glad tidings of which will be declared in the days of the voice of the seventh angel, appears plainly from this passage in the next or eleventh chapter: "And the seventh angel sounded, and there were great voices in heaven, saying, *The kingdoms of this world are become the kingdoms of our Lord and of his Christ, and he shall reign for ever and ever:* And the four-and twenty elders fell upon their faces, and worshipped God, saying, We give thee thanks, O Lord God Almighty, which art, and wast, and art to come, because thou hast taken to thee thy great power, and *hast begun thy reign*," verses 15—17. This mystery is described in Daniel almost in the same words as here in the Apocalypse: "And I heard the man clothed in linen, when he held up his right hand and his left hand unto heaven, and sware by him that liveth for ever, that it shall be for a time, times,

and a half;" when all these things are to be finished: he said, "Go thy way, Daniel: for the words are closed up and sealed till the *time of the end*," Dan. xii. 7, 9; till the time of the end means till this time. That then the Son of Man will receive the kingdom, he foretells in these words: "I saw in the night visions, and behold, one like the *Son of Man* came with the clouds of heaven; and there was given to him dominion, and glory, and a kingdom, that all people, nations, and languages, should serve him: his dominion is an everlasting dominion, which shall not pass away, and his *kingdom* that which shall not be destroyed," Dan. vii. 13, 14. That to declare glad tidings signifies the Lord's advent, and then his kingdom, is plain from these passages: "O Zion, *that bringest glad tidings*, get thee up into the high mountain: O Jerusalem, *that bringest glad tidings*, lift up thy voice with strength; say unto the cities of Judah, Behold your God! Behold, the Lord Jehovah will come with a strong hand, and his arm shall rule for him," Isaiah xl. 9—11. "How beautiful upon the mountains are the feet of him that *bringeth glad tidings*, that publisheth peace, that *bringeth glad tidings* of good, that publisheth salvation, that saith unto Zion, Thy God reigneth," Isaiah lii. 7, 8; Nahum i. 15. "Sing unto Jehovah, bless in his name, *declare the glad tidings* of his salvation from day to day, for Jehovah cometh," Psalm xcvi. 2, 13. "The spirit of the Lord Jehovah is upon me, because Jehovah hath anointed me to *preach glad tidings* unto the meek—to proclaim liberty to the captives—to proclaim the acceptable year of Jehovah," Isaiah lxi. 1, 2. The angel said unto Zacharias, Behold, thy wife shall bear a son, who shall go before the Lord God in the spirit and power of Elias, and to prepare a people for the Lord: "I am Gabriel, and am sent to *show thee these glad tidings*," Luke i. 13, 17, 19. The angel said to the shepherds, "Fear not; behold, I *bring you glad tidings* of great joy, for unto you is born in the city of David this day a Saviour, who is Christ the Lord," Luke ii. 10, 11. The Lord *preached the glad tidings* of the kingdom of God, Matt. iv. 23; xi. 5; Mark i. 15; Luke vii. 22; viii. 1; ix. 1, 2; and John the Baptist, Luke iii. 18. Jesus also commanded his disciples, "Go ye into all the world, and *preach the gospel* to every creature," Mark xvi. 15. This also is *the everlasting gospel*, which the angel flying in the midst of heaven had to *preach* unto them that dwell on the earth, Apoc. xiv. 6. It is said that the mystery of God will be consummated, by which is meant, that now will be fulfilled that which before had not been fulfilled, that is, that the kingdom will be the Lord's; for it was not fulfilled by the Jews, because they did not acknowledge the Lord; nor by the Christians, for these have not acknowledged the Lord to be the God of heaven and earth, as to the Humanity, for they make his Humanity like that of another man, wherefore they do not immediately approach him, when yet he is Jehovah who came into the world.

479. *And the voice which I heard from heaven spake unto me again, and said, Go, take the little book, which is open in the hand of the angel who is standing upon the sea and upon the earth*, signifies a command from heaven, that they should admit that doctrine concerning the Lord, but that it should be made manifest by John, how it would be received in the church, before they who are meant by the dragon, the beast, and the false prophet are removed. By the voice which he heard from heaven now again talking with him, is meant the voice which told him to seal up the things which the seven thunders uttered, and not to write them, verse 4, by which is signified that the doctrine concerning the Lord would not be received till after they who are meant by the dragon, the beast, and the false prophet, should be cast out of the spiritual world, because there would be danger were it to be received before, as may be seen above, n. 473; that this is the case, is now made manifest by John, by his eating up the little book, as presently follows. That by the little book is meant the doctrine concerning the Lord, may be seen, n. 469, 472; and that by the angel who stood upon the sea and upon the earth is understood the Lord, n. 465, 470.

480. *And I went unto the angel, and said unto him, Give me the little book*, signifies a motion or inclination of the mind, with many in the church, to receive the doctrine. This is signified, because by John is here manifested the way in which the doctrine concerning the Lord is received by many in the church, as just observed; a motion or inclination of the mind with these to receive this doctrine is meant, because an inclination was apparent in John, in that he went and asked for it. As these things involve such a meaning, therefore John was first told to take the little book; he then went and asked for it; then the angel said that he would give it him, but that it would make his belly bitter; and, lastly, it is said that it was given him, and that it so came to pass; all these circumstances being significative.

481. *And he said unto me, Take it, and eat it up; and it shall make thy belly bitter, but it shall be in thy mouth sweet as honey*, signifies that reception from acknowledgment that the Lord is the Saviour and Redeemer, is grateful and pleasing, but that the acknowledgment that he alone is the God of heaven and earth, and that his Humanity is Divine, is unpleasing and difficult to receive by reason of falsifications. By taking the little book, is signified to receive the doctrine concerning the Lord; by eating it up, is signified to acknowledge it; by making the belly bitter, is signified that it will be unpleasant and difficult by reason of falsifications, for bitter signifies truth falsified,

n. 411; by being in the mouth sweet as honey, is signified that the reception of it at first is grateful and pleasant. These things that are now applied to the doctrine, which is meant by the little book that was open in the hand of the angel, n. 409, 472, signify that reception from acknowledgment that the Lord is the Saviour and Redeemer, is grateful and pleasing; but that the acknowledgment that he alone is the God of heaven and earth, and that his Humanity is Divine, is unpleasing and difficult by reason of falsifications. The falsifications, by which that doctrine is rendered disagreeable and difficult of reception, consist principally in not acknowledging the Lord to be one with the Father, although he himself so taught; and in not acknowledging his Humanity to be Divine, which, nevertheless, is the Son of God, Luke i. 35; and thus it may be said, that they have made God three, and the Lord two; not to mention the falses continued from them: from these falses flows the doctrine of faith alone, and faith alone afterwards confirms those falses. That in consequence of these falses, so great a bitterness and repugnance exists, that they cannot, after death, even name the Divine Humanity from any acknowledgment in thought, may be seen above, n. 294.

482. *And I took the little book out of the angel's hand, and ate it up: and it was in my mouth sweet as honey, and when I had eaten it my belly was bitter*, signifies that so it came to pass, and was thus manifested what reception that doctrine would meet with, before they who are meant by the dragon, the beast, and the false prophet, were removed. As this is a necessary consequence of what was said above, it needs no further explanation. It is written that the prophet Ezekiel was also commanded to eat the volume of the book, and that in his mouth it was *sweet as honey*, Ezek. ii. 8—10; iii. 1—4.

483. *And he said unto me, Thou must prophesy again before many peoples, and nations, and tongues, and many kings*, signifies that this is the case, because the quality of those who are principled in faith alone must be further shown. That this is signified, appears from what follows, down to chap. xvii., which treats of those who are in faith alone; and afterwards of the Roman Catholic religion, and then of the expulsion of the dragon, the beast, and the false prophet, into hell, and thus concerning the New Church, in which the Lord alone will be worshipped. To prophesy signifies to teach, n. 8, 133, therefore to prophesy again signifies to teach further; by peoples are signified those who are in the truths or falses of doctrine; and by nations, those who are in the good or evil of life, as will be seen presently; by tongues are signified those who are exteriorly in such things, n. 282; and by kings are signified those who are interiorly in them; for by kings are signified those who are in truths derived from good; and, in the opposite sense, those who

are in falses derived from evil, and, abstractedly, truths from good or falses from evil, as may be seen, n. 20, 664, 704, 720, 830, 921; and since they who are principled in interior falses are specifically treated of in what follows, it is said, "and many kings," by which are signified falses of evil in great abundance. Peoples, nations, tongues, and kings, are mentioned for the sake of comprehending all who are such in the church. John being told that he must prophesy again, signifies that it is necessary to teach further what is the quality of those who are in faith alone, to the end that their falses may be detected, and thus abolished; inasmuch as no falsity is ever abolished before it is detected. That peoples signify those who are in truths or falses of doctrine, and nations, those who are in good or evil of life, may appear from many passages in the Word, where peoples and nations are mentioned; but in confirmation of this, only those passages shall be here adduced, where peoples and nations occur together, from which this inference may be drawn, seeing that in the Word throughout, both generally and particularly, there is a marriage of the Lord and the church, and thence a marriage of good and truth; and peoples relate to truth, and nations to good. That there is such a marriage in all and every particular of the Word, may be seen in *The Doctrine of the New Jerusalem concerning the Sacred Scripture*, n. 80—90. The passages in the Word are as follow: "Ah sinful *nation*, a *people laden with iniquity*," Isaiah i. 4. "I will send him against a hypocritical *nation*, and against the *people* of my wrath," Isaiah x. 6. Jehovah smote the *peoples* in wrath, he ruled the *nations* in anger, Isaiah xiv. 6. "Go to a *nation* scattered and peeled—to a *people* terrible from their beginning," Isa. xviii. 2. "Therefore shall the strong *people* glorify thee, the city of the terrible *nations* shall fear thee," Isaiah xxv. 3. Jehovah will destroy the covering which is cast over all *peoples*, and the vail that is spread over all *nations*, Isaiah xxv. 7, 8. "Come near, ye *nations*, and hear, ye *people*," Isaiah xxxiv. 1. "I will give thee for a covenant to the *peoples*, and a light to the *nations*," Isaiah xlii. 6. "Behold, I will lift up my hand to the *nations*, and set up my standard to the *peoples*," Isaiah xlix. 22. "Let all the *nations* be gathered together, and let the *peoples* be assembled," Isaiah xliii. 9. "Behold, I have given him for a witness to the *peoples*, a leader and commander to the *nations*," Isaiah lv. 4, 5. "Behold, a *people* cometh from the north country, and a great *nation* from the sides of the earth," Jerem. vi. 22, 23. "Many *peoples* shall come, and strong *nations* to seek Jehovah of Hosts in Jerusalem," Zech. viii. 22. "Jehovah bringeth the counsel of the *nations* to nought, he maketh the devices of the *peoples* of none effect," Psalm xxxiii. 10. "Jehovah shall subdue the *peoples* under us, and the *nations* under our feet; Jehovah reigneth over the *nations*, the princes of the *peoples* are gathered together," Psalm xlvii. 8, 9. "Let the *peoples* praise thee, let the *nations* be glad, for thou shalt judge the *peoples* righteously, and govern the *nations* upon earth," Psalm lxvii. 3—5. "Remember me, O Jehovah, with the favour of thy *people*, that I may rejoice in gladness of thy *nations*," Psalm cvi. 4, 5. *All the peoples, nations, and tongues* of the Son of Man shall worship, Dan. vii. 14. Besides other places; as in Psalm xviii. 43; Isaiah ix. 2, 3; xi. 10; Ezek. xxxvi. 15; Joel ii. 17; Zeph. ii. 9; Apoc. v. 9; Luke ii. 30—32.

484. To the above I will add three Memorable Relations of what took place in the spiritual world. The first was as follows. I once heard a noise like the grinding of a mill; it was in the northern quarter. At first I wondered what it could mean, till I recollected that by a mill and by grinding, in the Word, is meant to collect from the Word what is serviceable to doctrine, n. 794. I advanced, therefore, towards the place from whence the noise came, and as I approached, the noise ceased: then I observed something like a roof above ground, the entrance to which was through a cave; on seeing which, I descended and entered; and lo, there was an apartment, in which I saw an aged person sitting, surrounded with books, with the Word before him, in which he was searching for what might be serviceable to his doctrine. There were papers lying about him, on which he wrote such passages as suited his purpose. And, in the next room, were a number of scribes, who collected the papers, and copied out their contents on a whole sheet. I inquired first, concerning the books which lay about him; he said, that they all treated of justifying faith: "Those from Sweden and Denmark," says he, "enter deeply into the subject; those from Germany somewhat deeper; those from England deeper still; and those from Holland the deepest of all;" he added withal, that notwithstanding the difference of their sentiments on other points, yet in the articles of justification and salvation by faith alone, they were all agreed. He then told me, that at that time he was collecting from the Word this chief article of justifying faith, viz., that God the Father fell away from grace towards mankind, by reason of their iniquities; and that, consequently, in order to effect their salvation, it was become indispensably necessary, that satisfaction, reconciliation, propitiation, and mediation, should be made by some person, who would take upon himself the sentence of wrath and justice, and that none could be found qualified for this purpose, but his only Son; and that when this purpose was effected, access was opened to God the Father, for his sake. He said, "I now see, and have long seen, that this is consistent with reason; for how could God the Father be approached, but by faith in the merit

of his Son? and now I have also found, that it is likewise consistent with Scripture." When I heard this, I was amazed at his saying that it was consistent with reason and Scripture, when yet it is contrary to both, as I plainly told him. He, then, in the heat of his zeal, replied, "How can you talk in this manner?" Wherefore I began to explain myself, by saying, "Is it not contrary to reason to conceive, that God ever fell away from grace towards mankind, and entirely cast them off? is not divine grace an attribute of the divine essence? Wherefore, to fall away from grace would be to fall away from his divine essence; and to fall away from his divine essence would be to be no longer God: for how can God be alienated from himself? Believe me, that grace on God's part, as it is infinite, so also is it eternal; it may indeed be lost on the part of man, if he will not receive it, but never on the part of God. If grace were to depart from God, there would be an end of the universal heaven and the whole race of mankind, insomuch that man would no longer be man in any respect whatever; wherefore, grace on God's part abides to all eternity, not only towards angels and men, but even towards the devil himself. Since this then is agreeable to reason, why do you assert, that the only access to God the Father is by faith in the merit of his Son, when yet there is perpetual access by grace? And why do you call it access to God the Father for the sake of his Son, and not access by his Son? Is not the Son the Mediator and Saviour? Why then do you not approach him as your Mediator and Saviour? Is he not God and Man? Who on earth approaches immediately any emperor, king, or prince, without having some person to introduce him? And did you never learn, that the Lord came into the world that he himself might introduce us to the Father? and that there is no possible access but by him? Search now the Scriptures, and you will there see that what I tell you is agreeable to them, and that the way which you talk of to the Father, is as contrary to Scripture as it is to reason. I assert, moreover, that it is great presumption to climb up to God the Father, and not by him who is in the bosom of the Father, and is alone with him. Did you never read John xiv. 6?" As I uttered these words, the old man was so much exasperated, that he sprang from his chair, and called to his scribes to turn me out of the house; and as I walked out of my own accord, he threw after me out of doors the first book that he could lay his hands on, which book happened to be the Word.

The second Memorable Relation. After I had retired, I heard a noise again like the collision of two mill stones against each other; but as I approached towards the place from whence it came, it ceased, and I saw a narrow gate leading obliquely downwards to a certain vaulted house, which was divided into small cells, in each of which sat two persons collecting passages from the Word in favour of faith alone; one collected, and the other transcribed, and this they did alternately. I went towards one of the cells, and stood at the door, and asked what they were collecting and writing; they said, "Concerning the act of justification, or concerning faith in act, which is the real justifying, vivifying, and saving faith, and the chief doctrine of all in Christendom." Then I said, "Tell me some mark or sign of that act, when that faith is introduced into the heart and soul of man." They replied, "The sign of that act is momentary, or instantaneous, when a man, under the anguish of condemnation for sin, thinks of Christ, as having taken away the condemnation of the law, and lays hold of this his merit with confidence, and, keeping it in his thoughts, approaches and prays to God the Father." Then I said, "Suppose it to be so, and that this act is instantaneous; yet how am I to conceive what is asserted of this act, that man contributes nothing towards it, any more than if he were a stock or a stone, and that he has no power to begin, will, understand, think, operate, co-operate, apply, and accommodate himself to this act? Tell me, how does this agree with what you said, that the act takes place when man is thinking about the justice of the law, and about the removal of its condemnation by Christ, in consequence of which he lays hold with confidence of his merit, and approaches and prays to God the Father with this in his thoughts? Are not all these things done by man as from himself?" They answered, "Not by man actively, but passively." I replied, "How can any one think, have confidence, and pray, passively? If you take away man's activity or re-activity, do you not also take away his capacity of reception, consequently all that belongs to him as man, and with it the act itself? And what does the act become in this case, but something purely ideal, or a mere creature of the imagination? I trust you do not believe with some, that such an act takes place only among the predestinate, who yet are utterly unconscious of any infusion of faith into themselves; and who might throw a cast of dice, in order to ascertain whether it be infused into them or no; wherefore, do you, my friends, believe, that man, in matters of faith, operates and co-operates as from himself, and that without such co-operation, your act of faith, which you call the chief doctrine of religion, is but a mere pillar or statue, like Lot's wife, tinkling like dry salt when scratched by a scribe's pen or finger-nail, Luke xvii. 32. I use this comparison, because as to that act, you make yourselves as mere statues." As I spake these words, one of them took up a candlestick, with intent to throw it in my face, but the candle suddenly going out, and it becoming dark in consequence, he threw it against the forehead of his own companion; at which I smiled and departed.

The third Memorable Relation. In the northern quarter of the spiritual world, hearing as it were the roaring of waters, I walked towards it, and as I approached, the roaring ceased, and I heard a buzzing noise like the distant voices of a multitude gathered together, and then there appeared a building full of chinks and clefts, encompassed with a mound of earth, from whence that buzzing issued. I went up to it, and seeing the porter, asked who were within the walls. He said, "The wisest of the wise, who are now debating together on subjects supernatural." He said this in the simplicity of his belief. And I said, "May I be permitted to enter?" "Yes," says he, "on condition thou wilt say nothing; for I have leave to admit Gentiles to stand with me at the door." So I went in, and lo, there was a circus, and in the centre a pulpit, where an assembly of the wise, so called, were discussing the mysteries of faith. The subject or proposition then in debate was, Whether the good which a man does in the state of justification by faith, or in its progression after the act, is the good of religion, or not. They were unanimous in defining the good of religion to be such good as contributes to salvation. The debate was warm, but victory inclined to the side of those who contended, that the good actions which a man does in the state or progression of faith, are only such as are moral, civil, and political, and which contribute nothing to salvation, since it is faith only that can do this. This opinion they confirmed by the following arguments: "How," said they, "can any good thing, proceeding from man's will, be conjoined with free grace? How can any work of man be connected with what is freely given? And is not salvation of free grace? How, again, can any good thing, proceeding from man, be conjoined with the merit of Christ, which is the only means of salvation? And how is it possible for man's operation to be conjoined with the operation of the Holy Ghost? Does not the Holy Ghost do all without the aid or assistance of man? Are not these three things alone conducive to salvation in the act of justification by faith? And do they not remain alone conducive to salvation in the state or progress of faith? Of consequence, the accessory good on man's part can in no wise be called the good of religion, which, as was observed, contributes to salvation, but ought rather to be called the evil of religion, whensoever it is done with a view to salvation." There were two Gentiles standing with the doorkeeper in the porch, who heard all this reasoning; and one of them said to the other, "These people have no religion at all; for who does not see that what is called religion consists in doing good to one's neighbour for the sake of God, consequently, with God, and from God?" And the other said, "Their faith has infatuated them." Then they asked the door-keeper, "Who are these people?" And he replied, "They are wise Christians." They replied, "Nonsense! thou art imposing upon us; by their manner of speaking we should take them for jugglers." I then departed; and some time after, when I looked at the place where that building was, behold! it was a stagnant pool.

These things, just as I have described them, were seen and heard by me when I was perfectly awake, both as to my body and my spirit: for the Lord has so united my spirit to my body that I am in both at one and the same time. My going to that building, and their then being engaged in debate on those subjects, with the other circumstances that have been described, were so ordered by the divine auspices of the Lord.

CHAPTER XI.

1. AND there was given me a reed like unto a rod: and the angel stood by, saying, Rise, and measure the temple of God, and the altar, and them that worship therein.

2. But the court which is without the temple leave out, and measure it not; for it is given unto the Gentiles: and the holy city shall they tread under foot forty and two months.

3. And I will give unto my two witnesses, and they shall prophesy a thousand two hundred and sixty days, clothed in sackcloth.

4. These are the two olive-trees, and the two candlesticks, standing before the God of the earth.

5. And if any one desire to hurt them, fire shall proceed out of their mouth, and shall devour their enemies; and if any one desire to hurt them, he must thus be killed.

6. These have power to shut heaven, that the rain fall not in the days of their prophecy: and have power over the waters to turn them into blood; and to smite the earth with every plague, as often as they will.

7. And when they shall have finished their testimony, the beast that ascendeth out of the bottomless pit shall make war with them, and shall overcome them, and kill them.

8. And their dead bodies shall lie in the street of the great city, which spiritually is called Sodom and Egypt, where also our Lord was crucified.

9. And they of the peoples, and tribes, and tongues, and

nations, shall see their dead bodies three days and a half, and shall not suffer their dead bodies to be put into monuments.

10. And they that dwell upon the earth shall rejoice over them and be glad, and shall send gifts one to another; because these two prophets tormented them that dwell upon the earth.

11. And after three days and a half, the spirit of life from God entered into them, and they stood upon their feet; and great fear fell upon them that saw them.

12. And they heard a great voice from heaven, saying unto them, Come up hither. And they ascended up to heaven in a cloud: and their enemies beheld them.

13. And the same hour there was a great earthquake, and the tenth part of the city fell, and in the earthquake were slain names of men seven thousand; and the remnant were affrighted, and gave glory to the God of heaven.

14. The second woe is past; behold, the third woe cometh quickly.

15. And the seventh angel sounded; and there were great voices in heaven, saying, The kingdoms of the world are become the kingdoms of our Lord and of his Christ, and he shall reign for ever and ever.

16. And the four-and-twenty elders, that sat before God on their thrones, fell upon their faces, and worshipped God,

17. Saying, We give thee thanks, O Lord God Almighty, who art, and who wast, and who art to come, because thou hast taken to thee thy great power, and hast begun to reign.

18. And the nations were angry; and thy wrath is come, and the time of judging the dead, and of giving reward unto thy servants the prophets, and to the saints, and to them that fear thy name, both small and great; and of destroying them that destroy the earth.

19. And the temple of God was opened in heaven; and there was seen in his temple the ark of his covenant; and there were lightnings, and voices, and thunderings, and an earthquake, and great hail.

THE SPIRITUAL SENSE.

THE CONTENTS OF THE WHOLE CHAPTER. The state of the church among the reformed is still treated of, as to the quality of those who are interiorly principled in faith alone, contrary to the two essentials of the New Church, which teach that the Lord is the only God of heaven and earth, that his Humanity is Divine; and that men ought to live according to the precepts of the decalogue. That these two essentials were declared to them, verses 3—6. But that they were totally rejected, verses 7—10. That they were raised up again by the Lord, verses 11, 12. That they who rejected them, perished, verse 13. That the state of the New Church was manifested from the new heaven, verses 15—19.

The Contents of each Verse. V. 1, "And there was given me a reed like unto a rod," signifies that the faculty and power of knowing and seeing the state of the church in heaven and in the world was given: "And the angel stood by, saying, Rise, and measure the temple of God, and the altar, and them that worship therein," signifies the Lord's presence and his command, that he should see and know the state of the church in the new heaven: v. 2, "But the court which is without the temple leave out, and measure it not," signifies that the state of the church on earth, such as it is at present, is to be removed, and not known: "For it is given unto the Gentiles," signifies, because the state of that church is destroyed and laid waste by evils of life: "And the holy city shall they tread under foot forty and two months," signifies that it would disperse every truth of the Word, even to nothing of the kind remaining: v. 3, "And I will give unto my two witnesses," signifies those who confess and acknowledge in their hearts that the Lord is the God of heaven and earth, and that his Humanity is Divine, and who are conjoined to him by a life according to the precepts of the decalogue: "And they shall prophesy a thousand two hundred and sixty days," signifies that these two articles, the acknowledgment of the Lord, and a life according to the commandments of the decalogue, which are the two essentials of the New Church, are to be taught until the end and the beginning: "Clothed in sackcloth," signifies lamentation in the mean time on account of the non-reception of truth: v. 4, "These are the two olive-trees, and the two candlesticks, standing before the God of the earth," signifies love and intelligence, or charity and faith, from the Lord with them: v. 5, "And if any one desire to hurt them, fire shall proceed out of their mouth, and shall devour their enemies," signifies that they who desire to destroy these two essentials of the New Church, will perish by reason of infernal love: "And if any one desire to hurt them, he must thus be killed," signifies that he who condemns them shall in like manner be condemned: v. 6, "These have power to shut heaven, that the rain fall not in the days of their prophecy," signifies that they who reject these two essentials cannot receive any truth from heaven: "And have power over the waters to turn them into blood," signifies that they who reject them falsify the truths of the Word: "And to smite the earth with every plague, as often as they will," signifies that they who desire to destroy them, will plunge themselves into all kinds of evils and falses, as often as and in proportion as they do so: v. 7, "And when they shall have finished their testimony," signifies that after the Lord taught these two essentials of the New Church: "The beast that ascendeth out of the bottomless pit shall make war with them, and shall overcome them, and kill them," signifies that they who are principled in the internals of the doctrine of faith alone will reject these two essentials: v. 8, "And their dead bodies shall lie in the street of the great city," signifies that they are totally rejected: "Which spiritually is called Sodom and Egypt," signifies two infernal loves, which are the love of dominion grounded in self-love, and the love of rule grounded in the pride of self-derived intelligence, which exist in the church where one God is not acknowledged, and the Lord not worshipped, and where they do not live according to the precepts of the decalogue: "Where also our Lord was crucified," signifies non-acknowledgment of the Lord's Divine Humanity, and, consequently, a state of rejection: v. 9, "And they of the peoples, and tribes, and tongues, and nations, shall see their dead bodies three days and a half," signifies when all they, who, until the end of the present church and the beginning of the New Church, have been and will be in falses of doctrine and evils of life from faith alone, have heard and shall hear of these two essentials: "And shall not suffer their dead bodies to be put into monuments," signifies that they condemned and will condemn them: v. 10, "And they that dwell upon the earth shall rejoice over them and be glad," signifies the delight of the affection of the heart and soul in the church among those who were in faith alone: "And shall send gifts one to another," signifies consociation through love and friendship: "Because these two prophets tormented them that dwell upon the earth," signifies that these two essentials of the New Church, by reason of their contrariety to the two essentials received in the Reformed Church, are held in contempt, dislike, and averison: v. 11, "And after three days and a half the spirit of life from God entered into them, and they stood upon their feet," signifies that these two essentials, during the commencement and progress of the New Church, will, with those who receive them, be vivified by the Lord: "And great fear fell upon them that saw them," signifies commotion of mind and consternation at divine truths: v. 12, "And they heard a great voice from heaven, saying unto them, Come up hither," signifies that these two essentials of the New Church were taken up by the Lord into heaven, from whence they came, and where they are, and the protection of them: "And they ascended up to heaven in a cloud," signifies the taking them up into heaven, and conjunction there with the Lord by the divine truth of the Word in its literal sense: "And their enemies beheld them," signifies that they who are in faith separated from charity heard them, but remained in their own falsities: v. 13, "And the same hour there was a great earthquake, and the tenth part of the city fell," signifies a remarkable change of state which then took place with them, and their separation from heaven, followed by a sinking down into hell: "And in the earthquake were slain names of men seven thousand," signifies that all those who were in the confession of faith alone, and therefore made no account of works of charity, perished: "And the remnant were affrighted, and gave glory to the God of heaven," signifies that they who saw their destruction acknowledged the Lord, and were separated: v. 14, "The second woe is past; behold the third woe cometh quickly," signifies lamentation over the perverted state of the church, and then the last lamentation, to be treated of presently: v. 15, "And the seventh angel sounded," signifies the exploration and manifestation of the state of the church after the consummation, at the coming of the Lord and of his kingdom: "And there were great voices in heaven, saying, The kingdoms of the world are become the kingdoms of our Lord and of his Christ, and he shall reign for ever and ever," signifies celebrations by the angels, because heaven and the church are become the Lord's, as they were from the beginning, and because now they are in subjection also to his Divine Humanity, consequently that now, both as to his Humanity and his Divinity, the Lord will reign over heaven and the church to eternity: v. 16, "And the four-and-twenty elders, that sat before God on their thrones, fell upon their faces, and worshipped God," signifies an acknowledgment by all the angels of heaven, that the Lord is the God of heaven and earth, and supreme adoration: v. 17, "Saying, We give thee thanks, O Lord God Almighty, who art, and who wast, and who art to come," signifies a confession and glorification by the angels of heaven, that it is the Lord who is, who has life and power from himself, and who rules all things, because he alone is eternal and infinite: "Because thou hast taken to thee thy great power, and hast begun to reign," signifies the new heaven and the New Church, where they acknowledge him to be the only God: v. 18, "And the nations were angry," signifies those who are in faith alone, and thence in evils of life, that they were enraged, and infested those who are against their faith: "And thy wrath is come, and the time of judging the dead," signifies their destruction, and the execution of the last judgment upon those who have not any spiritual life: "And of giving reward unto thy servants the prophets, and to the saints," signifies the felicity of life eternal to those who are in truths of doctrine from the Word, and in a life according to them: "And to them that fear thy name, both small and great," signifies who love the things which relate to the Lord in a lesser or greater degree: "And of destroying them that destroy the earth," signifies the casting of those into hell who have destroyed the church: v. 19, "And the temple of God was opened in heaven; and there was seen in his temple the ark of his covenant," signifies the new heaven, in which the Lord in his Divine Humanity is worshipped; and where they live according to the precepts of his decalogue, these constituting the two essentials of the New Church, whereby conjunction is effected: "And there were lightnings, and voices, and thunderings, and an earthquake, and great hail," signifies the ratiocinations, commotions, and falsifications of good and truth, that ensued in the spheres beneath (*in inferioribus*).

THE EXPLANATION.

485. *And there was given me a reed like unto a rod*, signifies that the faculty and power of knowing and seeing the state of the church in heaven and in the world was given by the Lord. By a reed is signified feeble power, such as man has from himself; and by a rod, or staff, is signified great power, such as man has from the Lord; therefore by a reed being given him like unto a rod, is signified power from the Lord. That it means the faculty and power of knowing and seeing the state of the church in heaven and in the world, is plain from what follows in this chapter to the end. That by a reed, or cane, is signified feeble power, such as man has from himself, is evident from these passages: "Lo, thou trustest in the *staff of this broken reed*, on Egypt; whereon when if a man lean it will go into his hand, and pierce it," Isaiah xxxvi. 6. "And all the inhabitants of Egypt shall know, that I am Jehovah, because they have been a *staff of reed* to the house of Israel; when they took hold of thee by the hand, thou didst break, and rend all their shoulder," Ezek. xxix. 6, 7. By Egypt is signified the natural man who trusts in his own strength, therefore he is called the staff of a bruised reed. By reed is signified feeble power, in Isaiah: "A bruised *reed* shall he not break, and the smoking flax shall he not quench," Isaiah xlii. 3. But by a rod, or a staff, is signified strong power, which is from the Lord; in the present instance, power to know the state of the church, because the temple and altar was measured with a rod; and by measuring is signified to know, and by the temple and altar is signified the church; as will be seen presently. A rod signifies power, because wood, of which walking-staves were made among those of the ancient church, signifies good; and because

a staff is instead of the right hand, and supports it, and by the right hand is signified power; hence it is, that a sceptre is a short staff, and by a sceptre is signified regal power; and a sceptre and staff are expressed by one and the same word in the Hebrew language. That a staff signifies power, is evident from these places: "Say, how is the *strong staff* broken, and the *beautiful rod*—come down from thy glory and sit in thirst," Jerem. xlviii. 17, 18. "Jehovah shall send the *rod of thy strength* out of Zion," Psalm cx. 2. "Thou didst strike through with his *staves* the head of his villages," Habak. iii. 14. "Israel is the *rod* of Jehovah's inheritance," Jerem. x. 16; li. 19. "Thy *rod* and thy *staff* they comfort me," Psalm xxiii. 4. "Jehovah hath broken the *staff*—of his shoulder," Isaiah ix. 4; xiv. 5; Psalm cxxv. 3. "My people ask counsel at their stocks, and their *staff* declareth unto them," Hosea iv. 12. "Jehovah doth take away from Jerusalem—the *staff* of bread, and all the *staff* of water," Isaiah iii. 1, 2; Ezek. iv. 16; v. 16; xiv. 13; Psalm cv. 16; Levit. xxvi. 26. By the staff of bread and water is signified the power of goodness and truth; and by Jerusalem, the church. By the rod of Levi, upon which was the name of Aaron, which blossomed in the tabernacle and yielded almonds, Numb. xvii. 2, 3, 7, 8, in a spiritual sense, nothing else is signified but the power of truth and good, because by Levi and Aaron was signified the truth and good of the church. That power is signified by a staff, is evident from the power of the staff or rod of Moses, in that by stretching forth his *rod* the waters were turned into blood, Exod. vii. 20. That frogs were made to come up over the land of Egypt, Exod. viii. 1, and following verses. That lice were caused to be produced, Exod. viii. 12, and following verses. That by the *rod* were caused thunderings and hail, Exod. ix. 23, and following verses. That locusts were made to come forth, Exod. x. 12, and following verses. That waters were made to gush out of the rock in Horeb, Exod. xvii. 5, and following verses; Numb. xx. 7—13. That the Red Sea was divided and turned back, Exod. xiv. 16, 21, 26. That by the *rod*, when lifted up in the hand of Moses, Joshua overcame the Amalekites, Exod. xvii. 9—12. That fire was made to issue from the rock by the *staff* of the angel, Judges vi. 21. From all these passages it appears, that by a rod, or staff, is signified power: likewise from other passages; as in Isaiah x. 5, 24, 26; xi. 4; xiv. 5; xxx. 31, 32; Ezek. xix. 10—14; Lament. iii. 1, 2; Micah vii. 14; Zech. x. 11; Numb. xxi. 18.

486. *And the angel stood by, saying, Rise, and measure the temple of God, and the altar, and them that worship therein,* signifies the Lord's presence and his command, that he should see and know the state of the church in the new heaven. By angel is meant the Lord, here as in n. 5, 415, and other places, be-

cause an angel never does any thing from himself, but only from the Lord; therefore he says, I will give my two witnesses, verse 3, and these were the Lord's witnesses. By standing by is signified the Lord's presence; and by saying is signified his command; by rise and measure are signified to see and know; that to measure signifies to know and scrutinize the quality of a state, will be seen below. By the temple, the altar, and them that worship therein, is signified the state of the church in the new heaven;—by the temple, the church as to truth of doctrine, n. 191; by the altar, the church as to the good of love, n. 392; and by them that worship is signified the church as to worship proceeding from these two sources. By them that worship is here signified adoration, which has relation to worship, because the spiritual sense is abstracted from persons, n. 78, 79, 96: that this is the case in the present passage, is evident from this circumstance also, that he was told to measure them that worship; for these three things constitute the church, viz., truth of doctrine, good of love, and worship proceeding from both. That it is the church in the new heaven which is meant, is plain from the last verse of this chapter, where it is said, that the temple of God was opened in heaven, and there was seen in his temple the ark of his covenant, verse 19. The reason why the measuring the temple is spoken of at the beginning of this chapter, is, in order that the state of the church in heaven, before it was brought into conjunction with the church in the world, might be seen and known: the church in the world is meant by the court without the temple, which was not to be measured, because it was given to the Gentiles, verse 2; and then it is described as the great city, which is called Sodom and Egypt, verses 7, 9; but after the fall of that great city, verse 13, it follows that the church was become the Lord's, verse 15, and subsequent verses. It must be observed, that there is a church in the heavens as well as on earth; and that they make one, like the internal and external with man; wherefore a church in the heavens is first provided by the Lord, and from it, or by it, a church on earth; thence, it is said, that the New Jerusalem came down from God out of the new heaven, chap. xxi. 1, 2. By the new heaven is meant the new heaven composed of Christians, which is frequently treated of in the following pages. To measure signifies to know and scrutinize the quality of any thing; because by a measure is signified the quality of a thing, or state; this is signified by all the measures of the New Jerusalem, chap. xxi.; and also by these words, which occur there: The angel having a golden reed, *measured* the city and the gates thereof; and he *measured* the wall, one hundred and forty-four cubits; the *measure* of a man, that is, of an angel, verses 15, 17; and as by the New Jerusalem is signified a New Church, it is plain that by measuring it, and the things relating to it, is signified to know its quality. To measure has a similar signification in Ezekiel, where it is said, That the angel *measured* the house of God, the temple, the altar, the court, and the chambers, xl. 3—17; xli. 1—5, 13, 14, 22; xlii. and xliii. And that he *measured* the waters, xlvii. 3—5, 9. Therefore it is said, Show the house of Israel the pattern, that they may be ashamed of their iniquities; and let them *measure* the pattern, and the goings out thereof, and the comings in thereof, and all the forms thereof, that they may keep the whole pattern, Ezek. xliii. 10, 11. The like is signified by measuring, in these passages: "I lifted up mine eyes, and behold, a man, in whose hand was a *measuring line*, and I said, Whither goest thou? and he said, *To measure Jerusalem*, Zech. ii. 1, 5, 6, 8. He stood and *measured* the earth, Habak. iii. 6. The Lord Jehovah " hath *measured* the waters in the hollow of his hand, and meted out heaven with a span, and weighed the mountains in scales, and the hills in a balance," Isaiah xl. 12. "Where wast thou when I laid the foundations of the earth? who laid the *measures* thereof, or who hath stretched the line upon it?" Job xxxviii. 4—6.

487. *But the court which is without the temple leave out, and measure it not*, signifies that the state of the church on earth, such as it is at present, is to be removed, and not to be known. By the court without the temple is signified the church on earth, this being without heaven or the temple, n. 486; by leaving it out is signified to remove it, in this instance, from heaven, because such is its state; and by not measuring it is signified not to scrutinize and know its quality, n. 486. The reason follows; namely, because it is given unto the Gentiles, and the holy city shall they tread under foot forty and two months. That by the court without the temple is here signified the church on earth such as it still is, appears from what follows in this chapter, where it is described as the great city, which spiritually is called Sodom and Egypt, in which the Lord's two witnesses lay dead, and which afterwards fell in a great earthquake, wherein were slain names of men seven thousand; besides other circumstances. By a court, in the Word in other places, is signified the external of the church; for there were two courts, through which it was necessary to pass, in order to go into the temple itself at Jerusalem; and because by the temple was signified the church as to its internal, therefore by the courts was signified the church as to its external; wherefore the strangers, who were from among the Gentiles, were admitted into the courts, but not into the temple itself. And as the external of the church is signified by a court, therefore also the church on earth is signified thereby, and also heaven in ultimates, because the church on earth is the entrance to heaven, and likewise heaven in ultimates. That is what is signified

by a court, in the following passages: "Blessed is the man whom thou choosest, that he may dwell in *thy courts;* we shall be satisfied with the goodness of thy house, even of thy holy temple," Psalm lxv. 5. "Praise ye the name of Jehovah, ye who stand in his house, in the *courts of the house* of our God," Psalm cxxxv. 1, 2. "How amiable are thy tabernacles, O Jehovah: my soul longeth, yea, even fainteth, for the *courts of Jehovah,*" Psalm lxxxiv. 1, 2. "Enter into his gates with thanksgiving, and into his *courts* with praise," Psalm c. 4. "The righteous shall flourish like the palm-tree, those that be planted in the house of Jehovah shall flourish in the *courts* of our God," Psalm xcii. 12, 13. "A day in thy *courts* is better than a thousand: I had rather be a door-keeper in the house of my God, than to dwell in the tents of wickedness," Psalm lxxxiv. 10; besides others; as in Psalm xcvi. 7; Isaiah i. 12; lxii. 9; Zech. iii. 7; Ezek. x. 3—5. Of the *courts* of the temple of Jerusalem, 1 Kings vi. 3, 36. Of the *courts* of the new temple, Ezek. xl. 17—31—44; xlii. 1—4; xliii. 4—7. And of the *court* without the tabernacle, Exod. xxvii. 9—18.

488. *For it is given unto the Gentiles,* signifies, because the state of that church is destroyed and laid waste by evils of life, as is evident from the signification of Gentiles, as denoting those who are in evils of life, and, abstractedly, evils of life, n. 147, 483.

489. *And the holy city shall they tread under foot forty and two months,* signifies that it would disperse every truth of the Word, even to nothing remaining. By the holy city is meant the holy Jerusalem; and by the holy Jerusalem is meant the New Church which is in truths of doctrine, for holy is predicated of divine truth, n. 173; and a city signifies doctrine, n. 194; therefore by treading that city under foot is signified to disperse the truths of its doctrine; by forty and two months is signified until there is an end, when there is no truth left; by truths of doctrine are meant truths from the Word, because the doctrine of the church, and all that relates to it, is thence derived. That they who are, at this day, in the internals of the church, have so dispersed the truths of the Word, and thence the doctrines of the church, and every thing relating to the church, is described in this chapter by the beast coming up out of the bottomless pit, in that he slew the two witnesses, verse 7, and may also be seen from the Memorable Relations from the spiritual world, annexed to each chapter. By forty and two months is signified to the end, and till nothing good or true is left in the church, because the same thing is signified by forty and two as by six weeks, for six times seven is forty-two, and by six weeks is signified what is complete to the end; for the number six has this signification, and a week signifies state, and the seventh week a holy state, which is a new state of the

church, when the Lord enters upon his reign. This number has a similar signification in the following passage: "And there was given unto the beast which came up out of the sea a mouth speaking great things and blasphemies, and power was given unto him to continue *forty-two months*," Apoc. xiii. 5, n. 583. The reason why six signifies what is complete to the end, is, because three has that signification, n. 505, and six is double that number, and a number doubled has the same signification as the simple number; besides, the same is signified by this number as by three and a half, because forty-two months make three years and a half. Months are mentioned because by a month is signified a full state; as in Isaiah lxvi. 23; Apoc. xxii. 1, 2; Gen. xxix. 14; Numb. xi. 18—20; Deut. xxi. 11, 13.

490. *And I will give unto my two witnesses*, signifies those who confess and acknowledge in their hearts that the Lord is the God of heaven and earth, and that his Humanity is Divine, and who are conjoined to him by a life according to the precepts of the decalogue. The reason why such persons are here understood by the two witnesses, is, because these two things constitute the two essentials of the New Church. That the first essential, that the Lord is the God of heaven and earth, and that his Humanity is Divine, is a testimony or witness, and consequently, that they are witnesses who confess and acknowledge it in their hearts, may be seen, n. 6, 846, and likewise from the following passages: "I am thy fellow-servant, of thy brethren that have the *testimony of Jesus; for the testimony of Jesus is the spirit of prophecy*," Apoc. xix. 10. The angels of Michael overcame the dragon by the blood of the Lamb and by the *Word of his testimony*: and the dragon "went to make war with the remnant of her seed, which keep the commandments of God, and have the *testimony of Jesus Christ*," Apoc. xii. 10 17. "The souls of them that were smitten with the axe, for the *testimony of Jesus*, and for the Word of God," Apoc. xx. 4 these are they who have acknowledged the Lord. It is called the testimony of Jesus, because the Lord testifies it from his Word, thus from himself, therefore he himself is called the *faithful and true witness*, Apoc. i. 5; iii. 14; and says, I *testify of myself, and my testimony* is true, because I know whence I came, and whither I go, John viii. 14; also, "When the Comforter is come, even the Spirit of Truth, he shall *testify* of me," John xv. 26. That the Comforter, the Spirit of Truth, which also is the Holy Spirit, is the proceeding Divinity, and that this is the Lord himself, may be seen in the *Doctrine of the New Jerusalem concerning the Lord*, n. 46—54. Now since the Lord himself is the witness, therefore also by witnesses are meant they who testify this from the Lord, as did John: Jesus said, "Ye sent unto John, and he bare *witness* unto the truth: but I receive not *testimony* from man," John v. 33. John came as a

witness, to bear witness of the light; he was not the light, but was to *bear witness* of the light. The Word which was with God, and which was God, was the true light, John i. 1, 2, and following verses, 14, 34. That the other essential of the New Church, which is conjunction with the Lord by a life according to the precepts of the decalogue, is a testimony, appears from the decalogue being called the testimony, as in these passages: "And thou shalt put into the ark the testimony which I shall give thee," Exod. xxv. 16. Moses put the *testimony* into the ark, Exod. xl. 20. The mercy-seat that is over the *testimony*, Levit. xvi. 13. Leave the rods of the tribes before the *testimony*, Numb. xvii.; besides other places, as in Exod. xxv. 22; xxxi. 7, 18; xxxii. 15; Psalm lxxviii. 5; Psalm cxxxii. 12. Something must here be said concerning conjunction with the Lord by a life according to the precepts of the decalogue. There are two tables upon which those precepts are written, one for the Lord, the other for man; what the first table contains, is, that a plurality of gods are not to be worshipped, but only one; and the second, that evils are not to be committed; therefore, when one God is worshipped, and man does not commit evils, a conjunction takes place; for in proportion as man desists from evils, that is, does the work of repentance, in the same proportion he is accepted of God, and does good from him. But who now is this one God? A trine or triune God is not one God, so long as this trine and triunity exists in three persons; but he, in whom a trine or triunity exists in one person, is one God, and that God is the Lord; enter into whatever intricacies of thought you please, yet will you never be able to extricate yourself and make out that God is one, unless he is also one in person. That this is the case, the whole Word teaches, both in the Old Testament and Prophets, and in the New Testament and Evangelists, as may be clearly seen in *The Doctrine of the New Jerusalem concerning the Lord*.

491. *And they shall prophesy a thousand two hundred and sixty days*, signifies that these two articles, the acknowledgment of the Lord, and a life according to the commandments of the decalogue, which are the two essentials of the New Church, are to be taught until the end and the beginning. That these two articles, the acknowledgment of the Lord, and a life according to the commandments of the decalogue, are the two essentials of the New Church, and are meant by the two witnesses, may be seen above, n. 490; and that to prophesy signifies to teach, n. 8, 133. By one thousand two hundred and sixty days, is signified until the end and the beginning, that is, until the end of the former church, thus the beginning of the New; the reason why this is signified by this number, is, because it has the same signification as three and a half, and by three and a half is signified an end and a beginning, n. 505; it has the same

signification as three and a half, because the number one thousand two hundred and sixty, when reduced into years, makes three years and a half. The like is signified by the same number in the next chapter: "And the woman fled into the wilderness, where she hath a place prepared of God, that they should feed her there a *thousand two hundred and sixty days,*" Apoc. xii. 6.

492. *Clothed in sackcloth,* signifies lamentation in the mean time on account of the non-reception of truth. By being clothed in sackcloth is signified lamentation on account of the devastation of truth in the church; for garments signify truths, n. 166, 212, 318, 378, 379: therefore to be clothed in sackcloth, which is not a garment, signifies lamentation because there is no truth, and where there is no truth there is no church. The children of Israel represented lamentation by various things, which, from correspondences, were significative, as by putting ashes on the head, by rolling themselves in the dust, by sitting a long time silent upon the ground, by shaving themselves, by mourning and howling, by tearing their garments, and also by putting on sackcloth, besides other particulars; and each of these signified some evil of the church among them, for which they were punished; and when they were punished, they represented repentance by such things, and on account of the representation of repentance, and, at the same time, of humiliation, they were heard. That lamentation on account of the devastation of truth in the church, was represented by putting on sackcloth, may be seen from the following passages: "The lion is come up from his thicket, he is gone forth from his place to make thy land desolate; for this *gird you with sackcloth,* lament and howl," Jerem. iv. 7, 8. "O daughter of my people, *gird thee with sackcloth,* and wallow thyself in ashes, for the spoiler shall suddenly come upon us," Jerem. vi. 26. "Woe unto thee, Chorazin and Bethsaida! for if the mighty works which have been done in you had been done in Tyre and Sidon, they would have repented in *sackcloth* and ashes," Matt. xi. 21; Luke x. 13. The king of Nineveh, when he had heard the words of Jonah, put off his robe from him, and covered him with *sackcloth,* and sat in ashes, and proclaimed a fast, and that man and beast should be *covered with sackcloth,* Jonah iii. 5, 6, 8; besides other places; as in Isaiah iii. 24; xv. 2, 3; xxii. 12; xxxvii. 1, 2; l. 3; Jerem. xlviii. 37, 38; xlix. 3; Lament. ii. 10; Ezek. vii. 17, 18; xxvii. 31; Dan. ix. 3; Joel i. 8, 13; Amos viii. 10; Job xvi. 15, 16; Psalm xxx. 12; Psalm xxxv. 13; Psalm lxix. 11, 12; 2 Sam. iii. 31; 1 Kings xxi. 27; 2 Kings vi. 30; xix. 1, 2.

493. *These are the two olive trees, and the two candlesticks, standing before the God of the earth,* signifies love and intelligence, or charity and faith, both from the Lord with them. By

an olive-tree is signified love and charity, as will be seen presently; and by candlesticks is signified illustration in truths, n. 43, and thence intelligence and faith, because from illustration in truth comes intelligence, and from intelligence comes faith. By standing before God is signified to hear and do his commandments, n. 366, here, therefore, that these two are with them from the Lord, who is the God of the earth, that is, in those who are principled in the two essentials of the New Church spoken of above; from which it is plain, that by the two witnesses being two olive-trees and two candlesticks, is signified that they were love and intelligence, or charity and faith, for these two constitute the church; love and charity its life, and intelligence and faith its doctrine. An olive signifies love and charity, because the olive-tree signifies the celestial church, and thence the olive, which is its fruit, signifies celestial love, which love is love to the Lord; hence it is, that this love is also signified by the oil, by which all the holy things of the church were anointed: the oil, which was called the oil of holiness, was produced from olives mixed with aromatics, Exod. xxx. 23—25; and also the lamps of the candlestick in the tabernacle were made to burn every evening with *olive oil*, Exod. xxvii. 20, 21; Levit. xxiv. 2. An olive-tree and olives have a like signification in Zechariah: There were two *olive-trees* by the candlestick, one upon the right side of the bowl, and the other upon the left, and two *olive berries:* these are the two sons of the *olive-tree standing before the Lord of the whole earth*, iv. 3, 11, 12, 14. In David: "I am like a *green olive-tree* in the house of God," Psalm lii. 8. And in Jeremiah: "Jehovah called thy name a *green olive-tree* fair and of goodly fruit," xi. 16, 17; besides other places. Since Jerusalem signified the church, therefore, also, many things that were in and about it signified such things as pertain to the church. Near it was also the Mount of Olives, which signified divine love, wherefore Jesus in the day-time was teaching in the temple, and at night he went out, and abode in the *Mount of Olives*, Luke xxi. 37; xxii. 39; John viii. 1. And Jesus discoursed with his disciples on *that mount* concerning the end of the world, and his coming at that time, Matt. xxiv. 3, and following verses; Mark xiii. 3, and following verses. And went likewise from *that mountain* to Jerusalem, and suffered, Matt. xxi. 1; xxvi. 30; Mark xi. 1; xiv. 16; Luke xix. 26, 37; and this according to the prediction in Zechariah: His feet shall stand in that day upon the *Mount of Olives*, which is before Jerusalem on the east, xiv. 4. Because the olive-tree signified the celestial principle of the church, therefore the cherubs in the midst of the temple of Jerusalem were made of the *wood of the olive-tree;* in like manner the doors of the entrance to the oracle, and the posts, 1 Kings vi. 23—33.

494. *And if any one desire to hurt them, fire shall proceed out of their mouth, and shall devour their enemies*, signifies that they who desire to destroy these two essentials of the New Church will perish from infernal love. To desire to hurt the two witnesses signifies a desire to destroy these two essentials of the New Church, which are the acknowledgment of the Lord as being the God of heaven and earth even as to his Humanity, and a life according to the commandments of the decalogue; that these are the witnesses, may be seen above, n. 490. Fire shall proceed out of their mouth, signifies infernal love; and shall devour their enemies, signifies that they who hurt them will perish by that love; but it is not here to be understood that fire will proceed out of the mouth of the witnesses, but from those who desire to destroy these two essentials of the New Church, which are meant by the witnesses, n. 490. Fire is infernal love; for he who does not live according to the commandments of the decalogue, and approach to God the Saviour and Redeemer, cannot be otherwise than in infernal love, and perish. This is similar to its being said, in other parts of the Word, that fire proceeds from Jehovah to consume the wicked; and that Jehovah acts from the fire of his wrath, anger, and fury; not to mention other expressions of a like kind, by which it is not meant that this comes from Jehovah, but from the infernal love of the wicked. Such expressions are used in the Word, because they are appearances; the Word, in its literal sense, being written according to correspondences and appearances. Since it is said, that fire should proceed out of their mouth, and that thereby it is to be understood that it proceeds from those who are in infernal love, some passages shall be adduced in which it is said that fire comes from Jehovah: The breath of Jehovah, like a *stream of brimstone*, doth kindle it. Isaiah xxx. 33. Smoke went up out of his nostrils, and *fire out of his mouth*, coals were kindled by it, Psalm xviii. 9. I will pour out upon them the indignation of mine anger, for in the *fire of my zeal* shall the whole earth be devoured, Zeph. iii. 8. "Behold, Jehovah shall come in *fire*, to render his anger with fury, and his rebuke with *flames of fire*," Isaiah lxvi. 15. Thou shalt be visited by Jehovah in a *flame of devouring fire*, Isaiah xxix. 6; xxx. 30; besides many others.

495. *And if any one desire to hurt them, he must thus be killed*, signifies that he who condemns them shall in like manner be condemned. By desiring to hurt them is here signified to condemn, because it follows he must thus be killed, and by being killed, in the Word, is signified to be killed spiritually, which is to be condemned; for the Lord says, With what judgment ye judge, ye shall be judged, Matt. vii. 1.

496. *These have power to shut heaven, that the rain fall not in the days of their prophecy*, signifies that they who reject these

two essentials, cannot receive any truth from heaven. By heaven is here meant the angelic heaven; consequently, by *rain*, the truth of the church from thence is signified; wherefore, by shutting heaven that the rain fall not, is signified that they are not able to receive any truth of the church from heaven; the truth of the church from heaven is the truth of doctrine from the Word. It is said that the witnesses had this power, but it is to be understood here as above, n. 494, that they have not the power to shut heaven, but that they shut heaven against themselves who reject these two essentials of the New Church, because they remain in their own falses. That rain signifies divine truth from heaven, appears from these passages: "My doctrine shall drop as the *rain*, my speech shall distil as the dew," Deut. xxxii. 2. If ye serve other gods, Jehovah will shut up the heaven, that there be no *rain*, Deut. xi. 11, 14, 16, 17. I will lay my vineyard waste, and "I will command the clouds, that they *rain no rain* upon it," Isaiah v. 6. "Therefore the *showers* have been withholden, and there hath been no *latter rain*; and thou hadst a whore's forehead, thou refusedst to be ashamed," Jerem. iii. 3. "For as the *rain* cometh down from heaven, so shall my Word be that goeth forth out of my mouth," Isaiah lv. 10, 11. "Ye children of Zion rejoice and be glad in Jehovah, for he hath given you the former *rain* moderately," Joel ii. 23. "Thou, O God, didst send a plentiful *rain*," Psalm lxviii. 9. "He shall come down like *rain* upon the mown grass, in his days shall the righteous flourish," Psalm lxxii. 6, 7. "Jehovah shall come unto us as the *rain*; as the *latter and former rain* unto the earth," Hosea vi. 3. "My speech dropped upon them, and they waited for me as for the *rain*, and they opened their mouth wide as for the *latter rain*," Job xxix. 22, 23. "Son of man, say unto her, Thou art the land that is not cleansed, nor *rained* upon in the day of indignation, there is a conspiracy of the prophets in the midst thereof," Ezek. xxii. 24, 25; besides other places; as in Isaiah xxx. 23; Jerem. v. 24; x. 12, 13; xiv. 3, 4; li. 16; Exek. xxxiv. 26, 27; Amos iv. 7, 8; Zech. x. 1; Psalm lxv. 10, 11; Psalm cxxxv. 7; 2 Sam. xxiii. 3, 4. An inundating rain denotes the devastation of truth, Ezek. xiii. 11, 13, 14; xxxviii. 22; and temptation, Matt. vii. 24—27.

497. *And have power over the waters to turn them into blood*, signifies that they who reject these two essentials falsify the truth of the Word. By waters are signified truths, n. 50; and by blood, the falsification of the truth of the Word, n. 379; therefore, by turning the waters into blood is signified to falsify the truths of the Word. This is to be understood in the same manner as before, namely, that they who reject the two essentials of the New Church can see nothing but their own falses,

and, if they confirm these by the Word, they then falsify its truths.

498. *And to smite the earth with every plague as often as they will*, signifies that they who desire to destroy these two essentials of the New Church will plunge themselves into all kinds of evils and falses, as often, and in proportion, as they do so. By the earth is signified the church, n. 285; and by a plague is signified evil and falsity, n. 456; hence by smiting the earth with every plague, is signified to destroy the church by all kinds of evils and falses. But this passage is to be understood in the same manner as the former, viz., that they who desire to smite these two essentials of the New Church with a plague, that is, to destroy them, which is done by evil through falses, will plunge themselves into all kinds of evils and falses; and as the natural sense is thus inverted while it is spiritual, therefore also this expression, "as often as they will," is inverted in like manner into this, *as often, and in proportion, as they* do this. The reason is, because in proportion as any one destroys these two essentials, in the same proportion he destroys the truths of the Word; and so far as he destroys the truths of the Word, so far he plunges himself into evils and falses; for these two essentials are the truths of the Word, as may appear manifestly from *The two Doctrines of the New Jerusalem;* one concerning *The Lord*, and the other concerning *The Doctrine of Life from the Precepts of the Decalogue*. This passage, which ascribes to the witnesses the power of smiting the earth with every plague as often as they will, is similar to many others in the Word, which attribute to Jehovah, that is, to the Lord, that he smites men with plagues, and that such is his will, when yet it must be understood that he neither smites them, nor is it his will to do so; as in Zechariah: "And this shall be the plague wherewith Jehovah will *smite* all the people that have fought against Jerusalem," xiv. 12. and following verses. And in Jeremiah: "I have *wounded* thee with the *wound* of an enemy, with the chastisement of a cruel one, for the multitude of thine iniquity," xxx. 14; likewise in many other places. See also above, n. 494.

499. *And when they shall have finished their testimony*, signifies that after the Lord has taught that he is the God of heaven and earth, and that conjunction is formed with him by a life according to the precepts of the decalogue. When they shall have finished, signifies after the Lord has taught; the two witnesses, indeed, taught, yet not from themselves, but from the Lord. That testimony signifies these two essentials, may be seen above, n. 490.

500. *The beast that ascendeth out of the bottomless pit shall make war with them, and shall overcome them, and kill them*, signifies that they who are principled in the internals of the

doctrine of faith alone will oppose them, and assault these two essentials of the New Church, and will reject them, and, as far as lies in their power, will cause others to reject them. By the beast that ascends out of the bottomless pit, are meant they who came up out of the bottomless pit, and appeared like locusts, chap. ix. 1—12. That these were they who are in the internals of the doctrine of faith alone, may be seen in the explanation there given; by making war is signified to oppose and assault these two essentials of the church, as will be seen presently; by overcoming and killing them is signified to reject and extirpate them in themselves, and, as far as lies in their power, to cause others to do the same. The reason why they who are principled in the internals of the doctrine of faith alone will impugn and reject these two essentials, is, because they have confirmed themselves in two things diametrically opposite to them,—first, that it is not the Lord, but God the Father, who is to be approached; and secondly, that a life according to the precepts of the decalogue is not a spiritual life, but only a moral and civil life, and this they confirm, that no one may believe that he can be saved by works, but by their faith alone. All they who have had these tenets strongly impressed upon their minds in schools and universities do not recede from them afterwards; and that for these three several reasons, which have not been made known till now: first, because they have entered, as to their spirit, into association with their life in the spiritual world, where there are many satans, who are delighted with nothing but falses, from whom they can no how be separated but by rejecting those falses; nor can this be done but by immediately approaching God the Saviour, and beginning a Christian life according to the precepts of the decalogue. The second reason is, because they believe that remission of sins, and consequent salvation, may take place in a moment in the act of faith, and afterwards in the state or in the progression by the same act continued, preserved, and retained, from the Holy Spirit, separate from the exercises of charity; and they who have once imbibed these doctrines afterwards make no account of sins before God, and so live in their uncleanness; and, because they have the art to confirm their tenets before the unlearned very ingeniously by falsifications of the Word, and before the learned by much sophistry, it is here said, that the beast which came up from the bottomless pit overcame and killed the two witnesses. But this is only exhibited among such as love to follow their own inclinations, being borne along by the delights of their lusts, and who, while thinking about salvation, nevertheless cherish those lusts in their hearts, and embrace their faith with both hands, seeing that they may be saved by uttering certain words with a tone of confidence, and need not attend to leading a life for the sake of God, but only for the sake of the world. The third reason is, that they who, in the early part of life, have imbibed the internals of that faith which are called the mysteries of justification, on being afterwards advanced to some dignified office in the ministry, do not think in their hearts about God and heaven, but about themselves and the world, retaining only the mysteries of their faith for the sake of character, that they may be honoured as wise men, and by reason of their wisdom, be thought worthy of being rewarded with riches. The reason why this is an effect of that faith, is, because there is nothing of religion in it; as may be seen by a reference to the third Memorable Relation, n. 484. That by wars, in the Word, are signified spiritual wars, which consist in impugning truth, and are conducted by reasonings from falses, is evident from these passages: "For they are the spirits of devils which go forth to gather them to the *battle* of that great day of God Almighty," Apoc. xvi. 14. "And the dragon was wroth with the woman, and went to make *war* with the remnant of her seed, which keep the commandments of God, and have the testimony of Jesus Christ," Apoc. xii. 17. "And it was given unto the beast of the dragon to make *war* with the saints," Apoc. xiii. 7. "Prepare ye *war* against the daughter of Zion, and let us go up at noon," Jerem. vi. 3—5. "Ye have not gone up into the gaps—to stand in the *battle* in the day of Jehovah," Ezek. xiii. 5. "In Salem also is the tabernacle of God, and his dwelling-place in Zion, there brake he the arrows of the bow, and the *battle*," Psalm lxxvi. 2, 3. "Jehovah shall go forth as a mighty man, he shall stir up his jealousy like a man of *war*," Isaiah xlii. 13; Psalm xxiv. 8. In that day Jehovah shall be for a spirit of judgment to him that sitteth in judgment, and for strength to them that *battle* to the gate," Isaiah xxviii. 6. "Deliver me from the evil man, preserve me from the violent man; continually are they gathered together for *war*;—they have sharpened their tongues like a serpent," Psalm cxl. 1—3. "Many shall come in my name, saying, I am Christ, and shall deceive many, and ye shall hear of *wars* and rumours of *wars*, see that ye be not troubled," Matt. xxiv. 6—8; Mark xiii. 7—9; Luke xxi. 9—11. The *wars* of the kings of the north, and of the south, and others, in Daniel, chap. x. xi. xii., signify no other than spiritual *wars*; besides the wars mentioned in other places; as in Isaiah ii. 3—5; xiii. 4; xxi. 14, 15; xxxi. 4; Jerem. xlix. 25, 26; Hosea ii. 18; Zech. x, 5; xiv. 3; Psalm xxxv. 3; Psalm xlvi. 9, 10. Since by wars, in the Word, are signified spiritual wars, therefore the ministry of the Levites was called military service, as appears from its being commanded that the Levites should be numbered, to perform *military service*, to do work in the tabernacle of the congregation, Numb. iv. 23, 35, 39, 43, 47. "This is the office of the Levites *to war in military service* of the tabernacle of the congregation; and from the age of fifty years they cease waiting upon the *military service* of the tabernacle, and shall serve no more," Numb. viii. 24, 25; see also above, n. 447, where it is proved from the Word that armies signify the goods and truths of the church, and, in the opposite sense, its evils and falses.

501. *And their dead bodies shall lie in the street of the great city*, signifies that the two essentials of the New Church are totally rejected by those who are interiorly principled in the falses of doctrine concerning justification by faith alone. By the bodies of the two witnesses are signified the two essentials of the New Church, which are the acknowledgment of the Lord as the only God of heaven and earth, and that there is conjunction with him by a life according to the precepts of the decalogue, n. 590, &c. By the street of the great city is signified the falsity of the doctrine concerning justification by faith alone; by a street is signified falsity, as will be seen presently; and by a city is signified doctrine, n. 194. It is called a great city, because it is a doctrine which prevails throughout the whole reformed Christian world among the clergy, though not in the same way among the laity. By streets, in the Word, almost the same is signified as by ways, because streets are ways in a city; but still by streets are signified the truths or falses of doctrine, by reason that a city signifies doctrine, n. 194; and by ways are signified the truths or falses of the church, because the earth signifies the church, n. 285. That streets signify truths or falses of doctrine, may be seen from the following passages: "And judgment is turned away backward, and justice standeth afar off: for truth is fallen in the *street*, and equity cannot enter," Isaiah lix. 14. "The chariots shall rage in the *streets*, they shall justle one against another in the *broad ways*," Nahum ii. 4. In the days of Jael the *ways* ceased, the *streets* ceased in Israel, Judges v. 6, 7. "How is the city of praise not left—therefore her young men shall fall in the *streets*," Jerem. xlix. 25, 26; l. 30. "They that did feed delicately are desolate in the *streets*. Their visage is blacker than a coal, they are not known in the *streets*. They have wandered as blind men in the *streets*. They hunt our steps, that we cannot go in our *streets*," Lament. iv. 5, 8, 14, 18. "I have cut off the nations, their towers are desolate, I made their *streets* waste," Zeph. iii. 6. Afterwards in sixty-two weeks the *streets of Jerusalem* "shall be built again even in troublous times," Dan. ix. 25. "The *street of the city* Jerusalem was pure gold, as it were transparent glass," Apoc. xxi. 21. "In the midst of the *street* of it, the tree of life bearing twelve fruits," Apoc. xxii. 1, 2; besides other places; as in Isaiah xv. 3; xxiv. 10, 11; li. 20; Jerem. v. 1; vi. 16; vii. 17; ix. 21; xi. 13; xvi. 24, 25, 31; xliv. 18; xlv. 9; Lament. ii. 11, 19; Ezek. xi. 6; xxvi. 11, 12; Amos v. 16; Zech. viii. 3—5; Psalm

cxliv. 13; Job xviii. 17. Since streets signify the truths of doctrine of the church, therefore it was the custom to teach in the *streets*, 2 Sam. i. 20. And it is said, "We have eaten and drunk in thy presence, and thou hast taught in our *streets*," Luke xiii. 26; and, therefore, hypocrites prayed in the corners of the *streets*, Matt. vi. 3, 5; and the master of the house commanded his servants to go into the *streets* and *lanes*, and bring in guests, Luke xiv. 21. "For the same reason, also, what is false and falsified is called mire, dirt, and dung, of the *streets*, Isaiah v. 25; x. 6; Micah vii. 10; Psalm xviii. 42. That the prophets who prophesied what was false, should be cast out into the *streets of Jerusalem*, and have none to bury them, Jerem. xiv. 16.

502. *Which spiritually is called Sodom and Egypt*, signifies two infernal loves, which are the love of dominion grounded in self-love, and the love of rule grounded in the pride of self-derived intelligence, which exist in the church where one God is not acknowledged, and the Lord is not worshipped, and where they do not live according to the commandments of the decalogue. By Sodom, in the spiritual sense, is signified the love of dominion grounded in self-love, as will be seen presently; and by Egypt, in the spiritual sense, is signified the love of rule grounded in the pride of self-derived intelligence, which, also, will be spoken of presently; and because these two loves are signified, therefore it is spiritually called Sodom and Egypt. The reason why these loves prevail in the church where one God is not acknowledged, and the Lord is not worshipped, and where they do not live according to the precepts of the decalogue, is, because man is born into those two loves, and comes into them as he grows up, and those loves cannot be removed but by God the Saviour, and by a life according to his commandments; and they cannot be removed by God the Saviour, unless he is approached: nor is a life according to his commandments possible, unless man is led by him; it is possible indeed to live according to the commandments, but not to live a life in which there is any thing of heaven and thence of the church. Such a life can only be given by him who is the life; that the Lord is that life, may be seen in John i. 1, 4; v. 26; vi. 33—35, and subsequent verses; xi. 25, 26; xiv. 6, 19; and in many other places. That the love of dominion grounded in self-love, and the love of rule grounded in the pride of self-derived intelligence, are the heads or sources of all infernal loves, and thus of all evils and of the falses resulting therefrom in the church, is unknown at this day; the delights of those loves, which surpass the delights of all the pleasures of the mind, are the causes of its not being known, when yet, spiritually, they are Sodom and Egypt. That Sodom is the love of dominion grounded in self-love, may appear from the description of Sodom in Moses, in that they wanted to

do violence to the angels who came into Lot's house; and in that fire and sulphur rained upon them out of heaven, Gen. xix. 1, and following verses. By fire and sulphur, that love with its concupiscences is signified. I saw the like things happen when the cities and societies of such persons were overthrown in the day of the last judgment, and their inhabitants cast into hell. These loves and their evils are signified by Sodom and Gomorrah, in these places: Isaiah i. 10; iii. 8, 9, 19; Jerem. xxiii. 14; xlix. 18; l. 37, 40; Lament. iv. 6; Ezek. xvi. 46—50; Amos iv. 11; Zeph. ii. 9, 10; Deut. xxix. 23; xxxii. 32; Matt. x. 14, 15; xi. 23; Mark vi. 11; Luke x. 10, 11, 13; xvii. 28, 29. That this love is signified by Sodom, is not known in the world; but keep this in mind and remember it when you enter into the world of spirits, as you will do after death, and you will be fully convinced of it. But it is to be observed, that there is a love of dominion grounded in self-love, and a love of dominion grounded in the love of uses; the latter is celestial, but the former infernal; therefore when one constitutes the head, the other constitutes the feet, that is, when the love of dominion grounded in self-love constitutes the head, then the love of dominion grounded in the love of uses, which is also the love of serving one's neighbour from the Lord, at first constitutes the feet, afterwards the soles of the feet, and, lastly, is trodden under foot; but when the love of dominion grounded in the love of uses, which, as was said, is a celestial love, constitutes the head, then the love of dominion grounded in self-love, which, as was observed, is an infernal love, at first constitutes the feet, afterwards the soles of the feet, and, finally, is trodden under foot. These two loves, however, are with difficulty distinguished by man in this world, because their external forms are alike; yet they may be distinguished by this circumstance, viz., that the above celestial love dwells in those who approach the Lord, and live according to the commandments of the decalogue; and that the above infernal love dwells in those who do not approach the Lord, nor live according to the commandments of the decalogue.

503. We shall now proceed to explain what is signified by Egypt in the Word. Egypt signifies the natural man in conjunction with the spiritual, and thus the affection of truth and thence science and intelligence; but, in the opposite sense, it signifies the natural man separated from the spiritual, and, in that case, the pride of self-derived intelligence, and consequent insanity in spiritual things. Egypt signifies the natural man in conjunction with the spiritual, and thus the affection of truth, and thence science and intelligence, in the following passages: "In that day shall five cities in the land of *Egypt* swear to Jehovah of hosts. In that day shall there be an altar to Jehovah in the midst of the land of *Egypt;* then shall Jehovah be known to *Egypt*, and the *Egyptians* shall know Jehovah in that day,"

Isaiah xix. 17—21. "In that day shall there be a highway out of *Egypt* to *Assyria*, and the *Egyptians* shall serve with the *Assyrians*. In that day shall *Israel* be the third with *Egypt* and *Assyria*, a blessing in the midst of the land; whom Jehovah of hosts shall bless, saying, Blessed be *Egypt* my people, and *Assyria* the work of my hands, and Israel mine inheritance," Isaiah xix. 23—25. Egypt there is the natural degree, Assyria is the rational degree, and Israel is the spiritual degree, and these three constitute a man of the church. Hence the king of *Egypt* was called the son of the wise, the son of ancient kings; and Egypt was called the stay of the tribes, Isaiah xix. 11, 13: and it is said of Solomon, that his wisdom excelled the wisdom of the *Egyptians*, 1 Kings iv. 30; and, that "he took *Pharaoh's daughter* to wife, and brought her into the city of David," 1 Kings iii. 1. And that he built *Pharaoh's daughter* a house beside the porch, 1 Kings vii. 8. For the same reason, also, Joseph was carried into *Egypt*, and was there made governor over all the land, Gen. xli. Since Egypt signified the natural man as to the affection of truth and thence science and intelligence, therefore Joseph the husband of Mary, being warned of an angel, departed into *Egypt* with the Lord who was then an infant, Matt. i. 14, 15; according to the prediction, "When Israel was a child then I loved him, and called my Son out of *Egypt*," Hosea xi. 1. "Thou hast caused a vine to come out of *Egypt*, thou hast planted it, and didst cause it to take deep root," Psalm lxxx. 8, 9; for man is born natural, becomes rational, and afterwards spiritual, thus is the vine out of Egypt planted and made to take root. For the sake of this representation, Abraham also journeyed into *Egypt*, Gen. xii. 10, and following verses. And Jacob was commanded to go with his sons into *Egypt*, and also abode there, Gen. xlvi. and following chapters. Thence, also, the land of Canaan, by which the church is signified, is described as extending as far as the river of *Egypt*, Gen. xv. 18; 1 Kings ii. 17, 18; Micah vii. 12. And *Egypt* is compared to the garden of Eden, the garden of God, Ezek. xxxi. 2, 8; Gen. xiii. 10. And the sciences of the natural man are called the desirable things of *Egypt*, Dan. xi. 43. And fine embroidered linen from *Egypt*, Ezek. xxvii. 7: besides other passages, where Egypt is favourably spoken of; as in Isaiah xlvi. 11, 12; Ezek. xxix. 13—16; xxxi. 1—8; Hosea xi. 11; Zech. x. 11; xiv. 16—18; Psalm lxviii. 31, 32; 2 Kings xvii. 36. But Egypt, in the opposite sense, signifies the natural man separated from the spiritual, and thus the pride of self-derived intelligence, and thence insanity in spiritual things, in these places: Because the heart of *Pharaoh* " is lifted up in his height, and he hath shot up his top among the thick boughs, strangers shall cut him off, and cast him forth. In the day when he went down to the grave, I covered the deep over him, thou shalt lie in the midst of the uncircumcised, Ezek. xxxi. 10—18. " The foundations of *Egypt* shall be overthrown; the pride of his strength shall come down, and his cities shall be laid waste in the midst of the desolate cities: I will send fire upon *Egypt*, and I will disperse *Egypt* among the nations, and will scatter them over the earth," Ezek. xxx. 1, to the end. " Woe to them that go down to *Egypt* for help, and look not unto the Holy One of Israel; now the *Egyptians* are men and not God, and their horses flesh, and not spirit," Isaiah xxxi. 1, 3. "*Egypt* riseth up as a flood, he saith, I will go up, I will cover the earth, and destroy the city: come up, ye horses, rage ye chariots, the sword shall devour you, and shall be made drunk with blood, for thou shalt not be cured," Jerem. xlvi. 2, 7, 8, 9. How say ye unto *Pharaoh*, I am the son of the wise, and the son of ancient kings; where now are thy wise men, let them tell thee; the princes of Zoan are become fools, they have seduced *Egypt*, the corner-stone of the tribes; there shall be unto *Egypt* no work that may make head and tail, Isaiah xix. 1—17. Prophesy against *Egypt*; " the great dragon, which lieth in the midst of his rivers; for he hath said, The river is mine, and I have made it for myself, therefore will I put hooks in thy jaws; and I will cause the fish of thy rivers to stick to thy scales, and I will leave thee in the wilderness: and therefore shall the land of *Egypt* be desolate and waste," Ezek. xxix. 1—12: besides other places; as in Isaiah xxx. 1, 7; Jerem ii. 17, 18, 36; xlii. 13—18; Ezek. xvi. 26, 28, 29; xxiii. 2—33; Hosea vii. 11, 13, 16; ix. 1, 3, 6; xi. 5; xii. 1, 2; Joel iii. 19; Lament. v. 2, 4, 6, 8; Deut. xvii. 16; 1 Kings xiv. 25, 26; 2 Kings xviii. 21. Because the Egyptians were of such a character, therefore they were deprived of all the goods and truths of the church; their devastations are described by the miracles performed there, which were plagues, and signified so many lusts of the natural man separated from the spiritual, which acts solely from self-derived intelligence and the pride thereof; the plagues significative of his lusts were, That the *waters in the river* were turned into blood, insomuch that the fish died, and the river stank, Exod. vii. That from the *rivers* and lakes *frogs* were produced over the land of *Egypt*. That the *dust of the earth* was turned into *lice*. That swarms of *noxious flies* were sent, Exod. viii. That *boils* breaking forth with blains were brought upon man and beast. That it *rained hail mingled with fire*, Exod. ix. That *locusts* were sent. That there was *darkness* in all the *land of Egypt*, Exod. x. That all the *first-born* in the *land of Egypt* died, chap. xi. And, finally, That the *Egyptians were drowned in the Red Sea*, Exod. xiv.; by which hell is signified. What these things specifically signify, may be seen in *The Arcana Cœlestia*, where they are explained. Hence it is evident, what is meant by the *plagues and diseases of Egypt*, Deut. vii. 15; xxviii. 60; what by being *drowned by the flood of Egypt*, Amos viii. 8; ix. 5; and whence it is that Egypt is called the *land of bondage*, Micah vi. 4; *the land of Ham*, Psalm cvi. 22; also *the iron furnace*, Deut. iv. 20; 1 Kings viii. 51. The reason why Egypt should signify not only intelligence but also insanity in spiritual things, is, because the Ancient Church, which extended through several kingdoms of Asia, was established also in Egypt, at which time the Egyptians excelled all others in cultivating the science of correspondences between spiritual things and natural, as appears from their hieroglyphics; but when that science was turned by them into magic, and became a foundation for idolatry, then their intelligence in things spiritual turned into insanity; for which reason, Egypt, in the opposite sense, signifies such insanity. From what has been said, it may now be seen, what is meant by the great city which is spiritually called Sodom and Egypt.

504. *Where also our Lord was crucified*, signifies non-acknowledgment of the Lord's Divine Humanity, and, consequently, a state of rejection. It is said in the church, that they crucify the Lord who blaspheme him; as do those also, who, like the Jews, deny his being the Son of God. The reason why they who deny the Lord's Humanity to be Divine are like the Jews, is, because every man considers the Lord as a man, and he who considers his Humanity as upon a level with that of another man cannot at the same time think of his Divinity, howsoever he may call his Humanity the Son of God born from eternity, and equal with the Divinity of the Father. When it is spoken and read, it is heard indeed, but still it is not at the same time believed; when the Lord is thought of as a material man like any other man, and retaining the like properties of the flesh, and as, in such case, his Divinity is removed and not regarded, therefore the same state is induced as if it were denied, for it is a denial of his Humanity being the Son of God, like that of the Jews, for which reason they crucified him. That the Lord's Humanity is nevertheless the Son of God, is expressly said in Luke i. 32, 35; Matt. iii. 16, 17; and in other places. From these considerations it appears, why the men of the church approach God the Father immediately, and many also the Holy Spirit immediately, but scarcely any one the Lord directly. Since the Jews, from a denial that the Lord was the Messiah, the Son of God, crucified him, therefore their Jerusalem is also called Sodom, Isaiah iii. 9; Jerem. xxiii. 14; Ezek. xvi. 46, 48. And the Lord says, "On the same day that Lot went out of *Sodom*, it rained fire and brimstone from heaven, and destroyed them all; even thus shall it be in the day when the Son of Man is revealed," Luke xvii. 29, 30. What is meant by fire and brimstone may be seen above, n. 452, 494.

505. *And they of the peoples, and tribes, and tongues, and*

nations, shall see their dead bodies three days and a half, signifies that when all they who, until the end of the present church and the beginning of the New Church, have been and will be in falses of doctrine and evils of life from faith alone, have heard and shall hear of these two essentials, which are the acknowledgment of the Lord and of works according to the decalogue. By peoples, and tribes, and tongues, and nations, are meant all of the reformed who have been and shall be in falses of doctrine, and thus in evils of life from faith alone; by peoples are signified those who are in falses of doctrine, n. 483; by tribes, falses and evils of the church, n. 349; by tongues, confession and reception thereof, n. 483; and by nations, those who are in evils of life, n. 483. Therefore, by these four are signified all and every one who have been and who will be such, thus all they who have been in that great city, and they that are like unto them, who will thenceforth come there out of the world. By their bodies, or those of the two witnesses, are signified the two essentials of the New Church above mentioned, n. 501; by seeing them is signified when they have heard and shall hear of them, because to see is said of their bodies, and to hear, of these two essentials; by three days and a half is signified to the end and beginning, that is, to the end of the present church and the beginning of the new. Now from collating what has been said into one sense, it is evident, that by these words, "They of the peoples, and tribes, and tongues, and nations, shall see their bodies three days and a half," the things above mentioned are signified in a spiritual sense. The reason why three days and a half signify to the end and beginning, is, because day signifies state; the number three, what is complete to the end; and a half, the beginning; for the same is signified by three days and a half as by a week, six days of which signify what is complete to the end, and the seventh day signifies what is holy; for the number 3½ is half of the number 7, which makes a week, and a double number, and the divided number of which it consists, signify the same thing. That three signifies a completion, thus to the end, may be seen from these passages in the Word: That "Isaiah walked naked and barefoot *three years*," Isaiah xx. 3. That Jehovah called Samuel *three times*, and Samuel ran *three times* to Eli, and that the *third time* Eli understood, 1 Sam. iii. 1—8. That Elijah stretched himself *three times* over the widow's son, 1 Kings xvii. 21. That Elijah commanded them to throw water upon the burnt-offering *three times*, 1 Kings xviii. 34. That Jesus said, "The kingdom of heaven is like unto leaven, which a woman took, and hid in *three measures* of meal, till the whole was leavened," Matt. xiii. 33. That Jesus said unto Peter, that he should deny him *thrice*, Matt. xxvi. 34. That the Lord asked Peter *thrice*, "Lovest thou me?" John xxi. 15—17. That "Jonah was in the belly of the fish *three days and three nights*," Jonah i. 17. That Jesus said the temple should be destroyed, and that he would build it up again in *three days*, Matt. xxvi. 6. That Jesus prayed *three times* in Gethsemane, Matt. xxvi. 39—44. That Jesus rose again on the *third day*, Matt. xxviii. 1: besides many others; as in Isaiah xvi. 14; Hosea vi. 2; Exod. iii. 18; x. 22, 23; xix. 1, 11, 15, 16, 18; Levit. xix. 23—25; Numb. xix. 12, to the end; xxxi. 19—25; Deut. xx. 2—4; xxvi. 12; Joshua i. 11; iii. 2; 1 Sam. xx. 5, 12, 19, 20, 35, 36, 41; 2 Sam. xxiv. 11—13; Dan. x. 2—4; Mark xii. 2, 4, 5, 6; Luke xx. 12, 18; xiii. 32, 33. Seven, as well as three, signifies what is full and complete; but seven is said of things holy, and three of things not holy.

506. *And shall not suffer their dead bodies to be put into monuments*, signifies that they condemned and will condemn them. By bodies are here signified the two essentials of the New Church, of which above, n. 505; and by not suffering them to be put into monuments, is signified to reject them as condemned. This is signified, because by being put into monuments, or buried, is signified resurrection and continuation of life, for then those things are committed to the earth which are from the earth, thus which are earthly and thence unclean; therefore by not being put into monuments, or not being buried, is signified to continue in things earthly and unclean, and for that reason to be rejected as damned. It was on this account that in the church established among the sons of Israel, which was a representative church, it was instituted, that they who were considered as damned, should be cast forth and not buried, as is evident from these words: Thus saith Jehovah concerning them, "they shall die of grievous deaths, they shall not be lamented; neither shall they be *buried*; they shall be as dung upon the face of the earth:—and their carcasses shall be meat for the fowls of heaven, and for the beasts of the earth," Jerem. xvi. 3, 4. The prophets that prophesy a lie "shall be cast out in the streets of Jerusalem, and shall have none to *bury* them," Jerem. xiv. 16. In that day "they shall bring out the bones of the kings of Judah, and the bones of his princes, and the bones of the priests, and the bones of the prophets—out of their graves:—they shall not be *gathered nor be buried*; they shall be for dung upon the face of the earth," Jerem. viii. 1, 2. That the dogs devoured "Jezebel in the portion of Jezreel, and there was none to *bury* her," 2 Kings ix. 10. "But thou art cast out of thy grave like an abominable branch; as a carcass trodden under feet," Isaiah xiv. 19, 20: besides other places; as in Jerem. xxv. 32, 33; xxii. 19; vii. 32, 33; xix. 11, 12; 2 Kings xxiii. 16.

507. *And they that dwell upon the earth shall rejoice over them and be glad*, signifies the delight, on that account, of the affection of the heart and soul in the church among those who

were in faith alone, as to doctrine and life. By the dwellers upon earth are meant they who are in the church, in the present case, they who are in the church where faith alone prevails; the earth signifies the church in which they are, n. 285; to rejoice and be glad signifies to enjoy the delight of the affection of the heart and soul; the delight of the affection of the heart having reference to the will, and the delight of the affection of the soul having reference to the understanding; for, in the Word, by heart and soul are meant the will and understanding of man: hence it is, that it is said to rejoice and be glad, although joy and gladness seem to be one and the same thing; but in these two expressions there is the marriage of the will and the understanding, which also is the marriage of good and truth, which exists in the whole and in every particular of the Word, as is shown in *The Doctrine of the New Jerusalem concerning the Sacred Scriptures*, n. 80—90. This is the reason why both these expressions, to rejoice and be glad, or joy and gladness, frequently occur in other parts of the Word, as in these passages: "They shall obtain *joy and gladness*," Isaiah xxxv. 10; li. 11. "*Joy and gladness* is cut off from the house of our God," Joel i. 16. The voice of *joy* and the voice of *gladness* shall cease, Jerem. vii. 34; xv. 10. "The fast of the tenth shall be for *joy and gladness*," Zech. viii. 19. "*Rejoice ye* with Jerusalem, *be ye glad* with her," Isaiah lxvi. 10. "*Rejoice and be glad*, O daughter of Edom," Lament. iv. 21. "Let the heavens *rejoice*, and the earth be *glad*," Psalm xcvi. 12. "Make me to hear *joy and gladness*," Psalm li. 8. *Joy and gladness* shall be found in Zion, Isaiah li. 3. "Thou shalt have *joy and gladness*, and many shall *rejoice* at his birth," Luke i. 14. "Then will I cause to cease the voice of *joy* and the voice of *gladness*, the voice of the bridegroom and the voice of the bride," Jerem. vii. 34; xvi. 9; xxv. 10; xxxiii. 10, 11. "Let all them that trust in thee *rejoice* and be *glad*," Psalm v. 11; Psalm lxx. 5. "But let the righteous be *glad* and *rejoice in gladness*," Psalm lxviii. 3. "*Be glad* in Jerusalem, *rejoice* for *joy* with her," Isaiah lxvi. 10.

508. *And shall send gifts one to another*, signifies consociation through love and friendship. To send gifts signifies to be associated by love and friendship, because a gift consociates, for it begets love and causes friendship; one to another, signifies mutually.

509. *Because these two prophets tormented them that dwell upon the earth*, signifies that these two essentials, one concerninging the Lord and concerning the Divine Humanity; and the other concerning a life according to the commandments of the decalogue, are contrary to the two essentials received in the church of the reformed, one of which relates to a trinity of persons, and the other to faith alone being saving without the

works of the law, and that by reason of this contrariety, those two essentials of the New Church, which is the New Jerusalem, are held in contempt, dislike, and aversion. That this is what is signified, when by the two prophets or witnesses are meant the two essentials of the New Church, and when by they that dwell upon earth are meant they who are principled in the two essentials of the Reformed Church, follows as a necessary consequence; by tormenting is signified to be held in contempt, dislike, and aversion.

510. *And after three days and a half the spirit of life from God entered into them, and they stood upon their feet*, signifies that these two essentials of the New Church, at the end of the former, and during the commencement and progress of the New Church, will, with those who receive them, be vivified by the Lord. By three days and a half is signified to the end and beginning, n. 505, thus from the end of the present church to the beginning of the new, in this case, with those among whom the New Church takes its rise and makes progress, because it is now said of the witnesses, that the spirit of life entered into them, and they stood upon their feet. By the spirit of life from God is signified spiritual life; and by standing upon their feet is signified natural life in accordance with spiritual life, and thus vivification from the Lord. The reason why this is signified, is, because by the spirit of life is meant the internal of man, which is called the internal man, which, considered in itself, is spiritual, for the spirit of man thinks and wills, and to think and will in itself is spiritual. By standing upon their feet is signified the external of man, which is called the external man, which is in itself natural; for the body speaks and acts what its spirit thinks and wills, and to speak and to act is natural: that feet signify things natural, may be seen, n. 49, 468. What is specifically meant by this expression, shall be explained:— every man who is reformed, is first reformed as to the internal man, and afterwards as to the external; the internal man is not reformed by merely knowing and understanding the truths and goods by which man is saved, but by willing and loving them; but the external man, by speaking and doing the things which the internal man wills and loves, and, in proportion as this takes place, in the same proportion man is regenerated. The reason why he is not regenerated before, is, because his internal is not before in the effect, but only in the cause, and, unless the cause be in the effect, it is dissipated;—it is like a house built upon ice, which sinks to the bottom when the ice is dissolved by the sun; in a word, it is like a man without feet to stand and walk upon: it is the same with the internal or spiritual man, if it is not grounded in the external or natural man. Such then is the signification of the two witnesses standing upon their feet after the spirit from God entered into them; and also

of similar expressions in Ezekiel: Jehovah "said unto me, Prophesy unto the wind.—So I prophesied, and *the spirit entered into them, and they stood upon their feet,*" Ezek. xxxvii. 9, 12. And again: A voice speaking unto me, said, "Son of man, stand upon thy feet,—and *the spirit entered into me,—and set me upon my feet,*" Ezek. ii. 1, 2. And again: "I fell on my face, then *the spirit entered into me, and set me upon my feet,*" iii. 23, 24. This is what is meant also by the Lord's words to Peter: Peter said, Thou shalt not wash my *feet* only, "but also my hands and my head. Jesus saith to him, He that is washed needeth not save to wash his *feet*, and is clean every whit," John xiii. 8, 10.

511. *And great fear fell upon them that saw them,* signifies commotion of mind and consternation at divine truths. Fear has various significations according to the thing which causes it; in the present instance, great fear signifies commotion of mind, and consternation at divine truths; for divine truths have these effects upon the wicked, for they terrify them when they at the same time hear of hell and eternal damnation; but that terror soon vanishes, together with the faith that there is any such thing as a life after death.

512. *And they heard a great voice from heaven, saying unto them, Come up hither,* signifies that these two essentials of the New Church were taken up by the Lord into heaven, whence they came, and where they are, and the protection of them. By a great voice from heaven is signified from the Lord, for a voice from heaven proceeds from no other source; come up hither, signifies their being taken up into heaven, whence they came, and where they are, and their protection.

513. *And they ascended up to heaven in a cloud,* signifies the taking them up into heaven, and conjunction there with the Lord by the divine truth of the Word in its literal sense. By ascending up to heaven is signified their being taken up by the Lord into heaven, as above, n. 512; in the present case, also, conjunction with the Lord there, because they ascended in a cloud, for by a cloud is signified the literal sense of the Word, n. 24, and by this there is conjunction with the Lord, and consociation with the angels, see *The Doctrine of the New Jerusalem concerning the Sacred Scripture,* n. 62—69.

514. *And their enemies beheld them,* signifies that they who are in faith separated from charity heard them, but continued in their own falsities. By seeing the two witnesses is signified to hear these two essentials of the New Church, and also to see them confirmed from the Word; because they saw them ascending in a cloud, and by a cloud is signified the literal sense of the Word, n. 24, 513; that, nevertheless, they did not receive them, but continued in their own falses, is evident from this circumstance, that no more is said than that they saw them,

and afterwards, that there was a great earthquake, in which they were destroyed. By enemies are meant they who were in the great city, which is spiritually called Sodom and Egypt, who were those that are in faith separated from charity, as may be seen above, n. 501, 502, and following numbers.

515. *And the same hour there was a great earthquake, and the tenth part of the city fell*, signifies a remarkable change of state which then took place with them, and their separation from heaven, followed by a sinking down into hell. The same hour signifies at the time when they saw the two witnesses ascend up to heaven, and nevertheless continued in their falses, as above, n. 314; for the two witnesses prophesied, that is, taught them, verse 3, and afterwards were slain, and revived again; they also saw them ascend up to heaven, and still did not recede from their falses, upon which the great earthquake took place. That the same thing happened with the *Two Doctrines of the New Jerusalem, one concerning the Lord, and the other concerning a Life according to the Commandments of the Decalogue*, may in some measure be seen in the Memorable Relations annexed to each chapter:—those two doctrines are the two witnesses here treated of. By an earthquake is signified a change of state, n. 331, here their destruction, because in that earthquake a tenth part of the city fell; by a tenth part is signified all therein, for ten signifies much and all, n. 101; a tenth part, or a tenth, in like manner, just as a fourth part or a fourth signifies the same thing as four, n. 322; and a third part or a third the same as three, n. 400. By falling is signified to sink down to hell, which takes place when they are torn from heaven; for the cities in the spiritual world, which are in evils and falses,—after they that dwell therein are visited, informed and warned, and still continue in their evils and falses,—are shook with an earthquake, by which a gulf is opened, into which they sink down, and then their inhabitants appear to themselves to be at the bottom, as it were, in a desert, whence they are severally removed to their places in hell; that it so happened to this city, will be seen below, n. 531.

516. *And in the earthquake were slain names of men seven thousand*, signifies that in that state all they who were in the confession of faith alone, and therefore made no account of works of charity, perished. By being slain is signified here, as before, to be slain spiritually, which is to perish as to the soul; by an earthquake is signified change of state among them, and their destruction, as above; by names of men seven thousand are signified all who were in the confession of faith alone, and for that reason made no account of works of charity, and therefore condemned those two holy essentials of the New Church; by names are signified they who are such, for a name signifies the quality of a man, n. 31, 122, 165; and by seven thousand

are signified all who were such, for the same is signified by seven thousand as by seven, just as twelve thousand has the same signification as twelve, n. 348. That seven signifies all, and all things, and is predicated of the holy things of heaven and the church, and, in an opposite sense, of the same when profaned may be seen, n. 10391.

517. *And the remnant were affrighted, and gave glory to the God of heaven*, signifies that they who had adjoined some goods of charity to faith, when they saw their destruction, acknowledged the Lord, and were separated. By the remnant are here meant they who adjoined some goods of charity to faith; by being affrighted is signified through fear, when they saw the destruction of the others; by giving glory to the God of heaven is signified to acknowledge the Lord as the God of heaven and earth; by giving glory is signified to acknowledge and worship; and by the God of heaven and earth is meant the Lord, because he is the God of heaven and earth, Matt. xxviii. 18. Inasmuch as these acknowledged the Lord through fear, they were separated, in order to their being explored for the purpose of ascertaining from what origin they did good, whether from themselves or from the Lord; all they do good from themselves who do not shun evils as sins, that is, who do not live according to the commandments of the decalogue; but they do good from the Lord, who shun the one and live according to the other.

518. *The second woe is past; behold, the third woe cometh quickly*, signifies lamentation over the perverted state of the church, and then the ultimate lamentation, to be treated of presently. That woe signifies lamentation over the perverted state of the church, may be seen above, n. 416; by the third woe is signified the ultimate lamentation, when it is complete and there is an end; for three and a third have that signification, n. 505; to come quickly signifies presently or hereafter, and hereafter means from chapter xii. to xvii., and, lastly, chapter xx., where the last judgment executed upon them is treated of.

519. *And the seventh angel sounded*, signifies the exploration and manifestation of the state of the church after the consummation, at the coming of the Lord and of his kingdom. By sounding with a trumpet is signified to explore and lay open the state of the church after its consummation, at the coming of the Lord and of his kingdom. The reason is, because this is signified by the seventh angel sounding; for by the six angels and their trumpets sounding, were signified explorations and manifestations of the state of the consummated church, as appears from the foregoing chapter, where its consummation only is treated of; but that now its state after consummation, which is the coming of the Lord and of his kingdom, is treated of, appears from what follows in this verse, and afterwards: in this

verse: "And the *seventh* angel sounded, and there were great voices in heaven, saying, The kingdoms of the world are become the kingdoms of our Lord and of his Christ, and he shall reign for ever and ever," &c. The reason why this manifestation is effected by the sounding of the seventh angel, is, because seven signifies the same as a week, and six days of the week are days of labour, and of man's proprium or selfhood, and the seventh is holy and the Lord's. That by consummation is meant the devastation of the church when there is no longer any truth of doctrine and good of life therein, thus when its end is accomplished, may be seen, n. 658, 750; and because then is the coming of the Lord and of his kingdom, therefore both, or the consummation of the age and the coming of the Lord, are mentioned together in Matthew xxiv. 3, and they are both also foretold in that chapter.

520. *And there were great voices in heaven, saying, The kingdoms of the world are become the kingdoms of our Lord and of his Christ, and he shall reign for ever and ever*, signifies celebrations by the angels, because heaven and the church are become the Lord's, as they were from the beginning, and because now they are in subjection also to his Divine Humanity, consequently that now, both as to his Humanity and his Divinity, the Lord will reign over heaven and the church to all eternity. There were great voices, signifies celebrations by the angels; saying, The kingdoms of the world are become the kingdoms of our Lord and of his Christ, signifies that heaven and the church are become the Lord's, as they were from the beginning, and that now they are subject also to his Divine Humanity; and he shall reign for ever and ever, signifies that the Lord, both as to his Humanity and his Divinity, will reign over them. That great voices in heaven signify celebrations of the Lord, because he has now taken to him his great power, appears from verse 17, where those great voices are specified. By the Lord is here meant the Lord from eternity, who is Jehovah; and by Christ is meant his Divine Humanity, which is the Son of God, Luke i. 32, 35. That the Lord as to his Divine Humanity also will reign, manifestly appears from these words: The Father hath given all things into the *hand of the Son*, John iii. 35. "The Father hath given the *Son power* over all flesh," John xvii. 2. Father, "*all mine are thine, and thine mine*," John xvii. 10. "*All power* is given unto me in heaven and in earth," Matt. xxviii. 18. Of his Divine Humanity he also said: That the Father and he are one. And that he is in the Father and the Father in him, John x. 30, 38; xiv. 5—12. To this may be added, that unless the Lord's Humanity is acknowledged to be Divine the church must perish, for in that case the Lord cannot be in man and man in the Lord, as he himself teaches, John xiv. 20; xv. 4—6; xvii. 9; and this conjunction

constitutes a man of the church, and thus the church. The reason why the Lord's Divine Humanity is meant by Christ, is, because Christ is the Messiah, and the Messiah is the Son of God, who was expected to come into the world. That Christ is the Messiah, appears from this: "We have found the *Messias*, which is, being interpreted, the *Christ*," John i. 41. "The woman said, I know that *Messias* cometh, which is called *Christ*," John iv. 25; for Messiah, in the Hebrew language, signifies the anointed, as Christ does in the Greek language. That the Messiah is the Son of God, appears from the following passages: The high-priest asked him, whether he was the *Christ* (Messiah) *the Son of God*, Matt. xxvi. 63; Mark xiv. 61; John xx. 31. "Thou art the *Christ the Son of God*, which should come into the world," John xi. 27. Peter said, "We believe and are sure that *thou art the Christ the Son of the living God*," John vi. 69. That the Lord as to His Divine Humanity is the Son of God, appears from this passage: The angel said unto Mary, "Thou shalt conceive in thy womb, and bring forth a son: he shall be great, and shall be called *The Son of the Highest*. The Holy Ghost shall come upon thee, and the power of the Highest shall overshadow thee; therefore, also, that holy thing which shall be born of thee, shall be called the *Son of God*," Luke i. 31, 35; and many others. From hence it is plain what is signified by their becoming the kingdoms of our Lord and of his Christ.

521. *And the four-and-twenty elders, that sat before God on their thrones, fell upon their faces and worshipped God*, signifies an acknowledgment by all the angels of heaven, that the Lord is the God of heaven and earth, and supreme adoration. By the four-and-twenty elders sitting on thrones are signified all in heaven, specifically in the spiritual heaven, n. 233, 251; and by falling upon their faces and worshipping God is signified supreme adoration, and acknowledgment that the Lord is the God of heaven and earth.

522. *Saying, We give thee thanks, O Lord God Almighty, who art, and who wast, and who art to come*, signifies a confession and glorification by the angels of heaven, that it is the Lord who is, who has life and power from himself, and who rules all things, because he alone is eternal and infinite. By giving thanks is signified an acknowledgment and glorification of the Lord; that the Son of Man, who is the Lord as to the Divine Humanity, is omnipotent, the Alpha and Omega, the beginning and the end, the first and the last, also who is, who was, and who is to come, may be seen above in the Apocalypse, chap. i. 8, 11, 17; ii. 8; iv. 8; and that thereby is signified that it is he who is, lives, and has power from himself, who rules all things, and is alone eternal and infinite, and God, may be seen above, n. 13, 29—31, 38, 57, 92.

523. *Because thou hast taken to thee thy great power, and*

hast begun to reign, signifies the new heaven and the new church, where they acknowledge him to be the only God, as he is and was. Because thou hast taken to thee thy great power, signifies divine omnipotence, which is his, and was his from eternity; and hast begun to reign, signifies that heaven and the church are now his, as before; by his kingdom is here meant the new heaven and new church, treated of in the Apocalypse, chap. xxi. xxii. The Apocalypse from beginning to end treats exclusively of the state of the former heaven and church, and of their abolition, and afterwards of the new heaven and new church, and of their establishment, in which one God will be acknowledged in whom there is a trinity, and that that God is the Lord. This the Apocalypse teaches from beginning to end; for it teaches that the Son of Man, who is the Lord as to the Divine Humanity, is the Alpha and the Omega, the beginning and the end, the first and the last, he that is, was, and is to come, and the Almighty, n. 522; and, lastly, that the New Church, which is the New Jerusalem, will be the church of the Lamb, that is, of his Divine Humanity, thus at the same time of the Divinity, from whence all things are, as is plain from the following passages: "Let us be glad and rejoice, for the *time of the Lamb's marriage is come, and his wife hath made herself ready*," Apoc. xix. 7. "And there came one of the seven angels, and said unto me, Come hither, I will show thee *the bride the Lamb's wife*; and he showed me that great city the Holy Jerusalem," Apoc. xxi. 9, 10. "I Jesus am the root and offspring of David, the bright and morning star; and the spirit and the *bride* say, Come, and let him that heareth say, Come," Apoc. xxii. 16, 17. There was given unto the Son of man dominion, and glory, and a kingdom; his dominion is an everlasting dominion, and his kingdom shall not be destroyed, Dan. vii. 14.

524. *And the nations were angry*, signifies those who are in faith alone, and thence in evils of life, that they were enraged, and infested those who are against their faith. By the nations are meant they who are in evils of life, and, abstractedly, evils of life, n. 147, 483, but here, they who are in faith alone, because these are here treated of, and these are in evils of life, because their religion inculcates that the law does not condemn them, provided they believe that Christ took away its condemnation. Their being angry signifies not only that they were enraged, but also that they infested those who are against that faith, as may appear from what follows concerning the dragon, chap. xii. 17, and afterwards.

525. *And thy wrath is come, and the time of judging the dead*, signifies their destruction, and the execution of the last judgment upon those who have not any spiritual life. By thy wrath is signified the last judgment, n. 340, thus their destruction; the reason why this is signified by the Lord's wrath, is, because it

seems to them as if the Lord cast them into hell from wrath, when nevertheless it is the wicked who cast themselves into hell; for it is like a malefactor's attributing his punishment to the law, or like a man's thrusting his hand into the fire, and ascribing to the fire the injury he receives; or like ascribing to the sword, held out merely in defence by another, its running him through the body, when he himself, in fact, runs against the point of it: thus it happens with every one who is against the Lord, and, out of wrath, rushes against those who are under the Lord's protection. By the dead who are to be judged, in a universal sense, are meant they who have died out of the world, but, in a proper sense, are meant they who have not any spiritual life, judgment being predicated of these, John iii. 18; v. 24, 29. The reason is, because they are called the living who have spiritual life; spiritual life exists with those only who approach the Lord, and at the same time shun evils as sins. They who have no spiritual life are understood in these passages: "They joined themselves also unto Baalpeor and ate the sacrifices of the *dead*," Psalm cvi. 28. "The enemy persecuteth my soul, he hath caused me to dwell in darkness as those who have been long *dead*," Psalm cxliii. 3. "To hear the groaning of the prisoner, and to loose those that are appointed to *death*," Psalm cii. 20. "I know thy works, that thou hast a name, that thou livest, and art *dead:* be watchful, and strengthen the things which are *ready to die*," Apoc. iii. 1, 2. The reason why these are meant by the dead, is, because spiritual death is understood; therefore also by the slain they are signified who die that death, n. 321, 325; and in other places. But they who have died out of the world are understood by the dead in these passages: "And the *dead* were judged according to those things which were written in the books," Apoc. xx. 12. "But the rest of the *dead* lived not again," Apoc. xx. 5. The reason is, because, by the first death there, is meant natural death, which is from the world; and by the second death is meant spiritual death, which is damnation.

526. *And of giving reward unto thy servants the prophets, and to the saints*, signifies the felicity of life eternal to those who are in truths of doctrine from the Word, and in a life according to them. By reward is signified the felicity of eternal life, as will be seen presently; by prophets are signified they who are in truths of doctrine from the Word, n. 8, 133; and by saints they who are in a life according to them, n. 173. By reward is here meant the felicity of eternal life, arising from the delight and pleasantness of the love and affection of good and truth; for every affection of love has its accompanying delight and pleasantness, and the affection of the love of good and truth has a delight and pleasantnesss such as the angels of heaven enjoy; and all affection continues with man after death: the

reason is, because affection is of the love, and love is the life of man, therefore the life of every one after death is such as his ruling love had been in the world; and the ruling love of truth and good exists with those who have loved the truths of the Word, and have lived according to them. Nothing else but the delight of goodness and the pleasantness of truth is meant by reward in the following passages: "Behold the Lord Jehovah will come with a strong hand, behold, his *reward* is with him," Isaiah xl. 10; lxii. 11. "And behold, I come quickly, and my *reward* is with me," Apoc. xxii. 12. "Surely my judgment is with Jehovah, and the *reward* of my work is with my God," Isaiah xlix. 4. "For I Jehovah love judgment, I will give the *reward* of their work," Isaiah lxi. 8. "Do good —hoping for nothing again; and your *reward* shall be great, and ye shall be the children of the Highest," Luke vi. 35; not to mention other places; as in Jeremiah xxxi. 16, 17; Matt. ii. 18; v. 2—6, 11, 12; x. 41, 42; Mark ix. 41; Luke vi. 22, 23; xiv. 12—14; John i. 35, 36.

527. *And to them that fear thy name, both small and great*, signifies, who love the things which are of the Lord in a greater or less degree. By fearing the name of the Lord is signified to love the things which are of the Lord; to fear signifies to love, and the name of the Lord signifies all things by which he is worshipped, n. 8; by small and great are signified they who fear the Lord in a lesser and greater degree. The reason why to fear here signifies to love, is, because every one who loves is also afraid of injuring him whom he loves: genuine love does not exist without such fear; therefore he who loves the Lord is afraid to do evils, because evils are contrary to him, being contrary to his divine laws in the Word, which are from him and thus himself; yea, they are contrary to his divine essence, which is that which wills to save all, for he is the Saviour, and cannot save man unless man lives according to his laws and commandments; and, what is more, he who loves evils also loves to do evil to the Lord, yea, to crucify him. This lies deeply hid in all evil, even among those who confess him with their lips in this world: this circumstance is unknown to men, but is well known to the angels. That to fear God signifies to love the things which are of God, by doing them, and by not willing to do those which are against him, appears from these passages: "What doth Jehovah God require of thee, but to *fear Jehovah thy God*, to walk in all his ways, and to *love him?*" Deut. x. 12. "Ye shall walk after Jehovah your God, and *fear him*, and keep his commandments," Deut. xiii. 4. "Thou shalt *fear* Jehovah thy God, him shalt thou serve, and to him shalt thou cleave," Deut. x. 20; vi. 2, 13, 14, 24; viii. 6; xvii. 19; xxviii. 58; xxxi. 12. "O that there were such a heart in them, that they would *fear me*, and keep all my command-

ments always," Deut. v. 29. "Teach me thy way, O Jehovah, unite my heart to the *fear of thy name*," Psalm lxxxvi. 11. "Blessed is every one that *feareth Jehovah*; that walketh in his ways," Psalm cxxviii. 1; Psalm cxii. 1; Jerem. xliv. 10. "If then I be a Father, where is mine honour? and if I be a master, where is *my fear?*" Mal. i. 6, ii. 5; Isaiah xi. 2, 3. "And I will give them one heart and one way, that they may *fear me* for ever, and I will put my *fear* in their hearts, that they depart not from me," Jerem. xxxii. 39, 40. "The *fear of Jehovah* is the beginning of wisdom," Psalm cxi. 10; besides other places; as in Isaiah vii. 13; xxv. 3; xxix. 13; l. 10; Jerem. xxxiii. 9; Psalm xxii. 23; Psalm xxxiii. 8, 10; Psalm xxxiv. 8, 10; Psalm lv. 19; Psalm cxv. 10, 11; Psalm cxlvii. 11; Apoc. xiv. 7; Luke i. 50. But the fear of God with the wicked is not love, but a dread of hell.

528. *And of destroying them that destroy the earth*, signifies the casting of those into hell who have destroyed the church. The reason why by destroying them which destroy the earth, is signified the casting of those into hell who have destroyed the church, is, because by the earth the church is signified, n. 285, and because it follows after these things: "And the time of the dead is come that they should be judged," by which is signified the execution of the last judgment upon those who have no spiritual life, n. 525, thus here, by the time is come of destroying them which destroy the earth, is signified the casting down into hell of those who have destroyed the church. The like is said of Lucifer, by whom Babylon is meant, in Isaiah: "Because thou hast destroyed thy earth and slain thy people," xiv. 20.

529. *And the temple of God was opened in heaven, and there was seen in his temple the ark of his covenant*, signifies the new heaven, in which the Lord in his Divine Humanity is worshipped; and where they live according to the commandments of his decalogue, which are the two essentials of the New Church, by which comes conjunction. By the temple of God is signified the Lord's Divine Humanity, likewise heaven, where angels dwell, and, also, the church upon earth; that these three are signified by the temple of God, and that they cannot be separated, may be seen, n. 191; but here, by the temple of God, is signified the Lord in his Divine Humanity in heaven where angels dwell, because it is called the temple of God in heaven. By the ark in the temple is meant the decalogue, for in the ark there were only the two tables on which the decalogue was written; by the temple being open is signified that these two, the Divine Humanity and the decalogue, which are the two essentials of the New Church, are now seen, and were seen after the wicked were cast into hell, n. 528. The reason why the ark of his covenant is said to be in his temple, is, because a covenant signifies conjunction, as will be seen below; but some-

thing shall first be said of the decalogue. What nation is there in the whole world which does not know that it is evil to murder, to commit adultery, to steal, to bear false witness? If mankind did not know these things, and if laws were not made to prevent these crimes, they must needs perish; for a society, commonwealth, and kingdom, would cease without such laws. Who can suppose that the Israelitish nation could have been so much more stupid than all others, as not to know that these things were evils? Therefore any one may wonder why these laws, universally known throughout the whole world, should have been promulgated by Jehovah himself from Mount Sinai in so miraculous a manner, and written with his own finger. But, let it be remembered, that they were promulgated in a miraculous manner by Jehovah himself, and written by his finger, to make known to them that those laws were not only civil and moral laws, but also spiritual laws, and that to act contrary to them, was not only to commit evil against a fellow-citizen and against society, but that it was also to sin against God: wherefore these laws, by being promulgated from Mount Sinai by Jehovah, were made laws of religion; for it is evident that whatsoever Jehovah God commands, he commands as a point of religion, and that it should be done for his sake, and for man's sake, that he might be saved. These laws, being the first-fruits of the church about to be established by the Lord among the Israelitish nation, and being, in a short summary, the complex of all things of religion whereby a conjunction of the Lord with man and of man with the Lord was given, surpassed every thing else in holiness. That they were most holy may appear from this testimony, as follows: That Jehovah himself, that is, the Lord, descended in fire, and that the mountain then smoked and quaked, "and that there were thunders, and lightnings, and a thick cloud, and the voice of a trumpet," Exod. xix. 16, 18; Deut. v. 19—23. That the people before the descent of Jehovah prepared and sanctified themselves three days, Exod. xix. 10, 11, 15. That bounds were set round the mount, that no one might come near to the border thereof, lest he should die, Exod. xix. 12, 13, 20—23; xxiv. 1, 2. That this *law* was written "upon two *tables* of stone, and that it was written with the finger of God," Exod. xxxi. 18; xxxii. 15, 16; Deut. ix. 10. That the face of Moses shone, when he brought those *tables* a second time down from the mount, Exod. xxxiv. 29—35. That those *tables* were deposited in the ark, Exod. xxv. 16; xl. 20; Deut. x. 5; 1 Kings viii. 9. That the place in the tabernacle, where the *ark* was, was called the Holy of Holies, Exod. xxvi. 33; and in other places. That the *ark*, from the *law* being contained in it, was called Jehovah there, Numb. x. 35, 36; 2 Sam. vi. 2; Psalm cxxxii. 28. That Jehovah spake with Moses over the *ark*, Exod. xxv. 22; Numb.

vii. 89. That on account of the holiness of that *law*, it was not permitted Aaron to enter within the vail, where the *ark* was, but with sacrifices and incense, lest he should die, Levit. xvi. 2—14, &c. That from the Lord's presence and power in the *law* which was in the ark, the waters of Jordan were divided, and so long as it rested in the midst of them, the people passed over on dry ground, Josh. iii. 1—17; iv. 5—20. That by carrying the *ark* round about Jericho, the walls thereof fell down, Josh. vi. 1—20. That Dagon, the god of the Philistines, fell down to the earth before the *ark*, and afterwards lay upon the threshold of the temple with his head broken off, 1 Sam. v. 3, 4. That the Ekronites and the Bethshemites were smitten on account of the *ark* to the number of several thousands, 1 Sam. v. and vi. That the *ark* was introduced by David into Sion with sacrifices and rejoicings, 2 Sam. vi. 1—19. That Uzzah, who then touched it, died, 2 Sam. vi. 6, 7. That the *ark* constituted the most sacred place or oracle in the temple of Jerusalem, 1 Kings vi. 19, &c.; viii. 3—9. That the *tables* upon which the *law* was written, were called the *tables* of the covenant, and that the *ark*, from them, was called the *ark* of the covenant, and the *law* itself the *covenant*, Numb. x. 33; Deut. iv. 13, 23; v. 2, 3; ix. 9; Josh. iii. 11; 1 Kings viii. 19, 21; and other places. By that law being called a covenant, conjunction is signified; the reason is, because covenants were entered into for the sake of love, of friendship, or consociation, and thus of conjunction; therefore it is said of the Lord, That he shall be for a *covenant* to the people, Isaiah xlii. 6; xlix. 8. And he is called *The Angel of the Covenant*, Malachi iii. 1. And his blood, *The Blood of the Covenant*, Matt. xxvi. 28; Zech. ix. 11; Exod. xxiv. 4—10. And therefore the Word is called *The Old and New Testament or Covenant.*

530. *And there were lightnings, and voices, and thunderings, and an earthquake, and great hail*, signifies the ratiocinations, commotions, and falsifications of good and truth that then ensued in the spheres beneath (*in inferioribus*). By lightnings, voices, and thunderings, are signified ratiocinations, n. 396; by earthquakes are signified changes of the state of the church, n. 331, here commotions; by great hail are signified falsifications of things true and good, n. 399. These things took place in the parts below, where the wicked still abode, before the last judgment was executed upon them; for it is said in the preceding verse (18): "And the time is come of judging the dead, and of destroying them which destroy the earth." Such things exist in the world of spirits, from the presence and influx of the heaven which is above them.

531. To the above I shall add this Memorable Relation. I was once seized suddenly with a disease that seemed to threaten

my life. I suffered excruciating pain all over my head; a pestential smoke ascended from that Jerusalem which is called Sodom and Egypt; half dead with the severity of my sufferings, I expected every moment would be my last. Thus I lay in my bed three days and a half; my spirit was reduced to this state, and, in consequence of it, my body. And then I heard the voices of persons about me, saying, "Lo, he who preached repentance for the remission of sins, and the Man Christ alone, lies dead in the streets of our city." And they asked some of the clergy whether he was worthy of burial? who answered, "No; let him lie to be looked at." And they passed to and fro, and mocked. All this befell me, of a truth, when I was writing the explanation of this chapter of the Apocalypse. Then were heard many shocking speeches of scoffers, who said, "How can repentance be performed without faith? and how can the man Christ be adored as God? Since we are saved of free grace without any merit of our own, what need is there of any faith but this, that God the Father sent the Son to take away the curse of the law, to impute his merit to us, and so to justify us in his sight, and absolve us from our sins by the declaration of a priest, and then give the Holy Ghost to operate all good in us? Are not these doctrines agreeable to Scripture, and consistent with reason also?" All this the crowd, who stood by, agreed to and applauded. I heard what passed without the power of replying, being almost dead; but after three days and a half my spirit recovered, and, being in the spirit, I left the street and went into the city, and said again, "Do the work of repentance, and believe in Christ, and your sins will be remitted, and ye will be saved; but otherwise ye will perish. Did not the Lord himself preach repentance for the remission of sins, and that men should believe in him? Did not he enjoin his disciples to preach the same? Is not a full and fatal security of life the sure consequence of this dogma of your faith?" But they replied, "What idle talk! Has not the Son made satisfaction? And does not the Father impute it to us, and justify us who have believed in it? Thus are we led by the spirit of grace: how then can sin have place in us, and what power has death over us? Do you comprehend this gospel, thou preacher of sin and repentance?" At that instant a voice was heard from heaven, saying, "What is the faith of an impenitent man, but a dead faith? The end is come, the end is come upon you that are secure, unblamable in your own eyes, justified in your own faith, ye devils!" And suddenly a deep gulf was opened in the midst of the city, which spread itself far and wide; and the houses fell one upon another, and were swallowed up; and presently water began to bubble up from the wide whirlpool, and overflowed the waste.

When they were thus overwhelmed, and, to appearance

drowned, I was desirous to know their condition in the deep; and a voice from heaven said to me, "Thou shalt see and hear." And straightway the waters, in which they seemed to be drowned, disappeared; for waters, in the spiritual world, are correspondences, and hence appear to surround those who are in falses. Then they appeared to me in a sandy place, where there were large heaps of stone, amongst which they were running, and lamenting that they were cast out of their great city; and they lifted up their voices, and cried, "Why has all this befallen us? Are we not, by our faith, clean, pure, just, and holy?" And others said, "Are we not, by our faith, cleansed, purified, justified, and sanctified?" And others said, "Are we not, by our faith, rendered such as to appear before God the Father, and to be seen and reputed clean, pure, just, and holy, and declared so before the angels? Are we not reconciled, propitiated, expiated, and thus absolved, washed, and cleansed from sins? And is not the curse of the law taken away by Christ? Why then are we cast down here as the damned? We have been told by a presumptuous preacher of sin in our great city, 'Believe in Christ and repent.' But have we not believed in Christ whilst we believed in his merits? And have we not done the work of repentance while we confessed ourselves sinners? Why then has all this befallen us?" But immediately a voice from one side said to them, "Do you know any one sin that is in you? Have you ever examined yourselves? Have you, in consequence, shunned any evil as a sin against God? For he who does not shun sin, remains in it; and is not sin the devil? Ye are therefore of the class of those of whom the Lord said, Then shall ye begin to say, We have eaten and drunk in thy presence, and thou hast taught in our streets; but he shall say, I tell you, I know you not, whence ye are; depart from me all ye workers of iniquity, Luke xiii. 26, 27, and of whom he spake in Matt. vii. 22, 23. Depart ye, therefore, every one to his own place; you see the openings into those caverns, enter, and there work shall be given each of you to do, and afterwards food in proportion to your work; but though you should refuse at present to enter, the calls of hunger will speedily compel you."

After this there came a voice from heaven to some on earth,* who were without that great city, and who are described also, verse 13, crying aloud, "Take heed to yourselves, take heed how you associate with such persons; can you not understand that evils, which are called sins and iniquities, render men impure and unclean? How can man be cleansed and purified from them, but by actual repentance, and by faith in Jesus Christ? Actual repentance consists in self-examination, in the knowledge and acknowledgment of sins, in owning to their guilt, in confessing them before the Lord, in imploring help

* By earth here is to be understood the earth in the spiritual world.

and power to resist them, thus in desisting from them, and in leading a new life, doing all these things as of yourselves: practise this once or twice a year, when you approach the holy communion, and afterwards when the sins, of which you owned yourselves guilty, recur; then say to yourselves, We will not consent to them because they are sins against God; this is actual repentance. Who cannot perceive that where a man does not search out and see his sins, he remains in them? for all evil is delightful to a man from his birth; it is delightful to him to take revenge, to commit whoredom, to defraud, to blaspheme, and especially to rule over others from self-love; is it not the delight arising from them which occasions their not being seen, and if you happen to be told that they are sins, does not that delight prompt you to make excuses for them? Nay more, do you not endeavour, by false reasonings, to make it appear that they are not sins, and thus continue in them, and practise them afterwards more than before, even till you no longer know what sin is, or whether there be any such thing or no? It is widely different with every one who performs actual repentance; the evils which he knows and acknowledges, he calls sins, and on that account begins to shun and turn away from them, and at last no longer to feel satisfaction in their delights; and in proportion as this is the case, he sees and loves what is good, and at length feels delight in it, which is the delight of the angels of heaven; in a word, so far as any one renounces the devil, so far is he adopted by the Lord, and by him is taught, guided, withheld from evil, and kept in good; this, and no other, is the way which leads from hell to heaven." It is surprising, that Protestants have a certain deep-rooted opposition and aversion to actual repentance, which is so obstinate, that they cannot force themselves to self-examination, neither can they look at their sins, nor confess them before God; for they are seized as it were with horror at the bare thought of such a duty. I have inquired of many in the spiritual world concerning this circumstance, who all told me that it was not in their power; and when they were informed that Roman Catholics practise such duties, that is, that they examine themselves and confess their sins openly before a monk, they have greatly wondered, more especially as the Reformed cannot do the same in private before God, although it is alike enjoined them before they approach the holy supper; some have inquired into the cause of this, and it was discovered that it was the doctrine of faith alone which induced such an impenitent state, and such a heart; and then it was given them to see that such of the Papists as worship Christ, and do not invoke saints, nor adore Christ's vicar, as he is called, or any one supposed to hold the keys from him, are saved.

After this, there was heard as it were a noise of thunder,

and a voice speaking from heaven, and saying, "We are astonished! say to the assembly of Protestants, Believe in Christ, and do the work of repentance, and you will be saved." And I said further, "Is not baptism a sacrament of repentance, and hence an introduction into the church? What else do the sponsors promise for the person to be baptized, but that he will renounce the devil and his works? Is not the holy supper a sacrament of repentance, and hence an introduction into heaven? for is it not declared to the communicants, that they must do the work of repentance before they approach? Does not the Catechism, which is the universal doctrine of the Christian church, insist on repentance? Is it not said in the six commandments of the second table, Thou shalt not do this and that evil, and not, Thou shalt do this and that good? hence you may understand, that in proportion as any one shuns evil, in the same proportion he loves good, and that before this he knows not what good is, nor even what evil is."

CHAPTER XII.

1. AND there appeared a great sign in heaven; a woman clothed with the sun, and the moon under her feet, and upon her head a crown of twelve stars.

2. And she, being with child, cried, travailing in birth and pained to be delivered.

3. And there appeared another sign in heaven; and behold, a great red dragon, having seven heads, and ten horns, and seven diadems upon his heads.

4. And his tail drew the third part of the stars of heaven, and cast them to the earth; and the dragon stood before the woman who was ready to be delivered, to devour her child as soon as it was born.

5. And she brought forth a male child, who was to rule all nations with a rod of iron: and her child was caught up unto God and to his throne.

6. And the woman fled into the wilderness, where she hath a place prepared of God, that they should feed her there a thousand two hundred and sixty days.

7. And there was war in heaven: Michael and his angels fought against the dragon; and the dragon fought and his angels,

8. And prevailed not, neither was their place found any more in heaven.

9. And the great dragon was cast out, that old serpent, called the Devil and Satan, which deceiveth the whole world;

he was cast out into the earth, and his angels were cast out with him.

10. And I heard a loud voice saying in heaven, Now is come salvation, and power, and the kingdom of our God, and the power of his Christ; for the accuser of our brethren is cast down, which accused them before our God day and night.

11. And they overcame him by the blood of the Lamb, and by the word of their testimony; and they loved not their lives unto the death.

12. Therefore rejoice, ye heavens, and ye that dwell in them. Woe to the inhabiters of the earth and of the sea, for the devil is come down unto you, having great wrath, because he knoweth that he hath but a short time.

13. And when the dragon saw that he was cast unto the earth, he persecuted the woman who brought forth the male child.

14. And to the woman were given two wings of a great eagle, that she might fly into the wilderness, into her place, where she is nourished for a time, and times, and half a time, from the face of the serpent.

15. And the serpent cast out of his mouth water as a flood after the woman, that he might cause her to be carried away of the flood.

16. And the earth helped the woman; and the earth opened her mouth, and swallowed up the flood which the dragon cast out of his mouth.

17. And the dragon was wroth with the woman, and went to make war with the remnant of her seed, who keep the commandments of God, and have the testimony of Jesus Christ.

18. And I stood upon the sand of the sea.*

THE SPIRITUAL SENSE.

THE CONTENTS OF THE WHOLE CHAPTER. The subject here treated of, is concerning the New Church and its doctrine: by the woman is here meant the New Church, and by the child which she brought forth, its doctrine: and, also, concerning those in the present church, who from doctrine believe in a trinity of persons, and in a duality of the person of Christ, likewise, and in justification by faith alone; these latter being meant by the dragon. Then follows the persecution of the New Church by these, on account of its doctrine, and its protection by the Lord, until, from being confined to a few, its reception, at length, extends to many.

* This verse, in the English translation, is the first clause of the first verse of the 13th chapter; but in the Greek Testament it is the last of the 12th chapter.

THE CONTENTS OF EACH VERSE. V. 1, "And there appeared a great sign in heaven," signifies revelation from the Lord concerning the New Church in the heavens and on earth, and concerning the difficult reception and resistance which its doctrine meets with: "A woman clothed with the sun, and the moon under her feet," signifies the Lord's New Church in the heavens, which is the new heaven, and the Lord's New Church about to be upon earth, which is the New Jerusalem: "And upon her head a crown of twelve stars," signifies its wisdom and intelligence from knowledges of divine good and divine truth derived from the Word: v. 2, "And she, being with child, cried, travailing in birth, and pained to be delivered," signifies the doctrine of the New Church about to come forth, and its difficult reception in consequence of the resistance it meets with from those who are understood by the dragon: v. 3, "And there appeared another sign in heaven," signifies revelation from the Lord concerning those who are against the New Church and its doctrine: "And behold, a great red dragon," signifies those in the Reformed Church, who make God three and the Lord two, and who separate charity from faith, and insist on the latter being competent to salvation without the former: "Having seven heads," signifies insanity from the falsification and profanation of the truths of the Word: "And ten horns," signifies much power: "And seven diadems upon his heads," signifies all the truths of the Word falsified and profaned: v. 4, "And his tail drew the third part of the stars of heaven, and cast them to the earth," signifies that by falsifications of the truths of the Word they have alienated all spiritual knowledges of good and truth from the church, and by applications to falses have entirely destroyed them: "And the dragon stood before the woman who was ready to be delivered, to devour her child as soon as it was born," signifies that they who are meant by the dragon will endeavour to extinguish the doctrine of the New Church at its birth: v. 5, "And she brought forth a male child," signifies the doctrine of the New Church: "Who was to rule all nations with a rod of iron," signifies which, by truths from the literal sense of the Word, and, at the same time, by rational arguments drawn from the light of nature, will convince all who are in dead worship through being principled in faith separated from charity, that are willing to be convinced: "And her child was caught up unto God and to his throne," signifies the protection of the doctrine by the Lord, and its being guarded by the angels of heaven: v. 6, "And the woman fled into the wilderness," signifies the church at first confined to a few: "Where she hath a place prepared of God, that they should feed her there a thousand two hundred and sixty days," signifies the state of the church at that time, while provision is making for its increase among many until it arrives at maturity: v. 7, "And there was war in heaven: Michael and his angels fought against the dragon, and the dragon fought and his angels," signifies the falses of the former church fighting against the truths of the New Church: v. 8, "And prevailed not, neither was their place found any more in heaven," signifies that they were convicted of being in falses and evils, but still remained in them, and that therefore they were torn from conjunction with heaven and cast down: v. 9, "And the great dragon was cast out, that old serpent, called the Devil and Satan," signifies this turning from the Lord to themselves, and from heaven to the world, and thence coming into the evils of their lusts and into falses: "Which deceiveth the whole world," signifies that they pervert all things of the church: "He was cast out into the earth, and his angels were cast out with him," signifies into the world of spirits, which is intermediate between heaven and hell, from whence there is immediate conjunction with men upon earth: v. 10, "And I heard a loud voice saying in heaven, Now is come salvation, and power, and the kingdom of our God and the power of his Christ," signifies the joy of the angels of heaven, because the Lord alone now reigns in heaven and in the church, and because they are saved who believe in him: "For the accuser of our brethren is cast down, which accused them before our God day and night," signifies that by the last judgment they are removed who opposed the doctrine of the New Church: v. 11, "And they overcame him by the blood of the Lamb, and by the word of their testimony," signifies victory by the divine truth of the Word, and by the acknowledgment of the Lord: "And they loved not their lives unto the death," signifies who loved not themselves more than the Lord: v. 12, "Therefore rejoice, ye heavens, and ye that dwell in them," signifies a new state of heaven, in that they are in the Lord and the Lord in them: "Woe to the inhabiters of the earth and of the sea! for the devil is come down unto you, having great wrath," signifies lamentations over those in the church who are in the falses of faith, and thence in evils of life, because they are in conjunction with the dragon: "Because he knoweth that he hath but a short time," signifies, because he knows that a new heaven is formed, and that thus there is about to be a New Church upon earth, and that then he with his like will be cast into hell: v. 13, "And when the dragon saw that he was cast unto the earth, he persecuted the woman who brought forth the man child," signifies that the dragonists in the world of spirits, immediately upon their being thrust down, began to infest the New Church on account of its doctrine: v. 14, "And to the woman were given two wings of a great eagle, that she might fly into the wilderness, into her place," signifies the divine circumspection over that church, and its protection, while as yet confined to a few: "Where she is nourished for a time, and times, and half a time, from the face of the serpent," signifies that by reason of the craftiness of seducers, provision is made with circumspection that its numbers may increase until it comes to maturity: v. 15, "And the serpent cast out of his mouth water as a flood after the woman, that he might cause her to be carried away of the flood," signifies ratiocinations from falses in abundance, with a view to destroy the church: v. 16, "And the earth helped the woman; and the earth opened her mouth, and swallowed up the flood which the dragon cast out of his mouth," signifies that those ratiocinations, in all their abundance, fall to nothing before the spiritual truths rationally understood, which the Michaels, of whom the New Church consists, can bring forward: v. 17, "And the dragon was wroth with the woman, and went to make war with the remnant of her seed, who keep the commandments of God, and have the testimony of Jesus Christ," signifies hatred kindled in those who think themselves wise from their confirmations of the mystical union of Divinity and Humanity in the Lord, and of justification by faith alone, against those who acknowledge the Lord alone to be the God of heaven and earth, and that the decalogue is the law of life; and their attempts on novitiates with intent to seduce them: v. 18, "And I stood upon the sand of the sea," signifies his spiritual-natural state.

THE EXPLANATION.

532. *And there appeared a great sign in heaven*, signifies revelation from the Lord concerning his New Church in the heavens and on earth, and concerning the difficult reception and resistance which its doctrine meets with. By a sign in heaven is here meant a revelation concerning things to come; and by a great sign appearing in heaven is meant a revelation concerning the New Church, for the woman clothed with the sun, which is the subject treated of in this chapter, signifies that church; the male child which she brought forth signifies its doctrine; her being pained to be delivered signifies its difficult reception; the dragon's desiring to devour the male child, and his persecuting the woman afterwards, signifies the resistance it meets with. This is what is to be understood by a great sign appearing in heaven. A sign is mentioned in reference to things to come, and then constitutes revelation; it refers also to truth, when it constitutes testification; and it also refers to the quality of any state and thing, when it constitutes manifestation. A sign refers to things to come, and then constitutes revelation, in the following passages: "They shall show us what shall happen, that we may know their latter end, or declare us things

for to come, show us *signs of the future*," Isaiah xli. 22, 23. "The disciples said unto Jesus, What shall be the *sign* of thy coming, and of the end of the world?" Matt. xxiv. 3; Mark xiii. 4; Luke xxi. 7. There shall be *signs* from heaven, and *signs* in the sun, the moon, and the stars," Luke xxi. 11, 25. "And then shall the *sign* of the Son of Man appear," Matt. xxiv. 3 It was said unto king Hezekiah, "This shall be a *sign* unto thee that Jehovah will do this thing, the shadow of the degrees in the sun-dial shall be brought back." Afterwards Hezekiah said, "What is the *sign* that I shall go up into the house of Jehovah?" Isaiah xxxviii. 7, 8, 22; and in other places. That a sign refers to truth, and then constitutes testification, and also to the quality of any state, when it constitutes manifestation, is evident from other passages in the Word.

533. *A woman clothed with the sun, and the moon under her feet*, signifies the Lord's New Church in the heavens, which is the new heaven, and the Lord's New Church about to be upon earth, which is the New Jerusalem. That the Lord's New Church is signified by this woman, results from all the particulars of this chapter being understood in a spiritual sense; that by a woman, in other parts of the Word also, the church is signified, may be seen, n. 434; and the church is signified, because the church is called the bride and wife of the Lord. The reason why she appeared clothed with the sun, is, because the church is principled in love to the Lord, for it acknowledges him, and does his commandments, and this is to love him, John xiv. 21—24; that the sun signifies love, see n. 53. The reason why the moon was seen under the woman's feet, is, because the church on earth is understood, which is not as yet conjoined with the church in the heavens, which is to be understood; by the moon is signified intelligence in the natural man, and faith, n. 423; and by appearing under the feet is signified that it is about to be upon earth; otherwise, by feet is signified the church itself when it is conjoined. It is to be observed, that there is a church in the heavens as well as on earth, for there also is the Word; there are temples also, and sermons delivered in them, and ministerial and priestly offices; for all angels there were once men, and their departure out of the world was only a continuation of their life; therefore they are also perfected in love and wisdom, every one according to the degree of the affection of truth and good which he took with him out of the world. The church among them is here understood by the woman clothed with the sun, who had upon her head a crown of twelve stars; but as the church in the heavens cannot subsist, except there be also a church on earth, which is in concordant love and wisdom, and as this was about to be, therefore the moon was seen under the feet of the woman, which here specifically signifies faith, such as it is at this day, in which there

is no conjunction. The reason why a church cannot subsist in the heavens unless there is a church on earth in conjunction with it, is, because heaven where angels are, and the church where men are, act as one, like the internal and external in man; and the internal in man cannot subsist in its state, unless an external be conjoined with it; for an internal without an external is like a house without a foundation, or like seed upon the ground and not in the ground, thus like any thing without a root; in a word, like a cause without an effect in which it may exist. From what has been said, it may be seen how absolutely necessary it is that there should be a church somewhere in the world, where the Word is, and where the Lord is known thereby.

534. *And upon her head a crown of twelve stars*, signifies its wisdom and intelligence from knowledges of divine good and divine truth derived from the Word. By the crown on her head is signified wisdom and intelligence, n. 189, 235, 252; by stars are signified the knowledges of divine good and divine truth derived from the Word, n. 51, 420; and by twelve are signified all things of the church, which have relation to its good and truth, n. 348; consequently, by a crown of twelve stars on the woman's head, is signified the wisdom and intelligence of the New Church from the knowledges of divine good and divine truth derived from the Word.

535. *And she, being with child, cried, travailing in birth, and pained to be delivered*, signifies the doctrine of the New Church about to come forth, and its difficult reception in consequence of the resistance it meets with from those who are understood by the dragon. To be with child signifies the birth of doctrine, because by the child which was in the womb, whose birth is treated of in verse 5, is signified the doctrine of the New Church; for nothing else is signified by being with child, or in travail, and bringing forth, in the spiritual sense of the Word, but to conceive and bring forth those things which relate to spiritual life, concerning which, presently. By "she cried, travailing in birth, and pained to be delivered," is signified the difficult reception of that doctrine, because of resistance from those who are understood by the dragon; this is plain from what follows in this chapter, as the dragon standing before the woman who was ready to be delivered, to devour her child, and afterwards pursuing her into the wilderness. That by being with child, travailing in birth, and bringing forth, nothing else is signified in the Word, appears from the following passages: Jesus said, "Except a man be *born again*, he cannot enter into the kingdom of God; that which is *born* of the flesh is flesh, but that which is *born* of the spirit is spirit," John iii. 3—6. "Sing, O barren, that didst not *bear*, cry aloud, thou that didst not *travail with child*, for more are the children of the desolate

than the children of the married wife," Isaiah liv. 1. "They have ceased until the *barren* hath *borne seven*, and she that had *many children* is waxed feeble," 1 Sam. ii. 5. By the barren are signified the Gentiles, who had no genuine truths, because they had not the Word; by the married wife and the mother of many children are signified the Jews who were in possession of the Word. "She that hath *borne seven* languisheth, she hath given up the ghost," Jerem. xv. 9; speaking also of the Jews. "We have *conceived*, we have been in *pain*, we have as it were brought forth wind, we have not wrought any deliverance in the earth," Isaiah xxvi. 16. "Before she travailed she *brought forth*, before her pain came *she was delivered* of a *man-child;* shall the earth be made to *bring forth* in one day, shall a nation be *born* at once? shall I bring to the *birth*, and not cause to *bring forth*, and *shut the womb?*" Isaiah lxvi. 7—10. "Thou, O earth, *bringest forth* at the presence of the Lord, at the presence of the God of Jacob," Psalm cxiv. 7. "This is the day of trouble, for the children are come to the *birth*, and there is not strength to *bring forth*," Isaiah xxxvii. 3. "Sin shall be in *travail*, and No shall be rent asunder," Ezek. xxx. 15, 16. "I have heard a voice as of a woman *in travail*, as of her that *bringeth forth* her first child, the voice of the daughter of Zion, she bewaileth herself, she spreadeth her hands, Woe is me, my soul is wearied because of murderers," Jerem. iv. 31. "Pangs and sorrows shall take hold of them, they shall be in pain as a *woman that travaileth*," Isaiah xiii. 6—8. "The iniquity of Ephraim is bound up, the sorrows of a *travailing woman* shall come upon him; he is an unwise son, for he should not stay long in the breaking forth of children," Hosea xiii. 12, 13. "Ephraim, thy glory shall fly away like a bird, from the *birth*, and from the *womb*, and from conception: give them, O Jehovah, a *miscarrying womb*, and dry breasts: even when they have conceived, I will slay the beloved of their *womb*," Hosea ix. 11, 12, 14, 16. In these passages also is described the difficulty of receiving the truths of doctrine from the Word, by many circumstances relating to pain in bringing forth, and in like manner in many other places. Moreover, Jehovah, that is, the Lord, is called the *Former from the womb*, Isaiah xliv. 2, 24; xlix. 1, 5; and by former from the womb is meant the reformer.

536. *And there appeared another sign in heaven*, signifies revelation from the Lord concerning those who are against the New Church and its doctrine. By a sign is signified revelation from the Lord, as above, n. 532. It is called another sign, because it is a revelation concerning those who will be against the New Church.

537. *And behold, a great red dragon*, signifies those in the Reformed Church who make God three, and the Lord two, and

separate charity from faith, and insist on the latter being competent to salvation without the former. Such are here meant, and in what follows, by the dragon; for they are against the two essentials of the New Church, which are, that God is one in essence and in person, in whom there is a trinity, and that the Lord is that God; also that charity and faith are a one as an essence and its form; and that none have charity and faith, but they who live according to the commandments of the decalogue, which say that evils are not to be done; and in proportion as any one does not commit evils, by shunning them as sins against God, in the same proportion he does the goods which relate to charity, and believes the truths which relate to faith. That they who make God three, and the Lord two, and who separate charity from faith, and consider the latter competent to salvation without the former, are opposed to those two essentials of the New Church, may be seen by any one who considers the matter. It is said, who make God three, and the Lord two, by whom are understood those who think of three persons as three Gods, and separate the Lord's Humanity from his Divinity: and who thinks otherwise, or can think otherwise, whilst, according to a formula of faith, he prays, "That God the Father for the sake of the Son would send the Holy Spirit?" Does he not pray to God the Father as to one God, and for the sake of the Son as another, and concerning the Holy Spirit as a third? From which it is evident that although in thought he makes three persons one God, still he divides them, that is, divides his idea into three gods, when he so prays; the same formula of faith also makes the Lord two, since the Lord's Humanity is then alone thought of, and not at the same time his Divinity, seeing that for the sake of the Son means for the sake of his Humanity which suffered on the cross. From what has been said, it may now appear who they are that are meant by the dragon, who fain would have devoured the woman's child, and afterwards pursued the woman into the wilderness on account of her child. The reason why he is called a great dragon, is, because all the Reformed Churches distinguish God into three persons, and make faith alone saving, except some here and there, who do not think alike concerning the trinity, and concerning faith: they who divide God into three persons, and adhere to these words of the Athanasian doctrine: "There is one person of the Father, another of the Son, and another of the Holy Ghost;" and also to these: "The Father is God, the Son is God, and the Holy Ghost is God:" these, I say, cannot make one God of three; they may indeed say that they are one God, but they cannot think so. In like manner they who think concerning the Lord's divinity from eternity as concerning the second person of the Divinity, and concerning his Humanity in time as concerning the humanity of another man, cannot do otherwise than make two of the Lord, although it is said in the Athanasian doctrine that his Divinity and Humanity are one person, united as the soul and body. The reason why the dragon is called red, is, because red signifies what is false from the evils of the concupiscences, which is the infernal false principle. Now because these two essentials of the doctrine of the Reformed Churches are falses, and as falses devastate the church, since they take away its truths and goods, therefore they were represented by a dragon; the reason is, because by a dragon, in the Word, is signified the devastation of the church; as may appear from the following passages: "I will make Jerusalem heaps, a *habitation of dragons*, and I will make the cities of Judah desolate," Jerem. ix. 11. "Behold, a great commotion out of the north country, to make the cities of Judah desolate, a *habitation of dragons*," Jerem. x. 22. "Hazor shall be a *habitation of dragons*, a desolation for ever," Jerem. xlix. 33. "That it may be a *habitation of dragons*, a court for owls," Isaiah xxxiv. 13. "In the *habitation of dragons* where each lay," Isaiah xxxv. 7. "I will go stripped and naked, I will make a wailing like the *dragons*, and mourning like the owls," Micah i. 8. "I cried, I am a brother to *dragons*, and a companion to owls," Job xxx. 28, 29. "The *wild beasts* shall cry in their desolate houses, and *dragons* in their pleasant palaces," Isaiah xiii. 22. "And Babylon shall become heaps, a *habitation of dragons*, an astonishment and a hissing," Jerem. li. 37. "Thou hast broken us in the place of *dragons*, and covered us with the shadow of death," Psalm xliv. 19, 20. "I have laid the mountains of Esau and his heritage waste for the *dragons of the wilderness*," Malachi i. 3; besides other places; as in Isaiah xliii. 20; Jerem. xiv. 6; Psalm xci. 13, 14; Deut. xxxii. 33. That by the dragon are here meant those who are in faith alone, and reject the works of the law as not conducive to salvation, has sometimes been proved to me in the world of spirits by lively experience; I have seen several thousands of them assembled together, when they have appeared at a distance like a dragon with a long tail, that seemed full of prickles like thorns, which signified falses. Once, also, there appeared a dragon still larger, who, raising his back and lifting up his tail towards heaven, endeavoured to draw down the stars from thence. Thus I have had ocular demonstration that no others are meant by the dragon.

538. *Having seven heads*, signifies insanity from the falsification and profanation of the truths of the Word. By the head is signified wisdom and intelligence, and, in an opposite sense, insanity; but by seven heads here, belonging to the dragon, is signified, properly, insanity from the falsification and profanation of the truths of the Word; for seven is predicated of things holy, and, in an opposite sense, of things profane, n.

173; therefore, it follows, that on his heads there appeared seven diadems, and by diadems are signified the truths of the Word, which are here falsified and profaned. That by the head is signified wisdom and intelligence, is plain from these passages: "I will give you wise men, and of understanding, and make them *rulers* over you," Deut. i. 13. "Jehovah hath closed your eyes, the prophets, and your *rulers*, the seers, hath he covered," Isaiah xxix. 10. By the *head* of Nebuchadnezzar's image, which consisted of pure gold, Dan. ii. 32, nothing else is signified but the wisdom of the first age, which prevailed among the men of the Most Ancient Church. By the head, in an opposite sense, is signified insanity and folly; in David: "God shall wound the *head* of his enemies, the hairy scalp of him who goeth on in his trespasses," Psalm lxviii. 21; nor is any thing else signified by the *head of the serpent*, which was to be trod under foot, Gen. iii. 15; and by smiting the *head* over many countries, Psalm cx. 6, 7; also by putting dust on the *head;* and by shaving the *head*, and putting the *hand on the head*, when they were ashamed, or grieved at having acted insanely, or contrary to wisdom, Isaiah vii. 20; xv. 2; Ezek. vii. 18; xxvii. 30; Jerem. ii. 37; xiv. 3, 4; Lament. ii. 10; 2 Sam. xiii. 19. Further, by seven heads is also signified insanity from the falsification and profanation of truths, in what follows, Apoc. xiii. 1, 3; xvii. 3, 7, 9.

539. *And ten horns*, signifies much power. A horn signifies power, n. 270; and ten signifies much, n. 101. The reason why it is said that the dragon has much power, is, because the salvation of man by faith alone, without the works of the law, which faith is meant by the dragon, captivates men's minds, and the result of this is, that confirmations exert a persuasive influence: it captivates, because man, on hearing that the damnation of the law is taken away, and the Lord's merit is imputed to him through faith therein alone, can indulge in the pleasures of his mind and body, without any fear of hell; hence comes the power which is signified by the ten horns of the dragon. That such has been his power, evidently appears from the reception of that faith everywhere throughout the reformed Christian world.

540. *And seven diadems upon his heads*, signifies all the truths of the Word falsified and profaned. By diadems, or precious stones, are signified the truths of the Word; specifically, the truths of the literal sense of the Word, but here, those truths falsified and profaned, from their being seen upon the seven heads of the dragon, by which is signified insanity from truths falsified and profaned, n. 538. That by diadems, or precious stones, are signified the truths of the the literal sense of the Word, may be seen in *The Doctrine of the New Jerusalem concerning the Sacred Scripture*, n. 43—45; where it is shown

that divine truths in their ultimates, which are the truths of the literal sense of the Word, are signified by the *twelve precious stones* in the breast-plate of Aaron, which was the Urim and Thummim, Exod. xxviii. 6, 15—21, 30; and by the *precious stones* in the garden of Eden, in which the king of Tyre is said to have been, Ezek. xxviii. 12, 13; also by the *twelve precious stones*, of which the foundations of the wall of the New Jerusalem consisted, Apoc. xxi. 17—20. The truths of the literal sense of the Word are signified by diadems, or precious stones, because all things of the literal sense of the Word are transparent in the sight of angels, by virtue of its spiritual sense, thus from the light of heaven, in which the spiritual truths of the Word are; for a stone, in the Word, signifies truth in ultimates; hence, a precious stone signifies that truth as being transparent. The reason why the truths of the Word, when falsified and profaned, are also called diadems, is, because they have a lustre from themselves, whether they be possessed by this person or that; in the same manner as diadems on earth, in whatever hands they may happen to be. It has sometimes been permitted me to see adulterous women, on their first coming from the earth into the world of spirits, decked with diadems; and Jews, likewise, selling diadems, which they had procured to themselves from heaven; from which circumstance it was plain, that evils and falses, with such, do not change the lustre and light of the truths of the Word. Therefore the like is signified by *the ten diadems* upon the horns of the beast which came up out of the sea, Apoc. xiii. 1; and by the *precious stones* on the woman who sat on the scarlet-coloured beast, Apoc. xvii. 3—5. That the truths of the Word are what are signified by diadems, appears manifestly in the Apocalypse, in that there were seen upon the head of him who sat upon the white horse, and whose name was the Word of God, *many diadems*, xix. 12, 13.

541. *And his tail drew the third part of the stars of heaven, and did cast them to the earth*, signifies that by falsifications of the truths of the Word they have alienated all spiritual knowledges of good and truth from the church, and, by applications to falses, have entirely destroyed them. By the tail, when the subject treated of relates to those who have confirmed heretical doctrines from the Word, are signified the truths of the Word falsified, n. 438; by stars are signified spiritual knowledges of good and truth, n. 51, 420; by the third part is signified all, n. 400, 505; and by drawing them from heaven, and casting them to the earth, is signified to alienate them from the church, and to destroy them utterly; for when they are drawn from heaven, they are also drawn from the church, because every truth of the Word is insinuated from the Lord through heaven into the man of the church; nor are truths drawn away

by any thing else but by falsifications of them in the Word, since there and thence are the truths of heaven and the church. That all the truths of the Word have been destroyed by those who are meant by the dragon spoken of above, n. 537, cannot be believed by any one in the world, and yet they have been so destroyed, as that not a single doctrinal truth remains; this matter was examined into, in the spiritual world, among the learned of the clergy, and was found to be the fact. The reasons I know, but I shall here mention only one of them;—they assert, that whatsoever proceeds from man's will and judgment is not good; and that therefore the goods of charity, or good works, being done by man, contribute nothing to salvation, but faith only; when, nevertheless, that alone, by virtue of which man is man, and by which he has conjunction with the Lord, is his having it in his power to do good and believe truth, as from himself, that is, as from his own will according to his own judgment; were this faculty to be taken away from him, all power of conjunction on the part of man with the Lord would also be taken away at the same time, and of the Lord with man; for it constitutes that power of reciprocation of love, which the Lord bestows on every one who is born a man, and which he also preserves in him to the end of his life, and afterwards to eternity. If this power were to be taken away from man, every truth and good of the Word would also be taken away, insomuch that the Word would be nothing but a dead letter and a blank book; for the Word teaches nothing else but the conjunction of man with the Lord by charity and faith, and both from man as from himself. They who are meant by the dragon spoken of above, n. 537, have broken this only bond of conjunction, by asserting that the goods of charity, or good works, which proceed from man, and his will and judgment, are only moral, civil, and political works, by which man has conjunction with the world, and none at all with God and with heaven; and when that bond is thus broken, there is then no doctrinal truth of the Word remaining; and if the truths of the Word are applied to confirm, that faith alone is saving without the works of the law, then they are all falsified; and if the falsification proceeds so far as to affirm, that the Lord has not commanded good works in the Word for the sake of man's conjunction with himself, but only for the sake of his conjunction with the world, then the truths of the Word are profaned; for thus the Word becomes no longer a Holy Book, but a profane one: but see the experience on this subject at the end of the chapter. The like things are signified by these words in Daniel, concerning the he-goat: *The he-goat with his horn cast down some of the host of heaven and of the stars to the ground, and stamped upon them; and he cast down truth to the ground,* viii. 10, 11.

542. *And the dragon stood before the woman who was ready to be delivered, to devour her child as soon as it was born*, signifies that they who are meant by the dragon will endeavour to extinguish the doctrine of the New Church at its birth. Who they are that are meant by the dragon may be seen above, n. 537; that by the woman is signified the New Church, n. 533; that by bringing forth is signified to receive the goods and truths of doctrine from the Word, n. 535; that by the child of which she was delivered is signified the doctrine of the New Church, will be seen in the next article. To devour signifies to extinguish, because by a child is signified doctrine; and when to devour is said in relation to the child, to extinguish is said in relation to doctrine. The reason why this was the case at the birth of the doctrine, is, because it is said, that the dragon stood before the woman, for to devour her child as soon as it was born.

543. *And she brought forth a male child*, signifies the doctrine of the New Church. By a son, in the Word, is signified the truth of doctrine, and also the understanding, and thence the thought, of truth and good; but by a daughter is signified the good of doctrine, as also the will, and thence the affection, of truth and good; and by a male child is signified truth conceived in the spiritual man, and born in the natural man. The reason is, because by generations and births, in the Word, are signified spiritual generations and births, all which in general relate to good and truth, n. 535; for nothing else is begotten and born of the Lord as a husband, and of the church as a wife. Now since by the woman who brought forth is signified the New Church, n. 533, it is plain that by the male child is signified the doctrine of that church. The doctrine here meant is *The Doctrine of the New Jerusalem*, published in London, 1758: as also *The Doctrines concerning the Lord*, concerning *The Sacred Scripture*, and concerning *A Life according to the Commandments of the Decalogue*, published in Amsterdam; for by doctrine are understood all the truths of doctrine, doctrine being the complex of them. When these doctrines were written, the dragonists stood around me, and endeavoured, with all their fury, to devour or to extinguish them; this strange circumstance it was permitted me to relate, because, of a truth, it so happened. The dragonists who stood around me were from all parts of the reformed Christian world. Seeing that a spiritual marriage gives birth to no other offspring, a male offspring denoting truth and good in the understanding and thence in the thought; and a female offspring denoting truth and good in the will, and thence in the affections; therefore, by a son, in the Word, is signified truth; by way of confirmation, some passages shall be adduced, from which this may in some measure be seen: "Lo, *sons* are an heritage of Jehovah, and the fruit of

the *womb* is his reward; as arrows in the hand of a mighty man, so are the *children of youth*," Psalm cxxvii. 3—5. "Make thee bald, and poll thee for the *sons of thy delight*, for they are gone from thee," Micah i. 16. "I saw two olive-trees upon the right side of the candlestick, and he said, These are the two *sons of the olive-tree* that stand by the Lord of the whole earth," Zech. iv. 11, 14. "My tabernacle is spoiled, *my sons* are gone forth from me, and they are not," Jerem. x. 20. "*My sons* are become desolate, because the enemy hath prevailed," Lament. i. 16. "*Thy sons*, O Jerusalem, have fainted, they lie at the head of all the streets," Isaiah li. 17, 18, 20. "The fathers shall eat the *sons* in the midst of thee, and the *sons* shall eat their fathers, and the whole remnant of thee will I scatter to all the winds," Ezek. v. 10. "The *son* shall be divided against the father, and the father against the *son*," Matt. x. 21; Mark xiii. 12; Luke xii. 53. "Thou hast taken the fair jewels of my gold, and hast made to thyself images of a *male*, and didst commit whoredom with them," Ezek. xvi. 17. Jesus said, "The seed are the *sons of the kingdom*, and the tares are the *sons of the evil one*," Matt. xiii. 38. That the Son of Man is the divine truth of the Word, thus the Lord, may be seen in *The Doctrine of the New Jerusalem concerning the Lord*, n. 19—28. In the passages quoted above, by sons, are meant they who are in truths of doctrine from the Word, and, abstractedly, the truths themselves; in like manner in other places; as in Isaiah xiii. 17, 18; xiv. 21—23; xliii. 6; xlix. 17, 22; li. 17, 18; lx. 9; Jerem. iii. 24, 25; v. 17; Ezek. xiv. 16—18, 20; xvi. 20, 26, 45; xx. 26, 31; xxiii. 37; Hosea xi. 9—11; Zech. ix. 13; Psalm cxliv. 11, 12; Deut. xxxii. 8. That by a daughter is signified the affection of the truth of the church, thus the church as to that affection, appears from so many passages in the Word, that to adduce them would fill several pages; nothing else is meant by the *daughter of Zion, the daughter of Jerusalem, the daughter of Judah, the daughter of Israel*. Some passages respecting the daughter of Zion may be seen adduced, n. 612. Who cannot see that not any daughter of Zion, Jerusalem, Judah, and Israel, so often mentioned in the Word, can possibly be meant?

544. *Who was to rule all nations with a rod of iron*, signifies which, by truths from the literal sense of the Word, and, at the same time, by rational arguments drawn from the light of nature, will convince all who are in dead worship through being principled in faith separated from charity, that are willing to be convinced. This refers to the doctrine of the New Church, because it is spoken of the male child, by whom that doctrine is signified, n. 543; to rule signifies to teach and instruct, n. 383; here, to convince those who are willing to be convinced; by nations are signified they who are in evils of life,

n. 483; here, they who are in dead worship through being principled in faith separated from charity, because these are here treated of; and these are in evils of life, for when charity is separated, there is not any good of life, and where good is not, there evil is. That to rule with a rod of iron signifies by the truths of the literal sense of the Word, and, at the same time, by rational arguments drawn from natural light, may be seen above, n. 148.

545. *And her child was caught up unto God and to his throne*, signifies the protection of the doctrine by the Lord, because it is for the use of the New Church, and its being guarded by the angels of heaven. By these words is signified the protection of the doctrine by the Lord, because it is said that the dragon stood before the woman who was ready to be delivered, to devour her child as soon as it was born; and by a child, and a male child, is signified the doctrine for the New Church, n. 542, 543. Being guarded by the angels is also signified, because it is said, that it was caught up unto God and to his throne; and by a throne is signified the angelic heaven, n. 14, 221, 222.

546. *And the woman fled into the wilderness*, signifies the church, which is the New Jerusalem, at first confined to a few. By the woman is signified the New Church, n. 533; and by a wilderness is signified where there are no longer any truths. That its being confined at first to a few is signified, because it follows, where she had a place prepared of God, that they should feed her there a thousand two hundred and sixty days, by which is signified its state at that time, that in the mean while an increase of its numbers may be provided for, until it comes to its appointed maturity, n. 547. By a wilderness, in the Word, is signified, I. The church devastated, or in which all the truths of the Word are falsified, such as it was among the Jews at the time of the Lord's advent. II. The church in which there are no truths, from not possessing the Word, such as it was among the well-disposed Gentiles in the Lord's time. III. A state of temptation, in which man is, as it were, without truths, because surrounded by evil spirits who induce temptations, and then, as it were, deprive him of truths. That by a wilderness is signified the church devastated, or the church in which all the truths of the Word are falsified, such as it was among the Jews in the Lord's time, appears from these passages: "Is this the man that made the earth to tremble, that did shake kingdoms, that made the world a *wilderness?*" Isaiah xiv. 16, 17; concerning Babel. "Thorns and briers are come up on the land of my people: the palace shall be a *wilderness*," Isaiah xxxii. 13, 14. "I beheld, and lo, the fruitful place was a *wilderness*, the whole land shall be desolate," Jerem. iv. 26, 27; earth is the church, n. 285. "The pastors have destroyed my vineyard, they have made my pleasant portion a *desolate wilderness*: the

spoilers are come in the *wilderness*," Jerem. xii. 10, 12. "A vine is planted in the *wilderness*, in a dry and thirsty ground," Ezek. xix. 13. "The fire hath consumed the habitations of the *wilderness*," Joel i. 19, 20. "The day of Jehovah cometh, the land is as the garden of Eden before them, but behind them a *desolate wilderness*," Joel ii. 3. "See ye the word of Jehovah; have I been a *wilderness* to Israel, or a land of darkness?" Jerem. ii. 31. "The voice of him that crieth in the *wilderness*, Prepare ye the way of Jehovah; make straight in the *desert* a highway for our God," Isaiah xl. 3; besides other places; as in Jerem. ii. 31; xxiii. 10; Lament. v. 18; Hosea ii. 2, 3; xiii. 15; Joel iv. 9; Malachi i. 3; Psalm cvii. 33, 34; Matt. xxiv. 26; Luke xiii. 35. That such also is the state of the church at this day, may be seen below, n. 566. II. That by a wilderness is meant the church in which there are no truths, from not possessing the Word, as among the well-disposed Gentiles in the Lord's time, appears from these places: "The spirit shall be poured upon us from on high, and the *wilderness* shall be a fruitful field, then judgment shall dwell in the *wilderness*," Isaiah xxxii. 15, 16. "I will open fountains in the midst of the valleys, and make the *wilderness* a pool of waters; I will plant in the *wilderness* the cedar shittim and the olive-tree," Isaiah xli. 18, 19. "He shall turn the *wilderness* into a standing water, and the dry ground into water springs," Psalm cvii. 35, 36. "I will make a way in the *wilderness*, and rivers in the *desert*, to give drink to my people, my chosen," Isaiah xliii. 19, 20. "Jehovah will make her *wilderness* like Eden, and her *desert* like the garden of Jehovah; joy and gladness shall be found therein," Isaiah li. 3. "The habitations of the *wilderness* distil," Psalm lxv. 12, 13. "Let the *wilderness* lift up its voice, let the inhabitants of the rock sing," Isaiah xlii. 10, 11. III. That by a wilderness is signified a state of temptation, in which man is as it were without truths, because surrounded by evil spirits, who induce temptation, and then as it were deprive him of truths, appears from Matt. iv. 1—3; Mark i. 12, 13; Luke iv. 1—3; Isaiah xl. 3; Jerem. ii. 2, 6, 7; Hosea ii. 13—16; Psalm cvii. 4—7; Deut. i. 31, 33; viii. 2—4, 15, 16; xxxii. 10.

547. *Where she hath a place prepared of God, that they should feed her there a thousand two hundred and sixty days*, signifies the state of the church at that time, while provision is making for its increase among many until it arrives at maturity. By place is signified state, n. 947; and by feeding, provision for its increase, for thus is the church fed; hence by having a place prepared of God that they should feed her, is signified the state of the church preparatory to its increase; by a thousand two hundred and sixty days is signified to the end and beginning, n. 491, that is, to the end of the former church and the

beginning of the new, the same as by a time, and times, and half a time, verse 14, n. 562; thus, also, to its appointed station, that is, until it exists as has been provided it should exist. It is of the Lord's divine providence, that the church should at first be confined to a few, and that its numbers should successively increase, because the falses of the former church must first be removed; for before this, truths cannot be received, since truths, which are received and implanted before falses are removed, do not remain, and they are also rejected by the dragonists; the like happened with the Christian church, which increased successively from a few to many. Another reason is, that a new heaven is first to be formed, which will act as one with the church on earth; therefore we read, that he saw *a new heaven, and the Holy Jerusalem coming down out of heaven from God*, Apoc. xxi. 1, 2. It is certain that a new church, which is the New Jerusalem, will exist, because it is foretold in the Apocalypse, chap. xxi. xxii.; and it is also certain that the falses of the former church are first to be removed, because they are what the Apocalypse treats of, as far as chapter xx.

548. *And there was war in heaven: Michael and his angels fought against the dragon; and the dragon fought and his angels*, signifies the falses of the former church fighting against the truths of the New Church. By war is signified spiritual war, which is of falsity against truth, and truth against falsity, n. 500, for no other war can take place in heaven, where this is said to have been waged; neither can it take place in heaven, when once formed of angels; but it was waged in the former heaven, which passed away, as appears, Apoc. xxi. 1, concerning which heaven, see the explanation there given; for that heaven passed away in consequence of the last judgment being executed on the dragon and his angels, which is also signified by the dragon's being cast down, and his place no more found in heaven, as appears from what follows. What the falses are, which are meant by the dragon, and which are to fight against the truths of the New Church, may be seen above, n. 537. By Michael is not meant any archangel; neither by Gabriel, nor Raphael, but ministries in heaven; the ministry signified by Michael is performed by those who prove from the Word, that the Lord is the God of heaven and earth, and that God the Father and He are one, as the soul and body are one; also that men ought to live according to the commandments of the decalogue, and that then they are gifted with charity and faith. Michael is also mentioned in Daniel, x. 13, 21; xii. 1; and thereby a similar ministry is understood, as appears from chap. ix. x. xi., and from the last verses of chap. xii. But by Gabriel is understood the ministry of those who teach from the Word, that Jehovah came into the world, and that the Humanity he there assumed is the Son of God, and divine; for which

reason, the angel who announced the same to Mary is called Gabriel, Luke i. 19, 26—35. They, also, who are engaged in those ministries, are named Michaels and Gabriels in heaven. By an angel, in the supreme sense, is meant the Lord; and, in a relative sense, the heaven of angels, as also an angelic society, as may be seen above, n. 5, 66, 258, 342, 344, 415, 465; but here, a ministry is signified, because they are mentioned by name; and, in Daniel, Michael is called a prince; and by a prince, in the Word, is signified a principal or leading truth, and by a king, truth itself, n. 20.

549. *And prevailed not, neither was their place found any more in heaven*, signifies that they were convicted of being in falses and evils, but still remained in them, and that therefore they were torn from conjunction with heaven and cast down. That this may be understood, something must first be said concerning the state of those who come into the other life after death. All in the other life are first instructed by angels, and conducted from one society to another, and explored whether they have any desire to receive heavenly truths, and live according to them; but still, all such as have confirmed themselves in falses in the world do not receive them; therefore they are sent to societies where they are who are in similar falses, which societies have no conjunction with heaven, but with hell; consequently, after a given time, in the world of spirits, they sink down into hell, and are sent away to their respective places, every one according to his evil and consequent falsity; this is what is to be understood by their being convicted of being in falses and evils, and still remaining in them, and that therefore they are torn from conjunction with heaven, and cast down. What their lot and condition is there, may be seen above, n. 153, 531.

550. *And the great dragon was cast out, that old serpent, called the Devil, and Satan*, signifies that they who are meant by the dragon turned from the Lord to themselves, and from heaven to the world, and thence became corporeally sensual, who could not but be in the evils of their concupiscences and thence in falses, and by separation from the Lord and heaven, became devils and satans. Who are meant by the dragon, may be seen, n. 537; these, inasmuch as they make God three, and the Lord two, and because they place the commandments of the decalogue among works which do not contribute to salvation, are called the old serpent, the devil, and Satan; and by a serpent is signified man, when he is corporeally sensual, n. 424, who turns from the Lord to himself, and from heaven to the world; and by the devil are signified they who are in the evils of concupiscences; and by Satan, they who are thence in falses, n. 97, 153 at the end, 856, 857. Such, also, was the serpent which seduced Eve and Adam, as appears from his description,

and the curse pronounced upon him, Gen. iii. 1—5, 14, 15. The dragon is here called the devil and Satan, but he is so called, because all in hell are devils and satans; and it is on this account that hell, in the aggregate, is so denominated.

551. *Which deceiveth the whole world*, signifies that they pervert all things of the church. By deceiving is signified to pervert, and by the world is signified the church; the same as by earth, n. 285. By the world is not signified the world of earths, but the church therein, in the following places: "The *earth* mourneth and fadeth away, the haughty people of the *world* do languish," Isaiah xxiv. 4. "The *earth* shall learn thy judgments, and the inhabitants of the *world* thy righteousness," Isaiah xxvi. 9. "Thou hast made the *earth* by thy power, thou hast prepared the *world* by thy wisdom," Jerem. x. 12; li. 15. "The foundations of the *world** were discovered at the blast of the breath of thy nostrils," Psalm xviii. 16. "The *earth* is Jehovah's and the fulness thereof, the *world* and they that dwell therein; he hath founded it upon the seas, and established it upon the floods," Psalm xxiv. 1, 2. "The heavens are thine, the *earth* also is thine, thou hast founded the *world* and the fulness thereof," Psalm lxxxix. 11. "He will make us inherit the throne of glory, for the pillars of the *earth* are Jehovah's, and he hath set the *world* upon them," 1 Sam. ii. 8. "Thou, O Babel, hast made the *world* a wilderness, thou hast destroyed thy *land*, and slain thy people," Isaiah xiv. 17, 20; besides other passages; as in Isaiah xviii. 3; xxvi. 18; xxvii. 6; xxxiv. 1; Nahum i. 5; Psalm ix. 8; Psalm lxxvii. 18; Psalm xcviii. 9; Lament. iv. 12; Job xviii. 18; Matt. xxiv. 14; Luke xxi. 26; Apoc. xvi. 14; but it is to be observed, that when the *world* and the *earth* are mentioned at the same time, the *world* signifies the church as to good, and the *earth* signifies the church as to truth.

552. *He was cast out into the earth, and his angels were cast out with him*, signifies that he was cast down into the world of spirits, which is intermediate between heaven and hell, from whence there is immediate conjunction with men upon earth. The reason why by the earth, upon which the dragon is said to have been cast out, is meant the world of spirits, is, because that world is immediately beneath the heavens, and when any one is cast down from heaven, he does not fall immediately into hell, but upon the earth of the world immediately beneath it, for that world is in the midst between heaven and hell, or below the heavens and above the hells. Many things concerning that world may be seen in the work *On Heaven and Hell*, n. 421—535. All who are in that world communicate immediately with men upon earth, consequently, the dragon and his angels communicate with those who are in falses, and thence in evils, through the received heresy of faith alone; on which

---

* Orbis—a *circle*, the *mixed globe of earth and water.*

account, it is said below, "Therefore rejoice, ye heavens, and ye that dwell in them; woe to the inhabiters of the *earth* and of the sea, for the devil is come down unto you, having great wrath, because he knoweth that he hath but a short time," verse 12 of this chapter. Also that " he pursued the woman into the wilderness, and went to make war with the remnant of her seed," verse 13—17. It is to be noted, that every man, as to his affections and consequent thoughts, is in society with those who are in the world of spirits, and mediately through them, with those who are either in heaven or in hell. The life of every man depends on that conjunction.

553. *And I heard a loud voice saying in heaven, Now is come salvation, and power, and the kingdom of our God and the power of his Christ*, signifies the joy of the angels of heaven, because the Lord alone now reigns in heaven and in the church, and because they are saved who believe in him. By a loud voice in heaven is signified the joy of the angels of heaven; for which reason it follows, "Therefore rejoice, ye heavens, and ye that dwell in them," verse 12; the voice also becomes great by reason of its being lifted up from joy of heart. Now is come salvation and power, signifies that now there is salvation from the Lord's divine power; and the kingdom of our God and the power of his Christ, signifies because the Lord alone reigns in heaven and in the church. That by God is understood the essential Divinity, from whom are all things, which is called Jehovah the Father; and by Christ, his Divine Humanity, which is called the Son of God, may be seen above, n. 500; and because the essential Divinity and the Lord's Divine Humanity are one, like soul and body, it follows that the Lord alone reigns. This is meant by the *gospel of the kingdom*, and by the *kingdom of God*, Matt. iii. 2; iv. 17, 23; vii. 21, 22; ix. 35; xi. 11; xii. 28; Mark i. 14, 15; ix. 1; xv. 43; Luke iv. 4; viii. 1; ix. 60; x. 8—11; xi. 17, 18, 20; xvi. 16; xxi. 30, 31; xxii. 18; xxiii. 50, 51. That the Lord has all power in heaven and earth, appears manifestly in Matthew xxviii. 18; John iii. 35; xvii. 2, 10. That they are saved who are in the Lord and the Lord in them, and that it is the Divine Humanity in which they are, John xiv. xv. xvii.; and that none are saved, but they that believe in him, appears from these passages: " As many as received him, to them gave he power to become the sons of God, even to them that *believe in his name*," John i. 12. "That whosoever *believeth in the Son*, should not perish, but have eternal life," John iii. 15. "God so loved the world, that he gave *his only-begotten Son*, that whosoever *believeth in him* may have everlasting life," John iii. 16. " He that *believeth in the Son* is not condemned, but he that believeth not is condemned already, because he hath not believed in the name of the only-begotten Son of God," John iii. 18. " He that *believeth in the*

Son, hath everlasting life, but he that believeth not the Son, shall not see life, but the wrath of God abideth on him," John iii. 36. " He that cometh to me shall never hunger, and he that *believeth in me* shall never thirst.—Verily I say unto you, he that *believeth in me* hath everlasting life," John vi. 33, 35, 47. " Unless ye *believe* that I am, ye shall die in your sins," John viii. 24. Jesus said, " I am the resurrection and the life, he that *believeth in me*, though he were dead, yet shall he live; whosoever liveth and *believeth in me*, shall never die," John xi. 25, 26: besides other places; as in John vi. 38—40; vii. 37, 38; viii. 12; xii. 36, 46. To believe in the Lord is to approach him immediately, and to have confidence that it is he who saves; and since no one can have this confidence who does not lead a good life, therefore this also is understood by believing in him, see above, n. 67.

554. *For the accuser of our brethren is cast down, which accused them before our God day and night*, signifies that by the last judgment they are removed who opposed the doctrine of the New Jerusalem. By the dragon being cast down is signified that they are removed who are meant by the dragon; that they were removed by being cast down from heaven into the world of spirits, and then into hell, which is their last judgment, was observed before. By brethren are meant they who are in the doctrine of the New Jerusalem, and in a life according to it; by accusing is signified to oppose the doctrine, to maintain that it is false, and to exclaim against it; and because they do this continually, as it were before God, the dragon is called the accuser of our brethren, accusing them before God day and night. This also the devil does when he tempts, for he brings forth various things out of man, which he calls falses, and condemns.

555. *And they overcame him by the blood of the Lamb, and by the Word of their testimony*, signifies victory by the divine truth of the Word, and thence by the acknowledgment that the Lord is the God of heaven and earth, and that the precepts of the decalogue are precepts of life according to which men ought to live. That the blood of the Lamb is the divine truth proceeding from the Lord, which is the divine truth of the Word, may be seen above, n. 379; that the testimony is the divine truth, above, n. 6, 16, and that it specifically consists in these two things, viz., that the Lord is the God of heaven and earth, and that the commandments of the decalogue are precepts of life, n. 490, 506; for which reason, the decalogue is also called the testimony, Exod xxv. 22; xxxi. 7, 18; xxxii. 15; Levit. xvi. 13; Numb. xvii. 19; Psalm lxxviii. 5; Psalm cxxxii. 12. Those at the present day, that are principled in faith alone, believe that, by the blood of the Lamb, is here meant the Lord's passion on the cross, and this because they make the Lord's pas-

sion on the cross the chief point of their solifidian dogma, saying, that thereby he transferred to himself the condemnation of the law, made satisfaction to the Father, and reconciled the human race to him; besides many other things. That this, however, is not the case, but that the Lord came into the world to subdue the hells and glorify his Humanity, and that the passion of the cross was the last combat, whereby he fully overcame the hells and fully glorified his Humanity, may be seen in *The Doctrine of the New Jerusalem concerning the Lord*, n. 12—14. Hence it may be seen, that by the blood of the Lamb is not here meant the passion of the cross according to the modern dogma. That by the blood of the Lamb is meant the divine truth proceeding from the Lord, which is the divine truth of the Word, may appear from this consideration, that the Lord is the Word; and because he is the Word, the divine truth therein is his blood, and the divine good therein, his body. This may be rendered evident at once, in the following manner:—Is not every man his own good and his own truth? And, since good has relation to the will, and truth to the understanding, every man is his own will and his own understanding. What else constitutes a man? Is not man, as to his essence, these two? But the Lord is good itself and truth itself, that is, divine good and divine truth, which two are also the Word.

556. *And they loved not their lives unto the death*, signifies who loved not themselves more than the Lord. By loving their lives is signified to love self and the world, for by the lives is signified man's own life, which every one has by birth, which consists in loving himself and the world above all things; therefore by not loving their lives is signified not to love self and the world, more than the Lord and the things which are of the Lord; unto death, signifies to be willing to die rather; consequently it is to love the Lord above all things, and our neighbour as one's self, Matt. xxii. 35—38; and to be willing to die rather than recede from those two loves. The same is signified by these words of the Lord: "He that findeth his *life*, shall lose it, and he that loseth *his life* for the sake of Jesus, shall find it," Matt. x. 39; Luke xvii. 33. "He that loveth his *life* shall lose it; but he that hateth his *life* in this world, shall keep it unto life eternal," John xii. 25. Jesus said, "If any man will come after me, let him deny himself; for whosoever will save *his life*, shall lose it; and whosoever will lose *his life*, for my sake, shall find it: What is a man profited, if he shall gain the whole world, and lose *his own soul?* or what shall a man give in exchange for *his soul?*" Matt. xvi. 24, 25; Mark viii. 35—37; Luke ix. 24, 25. By loving the Lord is meant to love to do his commandments, John xiv. 20—24. The reason is, because he himself is his own commandments, for they are from him, consequently he is in them, thus in the man in

whose life they are inscribed; and they are inscribed in man by willing and doing them.

557. *Therefore rejoice, ye heavens, and ye that dwell in them*, signifies a new state of heaven, in that they are in the Lord, and the Lord in them. By heavens is meant the heaven of Christians, in which the Lord alone is acknowledged as the God of heaven and earth; by rejoice is signified its new state, full of joy; by they that dwell in them are signified they who are in good, n. 380; and because all good is from the Lord, it signifies that they are in the Lord, and the Lord in them.

558. *Woe to the inhabiters of the earth and of the sea! for the devil is come down unto you, having great wrath*, signifies lamentations over those who are principled in the internals and externals of the doctrine of faith alone, and thence in evils of life, because their like are cast down from heaven into the world of spirits, and are thence in conjunction with men on earth, whom, out of hatred to the New Church, they excite to persevere in their falses and consequent evils. By woe to the inhabiters of the earth and of the sea is signified lamentation over those in the church who are influenced by the doctrine of faith alone; by woe is signified lamentation, n. 496; by inhabitants are signified they who are in the church whose doctrine is faith alone; by earth are meant they who are in its internals, and by sea they who are in its externals, n. 470; by great wrath is signified hatred against the New Church, because it denotes hatred against the woman, n. 525; to come down unto them signifies coming to those who are in the world of spirits, and as these are in conjunction with men upon earth, it also signifies to their like upon earth. That the dragon was cast out of heaven into the world of spirits, and that they who are in that world are in connexion with men upon earth, see above, n. 552. The dragon is here called the devil, because they are meant who from that heresy are in evils of life; and they are in evils of life from that heresy who live according to this tenet of their faith, that they have no sins who pray in confidence to God the Father, and that if they have they are remitted; all such, inasmuch as they do not examine themselves, know not any one sin that is in them, and at length do not even know what sin is, as may be seen above, n. 531. That by the dragon, as the devil, are meant they who are in the evils of their concupiscences, see n. 550. The reason why every man is in conjunction with those who are in the world of spirits, is, because man, as to the affections of his mind and the thoughts thence proceeding, is a spirit, therefore, as to such affections and thoughts, he is continually in conjunction with spirits who are in a similar affection, and thence in similar thoughts; there is such a conjunction, that if this bond was broken for a single moment, man would fall down dead. The church has hitherto

known nothing of this; nor that man, after death, is his own affection and consequent thought, therefore his own charity and consequent faith, and that no one can be faith separated from charity.

559. *Because he knoweth that he hath but a short time*, signifies, because he knows that a new heaven is formed, and that thus there is about to be a New Church upon earth, and that then he, with his like, will be cast into hell. This is signified, because the dragon knows that a new heaven is formed, for he was expelled from it, verse 8, 9; he knows also that there is about to be a New Church upon earth, from what is foretold in the Apocalypse, chap. xxi.; and he knows, likewise, that he and his like are then to be cast into hell, from what is also foretold, Apoc. xx. 1, 2, 10.

560. *And when the dragon saw that he was cast unto the earth, he persecuted the woman who brought forth the man child*, signifies that the dragonists in the world of spirits, immediately upon their being thrust down, began to infest the New Church on account of its doctrine. When the dragon saw that he was cast upon the earth, signifies that when the dragonists saw that they were separated from heaven, and in conjunction with men upon earth, n. 552, 558; he persecuted the woman, signifies that they immediately began to infest the Lord's church; that the woman whom he persecuted is that church, may be seen, n. 533; who brought forth a son, signifies on account of its doctrine; that the son, which the woman brought forth, is the doctrine of the New Church, see n. 535, 542, 543, 545.

561. *And to the woman were given two wings of a great eagle, that she might fly into the wilderness, into her place*, signifies the divine circumspection over that church, and its protection, while as yet confined to a few. By the woman is signified the New Church, n. 533; by wings are signified power and protection, n. 245; by an eagle is signified intellectual sight, and consequent thought, n. 245; by flying is signified seeing and circumspection, n. 245; by a wilderness is signified the church desolated, and thus among a few, n. 546; by her place is signified its state there; from which it follows, that by there being given to the woman two wings of a great eagle, that she might fly into the wilderness, into her place, is signified the divine circumspection over the New Church, and its protection, while as yet confined to a few.

562. *Where she is nourished for a time, and times, and half a time, from the face of the serpent*, signifies that by reason of the craftiness of seducers, provision is made with circumspection that its numbers may increase until it comes to maturity. By being nourished, when said of the New Church, is signified to provide for its increase, as above, n. 547; by a time, and times, and half a time, is signified to the end and beginning,

thus during its increase from a few to many, until it reaches its appointed station, as above, n. 547; by the face of the serpent is signified the subtle arts of seducers; by the face, subtle artfulness; and by the serpent, seducers. That by the serpent are signified seducers, is plain from the following passage in this chapter: "The great dragon was cast out, that old serpent, which *seduceth* the whole globe of earth," verse 9. And again: "He laid hold on the dragon, that old serpent, and cast him into the bottomless pit, that he should *seduce* the nations no more," Apoc. xx. 2, 3. The like is here meant as by the serpent who seduced Eve and Adam, of whom it is written: "And the *serpent was more subtle* than any beast of the field;—and the woman said to Jehovah, The *serpent seduced* me," Gen. iii. 1, 13. By face, in the Word, is signified that which is interior in man, because his face is the type of his mind formed to the correspondence; therefore, by the face of the serpent is signified anger, hatred, and subtlety. By a time, and times, and half a time, is signified the same here, as by a thousand two hundred and sixty days, verse 6, where it is said: "And the woman fled into the wilderness, where she hath a place prepared of God, that they should feed her *a thousand two hundred and sixty days*," which may be seen explained above, n. 547. The same is also signified by three days and a half, Apoc. xi. 9, 10; also by the three years and six months of famine, Luke iv. 25; and in Daniel, by a *stated time of stated times and a half*, and when he shall have accomplished to scatter the power of the holy people, Dan. xii. 7.

563. *And the serpent cast out of his mouth water as a flood after the woman, that he might cause her to be carried away of the flood*, signifies ratiocinations from falses in abundance, with a view to destroy the church. By the serpent is here signified, as above, the dragon which seduces; by the woman, the New Church, n. 533; by water are signified truths, and, in an opposite sense, falses, n. 50, 409; by a flood are signified truths in abundance, and in an opposite sense, falses in abundance, n. 409; out of the mouth of the serpent, signifies ratiocinations; therefore by casting out water as a flood, are signified ratiocinations from falses in abundance. The ratiocinations of those, who are meant by the dragon, are all grounded in fallacies and appearances, which, if confirmed, appear outwardly like truths, but within they conceal falses in abundance. This I can declare, that those in the church, who hereafter confirm themselves in faith alone, cannot recede from it, except by serious repentance, because they conjoin themselves with the dragonists, who now are in the world of spirits, giving rise to much tumult, where, out of hatred to the New Church, they infest all whom they meet; and as they are in conjunction with men on earth, as observed above, they will not suffer those who have once

been caught by their reasonings to disengage themselves, for they keep them bound in chains, as it were, and then blind their eyes so that they can no longer see any one truth in its light.

564. *And the earth helped the woman; and the earth opened her mouth, and swallowed up the flood which the dragon cast out of his mouth*, signifies that those ratiocinations, in all their abundance, fall to nothing before the spiritual truths rationally understood, which the Michaels, of whom the New Church consists, can bring forward. By the earth, which helped the woman, is signified the church as to doctrine, n. 285; and because the ratiocinations from falses, which the dragonists produce, are treated of, they are truths from the Word, by which the earth, that is, the church, helps the woman; by opening her mouth is signified to adduce those truths; by the flood which the dragon cast out of his mouth, are signified ratiocinations from falses in abundance, n. 563; by carrying away is signified to make them come to nothing; by the Michaels are meant the men of the New Church; by Michael, such as are wise therein; and by his angels, the rest of them. Since in the New Church this tenet is rejected, that the understanding is to be kept in subjection to faith, and in the place of it, it is a received maxim, that the truth of the church should be seen, in order that it may be believed, n. 224; and since truth cannot be seen otherwise than rationally, therefore it is said, from truths rationally understood. How can any man be led by the Lord, and conjoined with heaven, who shuts up his understanding against such things as relate to salvation and eternal life? Is it not the understanding which requires to be illuminated and instructed? And what is the understanding closed by religion, but thick darkness, and such darkness too as rejects from itself the light that would illuminate? Again, who can acknowledge truth and retain it, unless he sees it? What is truth not seen but a voice not understood, which, by sensual corporeal men, is usually retained in the memory, but not so by the wise? The wise, indeed, cast off empty or unmeaning words from the memory, that is, such as have not entered into their minds by being understood; as that one God consists of three persons, also that the Lord, born from eternity, is not one and the same with the Lord born in time, that is, that one Lord is God and not the other; and again, that a life of charity, which consists in good works, and likewise in repenting of evil works, contributes nothing to salvation; a wise man does not understand such things; therefore from his rationality he says, Is religion then of no consequence? Does not religion consist in shunning evil and doing good? Should not the doctrine of the church teach this, as well as a man ought to believe, that he may do the good things of religion from God?

565. *And the dragon was wroth with the woman, and went to make war with the remnant of her seed, who keep the commandments of God, and have the testimony of Jesus Christ*, signifies the burning hatred of those who think themselves wise from their confirmations of the mystical union of the Divinity and Humanity in the Lord, and of justification by faith alone, against those who acknowledge the Lord alone to be the God of heaven and earth, and that the decalogue is the law of life; and their attempts on novitiates with intent to seduce them. All this is contained in those few words, because it follows in a series from what went before, where it is said, that the earth helped the woman, and opened her mouth, and carried away the flood which the dragon cast out of his mouth, by which is signified that their reasonings from falses came to nothing, n. 564; consequently that their endeavours to destroy the New Church were vain; therefore by the dragon being wroth with the woman, is signified that he burned with hatred and breathed revenge against the church; by the dragon's wrath is signified hatred, n. 558; by making war is signified to assault and impugn by ratiocinations grounded in falses, n. 500; by the remnant of her seed which keep the commandments of God and have the testimony of Jesus Christ, are meant novitiates, who receive the doctrine concerning the Lord and the decalogue; what the testimony of Jesus Christ is, may be seen above, n. 6, 490. The reason why by the dragon are here meant those who think themselves wise from confirmations of the mystical union of the Lord's Divinity and Humanity, is, because these are proud of their own wisdom, and skilled in reasoning; and from pride proceeds hatred, and from hatred proceed revenge and wrath against those who are not of the same opinion. By the mystical union, which is also called the hypostatic union, are meant their fictions concerning the influx and operation of the Divinity upon the Lord's Humanity as upon another; not knowing that God and Man, or Divinity and Humanity in the Lord, are not two but one person, united like soul and body, according to the doctrine received throughout the whole Christian world, which has its name from Athanasius; but to adduce their notions respecting this mystical union would be an idle thing, because they are absurd. That by the seed of the woman are here meant those who are of the New Church, and are principled in the truths of its doctrine, may appear from the signification of seed, in the following passages: "Their *seed* shall be known among the Gentiles, and their offspring among the people, all that see shall acknowledge them, that they are the *seed* which Jehovah hath blessed," Isaiah lxi. 9. "They are the *seed* of the blessed of Jehovah," Isaiah lxv. 23. "As the new heavens and the new earth which I will make, shall remain before me, so shall your *seed* remain," Isaiah lxvi. 22.

"The *seed* which shall serve him, it shall be accounted to the Lord for a generation," Psalm xxii. 31. "I will put enmity between thee and the woman, and between *thy seed* and the *woman's seed*," Gen. iii. 15. "That he might seek a godly *seed*," Malachi ii. 15. "Behold the days come, when I will *sow* the house of Israel and the house of Judah with the *seed* of man," Jerem. xxxi. 27. "When thou shalt make his soul an offering for sin, he shall see *seed*," Isaiah liii. 10. "Fear not, for I am with thee, I will bring thy *seed* from the east," Isaiah xliii. 5, 6. "Thou shalt break forth on the right hand and on the left, and thy *seed* shall inherit the Gentiles," Isaiah liv. 3. "I had planted thee a noble vine, a *seed of truth*, how then art thou turned into the degenerate plant of a strange vine unto me," Jerem. ii. 21. "Their fruit shalt thou destroy from the earth, and their *seed* from among the children of men," Psalm xxi. 11. "Their *seed* are the children of the kingdom," Matt. xiii. 38. The same is signified by the *seed of Israel*, because Israel is the church, Isaiah xli. 8, 9; xliv. 3; Jerem. xxiii. 8; xxxi. 35, 36; and also by the *seed of David*, because David is the Lord, Jerem. xxx. 10; xxxiii. 22, 25, 26; Psalm lxxxix. 4, 5, 29; and by the *seed of the field*, because a field signifies the church in many places. But the contrary is signified by the *seed of the wicked*, Isaiah i. 4; xiv. 20; lvii. 3, 4; and by the *seed of the serpent*, Gen. iii. 15.

565½. *And I stood upon the sand of the sea*, signifies that his state was now spiritual-natural, such as prevails with those who are in the first or ultimate heaven. By the sand of the sea such a state is signified, because by the sea is signified the external of the church; this state is called spiritual-natural, such as exists with those who are in the first or ultimate heaven: he had been above in heaven previously, where he saw the dragon, his combat with Michael, his being cast out, and his persecution of the woman; but now, when the dragon is cast down, and continues to be treated of in what follows, John is let down in spirit, to the end that he may see more of the dragon beneath the heavens, and describe the same; in which state he saw two beasts come up, one out of the sea, and the other out of the earth, which he could not have seen from heaven, because it is not permitted any angel to look down from heaven into the lower regions, but if he chooses he may go down. It is to be observed, that in the spiritual world place corresponds to state, for no one can be anywhere else than where the state of his life is; and as John now stood upon the sand of the sea, it follows that his state now was spiritual-natural.

566. Here I will add this Memorable Relation. There arose a question among some spirits, whether a man can see any doctrinal theological truth in the Word, except from the Lord

In this they all agreed, that it could only be done from God, because "No man can receive any thing except it be given him from heaven," John iii. 27; for which reason it was made a question, whether it were possible without immediately approaching the Lord. On one side it was urged, that the Lord ought directly to be approached, because he is the Word; on the other it was maintained that a doctrinal truth might also be seen when God the Father was immediately approached; therefore the main point of debate at last rested here, whether it was admissible for any Christian to approach God the Father immediately, and thus climb above the Lord; and whether this was not a most indecent and rash insolence and boldness, because the Lord said, that no one cometh to the Father but by him, John xiv. 6. This they paid no attention to, but asserted that man can see doctrinal truth in the Word from his own natural light; this, however, was rejected: they therefore insisted that it might be seen by those who pray to God the Father; upon which, when a passage from the Word was read to them, they fell on their knees, and prayed that God the Father would enlighten them; and as to what had been read to them out of the Word, they said, that such and such truths might be thence collected, but these, in fact, were falsities; and this they repeated several times even to tediousness, till at length they were obliged to confess that it was not in their power. On the other hand, they who applied immediately to the Lord, could see truths, and explain them. After this dispute, there came up out of the abyss certain spirits, who appeared at first sight like locusts, but afterwards like men; they were some who in the world had directed their prayers to God the Father, and confirmed themselves in the doctrine of justification by faith alone, affirming that they could see in clear light, and this from the Word, that man is justified by faith alone without the works of the law. Being asked, "By what faith?" they replied, "By faith in God the Father." But after they were examined, it was signified to them from heaven, that they were not acquainted with a single doctrinal truth from the Word; to which they replied, that this truth however they saw in the clearest light; upon which they were told that they saw it in the light of infatuation; they asked, "What is the light of infatuation?" and were informed, "That the light of infatuation is the light arising from the confirmation of what is false, and that that light corresponds to the light in which owls and bats are, darkness being light to them, and light darkness." This was confirmed by what they themselves experienced, in that, when they looked up to heaven, which is light itself, they saw only darkness, and that when they looked down into the abyss from whence they came, they saw light. At this appeal to their own case they were much offended, and said, "At this rate light and darkness are nothing but states of the eye, in consequence of which light is said to be light and darkness darkness." But it was shown them, that the light by which they saw was the light of infatuation, arising from the confirmation of what is false, and that it was merely the activity of their minds excited by the fire of concupiscences, not unlike the light of cats, whose eyes appear like flame in the night-time, in consequence of their burning appetite for prey. On hearing these words, they replied with anger, that they were not cats, nor like cats, because they could see if they chose; but fearing to be asked why they did not choose, they retired, and sunk down into their own abyss and its light. They who dwell there, and such as resemble them, are called owls and bats.

When they were come to their companions in the abyss, and had told them what the angels had said, that they were ignorant of any doctrinal truth whatever, and had therefore called them owls and bats, it caused a tumult, and they said, "Let us pray to the Lord for permission to ascend, and we will prove clearly that we are in possession of many doctrinal truths, which the archangels themselves acknowledge;" and because they prayed to the Lord, permission was given; and they ascended, to the number of three hundred; and when they appeared above ground, they said, "We were held in great fame and reputation in the world, from understanding and teaching the mysteries of justification by faith alone, and from repeated confirmations, we not only saw it in the light, but in its meridian brightness, as we still continue to do in our cells; and yet we are informed by our companions who have been with you, that our light is not light, but darkness; by reason that we are not, as asserted by you, in possession of a single doctrinal truth from the Word. Now we know that every truth of the Word is luminous, and we have believed that our glittering light was from thence, when engaged in profound meditation upon these mysteries; therefore we will demonstrate to you that we have truths from the Word in great abundance." And then they said, "Have we not this truth, that there is a trinity, consisting of God the Father, God the Son, and God the Holy Ghost, and that this trinity is an object of faith? Have we not this truth, that Christ is our Redeemer and Saviour? Have we not this truth, that Christ alone is righteousness, and that he only has merit; and that he is unrighteous and wicked who would attribute to himself any part of his merit and righteousness? Have we not this truth, that no man can do any spiritual good from himself, but that all good, which is really such, is from God? Have we not this truth, that there is such a thing as meritorious and also hypocritical good, and that all such good is evil? Have we not this truth, that man from his own power cannot in the least contribute to his own salvation? Have we not this truth, that nevertheless works of charity should be done? Have we not this truth, that faith exists, and that it ought to be believed, and that every one obtains life according to his belief? not to mention many other truths from the Word: now which of you can deny any one of them? Yet you say, that in our schools there is not a single truth; is not this assertion grounded in prejudice and dislike?" But then it was given them for answer, "All that you have adduced, in themselves are truths, but you have falsified them by applying them to confirm a false principle; therefore they are with you, and in you, truths falsified, these being rendered false by that false principle; this we will prove to you by ocular demonstration. There is a place not far distant, into which the light flows immediately from heaven; in the midst of it there is a table, on which if any piece of paper be placed, having any truth from the Word written upon it, by virtue of that truth the writing instantly shines like a star: write therefore the truths you mentioned on a piece of paper, and place it on this table, and you will be convinced." They did so, and gave it to the person who had charge of the table, who placed it thereon, and then desired them to remove to a little distance, and look towards the table; they did so, and lo! the paper shone like a star; then said the keeper, "You see that these are truths which you have written on the paper; but come nearer, and fix your eyes attentively on the paper;" and they did so, and the light then suddenly disappeared, and the paper became black, as the smoke of a furnace. Then said the keeper, "Now touch the paper with your hands, but take heed not to touch any part of the writing;" and, as they did so, it took fire and was consumed. This sight made them hastily retire; and they were informed, that if they had touched the writing, they would have heard an explosion, and their fingers would have been burnt. Upon this it was remarked by those who were standing behind, "You see now, that the truths which you have abused to the confirmation of the arcana of your justifying faith, are in themselves truths, but in you they are truths falsified." They then looked upwards, and the heavens appeared to them like blood, and afterwards as thick darkness; and in the eyes of the angelic spirits, some of them looked like bats, some like owls, some like moles, and some like birds of night; and they fled away to their own regions of darkness, which shone in their eyes from the light of infatuation.

The angelic spirits who were present wondered that they had not known any thing of this place, or of the table it contained, before; and immediately a voice came to them from the southern quarter, saying, "Come up hither, and you shall see something still more wonderful." So they went, and entered into a room, the walls of which shone as with gold; where also they saw a table, on which lay the Word, decorated on all sides with precious stones in celestial arrangement. Then the angel who kept it said, "When the Word is opened, there beams from it a light of inexpressible brightness, and at the same time, from the precious stones, there is presented the appearance of a rainbow, as it were, encompassing the Word. When an angel from the third heaven approaches and looks at the Word as it lies open, the ground of the rainbow appears of a crimson colour; when an angel from the second heaven approaches and views it, the ground appears of a blue colour; when an angel from the ultimate or lowest heaven approaches and looks at it, the ground appears white; and when any good spirit comes and looks, there appears a variegation of the light like marble." The truth of all this was manifested to them by ocular demonstration. The angel who kept it added, "If any one approaches who has falsified the Word, the brightness at first disappears, and if he comes nearer, and fixes his eyes upon the Word, it seems covered with blood, and then he is admonished to depart, by reason of the danger." A certain person, however, who, in the world, had been a leading writer in favour of the doctrine of justification by faith alone, approached with great confidence, and said, "When I was in the world, I never falsified the Word; I laid equal stress on charity as on faith, and taught that man in the state of faith, in which he exercises charity and its works, is renewed, regenerated, and sanctified; and also that faith could not exist solitary, or without good works, any more than a good tree without fruit, or the sun without light, or the fire without heat; I also blamed those who asserted that good works were unnecessary, and that the commandments of the decalogue need not be observed; I also laid great stress on repentance, and thus, in a wonderful manner, applied all things in the Word to this single article of faith, which I discovered and demonstrated to be the only medium of salvation." Confident in the truth of his own assertion, that he had never falsified the Word, he approached the table, and, in spite of the angel's caution, touched the Word; when suddenly there issued fire and smoke from the Word, attended with a loud explosion, which cast him into a corner of the room, where he lay for the space of an hour, as if he were dead. The angelic spirits wondered at this, but they were informed, that this prelate had been more strenuous than others in exalting the good fruits of charity as proceeding from faith, but that, nevertheless, he meant no other than political works, which are also called moral and civil, and are performed for the sake of the world and prosperity therein, and not out of obedience to God and for the sake of salvation; and also that he had some idea of imperceptible works by the Holy Spirit, of which a man is not conscious, which are engendered in the act of faith during the state thereof.

The angelic spirits had then some conversation with each other about the falsification of the Word, and they agreed in this, that to falsify the Word is to take truths out of it, and apply them to confirm what is false, which is to extract truths from the Word and to destroy them; as, for example, to take this truth, that a man ought to love his neighbour, and from love do good to him for the sake of God and life eternal, and then to insist that it ought to be done, but not for the sake of salvation, because every good that comes from man is not good; this is to extract truth from the Word, and when it is so extracted, to destroy it; because the Lord in his Word enjoins every man, who would be saved, to do good to his neighbour as from himself; and yet to believe that he does it from the Lord.

CHAPTER XIII.

1. AND I saw a beast rise up out of the sea, having seven heads and ten horns, and upon his horns ten diadems, and upon his heads the name of blasphemy.

2. And the beast which I saw was like unto a leopard, and his feet were as the feet of a bear, and his mouth as the mouth of a lion; and the dragon gave him his strength, and his throne, and great power.

3. And I saw one of his heads as it were wounded to death; and his deadly wound was healed; and all the world wondered after the beast.

4. And they worshipped the dragon, which gave power unto the beast; and they worshipped the beast, saying, Who is like unto the beast? who is able to fight with him?

5. And there was given unto him a mouth speaking great things and blasphemies; and power was given unto him to continue forty-two months.

6. And he opened his mouth in blasphemy against God, to blaspheme his name, and his tabernacle, and them that dwell in heaven.

7. And it was given unto him to make war with the saints, and to overcome them: and power was given him over every tribe, and tongue, and nation.

8. And all that dwell upon the earth shall worship him whose names are not written in the book of life of the Lamb slain from the foundation of the world.

9. If any man have an ear let him hear.

10. He that leadeth into captivity shall go into captivity: he that killeth with the sword must be killed with the sword. Here is the patience and the faith of the saints.

11. And I beheld another beast coming up out of the earth: and he had two horns like a lamb, and he spake as a dragon.

12. And he exerciseth all the power of the first beast before him, and causeth the earth and them that dwell therein to worship the first beast, whose deadly wound was healed.

13. And he doeth great signs, so that he maketh fire come down from heaven on the earth in the sight of men.

14. And deceiveth them that dwell on the earth, by the means of those signs, which he had power to do in the sight of the beast; saying to them that dwell on the earth, that they should make an image to the beast which had the wound by a sword and lived.

15. And he had power to give breath unto the image of the beast, that the image of the beast should both speak, and cause that as many as would not worship the image of the beast should be killed.

16. And he caused all, both small and great, and rich and poor, free and bond, to receive a mark in their right hand, or in their foreheads.

17. And that no man might buy or sell, save he that had the mark, or the name of the beast, or the number of his name.

18. Here is wisdom. Let him that hath understanding count the number of the beast; for it is the number of a man; and his number is six hundred and sixty-six.

THE SPIRITUAL SENSE.

THE CONTENTS OF THE WHOLE CHAPTER. In this chapter the dragon continues to be treated of, and the doctrine and faith signified by him is described; what its quality is among the laity, and afterwards what its quality is among the clergy: by the beast which came up out of the sea, that doctrine and faith is described, as it exists with the laity, verse 1—10; and by the beast out of the earth, the same among the clergy, verse 11—17: lastly, concerning the falsification of the Word by the latter, verse 18.

THE CONTENTS OF EACH VERSE. V. 1, "And I saw a beast rise up out of the sea," signifies the laity in the churches of the Reformed, who are principled in the doctrine and faith of the dragon concerning God and salvation: "Having seven heads," signifies insanity arising from mere falses: "And ten horns," signifies much power: "And upon his horns ten diadems," signifies the power of falsifying many truths of the Word: "And upon his heads the name of blasphemy," signifies denial of the Lord's Divine Humanity, and doctrine of the church not drawn from the Word, but from self-derived intelligence: v. 2, "And the beast which I saw was like unto a leopard," signifies a heresy destructive of the church because derived from truths of the Word falsified: "And his feet were as the feet of a bear," signifies full of fallacies from the literal sense of the Word read but not understood: "And his mouth as the mouth of a lion," signifies reasonings from falses as from truths: "And the dragon gave him his strength, and his throne, and great power," signifies that this heresy prevails and reigns in consequence of its reception by the laity: v. 3, "And I saw one of his heads as it were wounded to death," signifies that the doctrine of faith alone does not acccord with the Word, in which works are so often enjoined: "And his deadly wound was healed," signifies the remedy applied on this account: "And all the world wondered after the beast," signifies that then this doctrine and faith was gladly received: v. 4, "And they worshipped the dragon which gave power unto the beast," signifies an acknowledgment that it is such as is laid down by the leaders and teachers, who have established its authority on the reception they have procured for it among the community at large: "And they worshipped the beast," signifies an acknowledgment on the part of the community, that it is holy truth: "Saying, Who is like unto the beast, who is able to fight with him?" signifies the excellence of that doctrine, because it cannot be contradicted by any one: v. 5, "And there was given unto him a mouth speaking great things and blasphemies," signifies that it teaches what is evil and false: "And power was given unto him to continue forty-two months," signifies the liberty of teaching and doing the evils and falses of that doctrine, even to the end of that church and the beginning of the new: v. 6, "And he opened his mouth in blasphemy against God, to blaspheme his name," signifies their sayings, which are scandals against the Essential Divinity and Divine Humanity of the Lord, and at the same time against every thing relating to the church derived from the Word, whereby the Lord is worshipped: "And his tabernacle, and them that dwell in heaven," signifies scandals against the Lord's celestial kingdom and against heaven: v. 7, "And it was given unto him to make war with the saints and to overcome them," signifies that they have impugned the divine truths of the Word, and cast them down to the ground: "And power was given him over every tribe, and tongue, and nation," signifies consequent dominion over all things of the church, both as to its doctrine and as to its life: v. 8, "And all that dwell upon the earth shall worship him, whose names are not written in the book of life of the Lamb," signifies that all acknowledged that heretical doctrine as holy in the church, except those who believed in the Lord: "Slain from the foundation of the world," signifies the Lord's Divine Humanity not acknowledged from the first establishment of the church: v. 9, "If any man have an ear let him hear," signifies that they should attend to this who desire to attain wisdom: v. 10, "He that leadeth into captivity shall go into captivity," signifies that he who by means of this heretical doctrine misleads others from believing well and living well, will himself be drawn into hell by his own evils and falses: "He that killeth with the sword must be killed with the sword," signifies that he who by means of falses destroys the soul of another, is himself destroyed by falses, and perishes: "Here is the patience and the faith of the saints," signifies that the man of the Lord's new church, by temptations from such things, is explored as to the quality of his life and faith: v. 11, "And I beheld another beast coming up out of the earth," signifies the clergy who are principled in the doctrine and faith of the dragon concerning God and salvation: "And he had two horns like a lamb, and he spake as a dragon," signifies that what they say, teach, and write is from the Word, as though it were the Lord's divine truth, and yet it is truth falsified: v. 12, "And he exerciseth all the power of the first beast before him," signifies that they confirmed these tenets, which thence derive their authority: "And causeth the earth and them that dwell therein to worship the first beast whose deadly wound was healed," signifies that from their being received by the community at large, it is established and confirmed that they ought to be acknowledged and held sacred in the church: v. 13, "And he doeth great signs," signifies testifications that the things they teach are true, although they are false: "So that he maketh fire come down from heaven on the earth in the sight of men," signifies attestations that their falsities are truths: v. 14, "And deceiveth them that dwell on the earth, by means of those signs, which he had power to do in the sight of the beast," signifies that by their testifications and attestations they lead the men of the church into errors: "Saying to them that dwell on the earth, that they should make an image to the beast, which had the wound by a sword and lived," signifies that they induce the men of the church to receive for doctrine, that faith is the only medium of salvation, for the reasons already mentioned: v. 15, "And he had power to give breath unto the image of the beast, that the image of the beast should both speak," signifies that it was permitted them to confirm that doctrine by means of the Word, whereby it does as it were receive life when it is taught: "And cause that as many as would not worship the image of the beast should be killed," signifies that they denounce damnation against those who do not acknowledge their doctrine of faith to be the holy doctrine of the church: v. 16, "And he caused all, both small and great, and rich and poor, free and bond," signifies all in that church, whatsoever may be their condition, learning, and intelligence: "To receive a mark in their right hand or in their foreheads," signifies that no one is acknowledged to be a reformed Christian unless he receives that doctrine in faith and love: v. 17, "And that no man might buy or sell, save he that had the mark or name of the beast, or the number of his name," signifies that it is not lawful for any one to teach from the Word, unless he acknowledges it, and swears to the belief and love thereof, or to something which amounts to the same: v. 18, "Here is wisdom," signifies that it is the part of a wise man, from what had been said and explained in this chapter, to see and understand the nature of the doctrine and faith of the clergy respecting God and salvation: "Let him that hath understanding count the number of the beast," signifies that he who is in illumination from the Lord, may know the nature and quality of the proofs they produce from the Word in confirmation of that doctrine and faith: "For it is the number of a man," signifies the quality of the Word and thence of the church: "And his number is six hundred and sixty-six," signifies this quality, that all the truth of the Word is falsified by them.

THE EXPLANATION.

567. *And I saw a beast rise up out of the sea*, signifies the laity in the churches of the Reformed who are principled in the doctrine and faith of the dragon concerning God and salvation. What the nature and quality of the faith of the dragon is, may be seen, n. 537: the same faith continues to be treated of in this chapter; and by this beast which was seen to rise out of the sea, is meant that faith among the laity; but by the beast which rose out of the earth, mentioned at verse 11, is meant that faith among the clergy. That the dragon continues to be treated of here is plain from the following passage in this chapter: that the dragon gave the beast which rose up out of the sea his strength, and throne, and great power, verse 2; and that they worshipped the dragon which gave power to the beast, verse 4; and of the beast which rose out of the earth, that he spake as the dragon, verse 11; and that he maketh all the power of the former beast before the dragon, verse 12. The reason why the laity are understood by the beast which rose out of the sea, and the clergy by the beast which rose out of the earth, is, because by the sea is signified the external of the church, and by the earth its internal, n. 398, and in other

places; and in the externals of church doctrine the laity are principled, but the clergy in its internals, on this account the beast which rose out of the earth is also called, in what follows, the false prophet. That they who are in the Reformed Churches are meant, is because the Reformed are treated of as far as chap. xvi. inclusive, and the Roman Catholics in chap. xvii. and xviii., and afterwards the last judgment, and finally the New Church. They appeared as beasts, because a dragon is a beast, and because a beast in the Word signifies man as to his affections; harmless and useful beasts signify man as to his good affections, and noxious and useless beasts signify man as to his evil affections; on which account the men of the church in general are called sheep, and a congregation of them, a flock, and their teacher is called a pastor: hence also it is, that the Word as to its power, affection, understanding, and wisdom, is described above, as four animals, which were a lion, a calf, an eagle, and a man, chap. iv., and that the intellectual knowledge of the Word is described by horses, chap. vi.; the reason is, because the affections of a man, in the spiritual world, appear at a distance as beasts, as has been before observed; and beasts, considered in themselves, are nothing but forms of natural affections, whereas men are not only forms of natural, but of spiritual affections at the same time. That men, as to their affections, are meant by beasts, may appear from these places: "Thou, O God, didst send a plentiful rain, whereby thou didst confirm thine inheritance, when it was weary; the *beast of thy congregation shall dwell* in it," Psalm lxviii. 9, 10. "Every *wild beast of the forest* is mine, the *cattle* upon a thousand hills. I know all the *fowls of the mountains*, and the *wild beast of the fields* are mine," Psalm l. 10. "Ashur is a cedar in Lebanon, of high stature, in his boughs the *fowls of the heavens* made their nests, and under his branches did all the *beasts of the field* bring forth their young, and under his shade dwelt all great nations," Ezek. xxxi. 2—6, 10, 13; Dan. iv. 7—13. "In that day I will make a covenant for them with the *beast of the field*, and with the *fowl of the heavens*, and I will betroth thee unto me for ever," Hos. ii. 18, 19. "Rejoice and be glad, be not afraid, ye *beasts of my fields*, for the pastures of the wilderness do spring," Joel ii. 21—23. "In that day there shall be a great tumult, Judah shall fight against Jerusalem, and there shall be a plague of the *horse*, of the *mule*, of the *camel*, and of every *beast;* then shall every one that is left go up to Jerusalem," Zech. xiv. 13—15. "The *fowl* shall summer upon them, and all the *beasts of the earth* shall winter upon them," Isaiah xviii. 6. "Thou son of man, speak unto the *fowl of every wing*, and unto every *beast of the field*, Assemble yourselves to my sacrifice upon the mountains of Israel; so will I set my glory among the heathen," Ezek. xxxix. 17—21

"Jehovah gathereth the outcasts of Israel; all ye *beasts* of the fields come to devour," Isaiah lvi. 8, 9. "Jehovah will destroy the Assyrian, and *flocks* shall lie down in the midst of her; all the *wild beasts of the nations*, both the *cormorant* and the *bittern*, shall lodge in the upper lintels of it," Zephan. ii. 13. "The sheep are scattered without a shepherd, and are meat for every *wild beast of the field*," Ezek. xxxiv. 5, 8. "I will cast thee forth upon the open field, and will cause all the *fowls of the heavens* to live upon thee, and I will fill the *beasts* of the whole earth with thee," Ezek. xxxii. 4: also v. 17; xxix. 5; xxxiii. 27; xxxix. 4; Jerem. xv. 3; xvi. 4; xix. 7; xxvii. 5, 8. "The enemy reproacheth Jehovah; O deliver not to the *beast* the soul of thy turtle-dove," Psalm lxxiv. 18, 19. "I saw in vision four *beasts* rise out of the sea, the first was like a *lion*, and had eagle's wings, the second was like a *bear*, the third like a *leopard*, and the fourth was terrible," Dan. vii. 3—5. "The spirit driveth Jesus into the wilderness, and he was with the *wild beasts*, and the angels ministered unto him," Mark i. 12, 13; he was not with beasts, but with devils, who are here meant by beasts; not to mention other passages where beasts and wild beasts are named, as in Isaiah xxxv. 9; xliii. 20; Jerem. xii. 4, 8—10; Ezek. viii. 10; xxxiv. 23, 25, 28; xxxviii. 18—20; Hosea iv. 2, 3; xiii. 8; Joel i. 16, 18, 20; Habak. ii. 17; Dan. ii. 37, 38; Psalm viii. 7—9; Psalm lxxx. 13; civ. 10, 11, 14, 20, 25; cxlviii. 7, 10; Exod. xxiii. 28—30; Levit. xxvi. 6; Deut. vii. 22; xxxii. 24; in all these places by beasts are signified men as to their affections. By *man* and *beast* together is signified man as to spiritual and natural affection; as in the following passages: Jerem. vii. 20; xxi. 6; xxvii. 5; xxxi. 27; xxxii. 43; xxxiii. 10—12; xxxvi. 29; l. 3; Ezek. xiv. 13, 17, 19; xxv. 13; xxxii. 13; xxxvi. 11; Zeph. i. 2, 3; Zech. ii. 7, 8; viii. 9, 10; Jonah iii. 7, 8; Psalm xxxvi. 6; Numb. xviii. 15. By all the beasts that were sacrificed were signified good affections; and likewise by the beasts used for food; but the contrary by such as were not to be used for food, Levit. xx. 25, 26.

568. *Having seven heads*, signifies insanity arising from mere falses, in like manner as by the seven heads of the dragon, n. 538.

569. *And ten horns*, signifies much power, in like manner as the horns of the dragon, which also were ten, n. 539.

570. *And upon his horns ten diadems*, signifies the power of falsifying many truths of the Word. By a horn is signified power, n. 539; by ten is signified much, n. 101; and by diadems are signified the truths of the Word falsified, n. 540; therefore by ten diadems upon his horns, is signified to have it in his power to falsify many truths of the Word. Of the dragon it is said that he had seven diadems on his heads, but of this

beast, that he had ten diadems on his horns; the reason is, because here it signifies the power of falsifying many truths of the Word, but there the falsification of all; for the laity are able, but do not do it; for they who are under the influence of falses and in the belief of them, are opposed to truths, consequently, when they see truths in the Word, they falsify them.

571. *And upon his heads the name of blasphemy*, signifies denial of the Lord's Divine Humanity and doctrine of the church not drawn from the Word, but from self-derived intelligence. By seven heads is signified insanity arising from mere falses, as above, n. 568; and this insanity speaks blasphemy, when it denies the Divinity of the Lord in his Humanity; and also when it does not deduce the doctrine of the church from the Word, but unfolds it from self-derived intelligence. As to the *first*, that it is blasphemy to deny the Lord's Divinity in his Humanity, the reason is this, that he who denies it is opposed to the faith received throughout the whole Christian world, named from Athanasius, where it is expressly said, that in Jesus Christ, God and Man, that is, Divinity and Humanity, are not two but one, and that they are one person, united like soul and body; therefore they who deny the Divinity in his Humanity, come near to the Socinians and Arians, especially when they think of the Lord's Humanity alone as of that of another man, and nothing at all of his Divinity from eternity. As to the *second* point, that it is blasphemy not to deduce the doctrine of the church from the Word, but to unfold it from self-derived intelligence, the reason is, because the church exists from the Word, and its quality is according to its understanding of the Word, as may be seen in the *Doctrine of the New Jerusalem concerning the Sacred Scripture*, n. 76—79; and the doctrine that faith alone, that is, faith without the works of the law, justifies and saves, is not from the Word, but from a single expression of Paul misunderstood, Rom. iii. 28, see n. 417; and all falsity of doctrine takes its rise from no other source than from self-derived intelligence; for what is more universally taught in the Word, than to shun evil and do good? and what is more evident than that God and our neighbour ought to be loved? And who can help seeing, that no one can love his neighbour, unless he lives according to the works of the law, and he who loves not his neighbour loves not God? for in the love of our neighbour the Lord conjoins himself with man, and man conjoins himself with the Lord, that is, the Lord and man are together in that love. And what is love to our neighbour but the shunning to do him evil, according to the commandments of the decalogue, Rom. xiii. 8—11? And in proportion as man is not willing to do evil to his neighbour, in the same proportion is he willing to do him good; hence it is evident that it is blasphemy to exclude the works of this law from salvation, as

they do, who make faith alone, which is faith separated from good works, by itself competent to salvation. By blasphemy (Matt. xii. 31, 32; Apoc. xvii. 3; Isaiah xxxvii. 6, 7, 23, 24) is meant to deny the Lord's Divinity, as the Socinians do, and to deny the Word; for they who thus deny the Lord's Divinity cannot enter heaven, for the Lord's Divinity is the all in all in heaven, and he who denies the Word denies all things of religion.

572. *And the beast which I saw was like unto a leopard*, signifies a heresy destructive of the church, because derived from the truths of the Word falsified. By beasts in general are signified men as to their affections, n. 567; and by a leopard is signified the affection or lust of falsifying the truths of the Word; and because it is a ferocious beast, and kills harmless animals, it signifies also a heresy destructive of the church. That a leopard signifies the truths of the Word falsified, is owing to its black and white spots, for by the black spots are signified falses, and by the white intermixed with them is signified truth; as therefore it is a fierce and murderous beast, it signifies the truths of the Word falsified and thus destroyed. Similar is the signification of a leopard in the following places: "Can the Ethiopian change his skin, or the *leopard his spots?* then may ye also do good that are accustomed to do evil," Jerem. xiii. 23. "The lion out of the forest shall slay them, and a wolf of the evening shall spoil them, a *leopard shall watch over their cities*, every one that goeth out thence shall be torn in pieces, because their transgressions are many, and their backslidings are increased," Jerem. v. 6; the leopard watching against their cities, means watching against the truths of doctrine. A city means doctrine, n. 194. "As they have forgotten me, therefore I will be unto them as a lion, as a *leopard by the way* will I observe them," Hosea xiii. 6, 7; a way also signifies truth, n. 176. "The wolf also shall dwell with the lamb, and the *leopard* shall lie down with the kid," Isaiah xi. 6; here the Lord's kingdom which is to come is treated of; a kid signifies the genuine truths of the church, and a leopard the same falsified. "The third beast which rose out of the sea was like a *leopard* which had upon the back of it four wings of a fowl," Dan. vii. 6; concerning the four beasts seen by Daniel, see below, n. 574.

573. *And his feet were as the feet of a bear*, signifies full of fallacies from reading the letter of the Word but not understanding it. By feet is signified the natural degree, which is the ultimate, upon which that heresy, meant by the leopard, subsists, and as it were walks, this being the literal sense of the Word, and by a bear are signified those who read the Word and do not understand it, whereby they involve themselves in fallacies; that these are signified by bears was clear to me from the

bears which I saw in the spiritual world, and from such there as were clad in bear skins, who had all read the Word indeed, but without seeing any doctrinal truth in it; also who had confirmed the appearances of truth therein, and thus were involved in fallacies. In that world there appear bears that are hurtful, and bears that are harmless, and some that are white; but they are distinguished by their heads, those which are harmless have heads like calves or sheep. Bears have such a signification in the following places: "He was unto me as a *bear* lying in wait, and as a lion in secret places, he hath turned aside my ways, he hath made me desolate," Lament. iii. 10, 11. "I will meet them as a *bear* that is bereaved of her whelps, and there will I devour them like a lion, the wild beast of the field shall tear them," Hosea xiii. 7, 8. "The calf and the young lion shall lie down together, and the cow and the *bear* shall feed," Isaiah xi. 6, 7. "The second beast which rose out of the sea was like to a *bear*, and it had three ribs in the mouth of it between the teeth of it," Dan. vii. 5. By the lion and the *bear*, which David took by the beard and smote, 1 Sam. xvii. 34—37, the same is signified; and likewise 2 Sam. xvii. 8. The *lion* and *bear* are mentioned in those places, because by a lion is signified falsity destroying the truths of the Word, and by a bear are signified fallacies, which are also destructive, but not in so great a degree; therefore it is said in Amos, "The day of Jehovah is darkness and not light, as if a man did flee from a *lion*, and a *bear* met him," v. 18, 19. We read in the second book of Kings, that Elisha was mocked of little children, and that they said unto him, "Go up, thou bald head; and there came forth two *she bears* out of the wood, and tare forty and two children of them," ii. 23, 24; this took place because Elisha represented the Lord as to the Word, n. 298; and because baldness signifies the Word devoid of its literal sense, thus not any thing, n. 47; and the number forty-two, blasphemy, n. 583; and bears signify the literal sense of the Word, read indeed, but not understood.

574. *And his mouth as the mouth of a lion*, signifies reasonings from falses as from truths. By mouth is signified doctrine, preaching, and discourse, n. 453, here, reasoning from falses of doctrine, because by the head, in which is the mouth, is signified insanity from mere falses, n. 568; by a lion is signified Divine Truth in power, n. 241, 471, but here falsity in power appearing like truth by reasonings, n. 573; hence by his mouth being as the mouth of a lion, are signified reasonings from falses as from truths. That a leopard, a bear, and a lion, signify such things, may appear from the beasts of the same kind that were seen by Daniel, of which it is thus written: "Four great beasts came up out of the sea, the *first was like a lion*, and had eagle's wings: I beheld till the wings thereof were plucked, and it was

lifted up from the earth, and made to stand upon the feet, as a man, and a man's heart was given to it. *The second beast was like a bear*, and it raised up itself on one side; and it had three ribs in the mouth of it, between the teeth of it; and they said, Arise, devour much flesh. The *third beast was like a leopard*, which had upon the back of it four wings as of a fowl, the beast had also four heads, and dominion was given to it. The *fourth beast* was dreadful, and terrible, and exceedingly strong, and it had great iron teeth, it devoured and brake in pieces, and stamped the residue with the feet of it," Dan. vii. 3—7; by these four beasts are described the successive states of the church, from its beginning to its end, even to its utter devastation as to every good and truth of the Word; after which is the Lord's advent. By the *lion* is signified the Divine Truth of the Word in its first state, and the restoration of the church thereby, which is understood by his being lifted up from the earth, and set erect upon his feet as a man, and a man's heart being given him. By the *bear* is described the second state of the church, when the Word is read indeed, but not understood: by the three ribs between his teeth are signified appearances and fallacies, and by much flesh is signified the sum of the literal sense of the Word. A third state of the church is described by the *leopard*, by which is signified the Word falsified as to its truths; by the four wings, as of fowls, on his back, are signified confirmations of what is false. The *fourth* or last state of the church is described by a *beast* dreadful and terrible, by which is signified the destruction of all truth and goodness, for which reason it is said that he crushed in pieces and devoured, and stamped the residue with his feet; lastly, the Lord's advent is described, and then the destruction of that church, and the establishment of a new one, from verse 9 to the end. These four beasts were seen by Daniel to rise out of the sea successively, but by John the three first beasts were seen united in one body, and also coming out of the sea; the reason is, because in Daniel successive states of the church are described by them, but here in the Apocalypse its ultimate state is described, in which all the former states exist together; but as the body of this beast appeared like a leopard, and its feet like a bear, and its mouth like a lion; the leopard and the bear have everywhere a like signification; but by a mouth like a lion are signified reasonings derived from falses, because it follows that "The beast out of his mouth spake blasphemies," verse 5, 6, and by his head is signified insanity from mere falses.

575. *And the dragon gave him his strength, and his throne, and great power*, signifies that this heresy prevails and reigns in consequence of its reception by the laity. By the dragon is signified that heretical doctrine, concerning which see n. 537; by this beast the laity are signified, n. 563, who do not speak

from themselves, but from their teachers, and as they constitute the people, it is evident that by reception from them that heresy prevails and reigns. This therefore is what is signified by the strength, throne, and great power which the dragon gave to this beast, and by what follows in verse 4, "And they worshipped the dragon, which gave power unto the beast." The dragon prevails and reigns by them, especially by means of this tenet of their religion, "That the understanding is to be kept in subjection to faith; and that is the faith which is not understood, and that in matters of a spiritual nature, faith in a thing which is understood is intellectual faith, destitute of any justifying virtue;" when these notions prevail among the laity, the clergy have power, veneration, and a sort of adoration on account of the divine things which they are supposed to know, and which are to be imbibed from their mouths. By strength is signified authority; by throne, government; and by great power, dominion.

576. *And I saw one of his heads as it were wounded to death*, signifies that the doctrine which is the head of all the rest, that man is justified and saved by faith alone without the works of the law, does not accord with the Word, in which works are so often enjoined. By one of his heads is signified the principal and fundamental article of the whole doctrine of the reformed church; for the beast had seven heads, by which is signified insanity from mere falses, n. 568, thus also all falses in the complex; for by seven in the Word are signified all, n. 10, 391; and as all the falses of their doctrine respecting salvation depend upon this one, that man is justified and saved by faith alone without the works of the law, this is what is here signified by one of the heads of the beast; by its being as it were wounded to death, is signified that it does not accord with the Word, where works are so frequently enjoined; for all church doctrine, which does not accord with the Word, is not sound, but labours under a deadly disease; for from the Word, and from no other source, the doctrine of the church is to be derived.

577. *And his deadly wound was healed*, signifies the remedy applied to this chief article of doctrine by their reasoning as follows: that no one can do good works from himself, and fulfil the law; and that on this account another medium of salvation is provided instead, which is faith in the righteousness and merit of Christ, who suffered for man, and thereby removed the sentence of the law. That this is their remedy for the wounded head, and is also applied, when by the wounded head is understood what goes before, n. 576, is well known, and therefore needs no further explanation.

578. *And all the world wondered after the beast*, signifies that then this faith was gladly received, and became the doctrine of the whole church, because they thus were not bondmen

under the law, but freemen under faith. And all the world wondered, signifies admiration that his deadly wound was healed, and thence reception gladly; by all the world is signified the whole church of the reformed, for the world or earth means the church, n. 285; therefore by all the world wondered after the beast is signified that this faith was gladly received, and became the doctrine of the whole church. It is gladly received, because they thus are not bondmen under the law, but freemen under faith; not knowing that the very reverse is true, viz., that they who think themselves free under faith, or from that faith, or through that faith, are slaves to sin, that is to the devil, for sin and the devil are one and the same; for thus they think that the law does not condemn, and therefore that to sin without being obnoxious to the sentence of the law constitutes freedom, provided they have faith; when nevertheless this is slavery itself; but man when he shuns sin, that is the devil, from being a slave becomes free. Here I will add this MEMORABLE CIRCUMSTANCE: I conversed in the spiritual world with certain doctors of the church, about what they meant by works of the law, and what by the law, under whose yoke, servitude, and sentence, they declared themselves not to be. They said they meant the works of the law of the decalogue; upon which I asked, "What are the things forbidden in the decalogue? are they not these: Thou shalt not kill; thou shalt not commit adultery; thou shalt not steal; thou shalt not bear false witness? Are these the works of the law, which you separate from faith, saying, that faith alone, without the works of the law, justifies and saves, and are these what Christ made satisfaction for?" And they replied, "They are." Upon this there was heard a voice from heaven, saying, "Who can be so senseless?" and instantly their faces were turned towards some diabolical spirits, among whom was Machiavel, and several of the order of Jesuits, who acknowledged all these things to be allowable, provided they do not expose themselves to the penalties of worldly laws; and they would have associated themselves with these, had not a society interposed to prevent them. It is said that all the world wondered after the beast; that after the beast means to follow and obey it, appears from these places: David hath "kept my commandments, and hath *walked after me* with all his heart," 1 Kings xiv. 8. "The sons of Jesse went *after Saul* to the war," 1 Sam. xvii. 13. "Thou shalt not go *after a multitude* to do evil; neither shalt thou speak in a cause to decline *after many*, to wrest judgment," Exod. xxiii. 2. "And walk not *after other gods*, whom ye know not," Jerem. vii. 9. "And they went *after other gods* to serve them," Jerem. xi. 10; Deut. viii. 19. "For all the men that go *after Baalpeor*, Jehovah thy God hath destroyed," Deut. iv. 3.

579. *And they worshipped the dragon, which gave power unto*

the beast, signifies an acknowledgment of the doctrine of justification by faith, without the works of the law, by leaders and teachers, who have established its authority on the reception they have procured for it among the community at large; by worshipping is signified to acknowledge it as holy in the church; by the dragon is signified the doctrine of justification and salvation by faith alone, without the works of the law, n. 537; by this beast is signified the community, because it denotes the laity, n. 567; by giving power is signified to establish its authority by its reception among the laity, n. 575.

580. *And they worshipped the beast*, signifies an acknowledgment on the part of the community that it is holy truth, that no one can do good works from himself, nor fulfil the law. To worship signifies to acknowledge it as holy in the church, as above, n. 579, here, to acknowledge it as a holy truth, that no one can do good works of himself, and fulfil the law; and these two being regarded as holy truths, it follows, that the works of the law are to be removed from faith, as not conducive to salvation; but that these truths, and many others, are falsified, may be seen above, n. 566: by the beast is here signified the same as by the dragon, on account of the reception and acknowledgment of the doctrine; therefore it is said that they worshipped the dragon, and worshipped the beast.

581. *Saying, Who is like unto the beast? who is able to fight with him?* signifies the excellence of that doctrine above all others, because it cannot be contradicted by any one. Who is like unto the beast, signifies an opinion of the excellence of that church above all others on account of its doctrine; by the beast is signified the community, thus the church, and abstractedly its doctrine; who is able to fight with him, signifies, who can deny that man is not able to do any spiritual good from himself, &c., as above, n. 566, and as this cannot be contradicted, are we not therefore saved by faith without the works of the law? But that this conclusion is absurd, yea, insanity itself, may be seen by every one who knows and understands any thing of the Word. Who is able to fight with him, also signifies that this doctrine has been so ingeniously and subtilly confirmed, and so fortified and guarded by its first leaders, and such as have since taught after them, that it cannot be impugned.

582. *And there was given unto him a mouth speaking great things and blasphemies*, signifies that it teaches what is evil and false. By a mouth speaking is signified doctrine, preaching, and discourse, n. 453; by speaking great things and blasphemies, is signified to teach what is evil and false; for great is predicated of good, and in an opposite sense of evil, n. 656, 663, 896, 898, and by blasphemies are signified truths of the Word falsified, thus, falses; what is here signified by blas-

phemies in particular, may be seen above, n. 571: the reason why it teaches what is evil, is, because it removes the works of the law, thus, the things which ought to be done, from salvation, and he who does this, is in spiritual evils, which are sins.

583. *And power was given unto him to continue forty-two months*, signifies the liberty of teaching and doing the evils and falses of that doctrine, even to the end of that church, and the beginning of the new. By power being given him, is signified the power of speaking great things and blasphemies, that is, of teaching and doing the evils and falses mentioned above, n. 582; forty-two months signify even to the end of the former church and beginning of the new, as above, n. 496; the same as is signified by three days and a half, n. 505; and by a time and times and half a time, n. 562; and also by a thousand two hundred and sixty, n. 491, forty-two months making three years and a half.

584. *And he opened his mouth in blasphemy against God, to blaspheme his name*, signifies their sayings, which are scandals, against the Essential Divinity and Divine Humanity of the Lord, and at the same time against every thing relating to the church derived from the Word, whereby the Lord is worshipped. He opened his mouth in blasphemy, signifies the things uttered, which are false; by a mouth is signified doctrine, preaching, and discourse, n. 453, thus, by opening the mouth, is signified to utter them; and blasphemies signify falsifications of the Word, and other things, as above, n. 571, 582, and in the present case, scandals, because it next follows, against God and his name; by God is signified the Lord's Divinity, as also in many other parts of the Apocalypse; and by his name is signified every thing by which the Lord is worshipped, likewise the Word, because worship is according to it, n. 81. That by the name of Jehovah, or of God, is signified the Lord's Divine Humanity, and at the same time the Word, likewise every thing by which he is worshipped, may further appear from the following passages: Jesus said, "Father, glorify *thy name;* then came a voice from heaven, saying, I have both glorified it, and will glorify it again," John xii. 28. Jesus said, "I have declared unto them *thy name*, and I will declare it," John xvii. 26. "Whatsoever ye shall ask in *my name*, that will I do, that the Father may be glorified in the Son; if ye shall ask any thing in *my name*, I will do it," John xiv. 13, 14. "In the beginning was the Word, and the Word was with God, and the Word was God. But as many as received him, to them gave he power to become the sons of God, even to them that believe on his *name;* and the Word was made flesh," John i. 1, 12, 14. Jesus said, "He that believeth not in him is condemned already, because he hath not believed in the *name of the only-begotten Son of God*," John iii. 18. By the *name of Jehovah God*, which

is not to be profaned, in the second commandment of the decalogue; and by the *name of the Father*, which is to be hallowed, in the Lord's prayer, nothing else is understood.

585. *And his tabernacle, and them that dwell in heaven*, signifies scandals against the Lord's celestial kingdom and against heaven. By a tabernacle nearly the same is signified as by a temple, viz., in a supreme sense, the Lord's Divine Humanity, and, in a relative sense, heaven and the church, n. 191, 529. But by a tabernacle, in this latter sense, is signified the celestial church, which is in the good of love from the Lord to the Lord; and by a temple, the spiritual church, which is in the truths of wisdom from the Lord; by them that dwell in heaven is signified heaven. The tabernacle signifies the celestial kingdom, because the Most Ancient Church, which was celestial, through being principled in love to the Lord, performed divine worship in tabernacles; and the Ancient Church, which was a spiritual church, performed divine worship in temples. Tabernacles were of wood, and temples of stone, and wood signifies good, and stone truth. That by a tabernacle is signified the Lord's Divine Humanity as to Divine Love, likewise heaven and the church, which are in love to the Lord, may appear from the following passages: "Jehovah, who shall abide in thy *tabernacle;* who shall dwell in thy holy hill? he that walketh uprightly, and worketh righteousness, and speaketh the truth in his heart," Psalm xv. 1, 2. "Jehovah shall hide me in his *tent*, in the secret of *his tabernacle* shall he hide me, he shall set me upon a rock," Psalm xxvii. 4, 5. "I will abide in thy *tabernacle* for ever," Psalm lxi. 4. "Look upon Zion, the city of our solemnities, thine eye shall see Jerusalem, a quiet habitation, a *tabernacle* that shall not be taken down." Isaiah xxxiii. 20. "Jehovah that spreadeth out the heavens as a *tabernacle* to dwell in," Isaiah xl. 22. "Because thou hast made even the Most High thy habitation, neither shall any plague come nigh thy *tabernacle*," Psalm xci. 9, 10. "Jehovah hath set his *tabernacle* amongst you, and will walk among you," Levit. xxvi. 11, 12. "Jehovah forsook the *tabernacle* of Shiloh, the *tent* which he placed among men," Psalm lxxviii. 60. "I heard a great voice out of heaven, saying, Behold, the *tabernacle* of God is with men, and he will dwell with them," Apoc. xxi. 3. "My *tabernacles* are spoiled," Jerem. iv. 20; x. 20. "He shall pluck thee out of the *tabernacle*, and root thee out of the land of the living," Psalm lii. 5; besides other places, as Isaiah xvi. 5; liv. 2; Jerem. xxx. 18; Lament. ii. 4; Hosea ix. 6; xii. 9; Zech. xii. 7. Since the Most Ancient Church, which was a celestial church, by reason of its love to the Lord, and consequent conjunction with him, celebrated divine worship in *tabernacles*, therefore the Lord commanded Moses to build a *tabernacle*, in which all things of heaven and the church

were represented; which was so holy, that it was not lawful for any one to go into it, except Moses, Aaron, and his sons; and if any one of the people entered he would die, Numb. xvii. 12, 13; xviii. 1, 22, 23; xix. 14—19; in the inmost part of it was the ark, in which were the two tables of the decalogue, over which was the mercy-seat and the cherubims; and without the vail was the table for the show-bread, the altar of incense, and the candlestick with seven lamps; all which were representatives of heaven and the church; it is described, Exod. xxvi. 7—16; xxxvi. 8—37; and we read that the pattern thereof was shown to Moses on Mount Sinai, Exod. xxv. 9; xxvi. 30; and whatsoever is given to be seen from heaven, the same is representative of heaven, and thence of the church. In memory of the most holy worship of the Lord in tabernacles by the most ancient people, and of their conjunction with him by love, *the feast of tabernacles* was instituted, as mentioned in Levit. xxiii. 39—44; Deut. xvi. 13, 14; Zech. xiv. 16, 18, 19.

586. *And it was given unto him to make war with the saints, and to overcome them*, signifies that they have impugned the divine truths of the Word, and cast them down to the ground. By war is signified spiritual war, which is that of falsity against truth, and of truth against falsity, n. 500, hence to make war is to impugn; by saints are meant they who are in divine truths from the Lord through the Word, and thence, abstractedly from persons, divine truths, n. 173; therefore by overcoming them is signified to cause that truths should not prevail, thus to overthrow them. The like is signified by these words in Daniel: "The fourth beast that came up out of the sea, which had a mouth speaking great things, *made war with the saints and prevailed*," vii. 21; and also by these: "The he-goat ran at the ram, and cast him to the ground, and stamped upon him; and magnified himself even to the prince of the host, and the place of his sanctuary was cast down: and *he cast down the truth to the ground*," viii. 5—7, 11, 12; that by the he-goat is meant faith separated from charity, may be seen in *The Doctrine of the New Jerusalem concerning Faith*, n. 61—68. In like manner by these words: A king shall arise "of a fierce countenance, and understanding dark sentences; *he shall destroy the mighty, and the holy people*, and he shall stand up against the Prince of princes; and he shall cause craft to prosper in his hand," Dan. viii. 23—25; that this king is the he-goat, is said verse 21 of the same chapter. The like is also signified by the beast that ascended out of the bottomless pit, and *made war with the two witnesses, and overcame and killed them*, Apoc. xi. 7, n. 500; the reason why they overcame, is, because the laity do not discern their artifices, which they call mysteries, for they conceal them under appearances and fallacies; therefore they said, "Who is like unto the beast? who is

able to fight with him?" verse 4, n. 579, 580, 581. That by saints are meant those who are in truths from the Lord through the Word, may appear from the places adduced above, n. 173, and also from the following: Jesus said, "Father, *sanctify them through thy truth, thy Word is truth. And for their sakes I sanctify myself, that they also might be sanctified through the truth; I in them, and thou in me,*" John xvii. 17, 19, 23. "Jehovah came from Sinai, he shined forth from Mount Paran, and he came with ten thousands of *saints,* from his right hand went a fiery law for them, all *his saints* are in thy hand; every one *shall receive of thy words,*" Deut. xxxiii. 2, 3; from which it is plain, that they are called saints who are in divine truths from the Lord through the Word: also, that they *who live according to the commandments*, that is, according to the truths of the Word, were the *saints of Jehovah*, Levit. xix. 2; Deut. xxvi. 18, 19; and that if they did the covenant, they were a *holy nation*, or nation of saints, Exod. xix. 5, 6: the decalogue or ten commandments is the covenant which they were to do or keep, n. 60; thus the place in the tabernacle, where the ark was, in which the decalogue was deposited, was called the *holy of holies*, Exod. xxvi. 33, 34. They are called saints who live according to the truths of the Word; not that they are holy, but the truths in them are holy, and they are holy when they are in them from the Lord; and the Lord is in them when the truths of his Word are in them, John xv. 7. By virtue of truths from the Lord the *angels are called holy*, Matt. xxv. 31; Luke ix. 26; and in like manner the *prophets*, Luke i. 70; Apoc. xviii. 20; xxii. 6; and the *apostles*, Apoc. xviii. 20. It is for this reason that the temple is called the *temple of holiness*, Psalm v. 7; lxv. 4; and *Sion, the mountain of holiness*, Isaiah lxv. 11; Jerem. xxxi. 23; Ezek. xx. 40; Psalm ii. 6; iii. 4; xv. 1· and *Jerusalem the holy city*, Isaiah xlviii. 2; lxiv. 10; Apoc. xxi. 2, 10; Matt. xxvii. 53. And the *church, the holy people*, Isaiah lxii. 12; lxiii. 18; Psalm cxlix. 2; and also the *kingdom of saints*, Dan. vii. 18, 22, 27. The reason why they were called holy, is, because angels, in an abstract sense, signify divine truths from the Lord; prophets, truths of doctrine; apostles, truths of the church; the temple, heaven and the church as to divine truth; and, in like manner, Sion, Jerusalem, the people and kingdom of God: that no one is holy from himself, not even the angels, may be seen in Job xv. 14, 15, but from the Lord, because the Lord alone is holy, Apoc. xv. 4, n. 173.

587. *And power was given him over every tribe, and tongue, and nation*, signifies consequent dominion over all things of the church, both as to its doctrine and as to its life. By power is signified dominion as above, n. 575; by tribe is signified the church as to its truths and goods, and, in an opposite sense, as

to its falses and evils, n. 20, 349; by tongue is signified its doctrine, n. 282, 483, and by nation is signified a life according to such doctrine, n. 483.

588. *And all that dwell upon the earth shall worship him, whose names are not written in the book of life of the Lamb*, signifies that all acknowledged that heretical doctrine, which is meant by the dragon and the beast, as holy in the church, except those who believed in the Lord. To worship signifies to acknowledge as a sacred principle of the church, as above, n. 579, 580; by all that dwell upon the earth, are signified all of the Reformed Church, as in n. 558; by names not written in the Lamb's book of life, is signified, except those who believe in the Lord; by names, they are signified as to their quality, n. 81, 122, 165; by the book of life is signified the Word of the Lord, and all doctrine respecting him, n. 256, 257, 259, 469; and as all church doctrine from the Word refers to this point, that the Lord is to be believed in, therefore this is here understood by name written in the Lamb's book of life. Concerning faith in the Lord, see above, n. 67 and 533.

589. *Slain from the foundation of the world*, signifies the Lord's Divine Humanity not acknowledged from the first establishment of the church. By the Lamb slain is signified that the Lord's Divine Humanity is not acknowledged, may be seen above, n. 59, 269, where these words are explained: "I am the First and the Last, and am he that liveth, and was *dead*, and behold I am alive for evermore, i. 17, 18; and the following: "And I beheld, and lo, in the midst of the throne, a lamb standing as it were *slain*; and they sung a new song, saying, Thou art worthy to take the book, for thou wast slain, and hast redeemed us to God," v. 6, 9; from the foundation of the world, signifies from the establishment of the church, both Jewish and Christian; that the Jews did not acknowledge the Lord's Divine Humanity, is well known; that the Roman Catholics do not, is also well known; and that the Reformed do not, may be seen above, n. 294. By the foundation of the world is not here meant the creation of the world, but the establishment of the church; for by the world, in the most extensive sense, is meant the whole world, and the good as well as the wicked that are therein, and sometimes the wicked only; but in a less extensive sense, by the world is meant the same as by the globe and the earth, thus the church; that by the globe is signified the church, may be seen, n. 551, and the same by the earth, n. 285; that by laying the foundation of the globe and the earth is signified to establish the church, and that by the founding and foundation thereof, its establishment is signified, may appear from Isaiah xxiv. 18; xl. 21; xlviii. 12, 13; li. 16, 17; lviii. 12; Jerem. xxxi. 37; Mic. vi. 1, 2; Zech. xii. 1; Psalm xviii. 7, 15; xxiv. 1, 2; lxxxii. 5; lxxxix. 11. That

the world also signifies the church, may be seen in Matt. xiii. 37—39; Joel i. 9, 10; and that the Lord from faith in him is called the Saviour of the world, John iii. 16—19; iv. 42; vi. 33, 51; viii. 12; ix. 4, 5; xii. 46, 47. That the world also means the people of the church, John xii. 19; xviii. 20. From hence it may be seen what is signified by the foundation of the world; also in Matt. xxv. 34; Luke xi. 50; John xvii. 24; Apoc. xvii. 11.

590. *If any man have an ear, let him hear*, signifies that they should attend to this, who desire to attain wisdom. That by having an ear to hear is signified to perceive and obey, and also to attend, may be seen above, n. 87; that it also means those who desire to attain wisdom, follows of course. Here it is said, "If any man have an ear let him hear," in order that they may attend to what goes before, and that otherwise they are not wise.

591. *He that leadeth into captivity shall go into captivity*, signifies that he who by means of this heretical doctrine misleads others from believing well and living well, will himself be drawn into hell by his own evils and falses. By leading into captivity is signified to persuade and draw over to his own party, that they may consent to and become adherents to that heresy, which is understood by the dragon and the beast, and so to draw aside from believing well and from living well. By going into captivity is signified to be drawn into hell by his own falses and evils. By captivity is here meant spiritual captivity, which consists in being seduced, and so drawn away from truths and goods, into falses and evils. That by captivity in the Word is meant this spiritual captivity, may appear from the following passages: "Hear, I pray you, all people, and behold my sorrow, my virgins and my young men are gone into *captivity*," Lament. i. 18. "God forsook the tabernacle of Shiloh, the tent which he placed among men, and delivered his strength into *captivity*," Psalm lxxviii. 60, 61. "The wind shall eat up all thy pastors, and thy lovers shall go into *captivity*; surely then shalt thou be ashamed for all thy wickedness," Jerem. xxii. 22. "I will make mine arrows drunk with the blood of the slain and of the captives," Deut. xxxii. 42. "They stoop, they bow down together, and their soul is gone into *captivity*," Isaiah xlvi. 1, 2. "Jehovah hath sent me to bind up the brokenhearted, to proclaim liberty to the *captives*, and the opening of the *prison* to them that are bound," Isaiah lxi. 1; Luke iv. 18, 19. "I have raised him up in righteousness; and he shall let go my *captives*, not for price nor reward," Isaiah xlv. 13. "Thou hast ascended on high, *thou hast led captivity captive*," Psalm lxviii. 18. "Shall the lawful *captive* be delivered? Even the *captives* of the mighty shall be taken away, and the *prey* of the terrible shall be delivered," Isaiah xlix. 24, 25.

"Shake thyself from the dust, arise, sit down, O Jerusalem, loose thyself from the bands of thy neck, *O captive daughter of Zion*," Isaiah lii. 1, 2; not to mention others; as Jerem. xlviii. 46, 47; l. 33, 34; Ezek. vi. 1—10; xii. 1—12; Obad. i. 11; Psalm xiv. 7; l. 33, 34; liii. 6. By the captivities of the sons of Israel by their enemies, spoken of in the book of Judges, and 2 Kings xxx., and in the prophets, were represented, and consequently signified spiritual captivities, of which elsewhere. By those that are bound, or prisoners, the same is signified as by captives in the following passages: "By the blood of thy covenant I have sent forth thy *prisoners* out of the pit, wherein is no water," Zech. ix. 11. "Let the sighing of the *prisoner* come before thee," Psalm lxxix. 11. "And they shall be gathered together as *prisoners* are gathered in the pit, and shall be shut up as in the prison," Isaiah xxiv. 22. "That made the world as a wilderness, that opened not the house of his *prisoners*," Isaiah xiv. 17. "The King said, I was in *prison*, and ye came not unto me," Matt. xxv. 36. Jesus said, "Ought not this woman, being a daughter of Abraham, whom *Satan hath bound*, lo, these eighteen years, be *loosed from this bond* on the Sabbath day?" Luke xiii. 16.

592. *He that killeth with the sword, must be killed with the sword*, signifies that he who by means of falses destroys the soul of another, is himself destroyed by falses, and perishes. By a sword, a dagger, and a two-edged sword, is signified truth, and, in an opposite sense, falsity, both militant, n. 52, 836; therefore by killing and being killed is signified to destroy and be destroyed, or to ruin and to perish, which is effected by falses.

593. *Here is the patience and the faith of the saints*, signifies that the man of the Lord's New Church, by temptations derived from the spirits of the dragon, is explored as to the quality of his life and faith. By patience is here signified patience in temptations, and in such case exploration of man's quality as to life according to the Lord's commandments, and as to faith in the Lord; therefore it is said, here is patience and faith; by saints are signified they who are of the Lord's New Church, specifically they who are in divine truths therein, n. 586. Patience is predicated of temptations, whereby man is explored as to what he really is; likewise as in other parts of the Apocalypse, as in chap. i. 9; ii. 3, 19; iii. 10: that it means as to a life according to the Lord's commandments, and as to faith in him, is evident from these words, "They have no rest day nor night who worship the beast and his image, here is the *patience* of the saints; here are they that keep the commandments of God, and the faith of Jesus," Apoc. xiv. 11, 12.

594. *And I beheld another beast coming up out of the earth*, signifies the clergy in the churches of the reformed who are

principled in the doctrine and faith of the dragon concerning God and salvation. What the nature of the faith of the dragon is, may be seen above, n. 537. The laity are they who are meant by the beast which came up out of the sea, and the clergy by the beast which came up out of the earth; because by the sea is signified the external of the church, and by the earth its internal, n. 398, 567, and the laity are in the externals of church doctrine, and the clergy in its internals. That the clergy are now described, appears from all the particulars which follow, when understood in a spiritual sense; and manifestly from this circumstance, that this beast is also called the false prophet, Apoc. xvi. 13; xix. 20; xx. 10; and especially from the following passage: "And the beast was taken, and with him the *false prophet* that wrought miracles before him, with which he deceived them that had received the mark of the beast, and them that worshipped his image," xix. 20; that this beast wrought signs before the other, by which he seduced them, is said in this chapter in these words: "And he doeth great wonders, and deceiveth them that dwell on the earth, by the means of those miracles which he had the power to do in the sight of the beast, saying to them that dwell on the earth, that they should make an image to the beast, and worship it," verses 13—15.

595. *And he had two horns like a lamb, and he spake as a dragon,* signifies that what they say, teach, and write, is from the Word, as though it were the Lord's divine truth, and yet it is truth falsified. By horns is signified power, n. 270, 443, here the power of speaking, teaching, and writing, thus of reasoning and arguing; his having horns like a lamb, signifies that they propagate these their notions as though they were divine truths of the Lord, because they are derived from the Word: for by a lamb is meant the Lord as to his Divine Humanity, and likewise as to the Word, which is divine truth from divine good; hence it is that upon this beast, which is also the false prophet, n. 594, there appeared two horns like a lamb; but that they were divine truths falsified, is signified by his speaking as a dragon: that by those who are in the faith of the dragon concerning God and salvation all the truths of the Word are falsified, may be seen above, n. 565. That these two things are signified by this beast having two horns like a lamb and speaking like a dragon, appears evidently from these words of the Lord in Matthew: "If any man shall say unto you, Lo, here is Christ, or there, believe it not; for there shall arise false Christs and *false prophets,* and shall show great signs and wonders, insomuch that if it were possible, they shall deceive the very elect; *behold I have told you before,*" xxiv. 23—25. By Christ is signified the same as here by lamb, viz., the Lord as to the divine truth of the Word; therefore their saying, "Lo, here is Christ," signi

fies that they would say that this is the divine truth of the Word; but that the same would be falsified, is signified by these words, "If any one shall say unto you, Here is Christ, or there, believe it not, for there shall arise false Christs and false prophets." That these are they concerning whom the Lord utters this prediction, is plain from this consideration, that it is said they would show great signs and wonders, and would deceive, if possible, the elect; the same as is said of this beast, which is the false prophet, in verses 13, 14, of this chapter. The things which the Lord foretold in that chapter of Matthew relate to the last time or state of the church, which is there meant by the consummation of the age.

596. *And he exerciseth all the power of the first beast before him*, signifies that they confirmed the tenets which are signified by the dragon, and are received by the laity, and that they thence derive their influence and authority. That this is signified, may be seen from the explanation above concerning the power given by the dragon to the beast which rose out of the sea, n. 575, 579; and as this beast, which is the false prophet, exercised that power before the dragon, nothing else is signified than that they caused them to prevail by their confirmations.

597. *And causeth the earth and them that dwell therein to worship the first beast whose deadly wound was healed*, signifies that thus by their confirming arguments they have established this tenet, that it is to be acknowledged as a doctrine sacred in the church, that since no one can do good works from himself and fulfil the law, the only medium of salvation is faith in the righteousness and merit of Christ, who suffered for man, and thereby took away the sentence of the law. It is unnecessary to explain this any further, because it follows from the explanations given in n. 566, 577—582: by the earth and them that dwell therein, are signified the churches of the reformed as above; to worship signifies to acknowledge a thing to be sacred in the church, as appears also above; in the present instance it signifies to acknowledge as sacred that which is understood by the beast which rose out of the sea, after his death-wound was healed; and this has been explained already.

598. *And he doeth great signs*, signifies testifications that the things they teach are true, although they are false. By signs are signified testifications that things are true, because formerly signs were wrought to bear testimony to the truth; but after the cessation of signs and miracles, their signification still continues, which is a testification of the truth; but in the present case by signs are signified testifications from the beast or false prophet, that his falses were truths, by reason that when they are confirmed they do not appear otherwise. That the testifications of a truth are signified by signs, may appear from the following passages: In the consummation of the age there

shall "arise false Christs and false prophets, and shall show *great signs and wonders*, insomuch that, if it were possible, they shall deceive the very elect," Matt. xxiv. 24; Mark xiii. 22. "And great *signs* shall there be from heaven, and there shall be *signs* in the sun, and in the moon; and upon the earth distress of nations, with perplexity, the sea and the waves roaring," Luke xxi. 11, 25. "Jehovah frustrateth the *signs* of the liars, and maketh the diviners mad, that turneth the wise men backward and maketh their knowledge foolish," Isaiah xliv. 25. "Learn not the way of the heathen, and be not dismayed at the *signs of the heavens*," Jerem. x. 2. "They are the spirits of devils working *miracles* to gather them to the battle of that great day," Apoc. xvi. 14. "And the beast was taken, and with him the false prophet that wrought *miracles* before him, with which he deceived them," Apoc. xix. 20. That signs were testifications of the truth of a thing, appears further from the following passages: The disciples said to Jesus, "what *sign* showest thou, that we may see and believe thee?" John vi. 30—33. The Jews, Scribes, and Pharisees sought a *sign* of the Lord, that they might know that he was the Christ, Matt. xii. 38—40; xvi. 1—4; Mark viii. 11, 12; Luke xi. 16, 29, 30; John ii. 16, 18, 19. The disciples said to Jesus, "What is the *sign* of thy coming and of the end of the world?" Matt. xxiv. 3; Mark xiii. 4. "If they will not believe thee, neither hearken to the voice of the *first sign*, that they will believe the voice of the *latter sign*," Exod. iv. 8: the voice of a sign is testification. "They showed his *signs* among them," Psalm cv. 27. "He said unto Ahaz, Ask thee a *sign* of Jehovah," Isaiah vii. 11, 14. "And this shall be a *sign* unto thee from Jehovah, behold I will bring again the shadow of the degrees, which is gone down in the sun-dial of Ahaz," Isaiah xxxviii. 7, 8. "Hezekiah also had said, What is the *sign*, that I shall go up to the house of Jehovah?" Isaiah xxxviii. 22. "And this shall be a *sign* unto you, saith Jehovah, that I will punish you in this place, that ye may know that my words shall surely stand against you for evil," Jerem. xliv. 29, 30. "O Jehovah, show me a *sign* for good, that they which hate me may see it and be ashamed," Psalm lxxxvi. 17. "Let them bring them forth and show us what shall happen, that we may consider them; show a *sign* of what is to come hereafter, that we may know that ye are gods," Isaiah xli. 22, 23. "Thine enemies roar in the midst of thy congregations, they have set up *their ensigns for signs*," Psalm lxxiv. 3, 4, 9; besides other places, as Isaiah xlv. 11, 13; Jerem. xxxi. 20, 21; Ezek. iv. 3; Psalm lxv. 7, 8; Psalm lxxviii. 42, 43; Exod. iv. 3; Numb. xiv. 11, 22; Deut. iv. 34; xiii. 2—4; Judges vi. 17, 21; 1 Sam. ii. 34; xiv. 10; Mark xvi. 17, 18, 20; Luke ii. 11, 12, 16. The same is signified by the *sign of the covenant*, Gen. ix. 13; xvii. 11; Ezek. xx. 12, 20. Hence it may clearly be seen, that by the great signs which this beast of the dragon works, are not meant signs, but the testifications by them that what they teach are truths; for every heretic who has confirmed himself in falses, after confirmation, strives to prove that his falses are truths; for then he no longer sees truths, inasmuch as the confirmation of falsity is the negation of truth, and when a truth is denied it loses its light; and so far as falses shine from the light of confirmation, which is an infatuating light, so far the light of truth is turned into darkness, as may be seen above, n. 566.

599. *So that he maketh fire come down from heaven on earth in the sight of men*, signifies attestations that their falsities are truths of heaven, and that they who receive them are saved, and that they who do not receive them perish. The reason why this is signified by these words, is, because the greatest signs were wrought by fire from heaven; whence it was a common saying among the ancients in confirmation of any thing, when the matter in question was concerning the testification of truth, that they could bring down fire from heaven to testify it; by which was signified that they could testify even to that extent. That the truth was also testified by fire from heaven, appears from the following passages: That the burnt-offering which was offered by Aaron was *consumed by fire* from heaven, Levit. ix. 24, and in like manner the *burnt-offering* which was offered by Elijah, 1 Kings xviii. 38. Fire from heaven, in an opposite sense, was a sign testifying that they were in evils and thence in falses, and that they would perish; but this fire was a consuming fire; as for instance, The *fire from heaven* that consumed the two sons of Aaron, Levit. x. 1—6. That which *consumed* two hundred and fifty men, Numb. xxvi. 10. That which *consumed* the uttermost parts of the camp, Numb. xi. 1—4. That which twice *consumed* fifty men sent by the king to Elijah, 2 Kings i. 10, 12. The *fire* and *brimstone* which came down from heaven upon Sodom, Gen. xix. 24, 25. The *fire* from heaven which consumed those who compassed the camp of the saints and the beloved city, concerning which see Apocalypse xx. 9. The disciples being angry with the impenitent, said to Jesus, "Lord, wilt thou that we command *fire* to come down from heaven and consume them?" Luke ix. 54. These passages are adduced to show that fire from heaven signifies a testification, yea, an attestation, that truth is truth, and, in an opposite sense, that falsity is truth, as in the present instance. Fire also signifies celestial love, and thus zeal for the truth, and, in an opposite sense, infernal love, and thence zeal for falsehood, n. 468, 494.

600. *And deceiveth them that dwell on the earth, by the means of those signs which he had power to do in the sight of the beast*, signifies that by their testifications and attestations they lead the men of the church into errors. To seduce signifies to lead

into errors; by them that dwell on the earth are signified the men of the Reformed Church, as above, n. 578, 588, 597; by the signs which it was given him to do before the beast, are signified testifications, or asseverations and attestations, n. 598, 599: by the beast which rose out of the sea, before whom the signs were done, is signified the faith of the dragon among the laity, n. 567; and by the beast which rose out of the earth and did the signs, and which in other places is called the false prophet, is signified the faith of the dragon among the clergy, n. 594. The like is said by the Lord in Matthew xxiv. 24—26.

601. *Saying to them that dwell on the earth, that they should make an image to the beast, which had the wound by a sword and lived*, signifies that they induce the men of the church to receive for doctrine, that faith is the only medium of salvation, because no one can do good from himself but what is meritorious, and because no one can fulfil the law, and so be saved. By them that dwell on the earth, are meant the men of the Reformed Church, as above, n. 600; by an image is signified the doctrine of that church, as will be seen presently; and by the image of the beast, which had the wound by a sword and lived, is signified this doctrine, that faith is the only medium of salvation, because no one can do good from himself but what is meritorious, and because no one can fulfil the law, and so be saved, as above, n. 576, 577, &c. Every church appears before the Lord as a man; if it is in truths from the Word, it appears as a beautiful man, but if it is in truths falsified, it appears as a man-monster: the church so appears from its doctrine and from a life according to it; from which it follows, that the doctrine of a church constitutes its image. This may also be seen from the following consideration: every man is his own good and truth, or his own evil and falsity, man being truly a man from no other ground; consequently it is doctrine and conformity of the life to it which makes the image of a man of the church, the image being that of a beautiful man, if the doctrine and the life according to it be formed from genuine truths of the Word; but it is the image of a man-monster, if formed from falsified truths of the Word. Man, indeed, in the spiritual world, appears like some animal; but it is his affection which has this appearance at a distance: they who are in truths and goods from the Lord, appear as lambs and doves, but they who are in falsified truths and adulterated goods, appear as owls and bats; they who are in faith separated from charity, as dragons and goats; they who are in falses from evil, appear as basilisks and crocodiles; and they who are such, and yet have confirmed the doctrinals of the church, have the appearance of fiery flying serpents. From these considerations it may be seen, that church-doctrine and conformity of life to it are meant by the image of the beast,

which they made for the dwellers upon earth. But what became of those who worshipped the image of the beast, may be seen, Apoc. xiv. 9—11; xix. 20, xx. 4. In a spiritual sense, images have a similar signification: in Exodus xx. 4, 5; Levit. xxvi. 1; Deut. iv. 16—18; Isaiah ii. 20; Ezek. vii. 20; xvi. 17; xxiii. 14—16. The idols and graven images of the ancients were images of their religion, on which account falses and evils of doctrine are signified by them, n. 459.

602. *And he had power to give breath unto the image of the beast, that the image of the beast should both speak,* signifies that it was permitted them to confirm that doctrine by means of the Word, whereby it does as it were receive life when it is taught. By his having power is signified that it was permitted; for all falses of doctrine, as well as evils of life, are of permission, concerning which see *The Angelic Wisdom concerning the Divine Providence*, n. 234—274, 275—285, 296 : by the image of the beast, that doctrine is signified, n. 601; by giving life to the image of the beast is signified to confirm it from the Word, for there is no spirit and life to any doctrine of the church from any other source; that the image of the beast might speak, signifies that so it may seem to have life when it is taught. The true reason why this is meant by giving spirit to the image of the beast, that it might speak, is, because in every particular of the Word there is spirit and life, for the Lord spake the Word, therefore he himself is in it, and he so spake the Word as that every thing therein should have communication with heaven, and through heaven with himself, there being a spiritual sense in it, whereby communication is effected; wherefore the Lord says, " The words that I speak unto you, they are *spirit and they are life,*" John vi. 63.

603. *And cause, that as many as would not worship the image of the beast should be killed,* signifies that they denounce damnation against those who do not acknowledge their doctrine of faith to be the holy doctrine of the church. To worship the image of the beast signifies to acknowledge their doctrine of faith as holy church-doctrine; for by worshipping is signified to acknowledge as a sacred principle of the church, n. 579, 580, 588, 597, and by the image of the beast is signified the doctrine, n. 601; by being killed is signified to be killed spiritually, which is to be damned, n. 325, and elsewhere; and as being killed signifies to be damned, it also signifies to be declared a heretic, and excluded from the communion with the church, for such a one, in their eyes, is considered as damned. This is done by the learned among the clergy, who have imbibed the mysteries of justification in schools and universities, especially they who are puffed up with a conceit of their own erudition in such things; these condemn all who do not think as they do, and so far as they dare, they fulminate against them. This I

can declare, that they who have imbibed these mysteries, and were in consequence in the pride of erudition, are so inveterate in the spiritual world against those who worship the Lord only, and do not acknowledge faith alone as the sole means of salvation, that they burn with wrath and fury when they see them, and also when they feel at a distance the divine sphere of the Lord and a sphere of charity encompassing them. Since they are such, the dragon is therefore described as a most inveterate enemy to them, as that he "stood before the woman which was ready to be delivered, for to devour her child as soon as it was born. And the serpent cast out of its mouth water as a flood after the woman, that he might cause her to be carried away of the flood. And the dragon was wroth with the woman, and went to make war with the remnant of her seed," Apoc. xii. 4, 15, 17. That "out of the mouth of the dragon, and out of the mouth of the beast, and out of the mouth of the false prophet," there came forth three unclean spirits like frogs, to gather them to the battle of the great day of God Almighty, Apoc. xvi. 13—16; the same in chap. xix. 19, 20, and xx. 8—10; as also that the beast that ascendeth out of the bottomless pit slew the two witnesses, and cast out their bodies into the street of the great city, which spiritually is called Sodom and Egypt, and suffered not their dead bodies to be put into graves, Apoc. xi. 7—9: by not suffering them to be put into graves is signified to reject them as condemned, n. 506.

604. *And he caused all, both small and great, and rich and poor, free and bond*, signifies all in that church, whatsoever may be their condition, learning, and intelligence. By small and great are here meant they who are in a greater or lesser degree of dignity, thus of whatever condition; by rich and poor are meant they who are more or less in knowledges and sciences, n. 206, thus of whatever degree of learning; by free and bond are meant they whose wisdom is from themselves and they whose wisdom is from others, n. 337, thus of whatever degree of intelligence; therefore by all, both small and great, rich and poor, free and bond, are meant all in that church whatever may be their condition, learning, and intelligence. These are the things that are understood in the spiritual sense.

605. *To receive a mark in their right hand or in their foreheads*, signifies that no one is acknowledged to be a reformed Christian unless he receives that doctrine in faith and love. By receiving a mark is signified to be acknowledged to be a reformed Christian, or of the confession which that doctrine teaches; a mark denotes such acknowledgment and confession; by the right hand is signified the all of man as to intellectual power, thus as to faith, for the right hand signifies the power of man, n. 457; by the forehead is signified the all of man as to voluntary power, thus as to love, for the forehead signifies love, n. 347.

606. *And that no man might buy or sell save he that had the mark, or name of the beast, or the number of his name,* signifies that it is not lawful for any one to teach from the Word, nor consequently to be inaugurated into the priesthood, honoured with the magisterial laurel, invested with the doctor's cap, and called orthodox, unless he acknowledges that doctrine, and swears to the belief and love thereof, or of that which is in agreement, or of that which is not at variance with it. By buying and selling is signified to acquire knowledges, here such as belong to that doctrine, and to teach them, as will appear presently; by a mark is signified the acknowledgment of being a reformed Christian, and confession that he is so, n. 605; by the name of the beast is signified the quality of the doctrine, by name the quality, n. 81, 122, 165, 584, and by the beast is signified the doctrine received by the laity, consequently by the community at large, n. 567; and as it is said, *or* the name of the beast, that which is in agreement with it and its quality is signified: by number is signified the quality of a thing, n. 448; and because it is said, *or* the number of his name, that which is not at variance with it and its quality is signified. It is so said, because the doctrine which is signified by the dragon and his beast, varies in the different kingdoms in which the Reformed Church exists; whilst it is the same as to this chief or leading tenet, THAT FAITH WITHOUT THE WORKS OF THE LAW JUSTIFIES AND SAVES. That to buy and sell signifies to procure knowledges, and teach them, in like manner to merchandise, trade, and gain, appears from the following passages: "Ho, every one that thirsteth, come ye to the waters, and he that hath no money, come ye, *buy* and eat; yea, come, *buy* wine and milk without money and without price," Isaiah lv. 1. "Ye have sold yourselves for nought, and ye shall be *redeemed* without money," Isaiah lii. 3. "With thy wisdom and with thine understanding hast thou gotten thee riches, and by thy great wisdom and by *thy traffic* hast thou increased thy riches," Ezek. xxviii. 5. Since by Tyre is signified the church as to the knowledges of things good and true, therefore it is said of Tyre, "All the ships of the sea were to carry on thy *merchandise:* Tarshish was thy *merchant* in silver: Javan, Tubal, and Mesheck, they were thy *merchants*, they traded in persons of men: Syria was thy *merchant* in emeralds: thy riches, thy *traffic,* thy *merchandise,* they that carry on thy *merchandise,* shall fall into the midst of the seas in the day of thy ruin," Ezek. xxvii. 1 to the end. "Howl, ye ships of Tarshish, for Tyre is laid waste, whose *merchants* are princes, and whose *traffickers* are the honourable of the earth," Isaiah xxiii. 1—8. The same is meant by trading, in the Lord's parable of the man who travelled into a far country, and gave his servants talents, that they might *trade* with them and *gain*, Matt. xxv. 14—20